S0-ADO-972

# SOMETHING ABOUT THE AUTHOR®

Something about the Author *was named an "****Outstanding Reference Source,****" the highest honor given by the American Library Association Reference and Adult Services Division.*

ISSN 0276-816X

# SOMETHING ABOUT THE AUTHOR®

Facts and Pictures about Authors
and Illustrators of Books for Young People

## volume 192

GALE
CENGAGE Learning™

Detroit • New York • San Francisco • New Haven, Conn • Waterville, Maine • London

**Something about the Author, Volume 192**

Project Editor: Lisa Kumar

Editorial: Dana Ferguson, Amy Elisabeth Fuller, Michelle Kazensky, Jennifer Mossman, Joseph Palmisano, Mary Ruby, Marie Toft

Permissions: Mollika Basu, Barb McNeil, Aja Perales

Imaging and Multimedia: Leitha Etheridge-Sims, Lezlie Light

Composition and Electronic Capture: Amy Darga

Manufacturing: Drew Kalasky

Product Manager: Janet Witalec



*Gale*
27500 Drake Rd.
Farmington Hills, MI, 48331-3535

LIBRARY OF CONGRESS CATALOG CARD NUMBER 62-52046

ISBN-13: 978-1-4144-2164-3
ISBN-10: 1-4144-2164-8

ISSN 0276-816X

This title is also available as an e-book.
ISBN-13: 978-1-4144-3844-3
ISBN-10: 1-4144-3844-3
Contact your Gale sales representative for ordering information.

Printed in the United States of America
1 2 3 4 5 6 7 12 11 10 09 08

# Contents

# Authors in Forthcoming Volumes

Below are some of the authors and illustrators that will be featured in upcoming volumes of *SATA*. These include new entries on the swiftly rising stars of the field, as well as completely revised and updated entries (indicated with *) on some of the most notable and best-loved creators of books for children.

**Istvan Banyai** ▮ An artist, designer, and animator, Hungarian-born Banyai has created animated short films for Nickelodeon and MTV Europe in addition to producing several innovative books for young children. In wordless books such as *Zoom* and *The Other Side,* Banyai mixes computer-generated images with freehand images, playing with perspective and challenging readers young and old with his complex, surrealistic design.

***Robert Burleigh** ▮ A writer of biographies and history as well as verse, Burleigh is noted for introducing topics from America's past to today's young readers in an accessible and effective manner. Often using a picture-book format, he presents facts about subjects that have ranged from Henry David Thoreau and Charles Lindbergh to Harry Houdini, Admiral Richard Byrd, and Jackie Robinson—in simple language and present-tense narration. His clipped, staccato texts, which help express the ideas, drama, and importance of each of his topics in an evocative fashion, are paired with illustrations by such noted artists as Lloyd Bloom, Ed Young, and Wendell Minor.

***Christopher Denise** ▮ Denise began his illustrating career after graduating from the Rhode Island School of Design, starting in newspapers and quickly finding his way into children's book illustration. Since his first illustration project, he has contributed art to books by popular writers such as Phyllis Root, Jane Yolen, and "Redwall" author Brian Jacques. In addition, Denise has collaborated with wife, writer Anika Denise, on the humorous counting book *Pigs Love Potatoes,* featuring the characteristic attention to detail and folktale elements that make his artwork so popular.

***Deborah Heiligman** ▮ A former children's book editor, Heiligman is the author of both fiction and nonfiction titles for younger readers. From biographies such as *Barbara McClintock: Alone in Her Field* and *Charles and Emma: The Darwins' Leap of Faith* to books about insects, titles for emergent readers, and a series of books about holidays throughout the world, she ranges widely in her focus and interests. Heiligman shares her knowledge of research tools in *The New York Public Library Kid's Guide to Research,* while her more fanciful side is revealed in books for beginning readers, such as *Fun Dog, Sun Dog* and *Honeybees.*

**Dean Lorey** ▮ Born in Michigan, Lorey is a Hollywood screenwriter who has also served as a producer and screenwriter for the Emmy Award-winning television show *Arrested Development.* In addition, he is the creator of the popular "Nightmare Academy" series of horror novels for middle-grade readers. Beginning with *Monster Hunters,* the series centers on Charlie Benjamin, a preteen who possesses an incredible power: the ability to summon creatures from the netherworld through his dreams.

***Walter Dean Myers** ▮ A versatile and prolific author whose award-winning books include the young-adult novels *Slam!* and *The Glory Field,* as well as nonfiction such as *Now Is Your Time! The African-American Struggle for Freedom,* Myers creates realistic novels, mysteries, adventure stories, fantasies, poetry, and picture books for readers of many ages. Despite his range, he is best known for the stories and novels he writes for middle-grade and teen readers. Featuring strong and resilient young characters, Myers' books focus on the positive aspects of contemporary urban life as well as on the roles played by African Americans throughout history.

**Tamara Petrosino** ▮ Quirky animal characters take center stage in Petrosino's colorful cartoon art. Since earning her degree at the prestigious Rhode Island School of Design, she developed a unique style of illustration that now features in a number of children's books. In addition to collaborating with author Dave Crawley on *Dog Poems* and *Cat Poems,* her watercolor-and-ink art also brings to life texts by Donna Jo Napoli, Harriet Ziefert, Stephen Krensky, Mark Shulman, and Siobhan Ciminera.

**Marc Rosenthal** ▮ Rosenthal is a designer, sequential artist, and illustrator whose work has appeared in such well-known publications as *Time, Newsweek,* and the *New Yorker.* He has also provided the art for several critically-acclaimed children's books, among them *First, Second* by Russian author Daniil Kharms and *Dig!* by the husband-and-wife team of Andrea Zimmerman and David Clemesha. His original, self-illustrated picture book, *Phooey!,* reveals his interest in 1940s comics, classic illustration, and architecture.

***Barbara Seuling** ▮ An illustrator and writing instructor as well as the author of fiction, nonfiction, and picture books for young readers, Seuling is best known for her "Freaky Facts" books, which provide trivia-minded middle graders with little-known facts, myths, and legends surrounding such subjects as sports, law, money, television, geography, the weather, the human body, and the presidency. Older children are the target audience of her nonfiction books, which focus on such topics as being handicapped and adjusting to a new stepfamily, while Seuling's popular activity books tap into favorite childhood subjects: monsters, ghosts, dinosaurs, crafts, and holidays.

**Rick Yancey** ▮ Yancey is a writer with a dual identity. Under the name Richard Yancey, he has penned adult novels such as the Southern gothic *A Burning in Homeland,* while younger readers know him as the author of YA adventure yarns. In *The Extraordinary Adventures of Alfred Kropp* Yancey's likable sixteen-year-old hero attempts to steal the magical sword Excalibur, the weapon of legendary Briton King Arthur, and his adventures continue in *Alfred Kropp: The Seal of Solomon.*

# Introduction

*Something about the Author* (*SATA*) is an ongoing reference series that examines the lives and works of authors and illustrators of books for children. *SATA* includes not only well-known writers and artists but also less prominent individuals whose works are just coming to be recognized. This series is often the only readily available information source on emerging authors and illustrators. You'll find *SATA* informative and entertaining, whether you are a student, a librarian, an English teacher, a parent, or simply an adult who enjoys children's literature.

## What's Inside *SATA*

*SATA* provides detailed information about authors and illustrators who span the full time range of children's literature, from early figures like John Newbery and L. Frank Baum to contemporary figures like Judy Blume and Richard Peck. Authors in the series represent primarily English-speaking countries, particularly the United States, Canada, and the United Kingdom. Also included, however, are authors from around the world whose works are available in English translation. The writings represented in *SATA* include those created intentionally for children and young adults as well as those written for a general audience and known to interest younger readers. These writings cover the entire spectrum of children's literature, including picture books, humor, folk and fairy tales, animal stories, mystery and adventure, science fiction and fantasy, historical fiction, poetry and nonsense verse, drama, biography, and nonfiction. Obituaries are also included in *SATA* and are intended not only as death notices but also as concise overviews of people's lives and work. Additionally, each edition features newly revised and updated entries for a selection of *SATA* listees who remain of interest to today's readers and who have been active enough to require extensive revisions of their earlier biographies.

## Autobiography Feature

Beginning with Volume 103, many volumes of *SATA* feature one or more specially commissioned autobiographical essays. These unique essays, averaging about ten thousand words in length and illustrated with an abundance of personal photos, present an entertaining and informative first-person perspective on the lives and careers of prominent authors and illustrators profiled in *SATA*.

## Two Convenient Indexes

In response to suggestions from librarians, *SATA* indexes no longer appear in every volume but are included in alternate (odd-numbered) volumes of the series, beginning with Volume 57.

*SATA* continues to include two indexes that cumulate with each alternate volume: the Illustrations Index, arranged by the name of the illustrator, gives the number of the volume and page where the illustrator's work appears in the current volume as well as all preceding volumes in the series; the Author Index gives the number of the volume in which a person's biographical sketch, autobiographical essay, or obituary appears in the current volume as well as all preceding volumes in the series.

These indexes also include references to authors and illustrators who appear in *Gale's Yesterday's Authors of Books for Children, Children's Literature Review,* and *Something about the Author Autobiography Series.*

## Easy-to-Use Entry Format

Whether you're already familiar with the *SATA* series or just getting acquainted, you will want to be aware of the kind of information that an entry provides. In every *SATA* entry the editors attempt to give as complete a picture of the person's life and work as possible. A typical entry in *SATA* includes the following clearly labeled information sections:

***PERSONAL:*** date and place of birth and death, parents' names and occupations, name of spouse, date of marriage, names of children, educational institutions attended, degrees received, religious and political affiliations, hobbies and other interests.

***ADDRESSES:*** complete home, office, electronic mail, and agent addresses, whenever available.

***CAREER:*** name of employer, position, and dates for each career post; art exhibitions; military service; memberships and offices held in professional and civic organizations.

***MEMBER:*** professional, civic, and other association memberships and any official posts held.

***AWARDS, HONORS:*** literary and professional awards received.

***WRITINGS:*** title-by-title chronological bibliography of books written and/or illustrated, listed by genre when known; lists of other notable publications, such as plays, screenplays, and periodical contributions.

***ADAPTATIONS:*** a list of films, television programs, plays, CD-ROMs, recordings, and other media presentations that have been adapted from the author's work.

***WORK IN PROGRESS:*** description of projects in progress.

***SIDELIGHTS:*** a biographical portrait of the author or illustrator's development, either directly from the biographee—and often written specifically for the *SATA* entry—or gathered from diaries, letters, interviews, or other published sources.

***BIOGRAPHICAL AND CRITICAL SOURCES:*** cites sources quoted in "Sidelights" along with references for further reading.

***EXTENSIVE ILLUSTRATIONS:*** photographs, movie stills, book illustrations, and other interesting visual materials supplement the text.

## How a *SATA* Entry Is Compiled

*SATA* editors examine a wide variety of published sources to gather information for an entry. Biographical and bibliographic sources are consulted, as are book reviews, feature articles, published interviews, and material sometimes obtained from the biographee's family, publishers, agent, or other associates. Whenever possible, the author or illustrator is sent a copy of the entry to check for accuracy and completeness.

Entries that have not been verified by the biographees or their representatives are marked with an asterisk (*).

## Contact the Editor

We encourage our readers to examine the entire *SATA* series. Please write and tell us if we can make *SATA* even more helpful to you. Give your comments and suggestions to the editor:

Editor
Something about the Author
Gale, Cengage Learning
27500 Drake Rd.
Farmington Hills MI 48331-3535

Toll-free: 800-877-GALE
Fax: 248-699-8070

# *Something about the Author* Product Advisory Board

The editors of *Something about the Author* are dedicated to maintaining a high standard of excellence by publishing comprehensive, accurate, and highly readable entries on a wide array of writers for children and young adults. In addition to the quality of the content, the editors take pride in the graphic design of the series, which is intended to be orderly yet inviting, allowing readers to utilize the pages of *SATA* easily and with efficiency. Despite the longevity of the *SATA* print series, and the success of its format, we are mindful that the vitality of a literary reference product is dependent on its ability to serve its users over time. As literature, and attitudes about literature, constantly evolve, so do the reference needs of students, teachers, scholars, journalists, researchers, and book club members. To be certain that we continue to keep pace with the expectations of our customers, the editors of *SATA* listen carefully to their comments regarding the value, utility, and quality of the series. Librarians, who have firsthand knowledge of the needs of library users, are a valuable resource for us. The *Something about the Author* Product Advisory Board, made up of school, public, and academic librarians, is a forum to promote focused feedback about *SATA* on a regular basis. The nine-member advisory board includes the following individuals, whom the editors wish to thank for sharing their expertise:

**Eva M. Davis**
*Youth Department Manager,*
*Ann Arbor District Library,*
*Ann Arbor, Michigan*

**Joan B. Eisenberg**
*Lower School Librarian,*
*Milton Academy,*
*Milton, Massachusetts*

**Francisca Goldsmith**
*Teen Services Librarian,*
*Berkeley Public Library,*
*Berkeley, California*

**Susan Dove Lempke**
*Children's Services Supervisor,*
*Niles Public Library District,*
*Niles, Illinois*

**Robyn Lupa**
*Head of Children's Services,*
*Jefferson County Public Library,*
*Lakewood, Colorado*

**Victor L. Schill**
*Assistant Branch Librarian/Children's Librarian,*
*Harris County Public Library/Fairbanks Branch,*
*Houston, Texas*

**Caryn Sipos**
*Community Librarian,*
*Three Creeks Community Library,*
*Vancouver, Washington*

**Steven Weiner**
*Director,*
*Maynard Public Library,*
*Maynard, Massachusetts*

# SOMETHING ABOUT THE AUTHOR

## ADDY, Sharon Hart 1943-

### Personal

Born February 3, 1943, in Oak Creek, WI; daughter of Earl (a bricklayer and janitor) and Gertrude (a caterer) Hart; married Gordon Addy (a hydraulic repairman), August 9, 1969; children: Mari Jo Burri, Jill. *Education:* University of Wisconsin, Whitewater, B.E., 1964. *Religion:* Roman Catholic. *Hobbies and other interests:* Gardening.

### Addresses

*Home and office*—Wisconsin Dells, WI. *E-mail*—haronaddy@maqs.net.

### Career

Freelance writer, speaker and teacher. Fifth-grade teacher in Stone Bank, WI, 1964-66, Commerce City, CO, 1966, and Oak Creek, WI, 1967-70; substitute teacher in Oak Creek, 1983-87; Community Newspapers, Inc., Milwaukee, WI, staff and features writer, 1985-90. Institute of Children's Literature, West Redding, CT, instructor, beginning 1995.

### Member

Society of Children's Book Writers and Illustrators.

***Sharon Hart Addy*** (Photograph by Brayer Photography reproduced by permission.)

### Awards, Honors

Archer/Eckbald Children's Picture Book Award, and Outstanding Achievement in Children's Literature selection, Wisconsin Library Association, both for *Right Here on This Spot;* Cooperative Children's Book Center Choices designation, for *A Visit with Great-Grandma;*

Betty Ren Wright Children's Picture Book Award honorable mention, and Bill Martin, Jr. Picture Book Award nomination, both 2003, both for *When Wishes Were Horses.*

## Writings

*We Didn't Mean To* ("Life and Living from a Child's Point of View" series), illustrated by Jay Blair, Raintree (Milwaukee, WI), 1981.

*A Visit with Great-Grandma,* illustrated by Lydia Halverson, Albert Whitman (Morton Grove, IL), 1989.

*Kidding around Milwaukee: What to Do, Where to Go, and How to Have Fun in Milwaukee,* John Muir (Santa Fe, NM), 1997.

*Right Here on This Spot,* illustrated by John Clapp, Houghton Mifflin (Boston, MA), 1999.

*When Wishes Were Horses,* illustrated by Brad Sneed, Houghton Mifflin (Boston, MA), 2002.

*In Grandpa's Woods,* illustrated by Tamlyn Akins, Trails Custom Publishing (Black Earth, WI), 2004.

*Lucky Jake,* illustrated by Wade Zahares, Houghton Mifflin (Boston, MA), 2007.

Contributor of short story "The Breakwater" to *Wisconsin Seasons: Classic Tales of Life Outdoors,* Cabin Bookshelf, 1998. Contributor of short stories, poems, and articles to children's magazines, including *Highlights for Children, Boy's Quest, Hopscotch, Fun for Kidz* and *Pennywhistle Press.*

## Sidelights

A lifelong resident of Wisconsin, Sharon Hart Addy is the author of such well-received picture books as *Right Here on This Spot* and *Lucky Jake.* Addy's works for young readers are often recognized for their humorous narratives. "I love to make people laugh," the author stated in an interview on the *Lori Calabrese* Web log. "Laughter breaks down barriers. It makes people feel good about themselves and the people they're with. Life can be a pretty heavy experience. Laughter makes things lighter and easier to bear."

A number of Addy's books also incorporate her love of history. "Using historical settings . . . takes people out of their lives and connects them with the people who came before us," she remarked to Calabrese. "I firmly believe that 'history' is really 'his story' and 'her story'—the stories of individuals who faced the same personal and interpersonal conflicts and needs we struggle with today. The trappings of life change, but basic human needs don't. Humans scramble, not always visibly, to find physical and emotional comfort. How people in the past achieved that comfort changed the world and created the world we have today."

Addy's picture book *Right Here on This Spot* was described as a "lyrical homage to humankind's relationship to the land" by a contributor in *Publishers Weekly.* The book "grew from an idea for a magazine article," the author told *SATA.* "A children's magazine planned an issue on the Great Lakes. Since I live near Lake Michigan and find archaeology interesting, I contacted the Great Lakes Archaeological Research Center and set up an interview with the Center's archaeologist. The day we met he didn't have time to talk, so he handed me a report on one of his digs. The magazine rejected the article, but I never forgot what I read in the report. He excavated a spot just a few miles from my house and found evidence that humans hunted at the edge of Ice Age glaciers. I got to thinking about all the people who lived on the land we occupy today. The result was *Right Here on This Spot.*"

In *Right Here on This Spot,* a young narrator describes the historic artifacts that his grandfather finds on his cabbage farm, including a bone from a mastodon, an arrowhead, and a button from a U.S. soldier's Civil War uniform. "In Addy's stately text, spare language evokes the changes of seasons and of centuries," remarked the *Publishers Weekly* critic, and Hazel Rochman, writing in *Booklist,* praised the "simple poetic text" in Addy's tale.

*When Wishes Were Horses,* an "amusing twist on the traditional granted-wish-that-gets-out-of-control motif," according to *School Library Journal* critic Louise L. Sherman, centers on Zeb, a tired and overworked resident of Dry Gulch whose every desire suddenly comes true. While carrying a sack of flour, Zeb wishes for a horse to help ease his burden; before long, the town is filled with mares and stallions. "This cautionary tale, humorously told and illustrated, gets its message across gently and without didacticism," noted a contributor to *Kirkus Reviews.*

In *Lucky Jake,* a prospector's son learns to make the most of every opportunity. "As I was growing up, my mom taught me that you have to work for what you want," Addy remarked in her interview with Calabrese. "That idea seemed like an excellent theme for a story, so, mentally . . . I trolled through periods in history for a setting that would highlight that theme. The Gold Rush was perfect. Pa wants to strike it rich. Jake wants a pet, regular meals, and a few comforts of home."

Addy's tale focuses on Jake, a young gold panner who desperately hopes for a canine companion but settles for the only available pet: a pig. When the pig discovers some corn seeds in Pa's jacket, Jake plants and nurtures the corn, which attracts a goat that provides milk. Before long, Jake and Pa are feeding an army of hungry prospectors, and their fortunes soar. *Lucky Jake* earned strong reviews. "The sunny story is told in a deliberately deadpan, unruffled tone," noted *Horn Book* contributor Susan Dove Lempke, and a critic in *Publishers Weekly* stated that "perceptive readers will recognize their providence has quite a bit to do with gumption, ingenuity and a sense of fairness—and, yup, luck too."

Addy once told *SATA:* "One of my strongest memories from second grade is walking home from school thinking about becoming a writer. I wanted to write stories as wonderful as the ones I read.

"When I reached ninth grade, I discovered I could handle words pretty well. That year my English teacher accused me of plagiarism over my description of a leaf rustling down the street. Three years later, the same teacher sent an article I wrote for the school paper to the local newspaper. They published it with my byline.

"Unfortunately, by this point my dream of becoming a writer was supplanted by the practical decision to become an elementary school teacher. In college I kept my vision of writing to myself. Real writers certainly didn't spend as much time as I did on a single paragraph!

"After graduation from college, I taught fifth grade for several years, then married and left teaching to raise my family. I started writing while my girls watched *Sesame Street,* and I've been at it ever since. I write anything I get a good idea for—stories, articles, poetry, riddles, books.

"I wrote *We Didn't Mean To* after I learned that a series of books about problems children encounter could use a book on vandalism. *A Visit with Great-Grandma* grew out of an article I did as a feature writer for the local newspaper. My editor asked for a story about people who immigrated to America. The great-grandmas I interviewed didn't speak English very well, but they both enjoyed visiting with their great-grandchildren. I wondered how they communicated. As I played 'What if?' the story came together."

## Biographical and Critical Sources

*PERIODICALS*

*Booklist,* October 15, 1999, Hazel Rochman, review of *Right Here on This Spot,* p. 449; December 1, 2002, Kay Weisman, review of *When Wishes Were Horses,* p. 671; April 15, 2007, Ilene Cooper, review of *Lucky Jake,* p. 52.

*Horn Book,* July-August, 2007, Susan Dove Lempke, review of *Lucky Jake,* p. 375.

*Kirkus Reviews,* August 1, 2002, review of *When Wishes Were Horses,* p. 1120.

*Publishers Weekly,* September 27, 1999, review of *Right Here on This Spot,* p. 104; May 7, 2007, review of *Lucky Jake,* p. 58.

*School Library Journal,* November, 2002, Louise L. Sherman, review of *When Wishes Were Horses,* p. 110; July, 2007, Ieva Bates, review of *Lucky Jake,* p. 66.

*ONLINE*

*Cooperative Children's Book Center Web site,* http://www.education.wisc.edu/ccbc/ (August 15, 2008), Sharon Hart Addy."

*Lori Calabrese Web log,* http://loricalabrese.blogspot.com/ (April 30, 2008), Lori Calabrese, interview with Addy.

*Sharon Hart Addy Home Page,* http://www.sharonhartaddy.com (August 15, 2008).*

* * *

# ALDRIDGE, Sheila 1974-

## Personal

Born 1974, in Atlanta, GA; married; husband's name Gabe; children: Atticus. *Education:* Portfolio Center (Atlanta, GA), graduate, 2000.

## Addresses

*Home and office*—Atlanta, GA. *Agent*—Susan Wells & Associates, 5134 Timber Trail S., Atlanta, GA 30342. *E-mail*—Sheila_aldridge@yahoo.com.

## Career

Illustrator.

## Illustrator

Karen Rostoker-Gruber, *Food Fright!: A Mouthwatering Novelty Book,* Price Stern Sloan (New York, NY), 2003.

Fran Kennedy, *The Pickle Patch Bathtub,* Tricycle Press (Berkeley, CA), 2004.

Matthew Henry Hall, *Phoebe and Chub,* Rising Moon (Flagstaff, AZ), 2005.

Fran Kennedy, *The Just-Right, Perfect Present,* Tricycle Press (Berkeley, CA), 2007.

## Sidelights

Sheila Aldridge is an Atlanta, Georgia-based artist whose work can be found in picture books by Karen Rostoker-Gruber, Fran Kennedy, and Matthew Henry Hall. As she explained to *SATA,* "I was raised an only child who learned how to entertain herself quickly with a pen and a college-ruled notebook on long car rides with her parents who were selling property at the time. I made up my own books and illustrations and loved for my mom to tell me stories from when she was a little girl to retelling fairy tales."

Aldridge's first book-illustration project, the interactive *Food Fright!: A Mouthwatering Novelty Book,* pairs a humorous cast of ten monsters with a rhyming text by Rostoker-Gruber that finds the hungry creatures preparing a monstrous feast featuring eyeball stew and other delicacies. *Phoebe and Chub,* a whimsical fantasy by Hall, focuses on the magic of friendship, while Aldridge's collaboration with Kennedy draws on the author's rural roots and shows Aldridge's range as an artist.

In *The Pickle Patch Bathtub* Kennedy's folk-style story takes readers back to 1920s Missouri where a girl named Donna has grown too tall and gangly to fit into her farm family's tin washtub. Knowing that the family cannot afford such a luxury as a new bathtub, Donna and her siblings go into the cucumber-raising business, earning enough money to afford a satisfactory bathtub from the Sears & Roebuck mail-order catalogue. In keeping with the nostalgic-themed tale, Aldridge contributes oil-and acrylic collage paintings that "are filled with details of life on the farm," as a *Kirkus Reviews* writer observed. Also observing that the book's illustrations "are reminiscent of American folk art," Linda L. Walkins added in *School Library Journal* that *The Pickle Patch Bathtub* treats readers to an "engaging" story that "vividly bring[s] the past to life."

Aldridge and Kennedy team up again in creating *The Just-Right, Perfect Present,* which also centers on the relationships in Donna's close-knit farming family. At a celebration of Grandma and Grandpa's fiftieth wedding anniversary, family members gather at the family orchard and the grandchildren recite poems they have learned by heart. When Donna learns that the poem she has memorized is one that a younger relative also planned to recite, she finds the time to learn a much longer poem, thanks to her helpful siblings. Aldridge's "old-fashioned folksy paintings and hay-colored tones reinforce the . . . gentle mood" of Kennedy's simple story, concluded *School Library Journal* contributor Martha Simpson, and in *Kirkus Reviews* a critic noted that the collage illustrations in *The Just-Right, Perfect Present* are "rich in lemon/lime undertones" that add to the book's "old-fashioned, folksy feeling." "Well attuned to the tone" Kennedy infuses into her nostalgic story, Aldridge's illustrations "glow with a warm, nostalgic gold tone that suits . . . the . . . well-written text," according to *Booklist* contributor Carolyn Phelan.

## Biographical and Critical Sources

*PERIODICALS*

*Booklist,* July 1, 2007, Carolyn Phelan, review of *The Just-Right, Perfect Present,* p. 65.

***Three cousins take center stage in Sheila Aldridge's artwork for Frances Kennedy's* The Just-Right, Perfect Present.** 

*Kirkus Reviews,* April 1, 2004, review of *The Pickle Patch Bathtub,* p. 332; May 1, 2007, review of *The Just-Right, Perfect Present.*

*School Library Journal,* October, 2004, Linda L. Walkins, review of *The Pickle Patch Bathtub,* p. 120; November, 2007, Martha Simpson, review of *The Just-Right, Perfect Present,* p. 93.

*ONLINE*

*Sheila Aldridge Home Page,* http://www.sheilaaldridge.com (August 6, 2008).

* * *

# ALLEN, Alex B.
## See HEIDE, Florence Parry

* * *

# ANCONA, George 1929-

## Personal

Born Jorge Efrain Ancona, December 4, 1929, in New York, NY; son of Efrain José (an accountant and amateur photographer) and Emma (a seamstress) Ancona; married Patricia Apatow, March 4, 1951 (divorced, 1966); married Helga Von Sydow (a journalist), June 20, 1968; children: (first marriage) Lisa, Gina, Tomas; (second marriage) Isabel, Marina, Pablo. *Ethnicity:* "Mexican-American." *Education:* Attended Academia San Carlos, 1949-50, Art Students League, 1950-51, and Cooper Union, 1951-52. *Politics:* Democrat.

## Addresses

*Home and office*—35 Calle Enrique, Santa Fe, NM 87507. *E-mail*—geoancona@cybermesa.com.

## Career

Photographer, filmmaker, and author. *New York Times,* New York, NY, member of promotions department, 1950-51; *Esquire* magazine, New York, NY, art director, 1951-53; *Seventeen* magazine, New York, NY, head of promotion department, 1953-54; Grey Advertising, New York, NY, art director, 1954-57; Daniel & Charles, New York, NY, art director, 1957-61; George Ancona, Inc., New York, NY, photographer and filmmaker, 1961—. Instructor at Rockland Community College, School of Visual Arts, and Parsons School of Design; lecturer on film, design photography, and books.

## Member

Authors Guild.

## Awards, Honors

Art Director's Show award, 1959, 1960, 1967; Cine Golden Eagle Award, Council on Non-Theatrical Events, 1967, for film *Reflections,* and 1972, for film

***George Ancona*** (Photograph by Marina Ancona reproduced by permission.)

*Cities of the Web;* award from American Institute of Graphic Arts, 1967, 1968, 1974; Cindy Award, Industry Film Producers Association, 1967; Science Book Awards Nonfiction Younger Honor, New York Academy of Sciences, 1975, for *Handtalk,* and 1988, for *Turtle Watch;* Golden Kite Award, Society of Children's Book Writers and Illustrators, 1980, for *Finding Your First Job;* American Library Association Notable Book designation, and Notable Children's Trade Book in the Field of Social Studies designation, National Council for the Social Studies (NCSS)/Children's Book Council (CBC), 1986, both for *Sheep Dog;* Best Illustrated Children's Books of the Year citation, *New York Times,* 1987, for *Handtalk Birthday;* Carter G. Woodson Book Award for Outstanding Merit, NCSS, 1987, for *Living in Two Worlds;* Notable Children's Trade Book in the Field of Social Studies designation, NCSS/CBC, c. 1989, for *Spanish Pioneers of the Southwest;* Texas Blue Bonnet Award, c. 1989, for *The American Family Farm;* Notable Children's Trade Book in the Field of Social Studies designation, NCSS/CBC, c. 1990, for *Riverkeeper* and *Mom Can't See Me;* Pick of the Lists citation, American Booksellers Association, 1991, for *The Aquarium Book;* Children's Book of the Year citation, Bank Street College Children's Book Committee,

1993, for *Pablo Remembers;* Best 100 Children's Books citation, New York Public Library, 1993, for *Powwow;* John Burroughs Nature Books for Young Readers listee, 1993, for *Earth Keepers,* by Joan Anderson; Parents' Choice Award, 1994, for *The Piñata Maker/El piñatero;* Children's Book of the Year citation, Bank Street College Children's Book Committee, 1994, for *Twins on Toes;* Golden Duck Award for excellence in children's science fiction, 1994, for *Richie's Rocket;* Outstanding Science Trade Book for Children citation, National Science Teachers Association/CBC, 1995, for *The Golden Lion Tamarin Comes Home;* Americas Award for Children's and Young-Adult Literature, Consortium of Latin-American Studies Programs, 1998, and Pura Belpré Honor Book designation, Association for Library Service to Children/National Association to Promote Library and Information Services to Latinos and the Spanish Speaking, 2000, both for *Barrio; Washington Post*/Children's Book Guild Nonfiction Award, 2002, for body of work; Bank Street College Children's Book Committee Children's Book of the Year designation, Americas Award Commended designation, and Cooperative Children's Book Center Choice designation, all 2007, all for *Capoeira;* New Mexico Book Association Special Recognition award, 2008.

## Writings

*AND PHOTOGRAPHER*

*Monsters on Wheels,* Dutton (New York, NY), 1974.
*And What Do You Do?,* Dutton (New York, NY), 1976.
*I Feel: A Picture Book of Emotions,* Dutton (New York, NY), 1977.
*Growing Older,* Dutton (New York, NY), 1978.
*It's a Baby!,* Dutton (New York, NY), 1979.
*Dancing Is . . .,* Dutton (New York, NY), 1981.
*Bananas: From Manolo to Margie,* Clarion (New York, NY), 1982.
*Teamwork: A Picture Essay about Crews and Teams at Work,* Crowell (New York, NY), 1983.
*Monster Movers,* Dutton (New York, NY), 1983.
*Freighters,* Crowell (New York, NY), 1985.
*Sheep Dog,* Lothrop (New York, NY), 1985.
*Helping Out,* Clarion (New York, NY), 1985.
*Turtle Watch,* Macmillan (New York, NY), 1987.
*Riverkeeper,* Macmillan (New York, NY), 1990.
*The Aquarium Book,* Clarion (New York, NY), 1991.
*Man and Mustang,* Macmillan (New York, NY), 1992.
*My Camera,* Crown (New York, NY), 1992.
*Pablo Remembers: The Fiesta of the Day of the Dead,* Lothrop (New York, NY), 1993.
*Powwow,* Harcourt (San Diego, CA), 1993.
*Ser util,* Scholastic (New York, NY), 1993.
*The Golden Lion Tamarin Comes Home,* Macmillan (New York, NY), 1994.
*The Piñata Maker/El piñatero,* Harcourt (San Diego, CA), 1994.
*Ricardo's Day/El día de Ricardo,* Scholastic (New York, NY), 1995.
*Fiesta U.S.A.,* Dutton (New York, NY), 1995.
*Stone Cutters, Carvers, and the Cathedral,* Lothrop (New York, NY), 1995.
*Earth Daughter: Alicia of Acoma Pueblo,* Simon & Schuster (New York, NY), 1995.
*In City Gardens,* Celebrations Press (Glenview, IL), 1996.
*Mayeros: A Yucatec Maya Family,* Lothrop (New York, NY), 1997.
*Let's Dance!,* Morrow/Avon (New York, NY), 1998.
*Fiesta Fireworks,* Lothrop (New York, NY), 1998.
*Barrio: José's Neighborhood,* Harcourt (San Diego, CA), 1998.
*Carnaval,* Harcourt (San Diego, CA), 1999.
*Charro: The Mexican Cowboy,* Harcourt (San Diego, CA), 1999.
*Cuban Kids,* Marshall Cavendish (Tarrytown, MD), 2000.
*Harvest,* Marshall Cavendish (Tarrytown, MD), 2001.
*Come and Eat,* HarperCollins (New York, NY), 2001.
*Murals, Walls That Sing,* Marshall Cavendish (Tarrytown, MD), 2003.
*Capoeira: Game! Dance! Martial Art!,* Lee & Low (New York, NY), 2007.
*Self Portrait,* Robert C. Owen (New York, NY), 2007.

Authors works have been translated into Spanish.

*"HANDTALK" SERIES; AND PHOTOGRAPHER*

(With Remy Charlip and Mary Beth Miller) *Handtalk: An ABC of Finger Spelling and Sign Language,* Parents' Magazine Press (New York, NY), 1974.
(With Remy Charlip and Mary Beth Miller) *Handtalk Birthday: A Number and Story Book in Sign Language,* Four Winds Press (New York, NY), 1987.
(With Mary Beth Miller) *Handtalk Zoo,* Four Winds Press (New York, NY), 1989.
(With Mary Beth Miller) *Handtalk School,* Four Winds Press (New York, NY), 1991.

*"VIVA MEXICO!" SERIES; AND PHOTOGRAPHER*

*The Fiestas,* Marshall Cavendish (Tarrytown, MD), 2002.
*The Folk Arts,* Marshall Cavendish (Tarrytown, MD), 2002.
*The Past,* Marshall Cavendish (Tarrytown, MD), 2002.
*The People,* Marshall Cavendish (Tarrytown, MD), 2002.
*The Foods,* Marshall Cavendish (Tarrytown, MD), 2002.

*"SOMOS LATINOS" SERIES; AND PHOTOGRAPHER*

*Mi barrio/My Neighborhood,* Children's Press, 2004.
*Mi casa/My House,* Children's Press (Danbury, CT), 2004.
*Mi escuela/My School,* Children's Press (Danbury, CT), 2004.
*Mi familia/My Family,* Children's Press (Danbury, CT), 2004.
*Mis amigos/My Friends,* Children's Press (Danbury, CT), 2004.

*Mi musica/My Music,* Children's Press (Danbury, CT), 2005.

*Mis abuelos/My Grandparents,* Children's Press (Danbury, CT), 2005.

*Mis comidas/My Foods,* Children's Press (Danbury, CT), 2005.

*Mis fiestas/My Celebrations,* Children's Press (Danbury, CT), 2005.

*Mis juegos/My Games,* Children's Press (Danbury, CT), 2005.

*Mis quehaceres/My Chores,* Children's Press (Danbury, CT), 2005.

*PHOTOGRAPHER*

Barbara Brenner, *A Snake-Lover's Diary,* Scott Young Books, 1970.

Barbara Brenner, *Faces,* Dutton (New York, NY), 1970.

Barbara Brenner, *Bodies,* Dutton (New York, NY), 1973.

Louise Jackson, *Grandpa Had a Windmill, Grandma Had a Churn,* Parents' Magazine Press (New York, NY), 1977.

Jean Holzenthaler, *My Feet Do,* Dutton (New York, NY),

1979.Louise Jackson, *Over on the River,* Lothrop (New York, NY), 1980.

Sue Alexander, *Finding Your First Job,* Dutton (New York, NY), 1980.

Howard Smith, *Balance It,* Four Winds Press (New York, NY), 1982.

Maxine B. Rosenberg, *My Friend Leslie: The Story of a Handicapped Child,* Lothrop (New York, NY), 1983.

Joan Anderson, *First Thanksgiving Feast,* Clarion (New York, NY), 1984.

Maxine B. Rosenberg, *Being Adopted,* Lothrop (New York, NY), 1984.

Joan Anderson, *Christmas on the Prairie,* Clarion (New York, NY), 1985.

Maxine B. Rosenberg, *Being a Twin, Having a Twin,* Lothrop (New York, NY), 1985.

Joan Anderson, *The Glorious Fourth at Prairietown,* Morrow (New York, NY), 1986.

Maxine B. Rosenberg, *Making a New Home in America,* Lothrop (New York, NY), 1986.

Maxine B. Rosenberg, *Living in Two Worlds,* Lothrop (New York, NY), 1986.

Joan Anderson, *Pioneer Children of Appalachia,* Clarion (New York, NY), 1986.

Floreva G. Cohen, *My Special Friend,* Board of Jewish Education (New York, NY), 1986.

Sam and Beryl Epstein, *Jackpot of the Beagle Brigade,* Macmillan (New York, NY), 1987.

Joan Anderson, *Joshua's Westward Journal,* Morrow (New York, NY), 1987.

Maxine B. Rosenberg, *Artists of Handcrafted Furniture at Work,* Lothrop (New York, NY), 1988.

Maxine B. Rosenberg, *Finding a Way: Living with Exceptional Brothers and Sisters,* afterword by Stephen Greenspan, Lothrop (New York, NY), 1988.

Joan Anderson, *From Map to Museum: Uncovering Mysteries of the Past,* introduction by David Hurst Thomas, Morrow Junior Books (New York, NY), 1988.

Joan Anderson, *A Williamsburg Household,* Clarion (New York, NY), 1988.

Joan Anderson, *The American Family Farm: A Photo Essay,* Harcourt (San Diego, CA), 1989.

Marcia Seligson, *Dolphins at Grassy Key,* Macmillan (New York, NY), 1989.

Joan Anderson, *Spanish Pioneers of the Southwest,* Dutton (New York, NY), 1989.

Shirley Climo, *City! New York,* Macmillan (New York, NY), 1990.

Shirley Climo, *City! San Francisco,* Macmillan (New York, NY), 1990.

Joan Anderson, *Harry's Helicopter,* Morrow (New York, NY), 1990.

Sally Hobart Alexander, *Mom Can't See Me,* Macmillan (New York, NY), 1990.

Joan Anderson, *Pioneer Settlers of New France,* Dutton (New York, NY), 1990.

Maxine B. Rosenberg, *Brothers and Sisters,* Clarion (New York, NY), 1991.

Joan Anderson, *Christopher Columbus: From Vision to Voyage,* Dial (New York, NY), 1991.

Shirley Climo, *City! Washington, DC,* Macmillan (New York, NY), 1991.

Christine Loomis, *My New Baby-Sitter,* Morrow (New York, NY), 1991.

Bonnie Larkin Nims, *Just Beyond Reach and Other Riddle Poems,* Scholastic (New York, NY), 1992.

Sally Hobart Alexander, *Mom's Best Friend,* Macmillan (New York, NY), 1992.

Joan Anderson, *Earth Keepers,* Gulliver Green/Harcourt (San Diego, CA), 1993.

Mildred Leinweber Dawson, *Over Here It's Different: Carolina's Story,* Macmillan (New York, NY), 1993.

Joan Anderson, *Richie's Rocket,* Morrow (New York, NY), 1993.

Joan Anderson, *Twins on Toes: A Ballet Debut,* Lodestar (New York, NY), 1993.

Joan Anderson, *Sally's Submarine,* Morrow (New York, NY), 1995.

Joan Anderson, *Cowboys: Roundup on an American Ranch,* Scholastic (New York, NY), 1996.

Barbara Beasley Murphy, *Miguel Lost and Found in the Palace,* Museum of New Mexico Press (Santa Fe, NM), 2002.

Pat Mora, *Join Hands: The Ways We Celebrate Life,* Charlesbridge (New York, NY), 2008.

*OTHER*

Also author of film scripts, including *Doctor* and *Dentist,* two short films for *Sesame Street; Faces* and *The River,* for children; *Getting It Together,* a documentary film about the Children's Television Workshop and Neighborhood Youth Corps; *Cities of the Web,* produced by Macmillan; *Looking for Pictures, Looking for Color,* and *Seeing Rhythm,* a series; *Reflections,* produced by American Crafts Council; *The Link,* produced by Orba Corporation; and *Expansion,* produced by Diamond International Corporation.

## Sidelights

George Ancona is renowned for creating vivid photo essays that allow children to immerse themselves in new ideas and cultures, to appreciate labor that so often goes unnoticed behind the scenes of daily life, and to accept themselves as well as others. Many of his images, as well as his writings, also celebrate his own Mexican heritage and the Spanish language. Ancona keeps the interests of his readers in mind while he works; as he explained in an essay for *Something about the Author Autobiography Series* (*SAAS*), he attempts to convey "the same feeling I had when my father would show me . . . big ships. It's like seeing something awe-inspiring and you just have to say, 'WOW.'"

Ancona once told *SATA* about his childhood: "My parents had come from Yucatan in Mexico, and I was raised a Mexican, learning to speak Spanish first. My father wanted me to grow up in the American way so we never lived in a Latin barrio. Instead I grew up the only Latin in an Italian neighborhood. There I acquired my English, work skills, street wisdom, and a godfather.

"Growing up in Coney Island, my world consisted of the contrast between the fantasies of the amusement rides and the limitless space of the sea. Summers were spent in a bathing suit running with a pack of boys through the streets to the beach, swimming out beyond the third barrel, straining the sands for coins, and sneaking into the amusement parks. From the age of twelve, I worked weekends and summers for a variety of craftsmen: an auto mechanic, a carpenter, and in the amusement parks. I would, also, make money with a friend by collecting junk and scrap paper in an old push cart. When loaded with newspaper it took both of us to raise it on its two big wheels and push it to the junk dealer. This way we always had money for the movies and a hot dog."

Ancona began to express his creativity as an artist while he was still young. "My father's hobby was photography and it was my first introduction to the making of images. . . . It was at home that I began to draw by copying photographs." Later, at Mark Twain Junior High School, he began to gain an interest in graphic design. "It was the sign-painting teacher who got me interested in lettering and painting the sets for the dramatic performances. When I graduated, I was given the Sign Painting Medal. In Lincoln High School, I had the good fortune of studying design with Mr. Leon Friend, who had organized an extra-curricular group called the Art Squad," Ancona recalled. He excelled under the direction of the Art Squad and its alumni, and won a scholarship to the Art Students League in New York City. He also met Rufino Tamayo, a renowned Mexican artist, who invited Ancona to visit him in Mexico.

Ancona accepted Tamayo's invitation, and Tamayo arranged for the young artist to spend six months painting at the Academy of San Carlos in Mexico. There, Ancona met José Clemente Orozco, a famous Mexican muralist; Igor Stravinsky, the composer; Diego Rivera, another great Mexican muralist; and Frida Kahlo, Rivera's wife and a painter and artist in her own right. Ancona also journeyed to Merida, in the Yucatan, to meet relatives from both sides of his family. Traveling further into the Yucatan, he spent the night at the Mayan ruins of Chichen Itza.

When his money ran out, Ancona returned to the United States to attend the Art Students League. He stayed for the duration of his scholarship, nine months, and then went to work as an artist's apprentice. Although he tried to attend school at Cooper Union at night, a new job in the promotion department at the *New York Times* left him exhausted. He decided to forgo school and concentrate on work. Around the same time, he also decided to marry his first wife, Patricia Apatow. Ancona went on to work as a staff designer at *Esquire* magazine, as an art director for *Apparel Arts* magazine, and then as art director of the promotion department for *Seventeen* magazine. Ancona recalled in his *SAAS* essay that the job at *Seventeen* "gave me my first taste of advertising. I enjoyed the challenge of blending images with words to create forceful messages."

Ancona moved on again to become an art director for the NBC television and radio networks, to work in fashion photography, and to try his hand at filmmaking. "The film experiences and my early attempts at photography seemed to be leading me into a different career direction. Having started out as someone who loved to draw and paint, I was spending more and more time with film and still cameras." At thirty years old, Ancona felt he had to make a decision about his career: "It was now or never so I took the plunge," he wrote in *SAAS*. He quit his job and began his career as a freelance photographer by taking photographs for *Vogue Children.* In addition, he made films for *Sesame Street* and filmed the children's series *Big Blue Marble.* As he worked, he traveled to Brazil, Pakistan, Hong Kong, Japan, Iceland, Tunisia, and Switzerland. It was during this time that Ancona and his first wife divorced. Ancona's three children, Lisa, Gina, and Tomas, stayed with him, and he later married Helga Von Sydow. With Von Sydow, Ancona had three more children: Isabel, Marina, and Pablo. By 2008 he could also boast four grandchildhren and three great grandchildren.

Ancona created his first children's book photographs in 1970. "My introduction to children's books was totally unexpected," he later revealed. Barbara Brenner, Ancona's friend and an established writer, asked him if he would be interested in making photographs to illustrate one of her books. "Since I had never done a children's book, I said yes." *Faces, Bodies,* and *A Snake-Lover's Diary* resulted. Later, when the editor of Brenner and Ancona's books suggested that he write the text as well as illustrate a book, Ancona "gulped hard" and said he "would try." Ancona's interest in "watching construction sites and huge machinery" and "several months photographing" led to the creation of his first book,

***Scene from Ancona's photo-essay picture book* Powwow, *which introduces young readers to Native American rituals and culture.*** (Copyright © 1993 by George Ancona. Reprinted by permission of Houghton Mifflin Harcourt Publishing Company. This material may not be reproduced in any form or by any means without the prior written permission of the publisher.)

*Monsters on Wheels.* This detailed book describes machines that "push, lift, crush, and haul," from cranes to the Lunar Roving Vehicle that explored the moon. John S. Radosta, writing in the *New York Times Book Review,* characterized *Monsters on Wheels* as "excellent."

*Monster Movers* features sixteen machines, from a walking dragline to a clamshell bucket loader, that move mountains of coal, grain, and cargo over land, onto ships, and off ships. One of these machines, a crawler-transporter, is pictured moving the U.S. Space Shuttle. "Once again Ancona has mixed striking photographs, a lucid text and a fascinating subject with winning results," Connie Tyrrell Burns commented in *School Library Journal.* Like *Monsters on Wheels* and *Monster Movers, Freighters* presents various machines that help people work. In *Freighters* Ancona focuses on the people who control the machines as well as on the machines; with his camera, he follows the qualifications, training, and daily routine of a freighter crew. Many of his books are entirely devoted to workers and the jobs they perform. Even *Sheep Dog,* which features a very intelligent breed of dogs, is about an important kind of work: guarding and herding sheep.

According to *School Library Journal* reviewer Andy Ward, *And What Do You Do?* presents twenty-one jobs, including carpenter, costume designer, dental assistant, barber, and nurse through "outstanding photographs" and a "lucid writing style." Denise M. Wilms noted in *Booklist* that Ancona's photographs feature "men and women of varying racial and ethnic backgrounds" and that there is a "conscious attempt to avoid stereotyping." *Teamwork: A Picture Essay about Crews and Teams at Work* follows the efforts of mountain climbers, a nursing crew, a sailing crew, a film crew, and other team-based workers. Like *And What Do You Do?,* the women and men in *Teamwork* are not cast in stereotypical roles.

Ancona has also made photo essays focusing on specific jobs. *Man and Mustang* shows how feral horses are captured, transported, and tamed by prison inmates for the Bureau of Land Management. *Stone Cutters, Carvers, and the Cathedral* illuminates an esoteric and fascinating profession. With black-and-white photographs and text, *Riverkeeper* follows John Cronin, the riverkeeper of the Hudson River in New York as he works to protect the water, plants, and wildlife. Ancona demonstrates that Cronin cannot fight pollution from the seat of his powerboat, named *Riverkeeper;* as a representative of the Hudson River Fishermen's Association, he must deal with corporate polluters and a host of government agencies to ensure the water's cleanliness. According to Mary M. Burns in *Horn Book,* Ancona provides a "balanced, rational presentation" which "speaks directly to our times in a manner as informative as it is appealing." Betsy Hearne of *Bulletin of the Center for Children's Books* concluded that *Riverkeeper* "will energize kids" to view its subject "in the light of ecological responsibility."

Looking forward to a satisfying career and an understanding of the world of work is just one aspect of childhood. Ancona has dealt with a variety of other childhood concerns and interests in his work. *Helping Out,* according to a *Publishers Weekly* critic, is based on a "stimulating" idea—children can help out (washing cars, planting seeds, doing chores) to the satisfaction of all. The children featured in Ancona's black-and-white pictures smile and, as the reviewer noted, "show clearly that they like what they're doing."

Children are fascinated with babies, as the nursery school teachers told Ancona in requesting a book discussing babies and how they grow. Ancona met this need by staying home to photograph the first twelve months in the life of his son Pablo As he noted in a *Junior Literary Guild* article, the text of *It's a Baby!* "grew out of the questions children would ask" about Pablo when they saw him. This book shows the boy nursing, playing, climbing, and taking his first steps. In *Horn Book,* Kate M. Flanagan described Ancona's black-and-white photographs as "exquisite."

Ancona's photographs have also helped children learn to accept themselves and others by bringing life to books featuring physically challenged children and adults. *Mom Can't See Me* and *Mom's Best Friend,* both by Sally Hobart Alexander, show how a blind woman lives a fulfilling life; *Finding a Way: Living with Exceptional Brothers and Sisters,* by Maxine B. Rosenberg, demonstrates how children can help physically challenged siblings in a caring, positive manner. The "Handtalk" series has been especially popular. In *Handtalk Zoo,* with a text by Mary Beth Miller, children visit the zoo and communicate in sign language. Ancona's color photographs clearly show the signs the children make, as well as capturing hands in rapid movement. As Hanna B. Zeiger observed in *Horn Book,* some "photos of signs capture very clearly the essence of the animal" the children are viewing. In the words of *School Library Journal* contributor Susan Nemeth McCarthy, *Handtalk Zoo* introduces children to sign-language vocabulary in a "creative and exuberant manner."

Ancona's travels to countries around the world have provided him with alternate settings to explore his favorite topics: machines, working and occupations, and nature. He was inspired to write *Bananas: From Manolo to Margie* while visiting a Honduran village. This book demonstrates how bananas are cultivated on a Honduran plantation, picked by plantation workers, and sent on a two-week trip to a grocery store in the United States, where Margie and her mother buy some. The mostly black-and-white photos focus on the equipment used in picking and transporting banans as well as on the people who operate it. They also feature the families of the plantation workers. The photos in *Bananas* are "fair: workers live poorly and work hard," as Terry Lawhead noted in *School Library Journal.* As Zena Sutherland observed in the *Bulletin of the Center for Children's Books,* information about the plantation workers is offered, although the text does not really discuss the "personal lives" of Margie and the transportation and marketing workers.

*Turtle Watch* follows the efforts of oceanographers attempting to replenish the sea turtle population in northeastern Brazil. During nesting season, both oceanographers and the people of Praia do Forte have important responsibilities. The local people, especially fishermen, must encourage one another to leave the eggs and turtles they find instead of selling them. Oceanographers must observe female turtles laying eggs, recover the eggs for safe hatching, and then, after the baby turtles emerge from their eggs, help them make their way to the ocean. According to Karey Wehner, writing in *School Library Journal,* in *Turtle Watch* "Ancona conveys some of the excitement and wonder scientists must feel when observing animals firsthand, in the field." Ancona noted in *Junior Literary Guild* that photographing the turtles was difficult. "We would arrive either too early or too late to see them emerge from the sea." Although it took a long time for Ancona to finally get his photos, he did not mind because "Brazil is a wonderful place to be stranded in." Ancona returned to Brazil to research and take photos for his book on the Golden Lion Tamarin monkey.

*Pablo Remembers: The Fiesta of the Day of the Dead* features a Mexican family as they prepare for and enjoy the festival of the Day of the Dead. As Ancona wrote in *SAAS,* "It is a time for family reunions, meals, and an evening spent in the cemetery among flowers and candles on the decorated tombs of departed relatives." He continued, "In the streets, people parade in costume and recite satiric poems in front of their neighbors' houses." During the festival's three days (All Hallows Eve, All Saints Day, and All Souls Day), which honor the dead in a combination of Aztec and Catholic traditions, altars are decorated, children eat candy skulls, and Pablo takes time to remember his deceased grandmother. According to *Bulletin of the Center for Children's Books* contributor Roger Sutton, the "photography has the intimacy of high-quality family snapshots." Margaret A. Bush concluded of *Pablo Remembers* in *Horn Book* that the "beautiful book" serves as a fitting "tribute to Mexican home life."

*The Piñata Maker/El piñatero* also focuses on life in Mexico, but its text is written in both Spanish and English. Ancona follows Don Ricardo Nuñez Gijon—better known as Tio Rico in the village—as he carefully crafts fantastic, delightful piñatas. Ancona's photos demonstrate how Tio Rico makes a paste out of old newspapers and paper bags, and then shapes the paste into the form of a carrot, swan, star, or other figure. The next series of photos demonstrates how Daniela, a young girl, chooses a piñata for her birthday party, and how her guests crack it open and spill the candy. "Ancona has created an authentic, detailed account of one aspect of Mexican culture which has particularly wide appeal to children," wrote Maeve Visser Knoth in *Horn Book.* According to Ann Welton in *School Library Journal,* the "balance between text and illustration is masterful."

One problem Ancona had once he had created *Pablo Remembers* and *The Piñata Maker,* as he wrote in *SAAS,* was saying good-bye to the friends he had made. "The departure is very sad for me because these people have become part of my life and I don't know if I will ever see them again. . . . Someday I would like to take as much time as it would take to visit all the people I have gotten to know through my travels and books."

Ancona did not have to travel far to meet the people he photographed for *Powwow.* With color photographs and a thoughtful introduction, he provides what *School Library Journal* reviewer Lisa Mitten described as an "exquisite kaleidoscope of Native-American music, customs, and crafts." The Crow Fair in Montana provides an opportunity for people from various tribes, including the Crow, Lakota, Cheyenne, Cree, and Ojibwa, to

***In his photo-essay* Charro: The Mexican Cowboy *Ancona draws on his Mexican roots.*** 

dance traditional, fancy, grass, and jingle-dress dances competitively. Ancona follows the celebration as it progresses from parade to dance; he focuses his camera on the people watching the dances as well as on the dancers themselves. As Bush noted in *Horn Book,* in *Powwow* Ancona's camera records "the ironies of traditional cultural practice in the modern setting" and "conveys the universal appeal of spectacle and celebration."

Ancona returns to Mexican-American themes with *Fiesta U.S.A.,* a book dealing with four of the holidays most celebrated by Latinos in North America. Featured holidays include El Día de los Muertos, or Day of the Dead; Los Matachines, celebrated on New Year's Day; La Fiesta de los Reyes Magos, or Three Kings' Day; and Los Posadas, a re-enactment of Mary and Joseph's hunt for accommodations in Bethlehem. Ancona takes readers to a New Mexican pueblo in *Earth Daughter: Alicia of Acoma Pueblo,* an "attractive photo-essay," according to *Booklist* critic Stephanie Zvirin. Here young Alicia, who is learning to throw pottery, introduces readers to the simple life of her small town, which dates to the Spanish conquest. Traveling farther south to the Yucatan Peninsula and his own heritage, Ancona features Mayan culture in *Mayeros: A Yucatec Maya Family,* with color photographs of not only people of the region, but also of their ancient artwork and temples. "Ancona ably interweaves the history of . . . the ancient Mayeros with the daily life of their descendants," claimed Karen Morgan in *Booklist.* Frances E. Millhouser, writing in *School Library Journal,* praised Ancona's "involving text" as well as the manner in which he "seamlessly interspersed" more factual information into the narrative of the present-day family. Millhouser concluded, "Ancona provides a unique perspective on the vibrant survival of an enduring way of life."

More Hispanic themes are served up in *Fiesta Fireworks,* in which Ancona follows Caren and her family of fireworks makers in Tultepec, a town near Mexico City, as they create the fireworks display for the annual festival of San Juan de Dios. Phelan found that the book "captures the excitement of a fiesta," while *School Library Journal* critic Selene S. Vasquez called *Fiesta Fireworks* in which Ancona follows Caren and her family of fireworks makers in Tultepec, a town ne "an informative tribute to an enduring Mexican tradition." Ancona deals with a year in the life of a Mexican-American youth in San Francisco's Mission District in *Barrio: José's Neighborhood.* José strolls through this barrio and enjoys sights from a soccer game to a colorful mural as well as the traditional celebrations that mark the year. Annie Ayres, writing in *Booklist,* called the book "a fond and fascinating photo-essay focusing on the richness of the Latino experience." Similarly, Dina Sherman observed in *School Library Journal* that the "title successfully captures images of a particular place as seen through the eyes of a child." *Charro: The Mexican Cowboy* is set in Guadalajara, Mexico, on the day of a local rodeo, or *charreada.* Ancona focuses on the riding and roping skills of the cowboys who take part in the event, and his color photographs also highlight the scene, complete with mariachi bands and the fancy dress of both men and women. Helen Rosenberg, in *Booklist,* called Ancona's book "beautiful and informative" and predicted that it "will satisfy any reader interested in the ways of today's cowboys." A reviewer for *Publishers Weekly* praised Ancona's "energetic" photographs, while Ruth Semrau, writing in *School Library Journal,* similarly noted that "Ancona's pictures just keep getting better and better." Reviewing the book for the *Bulletin of the Center for Children's Books,* Deborah Stevenson concluded that "young buckaroos who enjoy a rodeo will be intrigued by this southern alternative."

Ancona deals with themes ranging from festivals to Caribbean children to Mexican field workers in *Carnaval, Cuban Kids,* and *Harvest.* In *Carnaval,* he documents celebrations in the Brazilian town of Olinda in an "appealing picture-book format" with "accessible, lively text," according to Sherman. Similarly, a contributor for *Hungry Mind Review* noted that "full-page photographs bring all the wonder and energy of carnival to life." Paul Kelsey, writing in *School Library Journal,* concluded that *Carnaval* is "an excellent introduction in an inviting and visually pleasing format." Ancona illustrates life in Cuba through his photos of students in *Cuban Kids,* "a very fine portrait of modern Cuba," according to *Booklist* critic Denia Hester, who also praised the "well-written text." Marilyn Long Graham, writing in *School Library Journal,* deemed *Cuban Kids* "upbeat and positive." With *Harvest,* "Ancona puts a face on Mexican migrant workers," explained Ilene Cooper in a *Booklist* review. With photos and text, he shows the hard work these people do, picking produce on various West Coast farms. At the same time, the author/illustrator also introduces young readers to a wide variety of crops and to the work of labor organizer Cesar Chavez.

Ancona travels from the farm to the world of art in *Murals, Walls That Sing,* which focuses on prehistoric wall paintings in France, Mexican church murals, and modern graffiti in Harlem. He not only deals with the use of materials in the execution of these very public works of art, but through a combination of close-up and wide-angle shots, lets readers see the work in relation to the architecture they adorn. Once again, Ancona's work elicited praise from reviewers. Susannah Price, writing in *School Library Journal,* called the title an "eye-catching book [that] just might whet the appetite of budding artists." In *Booklist* Gillian Engberg also felt that "the beautiful, sharp color photos and the unusual subject will attract plenty of browsers," while a *Kirkus Reviews* critic deemed *Murals, Walls That Sing* "a unique chronicle of our country's diversity and an engaging look at the connection between the arts and activism."

Ancona celebrates Mexico in the five-volume set, "Viva Mexico!," whose titles include *The Fiestas, The Folk*

***Cover of* Capoeira, *a nonfiction picture book focusing on a unique Brazilian sport that features both photos and text by Ancona.*** (Copyright © 2007 by George Ancona. Reproduced by permission of Lee & Low Books, Inc.)

*Arts, The Foods, The Past,* and *The People.* Blending clear color photos with his typical incisive text, Ancona views these various aspects of contemporary Mexican life in works that provide a "visual feast," as *Booklist* critic Annie Ayres commented of the series. Reviewing *The Past, The Foods,* and *The People* in *School Library Journal,* Coop Renner called the books "breezy and upbeat," while Mary Elam, writing in the same journal, found *The Fiestas* and *The Folk Arts* to be "beautifully illustrated volumes," that "contain a wealth of information."

Ancona turns to Latinos living in the United States in the eleven-volume "Somos Latinos" series. Each volume is told from a child's point of view and covers an aspect of daily life, including school, family, and friends. Ancona's photographs illustrate the text, sometimes supplemented with children's drawings. Ann Welton noted in *School Library Journal* that "from city to country life, schools to dances, Latino life is presented in its great variety."

*Capoeira: Game! Dance! Martial Art!* examines a martial art developed in Brazil that has become increasingly popular in the United States as well. A mixture of fighting, dance, and game, capoeira involves a series of movements set to music. Several schools of capoeira have evolved over the centuries, and Ancona explains the differences between them. His photographs show how capoeira students learn the basic moves of the sport. Alana Abbott, writing in *School Library Journal,* concluded: "Action-packed pictures of capoeiristas—people who play capoeira—in both the United States and Brazil make this an eye-catching title." A critic in *Kirkus Reviews* believed that the book was "for martial-arts fans, armchair travelers and anyone who wants to view a new way of having fun."

In *Self Portrait,* Ancona gives a brief overview of his life and career, taking readers behind the scenes of his work as a writer and illustrator of children's books. "Kids will learn about the entire process," according to the reviewer for *Children's Bookwatch.*

Aspiring photographers who admire Ancona's work may enjoy *My Camera,* which demonstrates how to use a 35mm camera like the one Ancona uses. He describes how to compose pictures, how to use the flash, and how to put together albums, photo essays, and storyboards. Ancona also includes a diagrammatic and textual explanation of how a camera works. "Evidence of Ancona's photographic talent and teaching ability radiates from every page," remarked Nancy E. Curran in the *School Library Journal.*

A thorough understanding of the technical issues involved in photography is just one aspect of any photographer's success. Ancona once revealed for *SATA* readers the character trait that has stimulated his achievements: "Curiosity is the biggest element in my work. . . . I think people are fascinating and I love to find myself in strange places, meeting people, getting to know them, and learning about them. This helps me to learn about myself. Photographing, filming, or writing about someone or someplace is my way of feeling alive and in touch with the world around me. I believe that work does this for many people. Whether it is baking bread, building a house, driving a truck, or singing a song, people reach each other each in their own way. I think that's what living is all about." In an interview with Rosalinda B. Barrera for *Language Arts,* Ancona elaborated on his career in creating children's books: "If I weren't doing books, I'd probably be in school teaching. I like kids, and I love watching them develop and explore. They are a wonderful community to photograph." He further explained: "So, doing children's books keeps me in touch and I can still apply my craft, my love for imagery, and share it with others."

On his home page, Ancona noted: "It is very gratifying to be invited to speak at schools and conferences around the country and abroad. It warms my heart to see my well-worn books in classrooms and libraries. When teachers praise my books and kids run up to me to tell me my books are 'cool,' I figure I must be doing something right."

## Biographical and Critical Sources

*BOOKS*

Ancona, George, *Self Portrait,* Robert C. Owen (New York, NY), 2007.

Ancona, George, essay in *Something about the Author Autobiography Series,* Volume 18, Gale (Detroit, MI), 1994.

*St. James Guide to Children's Writers,* 5th edition, St. James Press (Detroit, MI), 1999.

*PERIODICALS*

*Booklist,* July 1, 1976, Denise M. Wilms, review of *And What Do You Do?,* p. 1525; October 1, 1995, Annie Ayres, review of *Fiesta U.S.A.,* pp. 305-306; October 15, 1995, Stephanie Zvirin, review of *Earth Daughter: Alicia of Acoma Pueblo,* p. 397; April 15, 1997, Karen Morgan, review of *Mayeros: A Yucatec Maya Family,* p. 1420; April, 1998, Carolyn Phelan, review of *Fiesta Fireworks,* p. 1323; September 1, 1998, Ellen Mandel, review of *Let's Dance!,* p. 121; December 1, 1998, Annie Ayres, review of *Barrio: José's Neighborhood,* p. 662; May 15, 1999, Helen Rosenberg, review of *Charro: The Mexican Cowboy,* p. 1689; November 15, 1999, Chris Sherman, review of *Carnaval,* p. 617; December 15, 2000, Denia Hester, review of *Cuban Kids,* p. 811; January 1, 2002, Ilene Cooper, review of *Harvest,* pp. 846-847; March 1, 2002, review of "Viva Mexico!" series, pp. 1121-1132; April 15, 2003, Gillian Engberg, review of *Murals, Walls That Sing,* p. 1467; April 15, 2007, Gillian Engberg, review of *Capoeira: Game! Dance! Martial Art!,* p. 45.

*Black Issues Book Review,* May-June, 2007, review of *Capoeira,* p. 30.

*Bulletin of the Center for Children's Books,* January, 1983, Zena Sutherland, review of *Bananas,* p. 81; July-August, 1990, Betsy Hearne, review of *Riverkeeper,* p. 259; May, 1993, Roger Sutton, review of *Powwow,* p. 276; December, 1993, Roger Sutton, review of *Pablo Remembers: The Fiesta of the Day of the Dead,* p. 114; May, 1999, Deborah Stevenson, review of *Charro,* pp. 306-307.

*Childhood Education,* fall, 2003, Gina Hoagland, review of *Murals, Walls That Sing,* p. 38.

*Children's Bookwatch,* June, 2007, review of *Self Portrait.*

*Horn Book,* February, 1980, Kate M. Flanagan, review of *It's a Baby!,* p. 7; November-December, 1989, Hanna B. Zeiger, review of *Handtalk Zoo,* p. 775; May-June, 1990, Mary M. Burns, review of *Riverkeeper,* p. 345; May-June, 1993, Margaret A. Bush, review of *Powwow,* p. 343; March-April, 1994, Margaret A. Bush, review of *Pablo Remembers,* pp. 213-214; July-August, 1994, Maeve Visser Knoth, review of *The Piñata Maker/El piñatero,* p. 469; November-December, 1995, Elizabeth S. Watson, review of *Fiesta U.S.A.,* pp. 728-729; May-June, 1998, Margaret A. Bush, review of *Fiesta Fireworks,* pp. 353-354.

*Hungry Mind Review,* fall, 1999, review of *Carnaval,* p. 34.

*Junior Literary Guild,* September, 1979, interview with Ancona; October, 1987-March, 1988, review of *Turtle Watch,* p. 25.

*Kirkus Reviews,* March 15, 2003, review of *Murals, Walls That Sing,* p. 458; May 1, 2007, review of *Capoeira;* June 15, 2008, review of *Join Hands: The Ways We Celebrate Life.*

*Language Arts,* October, 1997, Rosalinda B. Barrera, "Profile—George Ancona: Photographer and Writer," pp. 477-481.

*New York Times Book Review,* January 19, 1975, John S. Radosta, review of *Monsters on Wheels,* p. 8.

*Publishers Weekly,* July 19, 1985, review of *Helping Out,* p. 53; June 7, 1999, review of *Charro,* p. 85; December 20, 1999, review of *Carnaval,* p. 82.

*School Library Journal,* September, 1976, Andy Ward, review of *And What Do You Do?,* p. 109; January, 1983, Terry Lawhead, review of *Bananas,* pp. 69-70; February, 1984, Connie Tyrrell Burns, review of *Monster Movers,* p. 65; October, 1987, Karey Wehner, review of *Turtle Watch,* p. 131; October, 1989, Susan Nemeth McCarthy, review of *Handtalk Zoo,* pp. 99-100; February, 1993, Nancy E. Curran, review of *My Camera,* p. 95; April, 1993, Lisa Mitten, review of *Powwow,* pp. 125-126; April, 1994, Ann Welton, review of *The Piñata Maker/El piñatero,* p. 116; November, 1995, Rose Zertuche Trevino, review of *Fiesta U.S.A.,* p. 136; December, 1995, Darcy Schild, review of *Earth Daughter,* p. 94; June, 1997, Frances E. Millhouser, review of *Mayeros,* p. 105; March, 1998, Selene S. Vasquez, review of *Fiesta Fireworks,* p. 191; November, 1998, Kit Vaughan, review of *Let's Dance!,* p. 101; December, 1998, Dina Sherman, review of *Barrio,* p. 99; June, 1999, Ruth Semrau, review of *Charro,* p. 110; February, 2000, Paul Kelsey, review of *Carnaval,* p. 107; January, 2001, Marilyn Long Graham, review of *Cuban Kids,* p. 112; February, 2002, Mary Elam, reviews of *The Folk Arts* and *The Fiestas,* pp. 138-139; March, 2002, Coop Renner, reviews of *The Foods, The Past,* and *The People.* pp. 240-241; April, 2002, Louise L. Sherman, review of *Harvest,* p. 162; July, 2002, Francisca Goldsmith, review of *Miguel Lost and Found in the Palace,* p. 123; May, 2003, Susannah Price, review of *Murals, Walls That Sing,* p. 161; May, 2005, Ann Welton, reviews of *Mi barrio/My Neighborhood, Mi casa/My House, Mi escuela/My School, Mi familia/My Family,* and *Mis amigos/My Friends,* p. 118; February, 2006, Maria Otero-Boisvert, reviews of *Mi musica/My Music, Mis abuelos/My Grandparents, Mis comidas/My Foods, Mis fiestas/My Celebrations, Mis juegos/My Games,* and *Mis quehaceres/My Chores,* p. 126; June, 2007, Alana Abbott, review of *Capoeira,* p. 129.

*ONLINE*

*George Ancona Home Page,* http://www.georgeancona.com (August 12, 2008).

*Scholastic Author Studies Web site,* http://www2.scholastic.com/ (May 22, 2003), interview with Ancona.

* * *

# ANGEL, Ann 1952-

## Personal

Born 1952, in WI; married, husband's name, Jeff; children: four. *Education:* Mount Mary College, B.A. (education), 1975; Marquette University, M.A. (journalism); Vermont College of Fine Arts, M.F.A. (writing), 1999. *Hobbies and other interests:* Cooking, traveling.

## Addresses

*Home*—WI. *Office*—Mount Mary College, 2900 N. Menomonee River Pkwy., Milwaukee, WI 53222-4597. *E-mail*—aangel@aol.com.

## Career

Writer, journalist, and educator. *Milwaukee Sentinel,* Milwaukee, WI, reporter; Mount Mary College, Milwaukee, assistant professor of English, 1989—. Has also worked as a junior-high-school teacher.

## Member

Society of Children's Book Writers and Illustrators.

## Awards, Honors

Arthur Tofte Juvenile Book Award, Council for Wisconsin Writers, 1989, for *John Glenn: Space Pioneer.*

## Writings

*FICTION*

*Real for Sure Sister,* illustrated by Joanne Bowring, Perspectives Press (Ft. Wayne, IN), 1988.

(Editor) *Such a Pretty Face: Short Stories about Beauty,* Amulet Books (New York, NY), 2007.

*NONFICTION*

*John Glenn: Space Pioneer,* Fawcett Columbine (New York, NY), 1990.

*Lech Walesa: Champion of Freedom for Poland,* Gareth Stevens (Milwaukee, WI), 1992.

*Louis Pasteur: Leading the Way to a Healthier World,* Gareth Stevens (Milwaukee, WI), 1992.

(Editor) *America in the Twentieth Century: 1900-1909,* Marshall Cavendish (North Bellmore, NY), 1995.

(Editor) *America in the Twentieth Century: 1910-1919,* Marshall Cavendish (North Bellmore, NY), 1995.

*Milwaukee: City Smart Guidebooks,* John Muir Publications (Santa Fe, NM), 1997.

*Robert Cormier: Author of The Chocolate War,* Enslow Publishers (Berkeley Heights, NJ), 2008.

*Amy Tan: Weaver of Asian-American Tales,* Enslow Publishers (Berkeley Heights, NJ), 2009.

Editor of "Sight and Sounds" books, Western Publishing, 1998-99; writer and editor for Raintree Books and Gareth Stevens. Contributor to periodicals, including *ALAN Review.* Contributing editor, *MetroParent* (Milwaukee, WI).

## Sidelights

Ann Angel, a former journalist who teaches writing at Mount Mary College, is the author of several works of nonfiction, including biographies of Robert Cormier and Amy Tan. Angel also served as the editor of *Such a Pretty Face: Short Stories about Beauty,* a collection featuring tales from such acclaimed young-adult writers as Chris Lynch and Jacqueline Woodson. "Writing and reading for me are all about finding connections," Angel stated in an essay on the *Wordswimmer* Web log. "This is probably why anthologies have always fascinated me. Each anthology, usually centered on a single and specific theme, allows a reader to explore the world from a variety of perspectives. Anthologies let us hear the many voices that inhabit the world. They show us life through the eyes and ears, the senses and thoughts, of a variety of characters."

*Such a Pretty Face* "challenges the myths and expectations surrounding the stronghold of physical beauty," observed *School Library Journal* contributor Dianne P. Tucillo. In "Bad Hair Day," a humorous story by Lauren Myracle, a homecoming queen sprouts an unruly chin hair, while Tim Wynne-Jones' "Bella in Five Acts" concerns an undersized boy's efforts to save a suicidal girl. "In each story," remarked *Journal of Adolescent & Adult Literacy* reviewer Candis McGovern, "different and identifiable characters are confronted with having to make their own definition of beauty in the face of others' standards and, furthermore, are forced to look within for the truth of their own personal beauty." "The stories encompass a range of mood and style, but all address issues of self-discovery and looking beneath the surface," Lauren Adams similarly noted in *Booklist.*

***Cover of Ann Angel's* Such a Pretty Face*, which contains stories that force readers to reconsider the cost of physical beauty.*** (Amulet Books, 2007. Reproduced by permission.)

## Biographical and Critical Sources

*PERIODICALS*

*Booklist,* July 1, 2007, Gillian Engberg, review of *Such a Pretty Face: Short Stories about Beauty,* p. 32.

*Horn Book,* May-June, 2007, Lauren Adams, review of *Such a Pretty Face,* p. 276.

*Journal of Adolescent & Adult Literacy,* March, 2008, Candis McGovern, review of *Such a Pretty Face,* p. 521.

*Kirkus Reviews,* May 1, 2007, review of *Such a Pretty Face.*

*School Library Journal,* January, 2008, Dianne P. Tucillo, review of *Such a Pretty Face,* p. 114.

*ONLINE*

*Ann Angel Home Page,* http://www.annangelwriter.com (August 10, 2008).

*Ann Angel Web log,* http://www.annangelwriter.com/blog/ (August 10, 2008).

*Cynsations Web site,* http://cynthialeitichsmith.blogspot.com/ (August 29, 2007), Cynthia Leitich Smith, "Author Interview: Ann Angel on *Such a Pretty Face: Short Stories about Beauty.*"

*Wordswimmer Web log,* http://wordswimmer.blogspot.com/ (May 5, 2007), "One Writer's Process: Ann Angel."

* * *

## AUTH, Tony 1942-
## (William Anthony Auth, Jr.)

### Personal

Born May 7, 1942, in Akron, OH; son of William Anthony (an executive with Firestone Tire and Rubber Co.) and Julia Kathleen (a homemaker) Auth; married Eliza Drake (an artist), August 28, 1982; children: Kathleen. *Education:* University of California, Los Angeles, B.A., 1965. *Hobbies and other interests:* "I read fiction for enjoyment. I'm a big fan of children's books, and also science fiction and fantasy. I like Ursula Le Guinn, among others. I swim, travel, watch movies, read books, and spend time with friends."

### Addresses

*Home and office*—Philadelphia, PA. *Office*—Philadelphia Inquirer, 400 N. Broad St., Philadelphia, PA 19130. *Agent*—Toni Mendez, 141 E. 56th St., New York, NY 10022. *E-mail*—tauth@phillynews.com.

## Career

Rancho Los Amigos Hospital, Downey, CA, chief medical illustrator, 1964-70; *Philadelphia Inquirer,* Philadelphia, PA, editorial cartoonist, 1971—; illustrator of children's books, 1984—.

## Member

Association of American Editorial Cartoonists.

## Awards, Honors

Overseas Press Club Award, 1975, 1976, 1985, all for editorial cartoons; Pulitzer Prize, Society of Professional Journalists Award, Sigma Delta Chi Award, and Columbia University Trustees Award, all 1976, all for editorial cartooning; Herblock Prize, 2005.

## Writings

*SELF-ILLUSTRATED*

*Behind the Lines: Cartoons,* Houghton Mifflin (Boston, MA), 1977.
*The Gang of Eight,* Faber & Faber (Boston, MA), 1985.
*Lost in Space: The Reagan Years,* Andrews McMeel (Kansas City, MO), 1988.
*Sleeping Babies,* Golden Book (New York, NY), 1989.

*ILLUSTRATOR*

Stephen Manes, *That Game from Outer Space: The First Strange Thing That Happened to Oscar Noodleman,* Dutton (New York, NY), 1983.
Nathan Zimelman, *Mean Murgatroyd and the Ten Cats,* Dutton (New York, NY), 1984.
Chaim Potok, *The Tree of Here,* Alfred A. Knopf (New York, NY), 1993.
Linda K. Harris, *Kids' Talk,* Andrews McMeel (Kansas City, MO), 1993.
Chaim Potok, *The Sky of Now,* Alfred A. Knopf (New York, NY), 1995.
Barry Yourgrau, *My Curious Uncle Dudley,* Candlewick Press (Cambridge, MA), 2004.
Daniel Manus Pinkwater, *The Hoboken Chicken Emergency,* Atheneum Books for Young Readers (New York, NY), 2007.
Florence Parry Heide, *A Promise Is a Promise,* Candlewick Press (Cambridge, MA), 2007.
Joan Levine, *Topsy-Turvy Bedtime,* Candlewick Press (Cambridge, MA), 2008.
Douglas Rees, *Uncle Pirate,* Margaret K. McElderry Books (New York, NY), 2008.

## Sidelights

Winner of the Pulitzer Prize for editorial cartooning, Tony Auth studied biological illustration at the University of California, Los Angeles, and worked as a medical illustrator before he became a political cartoonist, inspired by the Vietnam War. "In my youth I had always thought that I would probably be a cartoonist," he once stated, "but I was totally apolitical, so that throughout high school and college the cartoons I was drawing were not political in nature at all, but social commentary. It was very rewarding suddenly to find that the same talents I was using in medical illustration, where I was in fact doing a lot of cartooning, could be turned toward politics."

"I became interested in political cartoons when I was in the sixth or seventh grade," Auth once recalled, "and started noticing drawings by Bruce Russell and Karl Hubenthal who were in Los Angeles at the time. But I lost interest because I was only superficially interested in politics and had no real depth of knowledge. Later, I was influenced by people like Paul Conrad, Pat Oliphant, Ronald Searle, as well as the children's book illustrators Tomi Ungerer and Maurice Sendak. I find there's a lot of overlap; Ernest Shepard's work and Hans-Georg Rauch's work have been very significant to me."

*Behind the Lines: Cartoons,* Auth's first book, was published in 1977. He soon became interested in doing illustrations for children's books. "I got my agent in New York to pick out some of my cartoons that are in the style I would like to use for children's books, and she approached various publishers. I'd nursed the desire for a while and done a lot of watercolors, trying to prepare myself for this kind of work."

Auth's illustrations for children's books, which include collaborations with Chaim Potock, Daniel M. Pinkwater, and Florence Parry Heide, have won praise from reviewers. He worked with Potok on two books, *The Tree of Here,* and *The Sky of Now.* Reviewing the latter title, which is a story about a boy's fear of heights, Julie Corsaro noted in *Booklist* that Auth's pastel wash-and-line pictures "are spare yet evocative." In Nathan Zimelman's *Mean Murgatroyd and the Ten Cats,* Auth brings to life the tale of a cat-hating dog and the little girl who foils him. Olga Richard and Donnarae MacCann, reviewing for the *Wilson Library Bulletin,* cited the book's illustrations as "an example of how humor and stylistic originality can blend. Auth's art is spontaneous, fresh, bold. He combines color and line in a unique manner" that "brings tremendous action and energy to the illustration."

In *My Curious Uncle Dudley,* Auth teams with Barry Yourgrau to tell of Duncan Peckle, a young boy who is sent to spend the summer with his beloved Uncle Dudley. Dudley not only tells wildly entertaining stories, but he also claims to practice real magic. It takes Duncan some time to see through Uncle Dudley's imaginative claims. "Witty, cartoonlike illustrations support the nostalgic feel of the story," Debbie Carton wrote in *Booklist,* the critic adding that Auth's art "captures the innocence and quiet of a small rural town

***Tony Auth's engaging cartoon art pairs with a humorous story by Florence Parry Heide in* A Promise Is a Promise.** (Illustrations copyright © 2007 by Tony Auth. Reproduced by permission of the publisher Candlewick Press, Inc., Somerville, MA.)

from times past." A critic for *Kirkus Reviews* found that "Auth's pen-and-ink illustrations help to ground the story in time . . . and offer amusing glimpses of characters and events." "Auth's illustrations complement the fun and whimsy of the story," according to Edith Ching in *School Library Journal.*

Auth has also illustrated Joan Levine's *Topsy-Turvy Bedtime,* in which young Arathusela must put her stubborn parents to bed. The adults want to stay up longer to watch television, get a drink of water, and have stories read to them, and their continuing efforts to stay up quickly test the girl's patience. After she finally puts them to sleep, Arathusela finds that she is lonely all by herself. "Auth's fluidly rendered line-and-watercolor cartoon characters . . . reflect a wide range of emotion—from surprise to frustration to glee," wrote Patricia Austin in *Booklist.*

Auth encourages budding cartoonists when he feels they have talent. "I try to be as honest with them as I possibly can," he explained. "A lot of kids . . . are under the illusion that they're very talented because their parents or their friends have been saying, 'Boy, that's pretty good.' They haven't been subjected to any sort of professional criticism at all. So I try to disillusion them as kindly as I can. . . . On the other hand, occasionally someone will come through who is very talented, and I encourage him or her to keep working on whatever I sense needs work. A lot of people like the idea of being a cartoonist but haven't really decided what kind of cartoonist. They don't realize that cartooning is very specialized. So I try to find out where their inclination is, find out what direction it might lead them, and give them appropriate advice."

"Cartooning is an excellent medium for making one point at a time," Auth once commented of his field, "and the point is usually one that I anticipate will provoke a reaction of sadness or joy or laughter or nostalgia or any number of things . . . . I tend to think of information as being a torrent of particles: some of it is public relations material; some of it is half-truths; some honest. Everybody's putting out information, and people get subjected to a torrent of it and then form an opinion of what's going on. I contribute one particle a day to the torrent."

Auth feels it is important to be emotionally involved in an issue to do a good cartoon. "If you don't feel strongly about what you're drawing, I think the work shows that lack of interest, and that's what we call hack work. You're not into it anymore; you're cranking out stuff because you have a job.

## Biographical and Critical Sources

*PERIODICALS*

*Booklist,* January 1, 1996, Julie Corsaro, review of *The Sky of Now,* p. 848; September 15, 2004, Debbie Carton, review of *My Curious Uncle Dudley,* p. 246; June 1, 2008, Patricia Austin, review of *Topsy-Turvy Bedtime,* p. 92.

*Kirkus Reviews,* July 15, 2004, review of *My Curious Uncle Dudley,* p. 695; May 1, 2007, review of *A Promise Is a Promise.*

*Publishers Weekly,* August 30, 1993, review of *The Tree of Here,* p. 96; November 27, 1995, review of *The Sky of Now,* p. 69; July 26, 2004, review of *My Curious Uncle Dudley,* p. 55; May 21, 2007, review of *A Promise Is a Promise,* p. 53.

*School Library Journal,* January, 2005, Edith Ching, review of *My Curious Uncle Dudley,* p. 100; June, 2007, Catherine Callegari, review of *A Promise Is a Promise,* p. 107.

*Wilson Library Bulletin,* May, 1985, Olga Richard and Donnarae MacCann, review of *Mean Murgatroyd and the Ten Cats,* p. 609.

*ONLINE*

*The Galleries at Moore Web site,* http://www.thegalleriesatmoore.org/ (August 20, 2008), "Tony Auth."*

* * *

## AUTH, William Anthony, Jr.

See AUTH, Tony

# B

## BAKER, Barbara 1947-

### Personal
Born 1947.

### Addresses
*Home and office*—New York, NY. *E-mail*—BarbaraABaker@yahoo.com.

### Career
Writer and educator. Teaches at a day care center in New York, NY.

### Writings

*Third Grade Is Terrible,* illustrated by Roni Shepherd, Dutton (New York, NY), 1989.
*N-O Spells No!,* illustrated by Nola Langner Malone, Dutton (New York, NY), 1990.
*Oh, Emma,* illustrated by Catherine Stock, Dutton (New York, NY), 1991.
*Staying with Grandmother,* illustrated by Judith Byron Schachner, Dutton (New York, NY), 1994.
*The William Problem,* illustrated by Ann Iosa, Dutton (New York, NY), 1994.
*Little Martin,* illustrated by Vera Rosenberry, Dutton (New York, NY), 2003.
*Anna's Book,* illustrated by Catharine O'Neill, Dutton (New York, NY), 2004.
*Anna Shares,* illustrated by Catharine O'Neill, Dutton (New York, NY), 2004.

*"DIGBY AND KATE" SERIES*

*Digby and Kate,* illustrated by Marsha Winborn, Dutton (New York, NY), 1988.
*Digby and Kate Again,* illustrated by Marsha Winborn, Dutton (New York, NY), 1989.
*Digby and Kate and the Beautiful Day,* illustrated by Marsha Winborn, Dutton (New York, NY), 1998.
*Digby and Kate 1, 2, 3,* illustrated by Marsha Winborn, Dutton (New York, NY), 2004.

*"SATURDAY" SERIES*

*One Saturday Morning,* illustrated by Kate Duke, Dutton (New York, NY), 1994.

***Cover of Barbara Baker's* Digby and Kate 1, 2, 3, *featuring artwork by Marsha Winborn.*** (Illustration copyright © 2004 by Marsha Winborn. Reproduced by permission of Dutton Children's Books, a division of Penguin Putnam Books for Young Readers.)

*One Saturday Afternoon,* illustrated by Kate Duke, Dutton (New York, NY), 1999.

*One Saturday Evening,* illustrated by Kate Duke, Dutton (New York, NY), 2007.

## Sidelights

Barbara Baker is the author of a number of well-received chapter books and easy readers. Baker's "Digby and Kate" series centers on the relationship between a frisky dog named Digby and his neighbor and best friend, Kate, a cat. The opening work in the series, *Digby and Kate,* collects six tales in which the pair prepares lunch together, paints a room in Digby's house, and exchanges gifts. Kimberly Olson Fakih, writing in *Publishers Weekly,* stated that "this well-produced book is packed with child appeal." In *Digby and Kate 1, 2, 3,* the companions learn to resolve simple conflicts, such as the one that arises when Digby insists that Kate should make friends with a mouse instead of catching him. The five stories "have a simple narrative appeal that will engage beginning readers," noted *School Library Journal* contributor Robyn Walker.

A family of bears is the focus of Baker's "Saturday" series of books. In *One Saturday Morning,* the author introduces Mama and Papa Bear and their four lively youngsters, each of whom has a busy day planned. "Beginning readers will enjoy the humor of familiar family situations," remarked *Booklist* reviewer Chris Sherman. *One Saturday Afternoon* also follows the fun-filled activities of Jack, Lily, Daisy, and Rose Bear. "Short sentences, concise chapters, and the right amount of repetition" make *One Saturday Afternoon* appropriate for early readers, observed Susan Dove Lempke in *Booklist.* Mama and Papa Bear try to prepare their young ones for bed in *One Saturday Evening.* Erika Qualls, writing in *School Library Journal,* described the tale as "very satisfying," and *Booklist* critic Gillian Engberg called the work "a strong choice for the just-literate crowd."

In *Staying with Grandmother,* a "warm and comforting" story according to *School Library Journal* critic Sharon McElmeel, young Claire approaches an extending stay at her grandma's house with trepidation until she adjusts to her new surroundings. *Little Martin,* another easy reader, concerns a rambunctious preschooler who delights in making messes and confounding his mother. Though some reviewers found the toddler's actions unappealing, a *Kirkus Reviews* contributor observed that "Martin is a reprobate, fielding the consequences of his acts like a major leaguer, then tossing them right back at you."

A lovable but strong-willed toddler is the subject of *Anna's Book* and *Anna Shares,* two picture books written by Baker. In the former, Anna chooses an unusual reading partner after her mother must tend to the laundry, and in the latter, the little girl spoils a play date when she refuses to share a plate of cookies. Carolyn Phelan, writing in *Booklist,* praised the "simple narrative appeal and visual charm" of the stories, and *School Library Journal* reviewer Martha Topol commented that the works "are simple and repetitive and cover topics that will have meaning for the intended audience."

***Artist Kate Duke teams up with Baker and creates watercolor images for* One Saturday Afternoon.** (Illustration copyright © 1999 by Kate Duke. Reproduced by permission of Puffin Books, a division of Penguin Putnam Books for Young Readers.)

In the chapter book *Oh, Emma,* a nine year old has a difficult time dealing with her younger brother and sister. "The depiction of the siblings' interaction is realistic and well conveyed," Ruth Semma wrote in *School Library Journal.* Third-grader Liza Farmer finds herself aligned with the school nerd in *The William Problem,* another chapter book. "Baker's short sentences and familiar situations should appeal to new readers," Ilene Cooper stated in a characteristic review of the author's work for *Booklist.*

## Biographical and Critical Sources

*PERIODICALS*

*Booklist,* October 1, 1994, Ilene Cooper, review of *The William Problem,* p. 325; January 1, 1995, Chris Sherman, review of *One Saturday Morning,* p. 827; May

15, 1999, Susan Dove Lempke, review of *One Saturday Afternoon,* p. 1704; February 1, 2004, Carolyn Phelan, reviews of *Anna's Book* and *Anna Shares,* p. 978; September 1, 2004, Carolyn Phelan, review of *Digby and Kate 1, 2, 3,* p. 128; July 1, 2007, Gillian Engberg, review of *One Saturday Evening,* p. 66.

*Kirkus Reviews,* February 1, 2003, review of *Little Martin,* p. 226; December 15, 2003, reviews of *Anna's Book* and *Anna Shares,* p. 1445; July 1, 2007, review of *One Saturday Evening.*

*Publishers Weekly,* March 11, 1998, Kimberly Olson Fakih, review of *Digby and Kate,* p. 103; January 6, review of *Little Martin,* p. 59; March 1, 2004, "Toddler Times," reviews of *Anna's Book* and *Anna Shares,* p. 71.

*School Library Journal,* November, 1998, Sharron McElmeel, review of *Digby and Kate,* p. 83; February, 1992, Ruth Semrau, review of *Oh, Emma,* p. 70; May, 1994, Sharron McElmeel, review of *Staying with Grandmother,* p. 84; November, 1994, Gale W. Sherman, review of *One Saturday Morning,* p. 72; March, 2003, Elaine Lesh Morgan, review of *Little Martin,* p. 176; February, 2004, Martha Topol, review of *Anna's Shares,* p. 102; August, 2004, Robyn Walker, review of *Digby and Kate 1, 2, 3,* p. 82; August, 2007, Erika Qualls, review of *One Saturday Evening,* p. 76.

*ONLINE*

*Barbara Baker Web log,* http://barbarabakerbooks.blogcity.com/ (August 10, 2008).*

* * *

## BARRON, T.A. 1952-
## (Thomas Archibald Barron, Tom Barron)

### Personal

Born March 26, 1952, in Boston, MA; son of Archibald (a hotel operator) and Gloria (a geologist and museum founder) Barron; married Currie Cabot; children: three boys, two girls. *Education:* Princeton University, B.A., 1974; Oxford University, graduated 1978; Harvard University, M.B.A. and J.D., both 1982. *Hobbies and other interests:* Reading, traveling, hiking, "playing any sports that my kids like to play."

### Addresses

*Office*—545 Pearl St., Boulder, CO 80302.

### Career

Author and environmentalist. Worked variously as president of a venture capital firm, general partner of Sierra Ventures, and chairman of Swiss Army Corporation, New York, NY, until 1989; full-time writer, 1989—. Founder, Princeton University Environmental Studies Program; former trustee, Princeton University; trustee, Nature Conservancy of Colorado. Presenter at workshops in environmental preservation and restoration for Wilderness Society and other groups; speaker at conferences on literature, education, and the environment as well as at schools and libraries.

### Member

Wilderness Society (member of board).

### Awards, Honors

Best Books of the Year designation, *Parents* magazine, 1992, Best Books for the Teen Age designation, New York Public Library, 1993, and Young Adult Choice listee, International Reading Association, 1994, all for *The Ancient One;* Colorado Book Award, 1995, Texas Lone Star Book Award, 1997, and Utah Book Award, Children's Literature Association of Utah, 1998, both for *The Merlin Effect;* Robert Marshall Award, Wilderness Society, 1997, for environmental work; Not Just for Children Anymore Award, Children's Book Council, 1997, and Oppenheim Portfolio Gold Award, 2000, both for *The Lost Years of Merlin;* Not Just for Children Anymore Award, 1998, for *The Seven Songs of Merlin;* Best Fantasy Books listee, *Booklist,* 1999, for *The Fires of Merlin;* Colorado Book Award nominee, 2000, for *The Mirror of Merlin, The Wings of Merlin,* and *The Fires of Merlin;* Nautilus Visionary Book Award Grand Prize, 2001, and Bank Street College of Education Best Books designation, 2002, both for *The Wings of Merlin;* Bank Street College of Education Best Book designation, 2002, and Massachusetts Children's Book Award nominee, 2004, both for *Tree Girl;* Colorado Book Award nominee, and Nautilus Visionary Book Award Grand Prize, both 2005, both for *Child of the Dark Prophecy;* Nautilus Visionary Book Award finalist, and Arkansas Diamond Award nomination, both 2005, both for *High as a Hawk;* Colorado Book Award finalist, and Nautilus Visionary Book Award Grand Prize, both 2007, both for *The Eternal Flame;* Colorado Book Award finalist, Nautilus Visionary Book Award Gold Medal, and *Storytelling World* Award for Young Readers, all 2008, all for *The Day the Stones Walked*; Wilderness Society award for conservation work.

### Writings

*FOR CHILDREN*

*Where Is Grandpa?* (picture book), illustrated by Chris K. Soenpiet, Philomel (New York, NY), 2000.

*Tree Girl* (middle-grade novel), Philomel (New York, NY), 2001.

*High as a Hawk: A Brave Girl's Historic Climb* (picture book), Philomel (New York, NY), 2004.

*The Day the Stones Walked: A Tale of Easter Island* (picture book), illustrated by William Low, Philomel (New York, NY), 2007.

*Basilgarrad: Merlin's Dragon* (first volume in "Merlin's Dragon" trilogy), Philomel (New York, NY), 2008.

Contributor to periodicals, including *Book Links, Parents',* and *Voice of Youth Advocates.* Some work appears under name Tom Barron.

Author's books have been translated into several languages, including German and Spanish.

*"ADVENTURES OF KATE" SERIES*

*Heartlight,* Philomel (New York, NY), 1990.
*The Ancient One,* Philomel (New York, NY), 1992.
*The Merlin Effect,* Philomel (New York, NY), 1994.

*"LOST YEARS OF MERLIN" SERIES*

*The Lost Years of Merlin* (also see below), Philomel (New York, NY), 1996.
*The Seven Songs of Merlin* (also see below), Philomel (New York, NY, 1997.
*The Fires of Merlin* (also see below), Philomel (New York, NY), 1998.
*The Mirror of Merlin,* Philomel (New York, NY), 1999.
*The Wings of Merlin,* Philomel (New York, NY), 2000.
*A T.A. Barron Collection* (omnibus; includes *The Lost Years of Merlin, The Seven Songs of Merlin,* and *The Fires of Merlin*), Philomel Books (New York, NY), 2001.

*"GREAT TREE OF AVALON" TRILOGY*

*Child of the Dark Prophecy,* Philomel (New York, NY), 2004.
*Shadow on the Stars,* Philomel (New York, NY), 2005.
*The Eternal Flame,* Philomel (New York, NY), 2006.

*OTHER*

*To Walk in Wilderness: A Rocky Mountain Journal* (adult nonfiction), photographs by John Fielder, Westcliffe Publishers (Englewood, CO), 1993.
(With Enos Mills and John Fiedler) *Rocky Mountain National Park: A 100-Year Perspective* (adult nonfiction) , photographs by Mills and Fielder, Westcliffe Publishers (Englewood, CO), 1995.
*The Hero's Trail: A Guide for a Heroic Life,* Philomel (New York, NY), 2002.

## Adaptations

The "Lost Years of Merlin" books were released on audio cassette by Listening Library, beginning 2001; the "Great Tree of Avalon" books were released on audio cassette by Listening Library, beginning 2004.

## Sidelights

A popular, prolific American author of fiction for children and young adults as well as of informational books for adults, T.A. Barron is regarded as both a master storyteller and a gifted nature writer. As a fantasist, he has been compared favorably to such writers as J.R.R. Tolkien, T.H. White, Lloyd Alexander, and, especially, Madeleine L'Engle. Barron is perhaps best known as the author of the coming-of-age fantasy series "Adventures of Kate," "Lost Years of Merlin," "Great Tree of Avalon," and "Merlin's Dragon." In addition, he has received praise for his autobiographical picture book *Where Is Grandpa?,* which describes how a boy adjusts to the death of his beloved grandfather, and the inspiring *The Hero's Trail: A Guide for a Heroic Life.* In addition, Barron has been lauded for the prose and poetry he has contributed to the nature books *To Walk in Wilderness: A Rocky Mountain Journal* and *Rocky Mountain National Park: A 100-Year Perspective.*

Thematically, Barron is noted for addressing issues that relate directly to both his young audience and to the universal human condition. He explores such themes as the connections among people, cultures, and other forms of life; the ultimate meaning of existence; the power of love; death as part of a grand design; the bond between generations; the need to preserve the environment; and the acceptance of the light and darkness within ourselves. In the "Adventures of Kate," "Lost Years of Merlin," and "Great Tree of Avalon" series, he takes his young protagonists on both literal and figurative journeys. Each teen faces enormous—and often dangerous—obstacles that require him or her to make difficult, sometimes life-threatening, decisions. These choices lead ultimately to a greater sense of self-confidence and maturity as well as to a deeper sense of how each person can contribute to the world. As a writer, Barron characteristically favors a clear, lyrical prose style. He is commended for his use of descriptive language; for his creation of exciting plots which often include twists at the end; and for his inclusion of strong female and sensitive male characters. Although some observers have criticized Barron for overwriting, most critics applaud him as a talented storyteller whose well-crafted blend of adventure, fantasy, and spirituality has led to the creation of insightful, moving books.

Barron credits his parents and several of his teachers with fostering his love of nature and interest in traditional cultures. His father was owner and operator of the historic Alamo Hotel in Colorado Springs, and his first memory is being carried on his father's shoulders to an old chestnut tree near his home. In an article for *Book Links,* Barron wrote: "I remember him lifting me up to peer into a dark hole in the trunk. To my surprise, a family of baby raccoons, their eyes as bright as lanterns, peered back at me. Whenever I think of that man, I think of all the places that he shared. And the memories, like the eyes of those raccoons, are lantern-bright. Small wonder that, for me, place is far more than landscape." Barron would later use his father, and the man's passing, as the basis for *Where Is Grandpa?*

After the youngest of Barron's six brothers and sisters started school, his mother Gloria returned to college to study geology. She eventually founded the Touch Museum, a hands-on nature museum for children, at the Colorado School for the Deaf and Blind. To honor her efforts and her example, in 2001, Barron established the Gloria Barron Young Heroes Prize, an award that celebrates the young people of Colorado who make a major contribution to that state or to the world.

Although he enjoyed reading world mythology, sports stories, and biographies, Barron's earliest writings were nature journals; at the age of nine, for example, he wrote "Autobiography of a Big Tree," the story of the old chestnut tree in which the family of raccoons had lived that his father had shown him. When his family moved to a ranch, Barron continued writing outside under the ponderosa. In middle school, he wrote, illustrated, and published his own humor magazine, *The Idiot's Odyssey.*

Barron also enjoyed outdoor pursuits, especially hiking and camping. He joined the Boy Scouts of America, worked summers as a counselor at a local scout camp, and became an Eagle Scout. After winning a national speech competition sponsored by the Scouts, he was sent to Washington, DC, to meet the president of the United States. After graduating from high school, he attended Princeton University, where he continued to write. "Then," he wrote on his home page, "I encountered Tolkien, and a new world opened before my eyes." Barron founded two literary publications at Princeton. As a senior, he won the Pyne Prize, the university's highest honor for an undergraduate; the prize honors outstanding service to Princeton by one of its students. After winning a Rhodes scholarship, Barron set off for Oxford University in England.

At Oxford, Barron studied, but took time out to write stories and poems while sitting under an English oak that he dubbed "Merlin's Tree." He took a year off from school to travel, exploring the British Isles, riding the Trans-Siberian railway, going to the Arctic, living in Africa, India, and Nepal, and helping to build thatched roofs on homes in a remote Japanese village, among other adventures. After returning to Oxford, he wrote his first novel, and collected more than forty rejection letters for it. Once back in the United States, he enrolled in law school at Harvard University, hoping to become an environmental lawyer. He changed his mind, however, and earned his MBA, then moved to New York City to work as a venture capitalist, acquiring small and medium-sized businesses for his firm.

While working in New York, Barron married Currie Cabot, a woman whom he had met while cross-country skiing in the Catskill Mountains and with whom he has since raised five children. He also continued to write, even stopping to jot a few lines while running the Boston Marathon. He sent the manuscript of his first novel for young people, *Heartlight,* to L'Engle, the author who most influenced him and to whom he is often compared. L'Engle saw promise in the manuscript and passed it on to her agent. With the encouragement of his wife, in 1989 Barron resigned from his firm and moved his family to a Colorado ranch so that he could become a full-time writer. *Heartlight* was published the following year.

*Heartlight* became the first novel in Barron's "Adventures of Kate" series, and is followed by *The Ancient One* and *The Merlin Effect.* The series blends such elements as science fiction, history, mythology, metaphysics, and ecology into contemporary adventures that feature thirteen-year-old Kate Prancer Gordon, a courageous, resourceful teen. In *Heartlight,* Kate and her beloved grandfather, a renowned astrophysicist who has done research on the nature of light and its relationship to the human soul, travel to a distant galaxy by liberating their souls (or "heartlights") in order to find out why the Earth's sun is losing power. They discover that the star Trethonial, which should have become a black hole, has begun to drain the energy from other suns in order to survive. Kate and her grandfather also battle a demonic force that is seeking eternal life. The Darkness, a dark cloud, fights with the Pattern, the force that keeps the universe in balance, before order is restored. A critic in *Publishers Weekly* wrote that *Heartlight* "shines as a bold, original effort worthy of repeat readings."

In *The Ancient One,* Kate and her great-aunt Melanie work to save a forest of redwood trees from being cut down; the forest is located in an Oregon logging town established on Native American holy ground. After Kate is transported 500 years into the past, she encounters the Halamis, a tribe of Native Americans who are facing a volcanic eruption that will wipe them out. The eruption is being caused by Gashra, an evil being that wants to rule the world. Kate enlists the help of the Ancient One, the oldest living tree in the forest, to save the Halami and the redwood forest and return to her own time. Kate must risk her life to restore balance; in addition, she must learn to become a tree. She succeeds, sending Gashra back into the earth, but returns to the present just in time to see a logger felling the Ancient One right before a protective injunction is put into place.

In the final book of the series, *The Merlin Effect,* Kate accompanies her father, a leading Arthurian scholar, to the coast of Baja, California where he hopes to locate one of Merlin's lost treasures, a drinking horn that has powers of immortality and is believed to be on a sunken Spanish galleon. After Kate saves a whale that gets tangled in the expedition's equipment, she is sucked into a whirlpool that takes her to the ocean's floor. She and her companions engage in a battle with the enchantress Nimue and her army of sea demons, who want to use the horn for their own evil purposes. In order to save herself, her father, his friends, and the Horn of Merlin, Kate must find a way to regain her free will. While noting that Barron's plot is at times "too incred-

*Cover of* The Merlin Effect, *the closing volume of T.A. Barron's "Adventures of Kate" series, featuring artwork by Yvonne Gilbert.* (Ace Books, 2004. Used by permission of Penguin Group (USA) Inc.)

ible," *Booklist* critic Sally Estes praised *The Merlin Effect* as a "fast-paced adventure tale" that is "steeped in Arthurian legend."

In the "Lost Years of Merlin" series, which includes *The Lost Years of Merlin, The Seven Songs of Merlin, The Fires of Merlin, The Mirror of Merlin,* and *The Wings of Merlin,* Barron focuses on the teenage years of the legendary magician, a period that is not represented in traditional Arthurian literature. He describes Merlin's search for identity and inner balance as well as his adventures with both human characters—such as Ector, the boy destined to become King Arthur—and supernatural characters, such as spirits, ogres, dwarves, and shape-shifters. In an interview with Ken Trainer in the *Chicago Parent,* Barron said that Merlin is "a boy who has enormous struggles to learn the basic lessons of wisdom, truth, humility, power, and love. Merlin's journey is a metaphor for the hero that's in every one of us." Writing on his home page, Barron concluded that Merlin's story "is, in truth, a metaphor—for the idea that all of us, no matter how weak or confused, have a magical person down inside, just waiting to be discovered."

In the series opener, twelve-year-old Emrys is washed up on a Welsh beach with a woman who claims to be his mother. The boy has lost all of his memories, including knowing his real name; his mother, the witch Branwen, refuses to tell him about his past. Drawing on the magical powers he learns that he has, Emrys defends Branwen against a vicious young mob by burning its leader, Dinatius, through telekinesis. When he leaps into the fire to save the boy, Emrys loses his own eyesight and vows never again to use his powers in anger. After developing second sight to replace his lost eyesight, Emrys sets off on a journey to find out who he really is. Reaching Fincayra, an enchanted island that connects Heaven and the Otherworld, he embarks on a dangerous quest to save Fincayra from a blight caused by a pact between its king, Stangmar, and the evil Rhita Gawr, a warlord of the spirit world whose glance means certain death. By novel's end Emrys learns that Stangmar is really his father; that his mother's real name is Elen; that he has a sister, Rhia; and that he is really Merlin. Noting Barron's skill for bringing to life "a magical land populated by remarkable beings," Estes predicted that *The Lost Years of Merlin* "will enchant readers."

In *The Seven Songs of Merlin,* thirteen-year-old Merlin is entrusted with healing the barren lands of Fincayra. When he uses his powers irresponsibly as a means to bring his mother to the island, Elen is stricken with a death shadow—a shadow meant for her son—by Rhita Gawr. In order to save his mother's life, Merlin must find and master the Seven Songs of Wisdom; in addition, he must go to the Otherworld and find the magic antidote to the death shadow. On this search he encounters giants and monsters and kills the ogre that took the life of his grandfather Tuatha, a great but arrogant wizard. Merlin also finds the magic sword Excalibur, which one day will belong to King Arthur. Through these adventures, the teen learns about responsibility, intuition, and the worth of all living things.

"With each book, Barron's 'Lost Years of Merlin' saga just keeps getting richer in characterization, ambience, and Celtic lore," proclaimed Estes in her *Booklist* review of *The Fires of Merlin.* Now fourteen, Merlin has by now earned his wizard's staff and is learning the ways of a wizard. However, his powers are still new. The last dragon emperor, Valdearg—called Wings of Fire—was put to sleep by Merlin's grandfather, the wizard Tuatha. When the eggs containing the dragon's last offspring are destroyed, Valdearg awakes and is led to believe that Merlin is the culprit. Meanwhile, the evil Rhita Gawr has made a deal with dwarf queen Umalda to steal Merlin's magic in return for a promise of safety for the dwarves. In order to confront the dragon, Merlin must face a series of dangers and fight the fires within himself by tapping into the source of his magic: his compassion and his readiness to sacrifice himself for the common good. Ultimately, his practical knowledge of herbs and his compassion in saving Valdearg's last surviving hatchling allow the teen to succeed in his quest.

As *The Mirror of Merlin* opens, fifteen-year-old Merlin is deep in the Haunted Marshes of Fincarya, searching for his stolen sword. The theft of his sword is a trap set by the sorceress Nimue, and she infects the teen with a deadly and incurable condition. Fortunately, Merlin meets Ector, a boy who believes that his own master can cure the teen's illness. Traveling through the Mists of Time into the future and encountering a magic mirror, an ailing Merlin meets his much-older self, trapped in the Crystal Cave by Nimue. Before he can return to his own time, the teen must confront his deepest fears but also accept the choices open to him. Inspired by his future, he envisions the Round Table of King Arthur and his knights and forecasts a society based on justice.

The "Lost Years of Merlin" series culminates with *The Wings of Merlin,* in which Rhita Gawr and his henchmen are preparing to invade Fincayra. Within a two-week time frame, Merlin must convince the squabbling Fincaryran creatures and races to put aside their mistrust of each other and band together to battle the coming evil. Meanwhile, Slayer, a masked warrior with swords for arms, attacks orphaned children in an attempt to lure the young sorcerer into a duel to the death. After Stangmar escapes from his imprisonment, he saves Merlin and Elen from Slayer before sustaining fatal injuries. As he dies, Stangmar is forgiven by Elen, although Merlin cannot bring himself to forgive the father who tried to kill him. In their quest for safety, Merlin, Elen, and a large group of children go to the Forgotten Island, a place considered fearsome by Fincayrans. Slayer follows them there and reveals himself to be Dinatius, Merlin's boyhood nemesis and a friend of Rhita Gawr Merlin eventually defeats Slayer and decides to spare his life, an act of mercy that brings about the rejoining of the Forgotten Island with Fincayra. After a victory against Rhita Gawr, a cosmic shift occurs: Fincayra and the Otherworld meld into a single world while the Forgotten Island becomes Avalon. Merlin learns his true name—Ole Eopia, which means "man of many worlds and many times"—and is able to whisper words of forgiveness to the dead Stangmar. Now he must make his hardest decision yet: to leave his beloved Fincayra for the earthly island of Britannia, where he will become mentor to King Arthur as well as the celebrated wizard of story and song.

The transformed Forgotten Island is the setting of Barron's "Great Tree of Avalon" series, which includes *Child of the Dark Prophecy, Shadow on the Stars,* and *The Eternal Flame.* In *Child of the Dark Prophecy* Merlin rescues a young orphaned boy living in the seven-rooted Great Tree that bridges Earth and heaven after kidnappers kill both the boy's parents. Raised by a foster mother, the boy, Scree, grows up with his foster

*Cover of Barron's* **The Eternal Flame,** *part of the "Great Tree of Avalon" series, featuring artwork by David Elliot.* (Ace Books, 2007. Used by permission of Penguin Group (USA) Inc.)

brother Tamwyn, the grandson of Merlin. Although they have been separated, Scree and Tamwyn attempt to seek each other out in their late teens. Meanwhile, Elli, an orphan apprenticed to a powerful priestess who can channel the Lady of the Lake, must help her mistress locate Merlin's true heir in order to save Avalon from the fate decreed in the Dark Prophecy. The novel's "captivating supporting cast of sprites, fairies and assorted changelings will keep the pages turning," predicted a *Publishers Weekly* critic, and in *Booklist* Estes cited Barron's skill in "creating an elaborate, richly detailed world" in a story "liberally laced with humor and wit."

In *Shadow on the Stars* each of the three protagonists continue to follow his or her fate, while also questioning whether he or she is destined to save Avalon or destroy it as the child of the Dark Prophecy. Tamwyn uses his ability to understand the forest creatures by becoming a nature guide, but is called up to the forest heights. Scree recovers from battle injuries and attempts to marshall a force of Bram Kaie eaglefolk to defend the threatened Avalon, while Elli takes over the role of priestess to the Lady of the Lake. Dubbed by Estes a "fitting finale" to the "Great Tree of Avalon" series, *The Eternal Flame* finds Rhita Gawr continuing his effort to destroy Avalon by searching for ways his minions can invade the sacred place. While Scree hones his skills as a warrior, Elli braves the dark, deep place called Shadowroot in order to destroy a magic crystal before its powers can be used by Rhita Gawr. Meanwhile Tamwyn climbs to the top of the Great Tree in an effort to rekindle the stars and battle the forces of the evil one.

Noting the intersection of the "Great Tree of Avalon" books and the "Lost Years of Merlin" books, Connie Tyrrell Burns commented in *School Library Journal* that Barron's more-recent saga features a "fully realized universe replete with a large cast of characters" and a plot "laced with some humor, gory battles, and many magical elements." While some critics found the series overwritten, Estes begged to differ, writing that in *Shadows on the Stars* "Barron infuses the story with humor" and creates a "dynamic fantasy adventure [that] will leave readers wanting more."

In addition to his fantasy series, Barron has also written a number of standalone titles. In his picture book *Where Is Grandpa?,* illustrated by Chris K. Soenpiet, he uses the concept of nature to explain the cycle of life by depicting a young boy sitting with his family on the day that his grandfather has passed away. Each member of the family shares a memory of Grandpa, but the boy stays silent. Learning that his elderly relative is now in heaven, the boy decides that, for Grandpa, heaven is the world of nature and that his grandfather will remain with him in all of the places that they shared. Writing in *School Library Journal,* Virginia Golodetz called *Where Is Grandpa?* a "helpful introduction to death and the grieving process," while a critic in *Publishers Weekly* dubbed it a "useful springboard for dialogue between bereaved adults and children." Another picture book, the environmentally themed *The Day the Stones Walked: A Tale of Easter Island,* features a fictional story that takes readers back to ancient times and the people who carved the huge stone statues that have continued to mystify historians. Praising Barron's ability to "ably balanc[e] . . . fact and legend," a *Publishers Weekly* contributor cited *The Day the Stones Walked* as a "dramatic, crisply told tale."

Young female protagonists take center stage in both *Tree Girl* and *As High as a Hawk: A Brave Girl's Historic Climb.* In *Tree Girl* nine-year-old Rowanna lives in the forest with her aged guardian, and her questions about her past are met with warnings about the evil creatures that live in the darkest parts of the wood. Pulled by the lure of the captivating High Willow, the girl ignores her guardian's warning, and enters the world of the forest spirits. According to *Booklist* critic Carolyn Phelan, *Tree Girl* will find a readership among teens who enjoy "underlying themes of self reliance, rebellion, and the search for self-knowledge." In *As High as a Hawk* Barron retells a true story about an eight-year-old girl named Harriet Peters who in 1905 climbed to the top of one of Colorado's Rocky Mountain peaks, accompanied by her father and naturalist Enos Mills. With its paintings by Ted Lewin, the book features what *School Library Journal* critic Laurie Edwards described as a "poignant tale" recounted in Barron's "lyrical language." Edwards added that Lewin's "dramatic artwork" contributes to a "gripping saga [that] is sure to be a crowd-pleaser," while in *Kirkus Reviews* a contributor dubbed *High as a Hawk* "a fine, unusual, and inspiring read."

*The Hero's Trail* uses what *Booklist* contributor Shelle Rosenfeld described as "eloquent, engaging prose" to present examples from both history and legend of lives well lived. Barron's examples, which range from Prometheus and Merlin to former slave Harriet Tubman, athlete Lance Armstrong, and physicist Stephen Hawking, are framed against a conversation between Barron and a young hiker as they share a trek through the wilderness. Noting that the book "can serve as an inspiring resource for triumphing over difficulties," Rosenfeld deemed *The Hero's Trail* "a boon for educators as well as for readers," and in *School Library Journal* Wendy Lukehart concluded that Barron's "stories are well worth sharing."

***William Low creates dramatic artwork for Barron's picture book* The Day the Stones Walked, *which introduces readers to the mystery of Easter Island.*** (Illustration copyright © 2007 by William Low. Reproduced by permission of Philomel Books, a division of Penguin Putnam Books for Young Readers.)

Discussing his work as a writer, Barron told Antoinette Botsford of the *NAPRA Review* that his goal is to "give people a sense of their own wondrous gifts." On his home page, the author also discussed why he writes mythic quest novels and fantasy rather than realistic or historical fiction. "I write books I would like to read," Barron explained. "That means each story must have a character, a relationship, a place, a dilemma, and an idea that I care about. A lot. I like a story where an individual must deal with personal issues as well as overarching issues. The mythic quest—call it fantasy if you prefer—allows me to incorporate all of these qualities." In an interview with Estes, Barron added that since becoming a full-time writer, "I haven't had a moment of regret. I feel very, very lucky to get to follow my deepest passion in life."

## Biographical and Critical Sources

*PERIODICALS*

*Booklist,* November 1, 1994, Sally Estes, review of *The Merlin Effect,* p. 491; September 1, 1996, Sally Estes, review of *The Lost Years of Merlin,* p. 118; September 1, 1998, Sally Estes, review of *The Fires of Merlin,* p. 107; April 15, 2001, Sally Estes, interview with Barron, p. 1560; March 1, 2004, Ilene Cooper, review of *High as a Hawk: A Brave Girl's Historic Climb,* p. 1204; September 1, 2004, Sally Estes, review of *Child of the Dark Prophecy,* p. 122; September 15, 2005, Sally Estes, review of *Shadows on the Stars,* p. 55; September 1, 2006, Sally Estes, review of *The Eternal Flame,* p. 108.

*Chicago Parent,* March, 1999, Ken Trainer, "Teaching the Difference between Celebrities and Heroes."

*Cincinnati Enquirer,* October 29, 1999, Sara Pearce, "Youngsters Can Find Magic in 'Merlin'."

*Denver Post,* October 28, 1998, Claire Martin, "Colorado Author Is Living His Dream."

*Emergency Librarian,* Volume 24, number 4, 1997, Kylene Beers, "Where Fantasy Flies" (interview), pp. 61-63.

*Kirkus Reviews,* December 1, 1999, review of *Where Is Grandpa?,* p. 1880; August 15, 2002, review of *The Hero's Trail: A Guide for a Heroic Life,* p. 1215; April 1, 2004, review of *High as a Hawk,* p. 324; September 15, 2004, review of *Child of the Dark Prophecy,* p. 910; May 1, 2007, review of *The Day the Stones Walked: A Tale of Easter Island;* August 1, 2008, review of *Merlin's Dragon.*

*Kliatt,* March, 2003, Donna L. Scanlon, review of *The Wings of Merlin,* p. 30; September, 2004, Michele Winship, review of *Child of the Dark Prophecy,* p. 4; September, 2006, Deirdre Root, review of *The Eternal Flame,* p. 6.

*NAPRA Review,* April, 1997, Antoinette Botsford, "Merlin in Our Midst."

*Parents',* November, 1998, T.A. Barron, "Merlin's Message."

*Publishers Weekly,* June 29, 1990, review of *Heartlight,* p. 102; August 12, 1996, review of *The Lost Years of Merlin,* p. 84; July 21, 1997, review of *The Seven Songs of Merlin,* p. 202; January 11, 2000, review of *Where Is Grandpa?,* p. 103; October 15, 2001, review of *Tree Girl,* p. 72; June 21, 2004, review of *High as a Hawk,* p. 62; October 25, 2004, review of *Child of the Dark Prophecy,* p. 48; May 28, 2007, review of *The Day the Stones Walked,* p. 62.

*School Library Journal,* February, 2000, Virginia Golodetz, review of *Where Is Grandpa?,* p. 91; October, 2001, Connie Tyrell Burns, review of *Tree Girl,* p. 148; December, 2002, Wendy Lukehart, review of *The Hero's Trail,* p. 153; October, 2004, Beth Wright, review of *Child of the Dark Prophecy,* p. 154; December, 2005, Connie Tyrrell Burns, review of *Shadows on the Stars,* p. 140; November, 2006, Tim Wadham, review of *The Eternal Flame,* p. 129; July, 2007, Kirsten Cutler, review of *The Day the Stones Walked,* p. 67.

*Voice of Youth Advocates,* April, 1999, T.A. Barron, "Vision, Voice, and the Power of Creation: A Young-Adult Author Speaks Out."

*ONLINE*

*T.A. Barron Home Page,* http://www.tabarron.com (August 15, 2008).

*BookPage,* http://www.bookpage.com/ (July 24, 2001), "Meet the Kids' Author: T.A. Barron."

*NAPRA—ALA Web site,* http://www.napra.com/ (July 21, 2001), Antoinette Botsford, "To Think as a Tree, to Act as a Man."

*Natural Resources Defense Council Web site,* http://www.ndrc.org/ (July 24, 2001), "T.A. Barron."*

* * *

## BARRON, Thomas Archibald
## See BARRON, T.A.

* * *

## BARRON, Tom
## See BARRON, T.A.

* * *

## BARYSHNIKOV, Mikhail 1948-

### Personal

Born January 27, 1948, in Riga, Latvia, USSR; immigrated to Canada, 1974; immigrated to United States, 1974; naturalized U.S. citizen, 1986; son of Nikolai and Alexandra Baryshnikov; companion of Jessica Lange (an actress), mid-1970s-early 1980s; companion of Lisa Rinehart (a dancer), early 1980s—; children: (with Lange) Aleksandra; (with Rinehart) Sofia, Anna, Peter. *Education:* Trained in ballet at School of Theatre Opera

Ballet (Riga); Agrippina Vaganova Choreographic Institute, graduated 1967. *Hobbies and other interests:* Fishing.

## Addresses

*Home and office*—New York, NY.

## Career

Dancer, choreographer, actor, and author. Kirov Ballet, Leningrad, USSR, soloist, 1969-74; American Ballet Theatre, New York, NY, principal dancer, 1974-78, 1979-90, director designee, 1979-80, artistic director, 1980-89; New York City Ballet, principal dancer, 1978-79; White Oak Dance Project, director and dancer, 1990-2003; Baryshnikov Center for Dance, New York, NY, founder, 2004. Guest artist with numerous groups, including National Ballet of Canada, Royal Ballet, Hamburg Ballet, Ballet Victoria, Stuttgart Ballet, Vienna Opera Ballet, Alvin Ailey Company, Eliot Feld Ballet, Martha Graham Dance Company, and Mark Morris Dance Company. Performer in numerous television programs or specials, including *The Nutcracker, In Performance at Wolf Trap, Live from Lincoln Center, Baryshnikov at the White House, Baryshnikov on Broadway, Baryshnikov in Hollywood,* and *Baryshnikov by Tharp.* Actor in motion pictures, including *The Turning Point,* 1977, *White Nights,* 1987, and *Dancers.* Choreographer of full-length ballets, including *The Nutcracker,* 1976, *Don Quixote (Kitri's Wedding),* 1978, *Cinderella,* 1984, and *Swan Lake,* 1989. Performer on stage, including in *Forbidden Christmas; or, The Doctor and the Patient,* 2004. Co-owner, Russian Samovar (restaurant), New York, NY.

## Awards, Honors

Gold Medal, Varna Dance Competition, 1966; Gold Medal, First International Ballet Competition, 1969, and Nijinsky prize, Paris Academy of Dance, 1969, both for performance in *Vestris;* Academy Award nomination for best supporting actor, Academy of Motion Picture Arts and Sciences, 1977, for *The Turning Point;* award from *Dance* magazine, 1978; D.F.A. from Yale University, 1979; Kennedy Center Honor, 2000; Jerome Robbins Prize, 2004; National Arts Award, 2005; George and Judy Marcus Prize for Lifetime Achievement, 2006; honorary degrees from New York University, 2006, Shenandoah University Conservatory, 2007, and Montclair State University, 2008; Commonwealth Award; Chubb fellowship, Yale University.

## Writings

*Baryshnikov at Work: Mikhail Baryshnikov Discusses His Roles,* photographs by Martha Swope, edited by Charles Engell France, Alfred A. Knopf (New York, NY), 1976.

***Mikhail Baryshnikov, and partner, performing in Washington, DC, 1979.*** (Library of Congress.)

(Author of introduction and commentary) *Baryshnikov in Color,* edited by Charles Engell France, Harry Abrams (New York, NY), 1980.

Peter Anastos, *The Swan Prince: A Fairy Tale,* Bantam Books (New York, NY), 1987.

(Author of foreword) *Reinventing Dance in the 1960s: Everything Was Possible,* edited by Sally Banes, University of Wisconsin Press (Madison, WI), 2003.

(With Vladimir Radunsky) *Because . . . ,* illustrated by Radunsky, Atheneum Books for Young Readers (New York, NY), 2007.

## Sidelights

Mikhail Baryshnikov is widely hailed as one of ballet's greatest performers of all time. Born in 1948 in the former Soviet Union, he began dance studies at age nine and became a principal dancer for the prestigious Kirov Ballet in 1969. Because he had a stellar career in the communist USSR, Baryshnikov was given many comforts not available to most Soviets, and he toured widely outside the country before defecting to the West in the mid-1970s. North American critics found in the Soviet dancer an unequaled combination of acting and athletic talents. Unlike most dancers, Baryshnikov's dramatic expressions on stage were hailed as utterly convincing and stirring, while his technical capabilities—including his extraordinary leaping capacity—continue to be unmatched. As a dancer, as well as an artistic director, Baryshnikov has continued to push for innovation in the dance by promoting performance opportunities for younger dancers, injecting minimalism and improvisation into his performances, and cofounding the White Oak Dance Company with choreographer Mark Morris.

***Joining Baryshnikov as coauthor, Vladimir Radunsky captures the optimistic energy in the inspirational short story* Because. . . .** (Illustration copyright © 2007 by Vladimir Radunsky. Reprinted with the permission of Atheneum Books for Young Readers, an imprint of Simon & Schuster Children's Publishing Division.)

In addition to his successes on stage (he has danced over one hundred different works during his long career), Baryshnikov has also acted in several films, and his public appearances have made him well known as a celebrity. In 2007 he shared his love of the dance and his belief in life's possibilities in the pages of *Because . . . ,* a picture book featuring illustrations by coauthor Vladimir Radunsky. In the book, a young red-haired narrator describes what it is like to spend each day with his quirky grandmother. The agility and grace of the stout woman, as well as her obvious zest for life as she leaps, spins, cartwheels, and prances through the week, cause the boy embarrassment. Her activities also prompt others to question how she can sustain such energy, and her answer to such questions is always that she is a dancer. Praising the "buoyant" illustrations created by Radunsky, Jennifer Mattson added in *Booklist* that "young readers will respond to [the book's] . . . worthwhile, inclusive message about joy in physical movement." In *School Library Journal* Suzanne Myers Harold dubbed *Because . . .* "a playful book about being true to oneself regardless of how others react," and in *Publishers Weekly* a critic cited the author's "casual text" as positive and inspiring. "Radunsky's trademark offbeat artistry makes him a perfect partner in this charming pas de deux," concluded a *Kirkus Reviews* critic of Baryshnikov's picture-book debut.

## Biographical and Critical Sources

*BOOKS*

Alovert, Nina, *Baryshnikov in Russia,* translated by Irene Huntoon, Henry Holt (New York, NY), 1984.

Aria, Barbara, *Misha: The Mikhail Baryshnikov Story,* St. Martin's Press (New York, NY), 1989.

Glassman, Bruce, *Mikhail Baryshnikov,* Silver Burdett (Englewood Cliffs, NJ), 1990.

Goodman, Saul, *Baryshnikov: A Most Spectacular Dancer,* Harvey House (New York, NY), 1979.

Klein, Norma, *Baryshnikov's Nutcracker,* Putnam (New York, NY), 1983.

Smakov, Gennady, *Baryshnikov: From Russia to the West,* Farrar, Straus (New York, NY), 1981.

*PERIODICALS*

*Dance,* March, 1994, Hilary Ostlere, profile of Baryshnikov, p. 38; May, 1998, Hilary Ostlere, interview with Baryshnikov, p. 44.

*Kirkus Reviews,* May 1, 2007, review of *Because* . . .
*New Yorker,* January 19, 1998, Joan Acocella, "The Soloist," p. 44.
*Publishers Weekly,* April 2, 2007, review of *Because* . . . , p. 55.
*School Library Journal,* May, 2007, Suzanne Myers Harold, review of *Because* . . . , p. 84.

*ONLINE*

*While Oak Dance Project Web site,* http://www.whiteoak danceproject.com/ (August 15, 2008).*

* * *

## BAUER, Marion Dane 1938-

### Personal

Born November 20, 1938, in Oglesby, IL; daughter of Chester (a chemist) and Elsie (a kindergarten teacher) Dane; married Ronald Bauer (an Episcopal priest), June 25, 1959 (divorced); children: Peter Dane, Elisabeth Alison. *Education:* Attended La Salle-Peru-Oglesby Junior College, 1956-58, and University of Missouri, 1958-59; University of Oklahoma, B.A., 1962. *Religion:* Unitarian Universalist.

### Addresses

*Home and office*—Eden Prairie, MN. *E-mail*—mdb@mariondanebauer.com.

### Career

Educator and author. High-school teacher, Waukesha, WI, 1962-64; Hennepin Technical Center, Minneapolis, MN, instructor in creative writing for adult education program, 1975-78; instructor at University of Minnesota Continuing Education for Women, 1978-85, and Institute for Children's Literature, 1982-85; Crestwood House, editor, 1989; Vermont College of Norwich University (now Vermont College of Fine Arts), faculty chair of MFA program in writing for children, 1997-2000, faculty member, 1997—.

### Member

Authors Guild, Authors League of America, Society of Children's Book Writers and Illustrators.

### Awards, Honors

American Library Association (ALA) Notable Book Award, 1976, and Japanese Library Association Award, both for *Shelter from the Wind;* Golden Kite Honor Book Award, Society of Children's Book Writers, 1977, for *Foster Child;* Jane Addams Peace Association Children's Book Award, 1984, for *Rain of Fire;* Notable Children's Book Award, ALA, and Best Books list,

***Marion Dane Bauer*** (Reproduced by permission.)

*School Library Journal,* both 1986, *Booklist* Editors' Choice, Newbery Honor Book Award, and British Children's Book Award runner-up, all 1987, Golden Archer Award, 1988, Flicker Tale Children's Book Award, William Allen White Award, and West Virginia Children's Book Award, all 1989, all for *On My Honor;* Children's Book of Distinction, *Hungry Mind Review,* 1992, for *Face to Face;* Notable Children's Book citation, ALA, 1992, for *What's Your Story?;* Pick of the Lists citation, American Booksellers Association, and *School Library Journal* Best Books citation, both 1995, both for *A Question of Trust;* Best Book for Young Adults designation, and Recommended Book for Young Adult Readers citation, ALA, Minnesota Book Award for older children, and Gay/Lesbian/Bisexual Book Award for Literature, all for *Am I Blue?;* Minnesota Book Award for Children, Outstanding Achievement in Children's Literature designation, Wisconsin Library Association, Society of School Librarians International Honor Book, Charlotte Zolotow Award highly commended title, and ABC Choices for Children, all 1998, all for *If You Were Born a Kitten;* Kerlan Award, Kerlan Collection, University of Minnesota, 1996; 100 Best Books listee, New York Public Library, 1999, for *An Early Winter;* Rebecca Caudill Award nomination, 2002, Children's Crown Award, 2005, and Gorgia Book Award, 2006, all for *Runt.*

## Writings

*MIDDLE-GRADE NOVELS*

*Shelter from the Wind,* Seabury Press (New York, NY), 1976.
*Foster Child,* Seabury Press (New York, NY), 1977.
*Tangled Butterfly,* Clarion Books (New York, NY), 1980.
*Rain of Fire,* Clarion Books (New York, NY), 1983.
*Like Mother, like Daughter,* Clarion Books (New York, NY), 1985.
*On My Honor,* Clarion Books (New York, NY), 1986.
*Touch the Moon,* illustrated by Alix Berenzy, Clarion Books (New York, NY), 1987.
*A Dream of Queens and Castles,* Clarion Books (New York, NY), 1990.
*Face to Face,* Clarion Books (New York, NY), 1991.
*Ghost Eye,* illustrated by Trina Schart Hyman, Scholastic (New York, NY), 1992.
*A Taste of Smoke,* Clarion Books (New York, NY), 1993.
*A Question of Trust,* Scholastic (New York, NY), 1994.
*An Early Winter,* illustrated by Susan Winter, Clarion (New York, NY), 1999.
*Runt,* Clarion (New York, NY), 2002.
*Land of the Buffalo Bones: The Diary of Mary Ann Elizabeth Rodgers, an English Girl in Minnesota* ("Dear America" series), Scholastic (New York, NY), 2003.
*The Double Digit Club,* Holiday House (New York, NY), 2004.
*A Bear Named Trouble,* Clarion Books (New York, NY), 2005.

*PICTURE BOOKS*

*When I Go Camping with Grandma,* illustrated by Allen Garns, BridgeWater Books (Mahwah, NJ), 1995.
*If You Were Born a Kitten,* illustrated by JoEllen McAllister Stammen, Simon & Schuster (New York, NY), 1997.
*Sleep, Little One, Sleep,* illustrated by JoEllen McAllister Stammen, Clarion (New York, NY), 1999.
*Jason's Bears,* illustrated by Kevin Hawkes, Hyperion (New York, NY), 2000.
*Grandmother's Song,* illustrated by Pamela Rossi, Simon & Schuster (New York, NY), 2000.
*If You Had a Nose like an Elephant's Trunk,* illustrated by Susan Winter, Holiday House (New York, NY), 2001.
*My Mother Is Mine,* illustrated by Peter Elwell, Simon & Schuster (New York, NY), 2001.
*The Kissing Monster: A Lift-the-Flap Story,* illustrated by Kathi Couri, Little Simon (New York, NY), 2002.
*Love Song for a Baby,* illustrated by Dan Andreasen, Simon & Schuster (New York, NY), 2002.
*Uh-Oh!: A Lift-the-Flap Story,* illustrated by Valeria Petrone, Simon & Schuster (New York, NY), 2002.
*Why Do Kittens Purr?,* illustrated by Henry Cole, Simon & Schuster (New York, NY), 2003.
*Toes, Ears, and Nose!,* illustrated by Karen Katz, Simon & Schuster (New York, NY), 2003.
*A Recipe for Valentine's Day: A Rebus Lift-the-Flap Story,* Little Simon (New York, NY), 2005.
*Waiting for Christmas,* Little Simon (New York, NY), 2005.
*If Frogs Made Weather,* Holiday House (New York, NY), 2005.
*Easter Is Coming,* illustrated by Jayoung Cho, Little Simon (New York, NY), 2005.
*I'm Not Afraid of Halloween!: A Pop-Up and Flap Book,* illustrated by Rusty Fletcher, Little Simon (New York, NY), 2006.
*Baby Bear Discovers the World,* photographs by Stan Tekiela, Adventure Publications, 2007.
*The Very Best Daddy of All,* illustrated by Leslie Wu, Aladdin (New York, NY), 2007.
*A Mama for Owen,* illustrated by John Butler, Simon & Schuster Books for Young Readers (New York, NY), 2007.
*Some Babies Are Wild,* photographs by Stan Tekiela, Adventure Publications, 2007.
*One Brown Bunny,* illustrated by Ivan Bates, Orchard Books (New York, NY), 2008.
*The Christmas Baby,* illustrated by Richard Cowdrey, Simon & Schuster Books for Young Readers (New York, NY), 2008.
*The Longest Night,* illustrated by Ted Lewin, Holiday House (New York, NY), 2009.
*Thank You for Me,* illustrated by Kristina Stephenson, Simon & Schuster Books for Young Readers (New York, NY), 2010.

*YOUNG-ADULT FICTION*

*Killing Miss Kitty, and Other Sins,* Clarion Books (New York, NY), 2007.

*READERS*

*Alison's Wings,* illustrated by Roger Roth, Hyperion (New York, NY), 1996.
*Turtle Dreams,* illustrated by Diane Dawson Hearn, Holiday House (New York, NY), 1997.
*Alison's Fierce and Ugly Halloween,* illustrated by Laurie Spencer, Hyperion (New York, NY), 1997.
*Alison's Puppy,* illustrated by Laurie Spencer, Hyperion (New York, NY), 1997.
*Beyond the Playhouse Wall,* Scholastic (New York, NY), 1997.
*Bear's Hiccups,* illustrated by Diane Dawson Hearn, Holiday House (New York, NY), 1998.
*Christmas in the Forest,* illustrated by Diane Dawson Hearn, Holiday House (New York, NY), 1998.
*Frog's Best Friend,* illustrated by Diane Dawson Hearn, Holiday House (New York, NY), 2002.
*The Blue Ghost,* illustrated by Suling Wang, Random House (New York, NY), 2005.
*The Secret of the Painted House,* illustrated by Leonid Gore, Random House (New York, NY), 2007.
*The Red Ghost,* illustrated by Peter Ferguson, Random House (New York, NY), 2008.
*The Green Ghost,* illustrated by Peter Ferguson, Random House (New York, NY), 2008.

*JUVENILE NONFICTION*

*Rain,* illustrated by John Wallace, Aladdin (New York, NY), 2003.
*Snow,* illustrated by John Wallace, Aladdin (New York, NY), 2003.
*Clouds,* illustrated by John Wallace, Aladdin (New York, NY), 2004.
*Wind,* illustrated by John Wallace, Aladdin (New York, NY), 2004.

*"WONDERS OF AMERICA" SERIES; JUVENILE NONFICTION*

*The Rocky Mountains,* Aladdin (New York, NY), 2006.
*Niagara Falls,* illustrated by John Wallace, Aladdin (New York, NY), 2006.
*The Grand Canyon,* illustrated by John Wallace, Aladdin (New York, NY), 2006.
*The Statue of Liberty,* illustrated by John Wallace, Aladdin (New York, NY), 2007.
*Mount Rushmore,* illustrated by John Wallace, Aladdin (New York, NY), 2007.
*The Mighty Mississippi,* illustrated by John Wallace, Aladdin (New York, NY), 2007.
*Yellowstone,* illustrated by John Wallace, Aladdin (New York, NY), 2008.

*"NATURAL DISASTERS" SERIES; JUVENILE NONFICTION*

*Volcano!,* illustrated by John Wallace, Aladdin (New York, NY), 2008.
*Flood!,* illustrated by John Wallace, Aladdin (New York, NY), 2008.
*Earthquake!,* illustrated by John Wallace, Aladdin (New York, NY), 2009.

*OTHER*

*What's Your Story?: A Young Person's Guide to Writing Fiction,* Clarion Books (New York, NY), 1992.
(Editor and contributor) *Am I Blue?: Coming out from the Silence* (short stories), HarperCollins (New York, NY), 1994.
*A Writer's Story: From Life to Fiction,* Clarion Books (New York, NY), 1995.
*Our Stories: A Fiction Workshop for Young Authors,* Clarion Books (New York, NY), 1996.

Also author of *God's Tears: A Woman's Journey,* a chancel drama performed as a one-woman show. Contributing editor of stories and articles to periodicals, including *Cricket, Horn Book, ALAN Review, Writers' Journal, School Library Journal,* and *Boy's Life.*

Bauer's work has been translated into more than a dozen languages.

## Adaptations

An *ABC Afterschool Special* titled *Rodeo Red and the Runaway* was based on *Shelter from the Wind.*

## Sidelights

Marion Dane Bauer is the award-winning author of middle-grade novels, chapter books, picture books, and nonfiction works. Although she sometimes focuses her fiction for young teen readers on fantastic themes and situations, books such as *Shelter from the Wind, Rain of Fire, On My Honor, An Early Winter,* and *Killing Miss Kitty, and Other Sins* focus on young people persevere by confronting problems that have no easy solutions. These books are often drawn from personal experiences and feature places where Bauer has lived or visited often; as a result, her prose is enriched by her inclusion of subtle detail.

In addition to her work for older readers, Bauer has increasingly written for a younger audience: the result includes easy-reading chapter books such as the "Alison" series, nonfiction in her "Wonders of America" series; beginning readers; and picture books such as *My Mother Is Mine, If You Were Born a Kitten, If Frogs Made Weather,* and *The Very Best Daddy of All.* A prolific writer, she has also penned several how-to books for would-be young writers, including the well-received *What's Your Story?: A Young Person's Guide to Writing Fiction,* and edited the award-winning short-story anthology *Am I Blue?: Coming out from the Silence.* In all her genres, Bauer's enthusiasm for the written word is evident. At its best, noted Karin Snelson in *Booklist,* the author's prose "communicates that all is right with the world."

Bauer grew up in a small Illinois prairie town and experienced a childhood that she once described as "idyllic." As she gained maturity, there was less and less time for Bauer to spend on her writing; first came college, then marriage and a family and teaching English. Writing remained Bauer's self-proclaimed "secret vice" until her daughter began grade school. After educating herself on the writing process, she began work on *Foster Child,* a middle-grade novel loosely based on her experiences as a foster parent.

The publication of the early novels *Shelter from the Wind* and *Foster Child* gave Bauer the boost of confidence she needed to commit herself to writing. In *Shelter from the Wind,* Stacy is at odds with her pregnant stepmother who steals the attention of Stacy's father. Running away from home, the girl discovers she is ill-prepared for such a momentous change. Wandering on the Oklahoma prairie, she is taken in by Old Ella, and when Ella is injured in a fall Stacy must take charge. Another early novel, *Rain of Fire,* focuses on a young boy's relationship with his older brother who has just returned from action in World War II. *Rain of Fire* was lauded by a reviewer for the *Bulletin of the Center for Children's Books* as "serious, but not somber, beautifully laminated and perceptive in unfolding the intricacies of human relationships . . . it has good pace and momentum within its tight frame." Also reviewing the novel, a critic for *Publishers Weekly* commented that Bauer "has the notable ability to relate a story so that it never deviates from the viewpoint of the child," while a *Booklist* contributor declared that the author's "characters and the dilemmas she creates for them grow in power" as the book "builds to its riveting conclusion."

*On My Honor* also explores human reaction to tragedy. When two friends impulsively swim in a forbidden and dangerous river and one boy drowns, the survivor must make some difficult decisions at a very confusing moment. Claudia Lepman-Logan, writing in *Horn Book,* noted that the moral dilemma at the core of Bauer's middle-grade novel makes for "an exciting reading experience," largely due to the book's "richness and strength." *On My Honor* was a personal triumph for Bauer as well, for she was just going through a painful divorce after nearly three decades of marriage. After the publication of the novel, she poured renewed energy into her writing, soon breaking through to new levels of popularity and critical success and paving the way to becoming a completely self-supporting writer.

In the middle-grade novel *Face to Face* thirteen-year-old Michael is reunited with his long-lost father on a rafting trip in Colorado, but soon learns that the man he has distantly idealized is far different from what he has imagined. Reviewing the book in *Kliatt,* Elaine S. Patterson dubbed it "an excellent read" that discusses a common problem for children of broken homes: "unrealistic ideas about an absent parent and the inability to accept stepparents." Another broken family is at the heart of *A Question of Trust,* in which the parents of Brad and Charlie have recently separated. The brothers refuse to have anything to do with their mother, hoping this will make her come home, while a subplot details their care for a stray cat and its kitten despite their father's objections. Ilene Cooper, writing in *Booklist,* noted that Bauer "writes with an intensity and honesty that propel readers through the story, stirring their feelings, too. She makes them see how much love and hate are intertwined."

With *An Early Winter* Bauer describes a boy's encounter with Alzheimer's disease. Tim refuses to admit anything is wrong with his beloved grandfather, but when the two go on a fishing trip together he is forced to confront the truth. A *Kirkus Reviews* contributor remarked that "Tim's experience with his grandfather may convince readers with Alzheimer's-stricken relatives that denial serves no purpose." In *Booklist,* Susan Dove Lempke maintained that Bauer "also develops a delicately layered story about blame and truth. . . . With its humane, complicated characters, this makes a good choice for discussion."

In *The Double-Digit Club* nine-year-old Sarah is bereft one summer when best friend Paige chooses membership in a club of older girls over spending time with her. In a funk, Sarah spends time reading or at Mrs. Berglund's house next door. Nosing through Mrs. B.'s possessions, she "borrows" the blind woman's antique doll in the hopes she can use it to lure Paige back to best-friend status. When her scheme backfires, Sarah confronts what a *Kirkus Reviews* writer described as "a classic Bauer struggle with conscience," and her struggle is "thoroughly believable." In *Publishers Weekly* a critic praised *The Double-Digit Club* as a "compassionately wrought coming-of-age story [that] features a bossy but likable heroine."

Shifting her focus to the natural world in *Runt,* Bauer explores life within a wolf pack from the point of view of one of its smallest members. Born last, and not as physically adept as his siblings, Runt struggles to gain his father's attention and improve his standing in the pack. Instead all seems to go amiss, culminating with human intervention to help the wolf cub survive an attack by a porcupine. Eventually, however, fate provides Runt with a chance to show his usefulness to his family. Although the wolf characters speak to one another, Bauer's tale is closely based upon actual wolf-pack biology and on the observations scientists have made in the wild. This YA title was well reviewed, with Julie Cummins in *Booklist* calling it a "compelling, poignant story" and a *Publishers Weekly* reviewer commending it

***Bauer captures a teen's coming of age in the 1950s Midwest in the five interlinking short stories comprising* Killing Miss Kitty and Other Sins.** (Photograph copyright © 2007 by Media Bakery. Reprinted by permission of Clarion Books, an imprint of Houghton Mifflin Harcourt Publishing Company. All rights reserved.)

as a "tightly plotted, swiftly paced tale." Several reviewers felt that *Runt* would increase readers' sympathy for and understanding of wild wolves. As *School Library Journal* correspondent Terrie Dorio concluded, "Bauer portrays the wolves' place in the natural world with compassion, respect, and warmth."

A collection of five interlinking short stories, *Killing Miss Kitty and Other Sins* returns readers to the Midwest of the 1950s, as eleven-year-old Claire attempts to deal with sexual confusion, racial issues, differences of religious faith, and problems with her parents. Inspired by Bauer's own experiences growing up, the volume features a "sympathetic" narrator "whose inability to acknowledge her heart's truth will resonate with questioning teens," according to *Booklist* critic Jennifer Mattson. Although noting that the novel's intended audience is uncertain, Faith Brautigam concluded in *School Library Journal* that *Killing Miss Kitty, and Other Sins* features writing that is "thought-provoking and beautifully literary." In *Kirkus Reviews* the critic found the stories mature in theme, featuring "skilled and graceful writing," and "tinged with nostalgia and a world long gone."

Among Bauer's middle-grade novels is a contribution to the "Dear America" series—a fictional book in diary form that features actual historical events. Bauer's initial contribution to the series, *Land of the Buffalo Bones: The Diary of Mary Elizabeth Rogers, an English Girl in Minnesota,* is based on actual events from Bauer's family history. In the novel, fourteen-year-old Polly Rodgers arrives in Minnesota with her pastor father and a congregation of families that have followed him from England to America. Full of unbridled optimism, the settlers soon discover that their new land is hardly a paradise; it is a hostile environment of extreme temperatures, insect plagues, and poverty. Eva Mitnick, writing in *Booklist,* described the work as "an engrossing look at the hardships faced by many pioneers."

Since the early 1990s, Bauer has expanded her writing repertoire to include nonfiction as well as picture books and chapter books for younger readers. In *The Red Ghost* and *The Blue Ghost* she mixes easy vocabulary with a scary story that features a "perfect formula" for attracting "transitional readers," according to a *Kirkus Reviews* writer. Her "Alison" early-chapter-book series for beginning readers focuses on a spunky young girl who is up for most sorts of challenges. Reviewing *Alison's Fierce and Ugly Halloween,* in which the heroine is having trouble scaring people with her Halloween outfit, Rochman noted that Bauer's "simple words make this an appealing easy reader about a girl who wants to get beyond cute stereotypes."

Bauer's "Wonders of America" nonfiction series features artwork by John Wallace and includes books on some of the most fascinating sites in North America, from Mount Rushmore to the Grand Canyon. Budding bookworms are also treated to the Bauer style in titles

***Cover of* The Blue Ghost, *one of a series of middle-grade novels by Bauer, featuring artwork by Carol Heyer.*** (Illustration copyright © 2005 by Carol Heyer. Used by permission of Random House, an imprint of Random House Children's Books, a division of Random House, Inc.)

including *Turtle Dreams, Bear's Hiccups,* and *Christmas in the Forest.* Rochman concluded in a *Booklist* review of *Turtle Dreams* that young readers "will see that simple words can make you think and take you far," and Shelley Townsend-Hudson wrote in *Booklist* that *Christmas in the Forest,* in which Cat and Mousling become unlikely friends, is "perfect for new readers." The beginning reader *Frog's Best Friend,* which finds Frog hoping that Turtle will be his very best friend, was praised by Cooper who wrote in *Booklist* that Bauer's "text is meaty enough to involve children [with some] . . . reading under their belts."

In the picture-book arena, *If You Were Born a Kitten* features a text that a critic for *Publishers Weekly* described as "lovingly maternal, soothing and perfect for bedtime." In *Love Song for a Baby* Bauer's "quiet but powerful" text pairs with "stunning" artwork by Dan Andreasen, according to *Booklist* critic Kathy Broderick, while a *Kirkus Reviews* writer concluded that the provocatively titled *If Frogs Made Weather* "introduces a thought-provoking theme for young poetry readers."

In *What's Your Story?* Bauer provides practical suggestions on focusing story ideas, on plot and character de-

***Cover of Bauer's teen anthology* Am I Blue?, *featuring cover art by Beck Underwood.*** (Art © 1994 by Beck Underwood. Copyright © 1995 by HarperCollins Publishers. Used by permission of HarperCollins Children's Books, a division of HarperCollins Publishers.)

velopment, and on revision. Cathi Dunn MacRae, writing in the *Wilson Library Bulletin,* called the how-to "a model of lucid organization, written as elegantly as [Bauer's] YA novels." Other Bauer books on writing include *A Writer's Story: From Life to Fiction* and *Our Stories: A Fiction Workshop for Young Authors,* the latter which pairs short stories by young writers with Bauer's critiques and commentary. A collection of short stories on gay and lesbian themes, *Am I Blue?* contains stories from fifteen popular YA writers, including Bauer, all of which explore the concerns of adolescents who are homosexual. *Booklist* correspondent Stephanie Zvirin called the anthology "wonderfully diverse in tone and setting" while Katherine Paterson concluded in the *Washington Post Book World* that "when a book that sets out to do good turns out to be as good as this one, we are all the winners."

In her writing, Bauer is careful to include moral choices in each of her books. "To have hope [children] must believe that the choices they make matter, that they have the power to change human history," the author once told *Horn Book.* She added that she is "convinced that one of the most fundamental experiences of being human is the discovery each of us makes in our cribs: that we are alone. . . . Fiction can cut through our isolation . . . because fiction can move us inside another human being, allow us to share the thoughts and feelings and to see the world through those other eyes."

As Bauer explained to *SATA,* Bauer's stories "are meant to ask unanswerable questions, to share pain, to test insights, and most of all, to make connections." "I am always writing toward that moment when a reader will say, 'But I thought I was the only one who felt that, thought that, wanted that'," she added, "and when that moment comes, my story has found its reason for being."

## Biographical and Critical Sources

*BOOKS*

Brown, Jean, and Elaine Stephens, *Teaching Young Adult Literature: Sharing the Connection,* Wadsworth (Belmont, CA), 1995.

Fisher, Bonnie, *Social Influences on the Writing of Marion Dane Bauer and Katherine Paterson: Writing as a Social Act,* Edwin Mellen Press (Lewiston, NY), 2001.

*St. James Guide to Young Adult Writers,* 2nd edition, St. James Press (Detroit, MI), 1999.

*PERIODICALS*

*Booklist,* September 15, 1983, review of *Rain of Fire,* p. 162; January 15, 1994, Ilene Cooper, review of *A Question of Trust,* p. 924; May 1, 1994, Stephanie Zvirin, review of *Am I Blue?: Coming out from the Silence,* p. 1598; September 1, 1997, Hazel Rochman, review of *Alison's Fierce and Ugly Halloween,* p. 137; February 1, 1998, Hazel Rochman, review of *Turtle Dreams,* p. 925; May 1, 1998, Lauren Peterson, review of *Bear's Hiccups,* p. 1524; December 1, 1998, Shelley Townsend-Hudson, review of *Christmas in the Forest,* pp. 665-666; December 1, 1999, Susan Dove Lempke, review of *An Early Winter;* September 15, 2001, Helen Rosenberg, review of *If You Had Nose like an Elephant's Trunk,* p. 230; May 1, 2002, Ilene Cooper, review of *Frog's Best Friend,* p. 1530; September 1, 2002, Kathy Broderick, review of *Love Song for a Baby,* p. 134; October 15, 2002, Julie Cummins, review of *Runt,* p. 406; January 1, 2003, Karin Snelson, review of *Why Do Kittens Purr?,* p. 904; May 15, 2003, Eva Mitnick, review of *Land of the Buffalo Bones: The Diary of Mary Elizabeth Rogers, an English Girl in Minnesota,* p. 1665; February 1, 2004, Hazel Rochman, review of *Clouds,* p. 978; September 1, 2005, Shelle Rosenfeld, review of *The Blue Ghost,* p. 128; February 15, 2007, Jennifer Mattson, review of *Killing Miss Kitty, and Other Sins,* p. 87; May 1, 2007, Carolyn Phelan, review of *The Secret of the Painted House,* p. 48; April 15, 2008, Ilene Cooper, review of *The Red Ghost,* p. 45; May 15, 2008, Carolyn Phelan, review of *Yellowstone,* p. 46.

*Bulletin of the Center for Children's Books,* November, 1983, review of *Rain of Fire;* October, 1999, review of *An Early Winter,* p. 46; January, 2004, Elizabeth Bush, review of *Snow,* p. 179; April, 2004, Hope Morrison, review of *The Double-Digit Club,* p. 315; October, 2007, Hope Morrison, review of *The Secret of the Painted House,* p. 73.

*Horn Book,* November-December, 1987, Marion Dane Bauer, "Peace in Story, Peace in the World"; January-February, 1989, Claudia Lepman-Logan, "Books in the Classroom: Moral Choices in Literature," pp. 108-111; January-February, 1994, Elizabeth S. Watson, review of *A Taste of Smoke,* p. 68; July-August, 1994, Maeve Visser Knoth, review of *A Question of Trust,* p. 448.

*Kirkus Reviews,* July 1, 1999, review of *An Early Winter,* p. 1050; October 1, 2002, review of *Runt,* p. 1463; February 15, 2003, review of *Why Do Kittens Purr?,* p. 299; February 15, 2004, review of *The Double-Digit Club,* p. 173; April 1, 2005, review of *If Frogs Made Weather,* p. 412; July 1, 2005, review of *The Blue Ghost,* p. 73; May 1, 2007, review of *Killing Miss Kitty, and Other Sins;* June 1, 2007, review of *The Secret of the Painted House;* March 15, 2008, review of *The Red Ghost.*

*Kliatt,* July, 1993, Elaine S. Patterson, review of *Face to Face,* p. 5.

*Publishers Weekly,* November 25, 1983, review of *Rain of Fire,* p. 64; October 6, 1997, review of *If You Were Born a Kitten,* p. 82; April 3, 2000, review of *Jason's Bear,* p. 79; March 26, 2001, review of *My Mother Is Mine,* p. 91; July 8, 2002, review of *Love Song for a Baby,* p. 48; October 14, 2002, review of *Runt,* p. 84; December 9, 2002, review of *Why Do Kittens Purr?,* p. 82; April 5, 2004, review of *The Double-Digit Club,* p. 62.

*School Library Journal,* April, 2001, Linda Ludke, review of *My Mother Is Mine,* p. 98; September, 2001, Shara Alpern, review of *If You Had a Nose like an Elephant's Trunk,* p. 183; June, 2002, Sandra Welzenbach, review of *Frog's Best Friend,* p. 87; September, 2002, Terrie Dorio, review of *Runt,* p. 219; March, 2003, Carolyn Janssen, review of *Why Do Kittens Purr?,* p. 176; June, 2004, Martha Topol, review of *The Very Best Daddy of All,* p. 96; August, 2005, Elaine E. Knight, review of *The Blue Ghost,* p. 84; July, 2006, Susan E. Murray, review of *The Grand Canyon,* p. 90; May, 2007, Farida S. Dowler, review of *The Mighty Mississippi,* p. 114; May, 2007, Faith Brautigam, review of *Killing Miss Kitty, and Other Sins,* p. 129; August, 2007, Debbie Whitbeck, review of *The Secret of the Painted House,* p. 76; December, 2007, Colleen D. Bocka, review of *Mount Rushmore,* p. 104; April, 2008, Debbie S. Hoskins, review of *The Red Ghost,* p. 102.

*Washington Post Book World,* September 9, 1994, Katherine Paterson, "Easing Troubled Hearts."

*Wilson Library Bulletin,* Cathi Dunn MacRae, review of *What's Your Story?: A Young Person's Guide to Writing Fiction,* p. 104.

*ONLINE*

*Marion Dane Bauer Home Page,* http://www.mariondanebauer.com (August 25, 2008).*

## BIGGS, Brian 1968-

### Personal

Born 1968, in AR; children: one son, one daughter. *Education:* Graduated from Parsons School of Design. *Hobbies and other interests:* Music, bicycles, food.

### Addresses

*Office*—P.O. Box 25922, Philadelphia, PA 19128. *Agent*—Steven Malk, Writers House, 3368 Governor Dr., Ste. 224F, San Diego, CA 92122; smalkwritershouse.com *E-mail*—brian@mrbiggs.com.

### Career

Designer, illustrator, cartoonist, and animator. Has designed puzzle games for Cranium and Mudpuppy, bike helmets for Bell Sports, and greeting cards for Peaceable Kingdom Press.

### Awards, Honors

Nominated for Harvey and Eisner awards; *Print* Regional Design Annual selection, 1999, 2001, 2003; Christopher Award, 2005, for *Shredderman: Secret Identity.*

### Writings

*GRAPHIC NOVELS*

*Frederick and Eloise: A Love Story,* Fantagraphics (Seattle, WA), 1993.

*Dear Julia,* Top Shelf Productions (Portland, OR), 2000.

*ILLUSTRATOR*

Stephen Mooser, *Follow That Flea!,* Grosset & Dunlap (New York, NY), 2005.

Stephen Mooser, *Smell That Clue!,* Grosset & Dunlap (New York, NY), 2006.

Garth Nix, *One Beastly Beast: Two Aliens, Three Inventors, Four Fantastic Tales,* HarperCollins (New York, NY), 2007.

Lynn Brunelle, *Camp Out!: The Ultimate Kids' Guide from the Backyard to the Backwoods,* Workman Publishing (New York, NY), 2007.

Judy Sierra, *Beastly Rhymes to Read after Dark,* Knopf (New York, NY), 2008.

Cynthia Rylant, *Brownie and Pearl Step Out,* Harcourt (Orlando, FL), 2009.

Cynthia Rylant, *Brownie and Pearl Get Dolled Up,* Harcourt (Orlando, FL), 2009.

Contributor of illustrations to periodicals, including *San Francisco Chronicle, New York Times, Nickelodeon, Wired, Philadelphia Weekly,* and *Village Voice.*

*ILLUSTRATOR; "SHREDDERMAN" SERIES*

Wendelin Van Draanen, *Secret Identity,* Knopf (New York, NY), 2004.
Wendelin Van Draanen, *Attack of the Tagger,* Knopf (New York, NY), 2004.
Wendelin Van Draanen, *Meet the Gecko,* Knopf (New York, NY), 2005.
Wendelin Van Draanen, *Enemy Spy,* Knopf (New York, NY), 2005.

*ILLUSTRATOR; "ROSCOE RILEY RULES" SERIES*

Katherine Applegate, *Never Glue Your Friends to Chairs,* HarperCollins (New York, NY), 2008.
Katherine Applegate, *Never Swipe a Bully's Bear,* HarperCollins (New York, NY), 2008.
Katherine Applegate, *Never Swap Your Sweater for a Dog,* HarperCollins (New York, NY), 2008.
Katherine Applegate, *Never Swim in Applesauce,* HarperCollins (New York, NY), 2008.
Katherine Applegate, *Never Walk in Shoes That Talk,* HarperCollins (New York, NY), 2009.

## Adaptations

*Dear Julia* was adapted as a live-action film, 2002.

## Sidelights

Brian Biggs is a designer, cartoonist, and animator who has provided the illustrations for a number of highly regarded children's books. A graduate of Parsons School of Design, Biggs lived and worked in Paris and San Francisco before settling in Philadelphia, where he now keeps a studio. He has designed bike helmets, greeting cards, and puzzles, among other projects, and his artwork has appeared in such publications as the *New York Times, Village Voice,* and *Wired.* As Biggs noted in an essay on the *One Book Two Book* Web log, "I like having several projects into which I can sink my teeth, and I love the fact that at any time the phone could ring and my life and career get turned upside-down. In a good way."

In 1993 Biggs made his literary debut with *Frederick and Eloise: A Love Story,* a haunting graphic novel set in Paris. Three years later he produced another graphic novel, *Dear Julia,* which centers on Boyd Solomon, a man obsessed with birds and flight. "The way Biggs delivers almost everything through Boyd's shaky state-of-mind makes for a fascinating narrative," Eric Reynolds remarked in a *Comics Journal* review of *Dear Julia.*

Biggs entered the world of children's literature when he was assigned to illustrate Wendelin Van Draanen's "Shredderman" series for middle-grade readers. *Secret Identity* introduces Nolan Byrd, an undersized and nerdy fifth grader who becomes an Internet sensation after he launches shredderman.com, a Web site devoted to tracking the comings and goings of school bully Bubba Bixby. "Droll, black-and-white cartoons are a perfect accompaniment to the clever text," wrote *School Library Journal* reviewer Edward Sullivan. In *Attack of the Tagger,* Nolan is determined to reveal the identity of a graffiti artist who is vandalizing buildings in Cedar Valley, but his Shredderman alter-ego inadvertently becomes the chief suspect in the case. According to *School Library Journal* critic Christine McGinty, Biggs's pictures "capture the humor and action of the straightforward plot."

***Brian Biggs creates his characteristic scratch-line cartoon drawings to capture the action in Stephen Mooser's easy-reading* Goofball Malone, Ace Detective.** (Illustration copyright © 2006 by Brian Biggs. Reproduced by permission of Grosset & Dunlap, a division of Penguin Putnam Books for Young Readers.)

*Meet the Gecko,* the third title in Van Draanen's series, centers on Nolan's relationship with Chase Morton, the star of his favorite television show. After Nolan's father, a journalist, arranges for his son to meet with his idol, Nolan learns that Chase is being harassed by an unethical photographer known as "The Mole," and he uses his Shredderman site to expose the culprit. A critic in *Kirkus Reviews* noted that readers "will enjoy the humor, swift pacing, and Biggs's heavy-line cartoon illustrations." In *Enemy Spy,* Nolan joins forces with Bubba to investigate an spy ring operating in their town. In *School Library Journal* Kim Carlson praised "the black-and-white cartoons scattered throughout."

Biggs has also illustrated *One Beastly Beast: Two Aliens, Three Inventors, Four Fantastic Tales,* a work by celebrated Australian author Garth Nix. He "renders even the most monstrous creatures as ludicrous rather than gruesome in his lighthearted cartoons," commented a *Publishers Weekly* critic. Carolyn Phelan, writing in *Booklist,* stated that Biggs's "droll ink drawings with gray washes illustrate these fresh, childlike, and engaging stories." *Beastly Rhymes to Read after Dark,* a collection by Judy Sierra, contains poems about werewolves and tapeworms. "Biggs contributes loud, crowded cartoon illustrations in appropriately queasy colors," a critic in *Kirkus Reviews* noted.

## Biographical and Critical Sources

*PERIODICALS*

*Booklist,* September 1, 2004, Jennifer Mattson, review of *Attack of the Tagger,* p. 125; February 1, 2005, Todd Morning, review of *Meet the Gecko,* p. 962; August, 2005, Carolyn Phelan, review of *Enemy Spy,* p. 2030; July 1, 2007, Carolyn Phelan, review of *One Beastly Beast: Two Aliens, Three Inventors, Four Fantastic Tales,* p. 62.

*Kirkus Reviews,* December 15, 2004, review of *Meet the Gecko,* p. 1210; June 15, 2008, review of *Beastly Rhymes to Read after Dark.*

*Publishers Weekly,* August 6, 2007, review of *One Beastly Beast,* p. 189.

*School Library Journal,* May, 2004, Edward Sullivan, review of *Secret Identity,* p. 158; November, 2004, Christine McGinty, review of *Attack of the Tagger,* p. 156; January, 2005, Jennifer Cogan, review of *Meet the Gecko,* p. 138; May, 2005, Jennifer Ralston, review of *Secret Identity,* p. 50; July, 2005, Kim Carlson, review of *Enemy Spy,* p. 110; September, 2007, Elaine E. Knight, review of *One Beastly Beast,* p. 173.

*ONLINE*

*Brian Biggs Home Page,* http://www.mrbiggs.com (August 10, 2008).

*Comics Journal Online,* http://www.tcj.com/ (July 11, 2006), Eric Reynolds, review of *Dear Julia.*

*One Book Two Book Web site,* http://www.onebooktwobook.com/ (October 19, 2007), "Friday Fifteen: Brian Biggs."

*On My Desk Web site,* http://on-my-desk.blogspot.com/ (February 18, 2007), "Brian Biggs."

*Phillyist Web site,* http://phillyist.com/ (June 9, 2008), "Artist: Brian Biggs."

*Pop-Culture-Corn Web site,* http://www.popculturecorn.com/ (June 2, 2000), Matt Springer, "Q/A with Brian Biggs."

* * *

# BRYAN, Sean

## Personal

Married; wife's name Emily; children: Emily. *Education:* College graduate.

## Addresses

*Home*—CT.

## Career

Author and creative director at an advertising agency, New York, NY.

## Awards, Honors

Blue Ribbon designation, *Bulletin of the Center for Children's Books,* 2005, for *A Boy and His Bunny.*

## Writings

*FOR CHILDREN*

*A Boy and His Bunny,* illustrated by Tom Murphy, Arcade (New York, NY), 2005.

*A Girl and Her Gator,* illustrated by Tom Murphy, Arcade (New York, NY), 2006.

*A Bear and His Boy,* illustrated by Tom Murphy, Arcade (New York, NY), 2007.

*The Juggling Pug,* illustrated by Tom Murphy, Arcade (New York, NY), 2008.

## Sidelights

Working for a New York City advertising agency by day, Sean Bryan has also established a second career in children's books as the author of picture books such as *A Bear and His Boy* and *The Juggling Pug,* the latter which stars a mischievous, fawn-colored pug dog in an entertaining lesson about good behavior.

Bryan made his picture-book debut with *A Boy and His Bunny,* the first of several collaborations with artist Tom Murphy. In the book, a young boy wakes up one morning to find a fluffy bunny named Fred perched on top of his head. As the boy goes through his day, his mother's concern changes to acceptance as Fred explains that having a bunny on one's head imposes no limitations. Two follow-up volumes, *A Girl and Her Gator* and *A Bear and His Boy,* continue the theme of accepting differences. In *A Girl and Her Gator* the sister of the boy from *A Boy and His Bunny* is surprised to find an alligator on her head. The tables turn in *A Bear and His Boy* as a busy bear named Mack wakes up to find a young boy on his shoulders and eventually learns to slow down and enjoy life's simple and sometimes silly moments.

In *School Library Journal,* Blair Christolon called *A Boy and His Bunny* a "quirky and imaginative tale" that "warrants repeated readings," and a *Kirkus Reviews* writer predicted that Bryan's story is "likely to tickle many a preschool listener's ribs." "Repetition . . . paired with the singsong rhyme makes Bryan's slight and silly story great fun to read aloud," concluded

***Sean Bryan's stories about accepting and embracing differences include* A Bear and His Boy, *featuring art by frequent collaborator Tom Murphy.***
(Illustration copyright © 2007 by Tom Murphy. Courtesy of Arcade Publishing.)

Catherine Callegari in her *School Library Journal* review of *A Girl and Her Gator,* while in the same periodical Debbie Lewis O'Donnell wrote that *A Bear and His Boy* is "outstanding in its simplicity" and features "spare" illustrations by Murphy that "are a perfect complement" to Bryan's whimsical tale.

## Biographical and Critical Sources

*PERIODICALS*

*Kirkus Reviews,* January 1, 2005, review of *A Boy and His Bunny,* p. 49; March 1, 2006, review of *A Girl and Her Gator,* p. 227; March 15, 2008, review of *The Juggling Pug;* April 1, 2007, review of *A Bear and His Boy.*

*Publishers Weekly,* January 31, 2005, review of *A Boy and His Bunny,* p. 66.

*School Library Journal,* June, 2005, Blair Christolon, review of *A Boy and His Bunny,* p. 106; August, 2006, Catherine Callegari, review of *A Girl and Her Gator,* p. 76; April, 2007, Debbie Lewis O'Donnell, review of *A Bear and His Boy,* p. 96.

*ONLINE*

*Arcade Publishing Web site,* http://www.arcadepub.com/ (August 15, 2008), "Sean Bryan."*

# BUSBY, Ailie

## Personal

Born in England. *Education:* Attended Nene College; Cambridge School of Art, degree (illustration and design).

## Addresses

*Home*—England.

## Career

Author and illustrator.

## Writings

*SELF-ILLUSTRATED*

*Hey, Diddle, Diddle,* Barron's Educational Series (Hauppauge, NY), 2000.

*Rosie's Zoo,* Scholastic (London, England), 2001.

*As Big as a Pig,* Barron's Educational Series (Hauppauge, NY), 2001.

*Christmas Is Coming: Favorite Christmas Rhymes to Read and Sing Again and Again!,* Barron's Educational Series (Hauppauge, NY), 2001.

*Lulu's Shoes,* Walker & Co. (New York, NY), 2008.

*ILLUSTRATOR*

Francesca Simon, *Camels Don't Ski,* Levinson Books (London, England), 1998.

Elizabeth Arnold, *Thief in the Garden,* Mammoth (London, England), 1999.

Fiona Waters, *Time for a Rhyme,* Orion Children's (London, England), 1999.

Elizabeth Laird, *King of the Supermarket,* Little Hippo (London, England), 1999.

Elizabeth Arnold, *The Triple Trouble Gang,* Mammoth (London, England), 2000.

Pippa Goodhart, *Kind of Twins,* Egmont (London, England), 2001.

Sue Ellis and Myra Barrs, selectors, *Don't Hit Your Sister, and Other Family Poems,* Walker (London, England), 2001.

Jenny Nimmo, *Beak and Whisker,* Egmont (London, England), 2002.

Simon Puttock, *Who's the Boss, Rhinoceros!,* Egmont (London, England), 2002.

Pippa Goodhart, *Friends Forever,* Egmont (London, England), 2003.

Pat Thomason, *Drat That Fat Cat!,* Arthur A. Levine Books (New York, NY), 2003.

Ivor Baddiel and Sophie Jubb, *Cock-a-Doodle Quack! Quack!,* Picture Corgi (London, England), 2006, David Fickling Books (New York, NY), 2007.

J. Patrick Lewis, *The Kindergarten Cat,* Schwartz & Wade Books (New York, NY), 2009.

## Biographical and Critical Sources

*PERIODICALS*

*Booklist,* January 1, 2004, GraceAnne A. DeCandido, review of *Drat That Fat Cat!,* p. 883.

*Horn Book,* January-February, 2004, Susan Dove Lempke, review of *Drat That Fat Cat!,* p. 73.

*Kirkus Reviews,* November 1, 2003, review of *Drat That Fat Cat!,* p. 1314.

*Publishers Weekly,* January 5, 2004, review of *Drat That Fat Cat!,* p. 59; April 2, 2007, review of *Cock-a-Doodle Quack! Quack!,* p. 56.

*School Library Journal,* December, 2003, Blair Christolon, review of *Drat That Fat Cat!,* p. 128; March, 2007, Rachel G. Payne, review of *Cock-a-Doodle Quack! Quack!,* p. 150.*

# C

## CARLSON, Kirsten 1968-
## (Kirsten M. Carlson)

### Personal
Born 1968; married. *Education:* University of Missouri, Columbia, B.S. (biology; with honors), 1990; graduate study at California State University (marine science); University of California, Santa Cruz, certificate in scientific illustration, 1995.

### Addresses
*Home and office*—Stuttgart, Germany. *E-mail*—kc@kirstencarlson.net.

### Career
Illustrator and graphic designer. Monterey Bay Aquarium, Monterey, CA, Web and graphic designer. *Exhibitions:* Work included in exhibitions for Guild of Natural Science Illustrators (Lisbon, Portugal) and for art shows in Monterey, CA, and Gig Harbor, WA.

### Member
Society of Children's Book Writers and Illustrators, Guild of Natural Science Illustrators, National Marine Educators Association.

### Awards, Honors
First Place Award for Realistic Portfolio, Society of Children's Book Writers and Illustrators, 2003, 2004.

### Illustrator
David A. Ufer, *The Giraffe Who Was Afraid of Heights,* Sylvan Dell Pub. (Mt. Pleasant, SC), 2006.

Ron Hirschi, *Ocean Seasons,* Sylvan Dell Pub. (Mt. Pleasant, SC), 2007.

Mary M. Cerullo and Beth E. Simmons, *Sea Secrets: Tiny Clues to a Big Mystery,* Moonlight Publishing (Lafayette, CO), 2008.

Contributor of artwork to periodicals, including *National Geographic* and *Phycologia.*

### Sidelights
Kirsten Carlson is an illustrator who combines her love of animals and nature using science, art, and design. Her creativity arises from direct experiences in nature, often observing animals and sketching them in the field. Back in the studio, she researches her subject using a variety of resources, including numerous visits to the local library and museums and talking with experts. In her classroom visits Carlson shares more about the subjects of her children's books, divulging behind-the-scenes secrets and introducing students to activities that combine both science and art. Her illustration projects include *Ocean Seasons* by Ron Hirschi and *The Giraffe Who Was Afraid of Heights,* a picture book with a text by David A. Ufer.

### Biographical and Critical Sources

*PERIODICALS*

*Children's Bookwatch,* September, 2006, review of *The Giraffe Who Was Afraid of Heights.*

*School Library Journal,* August, 2006, Maryann H. Owen, review of *The Giraffe Who Was Afraid of Heights,* p. 99.

*ONLINE*

*Kirsten Carlson Home Page,* http://www.kirstencarlson.net (August 4, 2008).

*Sylvan Dell Publishing Web site,* http://www.sylvandellpublishing.com/ (August 4, 2008), "Kirsten Carlson."

## CARLSON, Kirsten M.
## See CARLSON, Kirsten

* * *

## CARTER, Don 1958-

### Personal

Born 1958, in Hartford, CT; married; wife's name Catherine; children: Grayson, Phoebe. *Education:* Attended Paier College of Art, 1976-80. *Hobbies and other interests:* Jazz.

### Addresses

*Home*—West Hartford, CT. *Office*—Adams & Knight, 80 Avon Meadow Ln., Avon, CT 06001. *Agent*—Elizabeth Harding, Curtis Brown Ltd., 10 Astor Place, New York, NY 10003. *E-mail*—don@adamsknight.com.

### Career

Illustrator and art director. Tryol & Mikan, art director, 1980-81; Lardis, McCurdy & Company, art director, 1981-85; Naftzger & Kuhe, associate creative director, 1985-86; Mintz & Hoke, creative director, 1986-2001; Adams & Knight Advertising, Avon, CT, creative director, 2001—. Creator of *Happy Monster Band* (animated television series), Playhouse Disney, 2007—.

### Member

Advertising Club of Connecticut.

### Awards, Honors

Original Art Exhibit inclusion, Society of Illustrators, 2000, and 100 Titles for Reading and Sharing designation, New York Public Library, both for for *Wake Up House!;* awards for advertising art direction and copywriting from institutions including The One Show, CLIO, Connecticut Art Directors Club, and Advertising Club of Connecticut.

### Writings

*SELF-ILLUSTRATED*

*Get to Work, Trucks!,* Roaring Brook Press (Brookfield, CT), 2002.

*Heaven's All-Star Jazz Band,* Knopf (New York, NY), 2002.

*Send It!,* Roaring Brook Press (New Milford, CT), 2003.

*Old MacDonald Drives a Tractor,* Roaring Brook Press (New Milford, CT), 2007.

*ILLUSTRATOR*

Dee Lillegard, *Wake Up House!: Rooms Full of Poems,* Knopf (New York, NY), 2000.

***Don Carter (self-portrait)*** (Reproduced by permission.)

Donna Conrad, *See You Soon, Moon,* Knopf (New York, NY), 2001.

Dee Lillegard, *Hello School!: A Classroom of Poems,* Knopf (New York, NY), 2001.

Carter's work has also appeared in *Sesame Street* and *Nick Jr.* magazines.

### Sidelights

Don Carter, the creative director for a Connecticut advertising agency, has served as the illustrator for books that include Dee Lillegard's *Wake Up House!: Rooms Full of Poems* and *Old MacDonald Drives a Tractor,* a self-illustrated title. Carter is also the creator of *Happy Monster Band,* an animated television series for Playhouse Disney.

Describing his journey from advertising executive to children's book illustrator, Carter once told *SATA:* "I developed what I thought was a unique 3-D illustration style with the hopes of illustrating for the advertising field. I was already working in the business as an art director, so it seemed like it would be an easy transition. Without an agent or any serious marketing, my hopeful career went nowhere, so I shelved my portfolio and moved on.

***Carter's stylized art energizes Dee Lillegard's poetry collection* Wake Up House!** (Illustration copyright © 2000 by Don Carter. Used by permission of Alfred A. Knopf, an imprint of Random House Children's Books, a division of Random House, Inc.)

"Many years later, a local artist's representative reignited my interest in illustrating. I was designing a lot of posters for local theater groups at the time, and whenever I could, I would work on my own illustrations. There was no money to pay an illustrator, so it was a good way for me to at least get some printed samples of my own. Hoping the rep might be able to get me some paying jobs, I pulled together a bunch of the samples, and just for kicks I dusted off my old 3-D portfolio and dragged it along. When he saw the 3-D samples, he went nuts. I remember him saying, 'Never mind pastels. I've got at least five guys doing pastels. This 3-D stuff . . . that's what you should be doing.'

"Not satisfied with the quality of my old samples, I developed a whole new portfolio in the 3-D style. The funny thing about it was, not until I had finished all the samples did I fully realize every piece could have easily been for a children's book. I had stuff like blue dogs, teapots with faces, and farm animals dressed as people. I had always had an interest in children's books, but never seriously considered illustrating for them because I had always heard it was next to impossible to break into the market. Now I had a portfolio full of colorful, whimsical illustrations that was pretty much limited to some kind of children's market. So I thought the next logical step was to try and illustrate for the children's magazines.

"I took out an ad in a new publication titled *Picturebook* that was marketed solely to the children's market. Perfect, I thought. I would just sit back and wait for the jobs to come to me. The phone rang maybe half a dozen times. Everyone loved the style, but I didn't get any jobs. The ad also came with five hundred reprints of my page. So I mailed a personalized note along with a copy of the reprint to every magazine, every publisher I could find. The phone started ringing almost immediately. I got several requests to see my portfolio, and *Sesame Street* magazine gave me my first job. I was on my way, or at least I thought I was. Knowing that art directors often filed samples for future jobs, I knew it would take a while for the mailings to bring in work. So I waited. And waited. Again, nothing. I needed to try something else.

"Earlier on I had joined the Graphic Artists' Guild, primarily to get a discount on my *Picturebook* ad. The discount was more than the membership dues, so what did I have to lose? The Guild had a yearly show at the Puck Building in New York City, where illustrators could exhibit their work. Art directors and designers from the advertising, editorial, and publishing fields were invited. I thought maybe it would be a good opportunity to get face to face with the people who actually hired illustrators.

"That night was a major turning point. Designers and art directors snatched up my reprints and asked to be put on my mailing list. One editor from a major children's book publishing house came back to my table probably three times to look at my work. At the end of the night, I came home knowing I had to stick with it.

"Several months later, I received a call from Random House. They asked if I could send my portfolio to their art director. One of their designers had seen my work at the show and had brought back my sample sheet. When they returned my portfolio to me, there was a Random House catalog enclosed. Attached was a yellow post-it note with the message, 'Your portfolio is terrific and I have you in mind for a project. I'll be in touch soon. . . .'

"What was the project? Was it a definite thing? How soon would they be in touch? I couldn't wait. I gave [the art director] a call the next week. That turned out to be my first book, *Wake Up House!* by Dee Lillegard.

In *Wake Up House!* Carter employs foam board, plaster, and acrylic paint to illustrate Lillegard's story of the ordinary things a preschooler encounters at home, including a bathroom mirror, a kitchen stove, a set of cabinets, a broom, and a washing machine. Hazel Rochman, writing in *Booklist,* stated that "Carter's clear, beautiful three-dimensional illustrations" are "as tactile and immediate as the words." Carter's distinctive illustrations also drew praise from a *Publishers Weekly* reviewer, who called his art "dynamic and distinctive."

Carter and Lillegard later collaborated on *Hello School!: A Classroom of Poems,* a verse collection about desks, scissors, water fountains, and other objects that students use. Sheryl L. Shipley, writing in *School Library Journal,* noted that Carter's artwork "will draw youngsters in," and *Booklist* reviewer Marta Segal commented that the illustrations "fairly leap off the pages."

Carter also provided the illustrations for Donna Conrad's debut picture book, *See You Soon, Moon.* In the work, a young boy notices that the moon follows his family as they drive through the countryside on their way to Grandma's house. A *Publishers Weekly* contributor applauded Carter's "eye-catching, irresistibly tactile 3-D illustrations" and the book's "simple, uncluttered layout, vibrant colors and textured cut-out shapes," and Marianne Saccardi, writing in *School Library Journal,* remarked that Carter's foam, plaster, and acrylic illustrations "are brimming with texture and saturated colors."

Discussing his artistic style and the process he uses to create his illustrations, Carter told *SATA:* "It's not based on anything I've ever seen. I used to do a lot of paper collage constructions in art school because I liked the crispness of the shadows each layer made. I guess my

*Cover of Carter's self-illustrated picture book* **Old MacDonald Drives a Tractor,** *which gives a well-known folk story a technological twist.* (Roaring Brook Press, 2007. Illustration copyright © 2007 by Don Carter. Reprinted by permission of Henry Holt & Company, LLC.)

present style is just an expansion of that with thicker layers and thicker shadows." Carter added, "My initial pencil sketches are very tight. So once they are approved I blow them up on a copier to full size as a template for the constructions. After I determine how many layers are needed, I cut the pieces out of foam board. They are then glued together and covered with plaster for texture. Once the plaster is dry, everything is coated with gesso and finally painted with acrylics. Sometimes I'll incorporate other dimensional items such as buttons, twigs, fabric, and bird seed into the constructions for added interest. Then the finished pieces are photographed with a 4x5 format camera."

Carter has also produced a number of self-illustrated titles. In *Get to Work, Trucks!* he depicts a busy day for the men and women behind the controls of a variety of machines, including a bulldozer, dump truck, loader, crane, and cement mixer. Carter's "text provides an incantatory thrum to fill the activity with primal purpose," remarked a *Kirkus Reviews* contributor, and a *Publishers Weekly* critic observed that "every spread looks like a toy-enacted scenario assembled by a young construction enthusiast."

A young boy imagines his late grandfather cavorting with such musical greats as Dizzy Gillespie and Thelonious Monk in *Heaven's All-Star Jazz Band.* According to Ilene Cooper in *Booklist,* Carter's illustrations possess "a naive, kidlike quality that will immediately appeal to the audience," and a *Publishers Weekly* contributor stated that his "distinctive, 3-D concoctions . . . successfully translate a lofty abstraction into a joyful feast for the senses." Writing in *School Library Journal,* Jane Marino complimented the marriage of text and art, noting that Carter combines "sound words, rhyme, and rhythm with stylized illustration to tell an imaginative tale and pay tribute to the music and its stars."

A package makes it way through the postal system, arriving just in time for a child's birthday, in *Send It!,* an "instructive book for preschoolers captivated by planes, trains, and automobiles," remarked *Booklist* critic Karin Snelson. The work follows the package's week-long voyage, showing it aboard a mail truck, a ship, and an airplane. "With engaging simplicity, this title delivers the goods," Luann Toth commented in *School Library Journal.* In *Old MacDonald Drives a Tractor* Carter offers his take on an old favorite. His illustrations "are as enticing as ever," observed a contributor in a *Kirkus Reviews* appraisal of the book.

## Biographical and Critical Sources

*PERIODICALS*

*Advertising Age,* July 31, 2006, Patricia Riedman, "Storyboards Find New Life as Storybook Illustrations," p. 21.

*Booklist,* February 1, 2000, Hazel Rochman, review of *Wake Up House!: Rooms Full of Poems,* p. 1026; August, 2001, Marta Segal, review of *Hello School!: A Classroom Full of Poems,* p. 2125; March 1, 2002, Marta Segal, review of *Get to Work, Trucks!,* p. 1140; November 15, 2002, Ilene Cooper, review of *Heaven's All-Star Jazz Band,* p. 608; December 15, 2003, Karin Snelson, review of *Send It!,* p. 752.

*Kirkus Reviews,* February 15, 2002, review of *Get to Work, Trucks!,* p. 251; May 1, 2007, review of *Old MacDonald Drives a Tractor.*

*Publishers Weekly,* February 14, 2000, review of *Wake Up House!,* p. 196; January 1, 2001, review of *See You Soon, Moon,* p. 91; January 14, 2002, review of *Get to Work, Trucks!,* p. 58; October 21, 2002, review of *Heaven's All-Star Jazz Band,* p. 741; October 6, 2003, review of *Send It!,* p. 82.

*School Library Journal,* December, 2000, review of *Wake Up House!,* p. 54; March, 2001, Marianne Saccardi, review of *See You Soon, Moon,* p. 195; July, 2001, Sheryl L. Shipley, review of *Hello School!,* p. 95; March, 2002, Gay Lynn Van Vleck, review of *Get to Work, Trucks!,* p. 173; November, 2002, Jane Marino, review of *Heaven's All-Star Jazz Band,* p. 112; December, 2003, Luann Toth, review of *Send It!,* p. 111; June, 2007, Kathleen Kelly MacMillan, review of *Old MacDonald Drives a Tractor,* p. 94.

*ONLINE*

*Connecticut Creatives Web site,* http://conncreatives.com/ (March 2, 2008), David Cushman, "Don Carter's Art Farm."

*Flickr,* http://www.flickr.com/ (August 28, 2008), "Don Carter."

* * *

## CHANDLER, Jennifer
See WESTWOOD, Jennifer

* * *

## CHIMA, Cinda Williams

### Personal

Married; husband a scientist; children: Eric, Keith. *Education:* Case Western Reserve University, B.A. (philosophy); University of Akron, M.A. (nutrition).

### Addresses

*Home and office*—OH. *Agent*—Christopher Schelling, Ralph M. Vicinanza, Ltd., 303 W. 18th St., New York, NY 10011. *E-mail*—cinda@cindachima.com.

### Career

Author, nutritionist, and educator. University of Akron, Akron, OH, instructor. Presenter at workshops and speaker at writers' conferences.

## Member

Society for Children's Book Writers and Illustrators, Science Fiction and Fantasy Writers of America, Poets and Writers League of Greater Cleveland.

## Awards, Honors

Booksense Summer Reading Pick, American Library Association Popular Paperbacks listee, and Great Lakes Book Award finalist, all 2006, and South Carolina Young Adult Book Award nominee, Abe Award nominee (IL), Garden State Teen Book Award nominee (NJ), and Isinglass Teen Book Award nominee (NH), all 2009, all for *The Warrior Heir;* New York Public Library Books for the Teen Age designation, 2008, for *The Wizard Heir.*

## Writings

*The Warrior Heir,* Hyperion Books for Children (New York, NY), 2006.
*The Wizard Heir,* Hyperion Books for Children (New York, NY), 2006.
*The Dragon Heir,* Hyperion Books for Children (New York, NY), 2008.

Contributor to books, including *A Cup of Comfort for Christmas,* edited by Coleen Sell, Adams Media (Avon, MA), 2003; and *A Cup of Comfort for Courage,* edited by Sell, Adams Media, 2004; *The World of the Golden Compass: The Otherworldly Ride Continues,* edited by Scott Westerfeld, BenBella Books, 2007. Contributor of nutrition column to Cleveland, OH, *Plain Dealer,* 2004-07.

***Cover of Cinda Williams Chima's novel* The Warrior Heir, *the first volume of her multi-novel fantasy saga.*** 

## Sidelights

Although trained as a nutritionist, Ohio-based novelist Cinda Williams Chima has channeled her curiosity and her many interests into a second career as a fantasy novelist. "I've spent a lot of time prowling through graveyards and digging through dusty old records, uncovering family stories," Chima explained to *Cynsations* online interviewer Cynthia Leitich Smith. "My roots are in the Appalachians of southern Ohio, and there's a strong history of magic there. My grandmother was supposed to have had the 'second sight'—she read the cards for people. When I was in college, I took an English literature tour to England: went to Stratford and the Lake District and the theatres in London. I incorporated elements of all of those things into [my fantasy novel] *The Warrior Heir,* and its sequel, *The Wizard Heir.*"

In *The Warrior Heir* Chima takes readers to Ohio, where high-school student Jack Swift lives in a small Midwestern town. When the teen neglects to take medicine he has been given since he can remember, the magic within him is exposed. Now a group of wizards recognize Jack as a Warrior Heir, a rare being capable of helping a wizard amass power and rise above the other wizards by fighting to the death in tournaments designed to allocate such power within the secret community known as Weirland. Now Jack's friends and relatives are revealed to be equally magical creatures, such as enchantresses, soothsayers, wizards, and enchanters, and they help the teen gain the fighting and magical skills that will help him meet his destiny. Noting that Jack's maturation is well portrayed, *Kliatt* contributor Michele Winship noted that in *The Warrior Heir* Chima "cleverly entwines ancient magic and contemporary adolescence in a coming-of-age story that works on both levels." Because "many details about the Weir are initially hidden from readers," Chima is able to reveal her story's intricacies in a way that is "involving and often surprising," in the opinion of *School Library Journal* reviewer Steven Engelfried, the critic dubbing Chima's novel "suspenseful and entertaining."

In *The Wizard Heir* Chima turns her focus to a teen wizard-in-training as he attempts to take control of his growing magical powers. Orphaned as an infant, Seph McCauley is sixteen years old when the sorcerer who has guarded the boy from the world of magic dies. Now alone, Seph is increasingly frightened by his growing power, power that proves destructive and even deadly because of Seph's inability to control it. After causing a destructive fire, the teen is sent to a school for troubled teens located in a remote area of Maine, and there Seph comes under the tutelage of the school's wizard headmaster. However, Seph soon begins to question his mentor's motives, and when he encounters several other powerful creatures, including Warrior Heir Jack Swift, he realizes that the powers he possesses may also lead to his demise.

Chima's saga continues in *The Dragon Heir,* in which the power struggle among the wizard houses continues and the search for a magical stone called the Dragonheart forces Seph, Jack, and several powerful friends into a battle with those who would usurp all power. In *School Library Journal,* Sharon Rawlings observed of *The Wizard Heir* that Chima's "exciting page-turner is darker than *The Warrior Heir* due to the introduction of several violent characters." A *Kirkus Reviews* contributor had a similar reaction to the novel, concluding that the fantasy "sequel improves on the original, leaving fans eager for the foreshadowed resolution." In *Booklist* Krista Hutley called Seph an "appealing" and resourceful protagonist, concluding that *The Wizard Heir* is an "absorbing, suspenseful" installment in Chima's Weirland saga.

According to a reviewer for the Cleveland, Ohio, *Plain Dealer,* Chima "is adept with teen culture" and her efforts to reference both "slasher-film references" and "the works of Shakespeare" in her fantasy novels "strengthens both her narrative voice and . . . adds subtly to the moral subtext" of her fiction.

## Biographical and Critical Sources

*PERIODICALS*

*Booklist,* April 1, 2006, Holly Koelling, review of *The Warrior Heir,* p. 31; May 15, 2007, Krista Hutley, review of *The Wizard Heir,* p. 59.

*Kirkus Reviews,* April 1, 2006, review of *The Warrior Heir,* p. 344; May 15, 2007, review of *The Wizard Heir.*

*Kliatt,* March, 2006, Michele Winship, review of *The Warrior Heir,* p. 8.

*Plain Dealer* (Cleveland, OH), August 10, 2008, review of *The Dragon Heir.*

*School Library Journal,* July, 2006, Steven Engelfried, review of *The Warrior Heir,* p. 98; December, 2006, Heather Dieffenbach, review of *The Warrior Heir,* p. 73; December, 2007, Sharon Rawlins, review of *The Wizard Heir,* p. 120.

*ONLINE*

*Cinda Williams Chima Home Page,* http://www.cindachima.com (August 10, 2008).

*Cynsations Web site,* http://cynthialeitichsmith.blogspot.com/ (September 26, 2006), Cynthia Leitich Smith, interview with Chima.

* * *

# CLEMESHA, David

## Personal

Born in Blackburn, England; married Andrea Zimmerman (a writer and illustrator); children: Alex, Christian, Chase. *Education:* University of California, Los Angeles, B.A.; San Diego State University, M.A. *Hobbies and other interests:* Movies, tennis, music, going to museums.

## Addresses

*Home*—San Diego, CA. *E-mail*—email@andreaanddavid.com.

## Career

Writer and illustrator. Former elementary schoolteacher.

## Awards, Honors

Blue Ribbon selection, *Bulletin of the Center for Children's Books,* 1999, One Hundred Picture Books Everyone Should Know citation, New York Public Library, and Notable Books for Children selection, American Library Association, 2000, all for *Trashy Town;* Oppenheim Toy Portfolio Gold Award, and Best Children's Books designation, Bank Street College of Education, both 2000, both for *My Dog Toby;* Oppenheim Toy Portfolio Gold Award, 2003, for *Digger Man.*

## Writings

*SELF-ILLUSTRATED; WITH WIFE, ANDREA ZIMMERMAN*

*Rattle Your Bones: Skeleton Drawing Fun,* Scholastic (New York, NY), 1991.

*Digger Man,* Holt (New York, NY), 2003.

*Fire Engine Man,* Holt (New York, NY), 2007.

*FOR CHILDREN; WITH ANDREA ZIMMERMAN*

*The Cow Buzzed,* illustrated by Paul Meisel, HarperCollins (New York, NY), 1993.

*Trashy Town,* illustrated by Dan Yaccarino, HarperCollins (New York, NY), 1999.

*My Dog Toby,* illustrated by True Kelley, Harcourt (San Diego, CA), 2000.

*Fire! Fire! Hurry! Hurry!,* illustrated by Karen Barbour, Greenwillow (New York, NY), 2003.

*Dig!,* illustrated by Marc Rosenthal, Harcourt (Orlando, FL), 2004.

*Manatee Mom,* illustrated by Michael-Che Swisher, Millbrook Press (Minneapolis, MN), 2006.

## Adaptations

*Trashy Town* was adapted for videocassette, Weston Woods, 2001.

## Sidelights

With his wife, Andrea Zimmerman, David Clemesha has written and illustrated a number of critically acclaimed picture books for beginning readers. Born in Great Britain, Clemesha moved to the United States with his family when he was sixteen years old, and after graduating from college he taught elementary school. Clemesha and Zimmerman share writing responsibilities on each of their works; for their self-illustrated titles, Clemesha creates pencil drawings that Zimmerman completes with acrylic paints.

Clemesha and Zimmerman's debut work, *Rattle Your Bones: Skeleton Drawing Fun,* appeared in 1991. The pair later collaborated on *The Cow Buzzed,* a humorous work about the common cold. When a bee sneezes as it visits a farm, its germs as well as its buzzing sound are transmitted to a cow. The bovine then sneezes and passes along its "moo" to yet another animal, confusing the farmer and creating havoc with the farm's feeding schedule. "Easygoing wit permeates this book, from

***Artist David Clemesha joins wife Andrea Zimmerman to coauthor numerous picture books, among them the boy-friendly*** **Fire Engine Man.** (Copyright 2007 by Andrea Zimmerman and David Clemesha. Reprinted by permission of Henry Holt and Company, LLC.)

***Featuring a text by the Clemesha-Zimmerman team,* Dig! *is brought to life in artwork created by Marc Rosenthal.*** (Illustration copyright © 2004 by Marc Rosenthal. Reproduced by permission of Harcourt.)

Clemesha's whimsical style to the surprise punchline," remarked a contributor in a *Publishers Weekly* review of *The Cow Buzzed.*

In *Trashy Town,* Clemesha and Zimmerman follow Mr. Gully, a trash collector, as he makes the rounds of the school, the park, and the doctor's office. "This overwhelmingly positive day-in-the-life gives an overdue salute to an unsung hero," a *Publishers Weekly* reviewer noted, and Nancy Vasilakis commented in *Horn Book* that the couple's "well-designed picture book does a lot with a simple concept."

A young girl and her basset hound are the focus of *My Dog Toby,* "an amusing introduction to the trials and rewards of training a pet," wrote Holly Belli in *School Library Journal.* When the youngster's friends and family doubt Toby's intelligence, the adoring owner becomes determined to prove them wrong. In *Booklist,* Carolyn Phelan called *My Dog Toby* "a warm, witty picture book celebrating the mutual devotion of dogs and their owners."

In *Fire! Fire! Hurry! Hurry!* Captain Kelly's brigade of firefighting animals must interrupt their spaghetti dinner to douse several blazes. The company, which includes a pink mouse and a green elephant, manages to rescue a flower shop, toy store, pet shop, and bakery before finally sitting down to a meal. Clemesha and Zimmerman "ably stoke children's admiration for firefighters without fanning any fears," observed a contributor to *Publishers Weekly,* and a critic in *Kirkus Reviews* described the tale as "a joyful celebration of team work that is sure to please the preschool set."

In *Dig!* the authors depict the activities of Mr. Rally and his dog, Lightning, as they tackle a number of dirty jobs aboard a huge yellow backhoe. "Sentences jounce along from one construction site to the next," remarked Jess Bruder in the *New York Times Book Review,* and *School Library Journal* critic Marian Creamer noted that "the pace, repetition, and word choices make the book appropriate for beginning readers." "Full of action and rhythm, this winning picture book . . . will delight preschoolers," predicted Gillian Engberg in *Booklist.*

Clemesha and Zimmerman also collaborate on *Digger Man,* a self-illustrated work that explores a young boy's dream of becoming a construction worker. "Details are perfect," remarked *School Library Journal* reviewer Andrea Tarr, and Ellen Mandel, commenting in *Booklist,* stated that "the joyful acrylic illustrations and the sparse, confident text will delight" young readers. In a companion volume, *Fire Engine Man,* the youngster imagines the day he and his infant brother will extinguish blazes and prepare meals for their colleagues. According to *Booklist* reviewer Shelle Rosenfeld, "vibrant, detailed, child-friendly art, along with the boy's simple narration, highlights . . . a caring sibling relationship."

## Biographical and Critical Sources

*PERIODICALS*

*Booklist,* May 1, 1993, Ilene Cooper, review of *The Cow Buzzed,* p. 1606; August, 1999, Linda Perkins, review of *Trashy Town,* p. 2067; May 1, 2000, Carolyn Phelan, review of *My Dog Toby,* p. 1666; September 1, 2003, Ellen Mandel, review of *Digger Man,* p. 132; May 15, 2004, Gillian Engberg, review of *Dig!,* p. 1627; May 1, 2007, Shelle Rosenfeld, review of *Fire Engine Man,* p. 101.

*Horn Book,* March, 1999, Nancy Vasilakis, review of *Trashy Town,* p. 204.

*Kirkus Reviews,* June 1, 1993, review of *The Cow Buzzed,* p. 730; September 1, 2003, review of *Digger Man,* p. 1133; April 15, 2007, review of *Fire Engine Man.*

*New York Times Book Review,* May 14, 2000, Adam Liptak, "It's a Dog's Life," p. 29; September 19, 2004, Jess Bruder, review of *Dig!*

*Publishers Weekly,* May 24, 1993, review of *The Cow Buzzed,* p. 84; April 26, 1999, review of *Trashy Town,* p. 82; May 10, 2004, review of *Dig!,* p. 57; September 15, 2003, review of *Digger Man,* p. 63.

*School Library Journal,* May, 1999, Lisa Dennis, review of *Trashy Town,* p. 102; May, 2000, Holly Belli, review of *My Dog Toby,* p. 159; April, 2003, Leslie Barban, review of *Fire! Fire! Hurry! Hurry!,* p. 144; December, 2003, Andrea Tarr, review of *Digger Man,* p.

131; July, 2004, Marian Creamer, review of *Dig!*, p. 90; July, 2007, Linda M. Kenton, review of *Fire Engine Man*, p. 88.

*ONLINE*

*Andrea Zimmerman and David Clemesha Home Page*, http://www.andreaanddavid.com (August 5, 2008).

* * *

## COLIN, Ann
## See URE, Jean

* * *

## COOK, Ande

### Personal

Married. *Education:* Attended art school. *Hobbies and other interests:* Nature, photography.

### Addresses

*Home*—Atlanta, GA; Blue Ridge, GA. *E-mail*—andecook@tds.net.

### Career

Illustrator and fine-arts painter. Formerly worked as a high-school art teacher; Georgia State University, former instructor in art education. High Museum of Art, Atlanta, GA, former director of teacher training; freelance illustrator. Georgia Council for the Arts, former artist-in-residence.

### Member

pARTicular Women Artists.

### Writings

*SELF-ILLUSTRATED*

*Art Starters: Fifty Nifty Thrifty Art Activities*, David Pub. (Worcester, MA), 1996.

*ILLUSTRATOR*

Debbie Trafton O'Neal, *O Christmas Tree*, Augsburg Fortress (Minneapolis, MN), 2003.

Christin Ditchfield, *Bible Heroes of the Old Testament*, Golden Books (New York, NY), 2004.

Joanne Barkan, *Firefly's First Flight*, Reader's Digest Books, 2005.

Suzan Nadimi, *The Rich Man and the Parrot*, Albert Whitman (Morton Grove, IL), 2007.

Contributor to periodicals, including *School Arts*.

### Biographical and Critical Sources

*PERIODICALS*

*Booklist*, April 1, 2007, Hazel Rochman, review of *The Rich Man and the Parrot*, p. 54.

*Kirkus Reviews*, March 15, 2007, review of *The Rich Man and the Parrot.*

*Publishers Weekly*, April 16, 2007, review of *The Rich Man and the Parrot*, p. 51.

*School Library Journal*, April, 2007, Catherine Threadgill, review of *The Rich Man and the Parrot*, p. 124.

*ONLINE*

*Ande Cook Home Page*, http://www.andecook.com (August 15, 2008).

*pARTicular Women Artists Web site*, http://www.particularwomen.org/ (August 15, 2008), "Ande Cook."*

* * *

## CRUM, Shutta 1951-

### Personal

Born 1951; married. *Education:* University of Michigan, B.A. (library science), M.A. (library science). *Hobbies and other interests:* Quilting, mosaics.

### Addresses

*Home and office*—P.O. Box 7444, Ann Arbor, MI 48107. *E-mail*—shutta@shuttacrum.com.

### Career

Writer. South Lyon District Library, South Lyon, MI, former library director; Ann Arbor District Library, Ann Arbor, MI, former children's librarian and storyteller, and manager of Northeast Branch Library. Teacher in Holly, MI, public high school; Washtenaw Community College, MI, former instructor.

### Awards, Honors

Children's Services Award of Merit, Michigan Library Association, 2002; One Hundred Books for Reading and Sharing designation, New York Public Library, 2003, and shortlisted for Kentucky Bluegrass Award, 2005, and South Carolina Junior Book Reward, 2006, both for *Spitting Image;* Best Children's Books of the

***Shutto Crum*** (Reproduced by permission.)

Year designation, Bank Street College, 2002, and Black-eyed Susan Award shortlist, both 2003, for *Who Took My Hairy Toe?;* Canada Our Choice designation, 2002, for *All on a Sleepy Night;* Oppenheim Toy Portfolio Platinum award, Bank Street College Best Children's Book of the Year, and Volunteer State Book Award, 2007, for *Fox and Fluff;* Great Lakes Book Awards shortlist, 2004, for *The House in the Meadow;* Canada Our Choice designation, 2003, and Chocolate Lily Young Readers' Award shortlist, 2005, both for *Click!;* one of eight authors invited to read at 2005 White House Easter Egg Roll; Best Children's Book of the Year designation, Bank Street College, 2005, and Georgia Picture Storybook Award shortilst, 2009, both for *My Mountain Song;* Chicago Public Library Best of the Best designation, 2005, International Reading Association/Children's Book Council Choice designation, 2006, and Young Hoosier Award shortlist, 2008, all for *Bravest of the Brave;* Cybil Award shortlist, 2008, for *A Family for Old Mill Farm.*

## Writings

*PICTURE BOOKS*

*Who Took My Hairy Toe?,* illustrated by Katya Krenina, Albert Whitman (Morton Grove, IL), 2001.

*All on a Sleepy Night,* illustrated by Sylvie Daigneault, Fitzhenry & Whiteside (Toronto, Ontario, Canada), 2001.

*Fox and Fluff,* Albert Whitman (Morton Grove, IL), 2002.

*The House in the Meadow,* illustrated by Paige Billin-Frey, Albert Whitman (Morton Grove, IL), 2003.

*Click!,* illustrated by John Beder, Fitzhenry & Whiteside (Toronto, Ontario, Canada), 2003.

*My Mountain Song,* illustrated by Ted Rand, Clarion Books (New York, NY), 2004.

*The Bravest of the Brave,* illustrated by Tim Bowers, Alfred A. Knopf (New York, NY), 2005.

*A Family for Old Mill Farm,* illustrated by Niki Daly, Clarion Books (New York, NY), 2007.

*Thunder-Boomer!,* illustrated by Carol Thompson, Clarion Books (New York, NY), 2009.

*OTHER*

*Spitting Image* (novel), Clarion Books (New York, NY), 2003.

Contributor of poetry for adults to magazines and professional journals.

## Adaptations

Some of Crum's books have been adapted as audiobooks. *My Mountain Song* was adapted by Toni Buzzeo for reader's theatre, *Library Sparks* magazine, 2007.

## Sidelights

Shutta Crum worked as a children's librarian and storyteller for twenty-five years. In addition to drawing from this experience to write a number of children's picture books, Crum is also the author of the novel *Spitting Image.*

Crum's first book, *Who Took My Hairy Toe?,* is based on an old folk tale. "It is a very old folk tale with a long oral tradition," she explained to Cynthia Leitich Smith in an online interview for *Cynsations.* "*Who Took My Hairy Toe?* is my version of that folk tale that has passed from one person to another for hundreds of years." The story involves a strange monster who is searching for his lost toe. According to DeAnn Tabuchi in *School Library Journal,* "the language begs to be read aloud, with a bit of a drawl, with just the right touch of spookiness." "The neat thing about *Who Took My Hairy Toe?,*" Crum told Smith, "is that it is perfect for young readers who want to be a little scared, but not TOO much! And the kids always ask; how did the monster lose his toe? That's a question I'm not ready to ask the monster yet."

For her first novel, *Spitting Image,* Crum takes readers back to 1967 and a poor rural area of Kentucky. Twelve-year-old Jessie Bovey lives with her single mother just outside of town. She is trying to control her anger, which gets her into fistfights whenever things do not go her way, and is also hoping to find out who her father was. Along the way, Jessie befriends a poverty worker who has been sent to help the town's poor. When the government worker's efforts lead the mass media to take notice of the little town, their coverage is insulting to the locals. "Through Jessie's authentic, resounding voice," wrote a critic for *Publishers Weekly,* "the author ably balances the humorous and the heart-wrenching as she presents an affecting portrait of memorable characters in trying times." Writing in *School Library Journal,* Cindy Darling Codell praised *Spitting Image* for having an "absorbing plot with an uplifting ending," dubbing it "a remarkable first novel." Hazel Rochman, writing in *Booklist,* found that, "woven in with all the local color details is the compelling drama of . . . [Jessie's] search for her father, told with truth, tears, laughter, and real surprise."

Brenda Gail is spending the summer with her grandparents in Crum's picture book *My Mountain Song.* After she learns that each person who lives in the mountains has a "mountain song" inside of them made up of all their favorite memories, Brenda begins to discover her own song. "Written in folksy language, the tender story is beautifully illustrated," according to Karen Hutt in *Booklist.* "Together," wrote Laurie Edwards in *School Library Journal,* "author and illustrator [Ted Rand] have created a delight for the senses that harmonizes the coziness of a close-knit family with the gentle ambience of old-fashioned farm life."

*Crum's* **A Family for Old Mill Farm** *features artwork by artist Niki Daly.* (Illustration copyright © by Niki Daly. Reprinted by permission of Clarion Books, an imprint of Houghton Mifflin Harcourt Publishing Company. All rights reserved.)

Featuring cartoon art by Niki Daly, *A Family for Old Mill Farm* was "probably the most difficult book I've ever written," Crum told Smith in an interview for *Cynsations.* "It took many months of rewrites, it took cutting up the manuscript and rearranging (by me and my editor), it took a grid outline used by my editor to keep track of where we were." The story concerns a young married couple and their son who are looking to buy a house in the country. Every house their real estate agent shows them proves to be a problem. Breezy Lake Lodge is much too windy, while Dry River Ranch has no water. Meanwhile, a raccoon real estate agent has been finding homes for his animal clients at the Old Mill Farm. Eventually, the human family ends up at the Old Mill Farm as well. In her review for *School Library Journal,* Linda L. Walkins concluded that Crum's story "does cleverly celebrate the importance of turning an unfamiliar house into a beloved home."

Crum discusses her passion for encouraging children to read in an interview with Toni Buzzeo for *Library Sparks* magazine. "By reading we come to know that even one small event can have great repercussions," she explained, "that we can't always predict how others will respond, and that how an event is perceived depends upon the perspective of the perceiver. Because of this, we begin to understand the world outside our small daily spheres. It may not always make sense to us, but we know it's there and we have begun to learn how to interact with it. By reading we learn what is expected of us and what we can expect. . . . hopefully, reading also instills in us an insatiable curiosity to find out more about the great going-on-and-on world beyond our own families and friends."

## Biographical and Critical Sources

*PERIODICALS*

*Booklist,* August, 2001, John Peters, review of *Who Took My Hairy Toe?,* p. 2124; September 15, 2002, Kathy Broderick, review of *All on a Sleepy Night,* p. 238; October 15, 2002, Lauren Peterson, review of *Fox and Fluff,* p. 411; March 1, 2003, Hazel Rochman, review of *Spitting Image,* p. 1206; April 1, 2003, Diane Foote, review of *The House in the Meadow,* p. 1400; February 15, 2004, Abby Nolan, review of *Click!,* p. 1061; May 1, 2004, Karen Hutt, review of *My Mountain Song,* p. 1562.

*Kirkus Reviews,* August 1, 2002, review of *Fox and Fluff,* p. 1125; February 1, 2003, review of *The House in the Meadow,* p. 228; April 15, 2003, review of *Spitting Image,* p. 605; May 1, 2004, review of *My Mountain Song,* p. 440; May 1, 2007, review of *A Family for Old Mill Farm.*

*Library Sparks,* August-September, 2007, Toni Buzzeo, interview with Crum.

*Publishers Weekly,* February 3, 2003, review of *The House in the Meadow,* p. 74; April 21, 2003, review of *Spitting Image,* p. 62; June 14, 2004, review of *My Mountain Song,* p. 63.

*Resource Links,* February, 2002, Gail Lennon, review of *All on a Sleepy Night,* p. 3.

*School Library Journal,* October, 2001, DeAnn Tabuchi, review of *Who Took My Hairy Toe?,* p. 137; May, 2002, Linda Ludke, review of *All on a Sleepy Night,* p. 111; December, 2002, Kristin de Lacoste, review of *Fox and Fluff,* p. 86; April, 2003, Linda M. Kenton, review of *The House in the Meadow,* p. 118; April, 2003, Cindy Darling Codell, review of *Spitting Image,* p. 157; February, 2004, Carolyn Janssen, review of *Click!,* p. 104; June, 2004, Laurie Edwards, review of *Mountain Song,* p. 104; July, 2004, Casey Rodini, review of *Spitting Image,* p. 60; April, 2005, Lisa Gangemi Kropp, review of *The Bravest of the Brave,* p. 96; June, 2007, Linda L. Walkins, review of *A Family for Old Mill Farm,* p. 96.

*ONLINE*

*Cynsations Web site,* http://cynthialeitichsmith.blogspot.com/ (August 30, 2005), Cynthia Leitich Smith, interview with Crum.

*Shutta Crum Home Page,* http://www.shuttacrum.com (August 13, 2008).

# D

## DEAN, David 1976-

### Personal

Born 1976. *Education:* Manchester Metropolitan University, B.A. (illustration), 1999, M.A. (communication design), 1999.

### Addresses

*Home and office*—Cheshire, England. *Agent*—The Organisation, 69 Caledonian Rd., London N1 9BT, England; infoorganisart.co.uk.

### Career

Illustrator, 1999—.

### Writings

*ILLUSTRATOR*

Richard Moverley, *The Reluctant Rajput,* Egmont (London, England), 2005, Crabtree Publishing (New York, NY), 2006.
Lauren St. John, *The White Giraffe,* Orion (London, England), 2006, Dial Books (New York, NY), 2007.
Lauren St. John, *Dolphin Song,* Dial Books (New York, NY), 2008.

Also illustrator of more than forty book covers.

### Sidelights

British illustrator David Dean has provided artwork for advertisements, magazines, and posters, as well as for more than forty book covers. "My work is colourful and lively with broad appeal," the artist remarked on his home page. Dean has also served as the illustrator for a number of children's books, including *The Reluctant Rajput* by Richard Moverley. The work concerns Bhupinder, a young boy living in rural India who dreams that he is a Rajput: an ancient warrior. Dean's "illustrations are suitable to the story and are appropriate for the age range but do not overdo the blood and

***David Dean created the artwork for Lauren St. John's picture book* The White Giraffe.** (Art © 2006 by David Dean. Reproduced by permission of Dial Books for Young Readers, a division of Penguin Putnam Books for Young Readers.)

gore referred to in the story," wrote John Dryden in the *Canadian Review of Materials.* "The illustrator has depicted Bhupinder's community well, and a lot of information can be grasped from the art."

Set in South Africa, Lauren St. John's *The White Giraffe* focuses on eleven-year-old Martine, a British girl who is sent to live with her grandmother on a game reserve after her parents are killed in a fire. Told by a Zulu healer that she possesses mystical gifts, Martine then encounters a legendary white giraffe and attempts to save the creature from poachers. According to a reviewer in *Publishers Weekly,* "Dean contributes charming watercolor illustrations that open each chapter."

## Biographical and Critical Sources

*PERIODICALS*

*Booklist,* June 1, 2007, Anne O'Malley, review of *The White Giraffe,* p. 75.

*Canadian Review of Materials,* April 14, 2006, John Dryden, review of *The Reluctant Rajput.*

*Kirkus Reviews,* April 1, 2007, review of *The White Giraffe.*

*Publishers Weekly,* May 28, 2007, review of *The White Giraffe,* p. 63.

*School Library Journal,* June, 2007, Robyn Gioia, review of *The White Giraffe,* p. 162.

*ONLINE*

*Children's Illustrators Web site,* http://www.childrensillustrators.com/ (August 15, 2008), "David Dean."*

* * *

# DOWNHAM, Jenny 1964(?)-

## Personal

Born c. 1964, in England; married; children: two sons.

## Addresses

*Home*—England.

## Career

Author and actor. Tellers Theatre, London, England, actress, c. 1990s.

## Awards, Honors

London Writers' Competition first prize, 2003.

## Writings

*Before I Die,* David Fickling Books (New York, NY), 2007.

## Adaptations

*Before I Die* was adapted as an audiobook, read by Charlotte Parry, Listening Library, 2007.

## Sidelights

British writer Jenny Downham tackles a difficult theme in her first novel for teen readers: what a person does after learning that he or she has only months left to live. In *Before I Die* readers meet sixteen-year-old Tessa shortly after she has been told that the leukemia she was diagnosed with four years ago is now terminal. A strong character, Tessa decides to make the most out of every day she has left; with her best friend Zoey, she sets about listing the top ten things she most wants to accomplish or experience during what is left of her short life. While her parents' reactions range between denial (her overprotective dad) and disinterest (her emotionally distant mom), Tessa focuses on achieving each of her goals, and her record of her own progress serves as the novel's text. One goal stands out as most meaningful for the girl—to experience love—and this is accomplished through her relationship with Adam, the boy who lives next door.

***Cover of Jenny Downham's provocative and compelling young-adult novel* Before I Die.** (David Fickling Books, 2007. Reprinted by permission of David Fickling Books, an imprint of Random House Children's Books, a division of Random House, Inc.)

Calling Tessa's story "shockingly straightforward," a *Publishers Weekly* contributor added of *Before I Die* that in Downham's "wrenching and exceptionally vibrant" prose the author effectively portrays the teen's slow physical decline and her battle with a myriad conflicting emotions. In *Booklist* Hazel Rochman praised the use of the present tense, noting that the author's "clear, beautiful prose" will "draw readers deeply into the story" and inspire them to question what they would do in Tessa's place. Citing the novel's "inspired originality," John Burnham Schwartz added in his *New York Times Book Review* appraisal that *Before I Die* contains "as honest and indelible a portrait of a young adult at risk—no, beyond risk—as one is likely to find in recent literature."

In an interview with the *New York Times Book Review,* Downham discussed the focus and intent of her first novel, noting that she read widely on the medical aspects of her story in order that *Before I Die* portray the facts accurately. However, the novel "was never supposed to be a medical or hospital-based story," she added. "Tess has been sick for four years and has received a terminal diagnosis. She knows she will die. She lives with her condition. I wanted the reader to inhabit her body (by using first-person, present tense narrative) in the hope that they would have both a visceral and an emotional response. If Tessa's body does the talking—if the reader experiences a lumbar puncture or a hemorrhage with her—then it inevitably pushes the reader closer to the physical self. I wanted to achieve an immediacy between the body's decline and the words Tess uses to describe what's happening to her."

Downham, a former actor, draws on her stage training in her work as a writer. "I keep notebooks and journals and diaries for the characters, researching them as if I'm going to play them on stage . . . ," she explained in her interview for *Teenreads.com.* "It might not all get in the book, but it helps me to know who they are."

## Biographical and Critical Sources

*PERIODICALS*

*Booklist,* November 15, 2007, Hazel Rochman, review of *Before I Die,* p. 53.

*New York Times Book Review,* October 14, 2007, John Burnham Schwartz, review of *Before I Die,* and interview with Downham.

*Publishers Weekly,* August 6, 2007, review of *Before I Die,* p. 191.

*ONLINE*

*Teenreads Web site,* http://www.teenreads.com/ (September 1, 2007), interview with Downham.*

# DUKE, Kate 1956-

## Personal

Born August 1, 1956, in New York, NY; daughter of Robert (a lawyer) and Jeannette Duke; married Sidney Harris (a cartoonist), 1985. *Education:* Attended Duke University, 1975-76. *Hobbies and other interests:* Gardening, reading, cooking, visiting museums, mural-painting.

## Addresses

*Home*—New Haven, CT.

## Career

Children's book writer and illustrator, 1983—. Also lectures at schools and other educational institutions.

## Member

Society of Children's Book Writers and Illustrators, Writers Union, PEN, Authors Guild, Authors League of America.

## Awards, Honors

Library of Congress Book of the Year designation, Parents Choice Award, Remarkable Books for Literature designation, Children's Choice Award, International Reading Association/Children's Book Council (IRA/CBC), and *Boston Globe/Horn Book* Illustration Honor Book, all 1983, and Children's Picture Book of the Year award, *Redbook,* 1986, all for *The Guinea Pig ABC;* Children's Choice Award, IRA/CBC, 1985, for *Seven Froggies Went to School;* Year's Top Prizes selection, *Publishers Weekly,* 1986, for *Bedtime, Clean-up Day, At the Playground,* and *What Bounces?;* Pick of the Lists selection, American Booksellers Association, 1988, for *What Would a Guinea Pig Do?;* Children's Choice Award, IRA/CBC, 1989, for *It's Too Noisy!;* Children's Choice Award, IRA/CBC, and Children's Book of the Year designation, Bank Street Child Study Children's Book Committee, both 1992, both for *Aunt Isabel Tells a Good One;* Parents Choice Award, 1995, for *One Saturday Morning* by Barbara Baker; New Jersey Garden State Children's Book Award, and Garden State Teen Book Award in easy-to-read category, both 2002, both for *One Saturday Afternoon* by Baker.

## Writings

*SELF-ILLUSTRATED*

*The Guinea Pig ABC,* Dutton (New York, NY), 1983.

*Guinea Pigs Far and Near,* Dutton (New York, NY), 1984.

*Seven Froggies Went to School,* Dutton (New York, NY), 1985.

*What Would a Guinea Pig Do?,* Dutton (New York, NY), 1988.
*Roseberry's Great Escape,* Dutton (New York, NY), 1990.
*Aunt Isabel Tells a Good One,* Dutton (New York, NY), 1992.
*If You Walk down This Road,* Dutton (New York, NY), 1993.
*Aunt Isabel Makes Trouble,* Dutton (New York, NY), 1996.
*Archaeologists Dig for Clues,* HarperCollins (New York, NY), 1996.
*One Guinea Pig Is Not Enough,* Penguin Putnam (New York, NY), 1998.
*Twenty Is Too Many,* Penguin Putnam (New York, NY), 2000.
*The Tale of Pip and Squeak,* Dutton (New York, NY), 2007.

*"GUINEA PIG BOARD BOOKS" SERIES; SELF-ILLUSTRATED*

*What Bounces?,* Dutton (New York, NY), 1985.
*At the Playground,* Dutton (New York, NY), 1985.
*Bedtime,* Dutton (New York, NY), 1986.
*Clean-up Day,* Dutton (New York, NY), 1986.

*ILLUSTRATOR*

Raffi, *Tingalayo,* Crown (New York, NY), 1989.
Joanna Cole, *It's Too Noisy!,* HarperCollins (New York, NY), 1989.
Joanna Cole, *Don't Tell the Whole World!,* HarperCollins (New York, NY), 1990.
Barbara Brenner, *Good News!,* Bantam (New York, NY), 1991.
Miriam Schlein, *Let's Go Dinosaur Tracking!,* HarperCollins (New York, NY), 1991.
Joann Oppenheim, *Show-and-Tell Frog,* Bantam (New York, NY), 1993.
Barbara Baker, *One Saturday Morning,* Dutton (New York, NY), 1995.
William H. Hooks, *Mr. Garbage,* Bantam (New York, NY), 1996.
William H. Hooks, *Mr. Big Brother,* Bantam (New York, NY), 1999.
Barbara Baker, *One Saturday Afternoon,* Dutton (New York, NY), 1999.
Martha Lewis Lambert, *I Won't Get Lost,* HarperCollins (New York, NY), 2003.
Barbara Baker, *One Saturday Evening,* Dutton (New York, NY), 2007.

## Sidelights

An award-winning author and illustrator, Kate Duke creates imaginative and engaging picture books for children that introduce concepts ranging from the alphabet and mathematics to spatial relationships and the how-to's of creative writing. The characters in Duke's books are humorous and endearing animals of all sorts: pigs, mice, squirrels, a mole or two, and her trademark guinea pigs. Employing simple text in her own self-illustrated titles, Duke has also supplied vibrant, cartoon-like artwork for books by popular authors, including Raffi, Miriam Schlein, Barbara Baker, Joanna Cole, and Martha Lewis Lambert.

Duke uses her bemused and amusing guinea pigs in several picture books that have garnered much critical praise and drawn many fans at reading hour. "The heroes of Ms. Duke's stories are no ordinary guinea pigs," Rebecca Lazear Okrent noted in the *New York Times Book Review.* "They are whimsical creatures with serious ideas who always seem to be suppressing a giggle, especially in the face of disaster." Her audience includes both children and adults: "As in the best toddler books . . . there is humor here for both child and parent," Linda Wicher pointed out in a *School Library Journal* review of Duke's "Guinea Pig Board Books" series, and the same can be said for other books by Duke, with their vibrant, action-packed illustrations and frequently droll humor.

An early love of books spurred Duke's ambition to become a writer. "I was born in New York City and grew up there, the oldest of four children," she once told *SATA.* "Both my parents were and are great readers, and we children were always amply supplied with books. My experience of the world of literature was satisfying from the start, for my parents seemed to enjoy reading to me as much as I enjoyed being read to." Although she was an active child—often roller skating and riding bikes in the park across the street from her apartment building or in the country where she spent summers with her grandmother—Duke's favorite activity was reading. "I read in the summer and in the winter, in the city and in the country, in school and on vacation. I liked books that had adventures in them, and books with talking animals, and books that made me laugh. I still do!"

One of her favorite fictional characters was Doctor Doolittle: "I yearned passionately to be able to talk to animals as he did," Duke once told *SATA.* Another was Nancy Drew, and a third and the most influential was Harriet the Spy, "whose exploits prompted me at age eleven to start following pedestrians around my neighborhood, taking notes on their every 'suspicious' move. I think I owe Harriet my first conscious awareness of the act of writing as important and meaningful work." Accompanying this realization about words was another, equally important discovery. "At about that same time . . . sixth grade . . . I also discovered that I could draw," Duke once recalled. "In art class one day, the picture of a dog that I was copying from a how-to-draw book came out looking pretty much like a dog. Since my artistic abilities had not previously been particularly notable, I remember being quite surprised by this new development. Pleased, of course, but definitely surprised."

After finishing high school, Duke attended college for a couple of years; then she left school and "floundered around for a long while," she later described it, trying to figure out what she really wanted to do. Art classes in New York reminded her of how much she had enjoyed picture books as a child. "I got the idea that I could write stories to go with my pictures and turn them into books for children. I hoped that the children who read them would love them as much as I loved the books I had read as a child." Such aspirations eventually led to her first picture book, *The Guinea Pig ABC.* Different from other alphabet books, Duke's work is based on adjectives rather than nouns and carefully places the animal character within the shape of each letter so as to focus the eye of the child on it. For example, with the letter "K" for "kind," a solicitous guinea pig is leaning against the downward sloping extension of the letter, while an obviously sick guinea pig lies in bed, propped for support against the perpendicular spine of the letter. A contributor to *Kirkus Reviews* felt that the book was "wholly pleasing—a homespun, direct alternative to lots of artifice," and Selma G. Lanes, writing in the *New York Times Book Review,* called Duke's first book a "refreshingly different alphabet with heady possibilities." Ann A. Flowers, writing in *Horn Book,* noted that Duke's idea is "cleverly carried out" with "bright-colored illustrations," and that the "overall feeling is one of gaiety and happiness. . . . Destined perhaps to become a classic." *The Guinea Pig ABC* won the *Boston Globe/Horn Book* Illustration honor among many others awards, making it an auspicious debut for Duke.

Duke stuck with her guinea pigs, or "sprightly company of entertainers," as a *Publishers Weekly* reviewer described them, for her next picture book. *Guinea Pigs Far and Near* illustrates words of both physical and personal relationship, such as "apart," "far," "near," "beside," and "between." Each picture is a complete story that involves adventure, suspense, and humor. In the initial illustration, a female guinea pig gets on a railroad car with her brother in the car behind her. The two are separated when the coupling breaks, and their ensuing chase illustrates spatial relationships of far and near. Diane S. Rogoff, writing in *School Library Journal,* described *Guinea Pigs Far and Near* as "charming, entertaining and full of fun," but added that it could also be "very confusing to young people." Rogoff faulted the lack of a central character in the book, contending that children may have difficulty determining which character the featured word describes. Other commentators focused on Duke's humor and the quality of her illustrations, A critic in *Kirkus Reviews* called the book "sunny and good-humored, and quirky," while the reviewer in *Publishers Weekly* lauded Duke's "brightly colored, action-packed pictures."

Duke's third picture book uses frogs as an inspiration, telling the rhyming story of school-bound amphibians in *Seven Froggies Went to School.* Duke adapted an old poem for her text, sending her frogs to a bullrush-filled pond where a stern instructor puts his charges through their paces. Duke employs shades of green in her illustrations, creating "zippy little amphibians in waistcoated dress," according to Denise M. Wilms in *Booklist.* "The sense of fun is strong," Wilms concluded. A contributor in *Childhood Education* commented that "action abounds" in this text relating the "amusing antics" of the seven frogs who are learning about survival from Master Bullfrog. A critic to *Kirkus Reviews* found the illustrations "entertaining," but maintained that *Seven Froggies Went to School* "hasn't the conceptual eclat, or the masterly characterization, of [Duke's] previous entries."

Duke returned to her frisky and endearing guinea pigs with a set of four story board books, *Bedtime, Clean-up Day, At the Playground,* and *What Bounces?* "The irrepressible family of guinea pigs . . . star in the sunniest board books of the season," asserted a *Publishers Weekly* reviewer, who added: "This is the series for which Duke's pigs were born." The characters here represent a patient mother or a very active child with very simple, caption-like text. Daily activities are dealt with—cleaning up, going to bed, playing—as well as concepts, as in *What Bounces?* Here the young guinea pig climbs on a stool to explore the insides of the refrigerator, soon discovering that while balls bounce, eggs, milk, and butter most decidedly do not. A *Bulletin of the Center for Children's Books* contributor called the four-book set "funny" and "clever," while *Booklist* critic Ellen Mandel noted that the instructive nature of the books is

***Kate Duke's early work includes her self-illustrated* If You Walk down This Road.** (Copyright © 1993 by Kate Duke. Used by permission of Dutton Children's Books, a division of Penguin Putnam Books for Young Readers.)

***Duke's detailed cartoon art adds a whimsical air to Barbara Baker's picture book* One Saturday Morning.** (Copyright © 1994 by Kate Duke. Used by permission of Dutton Children's Books, a division of Penguin Putnam Books for Young Readers. )

"embellished by [Duke's] critters' perky personalities and by her own sense of humor," adding: "These four titles are especially engaging." Linda Wicher, in a *School Library Journal* review, concluded that the board books are "very nicely done," while in *Publishers Weekly* a critic noted that Duke's "sunny, delightfully childlike set . . . stands out in a crowded field."

Duke rejoins her anthropomorphic rodents in *What Would a Guinea Pig Do?,* providing further adventures in domesticity. "The irrepressible cast romps through each situation in merry mayhem," commented Starr LaTronica in a *School Library Journal* review of the book. "Duke's pigs make disasters look like terrific fun," noted a critic in *Publishers Weekly.* "The entire book is a joyful offering." Rebecca Lazear Okrent, writing in the *New York Times Book Review,* pointed out the subtle lessons to be learned in each of the characters' dilemmas: Once the guinea pigs clean their house, for instance, they have a party and then have to start cleaning all over again, a lesson in celebrating success. Okrent concluded: "The text is minimal and easy to read. The brightly colored illustrations . . . are cheerful and captivating. As in all the best books, the rules for living are discreet. You have to be looking for them."

A decade passed before Duke returned to her favorite creatures in *One Guinea Pig Is Not Enough,* "not a counting book, but an adding book," according to a critic for *Kirkus Reviews.* Here, Duke employs events that are propelled by numbers to introduce the concept of addition. As the numbers-driven scenario continues, the assembled guinea pigs grow to crowd size, frolicking and having a picnic in a volume "warm and playful from beginning to end," as a *Kirkus Reviews* contributor noted. A writer for *Publishers Weekly* felt that Duke "adds another feather to her cap" with this "exuberant and clever introduction to math," and April Judge, writing in *Booklist,* called *One Guinea Pig Is Not Enough* a "painless and fun-filled way to learn how to add."

Subtraction is at the heart of *Twenty Is Too Many.* Crowded in a tiny boat about to sink are a score of the "irrepressible and mathematically driven guinea pigs," as a contributor for *Publishers Weekly* wrote. Ten of them abandon ship and others set off on their own unique adventures. One group arrives at a desert island and discovers a buried treasure in between bouts of surfing. With each reduction, the correct formula is presented in the corner of the page to represent the mathematical result. Adele Greenlee, writing in *School Library Journal,* commended "the lively watercolors [that] offer humorous detail and foreshadow the action," while *Booklist* critic Marta Segal noted that *Twenty Is Too Many* "effortlessly and amusingly teaches simple math concepts." For Patricia Hohensee, reviewing the title in *Teaching Children Mathematics,* Duke's subtraction book is "absolutely delightful."

Other books by Duke feature different animals: mice in *Aunt Isabel Tells a Good One* and *Aunt Isabel Makes Trouble;* an adventurous pig in *Roseberry's Great Escape;* and a menagerie of rabbits, lizards, mice, squirrels, and owls in *If You Walk down This Road.* In the first title, a mouse child, Penelope, is staying overnight with her slightly bohemian Aunt Isabel. Duke's storytelling talents come to the fore in a story-within-a-story format in which the reader experiences not only the relationship between aunt and niece but also the adventurous tale Aunt Isabel creates with the child's

***In* Twenty Is Too Many *Duke creates an original self-illustrated counting story featuring an engaging cast of small critters.*** (Copyright © 2000 by Kate Duke. Reproduced by permission of Dutton Children's Books, a division of Penguin Putnam Books for Young Readers.)

assistance. "The framing story has an appealing warmth and is deftly interwoven with Aunt Isabel's tale so that both narratives move briskly," noted a *Kirkus Reviews* contributor, who added that the book "should be invaluable to creative-writing programs for young children." Writing in *Booklist,* Sheilamae O'Hara noted that *Aunt Isabel Tells a Good One* is "a fine book to enjoy on its own merits, but it will also be useful for teachers instructing primary students in the elements of creative writing." O'Hara also commented on Duke's "droll, neatly executed watercolor illustrations," describing them as "an integral part of the story." A reviewer in *Publishers Weekly* called Duke a "gifted artist," and favorably noted the "winsome borders, adorned with tiny, appropriate decorative touches."

Aunt Isabel is reprised in *Aunt Isabel Makes Trouble.* Again, young Penelope is visiting her aunt, and after a day of playing in the park, the niece wants a story from her aunt at naptime. Isabel accommodates with a tale about a mouse named Lady Penelope who has no money and is attempting to reach the prince's castle for his birthday. En route, she manages to foil a gang of cockroaches. Constant interruptions at the most exciting moments of the story by Penelope allow the niece to interact and to take the tale in new directions, ultimately telling the story her own way. A critic for *Kirkus Reviews* commented on the "chatty" and "lighthearted" narrative, as well as on the "good-humored twists and turns" of the plot. "Children," the same reviewer concluded, "will anticipate the satisfying outcome and surely applaud the mouse heroine." For Beth Tegart, writing in *School Library Journal,* Duke's story-within-a-story is both "clever and appealing," while her "charming" illustrations "complement the fast-paced, well-written text." A contributor for *Publishers Weekly* concluded that *Aunt Isabel Makes Trouble* "continues to celebrate the joys of storytelling while providing a splendid showcase for Duke's sunny, winningly detailed watercolors," and *Booklist* critic Stephanie Zvirin deemed Duke to be "in great form" with this "clever, funny, and inviting" tale.

With *If You Walk down This Road,* Duke introduces the anthropomorphic forest folk of Shady Green who are curious about and welcome some newcomers. "Soft watercolor illustrations burst with humorous detail and activity totally appropriate to the homes and residents" featured, noted Virginia Opocensky in *School Library Journal,* the critic adding that Duke's illustrations will "demand multiple readings." In *The Tale of Pip and Squeak,* Duke explores sibling rivalry through a pair of feuding mice brothers. Though they share an attic home, Pip and Squeak barely tolerate each other. Pip constantly complains about his brother's singing, while Squeak hates the smell of Pip's paints. As the duo prepares for an annual party, competitive instincts get the better of both, and before long their humble abode is in shambles. Pip and Squeak realize that they must pool their talents to make the shindig a success. Duke's "nimble narrative features plenty of peppy dialogue, yet the true charm of this tale is rooted in her whimsically detailed illustrations," wrote a contributor in *Publishers Weekly.* According to a critic in *Kirkus Reviews,* Duke's pictures "create a playful, lively environment for the reader to enjoy while learning about compromise."

Duke turned her hand to human protagonists with *Archaeologists Dig for Clues,* a "lively, informative title," according to *Booklist* critic Hazel Rochman. This book, part of a science series, presents a group of youngsters who go on an archaeological dig in a cornfield with the professional, Sophie, in charge. Together, they use painstaking techniques to sift through the materials dug up. No buried graves or treasures are discovered; instead the volunteers unearth rocks and dirt, the importance of which Sophie explains to them. As James E. Ayres pointed out in a *Science Books & Films* review, the dig is at "a 6,000-year-old prehistoric Archaic-period site," and the on-goings are "fairly and accurately depicted" in Duke's illustrated text. Scientific methods are introduced and explained, from the digging to the processing of artifacts. *Archaeologists Dig for Clues* "stresses the seriousness of the subject, while emphasizing the fun," continued Ayres. A contributor for *Kirkus Reviews* thought that "readers will feel as if they're taking an active part in an archaeological dig in this informative entry," and praised Duke's "inviting approach to a complex process." Rochman also observed that readers will become "totally involved" both in the process and the story, while Jackie Hechtkopf, writing in *School Library Journal,* dubbed the same book a "delightful cornucopia of information that students will return to again and again."

Duke has also illustrated several books by other authors, and her work on these has won praise similar to that for her own picture books. Her first collaborative effort was with Raffi in *Tingalayo,* a Caribbean tale about a rather mischievous donkey. A contributor for *Kirkus Reviews* applauded Duke's "vigorous black line and [use of] colors that evoke the Caribbean setting," while Debby Jeffery observed in *School Library Journal* that the illustrator's "colorful and humorous pictures expand the simple song."

Working with Joanna Cole on *It's Too Noisy!,* a retelling of a Yiddish folktale, Duke contributed "numerous watercolor illustrations [that] evoke a world where much more is happening than words can depict," according to Patricia Maclachlan in the *Los Angeles Times Book Review.* Cole and Duke paired together again on *Don't Tell the Whole World!,* another retelling of a comic folktale about a woman who has trouble keeping a secret. A contributor for *Publishers Weekly* thought that "Duke's pastel palette and affable characters lend snappy support to Cole's amusing text." Rochman also had praise for Duke's "ebullient, cartoon-style pictures," and in *School Library Journal* Judith Gloyer noted that her "watercolors reflect the gentle humor of the tale."

In *Booklist,* Denia Hester noted of *Let's Go Dinosaur Tracking!* by Miriam Schlein that "Duke's bright, play-

***Duke introduces a pair of fun-loving rodent characters in her self-illustrated* The Tale of Pip and Squeak.** (Copyright © 2007 by Kate Duke. Reproduced by permission of Dutton Children's Books, a division of Penguin Putnam Books for Young Readers.)

ful pen-and-watercolor illustrations are perfect for this not-so-serious science book." *One Saturday Morning,* Barbara Baker's popular story about the busy Saturday activities of the Bear family, has also been illustrated by Duke. Chris Sherman, reviewing the work in *Booklist,* asserted that "Duke's bright colors, which grace every page, enhance the warmth and bustle of the story." Gale W. Sherman, writing in *School Library Journal,* described *One Saturday Morning* as "a winner," noting that "Duke's watercolor-and-pen illustrations are filled with humor and will delight children."

Duke and Baker also team up for *One Saturday Afternoon,* detailing the after lunch activities of Mama and Papa Bear, as well as Lily, Rose, Daisy, and baby Jack. Lori Haas Weaver, writing in *School Library Journal,* felt that Duke's watercolor and pastel artwork contributes "a lively sense of animation to the story," while Lempke commented on the artist's "tender, mischievous" illustrations. The Bear family returns in *One Saturday Evening,* "a bedtime treat for parents and new readers alike," noted a *Kirkus Reviews* critic. As a busy day draws to a close, Mama Bear rewards herself with a relaxing bath, Papa drinks tea and reads a book, and the children prepare for bed. "Duke's expressive watercolors are endearing," remarked Erika Qualls in *School Library Journal.*

Working with Martha Lewis Lambert on *I Won't Get Lost,* Duke serves up "charming illustrations in pastel colors and with humorous details," according to Kristin de Lacoste in *School Library Journal.* Featuring Horatio Horndragon, a green and pink dragon, the story "may well help adults prove to youngsters the importance of memorizing their addresses and telephone number," as a contributor to *Publishers Weekly* explained. This same reviewer further commented that the illustrator adds "some fun details into the proceedings."

Duke, who lives in Connecticut, maintains a busy schedule to allow her to manage so many projects. "I work every day, from early morning to early afternoon," she once told *SATA*. "My studio is in the upstairs of my house, and it's there that I spend most of my time. My typewriter is there, and all my paints and paper, and a comfortable chair for me to sit in while I try to think of new ideas for books." But when time permits, Duke is out in her garden or off lecturing at schools. "Since writing and drawing are both solitary pursuits, I try to make a point of getting out into the real world. A little human contact is important to keeping one's equilibrium. Indeed, one of the great pleasures I have these days is in going out to visit schools and talk to children about what I do. These occasions are a chance to get in touch with my books' intended audience and to recharge my memories of what it was like to be a child. I don't have children of my own, so it's a real treat to be able to interact with them once in a while. I'm always cheered and inspired by their energy and imagination. Plus, they laugh at my jokes!" Duke also noted for *PBS Online* that her frequent visits to schools helps her in creating books for young readers: "I find out what makes children laugh, what doesn't make them laugh, what their current interests are. I am always cheered and inspired by their energy and imagination."

## Biographical and Critical Sources

*BOOKS*

*Authors of Books for Young People,* 3rd edition, Scarecrow (Metuchen, NJ), 1999.

*Children's Literature Review,* Volume 51, Gale (Detroit, MI), 1999.

*PERIODICALS*

*Booklist,* March 15, 1985, Denise M. Wilms, review of *Seven Froggies Went to School,* p. 1058; June 1, 1986, Ellen Mandel, review of "Guinea Pig Board Books," p. 1459; November 1, 1990, Hazel Rochman, review of *Don't Tell the Whole World!,* p. 525; January 1, 1992, Denia Hester, review of *Let's Go Dinosaur Tracking!,* p. 832; January 15, 1992, Sheilamae O'Hara, review of *Aunt Isabel Tells a Good One,* p. 950; January 1, 1995, Chris Sherman, review of *One Saturday Morning,* p. 827; October 15, 1996, Stephanie Zvirin, review of *Aunt Isabel Makes Trouble,* pp. 432, 434; December 1, 1996, Hazel Rochman, review of *Archaeologists Dig for Clues,* p. 662; February 1, 1998, April Judge, review of *One Guinea Pig Is Not Enough,* pp. 920-921; May 15, 1999, Susan Dove Lempke, review of *One Saturday Afternoon,* p. 1704; February 15, 2000, Hazel Rochman, review of *Mr. Big Brother,* p. 1124; July, 2000, Marta Segal, review of *Twenty Is Too Many,* p. 2038; July 1, 2007, Gillian Engberg, review of *One Saturday Evening,* p. 66.

*Bulletin of the Center for Children's Books,* July-August, 1986, review of "Guinea Pig Board Books," p. 206.

*Catholic Library World,* March, 1998, Rosanne Steitz, review of *Archaeologists Dig for Clues,* p. 67.

*Childhood Education,* January-February, 1986, review of *Seven Froggies Went to School,* p. 216.

*Growing Point,* July, 1987, Margery Fisher, review of *The Guinea Pig ABC,* p. 4838.

*Horn Book,* February, 1984, Ann A. Flowers, review of *The Guinea Pig ABC,* pp. 42-43; September, 1999, Mary M. Burns and Ann A. Flowers, "Whatever Happened to?," review of *The Guinea Pig ABC,* p. 574.

*Instructor,* September, 1997, Judy Freeman, review of *Aunt Isabel Tells a Good One,* p. 24.

*Journal of Adolescent and Adult Literacy,* May, 1997, review of *Aunt Isabel Tells a Good One,* p. 669.

*Kirkus Reviews,* November 1, 1983, review of *The Guinea Pig ABC,* p. 369; November 1, 1984, review of *Guinea Pigs Far and Near,* p. 88; March 1, 1985, review of *Seven Froggies Went to School,* p. J4; April 15, 1989, review of *Tingalayo,* p. 629; December 15, 1991, review of *Aunt Isabel Tells a Good One,* p. 1589; September 15, 1996, review of *Aunt Isabel Makes Trouble,* p. 1398; December 15, 1996, review of *Archaeologists Dig for Clues,* p. 662; December 15, 1997, review of *One Guinea Pig Is Not Enough,* p. 1833; March 1, 2007, review of *The Tale of Pip and Squeak,* p. 220; July 1, 2007, review of *One Saturday Evening.*

*Los Angeles Times Book Review,* December 17, 1989, Patricia Maclachlan, review of *It's Too Noisy!,* p. 7.

*New York Times Book Review,* October 9, 1983, Selma G. Lanes, review of *The Guinea Pig ABC,* p. 38; June 5, 1988, Rebecca Lazear Okrent, review of *What Would a Guinea Pig Do?,* p. 50.

*Publishers Weekly,* August 24, 1984, review of *Guinea Pigs Far and Near,* p. 80; May 30, 1986, review of "Guinea Pig Board Books," p. 60; January 29, 1988, review of *What Would a Guinea Pig Do?,* p. 429; October 12, 1990, review of *Don't Tell the Whole World!,* p. 63; November 29, 1991, review of *Aunt Isabel Tells a Good One,* p. 591; October 14, 1996, review of *Aunt Isabel Makes Trouble,* p. 83; June 12, 2000, review of *Twenty Is Too Many,* p. 71; February 26, 2001, review of *One Guinea Pig Is Not Enough,* p. 88; July 7, 2003, review of *I Won't Get Lost,* p. 71; April 23, 2007, review of *The Tale of Pip and Squeak,* p. 50.

*School Library Journal,* December, 1984, Diane S. Rogoff, review of *Guinea Pigs Far and Near,* pp. 69-70; October, 1986, Linda Wicher, review of "Guinea Pig Board Books," p. 159; June-July, 1988, Starr LaTronica, review of *What Would a Guinea Pig Do?,* p. 90; August, 1989, Debby Jeffery, review of *Tingalayo,* pp. 137-138; December, 1989, Karen James, review of *It's Too Noisy!,* pp. 93-94; December, 1990, Judith Gloyer, review of *Don't Tell the Whole World!,* p. 74; June, 1993, Virginia Opocensky, review of *If You Walk down This Road,* p. 72; November, 1994, Gale W. Sherman, review of *One Saturday Morning,* p. 72; October, 1996, Beth Tegart, review of *Aunt Isabel Makes Trouble,* pp. 91-92; February, 1997, Jackie Hechtkopf, review of *Archaeologists Dig for Clues,* p. 89; March, 1998, Jane Marino, review of *One Guinea Pig Is Not Enough,* p. 88; August, 1999, Lori Haas Weaver, review of *One Saturday Afternoon,* p. 124;

September, 1999, Jane Claes, review of *Mr. Big Brother,* p. 184; August, 2000, Adele Greenlee, review of *Twenty Is Too Many,* p. 153; August, 2003, Kristin de Lacoste, review of *I Won't Get Lost,* p. 136; May, 2007, Amelia Jenkins, review of *The Tale of Pip and Squeak,* p. 90; August, 2007, Erika Qualls, review of *One Saturday Evening,* p. 76.

*Science Books & Films,* June, 1997, James E. Ayres, review of *Archaeologists Dig for Clues,* p. 146.

*Teaching Children Mathematics,* April, 2001, Patricia Hohensee, review of *Twenty Is Too Many,* pp. 489-490.

*ONLINE*

*Connecticut Library Consortium Web site,* http://www.ctlibrarians.org/ (August 15, 2008), "About Kate Duke."

*Kate Duke Home Page,* http://www.kateduke.com (August 15, 2008).

*PBS Online,* http://www.pbs.org/ (January 10, 2004), "Writing & Spelling: Read Together with Kate Duke."*

# E-F

## EASTON, Kelly 1960-

### Personal

Born 1960, in Glendora, CA; married (divorced); married Michael Ruben (a therapist and social worker); children: (first marriage) Isabelle Easton Spivack, Isaac Easton Spivack; (second marriage) Mollie Ruben, Rebecca Ruben (stepchildren). *Education:* University of California, Irvine, B.A. (theater), 1985; University of California, San Diego, M.F.A. (playwriting), 1991.

### Addresses

*Home*—Jamestown, RI. *E-mail*—eastonka@hotmail.com.

### Career

Playwright, novelist, and educator. Kaiser Permanente, and Kaiser Permanente Hospice, San Diego, CA, consultant, 1990-93; University of North Carolina-Wilmington, lecturer in English and creative writing, 1993-2000; University of Rhode Island, Kingston, guest artist, 2000, and instructor in literature, 2007; Roger Williams University, Bristol, RI, adjunct professor of creative writing, 2002-04; Rhode Island College, Providence, adjunct professor in English, 2003; Hamline University, St. Paul, MN, assistant professor of writing, 2007—.

### Member

Society of Children's Writers and Illustrators.

### Awards, Honors

North Carolina Writers' Network Fiction Competition award, 1997, for "The Watcher of the Compound"; Robert Ruark Fiction Competition honorable mention, 1997, for "Sentences"; Sojourner Fiction Competition honorable mention, 1998, for "Air"; Golden Kite Honor Award, New York Public Library Books for the Teen Age selection, and American Library Association (ALA) Popular Paperbacks for Teens designation, all 2002, and Teen Readers BookSense Top Ten 76 List, 2003, all for *The Life History of a Star;* Julia Ward Howe Honor Award, Boston Authors' Club, 2003, and Great Reads for Middle Schoolers selection, ALA, both for *Walking on Air;* Quick Picks for Reluctant Readers selection, ALA, for *Aftershock;* Asian/Pacific American Literature Award, 2008, Rhode Island Middle School Book of the Year designation, Alliance for the Study and Teaching of Adolescent Literature, and Books for the Teen Age selection, New York Public Library, all for *Hiroshima Dreams;* New York Public Library Books for the Teen Age selection, 2008, for *White Magic.*

***Kelly Easton*** (Courtesy of Kelly Easton.)

### Writings

*NOVELS*

*The Life History of a Star,* Simon & Schuster (New York, NY), 2001.

*Trouble at Betts Pets,* Candlewick Press (Cambridge, MA), 2002.

*Canaries and Criminals,* Candlewick Press (Cambridge, MA), 2003.

*Walking on Air,* Margaret K. McElderry Books (New York, NY), 2004.

*Aftershock,* Margaret K. McElderry Books (New York, NY), 2006.

*White Magic: Spells to Hold You,* Wendy Lamb Books (New York, NY), 2007.

*Hiroshima Dreams,* Dutton (New York, NY), 2007.

*To Be Mona,* Margaret K. McElderry Books (New York, NY), 2008.

*The Outlandish Adventures of Liberty Aims,* Wendy Lamb Books (New York, NY), 2009.

*PLAYS*

*The Modern Heart and Housing,* produced at University of California—San Diego, 1990.

*Self Defense,* produced at University of California—San Diego, 1990.

*Three Witches,* produced in San Diego, CA, 1991.

*Ordinary Objects,* produced in New York, NY, 1991.

*It Falls like a Stone,* produced at Bard College (Annandale-on-Hudson, NY), 1995.

*OTHER*

Contributor of short fiction to books, including *Prairie Hearts: An Anthology of Women Writing about the Midwest,* 1996, and *What Are You Afraid of? An Anthology about Phobias,* Candlewick Press (Cambridge, MA), 2006. Contributor of fiction to periodicals, including *Paterson Literary Review, Kalliope, Sojourner, Blue Moon Review, Rio Grande Review, Washington Square, Iris, Connecticut Review, Frontiers,* and *Phoebe.*

## Sidelights

Kelly Easton, a playwright, novelist, and educator, is the author of several award-winning books for young adults that address a range of sensitive issues. As Easton remarked in a *TeensReadToo.com* interview, "Mark Twain said that 'Man is the only animal who blushes. Or needs to.' I write about the things we need to blush about: war, how religion can be misused, the need for people to be bullies. But I also write about all the aspects of teen life: relationships, clothes, music, the body's constant changes, pressures to have sex without love, friendship without devotion. My characters are survivors in one way or another and they all have a sense of humor."

The personal is interwoven with the political in Easton's debut novel. *The Life History of a Star* is a fictional first-person narrative in the form of a journal written by fourteen-year-old Kristin Folger during the school year 1973-74. Her diaries are filled with references to contemporary political upheavals, including the Watergate scandal that eventually brought down the presidency of Richard Nixon, and the kidnapping of Patricia Hearst, as well as television shows and popular music of the time. They are also a place where Kristin can express her mixed feelings about more personal issues, such as her developing body, the changes she sees in her friends, and the breakup of her parents' marriage. Most troubling of all is Kristin's brother David, who has lived like a ghost in the attic since his return from the Vietnam War. "The format makes this novel easy to read and it certainly allows readers to get to know Kristin, who comes through as very real teen," remarked Toni D. Moore in *School Library Journal.* "Anyone who reads this book will be able to identify with her," critic Lisa Marx likewise wrote in a review posted on *Teenreads.com.* By novel's end, Kristin's writing has helped her break through her own defenses, allowing her to grieve her losses and move on, observed Gillian Engberg in *Booklist.* The result is "an uneven but affecting first novel."

*Trouble at Betts Pets* centers on a homeless woman, a community garden, and the creeping gentrification of an old urban neighborhood. Aaron Betts, the novel's fifth-grade narrator, is a responsible twelve year old who works in his parents' pet store, and worries about the changes in his neighborhood as much as he frets over his assignment to a stuck-up rich girl for math tutoring. Then, when the survival of the family pet store is threatened by a thief, Aaron leaps into action to solve the mystery. "The protagonist is likable and believable, and shows quite a bit of moral fiber throughout the book," asserted Sharon R. Pearce in *School Library Journal.* While a contributor to *Publishers Weekly* felt that Easton had attempted too many subplots to resolve any of them satisfactorily, this critic also praised the author for "moments of delicious sarcasm, insight and verve." For *Booklist* reviewer Kathy Broderick, however, Easton's novel "teaches the children—and readers—about life, friendship, and loyalty."

In *Canaries and Criminals,* a sequel to *Trouble at Betts Pets,* Aaron finds himself at the center of a bizarre mystery. After he takes possession of a turtle with a map painted on its shell, Aaron receives a threatening note delivered via homing pigeon. When he refuses to divulge the creature's whereabouts, Aaron is kidnapped by a group of ex-convicts looking for a stash of money. "It's all handled with a light touch," noted a contributor in *Kirkus Reviews,* and Tina Zubak, writing in *School Library Journal,* remarked that the "fast-paced novel will appeal to kids who like funny stories tempered with sensitivity."

Set in 1931, *Walking on Air* concerns twelve-year-old June, the daughter of a embittered traveling preacher who forces her to perform as a tightrope-walker to attract crowds to his revival meetings. When her father is sent to jail for several months, June enjoys some semblance of a normal life with her frail mother and the family's mute assistant, Rhett. "Well researched Depression-era details heighten the desperation of

June's dysfunctional, secret-ridden family and their transient, hand-to-mouth existence," noted a contributor in *Publishers Weekly.* "Easton's writing is smooth, filled with rich descriptions and images," observed *School Library Journal* reviewer Lauralyn Persson, and *Booklist* critic Linda Perkins described June as "an engaging, compassionate character whose spirited account both amuses and inspires."

The traumatized survivor of a horrific car accident embarks on a cross-country odyssey in *Aftershock.* After his parents are killed in a crash in rural Idaho, seventeen-year-old Adam begins making his way back to Rhode Island, obtaining help from strangers despite his inability to talk. According to *Booklist* contributor Hazel Rochman, Easton's "contemporary road adventure is told with terse drama," and *School Library Journal* critic Vicki Reutter noted that "readers will be caught up in the teen's predicament."

In *White Magic: Spells to Hold You,* fifteen-year-old Vermont transplant Chrissie finds it difficult to adjust to life in fast-paced Los Angeles. Then she meets Yvonne and Karen, two classmates who practice witchcraft and invite her to join their coven. "Easton's book takes an adult view on teenage life that is surprisingly poignant and absorbing," remarked Cara Chancellor in *Kliatt,* and Heather Booth, writing in *Booklist,* stated of *White Magic* that the "search for belonging and friendship will capture teens."

*Hiroshima Dreams* focuses on the relationship between Lin, a shy but talented musician, and her Japanese grandmother, who witnessed the bombing of Hiroshima during World War II. The pair shares the gift of "second sight," and as Lin matures, she comes to appreciate her multi-racial background. "Easton's prose throughout is heartfelt and insightful," Marilyn Taniguchi remarked in *School Library Journal,* and *Kliatt* reviewer Claire Rooser observed that Lin's "voice as she tells the story is filled with wonder."

Easton once told *SATA:* "I fell in love with books after reading the 'Oz' series by L. Frank Baum, and knew that that was what I wanted to do with my life. The other thing that I wanted to be was a composer and a musician. My family was quite poor, though, and I knew I wouldn't be able to afford the necessary training. The only training you really need to be a writer is to read read read, and then to practice. It's a very democratic profession that way. I was eight or nine when I read Baum's imaginative series, but didn't get around to writing seriously until I was thirty. By then I had been an actor, a dancer, a police dispatcher, a waitress, and a student. My favorite children's book is *Holes.* I also love the works of Zilpha Keatly Snyder and Roald Dahl. All of these books have in common a strong feeling for humanity and a concern for how individuals can discover and express themselves when the odds are against them. These are the subjects about which I write.

"My happiest moments, as a writer, are when ideas flow, and also when children write to me and have enjoyed my books. The most common question children ask me is if I ever owned a pet store because the narrator of *Trouble at Betts Pets* does. I haven't owned a pet store, but as a child I wished I did. And I remembered how much I wanted a pet raccoon, and my mother, wisely, wouldn't let me have one. Raccoons do not make good pets. They're mean and mischievous. Now, I have two dogs and a turtle.

"Right now, I live on an island. It feels an ideal metaphor for being a writer. That is, you are so much on your own, but an island is rich with life, and abundant with plants, animals, stones, shells, even people. And writing is so much about just floating in your own mind. I often get ideas when I'm walking around the island or swimming in the ocean or bicycling. I also read a great deal, which is the most important thing a writer can do. I teach in universities, and enjoy how smart and talented the students are. Aside from that, I love to cook and eat, and above all, to play with my kids."

## Biographical and Critical Sources

*PERIODICALS*

*Booklist,* April 15, 2001, Gillian Engberg, review of *The Life History of a Star,* p. 1545; September 1, 2002, Kathy Broderick, review of *Trouble at Betts Pets,* p. 123; April 1, 2004, Linda Perkins, review of *Walking on Air,* p. 1360; December 15, 2006, Hazel Rochman, review of *Aftershock,* p. 41; September 15, 2007, Hazel Rochman, review of *Hiroshima Dreams,* p. 59; June 1, 2007, Heather Booth, review of *White Magic: Spells to Hold You,* p. 64.

*Childhood Education,* spring, 2002, Sylvia Loh, review of *The Life History of a Star,* p. 173.

*Horn Book,* September-October, 2007, Elissa Gershowitz, review of *White Magic,* p. 572.

*Jamestown Press* (Jamestown, RI), October 19, 2006, Sam Bari, "Author Kelly Easton Writes Another Winner."

*Kirkus Reviews,* September 15, 2003, review of *Canaries and Criminals,* p. 1173; November 1, 2006, review of *Aftershock,* p. 1122; July 15, 2007, review of *White Magic;* September 15, 2007, review of *Hiroshima Dreams.*

*Kliatt,* March, 2004, Claire Rosser, review of *Walking on Air,* p. 9; July, 2007, Cara Chancellor, review of *White Magic,* p. 12; September, 2007, Claire Rosser, review of *Hiroshima Dreams,* p. 10.

*Philadelphia Inquirer,* September 12, 2007, "*White Magic:* Her New Friends Are All Witches—But in a Good Way."

*Publishers Weekly,* March 19, 2001, review of *The Life History of a Star,* p. 101; April 15, 2002, review of *Trouble at Betts Pets,* p. 65; May 10, 2004, review of *Walking on Air,* p. 60; August 27, 2007, review of *White Magic,* p. 90.

*School Library Journal,* July, 2001, Toni D. Moore, review of *The Life History of a Star,* p. 106; April, 2002, Sharon R. Pearce, review of *Trouble at Betts Pets,* p. 146; April, 2004, Tina Zubak, review of *Canaries and Criminals,* p. 152; July, 2004, Lauralyn Persson, review of *Walking on Air,* p. 104; December, 2006, Vicki Reutter, review of *Aftershock,* p. 138; December, 2007, Marilyn Taniguchi, review of *Hiroshima Dreams,* p. 126; December, 2007, Ginny Collier, review of *White Magic,* p. 126.

*ONLINE*

*Teenreads.com,* http://www.teenreads.com/ (August 31, 2002), Lisa Marx, review of *The Life History of a Star.*

*Teensreadtoo.com,* http://www.teensreadtoo.com/ (August 5, 2008), interview with Easton.

*Washington Parent Online,* http://www.washingtonparent.com/ (August 31, 2002), review of *The Life History of a Star.*

* * *

## FELSTEAD, Cathie 1954-

### Personal

Born 1954, in Welwyn Garden City, Hertfordshire, England; partner of Paul Tucker; children. *Education:* Chelsea School of Art, degree (graphic design); Royal College of Art, M.F.A. (illustration), 1980.

### Addresses

*Home*—Ashwell, Hertfordshire, England.

### Career

Illustrator of books for children. Creator of art and design for advertising campaigns, packaging, posters, greeting cards, theatre, and television. *Exhibitions:* Work exhibited at Curwen Gallery, London, England, and other galleries in United Kingdom.

### Awards, Honors

Berger Prize; RCA traveling scholarship; Bronze Award, B&H Gold competition; Mother Goose Award runner up, for *A Caribbean Dozen;* three Oppenheim Toy Portfolio Gold awards.

### Illustrator

John Agard and Grace Nichols, editors, *A Caribbean Dozen: Poems from Caribbean Poets,* Candlewick Press (Cambridge, MA), 1994.

Judy Allen, editor, *Anthology for the Earth,* Walker Books (London, England), 1997.

*Creepy Crawlies* (pop-up book), HarperCollins (London, England), 1997.

*Egg Surprise* (pop-up book), Barron's Educational Series (Hauppauge, NY), 1997.

*Jumpers* (pop-up book), Barron's Educational Series (Hauppauge, NY), 1997.

*Seashore* (pop-up book), Barron's Educational Series (Hauppauge, NY), 1997.

Andrew Maxwell Hislop, editor, *A Book of Hearts,* Exley (New York, NY), 1998.

Reeve Lindbergh, *The Circle of Days,* Candlewick Press (Cambridge, MA), 1998.

*A Walker Treasury of First Rhymes,* Walker Books (London, England), 1999.

Brian Patten, *The Blue and Green Ark,* Scholastic Press (London, England), 1999.

Bill Martin, *Adam, Adam, What Do You See?,* Tommy Nelson (Nashville, TN), 2000.

Shirley Tulloch, *Who Made Me?,* Augsburg (Minneapolis, MN), 2000.

Sharon Phillips Denslow, *Big Wolf and Little Wolf,* Greenwillow Books (New York, NY), 2000.

Donna Jo Napoli, *Flamingo Dream,* Greenwillow Books (New York, NY), 2002.

Lisa Westberg Peters, *Earthshake: Poems from the Ground Up,* Greenwillow Books (New York, NY), 2003.

Lola M. Schaefer, *An Island Grows,* Greenwillow Books (New York, NY), 2006.

Jody Fickes Shapiro, *Family Lullaby,* Greenwillow Books (New York, NY), 2007.

Contributor of illustrations to books, including *South and North, East and West: The Oxfam Book of Children's Stories,* edited by Michael Rosen, Walker Books (London, England), 1992; *Under the Moon and Over the Sea: A Collection of Caribbean Poems,* edited by John Agard and Grace Nichols, Walker Books, 2002; and *Rudyard Kipling's Just So Stories,* Walker Books, 2005.

### Biographical and Critical Sources

*PERIODICALS*

*Booklist,* December 1, 1994, Julie Corsaro, review of *A Caribbean Dozen: Poems from Caribbean Poets,* p. 665; April, 1998, Susan Dove Lempke, review of *The Circles of Days,* p. 1325; April 15, 2000, Hazel Rochman, review of *Who Made Me?,* p. 1554; May 1, 2000, Carolyn Phelan, review of *Big Wolf and Little Wolf,* p. 1676; April 15, 2002, Ilene Cooper, review of *Flamingo Dream,* p. 1408; November 15, 2003, Carolyn Phelan, review of *Earthshake: Poems from the Ground Up,* p. 596; July 1, 2006, Carolyn Phelan, review of *An Island Grows,* p. 68.

*Horn Book,* July-August, 2002, Kitty Flynn, review of *Flamingo Dream,* p. 450; September-October, 2006, Danielle J. Ford, review of *An Island Grows,* p. 610.

*Kirkus Reviews,* March 15, 2002, review of *Flamingo Dream,* p. 421; December 15, 2002, review of *Under the Moon and Over the Sea: A Collection of Caribbean Poems,* p. 1844; June 1, 2006, review of *An Island Grows,* p. 579; April 15, 2007, review of *Family Lullaby.*

*Publishers Weekly,* November 28, 1994, review of *A Caribbean Dozen,* p. 62; March 23, 1998, review of *Circle of Days,* p. 95; December 20, 1999, review of *Who Made Me?,* p. 78; May 15, 2000, review of *Big Wolf and Little Wolf,* p. 116; March 11, 2002, review of *Flamingo Dream,* p. 72; May 21, 2007, review of *Family Lullaby,* p. 53.

*School Library Journal,* May, 2000, Laura Santoro, review of *Big Wolf and Little Wolf,* p. 140; August, 2000, Patricia Pearl Dole, review of *Who Made Me?,* p. 166; December, 2000, Patricia Pearl Dole, "What Do You See?," p. 134; May, 2002, Wendy Lukehart, review of *Flamingo Dream,* p. 124; September, 2003, Cris Riedel, review of *Earthshake,* p. 204; July, 2006, Heide Piehler, review of *An Island Grows,* p. 87; July, 2007, Amy Lilien-Harper, review of *Family Lullaby,* p. 84.

*ONLINE*

*Images of Delight Web site,* http://www.imagesofdelight.com/ (August 15, 2008), "Cathie Felstead."*

* * *

# FRANSON, Scott E. 1966-

## Personal

Born February 14, 1966; married; children: three daughters, one son. *Education:* Ricks College, A.A.; Art Center College of Design, B.F.A.; Utah State University, M.F.A. *Hobbies and other interests:* Doodling, reading, movies, creating artwork on the computer.

## Addresses

*Home and office*—P.O. Box 52, Rexburg, ID 83440-0052. *E-mail*—info@scottefranson.com.

## Career

Author and illustrator of children's books. Brigham Young University, Idaho, Rexburg, currently instructor in design and illustration. Freelance graphic designer in Minneapolis, MN, and Los Angeles, CA.

## Member

Society of Children's Book Writers and Illustrators.

## Writings

*SELF-ILLUSTRATED*

*Un-Brella,* Roaring Brook Press (New Milford, CT), 2007.

## Sidelights

Scott E. Franson told *SATA:* "I am blessed with two birthdays. My first birthday is February 14, 1966. I weighed 8 lb. 14 oz. and was twenty-one inches long. My second birthday or my re-birthday is May 26, 2008. On this birthday I weighed 185 lb. and was 75 inches long. This is a very special day for me because I received a liver transplant. Previous to the transplant I was very sick with liver disease and cancer. I waited for over a year before a compatible liver became available. I am grateful to an organ donor that I will never know who has given me a new life.

"Writing and illustrating books has been a dream of mine for a long time. I create the artwork for my books using the computer. It doesn't make the creation process faster, but it greatly increases the options.

"Images are the beginning of my creative process. An example of this is *Un-Brella.* I dreamed an image of a girl in rain clothes with an umbrella on a sunny day. From the umbrella there was a rain shower making puddles for her to splash in. I created the image and hung it on my wall where I could see it every day. The illustration didn't make it into the book, but it did spark the idea that led to my first published book."

## Biographical and Critical Sources

*PERIODICALS*

*Booklist,* June 1, 2007, Julie Cummins, review of *Un-Brella,* p. 86.

*Horn Book,* March-April, 2007, Vicky Smith, review of *Un-Brella,* p. 180.

*Kirkus Reviews,* March 1, 2007, review of *Un-Brella,* p. 221.

*School Library Journal,* April, 2007, Catherine Callegari, review of *Un-Brella,* p. 105.

*ONLINE*

*Scott E. Franson Home Page,* http://www.scottefranson.com (August 4, 2008).

* * *

# FULCHER, Jennifer
See WESTWOOD, Jennifer

# G

## GARDNER, Lyn

### Personal

Born in London, England; children: two daughters. *Education:* Graduated from Kent University.

### Addresses

*Office*—Guardian, 119 Farringdon Rd., London EC1R 3ER, England. *E-mail*—lyn.gardner@guardian.co.uk.

### Career

Author and journalist. *Independent,* London, England, reporter; *City Limits* (publishing cooperative), London, founding member and editor of theatre section; *Guardian,* London, theater critic. Also worked as a tea lady and a waitress.

### Writings

*Into the Woods,* illustrated by Mini Grey, David Fickling Books (New York, NY) 2006.

### Sidelights

Lyn Gardner, the theater critic for the London *Guardian,* is the author of *Into the Woods,* "a fast-paced and entertaining adventure filled with cheeky humor and wordplay," noted a reviewer in *Publishers Weekly.* Discussing the audience for the book on her Web log, Gardner stated that *Into the Woods* "is very much for 8-12 year olds. But I do hope that it's also a book that children and parents might want to read aloud to each other because it began as a bedtime story on a visit to see my children's American cousins."

*Into the Woods* follows the adventures of three sisters—strong-willed Storm, responsible Aurora, and precocious Anything—who live at Eden End, their dilapidated family estate. After her mother's death, Storm inherits a musical pipe with magical powers that is coveted by Dr. DeWilde, an evil-doer posing as a rat exterminator. Fleeing from DeWilde and his pack of wolves, the girls enter the woods surrounding their village, where they discover a fudge-covered gingerbread

***Cover of Lyn Gardner's novel* Into the Woods, *a middle-grade fantasy featuring artwork by Mini Grey.*** (Illustration copyright © 2006 by Mini Grey. Reproduced by permission of David Fickling Books, an imprint of Random House Children's Books, a division of Random House, Inc.)

house, a gemstone quarry worked by child slaves, and an ogress who turns out to be their long-lost great-grandmother.

*Into the Woods* garnered strong reviews. "Gardner's funky retelling of virtually every fairytale you can remember doesn't just borrow from Perrault and the Grimms but even, cheekily, inhabits Angela Carter's now-classic re-tellings," Kathryn Hughes remarked in the London *Guardian.* In *Books for Keeps* Adrian Jackson described the work as "part fairy tale . . ., part comedy caper and substantially high drama." Writing in *Horn Book,* Claire E. Gross also praised the story, commenting that Gardner's "vivid language is rich with imagery and metaphor that emerge naturally from the familiar pastoral setting but still achieve originality," and *School Library Journal* contributor Margaret A. Chang cited the author's "strong, descriptive style."

Although Gardner has learned, as she wrote on her Web log, that "being a first time children's author is no fairytale," she plans to continue writing for a young audience. After a slow start, the process of writing her first novel "became addictively good fun. The best days were when I found myself surprised by what I'd written. Four months later I wrote those glorious words 'The End.' I had for the first time actually finished a book. It was like moving into a brand-new house."

## Biographical and Critical Sources

*PERIODICALS*

*Booklist,* May 1, 2007, Kay Weisman, review of *Into the Woods,* p. 91.

*Books for Keeps,* September, 2006, Adrian Jackson, review of *Into the Woods.*

*Guardian* (London, England), October 14, 2006, Kathryn Hughes, "There and Back Again," review of *Into the Woods.*

*Horn Book,* July-August, 2007, Claire E. Gross, review of *Into the Woods,* p. 395.

*Kirkus Reviews,* May 15, 2007, review of *Into the Woods.*

*Observer* (London, England), October 22, 2006, Geraldine Bedell, "Welcome to the Post-apocalypse," review of *Into the Woods.*

*Publishers Weekly,* June 11, 2007, review of *Into the Woods,* p. 60.

*School Library Journal,* June, 2007, Margaret A. Chang, review of *Into the Woods,* p. 144.

*ONLINE*

*Lyn Gardner Web log,* http://blogs.guardian.co.uk/culture/ (August 15, 2008).*

* * *

# GRANDITS, John 1949-

## Personal

Born 1949; married; wife's name Joanne (a children's librarian).

## Addresses

*Home*—Red Bank, NJ. *Agent*—Andrea Cascardi, Transatlantic Literary Agency, 72 Glengowan Rd., Toronto, Ontario M4N 1G4, Canada.

## Career

Author and book and magazine designer.

## Awards, Honors

CCBC Choice designation, and American Library Association (ALA) Notable Book for Children designation and Quick Pick for Young Adults designation, all 2005, all for *Technically, It's Not My Fault;* Lee Bennett Hopkins Poetry Award Honor designation, 2008, for *Blue Lipstick.*

## Writings

*Pictures Tell Stories,* Open Court (Chicago, IL), 1995.

(Self-illustrated) *Technically, It's Not My Fault: Concrete Poems,* Clarion Books (New York, NY), 2004.

*Blue Lipstick: Concrete Poems,* Clarion Books (New York, NY), 2007.

*The Travel Game,* illustrated by R.W. Alley, Clarion Books (New York, NY), 2008.

Author of "Beatrice Black Bear" (monthly cartoon), for *Click* magazine.

## Sidelights

John Grandits started his career in children's book publishing as a book designer and an art director, and he has also worked as an art director at the highly praised *Cricket* magazine. However, he is best known to middle-grade and teen readers as the author of several verse novels featuring concrete poetry. A whimsical verse form, concrete poetry is comprised of words typeset on each page in such a way that they represent an object that is the subject of the same poem. For example, a poem about a snake might be typeset to twist and turn in a ropelike line across the page, visually mimicking the shape of a snake. In *Technically, It's Not My Fault: Concrete Poems* Grandits takes concrete poetry a step further, using colored fonts, drawings, and other visual elements to focus on a boy's troubles with his older sister. In *Blue Lipstick: Concrete Poems* he employs the same techniques, this time to present the siblings' conflicts from the older sister's perspective.

In *Technically, It's Not My Fault* eleven-year-old Robert shares the ups and downs of his day, including homework, basketball, friends, nonsensical musings, and his battles with his annoying older sister Jessie. Grandits' young narrator "emerges as the prototypical kids'-book kid: smart-mouthed, eternally at war with his sister, deeply in tune with the digestive process, and more interested in sports and video games than school," explained a *Kirkus Reviews* writer in appraising the poetry collection. The middle grader's humorous and often sarcastic musings are captured in a series of poems that, taken together, comprise what *Booklist* contributor Gillian Engberg described as a "highly creative collection" able to "convince readers that poetry can be loud, outrageous, gross fun." In *School Library Journal,* Marilyn Taniguchi praised the "brilliant" design of *Technically, It's Not My Fault,* adding that Grandits' "technical brilliance and goofy good humor [combine] to provide an accessible, fun-filled collection of poems" for middle-grade readers. Predicting that many readers "will appreciate the scatological wit" Robert employs, a *Publishers Weekly* critic dubbed Grandits' book "a technically (and imaginatively) inspired typeface experiment."

Turning to older readers, *Blue Lipstick* finds fifteen-year-old Jessie narrating her own perspective regarding high-school life and the annoyance of being Robert's sister. In addition to her typical teen fascination with boys, clothes, and makeup, Jessie also writes about her role on the volleyball team, her decision to become a vegetarian, her time practicing the cello, and her unique attitudes about life. In addition to using over fifty different fonts, unique page designs, and a graphic cover design, in *Blue Lipstick* Grandits presents readers with an intimate view of a creative, likeable, and strong-willed teen who "leaps right off the page, in turn feisty and insecure," in the opinion of *Horn Book* contributor Tanya D. Auger. The poet's "irreverent, witty collection should resonate with a wide audience," predicted Taniguchi, while in *Kirkus Reviews* a contributor dubbed Grandits' second collection of concrete verse a "a playfully worthy companion" to *Technically, It's Not My Fault.*

## Biographical and Critical Sources

*PERIODICALS*

*Booklist,* December 15, 2004, Gillian Engberg, review of *Technically, It's Not My Fault: Concrete Poems,* p. 739.

*Horn Book,* July-August, 2007, Tanya D. Auger, review of *Blue Lipstick: Concrete Poems,* p. 408.

*Kirkus Reviews,* October 15, 2004, review of *It's Not My Fault,* p. 1006; May 1, 2007, review of *Blue Lipstick.*

*Publishers Weekly,* December 6, 2004, review of *Technically, It's Not My Fault,* p. 61.

*School Library Journal,* December, 2004, Marilyn Taniguchi, review of *Technically, It's Not My Fault,* p. 161; July, 2007, Marilyn Taniguchi, review of *Blue Lipstick,* p. 115.

*ONLINE*

*Writing and Ruminating Web site,* http://kellyrfineman.livejournal.com/ (May 22, 2008), Kelly R. Fineman, interview with Grandits.*

# GREENHUT, Josh
## See MERCER, Sienna

* * *

# GREGORY, Jean
## See URE, Jean

* * *

# GREGORY, Nan 1944-

## Personal

Born 1944, in Boston, MA; married; children: one son. *Education:* University of British Columbia, B.A. *Hobbies and other interests:* Kayaking, drawing, watercolor painting, clowning.

## Addresses

*Home and office*—Vancouver, British Columbia, Canada.

## Career

Professional storyteller, 1984—; children's author, 1995—.

## Member

Writer's Union of Canada, Canadian Society of Children's Authors, Illustrators, and Performers, Vancouver Children's Literature Roundtable, Canadian Children's Book Centre, Children's Writers and Illustrators of British Columbia, Vancouver Society of Storytelling.

## Awards, Honors

Book of the Year for Children Award shortlist, Canadian Library Association, Ruth Schwartz Award shortlist, Our Choice Award, Canadian Children's Book Centre, Mr. Christie's Book Award, 1996, and Sheila A. Egoff Children's Literature Prize, 1996, all for *How Smudge Came;* Book of the Year for Children Award, Canadian Library Association, 2000, for *Wild Girl and Gran;* Christie Harris Illustrated Children's Literature Prize shortlist, and American Library Association Book of the Year shortlist, both 2003, both for *Amber Waiting;* Cooperative Children's Book Center Choices selection and Best Books for Kids and Teens selection, both 2008, both for *Pink.*

## Writings

*Moon Tales* (sound recording), First Avenue Press (Vancouver, British Columbia, Canada), 1989.

*How Smudge Came,* illustrated by Ron Lightburn, Red Deer Press (Red Deer, Alberta, Canada), 1995, Walker (New York, NY), 1997.

***Nan Gregory*** (Reproduced by permission of Nan Gregory.)

*Wild Girl and Gran,* illustrated by Ron Lightburn, Red Deer Press (Red Deer, Alberta, Canada), 2000.

*How Music Came to the World and Other Stories* (sound recording), Vancouver Society of Storytelling (Vancouver, British Columbia, Canada), 2000.

*Amber Waiting,* illustrated by Kady MacDonald Denton, Red Deer Press (Red Deer, Alberta, Canada), 2002.

*I'll Sing You One-O,* illustrated by Kady MacDonald Denton, Clarion Books (New York, NY), 2006.

*Pink,* illustrated by Luc Melanson, Groundwood Books (Toronto, Ontario, Canada), 2007.

## Adaptations

*How Smudge Came* was made into a motion picture, written, directed, and produced by Hilary Jones-Farrow, and released by Kineticvideo (Toronto, Ontario, Canada), 1997.

## Sidelights

Canadian Nan Gregory is a professional storyteller and the author of a number of award-winning works, including *How Smudge Came* and *Pink.* Gregory has performed in such diverse places as nursing homes, libraries, theaters, schools, museums, and parks. Her storytelling career has taken her across Canada and the United States, as well as to Japan and New Zealand. Additionally, Gregory is an accomplished artist who works in fabrics and paints.

Born in Boston, Massachusetts, in 1944, Gregory grew up in Victoria, British Columbia, Canada. She earned her bachelor's degree in theater from the University of British Columbia and became a professional storyteller in 1984. Gregory now makes her home in nearby Vancouver, and when she is not writing or storytelling, she enjoys taking long kayak trips along British Columbia's coast with her husband in the summer.

After working as a professional storyteller for ten years, Gregory was inspired in 1995 to try her hand at writing. The result was *How Smudge Came,* which won numerous awards. *How Smudge Came* is the story of Cindy, a developmentally disabled young woman, who finds a puppy and decides to keep him. She names the dog Smudge and takes him with her to work, where she is a cleaner at a hospice. The other workers, as well as the patients, love having the dog around. However, at the group home for adults where Cindy lives, she tries to hide Smudge, fearing that they will not let her keep him. Eventually, the supervisors do find the dog and take it to the animal shelter, assuming that Cindy is not capable of taking care of it. Cindy is heartbroken and tries to reclaim the dog at the shelter, only to be told to return the following week. When she goes back, the dog has already been claimed. The story ends happily when Cindy finds out that Smudge has been taken in by the hospice staff members, who allow Cindy to keep the dog there.

Calling the book "a beautifully constructed story," *Horn Book* reviewer Sarah Ellis observed the similarities between the dehumanizing restrictions the group home placed on Cindy and the prison-like atmosphere of the animal shelter where Smudge was taken. However, Ellis noted, Gregory provides a third place, that of the hospice, "where all the nonessential rules and regulations fall away." It is only in this environment, according to Ellis, that Cindy can finally "hear her own voice, the capable voice that tells her what she knows. . . . Friendship, respect, kindness. In the presence of an animal, we discover what is essential about ourselves." Writing in *Booklist,* reviewer Hazel Rochman claimed that *How Smudge Came* is unique in that the author shares the story from the perspective of a mentally challenged person rather than from a friend or relative, noting that the book "is remarkable in telling it as Cindy sees it." Rochman went on to comment favorably on the book's "wonderful ending, both surprising and convincing."

Five years later Gregory produced her next book, *Wild Girl and Gran.* Initially unsure about her grandmother coming to stay with her family, Wild Girl takes to Gran, a colorful creature herself, and the two spend hours together enjoying games in the outdoors. However, Gran's health begins to deteriorate, much to Wild Girl's distress as she feels helpless to stop it. Eventually, Gran must check into a hospital, where she eventually dies during the winter. Saddened by her loss, Wild Girl accompanies her mother on a walk in the spring to spread the dead woman's ashes among the wild flowers. Together, Wild Girl and her mother share stories about Gran, and slowly the youngster realizes how much Gran meant to her mother as well.

Valerie Nielsen, writing in the *Canadian Review of Materials,* called *Wild Girl and Gran* "a beautifully written story, the text closer to poetry than prose." *Resource Links* critic Heather Farmer commented on Gregory's use of "poetic language, contrasts, and repetition to create a story of exhilaration and uncomfortable reality and to illustrate the healing and empowering qualities of both nature and imagination." Farmer went on to recommend the book to readers looking "for a gentle, expressive story about death," while *Quill & Quire* contributor Sherie Posesorski deemed it "a beautifully apt metaphor for parental love as a safety net encouraging children to take risks and be adventurous."

A youngster's daydreams are the focus of Gregory's picture book *Amber Waiting.* Amber has just finished her morning session in kindergarten and is waiting for her father to pick her up. He is often late arriving, so Amber imagines flying him to the moon and telling him that she'll "be right back." Her father arrives an hour late and "smiles his famous smile" in an attempt to

***A child's travails in waiting for a ride home from day care are captured by Kady MacDonald Denton in her art for Gregory's* Amber Waiting.** (Red Deer Press, 2002. Illustration copyright © 2002 Kady MacDonald Denton. Reproduced by permission.)

make her feel better. But Amber needs to let her father know how lonely and scared she was. *Booklist* critic Carolyn Phelan called *Amber Waiting* "a subtle, sensitive picture book," and remarked that when the father is able to understand his daughter's pain, "their exchange is beautifully related . . . and children will find its emotional truth enormously satisfying." Writing in *Publishers Weekly,* a critic suggested that the "words and [Kady MacDonald Denton's] pictures do an equally fine job delivering this winning message in ways that both children and parents will understand—easily."

*I'll Sing You One-O,* a work for young adults, concerns twelve-year-old Gemma, a foster child who has been living happily on the Anderson Farm since the age of four. When the farmstead is sold, Gemma is forced to live with her aunt, uncle, and twin brother, none of whom she has ever met before. Unable to adjust to her new surroundings, a frustrated and homesick Gemma vows to return to the farm. After reading a book about saints, Gemma decides to assist a homeless woman in the hopes of acquiring a guardian angel that will reward her good deeds. Gemma's actions have unintended and even dangerous consequences, however, and her life is further complicated by a series of troubling nightmares.

"Gregory works a number of threads here, including a complex psychological mystery rooted in Gemma's past," remarked *Quill & Quire* reviewer Maureen Garvie, the critic adding that Gregory's debut novel "makes for an intense, and at times hair-raising, read." "Gemma's remarkably believable point of view allows readers to see her own raw emotions," Faith Brautigam stated in *School Library Journal,* and Phelan praised the "vivid portrayals and emotional nuance demonstrated throughout the story." Janis Flint-Ferguson, writing in *Kliatt,* also applauded Gregory's debut, commenting that "the characters are realistically portrayed and are not always likable, but the themes of family and identity are well developed." Flint-Ferguson described *I'll Sing You One-O* as "funny, poignant, and ultimately bittersweet."

A youngster envies her three well-heeled schoolmates and their seemingly perfect lives in *Pink,* "a tale that will capture children and adults alike," noted Jeannette Timmerman in the *Canadian Review of Materials.* Vivi yearns for the amenities that belong to Merillee, Miranda, and Janine, a trio of girls she calls the "Pinks" because they live in nice houses and adorn themselves in pink dresses, shoes, and coats. Unfortunately, Vivi's father, a truck driver, and mother, a cleaning woman, simply cannot afford the things their daughter desires. When Vivi spots a wondrous bridal doll dressed in pink in a store window, she becomes determined to own it. She earns the cash to purchase the doll by running errands for her neighbors, but when she mistakenly tells the "Pinks" about her plans, she must learn to cope with a tremendous disappointment. "Written with subtlety and tenderness but not a whiff of sentimentality, this picture book quietly depicts Vivi's intense longing," observed Phelan, and Susan Prior, writing in *Resource Links,* called *Pink* "a story about wanting something very badly, and for that reason, most children will probably be able to relate to it." As a *Publishers Weekly* contributor noted, Gregory's "heartrending reminder of what's truly important in life will likely linger."

## Biographical and Critical Sources

*BOOKS*

Gregory, Nan, *Amber Waiting,* illustrated by Kady MacDonald Denton, Red Deer Press (Red Deer, Alberta, Canada), 2002.

*PERIODICALS*

*Booklist,* March 15, 1996, Hazel Rochman, review of *How Smudge Came,* p. 1262; May 15, 2003, Carolyn Phelan, review of *Amber Waiting,* p. 1659; August 1, 2006, Carolyn Phelan, review of *I'll Sing You One-O,* p. 77; October 1, 2007, review of *Pink,* p. 57.

*Canadian Review of Materials,* May 23, 1997, Leslie Millar, review of *How Smudge Came;* p. 1262; January 18, 2002, Valerie Nielsen, review of *Wild Girl and Gran;* April 25, 2003, Alison Mews, review of *Amber Waiting;* August 31, 2007, Jeannette Timmerman, review of *Pink.*

*Horn Book,* September-October, 1996, Sarah Ellis, review of *How Smudge Came,* p. 632; July-August, 2006, Anita L. Burkam, review of *I'll Sing You One-O,* p. 441.

*Kirkus Reviews,* March 15, 2003, review of *Amber Waiting,* p. 467; July 1, 2006, review of *I'll Sing You One-O,* p. 678; July 15, 2007, review of *Pink.*

*Kliatt,* July, 2006, Janis Flint-Ferguson, review of *I'll Sing You One-O,* p. 10.

*Publishers Weekly,* April 7, 2003, review of *Amber Waiting,* p. 64; July 16, 2007, review of *Pink,* p. 163.

*Quill & Quire,* February, 1996, review of *How Smudge Came,* p. 41; December, 2000, Sherie Posesorski, review of *Wild Girl and Gran,* p. 29; September, 2006, Maureen Garvie, review of *I'll Sing You One-O.*

*Resource Links,* April, 1996, review of *How Smudge Came,* pp. 157-158; August, 1997, Nan Gregory, "From Passion to Story," pp. 256-259; April, 2001, Heather Farmer, review of *Wild Girl and Gran,* p. 3; April, 2003, Antonia Gisler, review of *Amber Waiting,* p. 2; December, 2006, Gail de Vos, review of *I'll Sing You One-O,* p. 34; February, 2008, Susan Prior, review of *Pink,* p. 2.

*School Library Journal,* August, 2001, Susan Hepler, review of *Wild Girl and Gran,* p. 147; July, 2003, Grace Oliff, review of *Amber Waiting,* p. 96; October, 2006, Faith Brautigam, review of *I'll Sing You One-O,* p. 156; November, 2007, Ieva Bates, review of *Pink,* p. 92.

*ONLINE*

*Canadian Society of Children's Authors, Illustrators, and Performers Web site,* http://www.canscaip.org/ (August 15, 2008), "Nan Gregory."*

## HARTUNG, Susan Kathleen

### Personal

Born in Ann Arbor, MI. *Education:* School of Visual Arts (New York, NY), B.F.A. (illustration), 1990.

### Addresses

*Home*—Brooklyn, MI. *E-mail*—mailbox@susanhartung.com.

### Career

Illustrator of children's books, 1993—. Has worked in advertising, design, and photography. Picture Book Artists Association, corporate cofounder and former vice president; University of Michigan School of Art and Design, interim lecturer. *Exhibitions:* Illustrations included in Society of Illustrators Original Art Exhibition, 1999, 2000, 2005; Bookman Gallery, 2000; Mill River Gallery, 2000; and Children's Hospital of Michigan, 2006. Work included in permanent collection at Mazza Museum, Findlay, OH.

### Member

Graphic Artist Guild, Society of Children's Book Writers and Illustrators, Picture Book Artists Association.

### Awards, Honors

Ezra Jack Keats Award, 1999, for *Dear Juno;* CBC Children's Choice designation, 2001, for *One Dark Night;* International Reading Association Children's Book Award, and Parents Choice Silver Honor Medal, both 2002, both for *One Leaf Rides the Wind.*

### Illustrator

Soyung Pak, *Dear Juno,* Viking (New York, NY), 1999.

Sigmund Brouwer, *The Little Spider,* Tyndale House (Wheaton, IL), 2001.

Lori Morgan, *I Went to the Beach,* R.C. Owen Publishers (Katonah, NY), 2001.

Hazel J. Hutchins, *One Dark Night,* Viking (New York, NY), 2001.

Karyn Henley, *Rag Baby,* Tyndale House (Wheaton, IL), 2002.

Celeste Davidson Mannis, *One Leaf Rides the Wind: Counting in a Japanese Garden,* Viking (New York, NY), 2002.

Julie Markes, *Where's the Poop?,* HarperFestival (New York, NY), 2004.

Dori Chaconas, *Christmas Mouseling,* Viking (New York, NY), 2005.

Lola M. Schaefer, *Mittens,* HarperCollins (New York, NY), 2006.

Lola M. Schaefer, *Follow Me, Mittens,* HarperCollins (New York, NY), 2007.

Lola M. Schaefer, *What's That, Mittens?,* HarperCollins (New York, NY), 2008.

Rita M. Bergstein, *Your Own Big Bed,* Viking (New York, NY), 2008.

### Sidelights

Susan Kathleen Hartung has been drawing avidly since she was a young child, and she finds great joy in earning her living as a book illustrator. Hartung established her reputation creating art for Soyung Pak's *Dear Juno,* a picture book that won the Ezra Jack Keats Award. Since then the artist has earned praise for creating detailed illustrations in such books as Hazel J. Hutchins's *One Dark Night,* Celeste Davison Mannis's *One Leaf Rides the Wind: Counting in a Japanese Garden,* Rita M. Bergstein's *Your Own Big Bed,* and Lola M. Schaefer's "Mittens" beginning reader series.

Hartung was born and raised in Ann Arbor, Michigan. "I started drawing as soon as I could hold a crayon," she recalled on her home page. "I drew all the time, on anything." By the time she went to high school she was sure that she wanted to be an artist. She attended the School of Visual Arts in Manhattan, majoring in illustration and graduating in 1990. After that she worked various part-time jobs while trying to make a name for herself in the picture-book market. Her big break came in 1998 when she contracted with Viking to provide the pictures for *Dear Juno.*

***Susan Kathleen Hartung creates Japanese-inspired artwork for Korean author Soyung Pak's picture book* Dear Juno.** (Illustration copyright © 1999 by Susan Kathleen Hartung. Reproduced by permission of Puffin Books, a division of Penguin Putnam Books for Young Readers.)

In *Dear Juno* Pak tells a story about a Korean American boy who learns to communicate with his far-away grandmother using drawings, photographs, and pressed leaves. Juno can't read, but he is still able to understand his grandmother's letters and to respond to them with pictures and photos that reveal his own feelings. Calling *Dear Juno* "a simple but moving story about communicating across distances," a *Publishers Weekly* reviewer described Hartung's illustrations as "well designed and touching."

Jonathan is glad to have shelter in Hutchins's *One Dark Night.* A violent thunderstorm is on the horizon, and as it approaches the boy sees a mother cat carrying a kitten and searching for safety. He lets the pair come inside, but the mother cat dashes outside again after depositing the kitten in the house. By the time the storm hits, two kittens are already inside, and Jonathan helps the mother cat carry her last baby to safety. Some critics particularly liked the way Hartung contrasts the growing menace of the storm with the interior of Jonathan's bright, comfortable home. A *Horn Book* reviewer, noting the "elemental power and high drama" of the story, observed that "art and text ably capture the atmosphere of a summer storm." In *School Library Journal,* Shara Alpern wrote that "the heart of this story is its illustrations," and went on to describe *One Dark Night* as a "wonderful read-aloud."

*One Leaf Rides the Wind* uses haiku and images from a Japanese garden to teach counting concepts. Guided by Mannis's text, young readers are encouraged to find the items they have counted hiding in a double-page spread. Marilyn Taniguchi, writing in *School Library Journal,* described the book as "elegantly and respectfully presented," particularly through Hartung's "pleasing and evocative" illustrations, created using oil paint glazes.

In Bergstein's *Your Own Big Bed* a young boy learns that many creatures—in the ocean, at the zoo, and on the family farm—grow bigger and change the way they spend their days and nights, including even human creatures like him. Calling *Your Own Big Bed* "a lovely, sensitive offering," *Booklist* critic Gillian Engberg added that "Hartung's careful blue palette portrays nighttime as restful and inviting rather than scary." Hartung's glazed oil paintings also bring to life Dori Chaconas's version of the nativity tale in *Christmas Mousling,* as a mother mouse searches for a warm nest for her newborn on a cold and snowy night. Reviewing *Christmas Mousling,* Engberg wrote that "Hartung's delicate, soft-toned illustrations . . . amplify the contrast between the blustery winter forest and the safety and warmth of the mange." Praising Chaconas's "repetitive text," a *Horn Book* contributor concluded that the illustrator's "blustery" images "convey . . . the wintry night and the warm and loving tableau in the stable."

In addition to picture books, Hartung has also created illustrations for several book series for young children. In the beginning readers *Mittens,* as well as *What's That, Mittens?* and *Follow Me, Mittens,* she follows the adventures of a curious young tiger kitten, producing what *School Library Journal* critic Elaine Lesh Morgan dubbed "simple and uncluttered" illustrations in muted tones. In *School Library Journal,* Gloria Koster noted of *What's That, Mittens?* that Hartung's "soft pastel illustrations are simple and uncluttered and enhance the quiet tone of" Schaefer's story, and a *Kirkus Reviews* writer described the series as "a sweet, sturdy addition to the growing array of very first readers." "Charming . . . illustrations expose Mittens's proud and confident personality," concluded Sarah Holla in a *School Library Journal* appraisal of *Follow Me, Mittens.*

## Biographical and Critical Sources

*PERIODICALS*

*Booklist,* November 15, 1999, Lauren Peterson, review of *Dear Juno,* p. 636; May 15, 2001, Shelle Rosenfeld, review of *One Dark Night,* p. 1758; October 15, 2005, Gillian Engberg, review of *Christmas Mouseling,* p. 55; April 15, 2006, Hazel Rochman, review of *Mittens,* p. 55; July 1, 2008, Gillian Engberg, review of *Your Own Big Bed,* p. 75.

*Horn Book,* July, 2001, review of *One Dark Night,* p. 440; November-December, 2005, review of *Christmas Mouseling,* p. 691.

*Kirkus Reviews,* August 1, 2002, review of *One Leaf Rides the Wind: Counting in a Japanese Garden,* p. 1136; November 1, 2005, review of *Christmas Mouseling,* p. 1191; May 15, 2006, review of *Mittens,* p. 523; April 15, 2007, review of *Mittens.*

*Publishers Weekly,* October 25, 1999, review of *Dear Juno,* p. 79; September 24, 2001, review of *The Little Spider,* p. 53; September 2, 2002, review of *One Leaf Rides the Wind,* p. 75; September 26, 2005, review of *Christmas Mouseling,* p. 85.

*School Library Journal,* June, 2001, Shara Alpern, review of *One Dark Night,* p. 118; October, 2002, Marilyn Taniguchi, review of *One Leaf Rides the Wind,* p. 149; June, 2006, Elaine Lesh Morgan, review of *Mittens,* p. 126; July, 2007, Sarah O'Holla, review of *Follow Me, Mittens,* p. 84; May, 2008, Gloria Koster, review of *What's That, Mittens?,* p. 108; July, 2008, Martha Simpson, review of *Your Own Big Bed,* p. 66.

*ONLINE*

*Susan Kathleen Hartung Home Page,* http://www.susanhartung.com (July 30, 2008).

* * *

# HATKOFF, Craig 1954-

## Personal

Born March 19, 1954; married Jane Rosenthal; children: Juliana Lee, Isabella. *Education:* Columbia University, M.B.A, 1978.

## Addresses

*Home*—New York, NY.

## Career

Investor, entrepreneur, and author. Victor Capital Group, New York, NY, founder and managing partner, 1989-97; Capital Trust, Inc., New York, NY, vice chairman, 1997-2000, member of board of directors, 1997—; Tribeca Film Festival, New York, NY, cofounder with wife, Jane Rosenthal, and Robert De Niro, 2001—; New York City School Construction Authority, New York, NY, trustee, 2002-05; Taubman Centers, Bloomfield Hills, MI, director, 2004—; Turtle Pond Publications, New York, NY, chairperson.

## Writings

(With daughter, Juliana Lee Hatkoff) *Good-bye Tonsils!,* illustrated by Marilyn Mets, Viking (New York, NY) 2001.

(With daughter, Isabella Hatkoff, and Paula Kahumbu) *Owen and Mzee: The True Story of a Remarkable Friendship* (originally published as an e-book), illustrated with photographs by Peter Greste, Scholastic (New York, NY) 2006.

(With Isabella Hatkoff and Paula Kahumbu) *Owen and Mzee: The Language of Friendship,* illustrated with photographs by Peter Greste, Scholastic (New York, NY) 2007.

(With Isabella Hatkoff and Paula Kahumbu) *Owen and Mzee: Best Friends,* illustrated with photographs by Peter Greste, Scholastic (New York, NY) 2007.

(With Isabella Hatkoff and Paula Kahumbu) *Owen and Mzee: A Day Together,* illustrated with photographs by Peter Greste, Scholastic (New York, NY) 2008.

(With daughters Isabella and Juliana Hatkoff, and Dr. Gerald R. Uhlich) *Knut: How One Little Polar Bear Captivated the World,* Scholastic (New York, NY) 2008.

Also author, with Juliana Hatkoff, of *Ladder 35 Engine 40,* eBookMall.

## Sidelights

Craig Hatkoff, an investment manager who lives in New York City, has written several children's books with his daughters Isabella and Juliana Hatkoff. Hatkoff is also recognized for his contributions to the Tribeca Film Festival, which he cofounded with his wife, Jane Rosenthal, and celebrated actor Robert De Niro. The festival, which originated in 2001 following the attacks on the World Trade Center, has attracted over two million attendees since its inception and has helped to revitalize Manhattan.

Hatkoff's first book for young readers, *Good-bye Tonsils!,* is based on a journal he began with the then-five-year-old Juliana to help her prepare for her first operation, a tonsillectomy. The story focuses on a girl who learns that her sore throats can be cured by a surgical procedure, and it follows her experiences at the doctor's office and the hospital. "The authors include all the necessary information regarding a tonsillectomy in a comforting yet straightforward story," noted Meghan R. Malone in *School Library Journal.* Amy Brandt, writing in *Booklist,* observed that the "age-appropriate explanations will reassure children readying themselves for surgery."

Hatkoff later collaborated with Isabella on *Owen and Mzee: The True Story of a Remarkable Friendship,* which describes the unlikely bond between an orphaned hippo and a 130-year-old tortoise. Following a devastating tsunami in December 2004, a 600-pound baby hippo became separated from its mother and found itself stranded on a coral reef. After being rescued, the hippo, which was given the name Owen, arrived at the Haller Park Animal Sanctuary in Kenya and quickly looked to an Aldabra tortoise named Mzee for protection. The pair soon began eating, swimming, and playing together. "We knew there was something very special about this story," Hatkoff stated in a *Playthings* interview with

Karyn M. Peterson. "Owen and Mzee give testament to the power of friendship. Their true story that borders on the unbelievable teaches us many beautiful lessons on many levels, including friendship, conservation and tolerance."

*Owen and Mzee: The True Story of a Remarkable Friendship* was completed with the help of Paula Kahumbu, the director of the nature preserve, and photojournalist Peter Greste. "This touching story of the power of a surprising friendship to mitigate the experience of loss is full of heart and hope," Wendy Lukehart commented in *School Library Journal.* According to *New York Times Book Review* contributor Sarah Ellis, "the heart of the book is the gracefully told tale of Owen's abandonment, rescue and remarkable new family."

In a follow-up, *Owen and Mzee: The Language of Friendship,* the Hatkoffs continue the story of the animal pair, noting that they have developed a system of rumbling sounds to communicate. They also question whether Owen will pose a danger to Mzee once he reaches his adult size. "The text is clearly written and accompanied by numerous high-quality, full-color photos," wrote Grace Oliff in *School Library Journal,* and a *Kirkus Reviews* critic stated that young readers will "be mesmerized, mystified and charmed."

Hatkoff, his two daughters, and Dr. Gerald R. Uhlich, a board member of Zoo Berlin, joined forces for *Knut: How One Little Polar Bear Captivated the World.* The work recounts the efforts of zookeeper Thomas Dorflein to nurture a baby polar bear whose mother rejected him. The heartwarming story captured the attention of

***Cover of Craig and Isabella Hatkoff's* Owen and Mzee: The Language of Friendship, *a book coauthored by Paula Kahumbu and featuring photographs by Peter Greste.*** (Copyright © 2005 by Peter Greste. Reprinted by permission of Scholastic Inc.)

people from around the world. "The informative narrative flows easily," a reviewer in *Publishers Weekly* remarked.

## Biographical and Critical Sources


*PERIODICALS*

*Booklist,* August, 2001, Amy Brandt, review of *Good-bye Tonsils!,* p. 2130; May 15, 2006, Jennifer Mattson, review of *Owen and Mzee: The True Story of a Remarkable Friendship,* p. 48.

*Kirkus Reviews,* December 15, 2006, review of *Owen and Mzee: The Language of Friendship,* p. 1269.

*New York Times Book Review,* May 14, 2006, Sarah Ellis, "Can't We All Just Get Along?," review of *Owen and Mzee: The True Story of a Remarkable Friendship,* p. 18.

*Publishers Weekly,* February 13, 2006, review of *Owen and Mzee: The True Story of a Remarkable Friendship,* p. 89; November 13, 2006, review of *Owen and Mzee: The Language of Friendship,* p. 56; October 8, 2007, review of *Knut: How One Little Polar Bear Captivated the World,* p. 52.

*School Library Journal,* August, 2001, Meghan R. Malone, review of *Good-bye Tonsils!,* p. 147; May, 2006, Wendy Lukehart, review of *Owen and Mzee: The True Story of a Remarkable Friendship,* p. 111; February, 2007, Grace Oliff, review of *Owen and Mzee: The Language of Friendship,* p. 108.

*ONLINE*

*Knut Web site,* http://www.knut.net/ (August 15, 2008).

*Owen and Mzee Web site,* http://www.owenandmzee.com/ (August 15, 2008).

*Playthings Web site,* http://www.playthings.com/ (July 10, 2007), Karyn M. Peterson, "Up Close: *Owen and Mizee* Author Craig Hatkoff."


*   *   *

# HEIDE, Florence Parry 1919- (Alex B. Allen, Jamie McDonald)

## Personal

Surname is pronounced "*high*-dee"; born February 27, 1919, in Pittsburgh, PA; daughter of David W. (a banker) and Florence (an actress, columnist, and drama critic) Parry; married Donald C. Heide (an attorney), November 27, 1943; children: Christen, Roxanne, Judith, David, Parry. *Education:* Attended Wilson College; University of California, Los Angeles, B.A., 1939. *Politics:* Republican. *Religion:* Protestant.

## Addresses

*Home and office*—Kenosha, WI.

***Florence Parry Heide*** (Reproduced by permission.)

## Career

Writer. Before World War II worked variously at Radio-Keith-Orpheum (RKO), and at advertising and public relations agencies, New York, NY; Pittsburgh Playhouse, Pittsburgh, PA, former public-relations director.

## Member

International Board on Books for Young People, American Society of Composers, Authors, and Publishers (ASCAP), Authors Guild, Authors League of America, Society of Children's Book Writers and Illustrators, Council for Wisconsin Writers, Children's Reading Round Table.

## Awards, Honors

Children's Book of the Year award, Child Study Association of America, 1970, for *Sound of Sunshine, Sound of Rain,* and 1972, for *My Castle;* American Institute of Graphic Arts selection as one of the fifty best books of the year, 1971, Children's Book Show selection, American Institute of Graphic Arts, 1971-72, Best Illustrated Children's Book citation, *New York Times,* 1971, Children's Book Showcase selection, 1972, Jugendbuch Preis for best children's book in Germany, 1977, graphic arts prize from Bologna Book Fair, 1977, Notable Book citation, American Library Association (ALA), 1978, and Best of the Best Books 1966-78 citation, *School Li-*

*brary Journal,* all for *The Shrinking of Treehorn;* second prize for juvenile fiction, Council for Wisconsin Writers, and Golden Kite honor book, Society for Children's Book Writers and Illustrators, both 1976, both for *Growing Anyway Up;* Golden Archer Award, 1976; Notable Book citation, ALA, 1978, for *Banana Twist,* 1981, for *Treehorn's Treasure,* 1982, for *Time's Up!;* Litt.D. from Carthage College, 1979; Charlie May Simon Award, 1980, for *Banana Twist;* first prize, Council for Wisconsin Writers, 1982, for *Treehorn's Treasure;* honorable mention, Council for Wisconsin Writers, 1982, for *Time's Up!;* Notable Book citation, ALA, and first prize, Council for Wisconsin Writers, both 1990, and Charlotte Award, New York State, 1991, all for *The Day of Ahmed's Secret;* Outstanding Children's Book Award, New Hampshire Writers and Publishers Project, 1992, Notable Children's Trade Book in the Field of Social Studies, NCSS, and Best Books designation, *Parent's* magazine, both 1992, and Children's Book of Distinction designation, *Hungry Mind Review,* and Rhode Island Children's Book Award master list inclusion, both 1993, all for *Sami and the Time of the Troubles.*

## Writings

*FOR CHILDREN*

*Benjamin Budge and Barnaby Ball,* illustrated by Sally Mathews, Four Winds (New York, NY), 1967.

(Under pseudonym Jamie McDonald, with Anne and Walter Theiss and others) *Hannibal,* illustrated by Anne and Walter Theiss, Funk, 1968.

*Maximilian Becomes Famous,* illustrated by Ed Renfro, McCall, 1970.

*Alphabet Zoop,* illustrated by Sally Mathews, McCall, 1970.

*Giants Are Very Brave People,* illustrated by Charles Robinson, Parents' Magazine Press, 1970.

*The Little One,* illustrated by Ken Longtemps, Lion, 1970.

*Sound of Sunshine, Sound of Rain,* illustrated by Ken Longtemps, Parents' Magazine Press, 1970.

*The Key,* illustrated by Ati Forberg, Atheneum (New York, NY), 1971.

*Look! Look! A Story Book,* illustrated by Carol Nicklaus, McCall, 1971.

*The Shrinking of Treehorn* (also see below), illustrated by Edward Gorey, Holiday House (New York, NY), 1971.

*Some Things Are Scary,* Scholastic (New York, NY), 1971, illustrated by Jules Feiffer, Candlewick Press (Cambridge, MA), 2000.

*Who Needs Me?,* illustrated by Sally Mathews, Augsburg, 1971.

*My Castle,* illustrated by Symeon Shimin, McGraw, 1972.

(With brother, David Fisher Parry) *No Roads for the Wind* (textbook), Macmillan (New York, NY), 1974.

*God and Me,* illustrated by Ted Smith, Concordia, 1975.

*When the Sad One Comes to Stay* (novel), Lippincott (Philadelphia, PA), 1975.

*You and Me,* illustrated by Ted Smith, Concordia, 1975.

*Growing Anyway Up,* Lippincott (Philadelphia, PA), 1975.

*Banana Twist,* Holiday House (New York, NY), 1978.

*Changes,* illustrated by Kathy Counts, Concordia, 1978.

*Secret Dreamer, Secret Dreams,* Lippincott (Philadelphia, PA), 1978.

*Who Taught Me? Was It You, God?,* illustrated by Terry Whittle, Concordia, 1978.

*By the Time You Count to Ten,* illustrated by Pam Erickson, Concordia, 1979.

*Treehorn's Treasure* (also see below), illustrated by Edward Gorey, Holiday House (New York, NY), 1981.

*The Problem with Pulcifer,* illustrated by Judy Glasser, Lippincott (Philadelphia, PA), 1982.

*The Wendy Puzzle,* Holiday House (New York, NY), 1982.

*Time's Up!,* illustrated by Marylin Hafner, Holiday House (New York, NY), 1982.

*Banana Blitz,* Holiday House (New York, NY), 1983.

*I Am,* Concordia, 1983.

*The Adventures of Treehorn* (includes *The Shrinking of Treehorn* and *Treehorn's Treasure*), illustrated by Edward Gorey, Dell (New York, NY), 1983.

*Treehorn's Wish* (also see below), illustrated by Edward Gorey, Holiday House (New York, NY), 1984, published as *Treehorn Times Three,* Dell (New York, NY), 1992 published as *The Treehorn Trilogy,* Harry N. Abrams (New York, NY), 2006.

*Time Flies!,* illustrated by Marylin Hafner, Holiday House (New York, NY), 1984.

*Tales for the Perfect Child,* illustrated by Victoria Chess, Lothrop (New York, NY), 1985.

*Grim and Ghastly Goings-On* (poems), illustrated by Victoria Chess, Lothrop (New York, NY), 1992.

*The Bigness Contest,* illustrated by Victoria Chess, Little, Brown (Boston, MA), 1994.

(With daughters, Judith Heide Gilliland and Roxanne Heide Pierce) *It's about Time!* (poems), illustrated by Cathryn Falwell, Clarion (New York, NY), 1999.

*A Promise Is a Promise,* illustrated by Tony Auth, Candlewick Press (Cambridge, MA), 2007.

*The One and Only Marigold,* illustrated by Jill McElmurry, Schwartz & Wade Books (New York, NY), 2009.

*WITH SYLVIA WORTH VAN CLIEF; FOR CHILDREN*

*Maximilian,* illustrated by Ed Renfro, Funk, 1967.

*The Day It Snowed in Summer,* illustrated by Ken Longtemps, Funk, 1968.

*How Big Am I?,* illustrated by George Suyeoka, Follett, 1968.

*It Never Is Dark,* illustrated by Don Almquist, Follett, 1968.

*Sebastian* (includes songs by Sylvia Worth Van Clief), illustrated by Betty Fraser, Funk, 1968.

*That's What Friends Are For,* illustrated by Brinton Turkle, Four Winds, 1968, illustrated by Holly Meade, Candlewick Press (Cambridge, MA), 2003.

*The New Neighbor,* illustrated by Jerry Warshaw, Follett, 1970.

(Lyricist) *Songs to Sing about Things You Think About,* illustrated by Rosalie Schmidt, Day, 1971.

(Lyricist) *Christmas Bells and Snowflakes* (songbook), Southern Music, 1971.
(Lyricist) *Holidays! Holidays!* (songbook), Southern Music, 1971.
*The Mystery of the Missing Suitcase,* illustrated by Seymour Fleishman, Albert Whitman (Morton Grove, IL), 1972.
*The Mystery of the Silver Tag,* illustrated by Seymour Fleishman, Albert Whitman (Morton Grove, IL), 1972.
*The Hidden Box Mystery,* illustrated by Seymour Fleishman, Albert Whitman (Morton Grove, IL), 1973.
*Mystery at MacAdoo Zoo,* illustrated by Seymour Fleishman, Albert Whitman (Morton Grove, IL), 1973.
*Mystery of the Whispering Voice,* illustrated by Seymour Fleishman, Albert Whitman (Morton Grove, IL), 1974.
*Who Can?* (primer), Macmillan (New York, NY), 1974.
*Lost and Found* (primer), Macmillan (New York, NY), 1974.
*Hats and Bears* (primer), Macmillan (New York, NY), 1974.
*Fables You Shouldn't Pay Any Attention To,* illustrated by Victoria Chess, Lippincott (Philadelphia, PA), 1978.

*WITH DAUGHTER ROXANNE HEIDE PIERCE; FOR CHILDREN*

*Lost!* (textbook), Holt (New York, NY), 1973.
*I See America Smiling* (textbook), Holt (New York, NY), 1973.
*Tell about Someone You Love* (textbook), Macmillan (New York, NY), 1974.
*Brillstone Break-In,* illustrated by Joe Krush, Albert Whitman (Morton Grove, IL), 1977.
*Face at Brillstone Window,* illustrated by Joe Krush, Albert Whitman (Morton Grove, IL), 1978.
*Fear at Brillstone,* illustrated by Joe Krush, Albert Whitman (Morton Grove, IL), 1978.
*A Monster Is Coming! A Monster Is Coming!,* illustrated by Rachi Farrow, Franklin Watts (New York, NY), 1980.
*Black Magic at Brillstone,* illustrated by Joe Krush, Albert Whitman (Morton Grove, IL), 1982.
*Time Bomb at Brillstone,* illustrated by Joe Krush, Albert Whitman (Morton Grove, IL), 1982.
*Timothy Twinge,* illustrated by Barbara Lehman, Lothrop (New York, NY), 1993.
*Oh Grow Up!: Poems to Help You Survive Your Parents, Chores, School, and Other Afflictions,* illustrated by Nadine Bernard Westcott, Orchard Books (New York, NY), 1996.
*Tio Armando,* illustrated by Ann Grifalconi, Lothrop (New York, NY), 1998.

*"SPOTLIGHT CLUB" SERIES: WITH ROXANNE HEIDE PIERCE*

*Mystery of the Melting Snowman,* illustrated by Seymour Fleishman, Albert Whitman (Morton Grove, IL), 1974.
*Mystery of the Vanishing Visitor,* illustrated by Seymour Fleishman, Albert Whitman (Morton, Grove, IL), 1975.
*Mystery of the Lonely Lantern,* illustrated by Seymour Fleishman, Albert Whitman (Morton Grove, IL), 1976.
*Mystery at Keyhole Carnival,* illustrated by Seymour Fleishman, Albert Whitman (Morton Grove, IL), 1977.
*Mystery of the Midnight Message,* illustrated by Seymour Fleishman, Albert Whitman (Morton Grove, IL), 1977.
*Mystery at Southport Cinema,* illustrated by Seymour Fleishman, Albert Whitman (Morton Grove, IL), 1978.
*I Love Every-People,* illustrated by John Sandford, Concordia, 1978.
*Body in the Brillstone Garage,* illustrated by Joe Krush, Albert Whitman (Morton Grove, IL), 1979.
*Mystery of the Mummy's Mask,* illustrated by Seymour Fleishman, Albert Whitman (Morton Grove, IL), 1979.
*Mystery of the Forgotten Island,* illustrated by Seymour Fleishman, Albert Whitman (Morton Grove, IL), 1979.
*Mystery on Danger Road,* illustrated by Joe Fleishman, Albert Whitman (Morton Grove, IL), 1983.

*WITH DAUGHTER JUDITH HEIDE GILLILAND; FOR CHILDREN*

*The Day of Ahmed's Secret,* illustrated by Ted Lewin, Lothrop (New York, NY), 1990.
*Sami and the Time of the Troubles,* illustrated by Ted Lewin, Clarion (New York, NY), 1992.
*The House of Wisdom,* illustrated by Mary GrandPré, DK Ink (New York, NY), 1999.

*UNDER PSEUDONYM ALEX B. ALLEN; FOR CHILDREN*

(With Sylvia Worth Van Clief) *Basketball Toss Up,* illustrated by Kevin Royt, Albert Whitman (Morton Grove, IL), 1972.
(With Sylvia Worth Van Clief) *No Place for Baseball,* illustrated by Kevin Royt, Albert Whitman (Morton Grove, IL), 1973.
(With son, David Heide) *Danger on Broken Arrow Trail,* illustrated by Michael Norman, Albert Whitman (Morton Grove, IL), 1974.
(With Sylvia Worth Van Clief) *Fifth Down,* illustrated by Dan Siculan, Albert Whitman (Morton Grove, IL), 1974.
(With David Heide) *The Tennis Menace,* illustrated by Timothy Jones, Albert Whitman (Morton Grove, IL), 1975.

## Adaptations

*It Never Is Dark* (filmstrip with cassette or record), BFA Educational Media, 1975; *Sound of Sunshine, Sound of Rain,* an animated short film, was produced by Filmfair in 1984 and nominated for an Academy Award from the Academy of Motion Picture Arts and Sciences. *Sami and the Time of the Troubles* was adapted as an audiobook by Houghton Mifflin, 2002.

## Sidelights

The stories of writer Florence Parry Heide reveal "an antic sense of humor that refuses to be cowed," Jane Yolen once wrote in the *New York Times Book Review.* In her many picture books, chapter books, novels for young adults, mysteries, and poetry collections, Heide blends tongue-in-cheek humor with an entertaining storyline. Best known for penning a series of adventures of an incredible shrinking boy named Treehorn that are brought to life by black-and-white illustrations by the late artist Edward Gorey, she also injects the same sort of humor into her writings about other youngsters in books such as *Banana Twist, Time Flies!, Some Things Are Scary, That's What Friends Are For,* and *A Promise Is a Promise.* Heide spoofs fables and advice to children in other easy readers and opens the door to madcap mayhem in the anti-cautionary *Tales for the Perfect Child.* She also has a serious side, however, and in books such as *When the Sad One Comes to Stay, Tio Armando, Secret Dreamer, Secret Dreams,* and *Sound of Sunshine, Sound of Rain,* she tackles such difficult themes as alienation, death of a relative, blindness, and mental disability.

A self-proclaimed late bloomer, Heide did not begin writing children's books until after her five children had started school. She quickly established a prolific and award-winning career, and in the course of over more than five decades of writing she has published dozens of titles. Well known for her ability to find humor in parent-child struggles, Heide is often praised by critics for her whimsical imagination and her exuberant, if sometimes irreverent, wit, as well as her strong characterizations and her keen perception of the colorful but often difficult and confusing life of a child. It is a testament to Heide's talent for communicating with young readers that many of her books, including *That's What Friends Are For* and *Some Things Are Scary,* have continued to remain in print, and have been re-illustrated for newer generations. "With a few simple, immediate words, Heide gets the child's voice," observed Rochman in a *Booklist* review of the new edition of *Some Things Are Scary.*

Many of Heide's novels have been collaborations, first with Sylvia Worth Van Clief, and then with three of her children, David, Roxanne, and Judith. These collaborative efforts have spawned two well-loved mystery series for reluctant readers, "The Spotlight Detective Club" and "Brillstone Apartments," as well as the award-winning picture books *The Day of Ahmed's Secret, Sami and the Time of the Troubles,* and *The House of Wisdom,* all of which focus on life in the Middle East.

Heide's own childhood, like those of many of her characters, instilled in her a strong sense of love, hope, and comedy as well as allowing her to experience the insecurities involved in adapting to circumstances beyond her control. Her mother, a successful actress, gave up her career to marry and raise children. When Florence was not quite three years old, her father, a banker, died. Her mother, faced with the immediate need to support her family, left her two children temporarily with her parents, and moved to Pittsburgh, where she established a photography studio and became a regular columnist and drama critic for the *Pittsburgh Press.* When Heide's mother was financially able, she brought her children to live with her in Pittsburgh. Missing the constant companionship of the bustling home of her grandparents and competing for time with her mother's two demanding careers, Florence was initially lonely and shy. Her memories of life in Pittsburgh include the anxious moments of a very sensitive adolescent, as well as many good times with friends and family. But throughout her childhood, Heide maintained her belief in the power of a cheerful spirit, a strength she attributes largely to her mother, who so courageously faced the unexpected disaster of her husband's death.

After receiving her bachelor's degree in English at the University of California, Los Angeles, Heide worked for a few years in New York and Pittsburgh in advertising. She then met and married Donald Heide, settling happily into family life. As Heide once noted in an essay for *Something about the Author Autobiography Series* (*SAAS*), "Even as a child, I always knew what I wanted to be when I grew up—a mother. I'd meet the right person, I'd have children, I'd live happily ever after. And I did, and I am."

When her children reached school age, Heide began to seek another vehicle for her energy. Her first attempt at a career was a joint venture into the hot fudge sauce business with her friend, Van Clief. The two women began daily experiments with hot fudge recipes, but, since neither of them enjoyed kitchen work the project was short-lived. Heide and Van Clief then turned to writing songs—Heide writing lyrics, Van Clief writing the music—but they could not find buyers for their work. When they began to write children's songs, however, they immediately found a market, and Heide settled upon what felt like a natural career: "Writing for children was an unexpected delight: I could reach my child-self (never long away or far from me) and I could reach the selves of other children like me. . . . Ideas flew into my head. I couldn't write fast enough to accommodate them. I wrote, and I wrote, and I wrote."

One of Heide's most popular and acclaimed works is *The Shrinking of Treehorn,* a story that has spawned several sequels. Treehorn is a very serious and competent boy who wakes up one morning to discover that he is shrinking. In dangling sleeves and dangerously long pants, he reports the strange phenomenon to his mother, father, principal, and teacher in turn. The familiar adult reaction to children's announcements ("Think of that," his mother responds. "I just don't know why this cake isn't rising the way it should." "We don't shrink in this class," his teacher admonishes), are both funny and painful. "That, indeed," remarked Caroline C. Hunt in a *Children's Literature* discussion of the book, "is a frequent problem of the child in the (adult) world: not to be noticed, not to be taken seriously." The inflexible structure of the adult world is accentuated by Gorey's two-dimensional, ordered, geometric line drawings, which interact as a "brilliant fugue with Heide's witty text," according to *Horn Book* contributor Gertrude

Herman. The reviewer concluded that *The Shrinking of Treehorn* demonstrates the apparent adult dictum that "wonders may occur, but they are not allowed to disturb this universe." Margery Fisher, reviewing the title in *Growing Point,* called Heide's story a "classic example of the deplorable lack of imagination and observation in grown-ups which constantly amazes the young."

The "Treehorn" sequels continue to juxtapose youthful wonder with the rigidity of adult order. In *Treehorn's Treasure,* no one pays any attention to the boy when he discovers a money tree in the backyard, and in *Treehorn's Wish,* his parents have forgotten his birthday and refuse to take any hints to rectify matters. Hunt observed that the "sequels explore the same idea of marginalization through different central metaphors," but felt that "the alternative metaphors have less immediate appeal than that of size alone."

Size rears its head again in *The Bigness Contest* in which Beasley the hippopotamus despairs that he is too large, until an aunt assures him that hippos are meant to be big. This aunt holds a bigness contest to bolster Beasley's spirits, and he is sure to win, until a huge cousin emerges from the water to take the title. Not to worry, for Beasley finds a second contest where he is certain to claim first prize: a laziness contest! "Beasley is a lovable character with a sincere heart," observed Lynn Cockett in a *School Library Journal* review. In *Booklist* Hazel Rochman concluded of *The Bigness Contest* that "silly humor can do a lot for self-image."

More inflexible adults trouble Noah, the main character in Heide's humorous books *Time's Up!* and *Time Flies!* The young boy has his hands full, both adapting to life in a new neighborhood and dealing with the thought of a new baby brother or sister. His mother, busy with her college work, leaves Noah to the care of his father, an efficiency fanatic who times the boy performing his chores. With parents who seem to make life more difficult for him, Noah finds the strength, both within himself and in people around him, to adapt to his circumstances. Reviewing *Time Flies!* in the *Bulletin of the Center for Children's Books,* Zena Sutherland noted that "Heide's at her best when she writes with a light, wry touch, and in this book that's maintained throughout."

Parents are similarly unhelpful in *The Problem with Pulcifer,* in which a boy who prefers reading to television becomes a subject of concern among his parents, teachers, and a psychiatrist. "A very funny book," *The Problem with Pulcifer* "is written with acidulated exaggeration but that has a strong unstated message," summarized a reviewer for the *Bulletin of the Center for Children's Books.* Jonah, the star of *Banana Twist* and *Banana Blitz,* is a boy who hopes to escape adult supervision altogether by applying for admission to a boarding school that promises a television set and refrigerator in every dorm room. His parents, on the other hand, are health-food fanatics who think television is the devil's doing. At his new school, Jonah hopes to satisfy his twin desires for non-stop television and banana splits. A reviewer for *Booklist* called *Banana Twist* a "laugh-filled story."

While adults are always in nominal control, the Pulcifers, Jonahs, and Noahs of Heide's books are by no means powerless. In a playful spoof on the struggle between parents and children, her *Tales for the Perfect Child* presents a series of manipulative, willful, and often deceitful children who manage to get their own way in spite of their less-calculating parents' authority. Sutherland, writing in the *Bulletin of the Center for Children's Books,* felt that "the bland, sly humor" of the seven gathered stores "is Heide at her best," and "the fact that her protagonists prevail over fate and mothers will undoubtedly win readers." More anti-cautionary advice is served up in *Fables You Shouldn't Pay Any Attention To,* which contains "seven brief morality spoofs glorifying greed, laziness, dishonesty, etc. in which the evil doer is always rewarded and the do-gooder suffers," as Laura Geringer described the book in *School Library Journal.* Yolen, writing in the *New York Times Book Review,* called the collection "offbeat, silly, and outrageous." Teaming up with daughter Roxanne Heide Pierce, Heide provides advice for young readers in *Oh, Grow Up! Poems to Help You Survive Parents, Chores, School, and Other Afflictions,* and with this one, the title tells it all. A reviewer for *Publishers Weekly* dubbed *Oh, Grow Up!* a "droll collection" that is "always full of fun."

Heide also employs humor in the service of dealing with childhood fears. In *Grim and Ghastly Goings-On* she uses poems to "indulge kids' delicious fear of monsters," according to Rochman. *Timothy Twinge,* also a rhyming story, deals with every childhood fear imaginable, from monsters to aliens, the last of which do come at night, but quiet Timothy's fears. Jacqueline Elsner, writing in *School Library Journal,* praised the book for allowing Timothy "to solve his problems without parental involvement." Heide and her daughters also employ rhyme in *It's about Time!,* an "inviting collection," according to Robin L. Gibson in *School Library Journal,* whose "overall tone is light and humorous."

Additionally, Heide has written numerous books for adolescents that directly confront pain and alienation. In her first novel, *When the Sad One Comes to Stay,* Sara—a young girl whose ambitious and rather insensitive mother has taken her away from her home with her kindhearted father—receives comfort and friendship from an eccentric old woman named Crazy Maisie. When a choice must be made between her mother and Crazy Maisie, Sara casts her lot with her mother—and with probable loneliness as well. Focusing on different manifestations of realities that are beyond one's control, Heide wrote *Sound of Sunshine, Sound of Rain* about a blind boy in order to help her readers understand what it would be like to be blind. In *Secret Dreamer, Secret*

***Heide joins daughter Judith Heide Gilliland in writing* Sami at the Time of the Troubles, *featuring evocative paintings by Ted Lewin.*** (Illustration copyright © 1992 by Ted Lewin. Reprinted by permission of Clarion Books, an imprint of Houghton Mifflin Harcourt Publishing Company. All rights reserved.)

*Dreams* she explores the consciousness of a mentally handicapped young woman who cannot communicate with anyone. Although these works do not offer happy or resolved endings, they have been commended by critics for their sensitive characterizations and realistic perspectives. Selma K. Richardson, writing in the *St. James Guide to Children's Writers,* commented on the quality of these books, writing that "keenly sensitive characterization and tight prose distinguish Heide's first-person narratives for emerging adolescents."

This same sensitivity to theme and subject appears in Heide's books for younger readers. In *Tio Armando,* she joins daughter Roxanne to tackle the difficult topic of death in a story about a beloved relative who passes away. A contributor for *Kirkus Reviews* called the picture book a "graceful chronicle of the last year in a beloved great-uncle's life," and further applauded the "unusually well-crafted" prose produced by the mother-daughter collaboration.

Mysteries comprise a significant percentage of Heide's published books, with many falling into her "Spotlight Detective Club" and "Brillstone Apartments" series. She began writing mysteries in order to draw in reluctant readers with easy, intriguing, and fast-paced plots, and the first mysteries were written with friend and partner Van Clief. When Van Clief died, Roxanne took her place and collaborated with her mother on the mystery series and several other projects. One of Heide's sons, David, and her other daughter, Judith Gilliland, have also co-authored books with her. In a *School Li-*

*brary Journal* review of *Body in the Brillstone Garage,* Robert E. Unsworth noted that there is "enough action to keep even reluctant readers turning pages."

Teaming up with daughter Judith Gilliland, who spent five years in the Middle East, Heide has produced several award-winning books set in that region. In the picture book *The Day of Ahmed's Secret,* a young Egyptian boy describes his daily life in Cairo and waits to share a surprise with his family in the evening: he is now able to write his name. Mary Lou Burket, reviewing the book in *Five Owls,* called *The Day of Ahmed's Secret* a "seamless evocation of a day of work for a boy in modern Cairo" that "has been sensitively written." Set in war-torn Lebanon, *Sami and the Time of the Troubles* follows the daily life of a boy living in troubled and dangerous times. "While the physical and emotional desolation of Sami's world is painfully felt," wrote *Horn Book* critic Ellen Fader, "children will be left with a sense of hope that Sami and the other young people of the city will be able to make a difference and stop the war." Geared for older readers and featuring what a *Publishers Weekly* contributor described as "lushly colored pastel" art by Mary GrandPré, *The House of Wisdom* which is set in Iraq during the ninth century. Ishaq, the son of a translator, roams the world searching for books of learning to bring back to his caliph's library, the House of Wisdom, in Baghdad. "The narrative transports readers to the Islamic Empire, at a time of dramatic academic and cultural growth," observed the reviewer for *Publishers Weekly.*

Whether writing of shrinking boys or wandering scholars, Heide's "particular strength lies in her delineation of character," as Richardson noted. Her underlying message, whether presented in humorous or dramatic form, is one of personal responsibility and empowerment. As Heide commented in *SAAS,* she wrote *When the Sad One Comes to Stay* "because I wanted you younger readers (yes, you) to understand that although you may feel you have no choices, that the decisions are made for you by the GrownUps: where you live and who you live with, how late you stay up, where you go to school, whether you're rich or poor—everything's decided by THEM! All but the most important thing: what kind of person you're going to be. And this is a choice you make each day."

## Biographical and Critical Sources

*BOOKS*

*Authors of Books for Young People,* 3rd edition, Scarecrow Press (Metuchen, NJ), 1990.

*Children's Books and Their Creators,* edited by Anita Silvey, Houghton Mifflin (Boston, MA), 1995.

Heide, Florence Parry, *The Shrinking of Treehorn,* Holiday House (New York, NY), 1971.

Richardson, Selma K., *St. James Guide to Children's Writers,* 5th edition, edited by Sara Pendergast and Tom Pendergast, St. James Press (Detroit, MI), 1999, pp. 489-492.

*PERIODICALS*

*Booklist,* February 15, 1982, review of *Banana Twist,* p. 762; September 15, 1992, Hazel Rochman, review of *Grim and Ghastly Goings-On,* p. 144; March 15, 1994, Hazel Rochman, review of *The Bigness Contest,* p. 1372; October 15, 2000, Hazel Rochman, review of *Some Things Are Scary,* p. 434; March 15, 2003, Karin Snelson, review of *That's What Friends Are For,* p. 1332.

*Bulletin of the Center for Children's Books,* October, 1982, review of *The Problem with Pulcifer;* December, 1984, Zena Sutherland, review of *Time Flies!,* p. 66; November, 1985, Zena Sutherland, review of *Tales for the Perfect Child,* p. 48; September, 1999, review of *The House of Wisdom,* p. 14; December, 2000, review of *Some Things Are Scary,* p. 146.

*Children's Literature,* 1995, Caroline C. Hunt, "Dwarf, Small World, Shrinking Child: Three Version of Miniature," pp. 127-135.

*Five Owls,* October, 1995, Mary Lou Burket, review of *The Day of Ahmed's Secret,* pp. 21-22.

*Growing Point,* November, 1989, Margery Fisher, review of *The Shrinking of Treehorn,* p. 5260.

***Heide and daughter Judith Heide Gilliland return readers to the Middle East in* The House of Wisdom, *a story brought to life in the art of Mary GrandPré.*** (Illustration copyright © 1999 by Mary GrandPré. Reprinted by permission of DK Publishing, a member of Penguin Group (USA) Inc.)

*Horn Book,* January, 1989, Gertrude Herman, "A Picture Is Worth Several Hundred Words," p. 104; July-August, 1992, Ellen Fader, review of *Sami and the Time of the Troubles,* pp. 445-446; September, 1999, review of *The Shrinking of Treehorn,* p. 581; January, 2001, Martha V. Parravano, review of *Some Things Are Scary,* p. 83.

*Kirkus Reviews,* March 1, 1998, review of *Tio Armando,* p. 339; April 15, 2003, review of *That's What Friends Are For,* p. 608; May 1, 2007, review of *A Promise Is a Promise.*

*New York Times Book Review,* October 18, 1981, Karla Kuskin, review of *Treehorn's Treasure,* p. 49; November 19, 2000, Jeanne B. Pinder, "Things That Go Squish in the Night," p. 44.

*Publishers Weekly,* February 5, 1996, review of *Oh, Grow Up!: Poems to Help You Survive Parents, Chores, School, and Other Afflictions,* p. 90; August 23, 1999, review of *The House of Wisdom,* p. 58; October 15, 2000, review of *Some Things Are Scary,* p. 76; May 5, 2003, review of *Hello Again,* p. 223; May 21, 2007, review of *A Promise Is a Promise,* p. 53.

*School Library Journal,* February, 1979, Laura Geringer, review of *Fables You Shouldn't Pay Any Attention To,* p. 56; November, 1980, Robert E. Unsworth, review of *Body in the Brillstone Garage,* p. 47; October, 1992, Nancy Menaldi-Scanlan, review of *Grim and Ghastly Goings On,* p. 88; November, 1993, Jacqueline Elsner, review of *Timothy Twinge,* p. 82; May, 1994, Lynn Crockett, review of *The Bigness Contest,* p. 95; May, 1999, Robin L. Gibson, review of *It's about Time!,* p. 107; July, 2002, Kathleen Kelly MacMillan, review of *Sami and the Time of the Troubles,* p. 64; May, 2003, Lauralyn Persson, review of *That's What Friends Are For,* p. 120; June, 2007, Catherine Callegari, review of *A Promise Is a Promise,* p. 107.

*ONLINE*

*Candlewick Press Web site,* http://www.candlewick.com/ (August 15, 2008), "Florence Parry Heide."*

* * *

## HIRSCHI, Ron 1948-

### Personal

Surname pronounced "Hershey"; born May 18, 1948, in Bremerton, WA; son of Glenn W. (a lumber mill mechanic) and Doris Hirschi; married Brenda Dahl (a grocery clerk), July 19, 1969; children: Nichol. *Education:* University of Washington, B.S., 1974, graduate research in wildlife ecology, 1974-76.

### Addresses

*Office*—P.O. Box 899, Hadlock, WA 9339. *E-mail*—whalemail@waypoint.com.

### Career

Washington Game Department, Seattle, biologist, 1976-81; North Kitsap Schools, Poulsbo, WA, counselor in Indian education program, 1984-85; author, 1985—; Point No Point Treaty Council, Kingston, WA, biologist, 1988-90. Northwest Coast Indian Tribes, consulting biologist.

### Member

National Marine Educators Association, Washington Science Teachers Association, Port Gamble S'Klallam Foundation (member of board).

### Awards, Honors

*Headgear* and *One Day on Pika's Peak* selected among Child Study Association's Children's Books of the Year, 1986; Outstanding Science Trade Book for Children, National Science Teachers Association, 1986, for *Headgear,* and 1987, for *City Geese, Who Lives in . . . the Forest?,* and *What Is a Bird?;* Washington Governos Writer Award, 1992, for *Seya's Song.*

### Writings

*FOR CHILDREN*

*Headgear,* photographs by Galen Burrell, Dodd (New York, NY), 1986.

*One Day on Pika's Peak,* photographs by Galen Burrell, Dodd (New York, NY), 1986.

*City Geese,* photographs by Galen Burrell, Dodd (New York, NY), 1987.

*What Is a Bird?,* photographs by Galen Burrell, Walker (New York, NY), 1987.

*Where Do Birds Live?,* photographs by Galen Burrell, Walker (New York, NY), 1987.

*The Mountain Bluebird,* Dodd (New York, NY), 1988.

*What Is a Horse?,* photographs by Linda Quartman Younker, Walker (New York, NY), 1989.

*Where Do Horses Live?,* photographs by Linda Quartman Younker, Walker (New York, NY), 1989.

*What Is a Cat?,* photographs by Linda Quartman Younker, Walker (New York, NY), 1991.

*Where Do Cats Live?,* photographs by Linda Quartman Younker, Walker (New York, NY), 1991.

*Harvest Song,* illustrated by Deborah Haeffele, Cobblehill (New York, NY), 1991.

*Loon Lake,* photographs by Daniel J. Cox, Cobblehill (New York, NY), 1991.

*Seya's Song,* illustrated by Constance R. Bergum, Sasquatch Books (Seattle, WA), 1992.

*Hungry Little Frog,* photographs by Dwight Kuhn, Cobblehill (New York, NY), 1992.

*Turtle's Day,* photographs by Dwight Kuhn, Cobblehill (New York, NY), 1994.

*Dance with Me,* photographs by Thomas D. Mangelsen, Cobblehill (New York, NY), 1995.

*When the Wolves Return,* photographs by Thomas D. Mangelsen, Cobblehill (New York, NY), 1995.

*People of Salmon and Cedar,* illustrated by Deborah Cooper, Cobblehill (New York, NY), 1996.

*When Morning Comes,* photographs by Thomas D. Mangelsen, Boyds Mills Press (Honesdale, PA), 2000.
*When Night Comes,* photographs by Thomas D. Mangelsen, Carline House (Honesdale, PA), 2000.
*Octopuses,* Carolrhoda Books (Minneapolis, MN), 2000.
*Whalemail,* illustrated by Evon Zerbetz, Island Heritage, 2001.
*Salmon,* Carolrhoda Books (Minneapolis, MN), 2001.
*Seals,* Benchmark Books (New York, NY), 2003.
*Dolphins,* Benchmark Books (New York, NY), 2003.
*Swimming with Humuhumu,* illustrated by Tammy Lee, Island Heritage, 2004.
*Who Lives in the Coral Reef?,* illustrated by Steve Sundram, Island Heritage, 2004.
*Searching for Grizzlies,* photographs by Thomas D. Mangelsen, Boyds Mills Press (Honesdale, PA), 2005.
*Ocean Seasons,* illustrated by Kirsten Carlson, Sylvan Dell Pub. (Mt. Pleasant, SC), 2007.
*Lions, Tigers, and Bears: Why Are Big Predators So Rare?,* photographs by Thomas D. Mangelsen, Boyds Mills Press (Honesdale, PA), 2007.
*Winter Is for Whales,* illustrated by Yuko Green, Island Heritage, 2007.
*Our Three Bears,* photographs by Thomas D. Mangelsen, Boyds Mills Press (Honesdale, PA), 2008.

Contributor to periodicals, including *Owl* and *Cobblestone.*

*"WHERE ANIMALS LIVE" SERIES*

*Who Lives in . . . the Forest?,* photographs by Galen Burrell, Dodd (New York, NY), 1987.
*Who Lives in . . . Alligator Swamp?,* photographs by Galen Burrell, Dodd (New York, NY), 1987.
*Who Lives in . . . the Mountains?,* photographs by Galen Burrell, Dodd (New York, NY), 1988.
*Who Lives on . . . the Prairie?,* photographs by Galen Burrell, Dodd (New York, NY), 1988.

*"WILDLIFE SEASONS" SERIES*

*Winter,* photographs by Thomas D. Mangelsen, Cobblehill (New York, NY), 1990.
*Spring,* photographs by Thomas D. Mangelsen, Cobblehill (New York, NY), 1991.
*Summer,* photographs by Thomas D. Mangelsen, Cobblehill (New York, NY), 1991.
*Fall,* photographs by Thomas D. Mangelsen, Cobblehill (New York, NY), 1991.

The titles in the "Wildlife Seasons" series have been translated into Spanish.

*"DISCOVER MY WORLD" SERIES*

*Forest,* illustrated by Barbara Bash, Bantam (New York, NY), 1991.
*Ocean,* illustrated by Barbara Bash, Bantam (New York, NY), 1991.
*Desert,* illustrated by Barbara Bash, Bantam (New York, NY), 1992.
*Mountain,* illustrated by Barbara Bash, Bantam (New York, NY), 1992.

*"ONE EARTH" SERIES*

*Where Are My Bears?,* photographs by Erwin and Peggy Bauer, Bantam (New York, NY), 1992.
*Where Are My Prairie Dogs and Black-footed Ferrets?,* photographs by Erwin and Peggy Bauer, Bantam (New York, NY), 1992.
*Where Are My Puffins, Whales, and Seals?,* photographs by Erwin and Peggy Bauer, Bantam (New York, NY), 1992.
*Where Are My Swans, Whooping Cranes, and Singing Loons?,* photographs by Erwin and Peggy Bauer, Bantam (New York, NY), 1992.
*Save Our Forests,* photographs by E. and P. Bauer and others, National Audubon Society (New York, NY), 1993.
*Save Our Oceans and Coasts,* photographs by E. and P. Bauer and others, Delacorte (New York, NY), 1993.
*Save Our Prairies and Grasslands,* photographs by E. and P. Bauer, Delacorte (New York, NY), 1994.
*Save Our Wetlands,* photographs by E. and P. Bauer, Delacorte (New York, NY), 1994.

*"HOW ANIMALS LIVE" SERIES*

*A Time for Babies,* photographs by Thomas D. Mangelsen, Cobblehill (New York, NY), 1993.
*A Time for Sleeping,* photographs by Thomas D. Mangelsen, Cobblehill (New York, NY), 1993.
*A Time for Playing,* photographs by Thomas D. Mangelsen, Cobblehill (New York, NY), 1994.
*A Time for Singing,* photographs by Thomas D. Mangelsen, Cobblehill (New York, NY), 1994.

*"WILDLIFE WATCHER'S FIRST GUIDE" SERIES*

*Faces in the Forest,* photographs by Thomas D. Mangelsen, Cobblehill (New York, NY), 1997.
*Faces in the Mountains,* photographs by Thomas D. Mangelsen, Cobblehill (New York, NY), 1997.

## Sidelights

Wildlife biologist and writer Ron Hirschi once recalled to *SATA:* "When I was growing up, I spent all my free time in the woods, at the beach, or out on the water in boats my father made for me. It was a wonderful childhood and a great way to learn about animals and their needs." As it would prompt his later choice of a career, so these early experiences of nature would also direct it toward becoming a children's author by inspiring such books as *One Day on Pika's Peak, When the Wolves Return,* and several nature guides for young people. With numerous books on plants, animals, and their habitats now to his credit, Hirschi has opened a wide window to the world of nature for young readers. As *School Library Journal* reviewer Eva Elisabeth Von Ancken commented of his contributions to the National Audubon Society-sponsored "One Earth" series for children, "books such as these may be vital steps in saving what remains of the Earth's once abundant species."

Hirschi believes that his desire to write children's books first became manifest while he was a student at the University of Washington, when he, his wife Brenda, and his young daughter Nichol would sometimes escape to the nearby mountains or, when free time was especially scarce, as far as a city park near campus. "The inspiration for my book *City Geese* came from those days spent feeding geese and watching them in their city home," he once recalled to *SATA*. Although it would be another decade before Hirschi began submitting work to publishers, he found himself "creating stories for my daughter as she turned one, then two, then quickly five, then. . . . I really became enchanted by children's books as I read stories to Nichol, stories by Russell Hoban and Leo Lionni and Brooke Goffstein. Without realizing it, I became a student of children's literature as I bought books for Nichol and read and reread them, carefully tracing the wonderful relationship between work and image."

***Ron Hirschi's text is paired with Dwight Kuhn's photographs in the nature-based picture book* Turtle's Day.** (Photograph © 1994 by Dwight Kuhn. Reproduced by permission of Cobblehill Books, a division of Penguin Putnam Books for Young Readers. )

After graduating from college in the mid-1970s, Hirschi worked as a biologist, which often found him out in the field studying relationships between plants and animals. "I spent a lot of time writing reports, too," he remembered, "especially reports that had an educational value. It seemed to me that there was a large gap between scientific knowledge and public knowledge." He used his writing skills to help bridge that gap, producing pamphlets, booklets, and eventually magazine articles. "First, a few articles were published in local newspapers and fishing magazines," the author explained. "I am very proud of some of those articles since they attempt to show people the relationships between their actions and environmental consequences."

An idea for an article he submitted to *Owl* magazine, a publication of the Canadian Young Naturalist Foundation, would eventually become Hirschi's first published book for children. "The idea I submitted to *Owl* was about horns and antlers. My editor thought it wasn't quite right for the magazine, but she liked the concept and wrote a few thoughts that triggered my imagination enough to rewrite the idea as a nonfiction book." That rejected idea became *Headgear,* which was published in 1986.

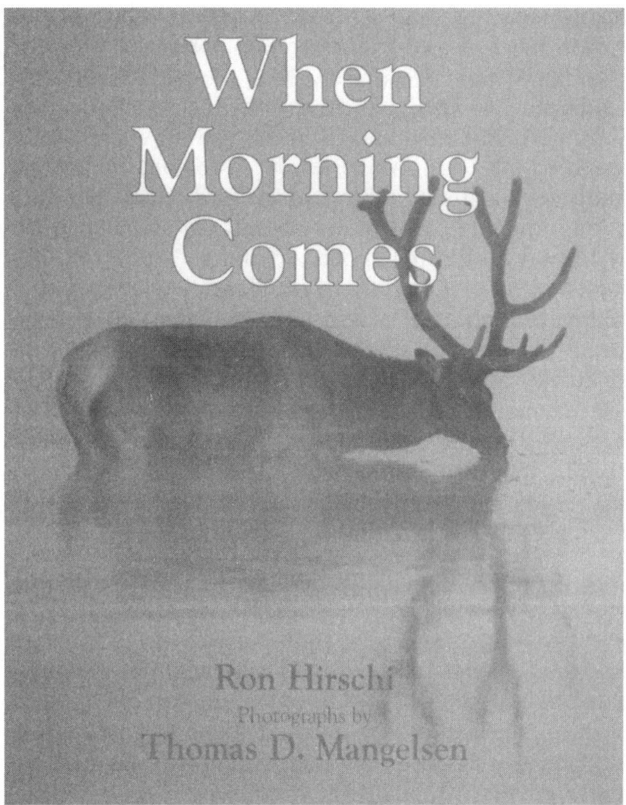


***Cover of Hirschi's inspirational picture book* When Morning Comes, *featuring photographs by Thomas D. Mangelsen.*** (Caroline House, 2005. Photograph copyright © 2000 by Thomas D. Mangelsen. Reproduced by permission.)

Hirschi's "Where Animals Live" series was based on a set of books he wrote for adults while he was employed in the Washington State Game Department. Including the titles *Who Lives in . . . the Mountains?* and *Who Lives on . . . the Prairie?,* the series is designed to appeal to a preschool audience, with its color photographs of animals in their habitats and a prose style that Nancy Vasilakis praised in a *Horn Book* review as "brief and expressive, never talking down to its young audience." Each volume includes a supplement for adults and older children that provides further information on the many animals that Hirschi features in each book—from such common creatures as a chipmunk to exotic birds like egrets and the gallinule. While noting the basic approach of the "Where Animals Live" books, Jacqueline Elsner commented in a *School Library Journal* review that Hirschi's work "is sure to inspire an appreciation for wildlife and conservation in the very young."

In addition to his "Where Animals Live" books, Hirschi has authored several other nature-book series, including "Discover My World," illustrated by artist Barbara Bash. Featuring titles like *Ocean, Forest,* and *Mountain,* each book is designed in a question-and-answer format. Detailed watercolor drawings of a particular animal's features—eyes, legs, teeth—encourage up-close observation by budding scientists so they can hypothesize what animal each picture represents, in answer to the question "Who am I,?" which is posed on every double-page spread. Other series by Hirschi include "The One Earth," which encourages young readers to actively engage in protecting and preserving the earth's endangered areas, and "Wildlife Seasons," each book of which documents the myriad of seasonal changes that occur in the natural world through beautiful color photographs by Thomas D. Mangelsen.

Picture books featuring animal characters in realistic natural settings are another way Hirschi has promoted a love of the natural world, especially to really young audiences. His *Hungry Little Frog* uses a tiny spring peeper's quest for dinner as the basis for a counting book: one ladybug, four strawberries, five robin's eggs, and so on. *Harvest Song* shows the passages of the seasons as viewed through the eyes of a young girl visiting her grandmother's farm, while *Turtle's Day,* illustrated with color photographs by nature photographer Dwight Kuhn, follows an eastern box turtle as he makes his daily rounds, scouting around for food, keeping out of the way of hungry bobcats, and righting himself after being turned over onto his back. "Hirschi conveys basic facts in a direct, lively manner that provides immediacy" to young readers, noted Diane Nunn in her review of *Turtle's Day* for *School Library Journal.*

Even after more than a decade as a prolific author, Hirschi is still surprised by the way new ideas spring up every day. Spending time in schools with students, watching the way kids respond to questions and talk about animals, has also inspired ideas that encourage young readers to participate more fully. "That is one reason I write books with questions as titles and the main reason the text often asks questions, too," the author explained.

For Hirschi, the most enjoyable part of writing a book is doing the research, which means spending lots of time in the mountains, at the beach, or in a boat. "Research for *The Mountain Bluebird* was especially enjoyable," Hirschi recalled, "since my wife came along much of the time. We traveled to Montana and Wyoming several times to watch bluebirds at their nests, during migration, and in the late days of summer." One of many well-illustrated books on birds that Hirschi has written, *The Mountain Bluebird* presents readers with a complete portrait of a bird whose numbers have been steadily decreasing due to the influence of mankind on its Rocky Mountain habitat. Praising the work as having "tremendous application as a reference tool," an *Appraisal* reviewer added that *The Mountain Bluebird* "is perfect for pleasure reading. Both young and old will enjoy the beauty of the bluebirds and their surroundings as portrayed in this wonderful book."

One of Hirschi's trips to Montana to watch bluebirds proved to be especially magical. Having camped in the Pryor Mountain range the night before, he and his wife awoke early and followed a flock of birds up a narrow canyon into the hills. "On our walk back we heard horses," the author remembered. "These weren't just any horses, though—they were wild horses, the first we had ever seen." Hirschi was overwhelmed by the experience of encountering such beautiful wild creatures, and would return to follow the Pryor Mountain horses, gathering information for his books *What Is a Horse?* and *Where Do Horses Live?* "As in my other books," the author maintained, "the horse books attempt to bring us a little closer—us, meaning the other creatures we share our world with as well as all the people, young and old."

In 1988 Hirschi accepted a job with Washington State's S'Klallam Indian Tribe. Acting to protect and help enforce the S'Klallam tribe's treaty rights to fish and wildlife in reservation areas, especially against the incursions by logging crews, he also continues to fight the deforestation along streams that threatens to destroy the habitat of trout, salmon, eagles, and other wildlife that live in such wooded areas. "The Klallam people lived in this area long before white people arrived," Hirschi explained, "and they have wonderful stories that tell of our relationship with animals and the land. As I listen to their stories, I realize the richness of their culture and I also realize how important it is to protect their way of life." Story is one way that the S'Klallam preserve their cultural traditions, and Hirschi reflects those rich traditions in *Seya's Song.* Using words of native S'Klallam speakers, a young girl describes the life cycle of the region's salmon against the changes wrought by the seasons and the activities of her tribe. With his characteristic fluid prose, which Janice Del Negro characterized in a *Booklist* review as "simple, poetic, and concrete," Hirschi paints a portrait of a rare Native-American culture and language that reflects its origins in nature.

In both *When Morning Comes* and *When Night Comes* Hirschi chronicles the activities of forest animals at both daybreak and nightfall. Illustrated with photographs by Thomas D. Mangelsen, the books present a variety of activities. Shelle Rosenfeld, writing in *Booklist,* praised "the simple, often poetic prose" of both books while Carolyn Angus noted in the *School Library Journal* that the books are enhanced by "Hirschi's spare lyrical text."

*Searching for Grizzlies* takes a look at the typical yearly cycle of the grizzly bears of Yellowstone National Park. It begins with their emergence from hibernation in the spring and ends with a final binge of eating in the fall, before hibernating for the winter again. Included are pages from the notebook journal Hirschi kept during a visit to Yellowstone. A critic for *Kirkus Reviews* believed that "Hirschi gives readers an up-close-and-personal look at grizzly bears," and Engberg concluded that *Searching for Grizzlies* was "excellent for classroom use or personal reading for young naturalists."

In *Ocean Seasons* Hirschi discusses the yearly cycle of seasons at sea. From one spring to the next, he explains the behaviors of fish, birds, and plants along the northern Pacific coast as the weather changes from warm to cold and back again. As on land, spring brings renewed plant growth in the ocean as well. Birds and fish breed in the springtime. Summer is a time of growth and activity. By fall, plankton growth falls off, and the food cycle begins to change. Fish begin to migrate south to warmer waters where the food is plentiful. "The lyrical text," Angela Leeper wrote in *ForeWord,* "not only describes the changes that occur throughout the year amidst the ocean's plants and animals but also how they form a food web." "*Ocean Seasons* provides a unique perspective on seasonal change," Judy Kraus noted in *Science and Children,* "and affords readers the opportunity to view a world they don't often see."

Hirschi looks at seven predatory animals—cougar, polar bear, lion, cheetah, tiger, grizzly bear, and killer whale—in *Lions, Tigers, and Bears: Why Are Big Predators So Rare?* Poaching and war, especially in Africa, have depleted the numbers of some predatory animals; poaching of tigers in Asia is particularly widespread. In other places, traditional habitats of such animals as the cougar have been taken over for farming and ranching, and Hirsch ultimately argues that the best way to save these animals is for humans to step in and protect them. The author's "approach is gentle and engaging," Anne Chapman Callaghan noted in *School Library Journal,* "but the urgency of his message is not lost—these animals need human help."

"When I think about the inspiration for my books, the connection with my childhood experiences always comes through," Hirschi explained to *SATA.* "But, my experiences as a biologist are also important in shaping the book themes. Now, I write nonfiction almost exclusively. I still pursue some fiction, but I remain a biologist and have a strong need to communicate through children's books all the ideas I have about our relationship with animals and the land."

## Biographical and Critical Sources

*PERIODICALS*

*Appraisal,* summer, 1990, review of *The Mountain Bluebird,* pp. 25-26.

*Audubon,* January-February, 2008, Julie Leibach, review of *Lions, Tigers, and Bears: Why Are Big Predators So Rare?,* p. 98.

*Booklist,* January 1, 1993, Janice Del Negro, review of *Seya's Song,* p. 806; December 15, 1993, Janice Del Negro, review of *A Time for Babies,* p. 757; March 15, 1994, Ellen Mandel, review of *Save Our Oceans and Coasts,* p. 1339; April 1, 1994, Mary Harris Veeder, review of *Turtle's Day,* pp. 1453, 1457; April 15, 1994, Mary Harris Veeder, reviews of *Save Our Prairies and Grasslands* and *Save Our Wetlands,* p. 1530; October 15, 1994, Deborah Abbott, reviews of *A Time for Singing* and *A Time for Playing,* p. 431; September 1, 1995, Mary Harris Veeder, review of *Dance with Me,* p. 79; September 15, 1997, Carolyn Phelan, reviews of *Faces in the Mountains* and *Faces in the Forest,* p. 237; July, 2000, Nora Jane Natke, review of *Octopuses,* p. 117; October 15, 2000, Shelle Rosenfeld, reviews of *When Morning Comes* and *When Night Comes,* p. 441; September 1, 2005, Gillian Engberg, review of *Searching for Grizzlies,* p. 126; October 15, 2007, Carolyn Phelan, review of *Lions, Tigers, and Bears,* p. 48.

*ForeWord,* July-August, 2007, Angela Leeper, review of *Ocean Seasons.*

*Horn Book,* January-February, 1988, Nancy Vasilakis, review of *Who Lives in . . . Alligator Swamp?,* p. 85.

*Kirkus Reviews,* September 1, 2005, review of *Searching for Grizzlies,* p. 974; May 1, 2007, review of *Ocean Seasons;* August 1, 2007, review of *Lions, Tigers, and Bears.*

*Publishers Weekly,* October 4, 1991, reviews of *Ocean* and *Forest,* p. 89; October 5, 1992, review of *Hungry Little Frog,* p. 69; November 9, 1992, review of *Seya's Song,* p. 82.

*School Library Journal,* January, 1988, Jacqueline Elsner, review of *Who Lives in . . . Alligator Swamp?,* pp. 72-73; November, 1990, p. 103; January, 1993, Eva Elisabeth Von Ancken, review of *Where Are My Bears?,* p. 92; February, 1994, p. 110; July, 1994, Diane Nunn, review of *Turtle's Day,* pp. 94-95; October, 1995, p. 148; December, 2000, Carolyn Angus, reviews of *When Morning Comes* and *When Night Comes,* p. 133; February, 2003, Pam Spencer Holley, review of *Seals,* p. 132; September, 2005, Patricia Manning, review of *Searching for Grizzlies,* p. 224; September, 2007, Anne Chapman Callaghan, review of *Lions, Tigers, and Bears,* p. 183.

*Science and Children,* April-May, 2008, Judy Kraus, review of *Ocean Seasons,* p. 67.

*Teacher Librarian,* June, 2008, John Peters, review of *Ocean Seasons,* p. 55.

*ONLINE*

*Ron Hirschi Home Page,* http://www.ronhirschi.com (August 14, 2008).

# HOGAN, Jamie

## Personal

Born in NH; married Marty Braun (an illustrator), 1988; children: Daisy. *Education:* Rhode Island School of Design, B.F.A. *Hobbies and other interests:* Skiing, motorcycling, beachcombing.

## Addresses

*Home and office*—Peaks Island, ME. *E-mail*—jamie@hoganbraun.com.

## Career

Illustrator. Teaches illustration at Maine College of Art, Portland; has also taught editorial illustration at Art Institute of Boston.

## Member

Graphic Artists Guild.

## Awards, Honors

Lupine Award Honor Book, Maine Library Association, 2007, for *Rickshaw Girl.*

## Writings

*ILLUSTRATOR*

Mitali Perkins, *Rickshaw Girl,* Charlesbridge (Watertown, MA), 2007.

Contributor of illustrations to periodicals, including *American Illustration, Boston Globe, Graphis, Print, Mother Jones,* and *Los Angeles Times.*

## Sidelights

Jamie Hogan, an illustrator based in Maine, often works in charcoal pencil, pastel, and paper collage. A graduate of the Rhode Island School of Design, Hogan has contributed to such publications as the *Boston Globe, Graphis,* and *Mother Jones.* She also teaches illustration at the Maine College of Art.

In 2007 Hogan provided the illustrations for *Rickshaw Girl,* an award-winning picture book by Mitali Perkins. *Rickshaw Girl* centers on Naima, a ten-year-old Bangladeshi girl who displays a talent for painting the traditional alpana patterns used to decorate homes during special celebrations. Hoping to assist her impoverished family, Naima disguises herself as a boy and attempts to drive her father's rickshaw, but her efforts end in disaster. The resourceful Naima must then use her artistic gifts to rectify her mistake.

Several critics praised Hogan's work in *Rickshaw Girl.* The illustrator's "bold black-and-white sketches show the brave girl, the beautiful traditional alpana painting and rickshaw art," Hazel Rochman commented in *Booklist.* "Black-and-white pastel drawings depict authentic *alpana* designs and also provide glimpses into Naima's dynamic world," remarked *Horn Book* contributor Norah Piehl. "Short chapters, well-delineated characters, soft black-line pastel illustrations, and a child-appropriate solution enrich this easy-to-read chapter book," Susan Hepler similarly noted in *School Library Journal.*

## Biographical and Critical Sources

*PERIODICALS*

*Booklist,* November 1, 2006, Hazel Rochman, review of *Rickshaw Girl,* p. 54.

*Horn Book,* May-June, 2007, Norah Piehl, review of *Rickshaw Girl,* p. 288.

*Kirkus Reviews,* December 1, 2006, review of *Rickshaw Girl,* p. 1225.

*School Library Journal,* April, 2007, Susan Hepler, review of *Rickshaw Girl,* p. 115.

***Cover of Mitali Perkins' picture book* Rickshaw Girl, *featuring artwork by Jamie Hogan.*** (Illustration copyright © 2007 by Jamie Hogan. Used with permission of Charlesbridge Publishing, Inc. All rights reserved.)

*ONLINE*

*Jamie Hogan Home Page,* http://www.hoganbraun.com (August 10, 2008).

*Jamie Hogan Web log,* http://www.jamiepeeps.blogspot.com/ (August 10, 2008).

* * *

# HORVATH, David 1972(?)-

## Personal

Born c. 1972; mother a toy designer; married Sun-Min Kim (an author and artist); children: Mini (daughter). *Education:* Parson's School of Design, degree. *Hobbies and other interests:* Collecting toys.

## Addresses

*Home and office*—Los Angeles, CA. *E-mail*—info@davidhorvath.com.

## Career

Art-toy designer, animator, and author/illustrator. Creator of character toys, including Uglydolls, Uglydog, Pounda, Noupa, and Littlebony. Toys International, Los Angeles, CA, manager, 2001-02; Prettyugly, Kenilworth, NJ, cofounder with wife, Sun-Min Kim, 2002.

## Awards, Honors

Specialty Toy of the Year award, Toy Industry of America, 2006, for Uglydolls.

## Writings

*Bossy Bear,* Hyperion (New York, NY), 2007.

*WITH WIFE, SUN-MIN KIM*

*How to Draw Uglydoll Kit: Ugly Drawings in a Few Easy Steps,* Walter Foster Books, 2006.

*The Ugly Guide to Things That Go and Things That Should Go but Don't,* Random House (New York, NY), 2008.

*Ugly Guide to the Uglyverse,* Random House (New York, NY), 2008.

*Ugly Guide to Being Alive and Staying That Way,* Random House (New York, NY), 2009.

*Chilly Chilly Ice-Bat,* Random House (New York, NY), 2009.

*ABC U Later,* Random House (New York, NY), 2009.

*1, 2, 3, 4 U,* Random House (New York, NY), 2009.

Also creator, with Kim, of animated films produced in Japan, including *Littlebony* and *Noupa.*

## Adaptations

Horvath and Kim's "Ugly" creatures have been adapted as stuffed toys and licensed for other items, including a card game.

## Sidelights

Anyone familiar with the names Peaco, Moxy, Ice-Bat, and Chunkanucka will also be familar with David Horvath, one half of the creative talent behind the Uglydoll phenomenon. Joined by wife and artist Sun-Min Kim, Horvath began designing the dolls in the early 2000s, and in 2002 the collectible art toys became available at upscale department stores, galleries, and museum stores in the United States. With an ever-growing following of fans and collectors, the dolls were even the focus of an Uglycon to celebrate the fifth year of their production! Because the dolls are handmade—Kim actually hand-sewed each one during their first eighteen months of production—each Uglydoll is unique and includes a small tag featuring the character's name, personality, and biography.

In addition to his work designing art toys, Horvath has also collaborated with Kim on several books for children, such as *The Ugly Guide to Things That Go and Things That Should Go but Don't, Chilly Chilly Ice-Bat,* and *ABC U Later.* With *Bossy Bear* Horvath has also produced his own original picture book featuring a cartoon bear who, with a crown atop his head, demands his own way from everyone around him. Helping to teach this pushy bear a lesson about sharing is a cast of colorful characters who, according to a *Publishers Weekly* contributor, "bear a striking resemblance to the plush dolls created by the author." Horvath's "crisp and spare" art "gives immediate appeal to this simple story," concluded Jayne Damron in her *School Library Journal* review of *Bossy Bear.*

## Biographical and Critical Sources

*PERIODICALS*

*Kirkus Reviews,* May 1, 2007, review of *Bossy Bear.*

*Publishers Weekly,* April 16, 2007, review of *Bossy Bear,* p. 49.

***David Horvath's characteristically curmudgeonly cast of characters enlivens his quirky self-illustrated picture book* Bossy Bear.** 

*School Library Journal,* June, 2007, Jayne Damron, review of *Bossy Bear,* p. 108.

*Time,* winter, 2006, Nadia Mustafa, review of *Who Are You Calling Ugly?,* p. 38.

*ONLINE*

*David Horvath Home Page,* http://www.davidhorvath.com (August 4, 2008).

*Ploom2,* http://www.ploom2.com/ (August 1, 2007), interview with Horvath.*

* * *

## HOSTA, Dar

### Personal

Surname pronounced "Hough-sta"; born September 21, in WI; daughter of an artist father and an educator mother; married; children: two sons. *Education:* University of Missouri-Columbia, B.A. (creative writing); Cleveland State University, secondary teaching certification.

### Addresses

*Office*—Brown Dog Books, P.O. Box 2196, Flemington, NJ 08822. *E-mail*—darhosta@mac.com.

### Career

Author, illustrator, and collage artist. *Exhibitions:* Works exhibited at art shows in New Jersey and Pennsylvania.

### Member

Society of Children's Book Writers and Illustrators, Teacher and Writers Collaborative, Independent Book Publishers Association.

### Awards, Honors

Teachers' Choice Award for the Family, *Learning* magazine, and Borders Original Voices Award nominee, both 2004, both for *I Love the Night;* Teachers' Choice Award, and Benjamin Franklin Award for Picture Books, both 2005, both for *I Love the Alphabet;* Teachers' Choice Award, National Arbor Day Foundation Media Award, and American Horticultural Society Growing Good Kids Book Award, all 2007, all for *If I Were a Tree.*

### Writings

*SELF-ILLUSTRATED*

*I Love the Night,* Brown Dog Books (Flemington, NJ) 2003.

***Dar Hosta*** (Photograph by Deborah Gichan courtesy of Dar Hosta.)

*I Love the Alphabet,* Brown Dog Books (Flemington, NJ), 2004.

*Mavis and Her Marvelous Mooncakes,* Brown Dog Books (Flemington, NJ), 2006.

*If I Were a Tree,* Brown Dog Books (Flemington, NJ), 2007.

*OTHER*

Contributor to periodicals, including *NJ SCBWI* magazine.

### Sidelights

Each of Dar Hosta's books is the result of many hours' work, from writing the story and creating the colorful collage art to publishing, promoting, and distributing the book. In creating her award-winning art, Hosta uses textured Japanese paper to create her collage shapes, and heavy watercolor paper as her background. Both papers are painted using vibrant and opaque acrylic paints, and the cut shapes are arranged on the watercolor paper and fastened using a dry-glue method. Hosta then details her collages with a variety of media, such as ink, oil pastel, and colored pencil. The most detailed collages, as well as her larger works of non-picture-book art, can take up to one hundred hours to complete.

"Collage artists like me are often called Mixed Media Artists because we do more than just glue pieces of paper and we use lots of different art supplies to make our art," Hosta explained on her home page. "Most of my book illustrations are done during the winter months when I am not tempted to putter around outside or when I am not playing around at the pool with my kids or on vacation! Winter is a great time to stay busy and cozy in a studio."

*I Love the Night,* Hosta's first original picture book, was designed as a bedtime story and features a gentle, rhyming text that describes the life of nocturnal animals. In contrast, *I Love the Alphabet* weaves an energetic sweep of letters from A to Z within a panorama of vivid collage images. "As fun as the rhymes are, Hosta's dynamic collage creations steal the show," noted *Booklist* critic Lauren Peterson in her review of *I Love the Alphabet,* while in *Publishers Weekly* a critic cited the author/illustrator for featuring "powerful visual" in her picture-book debut.

*Mavis and Her Marvelous Mooncakes* is an imaginative rhyming tale about a cat named Mavis Sugar who bakes a monthly mooncake, one slice per night, for fourteen days until it is finished and then eaten, one slice every night. But there is more than mere fantasy in Hosta's story about a moon made of cake. As Mavis's baking continues, readers learn about the nine phases of the moon, gaining an astronomy lesson in the process. "With beautiful use of color and texture, Hosta creates a cast of appealing animals and [an] atmospheric moonlit" setting in her tale, observed *School Library Journal* critic Amy Lilien-Harper. The story gains a "folksy, quilt-like feel" due to the author/illustrator's use of dark, saturated backgrounds and bright images, according to a *Kirkus Reviews* writer, the critic adding that Hosta's "pictures . . . pop off the pages." "Filled with stars and touched by moonlight," *Mavis and Her Marvelous Mooncakes* "charms more with each turn of the page," concluded *Booklist* contributor Ilene Cooper.

Hosta honors one of her favorite plants in her award-winning picture book *If I Were a Tree.* Long and narrow like the plant it describes, the book combines Hosta's rhyming text and vibrant collage art to follow each season in the life of various species of trees, and closes with a fact page giving further botanical information. Noting that the book "conveys both an environmental awareness and bits of natural science," a *Kirkus Reviews* writer dubbed *If I Were a Tree* "an effective consciousness-raiser" as well as a "pleasant" storyhour treat.

I am a bit of an accidental children's book creator," Hosta told *SATA.* "My journey began in language arts education in the public schools and, after the birth of my children, my longtime artistic hobbies evolved into freelance design and art work. With a background in creative writing, it was a small leap into my first, and experimental title, *I Love the Night,* after which I was hooked. I still spend a lot of time in schools and with kids, so I feel real lucky to be able to combine all the things I love to do into one job: teaching, writing, and art."

## Biographical and Critical Sources

*PERIODICALS*

*Booklist,* September 1, 2004, Lauren Peterson, review of *I Love the Alphabet,* p. 132; November 5, 2006, Ilene Cooper, review of *Mavis and Her Marvelous Mooncakes,* p. 53.

*Kirkus Reviews,* November 15, 2006, review of *Mavis and Her Marvelous Mooncakes,* p. 1175; May 1, 2007, review of *If I Were a Tree.*

*Publishers Weekly,* June 23, 2003, review of *I Love the Night,* p. 66.

*School Library Journal,* January, 2007, Amy Lilien-Harper, review of *Mavis and Her Marvelous Mooncakes,* p. 98.

*ONLINE*

*Brown Dog Books Web site,* http://www.browndogbooks.com/ (August 10, 2008), "Dar Hosta."

*Dar Hosta Home Page,* http://www.darhosta.com (August 4, 2008).

# J-K

## JUDGE, Lita

### Personal

Born in Ketchikan, AK; married; husband's name Dave. *Education:* Graduated from Oregon State University. *Hobbies and other interests:* Traveling, reading, gardening, yoga.

### Addresses

*Home*—Peterborough, NH. *Office*—Wilder Farm Studio, 77 Wilder Farm Rd., Peterborough, NH 03458. *E-mail*—Lita@litajudge.com.

### Career

Author and illustrator. Has worked as an environmental geologist and a paleobotanist.

### Member

Society of Children's Book Writers and Illustrators.

### Awards, Honors

New York Public Library 100 Books for Reading and Sharing selection, New York Public Library, and Gold Award winner, National Parenting Publications Awards, both 2007, Children's Book Award and Notable Book for a Global Society, both International Reading Association, Notable Children's Book selection, American Library Association, Jane Addams Children's Book Award Honor designation, Notable Children's Books in the Language Arts designation, National Council of Teachers of English, and *Storytelling World* Resource Award, all 2008, all for *One Thousand Tracings: Healing the Wounds of World War II.*

### Writings

*SELF-ILLUSTRATED*

*One Thousand Tracings: Healing the Wounds of World War II,* Hyperion Books (New York, NY), 2007.

(With Todd Chapman) *D Is for Dinosaur: A Prehistoric Alphabet,* Sleeping Bear Press (Chelsea, MI), 2007.

*ILLUSTRATOR*

Donna Jo Napoli, *Ugly,* Hyperion Books (New York, NY), 2006.

Helen Foster James, *S Is for S'mores: A Camping Alphabet,* Sleeping Bear Press (Chelsea, MI), 2007.

Donna Jo Napoli, *Mogo, the Third Warthog,* Hyperion Books (New York, NY), 2008.

### Sidelights

Lita Judge, a former environmental geologist and paleobotanist, now writes and illustrates children's books. "I've loved drawing from as early as I can remember," Judge remarked on her home page. "I especially loved drawing birds from life and dinosaurs from my imagination. Writing came later for me. I think my love of reading finally led me to want to write my own stories." Judge has provided the artwork for *Ugly,* an adaptation of Hans Christian Andersen's "The Ugly Duckling" by Donna Jo Napoli, as well as *D Is for Dinosaur: A Prehistoric Alphabet,* a title she coauthored with Todd Chapman.

In her self-illustrated *One Thousand Tracings: Healing the Wounds of World War II,* Judge describes her grandparents' effort to assist European survivors in the aftermath of war. "When I was cleaning out my grandmother's attic after her death, I found a dusty box stuffed with aged yellowed envelopes," Judge wrote on the *One Thousand Tracings* Web site. "I was intrigued when I lifted out the first envelope; it had a German stamp postmarked 1947 and inside were two paper foot tracings." Judge learned that her grandparents had founded The Action, a relief organization that provided food and clothing to more than 3,000 people in thirteen countries; the tracings helped volunteers determine the survivors' shoe sizes. "I wish my grandmother could have shared these memories with me, but I feel closer to her

***Lita Judge tells a story that focuses on the strength of a close-knit rural family during wartime in her self-illustrated* One Thousand Tracings.** (Art copyright © 2007 by Lita Judge. Reprinted by permission of Hyperion Books for Children. All rights reserved.)

now for having discovered the truth," Judge observed. "I wish I had known about it when she was alive so I could tell her how proud I am. Instead, I wrote my book as a tribute to her."

In *One Thousand Tracings* a six-year-old Midwestern girl and her mother take action after receiving a letter from a friend describing the horrific conditions in post-war Germany. The "narration offers a child's perspective on the tragedies and hope of the era, making the story especially accessible to young audiences," noted a critic in *Publishers Weekly.* Marianne Saccardi, writing in *School Library Journal,* commented that Judge's "soft-edged paintings are colorful and fluid and create a strong sense of time and place."

## Biographical and Critical Sources

*PERIODICALS*

*Booklist,* May 15, 2007, Hazel Rochman, review of *One Thousand Tracings: Healing the Wounds of World War II,* p. 47.

*Kirkus Reviews,* December 15, 2005, review of *Ugly,* p. 1326; June 15, 2007, review of *One Thousand Tracings.*

*Publishers Weekly,* February 6, 2006, review of *Ugly,* p. 70; June 11, 2007, review of *One Thousand Tracings,* p. 59.

*School Library Journal,* March, 2006, Susan Hepler, review of *Ugly,* p. 199; July, 2007, Marianne Saccardi, review of *One Thousand Tracings,* p. 92.

*ONLINE*

*Lita Judge Home Page,* http://www.litajudge.com (August 15, 2008).

*Lita Judge Web log,* http://wpblog.litajudge.com/ (August 15, 2008).

*One Thousand Tracings Web site,* http://tracings.litajudge.com/ (August 15, 2008).*

*　*　*

## KENNEDY, Frances 1937-

### Personal

Born 1937, in Sioux City, IA; daughter of Donna Delle Philp; married; husband's name Jim.

### Addresses

*Home*—Dubuque, IA.

### Career

Author. Taught elementary school in Dubuque, IA.

### Awards, Honors

Iowa Stories 2000 selection, for *The Pickle Patch Bathtub.*

### Writings

*The Pickle Patch Bathtub,* illustrated by Sheila Aldridge, Tricycle Press (Berkeley, CA), 2004.

*The Just-right, Perfect Present,* illustrated by Sheila Aldridge, Tricycle Press (Berkeley, CA), 2007.

### Adaptations

*The Pickle Patch Bathtub* was adapted for the stage by the Great Midwestern Educational Theatre Company, 2007.

### Sidelights

Frances Kennedy, a former elementary school teacher living in Iowa, is the author of the highly regarded picture book *The Pickle Patch Bathtub.* Based on a true story and set in the 1920s, *The Pickle Patch Bathtub* centers on Donna, a Missouri farm girl who has outgrown her family's washtub. When Donna's mother informs her that they do not have the money to purchase a new one, the youngster enlists her brothers and sisters to help her grow cucumbers and sell them to the local pickle factory. "Some old-fashioned lessons of delayed gratification and family cooperation are subtly conveyed," observed a critic in *Kirkus Reviews.* Linda L. Walkins, writing in *School Library Journal,* praised the combination of Kennedy's narrative and Sheila Aldridge's illustrations, stating that "both text and artwork vividly bring the past to life."

Donna and her family return in *The Just-right, Perfect Present,* "an engaging peek at family life in earlier days," according to a contributor in *Kirkus Reviews.* When her grandparents announce that they will be celebrating their fiftieth anniversary in their apple orchard, Donna chooses to recite a poem in their honor. When she learns that her cousin has selected the same verse, the girl is forced to learn a new poem, with unexpectedly delightful results. In *Booklist,* Carolyn Phelan remarked that Kennedy's tale "is infused with memory yet is never merely nostalgic."

## Biographical and Critical Sources

*PERIODICALS*

*Booklist,* July 1, 2007, Carolyn Phelan, review of *The Just-right, Perfect Present,* p. 65.

*Kirkus Reviews,* April 1, 2004, review of *The Pickle Patch Bathtub,* p. 332; May 1, 2007, review of *The Just-right, Perfect Present.*

*School Library Journal,* October, 2004, Linda L. Walkins, review of *The Pickle Patch Bathtub,* p. 120; November, 2007, Martha Simpson, review of *The Just-right, Perfect Present,* p. 93.

*ONLINE*

*Sioux City Journal.com,* http://www.siouxcityjournal.com/ (May 2, 2006), Dolly A. Butz, "Students Learn about Iowa as First Lady Gives Them Books."*

* * *

# KHING, T.T. 1933-
# (Thé Tjong-Khing)

## Personal

Born August 4, 1933, in Purworedjo, Java. *Education:* Attended Seri Rupa (Bandung, Java).

## Addresses

*Home and office*—Netherlands.

## Career

Illustrator, cartoonist, and graphic artist. Toodner Studios, Netherlands, draftsman, beginning 1956; freelance illustrator.

## Awards, Honors

Gouden Penseel award and Gouden Griffel award, both 1985, both for *Sophie Kleine and Lange Wapper* by Els Pelgrom; Gouden Penseel award, 2003, for *Het Woorden boek van Vos en Haas* by Sylvia Vanden Heede; Woutertje Pieterse Prijs, and Zilveren Penseel, both 2005, both for *Waar is de taart?*

## Writings

*Waar is de taart?,* Lannoo (Netherlands), 2004, translation published as *Where Is the Cake?,* Harry N. Abrams (New York, NY), 2007.

*Picknick met taart,* Lannoo (Netherlands), 2005, published as *Picnic with Cake,* Harry N. Abrams (New York, NY), 2009.

*De Sprookjesverteller,* Gottmer/Schuyt, 2007.

*ILLUSTRATOR*

Colin Dann, *De kieren van het Duitenbos,* Querido (Amsterdam, Netherlands), 1983.

Els Pelgrom, *Het Loterijbriefje,* Ploegsma, 1984.

Els Pelgrom, *Sophie Kleine and Lange Wapper,* Querido (Amsterdam, Netherlands), 1985.

Sylvia Vanden Heede, *Vos en Haas,* Lannoo (Netherlands), 1998.

Jacques Vriens, *Grootmoeder, wat heb je grote oren,* Ploegsma, 1998.

Antonie Schneider, *De wonderbare reis van de jongen,* Ploegsma, 1999.

Sylvia Vanden Heede, *Tot kijk, Vos en Haas,* Lannoo (Netherlands), 1999.

Sylvia Vanden Heede, *Vos en Haas op het eiland,* Lannoo (Netherlands), 2000.

Sylvia Vanden Heede, *Het Aa Bee See van Vos en Haas,* Lannoo (Netherlands), 2002.

Sylvia Vanden Heede, *Het Wordenboek van Vos en Haas,* Lannoo (Netherlands), 2003.

Henri van Daele, *En ze leefden nog lang en gelkukkig,* Davidsfonds, 2003.

Kolet Janssen, *Het grote avontuur van God en mens,* Davidsfonds, 2004.

Paul Biegel, *Swing,* Holland, 2004.

Henri van Daele, *Er was eens een prinses,* Davidsfonds, 2005.

Els Pelgrom, *Helden—Griekse mythen,* Lannoo (Netherlands), 2006.

Els Pelgrom, *Donder en blicksem,* Lannoo (Netherlands), 2007.

Illustrator for comic strip "Arman and Ilva," written by Olivier B. Bommelstrip. Contributor to books, including *Denkend aan Haarlem,* Gottmer/Schuyt, 1995; and *Lees dit neit!,* Lemniscaat, 1996. Contributor to periodicals, including *Haarlems Dagblad* and *Tina.*

## Biographical and Critical Sources

*PERIODICALS*

*Horn Book,* March-April, 2007, Joanna Rudge Long, review of *Where Is the Cake?,* p. 185.

*Kirkus Reviews,* March 1, 2007, review of *Where Is the Cake?,* p. 224.

*Publishers Weekly,* April 16, 2007, review of *Where Is the Cake?,* p. 50.

*ONLINE*

*T.T. Khing Home Page,* http://www.thethongkhing.nl (August 20, 2008).*

* * *

# KING-SMITH, Dick 1922-

## Personal

Born March 27, 1922, in Bitton, Gloucestershire, England; son of Ronald (a paper mill director) and Grace King-Smith; married Myrle England, February 6, 1943 (deceased, 2000); married; second wife's name Zona; children: Juliet Clare, Elizabeth Myrle, Giles Anthony Beaumont. *Education:* Attended Marlborough College, 1936-40; Bristol University, B.Ed., 1975.

## Addresses

*Home*—Avon, England. *Agent*—Caradoc King, A.P. Watt, 20 John St., London WC1N 2DR, England.

## Career

Author. Farmer in Gloucestershire, England, 1947-67; sold asbestos suits and worked in a shoe factory; Farmborough Primary School, near Bath, Avon, England, teacher, 1975-82; writer, 1978—. Writer and presenter of Yorkshire Television's *Tumbledown Farm* series for children, beginning 1983; presenter of *Rub-a-Dub-Dub* for TVAM and *Pob's Programme* for Channel 4. *Military service:* Grenadier Guards, 1941-46; became lieutenant; mentioned in dispatches.

## Member

Rare Breeds Survival Trust, Kelmscott Rare Breeds Foundation (director).

## Awards, Honors

*Guardian* Award runner-up, 1981, for *Daggie Dogfoot;* American Library Association Notable Book citations, 1982, for *Pigs Might Fly,* 1985, for *Babe: The Gallant Pig,* and 1987, for *Harry's Mad; Guardian* Award, 1984, for *The Sheep-Pig; Boston Globe/Horn Book* Honor Book, and Parents' Choice Award for Literature, both 1985, both for *Babe: The Gallant Pig;* Children's Author of the Year, British Book Awards, 1991; Reading Magic Award, *Parenting* magazine, 1995, for *Harriet's Hare;* honorary doctorate from University of Gloucestershire, 2004.

## Writings

*FOR CHILDREN*

*The Fox Busters,* illustrated by Jon Miller, Gollancz (London, England), 1978, Delacorte (New York, NY), 1988, reissued, Puffin (London, England), 2003.

*Daggie Dogfoot,* illustrated by Mary Rayner, Gollancz (London, England), 1980, published as *Pigs Might Fly,* Viking (New York NY), 1982.

*The Mouse Butcher,* illustrated by Wendy Smith, Gollancz (London, England), 1981, illustrated by Margot Apple, Viking (New York, NY), 1982.

*Magnus Powermouse,* illustrated by Mary Rayner, Gollancz (London, England), 1982, Harper (New York, NY), 1984.

*The Queen's Nose,* illustrated by Jill Bennett, Gollancz (London, England), 1983, Harper (New York, NY), 1985.

*The Sheep-Pig,* illustrated by Mary Rayner, Gollancz (London, England), 1983, reissued, Puffin (London, England), 2003, published as *Babe: The Gallant Pig,* Crown (New York, NY), 1985, reissued, Knopf (New York, NY), 2005.

*Harry's Mad,* illustrated by Jill Bennett, Gollancz (London, England), 1984, Crown (New York, NY), 1987.

*Saddlebottom,* illustrated by Alice Englander, Gollancz (London, England), 1985.

*Lightning Fred,* illustrated by Michael Bragg, Heinemann (London, England), 1985.

*Noah's Brother,* illustrated by Ian Newsham, Gollancz (London, England), 1986.

*Pets for Keeps* (nonfiction), illustrated by Alan Saunders, Penguin (London, England), 1986.

*H. Prince,* illustrated by Martin Honeysett, Walker Books (London, England), 1986.

*Yob,* illustrated by Abigail Pizer, Heinemann (London, England), 1986.

*E.S.P.,* illustrated by Peter Wingham, Deutsch (London, England), 1986.

*Dumpling,* illustrated by Jo Davies, Hamish Hamilton (London, England), 1986, reissued, Puffin (London, England), 2001.

*Farmer Bungle Forgets,* illustrated by Martin Honeysett, Walker (London, England), 1986.

*Town Watch* (nonfiction), illustrated by Catherine Bradbury, Penguin (London, England), 1987.

*Country Watch: Animals to Look out for in the Countryside* (nonfiction), illustrated by Catherine Bradbury, Penguin (London, England), 1987.

*Tumbleweed,* illustrated by Ian Newsham, Gollancz (London, England), 1987.

*The Hodgeheg,* illustrated by Linda Birch, Hamish Hamilton (London, England), 1987, new edition, illustrated by Ann Kronheimer, Puffin (London, England), 2003.

*Cuckoobush Farm,* illustrated by Kazuko, Orchard (London, England), 1987, Greenwillow (New York, NY), 1988.

*Friends and Brothers,* illustrated by Susan Hellard, Heinemann (London, England), 1987.

*Martin's Mice,* illustrated by Jez Alborough, Gollancz (London, England), 1988, Crown (New York, NY), 1989, new edition, illustrated by Ann Kronheimer, Puffin (London, England), 2004.

*George Speaks,* illustrated by Judy Brown, Viking (London, England), 1988, Roaring Brook Press (Brookfield, CT), 2002, new edition, illustrated by Ann Kronheimer, Puffin (London, England), 2004.

*The Jenius,* illustrated by Peter Firmin, Gollancz (London, England), 1988, reissued, Puffin (London, England), 2004, published as *Jenius: The Amazing Guinea Pig,* illustrated by Brian Floca, Hyperion (New York, NY), 1996.

*Emily's Legs,* illustrated by Katinka Kew, Macdonald (London, England), 1988.

*Water Watch* (nonfiction), illustrated by Catherine Bradbury, Penguin (London, England), 1988.

*Dodo Comes to Tumbledown Farm,* illustrated by John Sharp, Heinemann (London, England), 1988.

*The Greatest!,* Heinemann (London, England), 1988.

*The Toby Man,* illustrated by Ian Newsham, Gollancz (London, England), 1989, illustrated by Lynette Hemmant, Crown (New York, NY), 1991.

*Alice and Flower and Foxianna,* Heinemann (London, England), 1989.

*Beware of the Bull!,* Heinemann (London, England), 1989.

*Henry Pond Poet,* Hodder & Stoughton (London, England), 1989.

*Dodos Are Forever,* illustrated by David Parkins, Viking (London, England), 1989.

*Sophie's Snail,* illustrated by Claire Minter-Kemp, Delacorte (New York, NY), 1989.

*The Trouble with Edward,* Hodder & Stoughton (London, England), 1989.

*Ace: The Very Important Pig,* illustrated by Lynette Hemmant, Crown (New York, NY), 1990.

*Dick King-Smith's Alphabeasts,* illustrated by Quentin Blake, Gollancz (London, England), 1990, Macmillan (New York, NY), 1992.

*The Jolly Witch,* Simon & Schuster (London, England), 1990.

*Paddy's Pot of Gold,* illustrated by David Parkins, Crown (New York, NY), 1990.

*The Water Horse,* illustrated by David Parkins, Viking (London, England), 1990, Crown (New York, NY), 1998.

*The Whistling Pig,* Walker (London, England), 1990.

*Caruso's Cool Cats,* BBC/Longman (London, England), 1991.

*Horace and Maurice,* Doubleday (London, England), 1991.

*Lightning Strikes Twice,* Mammoth (London, England), 1991.

*Sophie's Tom,* illustrated by David Parkins, Candlewick Press (Cambridge, MA), 1991.

*The Cuckoo Child,* illustrated by Leslie Bowman, Hyperion (New York, NY), 1991.

*The Guard Dog,* illustrated by Jocelyn Wild, Corgi (London, England), 1991, reissued, Young Corgi (London, England), 2007.

*The Animal Parade: A Collection of Stories and Poems,* illustrated by Jocelyn Wild, Tambourine Books (New York, NY), 1992.

*Blessu and Dumpling,* Penguin (London, England), 1992.

*Farm Tales,* Mammoth (London, England), 1992.

*The Finger Eater,* Walker (London, England), 1992.

*The Ghost at Codlin Castle,* Viking (London, England), 1992.

*Jungle Jingles,* Corgi (London, England), 1992.

*Pretty Polly,* illustrated by Marshall Peck, Crown (New York, NY), 1992.

*Triffic Pig Book,* Gollancz (London, England), 1992, published as *Triffic, the Extraordinary Pig,* illustrated by Cary Pillo, Troll (Mahwah, NJ), 1998.

*The Topsy-turvy Storybook,* illustrated by John Eastwood, Gollancz (London, England), 1992.

*Dragon Boy,* illustrated by Jocelyn Wild, Viking (London, England), 1993.

*Horse Pie,* Doubleday (London, England), 1993.

*A Narrow Squeak, and Other Animal Stories,* Viking (London, England), 1993.

*Sophie Hits Six,* illustrated by David Parkins, Candlewick Press (Cambridge, MA), 1993.

*Lady Daisy,* illustrated by Jan Naimo Jones, Delacorte (New York, NY), 1993.

*The Invisible Dog,* illustrated by Roger Roth, Crown (New York, NY), 1993.

*Find the White Horse,* illustrated by Larry Wilkes, Chivers (London, England), 1993.

*All Pigs Are Beautiful,* illustrated by Anita Jeram, Candlewick Press (Cambridge, MA), 1993.

*The Merrythought,* illustrated by Mike Reid, Puffin (London, England), 1993.

*Uncle Bumpo,* Deutsch (London, England), 1993.

*Bobby the Bad,* illustrated by Julie Anderson, Deutsch (London, England), 1994.

*Connie and Rollo,* illustrated by Judy Brown, Doubleday (London, England), 1994.

*The Excitement of Being Ernest,* illustrated by Nigel McMullen, Simon & Schuster (London, England), 1994.

*The Swoose,* illustrated by Maire Corner, Hyperion (New York, NY), 1994.

*Happy Mouseday,* Doubleday (London, England), 1994.

*Harriet's Hare,* illustrated by Valerie Littlewood, Doubleday (London, England), 1994, illustrated by Roger Roth, Crown (New York, NY), 1995.

*Mr. Potter's Pet,* illustrated by Hilda Offen, Viking (London, England), 1994, illustrated by Mark Teague, Hyperion (New York, NY), 1996.

*Sophie in the Saddle,* illustrated by David Parkins, Candlewick Press (Cambridge, MA), 1994.

*Three Terrible Trins,* illustrated by Mark Teague, Crown (New York, NY), 1994.

*The Schoolmouse,* illustrated by Phil Garner, Viking (London, England), 1994, illustrated by Cynthia Fisher, Hyperion (New York, NY), 1995.

*Sophie's Adventures,* illustrated by David Parkins, Walker (London, England), 1995.

*Sophie Is Seven,* illustrated by David Parkins, Candlewick Press (Cambridge, MA), 1995.

*I Love Guinea Pigs,* illustrated by Anita Jeram, Candlewick Press (Cambridge, MA), 1995.

*King Max the Last: A Second Hodgeheg Story,* illustrated by Birch, Hamish Hamilton (London, England), 1995.

*Warlock Watson,* Hippo (London, England), 1995.

*All Because of Jackson,* illustrated by John Eastwood, Doubleday (London, England), 1995.

*The Stray,* illustrated by Wayne Parmenter, Crown (New York, NY), 1996.

*Dick King-Smith's Animal Friends: Thirty-one True Life Stories,* illustrated by Anita Jeram, Candlewick Press (Cambridge, MA), 1996.

*Sophie's Lucky,* illustrated by David Parkins, Candlewick Press (Cambridge, MA), 1996.

*Clever Duck,* illustrated by Mike Terry, Viking (London, England), 1996.

*Hogsel and Gruntel and Other Animal Stories,* illustrated by Liz Graham-Yooll, Gollancz (London, England), 1996, Orchard (New York, NY), 1999.

*Godhanger,* illustrated by Andrew Davidson, Doubleday (London, England), 1996.

*Mrs. Jollipop,* illustrated by Frank Rodgers, Macdonald (London, England), 1996.

*Treasure Trove,* illustrated by Paul Howard, Viking (London, England), 1996.

*Omnibombulator,* illustrated by Jim and Peter Kavanagh, Corgi (London, England), 1996.

*Fat Lawrence,* illustrated by Mike Terry, Puffin (London, England), 1997.

*Sophie's Further Adventures,* illustrated by David Parkins, Walker (London, England), 1997.

*Smasher,* illustrated by Michael Terry, Viking (London, England), illustrated by Richard Bernal, Random House (New York, NY), 1997.

*Animal Stories,* illustrated by Michael Terry, Puffin (London, England), 1997.

*The Spotty Pig,* illustrated by Mary Wormell, Farrar, Straus (New York, NY), 1997.

*A Mouse Called Wolf,* illustrated by Jon Goodell, Crown (New York, NY), 1997.

*Puppy Love,* illustrated by Anita Jeram, Crown (New York, NY), 1997.

*What Sadie Saw,* illustrated by Julie Anderson, Scholastic (London, England), 1997.

*The Crowstarver,* Doubleday (London, England), 1998, published as *Spider Sparrow,* illustrated by Peter Bailey, Crown (New York, NY), 2000.

*Mr. Ape,* illustrated by Roger Roth, Crown (New York, NY), 1998.

*How Green Was My Mouse,* illustrated by Robert Bartelt, Viking (London, England), 1998, published as *Charlie Muffin's Miracle Mouse,* illustrated by Lina Chesak, Crown (New York, NY), 1999.

*Poppet,* illustrated by Mike Terry, Puffin (London, England), 1999.

*The Merman,* illustrated by Roger Roth, Crown (New York, NY), 1999.

*The Witch of Blackberry Bottom,* illustrated by Ann Kronheimer, Viking (London, England), 1999, published as *Mysterious Miss Slade,* Crown (New York, NY), 2000.

*The Roundhill,* illustrated by Sian Bailey, Crown (New York, NY), 2000.

*Lady Lollipop,* illustrated by Jill Barton, Candlewick Press (Cambridge, MA), 2001.

*Chewing the Cud: An Extraordinary Life Remembered by the Author of Babe, the Gallant Pig* (autobiography), illustrated by Harry Horse, Viking (London, England), 2001.

*Billy the Bird,* illustrated by Susie Jenkin Pearce, Hyperion (New York, NY), 2001.

*Back to Front Benjy,* illustrated by Judy Brown, Puffin (London, England), 2001.

*The Big Book of Short Stories,* illustrated by Amanda Harvey, Viking (London, England), 2001.

*The Great Sloth Race,* illustrated by Tim Warnes, Puffin (London, England), 2001.

*Funny Frank,* illustrated by Roger Roth, Knopf (New York, NY), 2002.

*Titus Rules!,* illustrated by John Eastwood, Knopf (New York, NY), 2003.

*Clever Lollipop,* illustrated by Jill Barton, Candlewick Press (Cambridge, MA), 2003.

*The Adventurous Snail,* Doubleday (London, England), 2003.

*The Golden Goose,* illustrated by Ann Kronheimer, Puffin (London, England), 2003, Knopf (New York, NY), 2005.

*Aristotle,* illustrated by Bob Graham, Walker (London, England), 2003, published as *The Nines Lives of Aristotle,* Candlewick Press (Cambridge, MA), 2003.

*Here Comes Sophie,* illustrated by David Parkins, Walker (London, England), 2004.

*The Catlady,* illustrated by John Eastwood, Doubleday (London, England), 2004, Knopf (New York, NY), 2006.

*Hairy Hezekiah,* illustrated by Nick Breul, Doubleday (London, England), 2005, illustrated by Nick Bruel, Roaring Brook Press (New York, NY), 2007.

*Under the Mishmash Trees,* illustrated by Seb Burnett, Puffin (London, England), 2005, illustrated by Nick Bruel, Roaring Brook Press (New York, NY), 2008.

*The Twin Giants,* illustrated by Mini Grey, Candlewick Press (Cambridge, MA), 2007.

*Ninnyhammer,* Doubleday (London, England), 2007.

*The Mouse Family Robinson,* illustrated by Ben Cort, Puffin (London, England), 2007, illustrated by Nick Bruel, Roaring Brook Press (New York, NY), 2008.

*Clever Duck,* illustrated by Nick Bruel, Roaring Brook Press (New York, NY), 2008.

*Dinosaur Trouble,* illustrated by Nick Bruel, Roaring Brook Press (New York, NY), 2008.

Contributor to periodicals, including *Punch, Blackwood's,* and *Field.*

## Adaptations

*The Sheep-Pig* (also published as *Babe: The Gallant Pig*) was adapted for film as *Babe,* Universal Pictures/Kennedy Miller Productions, 1995; *The Water Horse* was adapted for film as *The Water Horse: Legend of the Deep* by Columbia Pictures, 2007. *Lady Daisy* was adapted to audio in 1996 by Listening Library. Chivers North America adapted the following to audio: *The Fox Busters,* 1987, *The Sheep-Pig, Magnus Powermouse,* and *Tumbleweed,* all 1988, and *Ace, the Very Important Pig,* 1991. Also adapted to audio were *The Hodgeheg* and *The Mouse Butcher,* 1989; *Jungle Jingles, The Schoolmouse,* and *Three Terrible Trins,* 1996; *The Stray,* 1997; *The Merman,* 1999; *Spider Sparrow,* 2000; and *The Witch of Blackberry Bottom,* 2001, and *The Water Horse,* 2008, among others.

## Sidelights

Take a cast of improbable animal protagonists, from pigs to mice and dogs; add a dose of anthropomorphism, a pinch of human affection, and a sprinkling of adversity to overcome. The result is the winning formula in the books of British author Dick King-Smith, a man perhaps best known for writing *Babe: The Gallant Pig,* the book from which the 1995 Academy Award-winning film *Babe* was adapted. With millions of copies of his books in print worldwide, King-Smith has become a one-man cottage industry in children's literature. "Helped by years of classical education in the best tradition of the English public-school system," wrote London *Guardian* contributor Julia Eccleshare, King-Smith's "stories have heroic resonances, as well as being written in perfectly shaped classical sentences, which makes them a joy to read—and especially out loud." Eccleshare further remarked, "More than that, [his books] are written with the humorous, civilised view of human or animal interaction so reflective of King-Smith himself."

Often compared to British writers of past generations, such as Beatrix Potter, Kenneth Grahame, E.B. White, and Rudyard Kipling, King-Smith mines the same vein of rich animal stories, never fearing to give his cast of pigs, dogs, hamsters, parrots, and other critters human characteristics while also making sure to retain the characteristics of the animal as well. "I allow them some human ones, especially speech, because it is such fun putting words into their mouths," King-Smith explained to a group of online grammar-school interviewers on *Young Writer.*

Most amazing about Kink-Smith's prodigious achievement is that he began writing for children relatively late in life, after pursuing careers in farming and teaching. He has been prolific since the late 1970s, and has earned acclaim for his works about animals, including *Pigs Might Fly, Babe: The Gallant Pig, Harry's Mad, The Water Horse,* and *Titus Rules!,* among a host of others. King-Smith is widely admired for a witty and often parodic writing style that appeals to both children and adults, as well as for his ability to portray his subjects affectionately without becoming too whimsical or sentimental. Combining exciting adventures with witty dialogue and subtly drawn but strong characters, King-

***Mary Rayner created art for Dick King-Smith's entertaining nature story* Pigs Might Fly, *a sequel to his perennially popular* Babe.** (Illustration copyright © 1980 by Mary Rayner. Used by permission of Viking Penguin, a division of Penguin Putnam Books for Young Readers.)

Smith presents his readers with specific moral lessons without being overly didactic. In his novels, animal protagonists—usually underdogs—manage to triumph through some extraordinary ability, supplemented by the help of friends. His humor ranges from high spirited to absurd and is often punctuated by wordplay.

"I write for the simplest and best of reasons—because I enjoy it," King-Smith once observed. "I write for children for a number of reasons: My level of humor is pretty childish (both my grandfathers were punsters of the worst kind, which is the best kind); I think I know what children like to read (teaching helps here); I like to write about animals (farming helps here), whereas adults on the whole prefer to read novels about people; I think an ounce of fantasy is worth a pound of reality; and anyway I wouldn't possibly write a modern sort of novel for grown people—I should get the giggles."

Born in 1922, in Bitton, Gloucestershire, England, King-Smith grew up in a "comfortably off West Country family," according to Eccleshare. The son of a paper mill director, his education was primarily in the classics, and he attended Marlborough College as a teen.

His early life also revolved around animals; "As a child I had pets—rabbits, tortoises, rats, mice—and a toy farm which I played with endlessly," he told Eccleshare. "It was a pretty eccentric collection—I never minded much what went with what, so I included a giraffe among the dairy herd—but it absorbed me completely." With the advent of World War II in 1939, King-Smith knew it was only a matter of time before he was called up, so he tried his hand at his dream—farming—while waiting. In 1940 he began a year of work on a farm where all the labor was done by men and animals, something of a relic even at the time.

When England entered the war, King-Smith served in the Grenadier Guards, and in 1943, while still in the service, he married his childhood sweetheart, Myrle England. Severely wounded while deployed to Italy, King-Smith became a lieutenant and served with distinction until 1946, when he left the military. With wife and children in tow and in need of an occupation, he took over a small farm owned by his father's paper mill, and for the next twenty years he and his family lived out King-Smith's dream of farming. Milk and eggs were the product of his farm; there were no great expectations for it. But farming had undergone a revolution during the war years; the age of mechanization had arrived. King-Smith began to gather a motley assortment of animals on the farm, just as with his youthful collection of animals. There was Ben the bull who made a heroic bid for freedom one day, a goat who enjoyed riding in the passenger seat of the farm van, and a bevy of pigs—one of King-Smith's favorite animals. "I ran my farm in much the same way [as the childhood animal collection]. I had animals that I liked," the author told Eccleshare. "Now I see that it was rather a stupid way to run a farm, but at the time I felt I didn't have to conform." In addition to housing this bizarre menagerie, the King-Smiths also ran their home as if from a different age, even hosting country balls in which male guests came dressed in white tie and tails.

In the end, the numbers did not tally. Over the years on Woodlands Farm, profits continually dropped. In 1967, after twenty years of farming, King-Smith had to call it quits. For a time he sold asbestos suits for firefighters, and then for three years worked in a shoe factory, until he finally went to university and earned a bachelor's degree in education. He would give teaching a go.

Thus began King-Smith's second career, at age fifty-three, as an elementary school teacher in the Farmborough Primary School near Bath, Avon, England. It was during his years of teaching that King-Smith began tinkering with stories, though he did not begin his career as a novelist until the mid-1970s. His teaching career provided insight into the type of material children like to read, and he received equal inspiration from his days as a farmer, for the tales he most enjoys creating concern farm animals. In 1978 King-Smith published his first book for children, *The Fox Busters,* which centers on a family of chickens who plot to drive the local foxes away from their hen house. Explaining the inspiration for this tale to *Young Writer,* King-Smith recalled that when he was a farmer a fox once killed many of his chickens. "One day, I thought, I'll have a go at writing a story where the weak are the winners, not the strong. About ten years later, I did have a go, and that became *The Fox Busters.*" Anne Carter, writing in the *Times Literary Supplement,* labeled *The Fox Busters* "a good, fast-moving story with sound characterization and an ability to be funny without condescension or whimsicality."

King-Smith continued to teach and write for several years, but as with farming, the numbers were his undoing as a teacher. He could not do long division, and so was moved from teaching middle graders to teaching younger children where he only had to manage simple addition. In 1982, at age sixty, he retired from teaching to write full time. Many of King-Smith's animal novels for children focus on "a single hero, whom we grow to love, [who] fights desperately against a terrifying enemy in a genuinely exciting plot, while the style, dialogue, and characterization remain light and playful," commented Stephanie Nettell in *Twentieth-Century Children's Writers.* For instance, Daggie Dogfoot, the piglet protagonist of *Pigs Might Fly* whose unusually webbed feet allow him to become a skilled swimmer, saves the entire farm, including the slaughterer, during a flood by swimming for help. His actions ensure that he will never be butchered by the farmer for food and serve to educate other characters metaphorically about inner values versus exterior appearances. About *Pigs Might Fly,* Arthur Arnold remarked in *Children's Literature in Education* that "King-Smith's writing stands comfortably alongside the more celebrated E.B. White's, sustained by his own inimitable wry sense of humour." Another of King-Smith's noteworthy animal books, *Harry's Mad,* chronicles the adventures of Madison, an intelligent, talking African gray parrot bequeathed by his American professor owner to a young English boy. Karla Kuskin observed in the *New York Times Book Review* that "King-Smith, as articulate in English as Madison is in American, is mostly to be congratulated. The characters in *Harry's Mad* have wit and are good, lively company."

King-Smith is perhaps best known for the award-winning *Babe,* the novel first published in England as *The Sheep-Pig* and on which the popular film of the same title was based. As Nettell wrote, in this book King-Smith "succeeds in balancing in one story the strongest qualities of all the others, and it is clearly right to award it that often overworked encomium, 'a modern classic.'" The story focuses on Babe, a piglet who is won at a fair by a farmer. Adopted by the mother sheepdog, Fly, Babe comes to understand that the best way to get sheep to obey is to speak politely to them. In the process, he saves the sheep from rustlers, not to mention saving his own life when the farmer realizes Babe is more valuable as a sheep-pig than as a meal. In fact, the farmer has so much confidence in Babe that he

*Cover of King-Smith's* Spider Sparrow, *featuring artwork by Brad Yeo.* (Illustration © 2000 by Andrew Davidson. Used by permission of Dell Publishing, a division of Random House, Inc.)

enters him in the local sheep-dog trials, which he wins. King-Smith's own experience as a farmer enables him to depict farm life with accuracy and affection.

Critics universally praised *Babe.* Nettell called it "deftly constructed, the animal and human characters are marvelously defined in dialogue, the suspense remains strong and quite unbullied by the joke, and the style is so clean and economic that our hero wins through to a frenzy of cheers without a hint of soppiness." In *Booklist* Denise M. Wilms was particularly impressed with the book's characterization. She wrote, "The relationship between Fly and Babe is fresh, and Babe's sensitivities, which are the key to his success, give the novel a richness that's impossible to resist." In the *Observer,* Naomi Lewis suggested that "the dialogue couldn't be bettered. There's a readymade classroom play here for the taking." Lewis's observation turned out to be prophetic indeed, though on a much greater scale than she imagined. In 1995, the film adaptation was nominated for several Academy awards and won the award for best visual effects. The success of the film led to a sequel, *Babe, Pig in the City,* a film not based on King-Smith's work.

More rich animal tales are served up in *The Animal Parade,* a compilation of stories and poems, including retellings of five of Aesop's fables. A *Publishers Weekly* critic found that book to be an "ideal compendium for introducing readers to animal tales." Teaming up with illustrator Quentin Blake, King-Smith produced the alphabet book, *Dick King-Smith's Alphabeasts,* an "entertaining and quotable" book, according to *Horn Book* contributor Ann A. Flowers. In *The Invisible Dog,* he tells a tale of a girl who desperately wants a dog, but whose parents can not afford to buy her one. Imagination takes over, and she enjoys the companionship of an invisible pooch until an unexpected inheritance allows her to purchase a real canine. Writing in *Publishers Weekly,* a reviewer dubbed this a book "chock-full of warmth, zany imagination and soft-hearted irony."

With *Ace: The Very Important Pig,* King-Smith provides something of a sequel to *Babe,* for the pig in question is Babe's great-grandson. Ace is a talking pig who enjoys watching educational television and visiting the local pub. Fame arrives, but does not go to Ace's head in this "winsome story . . . sure to warm hearts and bring smiles," according to a *Publishers Weekly* contributor.

King-Smith offers an amusing look at the Royal Family's pets in *Titus Rules!,* "a nimble blend of animal hijinks and gentle satire," a critic in *Publishers Weekly* remarked. One of the Corgi puppies that belong to Queen Elizabeth II, Titus earns his owner's respect by sniffing out a blaze and helping nab a thief. The author's "fast-moving, witty prose" garnered praised from *Booklist* contributor Shelle Rosenfeld.

Mice are at the center of *Three Terrible Trins,* the tale of an often-widowed mouse, Mrs. Gray, who vows never to marry again but instead devote herself to the upbringing of her three "trins" or triplets. "With his customary panache," wrote a reviewer for *Publishers Weekly,* "King-Smith grabs the reader's attention from his opening sentence" and incorporates the same "understated humor and rollicking pace." *Horn Book* contributor Ann Flowers called the book a "wildly comic view of the world in microcosm." More mice appear in *The Schoolmouse* in which a young mouse uses her reading skills to save her parents. "With a heroic main character that will surely remind kids of the lovely gray spider in *Charlotte's Web,* this is a fine book for instilling in children the importance of reading," wrote *Booklist* contributor Lauren Peterson. And in *Charlie Muffin's Miracle Mouse,* a lonely mouse farmer breeds a green mouse and wins best of show at the Grand Mouse Championship Show in an "offbeat, gently humorous story," according to *Booklist* critic Carolyn Phelan.

Not all of King-Smith's juvenile novels center on animal characters, however. Among the author's personal favorites are his tales of Sophie, a rambunctious young girl who wants to be a farmer. Inaugurated in 1989 with *Sophie's Snail,* the "Sophie" books take the girl from the age of four to eight. *Booklist* reviewer Mary Harris

Veeder compared Sophie to Beverly Cleary's invention for her spunk: "Think of Sophie as a slightly plump, more determined, British Ramona," wrote Veeder in a review of *Sophie Is Seven.* In *Sophie's Tom,* she befriends a cat named Tom who later, to everyone's surprise, produces a litter of kittens. Sophie has proved a winner with critics. Reviewing *Sophie's Tom* in *Publishers Weekly,* a contributor noted that "Sophie's spirit is sure to win readers' admiration." The reviewer also felt that the young girl's mischief "will keep laughs coming." *Horn Book* reviewer Ann Flowers felt that while "Tom is a terrific cat . . . it is Sophie who takes center stage in an endearing picture of a sturdy, self-reliant small girl." In *Sophie in the Saddle,* the protagonist gets hand-on practice with farming when she and her family vacation on a farm.In *Sophie's Lucky,* the now-eight-year-old heroine is close to achieving her agrarian dream when she goes to visit a relation in Scotland. In her *Booklist* review, Kay Weisman predicted that felt that *Sophie in the Saddle* will "charm young and old alike."

Fantasy takes the fore in many King-Smith titles. In *Paddy's Pot of Gold,* young Brigid inherits a pot of gold from the leprechaun Paddy O'Brien. When she turns eight, Brigid meets the leprechaun, visible only to herself. Soon they are friends, with Paddy teaching the young girl animal sounds, but the friendship ends when

*King-Smith's fanciful story* **The Water Horse** *features detailed drawings by artist David Parkins.* (Illustration copyright © 1990 by David Parkins. Used by permission of Random House Children' Books, a division of Random House, Inc.)

the leprechaun dies. Betsy Hearne, reviewing the book in *Bulletin of the Center for Children's Books,* found that it "makes cozy holiday reading." *The Water Horse* deals with the origins of the Loch Ness Monster in a "just-shy-of believable fantasy," according to a reviewer for *Publishers Weekly.* In *The Nine Lives of Aristotle,* Bella Donna, a kindly witch, adopts Aristotle, an accident-prone kitten who promptly squanders eight of his nine lives by falling down a chimney, plunging into rushing water, and fighting with an angry dog, among other incidents. Despite the feline's preoccupation with dangerous situations, "it's always clear from . . . King-Smith's understated text that this pet is in safe hands," observed Weisman. Good fortune shines upon a hapless farmer in *The Golden Goose,* an "engaging story," stated a critic in *Publishers Weekly.* Just when things look bleakest for John Skint, the owner of Woebegone Farm, the hatching of a golden gosling brings prosperity and happiness. "King-Smith's fans will appreciate his signature rural setting, full of genial livestock and good-natured incompetents," Weisman wrote.

Historical fantasy is at the heart of *The Roundhill,* the tale of a fourteen-year-old boy on holidays in 1936. On a pilgrimage to a local peak, the boy meets a mysterious young girl, Alice, who bears a striking resemblance to the main character in *Alice's Adventures in Wonderland.* A contributor to *Publishers Weekly* found this tale to be "served up with a measure of suspense and King-Smith's usual flair," resulting in "satisfying fare" for young readers. Reviewing the same novel in *School Library Journal,* Beth Wright concluded, "More than just a skillfully told ghost story, this is a thoughtful exploration of the transforming power of friendship, however unusual its circumstance." *Spider Sparrow* deals with a most unusual foundling who has the power to charm animals. *Horn Book* reviewer Kristi Beavin viewed this novel as a departure from the author's usual animal fantasies in that it deals in "the magic of the ordinary world." Set in the agrarian world of pre-World War II England, the book abounds in details with which King-Smith himself is all too familiar. Linda L. Plevak, writing in *School Library Journal,* called *Spider Sparrow* "heartwarming" and a book "filled with memorable characters." A reviewer for *Publishers Weekly* joined the chorus of praise for the novel, noting King-Smith's "pitch-perfect prose," and concluding, "Poignant and wise, this deeply moving tale is not to be missed." In *Billy the Bird,* young Mary Bird is amazed to discover that her little brother—who is seemingly a typical child in other respects—can fly when the moon is full. "King-Smith's fans will enjoy this . . . title and wish they could share the experience," wrote Anne Connor in a *School Library Journal* review.

The versatile King-Smith has also penned a number of books featuring elderly protagonists. In *The Stray,* a lady escapes from an old-folks home and is taken in by a family with five red-haired children, wins the lottery, and catches a burglar. A contributor to *Publishers Weekly* called this a "cozy, old-fashioned novel." *Mr. Ape* presents a crusty, aged male protagonist who turns his house into a mini-zoo, aided by a Gypsy boy and his father. When Mr. Ape's house is burned down, these two help him to save the animals. This novel found praise from a reviewer for *Publishers Weekly* who noted: "Once again adding a well-calculated measure of pathos to his comedy, King-Smith delivers another memorable animal tale." A chapter book set in 1901, *The Catlady* centers on Muriel Ponsonby, the eccentric owner of a variety of felines. Muriel believes her cats are the reincarnated souls of departed family and friends, and she even suspects one creature to be Queen Victoria. When Muriel passes away, her estate falls to her loyal helper, Mary, who receives a furry new guest six months later. According to Phelan, King-Smith "carries his readers along in a quietly engaging way."

In a departure from his fictional works, King-Smith recounts his path to becoming a writer in *Chewing the Cud: An Extraordinary Life Remembered by the Author of Babe, the Gallant Pig*. The work focuses on King-Smith's adult life, including his ill-fated attempts at farming. "As always, he employs a deft turn of phrase and plenty of humor," Weisman stated, and a *Publishers Weekly* critic wrote that the "pages reveal a gifted writer with an affection for animals and a simple country life, a passion for his work, and sheer goodness of heart." "We have already seen in his work that King-Smith has a skill, an eye and an ear that any author would be proud of, and that any reader can enjoy," observed London *Independent* contributor Nicolette Jones. "This collection of his reminiscences reminds us that the lasting pleasures of any existence are often the small ones. When they are related with modesty and joie de vivre, the effect is cheering and hopeful."

It continues to be the qualities of adventure, humor, and warmth of characterization that gain King-Smith legions of new fans. He once commented about his reasons for writing: "If there is a philosophical point behind what I write, I'm not especially conscious of it; maybe I do stress the need for courage, something we all wish we had more of, and I also do feel strongly for underdogs. As for trying to fill a need in children's literature, if I am, it is to produce books that can afford adults some pleasure when they read to their children. I write for fun." Into his eighties, King-Smith continues to pursue his third career as a writer diligently, rising early, writing by longhand, and retyping drafts in the afternoon. As he noted in an interview on the *Random House Web site* "I live in a beautiful old cottage in a tiny village; don't like nuts, turnips or pineapples; love the English countryside and would probably die immediately if forced to live in a town; and am a very happy man doing what is in effect my hobby for a living, i.e., writing stories for children."

## Biographical and Critical Sources

*BOOKS*

*Children's Literature Review,* Volume 40, Gale (Detroit, MI), 1996.

King-Smith, Dick, *Dick King-Smith's Animal Friends: Thirty-one True Life Stories,* Candlewick Press (Cambridge, MA), 1996.

King-Smith, Dick, *Puppy Love,* Candlewick Press (Cambridge, MA), 1997.

King-Smith, Dick, *Chewing the Cud: An Extraordinary Life Remembered by the Author of Babe, the Gallant Pig,* Viking (London, England), 2001.

Parker, Vic, *All about Dick King-Smith,* Heinemann (Oxford, England), 2004.

*St. James Guide to Children's Writers,* 5th edition, St. James Press (Detroit, MI), 1999.

*PERIODICALS*

*Booklist,* August, 1985, Denise Wilms, review of *Babe: The Gallant Pig;* April 1, 1994, Kay Weisman, review of *Sophie in the Saddle,* p. 1448; April 15, 1995, Lauren Peterson, review of *Harriet's Hare,* p. 1499; July 15, 1995, Marry Harris Veeder, review of *Sophie Is Seven,* p. 1880; October 15, 1995, Lauren Peterson, review of *The Schoolmouse,* p. 303; December 1, 1996, Ellen Mandel, review of *Dick King-Smith's Animal Friends,* p. 650; April 15, 1999, Carolyn Phelan, review of *Charlie Muffin's Miracle Mouse,* p. 1528; July, 2001, Carolyn Phelan, review of *Billy the Bird,* p. 2006; January 1, 2002, Ilene Cooper, review of *Funny Frank,* p. 858; February 15, 2002, Stephanie Zvirin, review of *George Speaks,* p. 1014; October 15, 2002, Kay Weisman, review of *Chewing the Cud: An Extraordinary Life Remembered by the Author of Babe, the Gallant Pig,* p. 398; February 1, 2003, Shelle Rosenfeld, review of *Titus Rules!,* p. 995; September 15, 2003, Kathleen Odean, review of *Clever Lollipop,* p. 240; December 1, 2003, Kay Weisman, review of *The Nine Lives of Aristotle,* p. 667; February 1, 2005, Kay Weisman, review of *The Golden Goose,* p. 958; January 1, 2006, Carolyn Phelan, review of *The Catlady,* p. 103; March 1, 2008, Suzanne Harold, review of *Dinosaur Trouble,* p. 67.

*Bulletin of the Center for Children's Books,* June, 1992, Betsy Hearne, review of *Paddy's Pot of Gold,* p. 266.

*Children's Literature in Education,* Volume 19, number 2, 1988, Arthur Arnold, review of *Pigs Might Fly,* p. 81.

*Horn Book,* September-October, 1992, Ann A. Flowers, review of *Dick King-Smith's Alphabeasts,* p. 595; March-April, 1993, Ann A. Flowers, review of *Sophie's Tom,* pp. 208-209; November-December, 1994, Ann A. Flowers, review of *Three Terrible Trins,* pp. 733-734; January-February, 2001, Kristi Beavin, review of *Spider Sparrow,* p. 122; January-February, 2005, Robin Smith, review of *The Golden Goose,* p. 95.

*Independent* (London, England), October 8, 2001, Nicolette Jones, "A Life with His Animals and Other Family," p. 5.

*New York Times Book Review,* May 17, 1987, Karla Kuskin, review of *Harry's Mad.*

*Observer* (London, England), December 11, 1983, Naomi Lewis, review of *The Sheep-Pig.*

*Publishers Weekly,* June 29, 1990, review of *Ace: The Very Important Pig,* p. 102; June 29, 1992, review of *Sophie's Tom,* p. 63; October 19, 1992, review of *The Ani-*

*mal Parade,* p. 79; May 31, 1993, review of *The Invisible Dog,* p. 55; October 17, 1994, review of *The Terrible Trins,* pp. 81-82; March 13, 1995, review of *Harriet's Hare,* p. 70; August 5, 1996, review of *The Stray,* p. 442; March 16, 1998, review of *Mr. Ape,* p. 64; July 6, 1998, review of *Animal Stories,* p. 61; July 13, 1998, review of *The Water Horse,* p. 78; December 6, 1999, review of *Spider Sparrow,* p. 77; June 26, 2000, review of *Mysterious Miss Slade,* p. 75; November 20, 2000, review of *The Roundhill,* p. 69; April 23, 2001, review of *Billy the Bird,* p. 78; December 10, 2001, review of *Funny Frank,* pp. 70-71; April 1, 2002, review of *George Speaks,* p. 83; September 30, 2002, Heather Vogel Frederick, "A Life Filled with Tails," p. 73, and review of *Chewing the Cud,* p. 73; November 25, 2002, review of *Titus Rules!,* p. 68; August 4, 2003, review of *The Nine Lives of Aristotle,* p. 80; February 14, 2005, review of *The Golden Goose,* p. 77; November 21, 2005, review of *The Catlady,* p. 48; August 6, 2007, review of *Hairy Hezekiah,* p. 189.

*School Library Journal,* July, 1992, Yvonne Frey, review of *Lady Daisy,* p. 62; April, 1993, Virginia Golodetz, review of *The Cuckoo Child,* p. 121; October, 1993, Kay McPherson, review of *All Pigs Are Beautiful,* p. 118; March, 2000, Linda L. Plevak, review of *Spider Sparrow,* p. 239; December, 2000, Beth Wright, review of *The Roundhill,* p. 145; June, 2001, Anne Connor, review of *Billy the Bird,* p. 121; November, 2002, Jennifer Ralston, review of *Chewing the Cud,* p. 189; October, 2003, Judith Constantinides, review of *Clever Lollipop,* p. 128, and Elaine E. Knight, review of *The Nine Lives of Aristotle,* p. 128; January, 2006, Debbie Whitbeck, review of *The Catlady,* p. 104; March, 2008, Kelly Roth, review of *Dinosaur Trouble,* p. 169.

*Times Literary Supplement,* July 7, 1978, Anne Carter, review of *The Fox Busters,* p. 770; October 17, 1986, Alice H.G. Phillips, review of *Noah's Brother.*

*ONLINE*

*British Broadcasting Corporation Web site,* http://www.bbc.co.uk/ (August 5, 2008), Clare Parrack, "How Babe Saved Dick King-Smith's Bacon."

*Guardian Online,* http://books.guardian.co.uk/ (November 10, 2001), Julia Eccleshare, "How to Make Millions from Pigs."

*Random House Web Site,* http://www.randomhouse.com/ (August 5, 2008), interview with King-Smith.

*Young Writer Web site,* http://www.mystworld.com/ (February 12, 2002), "Issue 4: Dick King-Smith."*

* * *

# KOELLER, Carol

## Personal

Married; children: two. *Education:* Attended college.

## Addresses

*Home and office*—Chicago, IL. *Agent*—Nicole and Jeremy Tugeau, 2225 Bellfield Ave., Cleveland Heights, OH 44106. *E-mail*—carolkoeller@comcast.net.

## Career

Illustrator. Formerly worked as a preschool teacher. Presenter at schools.

## Member

Society of Children's Book Illustrators and Writers, Picture Book Artists Association.

## Illustrator

Debra Pappas, *Mom, Dad, Come Back Soon,* Magination Press (Washington, DC), 2002.

Marc A. Neimroff, *All about Adoption: How Families Are Made and How Kids Feel about It,* Magination Press (Washington, DC), 2004.

Christine Taylor-Butler, *Ah-Choo,* Children's Press (New York, NY), 2005.

Sandy Riggs, *Nick Is Sick,* Barron's (Hauppauge, NY), 2006.

Michelle Medlock Adams, *Why I Thank You God,* Concordia Pub. House (St. Louis, MO), 2006.

Hope Vestergaard, *I Don't Want to Clean My Room: A Mess of Poems about Chores,* Dutton Children's Books (New York, NY), 2007.

Contributor of illustrations to periodicals, including *Ladybug, Babybug,* and *Highlights for Children.*

## Biographical and Critical Sources

*PERIODICALS*

*Kirkus Reviews,* February 15, 2008, review of *I Don't Want to Clean My Room: A Mess of Poems about Chores.*

*School Library Journal,* May, 2005, Laurel L. Iakovakis, review of *My Birthday Cake,* p. 83; July, 2007, Judith Constantinides, review of *I Don't Want to Clean My Room,* p. 95.

*ONLINE*

*Carol Koeller Home Page,* http://www.carolkoeller.com (August 4, 2008).

*Society of Children's Book Writers and Illustrators—Illinois Web site,* http://www.scbwi-illinois.org/ (August 4, 2008), "Carol Koeller."*

# L

## LEUCK, Laura 1962-

### Personal

Surname is pronounced "luke"; born July 9, 1962, in Toms River, NJ; daughter of John L. (a health care consultant) and Gwen (a homemaker) Yoder; married Arthur R. Leuck (a facilities manager), September 15, 1984; children: Matthew, Shane. *Education:* Monmouth College, B.A. *Hobbies and other interests:* Traveling, hiking, films, theatre.

### Addresses

*Home and office*—Princeton, NJ. *E-mail*—lauraleuck@patmedia.net.

### Career

Poet and author of children's books. Worked for *Asbury Park Press,* Neptune, NJ.

### Member

Authors Guild, Authors League of America, Society of Children's Book Writers and Illustrators, Electronic Writer's Association.

### Awards, Honors

Ben-Yitzhak Award, 1996, for *Sun Is Falling, Night Is Calling;* Children's Choice Award, 1999, for *My Monster Mama Loves Me So.*

### Writings

*Sun Is Falling, Night Is Calling,* illustrated by Ora Eitan, Simon & Schuster (New York, NY), 1994.

*My Brother Has Ten Tiny Toes,* illustrated by Clara Vulliamy, Albert Whitman (Morton Grove, IL), 1997.

*Teeny, Tiny Mouse: A Book about Colors,* illustrated by Pat Schories, BridgeWater Books (Mahwah, NJ), 1998.

*My Monster Mama Loves Me So,* illustrated by Mark Buehner, HarperCollins (New York, NY), 1999.

*Goodnight, Baby Monster,* illustrated by Nigel McMullen, HarperCollins (New York, NY), 2002.

*Jeepers Creepers: A Monstrous ABC,* illustrated by David Parkins, Chronicle Books (San Francisco, CA), 2003.

*One Witch,* illustrated by S.D. Schindler, Walker (New York, NY), 2003.

*My Beastly Brother,* illustrated by Scott Nash, HarperCollins (New York, NY), 2003.

*My Creature Teacher,* illustrated by Scott Nash, HarperCollins (New York, NY), 2004.

*Santa Claws: A Scary Christmas to All,* illustrated by Gris Grimley, Chronicle Books (San Francisco, CA), 2006.

*I Love My Pirate Papa,* illustrated by Kyle M. Stone, Harcourt (Orlando, FL), 2007.

*For Just One Day,* illustrated by Marc Boutavant, Chronicle Books (San Francisco, CA), 2009.

Contributor of poetry and stories to periodicals, including *Hopscotch* and *Turtle.*

Leuck's books have been translated into French.

### Sidelights

Through the use of verse, Laura Leuck creates picture books for young readers that teach children about the joy of language and illustrate basic concepts. While several of her books, such as *Teeny, Tiny Mouse: A Book about Colors* and *Sun Is Falling, Night Is Calling* feature simple, reassuring themes, Leuck also taps into children's love of less-reassuring stories in books such as *Goodnight, Baby Monster, My Creature Teacher,* and *Santa Claws: A Scary Christmas to All.*

In *Teeny, Tiny Mouse* Leuck employs a simple, repetitive text that describes a young mouse touring his home—actually a lavishly furnished doll's house—with his mouse mother in tow. *Children's Book Review Service* contributor Arlene Wartenberg dubbed the book "clever" in its interactive concept, as the pair travel from room to room, each time posing readers a color-

*Laura Leuck's quirky viewpoint is captured in Mark Buehner's monstrous illustrations for* **My Monster Mama Loves Me So.** (Illustration copyright © 1999 by Mark Buehner. Used by permission of HarperCollins Children's Books, a division of HarperCollins Publishers.)

related question. Noting that the "book invites sharing and further color exploration," *Christian Science Monitor* contributor Karen Carden commended *Teeny, Tiny Mouse* for its "clear concepts and reassuring repetition."

Leuck relates the rituals associated with night and getting ready for bed in *Sun Is Falling, Night Is Calling.* Such things as the moon in the sky, a bedtime story, a song, a teddy bear, and sweet dreams are described as a mother rabbit guides her young one towards sleep. "In spare, gently cadenced verse, newcomer Leuck beckons readers into the soothing rituals of nighttime," commented a *Publishers Weekly* reviewer, while *School Librarian* contributor David Lewis wrote that the book's rhythmic text, which describes "the gradual winding down of the toddler's day," is "genuinely charming."

Fuelled by Leuck's "well-cadenced, rhyming verse," in the opinion of *Booklist* contributor Carolyn Phelan, *I Love My Pirate Papa* follows a sword-carrying buccaneer and his son as they ply the seven seas in the father's ship, dig up a treasure chest on a secret island, and have a jolly time aboard ship with the father's rowdy but good-hearted pirate crew. According to Phelan, the acrylic illustrations by Kyle M. Stone "successfully balance the darkly alluring danger of piracy with the boy's buoyant good spirits," and in *School Library Journal* Judith Constantinides predicted that children's love of pirates ensures that *I Love My Pirate Papa* "will surely be met with delight by the youngest buccaneers."

In *My Monster Mama Loves Me So* Leuck spins a tender tale featuring a green, round-eyed, sharp-toothed monster that only a monster mother could love. A reviewer for *Early Childhood Educational Journal* deemed the story "captivating" and maintained that the humorously illustrated book "hits the spot," while in *School Library Journal,* Amy Lilien-Harper praised Leuck for providing story-time aficionados with "a reassuring message" packaged in "a funny, mildly scary story." A *Publishers Weekly* contributor had special praise for the author-illustrator collaboration, calling Mark Buehner's soft-edged illustrations "vibrant" and "cuddly," and predicting that Leuck's text, with its "tender tone," will make *My Monster Mama Loves Me So* a sure-fire "bedtime favorite for drowsy toddlers."

Monsters also figure in *Goodnight, Baby Monster* and *Jeepers Creepers: A Monstrous ABC,* the latter illustrated by David Parkins. In *Goodnight, Baby Monster,* which *School Library Journal* reviewer Rosalyn Pierini described as "a gentle, rhyming story chock-full of nighttime creatures both real and imaginary," Leuck uses poetic prose to offset imaginary terrors of the night and render them harmless, as a host of scary nocturnal creatures are revealed to be stuffed animals sharing the bed with a mother and child reading a good-night tale. Twenty-six monstrous children, arranged alphabetically according to type, march across the pages of *Jeepers Creepers.* The group gathers together for a fun-filled first day of school in this picture book that a *Kirkus Reviews* critic called a "cheerful offering" from Leuck.

*My Beastly Brother* and *My Creature Teacher* both feature quirky illustrations by artist Scott Nash and "a steady beat of humorous, monster-inspired verse," in the opinion of a *Publishers Weekly* critic, reviewing *My Beastly Brother.* Idiosyncratic illustrations by S.D. Schindler grace the pages of *One Witch,* a counting book with a difference. Readers learn the recipe for a distasteful witches' brew containing everything from straw-stuffed scarecrows to fish tails and bird claws through a rhyming text that a *Kirkus Reviews* contributor described as "jaunty." In *School Library Journal* James K. Irwin praised the story as "romping" and spiced with "plenty of alliteration," while in *Booklist,* Gillian Engberg deemed *One Witch* "a great choice for October preschool read-alouds."

Leuck teams up with quirky artist Gris Grimly to treat readers to a twisted version of a traditional holiday story in *Santa Claws.* Here, in a story that has been compared to filmmaker Tim Burton's *The Nightmare before Christmas,* she introduces monster siblings Zack and Mack. After decorating their living room with dead pine tree bones and other gruesome objects, hanging up their odoriferous stockings with care, and cooking up some poisonberry pie for a Santa-style snack, the boys crawl off to bed, leaving the room to the equally monstrous Santa who dashes through the night pulled by fire-breathing dragons. While writing that the story could have veered further into the creepy, *School Library Journal* contributor Maureen Wade praised Leuck's rhythmic text as "clever and amusing." Calling *Santa Claws* "mischievously macabre," a *Kirkus Reviews* writer had special praise for Grimly's "weirdly edgy but not too terribly scary illustrations."

## Biographical and Critical Sources

*PERIODICALS*

*Booklist,* June 1, 1994, Carolyn Phelan, review of *Sun Is Falling, Night Is Calling,* p. 1841; April 15, 1997, Julie Corsaro, review of *My Baby Brother Has Ten Tiny Toes,* p. 1436; September 1, 2003, Gillian Engberg, review of *One Witch,* p. 136; September 15, 2007, Carolyn Phelan, review of *I Love My Pirate Papa,* p. 72.

*Children's Book Review Service,* spring, 1998, Arlene Wartenberg, review of *Teeny, Tiny Mouse: A Book about Colors,* p. 136.

*Christian Science Monitor,* September 24, 1998, Karen Carden, "Bright Books Teach Smart Concepts," p. B9.

***Readers of Leuck's* Santa Claws *are treated to the offbeat vision of artist and illustrator Gris Grimly.*** (Illustration © 2006 by Gris Grimly. Used with permission of Chronicle Books, LLC, San Francisco. Visit ChronicleBooks.com.)

*Early Childhood Educational Journal,* winter, 1999, review of *My Monster Mama Loves Me So,* p. 106.

*Horn Book,* fall, 1997, Martha V. Parravano, review of *My Baby Brother Has Ten Tiny Toes,* p. 253.

*Kirkus Reviews,* July 1, 2003, review of *One Witch,* p. 912; August 1, 2003, review of *Jeepers Creepers: A Monstrous ABC,* p. 1019; November 1, 2006, review of *Santa Claws,* p. 1131; August 15, 2007, review of *I Love My Pirate Papa.*

*Publishers Weekly,* April 11, 1994, review of *Sun Is Falling, Night Is Calling,* p. 63; March 15, 1999, review of *Teeny, Tiny Mouse,* p. 61; September 27, 1999, review of *My Monster Mama Loves Me So,* p. 103; August 4, 2003, reviews of *One Witch,* p. 77, and *My Beastly Brother,* p. 79.

*School Librarian,* November, 1996, David Lewis, review of *Sun Is Falling, Night Is Calling,* p. 147.

*School Library Journal,* March, 1997, Patricia Pearl Doyle, review of *My Brother Has Ten Tiny Toes,* pp. 160-161; May, 1998, Jody McCoy, review of *Teeny, Tiny Mouse,* p. 120; January, 2000, Amy Lilien-Harper, review of *My Monster Mama Loves Me So,* pp. 106-107; September, 2002, Rosalyn Pierini, review of *Goodnight, Baby Monster,* p. 198; August, 2003, James K. Irwin, review of *One Witch,* p. 136; March, 2004, Nancy A. Gifford, review of *My Beastly Brother,* p. 172; July, 2004, Grace Oliff, review of *My Creature Teacher,* p. 81; October, 2006, Maureen Wade, review of *Santa Claws,* p. 97; September, 2007, Judith Constantinides, review of *I Love My Pirate Papa,* p. 169.

*Times Educational Supplement,* September 27, 1996, Ann Treneman, review of *Sun Is Falling, Night Is Calling,* p. 2.*

* * *

# LEVITIN, Sonia 1934-

***Sonia Levitin*** (Photograph by Rose Eichenbaum. Reproduced by permission. )

## Personal

Born August 18, 1934, in Berlin, Germany; immigrated to United States, 1938; daughter of Max (a manufacturer) and Helene Wolff; married Lloyd Levitin (a business executive), December 27, 1953; children: Daniel Joseph, Shari Diane. *Education:* Attended University of California, Berkeley, 1952-54; University of Pennsylvania, B.S., 1956; San Francisco State College (now University), graduate study, 1957-60. *Hobbies and other interests:* Hiking, piano, Judaic studies, travel, history, painting.

## Addresses

*Home and office*—Los Angeles, CA. *Agent*—Toni Mendez, Inc., 141 E. 56th St., New York, NY 10022. *E-mail*—slevitin@ucla.edu.

## Career

Writer and educator. Junior high school teacher in Mill Valley, CA, 1956-57; adult education teacher in Daly City, CA, 1962-64; Acalanes Adult Center, Lafayette, CA, teacher, 1965-72; teacher of creative writing, Palos Verdes Peninsula, CA, 1973-76, and University of California, Los Angeles Extension, 1978—; University of Judaism, instructor in American Jewish literature, 1989—. Founder of STEP (adult education organization), Palos Verdes Peninsula. Performed volunteer work, including publicity, for various charities and educational institutions.

## Member

Authors League of America, Authors Guild, PEN, Society of Children's Book Writers and Illustrators, California Writer's Guild, Moraga Historical Society (founder and former president).

## Awards, Honors

Charles and Bertie G. Schwartz Award for juvenile fiction, Jewish Book Council of America, 1970, and Notable Book citation, American Library Association (ALA), for *Journey to America;* Dorothy Canfield Fisher Award nomination, Georgia State Award nomination, and Mark Twain Award nomination, all for *Roanoke;* Notable Book citation, ALA, 1973, for *Who Owns the Moon?;* California Young Reader Medal award nomination in junior-high category, 1976, and Southern California Council on Literature for Children and Young People Award for fiction, 1981, both for *The Mark of Conte;* Golden Spur Award, Western Writers of America, 1978, and Lewis Carroll Shelf Award, both for *The No-Return Trail;* Children's Choice award, 1980, for *Nobody Stole the Pie;* Southern California Council on Literature for Children and Young People award for distinguished body of work, 1981; Notable Children's Trade Book designation, 1982, and Pick of the Lists, American Booksellers Association, both for *The Fisherman and the Bird;* Notable Children's Trade Book designation, 1982, for *All the Cats in the World;* Pick of the Lists, American Booksellers Association, 1982, for *The Year of Sweet Senior Insanity;* National Jewish Book Award in children's literature, 1987, and PEN Los Angeles Award for Young-Adult fiction, Sydney Taylor Award, Austrian Youth Prize, Catholic Children's Book Prize (Germany), Dorothy Canfield Fisher Award nomination, Parent's Choice Honor Book citation, and ALA Best Book for Young Adults designation, all 1988, all for *The Return;* Edgar Allen Poe Award, Mystery Writers of America, 1988, and Dorothy Canfield Fisher Award nomination and Nevada State Award nomination, both 1989, all for *Incident at Loring Groves;* Honor Book citation, Sydney Taylor Book Award, and Best Book for Young Adults, ALA-YASD, both 1989, Dorothy Canfield Fisher Award nomination, and Jefferson Cup Award finalist, all for *Silver Days;* Kansas State Reading Circle selection, 1993, and Recommended Book for Reluctant Young Adult Readers, YALSA, both for *The Golem and the Dragon Girl;* Pick of the Lists designation, American Booksellers Association, Riverside County Author's Award, 1993, and Georgia State Award nomination, all for *Annie's Promise;* Distinguished Body of Work Award, Southern California Council on Literature for Children and Young People, 1994; Recommended Books listee, National Conference of Christians and Jews, 1994, and outstanding book citation, *Voice of Youth Advocates,* Best Books for Young Adults designation, YALSA, Books for the Teen Age designation, New York Public Library, and South Carolina Junior Book Award nomination, all 1995, and Tennessee Book Award nomination in YA category, 1998-99, all for *Escape from Egypt;* Honor Book designation, Parents' Choice, Books for the Teen Age designation, New York Public Library, and Best of the Best Fiction, Pennsylvania Librarians Association, all for *Evil Encounter;* California Young Reader Medal finalist, 1996, and Show Me Readers Award nomination, Missouri Association of School Librarians, both for *Nine for California;* Edgar Allen Poe Award finalist, and Books for the Teen Age designation, New York Public Library, both for *Yesterday's Child;* Nebraska Golden Sower Award nomination, for *Boom Town;* Best Books designation, Bank Street College, 1998, and Sydney Taylor Award Honor Book designation, both for *The Singing Mountain;* Pick of the Lists selection, American Booksellers Association, 1999, for *The Cure;* Notable Book designation, *Smithsonian* magazine, for *Dream Freedom.*

## Writings

*FOR YOUNG ADULTS*

*Roanoke: A Novel of the Lost Colony,* illustrated by John Gretzer, Atheneum (New York, NY), 1973.

*The Mark of Conte,* illustrated by Bill Negron, Atheneum (New York, NY), 1976.

*Reigning Cats and Dogs* (nonfiction), illustrated by Joan Berg Victor, Atheneum (New York, NY), 1976.

*Beyond Another Door,* Atheneum (New York, NY), 1977.

*The No-Return Trail,* Harcourt (New York, NY), 1978.

*The Year of Sweet Senior Insanity,* Atheneum (New York, NY), 1982.

*Smile like a Plastic Daisy,* Atheneum (New York, NY), 1984.

*A Season for Unicorns,* Atheneum (New York, NY), 1986.

*The Return* (also see below), Atheneum (New York, NY), 1987.

*Incident at Loring Groves,* Dial (New York, NY), 1988.

*The Golem and the Dragon Girl,* Dial (New York, NY), 1993.

*Escape from Egypt,* Little, Brown (Boston, MA), 1994.

*Evil Encounter,* Simon & Schuster (New York, NY), 1996.

*Yesterday's Child,* Simon & Schuster (New York, NY), 1997.

*The Singing Mountain,* Simon & Schuster (New York, NY), 1998.

*The Cure,* Harcourt (New York, NY), 1999.

*Dream Freedom,* Silver Whistle (San Diego, CA), 2000.

*Clem's Chances,* Orchard Books (New York, NY), 2001.

*Room in the Heart,* Dutton (New York, NY), 2003.

*The Goodness Gene,* Dutton (New York, NY), 2005.

*Strange Relations,* Alfred A. Knopf (New York, NY), 2007.

*"PLATT FAMILY" TRILOGY*

*Journey to America,* illustrated by Charles Robinson, Atheneum (New York, NY), 1970.

*Silver Days,* Atheneum (New York, NY), 1989.

*Annie's Promise,* Atheneum (New York, NY), 1993.

*PICTURE BOOKS*

*Who Owns the Moon?,* illustrated by John Larrecq, Parnassus (Berkeley, CA), 1973.

*A Single Speckled Egg,* illustrated by John Larrecq, Parnassus (Berkeley, CA), 1976.

*A Sound to Remember,* illustrated by Gabriel Lisowski, Harcourt (New York, NY), 1979.

*Nobody Stole the Pie,* illustrated by Fernando Krahn, Harcourt (New York, NY), 1980.

*All the Cats in the World,* illustrated by Charles Robinson, Harcourt (New York, NY), 1982.

*The Fisherman and the Bird,* illustrated by Francis Livingston, Houghton Mifflin (Boston, MA), 1982.

*The Man Who Kept His Heart in a Bucket,* illustrated by Jerry Pinkney, Dial (New York, NY), 1991.

*A Piece of Home,* illustrated by Juan Wijngaard, Dial (New York, NY), 1996.

*Nine for California,* illustrated by Cat Bowman Smith, Orchard (New York, NY), 1996.
*Boom Town,* (sequel to *Nine for California*), illustrated by Cat Bowman Smith, Orchard (New York, NY), 1998.
*Taking Charge,* (sequel to *Boom Town*), illustrated by Cat Bowman Smith, Orchard (New York, NY), 1999.
*When Elephant Goes to a Party,* illustrated by Jeff Seaver, Rising Moon (Flagstaff, AZ), 2001.
*When Kangaroo Goes to School,* illustrated by Jeff Seaver, Rising Moon (Flagstaff, AZ), 2001.
*Junk Man's Daughter,* illustrated by Guy Porfirio, Sleeping Bear Press (Chelsea, MI), 2007.

*OTHER*

*Rita, the Weekend Rat* (fiction), illustrated by Leonard W. Shortall, Atheneum (New York, NY), 1971.
*Jason and the Money Tree* (fiction), illustrated by Pat Grant Porter, Harcourt (New York, NY), 1974.
(Under name Sonia Wolff) *What They Did to Miss Lily* (fiction for adults), Harper (New York, NY), 1981.
(Author of introduction) Yale Strom, *A Tree Still Stands: Jewish Youth in Eastern Europe Today,* Putnam (New York, NY), 1990.
*Adam's War* (for children), illustrated by Vincent Nasta, Dial (New York, NY), 1994.
*The Return* (musical; based on Leviton's novel of the same name), produced at Los Angeles Festival of New American Musicals, 2008.

Feature columnist for Sun Newspapers, Contra Costa, CA, and *Jewish Observer of the East Bay,* Oakland, CA. Contributor to periodicals, including *Christian Science Monitor, Ingenue, Parents', Reform Judaism, San Francisco, Scholastic, Smithsonian, Together, Woman's World,* and *Writer.*

## Sidelights

Sonia Levitin survived a difficult childhood to thrive as an award-winning children's author. Born to Jewish parents in 1934 amid the anti-Semitism of Nazi Germany, she soon fled with her family to the United States. There she grew up in poverty but went on to gain a college education and fulfill her girlhood dream of becoming a writer. After being honored by the Jewish Book Council of America in 1971 for her autobiographical first novel, *Journey to America,* she earned further awards for a wide variety of books, including the Western *No-Return Trail* and the murder mystery *Incident at Loring Groves.*

In the years before Levitin was born, her parents had become prosperous members of the German middle class. Her father, without benefit of higher education, was a skillful tailor and businessman who was able, with a few hasty scribbles, to prepare designs and budgets for his line of clothing. The family enjoyed such comforts as household servants and vacations at some of Germany's most popular resorts. All that changed dramatically after the Nazis took power in 1933 and began the campaign of anti-Jewish terror and murder now known as the Holocaust. To escape persecution, three-year-old Sonia and her family left their belongings and savings behind them and slipped into neighboring Switzerland. There she waited with her mother and two sisters for a year as refugees while her father went to America to arrange a home for them. Once the family settled in the United States, young Sonia's parents had to work mightily to recreate the family business; they were so busy that for several years she was raised largely by one of her sisters. Her mother, moreover, suffered terrible guilt from knowing that she had been unable to save several relatives from death at the hands of the Nazis.

"The Holocaust experience left its deep mark on me," Levitin once recalled. "It is agonizing for me as a Jew to realize that our people were almost exterminated; it is equally agonizing, as a human being, to have to admit to the evil that humans can do to one another." Al-

***Cover of Levitin's young-adult novel* The Singing Mountain, *featuring artwork by Andrea Eberbach.*** (Aladdin Paperbacks, 2000. Illustration copyright © 1998 by Andrea Eberbach. Reproduced by permission of Scott Hull Associates, Inc.)

though Levitin was forced to confront discrimination and suffering at an early age, she also learned the power of compassion, as her family was helped by a variety of non-Jews who sympathized with their plight. "To them I owe a great debt," Levitin wrote, "not the least of which is my optimistic belief that despite evil in the world, there is goodness in great measure, and that goodness knows no boundaries of religion or race."

For a few years Levitin's parents moved the family back and forth between New York City and Los Angeles in an effort to find a profitable living; finally they settled for good in southern California. Young Sonia became an avid reader and at age eleven wrote to Laura Ingalls Wilder, beloved author of the "Little House on the Prairie" novels, to confess that she wanted to become a writer. "To my great joy," she recalled, "[I] received a reply, which remains among my treasures to this day." As Levitin progressed through school she continued to be drawn to the arts, writing poems and short stories and learning how to paint and play the piano.

When Levitin was eighteen she enrolled at the Berkeley campus of the University of California, and almost immediately she met her future husband, a fellow student. They were married when she was nineteen. Once the couple completed their studies they settled in the San Francisco area, and after Levitin had taught school for a year she became pregnant and decided to stay home to raise her family. To make full use of her time she resolved to become a writer in earnest, and with encouragement from her husband she became a part-time writing student at nearby San Francisco State College. Her teacher was Walter Van Tilburg Clark, renowned for the moral insight of his Western novel *The Ox-Bow Incident.* Levitin fondly recalled the weekly meetings where Clark explained the strengths and weaknesses of her short stories: "Why had he accepted me [for his classes]? I asked him later, when we had become friends. Was my writing good? Not so much the writing style, he replied, but the subjects that I had chosen made him want me as a pupil. The subjects were thoughtful and serious, dealing with war, aging, love, sacrifice, freedom."

Levitin's career as a writer began modestly. To gain experience, she volunteered to do publicity for charities, including the writing of press releases. This work eased her into writing articles for magazines and columns for local newspapers. She also taught creative writing classes of her own. She remained frustrated, though, by her efforts to make an impact as a short-story writer. As an exercise, she started writing a longer narrative based on the tribulations that her family experienced when she was very young. This story, which she originally intended only for her own children, grew over the course of several years into *Journey to America,* a full-length novel for young people that was published to widespread praise in 1970. The book describes a year in the life of the fictional Platt family, Jewish refugees whose escape from Nazi Germany to the United States resembles Levitin's own. "With *Journey to America,*" Levitin once remarked, "I felt that my career was launched, and that I had found my niche. I loved writing for young people. I felt that in this genre I could be both gentle and serious, idealistic and pragmatic. I realized that I happen to possess a wonderful memory for the details of my own childhood, for smells and sights and sounds, how faces looked, how feelings felt, and what childhood was really all about."

Levitin went on to publish a new book almost every year, and she looked at growing up from many different points of view. Some of her books, including *Rita the Weekend Rat* and *The Mark of Conte,* are humorous stories loosely inspired by the antics of her own son and daughter. *Rita the Weekend Rat* is about a girl who thinks of her pet rat as her closest friend, and *The Mark of Conte* features an energetic high-school freshman who tries to outsmart the school computer and earn credit for two years of classes in one year's time.

Other books, in the spirit of *Journey to America,* are more serious works in which young people confront major challenges. *The No-Return Trail,* which won the prestigious Golden Spur Award, is a Western novel that breaks with tradition by stressing the heroism of a woman: the main character is a seventeen-year-old wife and mother who became the first female settler to cross the continent to California. The tale is based on a real wagon-train expedition from the 1840s and was researched in part through a local history society in Moraga, California, that Levitin founded with her husband. *Incident at Loring Groves,* which won the coveted Edgar Award for mystery fiction, is a novel about the moral dilemmas that teenagers face in the uncertain modern world. The story, again based on fact, describes the difficult choices faced by a group of irresponsible high-schoolers who discover that one of their classmates has been murdered—and then try to avoid telling the police for fear that their own drug abuse and vandalism will be exposed as well. A reviewer for *Publishers Weekly* hailed the book as "a searingly honest portrayal of adolescent society." "In each book I try to do something quite different from the previous work," Levitin once observed. "Themes and characters might repeat themselves, but I believe that my growth as a writer and as a person depends on accepting new challenges, deepening my experience and my efforts."

One theme that recurs in Levitin's work is the importance of her Jewish heritage. Nearly two decades after she wrote *Journey to America,* Levitin wrote a sequel—*Silver Days*—that follows the immigrant Platt family as it adjusts to life in the United States. When the mother of the family collapses with grief at news of the continuing Holocaust, she and the others find solace in carrying on the traditions of Judaism in their new homeland. "Our future," the father declares, "must have room in it for the past." *The Return,* a novel that won major awards in both America and Europe, recounts the

***Cover of Levitin's award-winning historical novel* The Return, *which focuses on an unusual group of religious refugees.*** (Copyright © 1988 by Sonia Levitin. Used by permission of Fawcett Books, a division of Random House, Inc.)

saga of an unusual group of refugees who arrived in Israel in the mid-1980s. They were the "black Jews" of Ethiopia, Africans who for centuries had observed Jewish religious traditions in almost complete isolation from fellow Jews and the rest of the world. Facing increasing discrimination in their native land, they were smuggled to their new home by the Israeli government through a secret military airlift. As a former refugee, Levitin was deeply moved by the operation and dropped her other writing projects to create a novel about it, journeying to Israel to interview the Ethiopians herself. Writing in the *New York Times Book Review,* Sheila Klass called the book "a remarkable fictional account," praised its evocation of Ethiopian Jewish culture, and declared: "*The Return'* is crammed with history, as Sonia Levitin, the author of other distinguished books for young people about Jewish history, here tells the story of an entire people."

Levitin's intense study of the Torah is evident in her historical novel *Escape from Egypt,* about the Jews' exodus from Egypt as seen through the eyes of Jesse, an Israelite slave, and the half-Egyptian girl Jennat, with whom he falls in love. Questions of love, duty, and faith intermingle with the action of Moses freeing the Israelites from the recalcitrant pharaoh in what a *Publishers Weekly* contributor labeled a "startling and searching" exploration that would "spur her audience to fresh appraisals of sacred history." "Working on this book was one of the most exhilarating experiences in my career," Levitin once explained, "for it brought together my love of research, the delight of rendering powerful and brilliant episodes described in the Bible, and exploring the questions that have engrossed mankind from the beginning of consciousness."

Levitin continued to explore what it means to be Jewish in her young adult novel *The Singing Mountain.* Told in alternating chapters by California natives Mitch and his cousin Carlie, the narrative follows Mitch's decision to study at a yeshiva in Jerusalem instead of attending college in the United States. As part of a coming-of-age novel, Levitin objectively presents both Orthodox and Reform Jewish practices. Commentators found much to like about the work. "This plot-driven novel bristles with questions about faith, love, family, acceptance, and self-determination," remarked *Booklist* critic Karen Simonetti. A *Publishers Weekly* reviewer added that Levitin uses a light touch and "maintains a remarkable evenhandedness with all her characters . . . as she presents conflicting points of view without favoring any one of them." *The Singing Mountain* "succeeds as a realistic and poignant portrayal of a young man's search for God and self, conveying both the struggle and joy of the continuous journey," concluded Lauren Adams in *Horn Book.*

*The Cure,* which a *Horn Book* contributor considered a "compelling interior tale of the little-known true horror that faced 'the other' during the Middle Ages," was likened to Lois Lowry's award-winning novel *The Giver* for its vision of a future society that limits freedoms to ensure social stability. When citizen Gemm 16884 finds himself attracted to music in a society that disallows music, he is considered a deviant and sent into the distant past to be cured of his malady. In fourteenth-century Europe, Gemm witnesses the persecution of Jews, who were made scapegoats for the plague that was terrorizing Europe. A *Publishers Weekly* critic maintained that the novel "handily combines futuristic science fiction and late-medieval Jewish history," and *Booklist* contributor Ilene Cooper asserted that "Gemm's experience in Strasbourg is carefully crafted and emotionally evocative." Similarly, a critic for *Kirkus Reviews* praised Levitin's "unusual mix of science and historical fiction," saying that the novel "pulsates with energy and freshness" and is "packed with spine-tingling historical detail."

Levitin examined another serious topic in *Dream Freedom.* In this novel, a boy and his classmates learn about present-day slavery in Sudan, and work to raise money to buy some of the slaves their freedom. The slaves' own stories are told in alternate chapters. Praising Levitin's "evocative language" and realistic detail, *Booklist* reviewer Shelle Rosenfeld observed that the author "offers perspective on what really matters: compassion, freedom, and how individuals can make a difference." Kathleen Isaacs expressed similar praise in *School Library Journal,* hailing the novel as a "moving narrative" that offers an "intense portrayal of the complex patterns of Sudanese society today and the issues surrounding buying back slaves."

In *Clem's Chances,* fourteen-year-old Clem Fontayne leaves Missouri for California in 1860, determined to find his father. His mother and sister have died, and Clem wants to find the only family he has left. Working for the Pony Express, he moves westward a little at a time. Along the way, he learns of the injustices that Native Americans, Mormons, and blacks have undergone on the frontier. "On his journey," wrote Kathryn Kosiorek in *School Library Journal,* "Clem grows from a daydreaming boy into a competent young man, and learns much about himself and his charming, intelligent, but irresponsible father." Shelle Rosenfeld in *Booklist,* found that "likable Clem's witty, folksy vernacular makes the story very engaging," and a critic for *Publishers Weekly* concluded that "Clem's folksy voice and resilient spirit are the novel's most memorable assets."

The Nazi occupation of Denmark during World War II is the backdrop of *Room in the Heart.* Jewish Julie and Christian Niels are teenagers caught up in the persecution of the Jews in Denmark. Niels distributes underground leaflets that detail Nazi crimes, while Julie and her family try to endure the persecutions they face. The story builds to a boatlift in which many of the country's Jews escape. "What will grab readers," Hazel Rochman wrote in *Booklist,* "is the picture of young people as survivors and heroic rescuers, the secrets and adventure, the fear and exhilaration." "The dangers of the time are never far from the surface," according to Lisa Prolman in *School Library Journal,* "and the story has immediacy because of the feelings readers will have for the characters." As a critic for *Publishers Weekly* concluded, "Levitin succeeds in illuminating a complex set of historical events."

Levitin turned to science fiction in *The Goodness Gene,* which is set some two hundred years in the future. Nutritional drinks have replaced the eating of actual food, machines provide all emotional and physical pleasure, and the mercy killing of children is commonplace. A benign dictator runs society and is raising his twin sons, Will and Berk, to be his heirs. During a trip to another part of the country, Will discovers that he and his brother are clones of Adolf Hitler. He also encounters a resistance group trying to restore society to its traditional ways, and finds that he sympathizes with their goals. Frances Bradburn, writing in *Booklist,* found that in *The Goodness Gene* "Levitin has created a future world only one step removed from our present." "The conclusion," wrote Susan L. Rogers in the *School Library Journal,* "is decisive, predictable, but still surprisingly moving and thought provoking."

In *Strange Relations,* fifteen-year-old Marne is looking forward to spending the summer with her Aunt Carole in Hawai'i. However, when she arrives, she discovers that Aunt Carole and her family are Hasidic Jews who take their faith very seriously. Marne, raised as a secular Jew, is first taken aback, but over the course of the summer, she comes to respect and appreciate her aunt's way of life. When her best friend comes to Hawai'i on vacation, Marne sees clearly how shallow her own way of life has been. Writing for *School Library Journal,* Susan Riley noted: "It's rare to find such well-developed characters, empathetic and sensitive religious treatment, and carefully crafted plotlines in one novel." "Too few novels give such a revealing, believable view of contemporary Jewish American kids wrestling with tradition and faith," Gillian Engberg wrote in *Booklist,* and a critic for *Publishers Weekly* concluded that Marne's "inner turmoil and emotional growth are skillfully and movingly wrought."

In addition to her acclaimed young-adult novels, Levitin has also written several picture books, including the historically themed *Nine for California* and its sequels, *Boom Town* and *Taking Charge. When Elephant Goes to a Party* and *When Kangaroo Goes to School* use humorous situations to present basic manners and social skills, while *Junk Man's Daughter* tells of an immigrant family who comes to America from Europe. In Levitin's story, Papa has promised that the streets are made of gold in America, but young Hanna despairs when the family finds itself living in poverty. Then Papa finds a profitable business: gathering and selling junk in the streets. At first the family gathers junk on foot, then they buy a horse-drawn wagon, and finally a truck. According to a critic for *Kirkus Reviews,* "Levitin's tale of a hardworking immigrant family pulling itself up to prosperity through hard times is inspiring."

Levitin once commented: "As time goes by I discover, somewhat to my surprise, that writing does not get any easier. It is still demanding and difficult work; at times I find it frustrating. I have a recurring dream where I stand before a large, oddly shaped room full of students, called to lecture to them, but the configuration of the room is such that I cannot possibly retain eye contact or voice contact with everyone. This is my struggle: I want to call out, reach everyone; I want to speak to them and to be heard. This is my mission, this is my goal with my books, to be a mind-bridge between people, among peoples of various colors, types, persuasions. Why else do I possess this intense interest about people and their past, their present desires and goals, their inclinations to do good, or to do evil?

"My writing is changing—it should with time. I am working with the same topics and themes, but delving deeper, I think, into my own experiences and beliefs, using them and blending them with fact and imagination to create stories that I hope will have the power to live and to persuade. I admit it, persuasion is surely the aim of the writer. Mine is to persuade beautifully, with clarity and in honesty. This demands self-examination and self-knowledge, both of which are attained only through a lifetime of effort—and then one is ever doubtful.

"All this sounds very serious; writing must also be fun. This is what I convey to my students. It must flow, laugh, sing, and dance with you. One is a writer purely by choice and from the love of it. It is well to remember that, and to glory in the independence and the sheer pleasure of being able to think and create and call it 'work.'

"Ideas abound. Right now, six various projects fill my desk space, and several more whisper in my mind for later development. One needs time, self-discipline, and a quiet, contemplative spirit in order to separate the valuable from the dross. I do take time to be silent each day, to meditate and sort out what is important, and what I shall use, how it fits together, what the universe has to tell me. Mysterious? No—it is simply—prayer.

"I should add, and not in jest, that it is very important to choose the right mate if one wishes to be a creative writer. I have been endowed with wonderful luck in that area. My husband knows when to listen well and to encourage, when to stand aside and say nothing, when to commiserate, when to celebrate with me. He sees my work as an important link between what the present reality is for us, and what we may yet leave behind. He understands the value of ideas and ideals. I know he would love me as well if I never wrote another book; the pressure is all mine, from within, the way it should be."

## Biographical and Critical Sources

*BOOKS*

*Children's Literature Review,* Volume 53, Gale (Detroit, MI), 1999.

*Contemporary Literary Criticism,* Volume 17, Gale (Detroit, MI), 1981.

*St. James Guide to Young Adult Writers,* second edition, St. James Press (Detroit, MI), 1999.

*Something about the Author Autobiography Series,* Volume 2, Gale (Detroit, MI), 1986.

*PERIODICALS*

*Booklist,* May 1, 1994, Ilene Cooper, review of *Escape from Egypt,* p. 1595; July, 1994, Stephanie Zvirin, review of *Adam's War,* p. 1949; February 15, 1998, Lauren Peterson, review of *Boom Town,* p. 1020; September 15, 1998, Karen Simonetti, review of *The Singing Mountain,* p. 221; April 15, 1999, Carolyn Phelan, review of *Taking Charge,* p. 1536; June 1, 1999, Ilene Cooper, review of *The Cure,* p. 1814; May 1, 2001, Amy Brandt, review of *When Elephant Goes to a Party,* p. 1691; November 1, 2000, Shelle Rosenfeld, review of *Dream Freedom,* p. 526; September 15, 2001, Shelle Rosenfeld, review of *Clem's Chances,* p. 223; February 15, 2002, Whitney Scott, review of *The Cure,* p. 1039; November 1, 2003, Hazel Rochman, review of *Room in the Heart,* p. 490; September 1, 2005, Frances Bradburn, review of *The Goodness Gene,* p. 111; June 1, 2007, Gillian Engberg, review of *Strange Relations,* p. 71; December 1, 2007, Hazel Rochman, review of *Junk Man's Daughter,* p. 48.

*Book Report,* September-October, 1999, Ron Marinucci, review of *The Cure,* p. 60; May, 2001, Ruie Chehak, review of *Dream Freedom,* p. 60.

*Bulletin of the Center for Children's Books,* January, 1999, Janice M. Del Negro, review of *The Singing Mountain,* p. 173.

*Children's Bookwatch,* August, 2007, review of *Strange Relations.*

*Horn Book,* March-April, 1998, Margaret A. Bush, review of *Boom Town,* p. 215; November, 1998, Lauren Adams, review of *The Singing Mountain,* p. 734; March, 1999, Margaret A. Bush, review of *Taking Charge,* p. 196; May, 1999, review of *The Cure,* p. 332; November-December, 2001, Betty Carter, review of *Clem's Chances,* p. 753; January-February, 2004, Susan P. Bloom, review of *Room in the Heart,* p. 85.

*Kirkus Reviews,* March 15, 1999, review of *The Cure;* September 1, 2001, review of *Clem's Chances,* p. 1294; October 1, 2003, review of *Room in the Heart,* p. 1226; September 1, 2005, review of *The Goodness Gene,* p. 976; May 15, 2007, review of *Strange Relations;* September 15, 2007, review of *Junk Man's Daughter.*

*Kliatt,* January, 2002, Claire Rosser, review of *Clem's Chances,* p. 6; September, 2005, Claire Rosser, review of *The Goodness Gene,* p. 10; May, 2007, Claire Rosser, review of *Strange Relations,* p. 15.

*New York Times Book Review,* May 17, 1987, Sheila Klass, "Waiting for Operation Moses," p. 36; May 17, 1998, Anne Scott MacLeod, "And No Television Either," p. 23.

*Publishers Weekly,* May 13, 1988, review of *Incident at Loring Groves,* p. 278; April 19, 1993, review of *Annie's Promise,* p. 63; March 28, 1994, review of *Escape from Egypt,* p. 98; June 13, 1994, review of *Adam's War,* p. 65; September 9, 1996, review of *Nine for California,* p. 83; September 7, 1998, review of *The Singing Mountain,* p. 96; April 12, 1999, review of *The Cure,* p. 76; November 6, 2000, review of *Dream Freedom,* p. 92; October 29, 2001, review of *Clem's Chances,* p. 64; September 8, 2003, review of *Room in the Heart,* p. 77; June 25, 2007, review of *Strange Relations,* p. 61.

*Reading Today,* October, 2000, Lynne T. Burke, review of *Dream Freedom,* p. 32.

*School Library Journal,* March, 1998, Steven Engelfried, review of *Boom Town,* p. 182; November, 1998, Elisabeth Palmer Abarbanel, review of *The Singing Mountain,* pp. 122-123; April, 1999, Beth Tegart, review of *Taking Charge,* p. 102; October, 2000, Kathleen Isaacs, review of *Dream Freedom,* p. 162; June, 2001, Patricia Pearl Dole, review of *When Elephant Goes to a Party,* p. 124; October, 2001, Kathryn Kosiorek, review of *Clem's Chances,* p. 165; December, 2001, Francisca Goldsmith, review of *The Cure,* p. 77; December, 2003, Lisa Prolman, review of *Room in the Heart,* p. 156; December, 2005, Susan L. Rogers, review of *The Goodness Gene,* p. 148; May, 2007, Susan Riley, review of *Strange Relations,* p. 138; April, 2008, Lucinda Snyder Whitehurst, review of *Junk Man's Daughter,* p. 115.

*Stone Soup,* November-December, 2001, Kat Clark, review of *Dream Freedom,* p. 34.

*Teacher Librarian,* June, 2008, Kathleen Odean, review of *Strange Relations,* p. 46.

*Voice of Youth Advocates,* June, 1999, Beth Karpas, review of *The Cure,* p. 123.

*ONLINE*

*Sonia Levitin Home Page,* http://www.sonialevitin.com (August 15, 2008).

* * *

## LYON, Elinor 1921-2008 (Elinor Bruce Lyon, Elinor Wright)

*OBITUARY NOTICE—*

See index for *SATA* sketch: Born August 17, 1921, in Guisborough, Yorkshire, England; died May 28, 2008. Children's author and illustrator. Lyon wrote twenty children's books, beginning in 1976, illustrating more than half of them with her own pen-and-ink drawings and watercolors. The books revolve around traditional middle-class themes of friendship, innocence, and honesty. They are stories of British youngsters pursuing their harmless adventures throughout the countryside of Wales and Scotland. Almost half of the novels feature the Scottish brother-sister team of Ian and Sovra. These stories enabled the author to reflect on her own Scottish ancestry and to offer young readers a peek at the Scottish highlands through landscape, history, and legend. The books were praised for their realism. The adventures were episodes that could happen to ordinary children who were observant and curious enough to uncover secrets and follow their instincts, but they were not without a certain amount of suspense. Lyon ceased writing in the mid-1970s and her books lay dormant for decades. In her later years, however, Lyon was able to see her books in print again, as a new generation discovered treasures such as *The House in Hiding* (1950; 2006). Other books that were popular in their day include *Wishing Water-Gate* (1949; 1976), *Daughters of Aradale* (1957; 1974), *Strangers at the Door* (1967), and *The Floodmakers* (1976).

*OBITUARIES AND OTHER SOURCES:*

*PERIODICALS*

*Times* (London, England), June 14, 2008, p. 86.

* * *

## LYON, Elinor Bruce
See LYON, Elinor

# M

## MacDONALD, Alan 1958-

### Personal

Born 1958, in Watford, England. *Education:* Attended Bangor University and Nottingham University. *Hobbies and other interests:* Soccer.

### Addresses

*Home*—Nottingham, England.

### Career

Writer, 1989—. Worked as a performer in a traveling theatre company; director of theatre productions; has also worked as an editor and in a day center.

### Writings

*BOOKS*

(With Stephen Stickley) *The Drama Recipe Book,* Minstrel, 1989.

(With others) *The Time of Your Life,* Inter-Varsity Press (Downers Grove, IL), 1989.

(With Tony Campolo) *The Career Starter Guide: Finding and Mastering Your First Job,* Frameworks (Leicester, England), 1990.

*Films in Close-up: Getting the Most from Film and Video,* Frameworks (Leicester, England), 1991, published as *Movies in Close-up: Getting the Most from Film and Video,* InterVarsity Press (Downers Grove, IL), 1992.

(With Janet Stickley) *The Essential Christmas Book,* Lion (Oxford, England), 1992, published as *The Family Christmas Book,* Lion (Batavia, IL), 1992.

*The Essential Easter Book,* Lion (Oxford, England), 1993, published as *The Family Easter Book,* Lion (Batavia, IL), 1993.

*Whispering in God's Ear: A New Collection of Poetry for Children,* illustrated by Susie Poole, Lion (Oxford, England), 1994.

*The Personality Potion,* illustrated by John Eastwood, Oxford University Press (Oxford, England), 1996.

*The Great Spaghetti Suit,* illustrated by Pat McCarthy, Oxford University Press (Oxford, England), 1996.

*Forgetful Little Fireman,* illustrated by Philip Hopman, Ladybird (Loughborough, England), 1997.

*Beware of the Bears!,* illustrated by Gwyneth Williamson, Little Tiger Press (Waukesha, WI), 1998.

*The King Next Door,* illustrated by Nick Ward, Lion (Oxford, England), 1998.

*The Pig in a Wig,* illustrated by Paul Hess, Macdonald Young (Hove, England), 1998, Peachtree Publishers (Atlanta, GA), 1999.

*The Goalie from Nowhere,* illustrated by Jane Cope, Oxford University Press (Oxford, England), 1998.

*The Wrong Letter,* illustrated by Judy Brown, Oxford University Press (Oxford, England), 1998.

*Leon Gets a Scarecut,* illustrated by Sally Anne Lambert, Macdonald Young (Hove, England), 1998.

*Leon's Fancy Dress Day,* illustrated by Sally Anne Lambert, Macdonald Young (Hove, England), 1998.

*The Not-so-wise Man,* illustrated by Andrew Rowland, Eerdmans (Grand Rapids, MI), 1999.

(Reteller) *The Magic Porridge Pot: Based on a Traditional Folk Tale,* illustrated by Tania Hurt-Newton, Ladybird (Loughborough, England), 1999.

*A Fish for Supper,* illustrated by Glummie Riday, Little Tiger Press (London, England), 1999.

*The Worst Team in the World,* illustrated by John Eastwood, Oxford University Press (Oxford, England), 1999.

*Henry VIII and His Chopping Block,* illustrated by Philip Reeve, Scholastic (London, England), 1999.

(Reteller) *The Gingerbread Man: Based on a Traditional Folk Tale,* illustrated by Anja Rieger, Ladybird (Loughborough, England), 1999.

*Al Capone and His Gang,* illustrated by Philip Reeve, Scholastic (London, England), 1999.

*Triffic Chocolate,* illustrated by Clive Goddard, Hippo (London, England), 2000.

*Football Stories That Really Happened,* Hippo (London, England), 2000.

*Oliver Cromwell and His Warts,* illustrated by Philip Reeve, Hippo (London, England), 2000.

*Titanic,* illustrated by Pete Smith, Scholastic (London, England), 2001.

(Adaptor) Robert Louis Stevenson, *Treasure Island,* Oxford University Press (Oxford, England), 2001.

(Adaptor) Robert Louis Stevenson, *Dr. Jekyll and Mr. Hyde,* Oxford University Press (Oxford, England), 2001.

*Snarlyhissopus,* illustrated by Louise Voce, Tiger Tales Books (Wilton, CT), 2002.

*The Great Brain Robbery,* illustrated by Lizzie Finlay, Scholastic (London, England), 2002.

*Scaredy Mouse,* illustrated by Tim Warnes, Little Tiger Books (London, England), 2002.

*High Five Henry,* illustrated by Phillippe Dupasquier, Oxford University Press (Oxford, England), 2002, published as *High Five Hank,* Picture Window Books (Minneapolis, MN), 2007.

*Mark's Dream Team,* illustrated by Clive Goodyer, Oxford University Press (Oxford, England), 2002.

*Queen Victoria and Her Amusements,* illustrated by Clive Goddard, Hippo (London, England), 2002.

*Yummy Scrummy,* illustrated by Judy Brown, Oxford University Press (Oxford, England), 2002.

*The Sand Witch,* illustrated by Chris Mould, Oxford University Press (Oxford, England), 2002, Picture Window Books (Minneapolis, MN), 2007.

*The Great Escape,* illustrated by Lizzie Finlay, Hippo (London, England), 2003.

*Tutankhamun's Tomb,* Scholastic (London, England), 2003.

*Miss Nile's Mummy Lessons,* illustrated by Kelly Waldek, Scholastic (London, England), 2003.

*Winston Churchill and His Great Wars,* illustrated by Clive Goddard, Hippo (London, England), 2004.

*The Spy from the Wreck,* Scholastic (London, England), 2005.

*The Sign of the Angel,* Scholastic (London, England), 2005.

*Wilfred to the Rescue* (based on Jill Barklem's "Brambly Hedge" series), illustrated by Lizzie Sanders, Atheneum (New York, NY), 2006.

*Fleas,* illustrated by David Roberts, Stripes (London, England), 2006.

*Nothing but Trouble,* illustrated by Pam Smy, A&C Black (London, England), 2006.

*Primrose in Charge,* illustrated by Lizzie Sanders, HarperCollins (London, England), 2007.

*Burp!,* illustrated by David Roberts, Stripes (London, England), 2007.

*Contest Crazy,* illustrated by Judy Brown, Picture Window Books (Minneapolis, MN), 2007.

*Cleaner Genie,* illustrated by Martin Remphry, Picture Window Books (Minneapolis, MN), 2007.

*Trolls Go Home!,* illustrated by Mark Beech, Bloomsbury (New York, NY), 2007.

*Trolls United!,* illustrated by Mark Beech, Bloomsbury (New York, NY), 2007.

*Trolls on Hols,* illustrated by Mark Beech, Bloomsbury (London, England), 2007, published as *Trolls on Vacation,* Bloomsbury (New York, NY), 2008.

*Goat Pie,* illustrated by Mark Beech, Bloomsbury (London, England), 2007.

*Custardly Wart: Pirate (Third Class),* illustrated by Mark Beech, Bloomsbury (London, England), 2008.

*Ditherus Wart: (Accidental) Gladiator,* illustrated by Mark Beech, Bloomsbury (London, England), 2008.

*Honesty Wart: Witch Hunter,* illustrated by Mark Beech, Bloomsbury (London, England), 2008.

*Sir Bigwart: Knight of the Wonky Table,* illustrated by Mark Beech, Bloomsbury (London, England), 2008.

*OTHER*

Writer of episodes for television series, including *Roly Mo Show,* BBC-TV, and *The Fimbles,* BBC-TV. Writer of stories for BBC Radio. Author of stage plays.

## Sidelights

Alan MacDonald is a prolific British author of fiction and nonfiction for young readers. Born in Watford, England, in 1958, MacDonald studied English and drama at Bangor University and joined a traveling children's theater company as a performer and writer. He also trained as a drama teacher at Nottingham University, and he has written stories and plays for BBC Ra-

***Cover of Alan MacDonald's quirky story* Trolls United, *featuring droll artwork by Mark Beech.*** (Illustration copyright © 2007 by Mark Beech. Reprinted by permission of Bloomsbury USA.)

dio as well as episodes of the *Roly Mo Show* and *The Fimbles* for BBC-TV.

One of MacDonald's early works, *Beware of the Bears!,* spoofs the classic Grimm Brothers tale "Goldilocks and the Three Bears." In MacDonald's version, the Bears return home to find that someone has been eating their porridge and sleeping in their beds. When the Bears later notice Goldilocks leaving another cottage, they decide to teach her a lesson and proceed to create a mess of their own, only to discover that the owner of the home isn't who they expected. According to Stephanie Zvirin in *Booklist, Beware of the Bears!* "is lots of silly fun."

A case of mistaken identity is the subject of *Snarlyhissopus,* another picture book. After Pelican spots a hippopotamus for the first time, she excitedly relates the encounter to Monkey but refers to the creature as a Spottyhippomus. Monkey creates further confusion when he tells Zebra about the ugly Woppabigamouse lurking about, and before long the entire jungle has been alerted to the presence of the fearsome Snarlyhissopus. "MacDonald's silly variations on Hippopotamus . . . good-naturedly prove that the time-tested game of 'Telephone' endures," wrote a contributor in *Publishers Weekly.*

In *Scaredy Mouse,* Squeak, a timid rodent, and his sister, Nibbles, decide to venture from their safety of their home beneath the stairs to nab a slice of chocolate cake. Before leaving, Squeak ties the end of a ball of string around this tummy so he won't get lost, and as the pair make their way to the kitchen, Squeak is certain that he spies the family's ginger cat around each corner. When the feline finally does appear, Squeak's stringy path comes in handy. A critic in *Kirkus Reviews* described *Scaredy Mouse* as an "amusing tale."

In *Wilfred to the Rescue,* a work based on Jill Barklem's "Brambly Hedge" series, Wilfred and his mouse family open their home to a family of voles after heavy rains flood the riverbank. During a game of hide-and-seek, a tiny vole falls asleep in a basket boat that begins to float away, prompting Wilfred and his friend, Horace, to board their raft and head downstream. MacDonald "offers a good story," Carolyn Phelan remarked in *Booklist,* and Maura Bresnahan, writing in *School Library Journal,* applauded "the book's gently paced plot and satisfying conclusion."

A trio of hairy, goat-eating trolls move into the cozy suburb of Biddlesden and make life difficult for their new neighbors, the Priddles, in *Trolls Go Home!* Young readers "will hear the messages about cultural tolerance, but it's the slapstick comedy that will draw readers" to the work, wrote *Booklist* critic Gillian Engberg. In a sequel, *Trolls on Hols,* Egbert, Nora, and Ulrik Troll sneak aboard the Priddles' van as they prepare for a vacation in Wales. "This is the type of light-hearted, well-plotted book that is often overlooked . . ., but is perfect for readers who hoot at Fungus the Bogeyman and who will one day discover P.G. Wodehouse," remarked Amanda Craig in the London *Times Online.*

## Biographical and Critical Sources

*PERIODICALS*

*Booklist,* May 15, 1998, Stephanie Zvirin, review of *Beware of the Bears!,* p. 1632; March 1, 2006, Carolyn Phelan, review of *Wilfred to the Rescue,* p. 100; May 1, 2007, Gillian Engberg, review of *Trolls, Go Home!,* p. 99.

*Kirkus Reviews,* February 15, 2002, review of *Scaredy Mouse,* p. 261; April 1, 2007, review of *Trolls, Go Home!*

*Publishers Weekly,* July 12, 1999, review of *The Pig in a Wig,* p. 94; February 4, 2002, review of *Snarlyhissopus,* p. 75.

*School Library Journal,* June, 2002, Roxanne Burg, review of *Scaredy Mouse,* p. 102; March, 2006, Maura Bresnahan, review of *Wilfred to the Rescue,* p. 198.

*ONLINE*

*Bloomsbury Web site,* http://www.bloomsbury.com/ (August 15, 2008), "Alan MacDonald."

*British Broadcasting Corporation Web site,* http://www.bbc.co.uk/bbc7/kids/ (August 15, 2008), "Alan MacDonald."

*London Times Online,* http://entertainment.timesonline.co.uk/ (August 18, 2007), Amanda Craig, "Holiday Horrors," review of *Trolls on Hols.**

* * *

## MARTIN, Ann M. 1955-

### Personal

Born August 12, 1955, in Princeton, NJ; daughter of Henry Read (a cartoonist) and Edith Aiken (a teacher) Martin. *Education:* Smith College, A.B. (cum laude), 1977. *Politics:* Democrat. *Hobbies and other interests:* "Reading and needlework, especially smocking and knitting."

### Addresses

*Home*—Woodstock, NY. *Agent*—Amy Berkower, Writers House, Inc., 21 W. 26th St., New York, NY 10010.

### Career

Elementary school teacher in Noroton, CT, 1977-78; Pocket Books, Inc., New York, NY, editorial assistant for Archway Paperbacks, 1978-80; Scholastic Book Services, New York, NY, copywriter for Teen Age Book

Club, 1980-81, associate editor, 1981-83, editor, 1983; Bantam Books, Inc., New York, NY, senior editor of Books for Young Readers, 1983-85; writer and freelance editor, 1985—. Founder of Lisa Libraries (charitable organization); founder of Ann M. Martin Foundation.

## Member

PEN, Authors Guild, Society of Children's Book Writers.

## Awards, Honors

New Jersey Author awards, New Jersey Institute of Technology, 1983, for *Bummer Summer,* 1987, for *Missing since Monday;* Children's Choice, 1985, for *Bummer Summer;* Child Study Association of America Children's Books of the Year selection, 1986, for *Inside Out,* 1987, for *Stage Fright, With You and without You,* and *Missing since Monday;* Keystone State Reading Award, 1998, for *Leo the Magnificat;* California Young Reader Medal nomination, 2000, and Washington Sasquatch Reading Award nomination, 2001, both for *P.S. Longer Letter Later;* Newbery Medal Honor Book, 2003, for *A Corner of the Universe.*

## Writings

*Bummer Summer,* Holiday House (New York, NY), 1983.

*Just You and Me,* Scholastic (New York, NY), 1983.

(With Betsy Ryan) *My Puppy Scrapbook,* illustrated by father, Henry Martin, Scholastic (New York, NY), 1983.

*Inside Out,* Holiday House (New York, NY), 1984.

*Stage Fright,* illustrated by Blanche Sims, Holiday House (New York, NY), 1984.

*Me and Katie (the Pest),* illustrated by Blanche Sims, Holiday House (New York, NY), 1985.

*With You and without You,* Holiday House (New York, NY), 1986.

*Missing since Monday,* Holiday House (New York, NY), 1986.

*Just a Summer Romance,* Holiday House (New York, NY), 1987.

*Slam Book,* Holiday House (New York, NY), 1987.

*Yours Turly, Shirley,* Holiday House (New York, NY), 1988.

*Ten Kids, No Pets,* Holiday House (New York, NY), 1988.

*Fancy Dance in Feather Town,* illustrated by Henry Martin, Western Publishing, 1988.

*Ma and Pa Dracula,* illustrated by Dirk Zimmer, Holiday House (New York, NY), 1989.

*Moving Day in Feather Town,* illustrated by Henry Martin, Western Publishing, 1989.

*Eleven Kids, One Summer,* Holiday House (New York, NY), 1991.

*Enchanted Attic,* Bantam (New York, NY), 1992.

*Rachel Parker, Kindergarten Show-off,* illustrated by Nancy Poydar, Holiday House (New York, NY), 1992.

*Chain Letter,* Scholastic (New York, NY), 1993.

(With Margot Becker) *Ann M. Martin: The Story of the Author of the Baby-Sitters Club,* Scholastic (New York, NY) 1993.

*Leo the Magnificat,* illustrated by Emily A. McCully, Scholastic (New York, NY), 1996.

(With Paula Danziger) *P.S. Longer Letter Later,* Scholastic (New York, NY), 1998.

(With Laura Godwin) *The Doll People,* Hyperion (New York, NY), 1999.

(With Paula Danziger) *Snail Mail No More,* Scholastic (New York, NY), 2000.

*Belle Teal,* Scholastic (New York, NY), 2001.

*A Corner of the Universe,* Scholastic (New York, NY), 2002.

(With Laura Godwin) *The Meanest Doll in the World,* illustrated by Brian Selznick, Hyperion (New York, NY), 2003.

*Here Today,* Scholastic (New York, NY), 2004.

(Editor, with David Levithan) *Friends: Stories about New Friends, Old Friends, and Unexpectedly True Friends,* Scholastic (New York, NY), 2005.

*A Dog's Life: The Autobiography of a Stray,* Scholastic (New York, NY), 2005.

*On Christmas Eve,* illustrated by Jon J. Muth, Scholastic (New York, NY), 2006.

(With Laura Godwin) *The Runaway Dolls,* illustrated by Brian Selznick, Hyperion (New York, NY), 2008.

*"BABY-SITTERS CLUB" SERIES*

*Kristy's Great Idea,* Scholastic (New York, NY), 1986.

*Claudia and the Phantom Phone Calls,* Scholastic (New York, NY), 1986.

*The Truth about Stacey,* Scholastic (New York, NY), 1986.

*Mary Anne Saves the Day,* Scholastic (New York, NY), 1987.

*Dawn and the Impossible Three,* Scholastic (New York, NY), 1987.

*Kristy's Big Day,* Scholastic (New York, NY), 1987.

*Claudia and Mean Janine,* Scholastic (New York, NY), 1987.

*Boy-Crazy Stacey,* Scholastic (New York, NY), 1987.

*The Ghost at Dawn's House,* Scholastic (New York, NY), 1988.

*Logan Likes Mary Anne!,* Scholastic (New York, NY), 1988.

*Kristy and the Snobs,* Scholastic (New York, NY), 1988.

*Claudia and the New Girl,* Scholastic (New York, NY), 1988.

*Good-bye Stacey, Good-bye,* Scholastic (New York, NY), 1988.

*Hello, Mallory,* Scholastic (New York, NY), 1988.

*Little Miss Stoneybrook . . . and Dawn,* Scholastic (New York, NY), 1988.

*Jessi's Secret Language,* Scholastic (New York, NY), 1988.

*Mary Anne's Bad-Luck Mystery,* Scholastic (New York, NY), 1988.

*Stacey's Mistake,* Scholastic (New York, NY), 1988.

*Claudia and the Bad Joke,* Scholastic (New York, NY), 1988.

*Kristy and the Walking Disaster,* Scholastic (New York, NY), 1989.
*Mallory and the Trouble with the Twins,* Scholastic (New York, NY), 1989.
*Jessi Ramsey, Pet-Sitter,* Scholastic (New York, NY), 1989.
*Dawn on the Coast,* Scholastic (New York, NY), 1989.
*Kristy and the Mother's Day Surprise,* Scholastic (New York, NY), 1989.
*Mary Anne and the Search for Tigger,* Scholastic (New York, NY), 1989.
*Claudia and the Sad Good-bye,* Scholastic (New York, NY), 1989.
*Jessi and the Superbrat,* Scholastic (New York, NY), 1989.
*Welcome Back, Stacey!,* Scholastic (New York, NY), 1989.
*Mallory and the Mystery Diary,* Scholastic (New York, NY), 1989.
*Mary Anne and the Great Romance,* Scholastic (New York, NY), 1990.
*Dawn's Wicked Stepsister,* Scholastic (New York, NY), 1990.
*Kristy and the Secret of Susan,* Scholastic (New York, NY), 1990.
*Claudia and the Great Search,* Scholastic (New York, NY), 1990.
*Mary Anne and Too Many Boys,* Scholastic (New York, NY), 1990.
*Stacey and the Mystery of Stoneybrook,* Scholastic (New York, NY), 1990.
*Jessi's Baby-Sitter,* Scholastic (New York, NY), 1990.
*Dawn and the Older Boy,* Scholastic (New York, NY), 1990.
*Kristy's Mystery Admirer,* Scholastic (New York, NY), 1990.
*Poor Mallory,* Scholastic (New York, NY), 1990.
*Claudia and the Middle School Mystery,* Scholastic (New York, NY), 1991.
*Mary Anne vs. Logan,* Scholastic (New York, NY), 1991.
*Jessi and the Dance School Phantom,* Scholastic (New York, NY), 1991.
*Stacey's Emergency,* Scholastic (New York, NY), 1991.
*Dawn and the Big Sleepover,* Scholastic (New York, NY), 1991.
*Kristy and the Baby Parade,* Scholastic (New York, NY), 1991.
*Mary Anne Misses Logan,* Scholastic (New York, NY), 1991.
*Mallory on Strike,* Scholastic (New York, NY), 1991.
*Jessi's Wish,* Scholastic (New York, NY), 1991.
*Claudia and the Genius of Elm Street,* Scholastic (New York, NY), 1991.
*Dawn's Big Date,* Scholastic (New York, NY), 1992.
*Stacey's Ex-Best Friend,* Scholastic (New York, NY), 1992.
*Mary Anne and Too Many Babies,* Scholastic (New York, NY), 1992.
*Kristy for President,* Scholastic (New York, NY), 1992.
*Mallory and the Dream Horse,* Scholastic (New York, NY), 1992.
*Jessi's Gold Medal,* Scholastic (New York, NY), 1992.
*Keep out, Claudia!,* Scholastic (New York, NY), 1992.
*Dawn Saves the Planet,* Scholastic (New York, NY), 1992.
*Stacey's Choice,* Scholastic (New York, NY), 1992.
*Mallory Hates Boys (and Gym),* Scholastic (New York, NY), 1992.
*Mary Anne's Makeover,* Scholastic (New York, NY), 1993.
*Jessi and the Awful Secret,* Scholastic (New York, NY), 1993.
*Kristy and the Worst Kid Ever,* Scholastic (New York, NY), 1993.
*Claudia's Friend,* Scholastic (New York, NY), 1993.
*Dawn's Family Feud,* Scholastic (New York, NY), 1993.
*Stacey's Big Crush,* Scholastic (New York, NY), 1993.
*Maid Mary Anne,* Scholastic (New York, NY), 1993.
*Dawn's Big Move,* Scholastic (New York, NY), 1993.
*Jessi and the Bad Baby-Sitter,* Scholastic (New York, NY), 1993.
*Get Well Soon, Mallory,* Scholastic (New York, NY), 1993.
*Stacey and the Cheerleaders,* Scholastic (New York, NY), 1993.
*Claudia and the Perfect Boy,* Scholastic (New York, NY), 1994.
*Dawn and the We Love Kids Club,* Scholastic (New York, NY), 1994.
*Mary Anne and Miss Priss,* Scholastic (New York, NY), 1994.
*Kristy and the Copycat,* Scholastic (New York, NY), 1994.
*Jessi's Horrible Prank,* Scholastic (New York, NY), 1994.
*Stacey's Lie,* Scholastic (New York, NY), 1994.
*Dawn and Whitney, Friends Forever,* Scholastic (New York, NY), 1994.
*Claudia and Crazy Peaches,* Scholastic (New York, NY), 1994.
*Mary Anne Breaks the Rules,* Scholastic (New York, NY), 1994.
*Mallory Pike, #1 Fan,* Scholastic (New York, NY), 1994.
*Kristy and Mr. Mom,* Scholastic (New York, NY), 1995.
*Jessi and the Troublemaker,* Scholastic (New York, NY), 1995.
*Stacey vs. the BSC,* Scholastic (New York, NY), 1995.
*Dawn and the School Spirit War,* Scholastic (New York, NY), 1995.
*Claudia Kishi, Live from WSTO,* Scholastic (New York, NY), 1995.
*Mary Anne and Camp BSC,* Scholastic (New York, NY), 1995.
*Stacey and the Bad Girls,* Scholastic (New York, NY), 1995.
*Farewell, Dawn,* Scholastic (New York, NY), 1995.
*Kristy and the Dirty Diapers,* Scholastic (New York, NY), 1995.
*Welcome to the BSC, Abby,* Scholastic (New York, NY), 1995.
*Claudia and the First Thanksgiving,* Scholastic (New York, NY), 1995.
*Mallory's Christmas Wish,* Scholastic (New York, NY), 1995.
*Mary Anne and the Memory Garden,* Scholastic (New York, NY), 1996.
*Stacey McGill, Super Sitter,* Scholastic (New York, NY), 1996.
*Kristy + Bart =?,* Scholastic (New York, NY), 1996.
*Abby's Lucky Thirteen,* Scholastic (New York, NY), 1996.
*Claudia and the World's Cutest Baby,* Scholastic (New York, NY), 1996.

*Dawn and Too Many Sitters,* Scholastic (New York, NY), 1996.

*Stacey's Broken Heart,* Scholastic (New York, NY), 1996.

*Kristy's Worst Idea,* Scholastic (New York, NY), 1996.

*Claudia Kishi, Middle School Drop Out,* Scholastic (New York, NY), 1996.

*Mary Anne and the Little Princess,* Scholastic (New York, NY), 1996.

*Happy Holidays, Jessi,* Scholastic (New York, NY), 1996.

*Abby's Twin,* Scholastic (New York, NY), 1997.

*Stacey the Match Whiz,* Scholastic (New York, NY), 1997.

*Claudia, Queen of the Seventh Grade,* Scholastic (New York, NY), 1997.

*Mind Your Own Business, Kristy!,* Scholastic (New York, NY), 1997.

*Don't Give up, Mallory,* Scholastic (New York, NY), 1997.

*Mary Anne to the Rescue,* Scholastic (New York, NY), 1997.

*Abby the Bad Sport,* Scholastic (New York, NY), 1997.

*Stacey's Secret Friend,* Scholastic (New York, NY), 1997.

*Kristy and the Sister War,* Scholastic (New York, NY), 1997.

*Claudia Makes up Her Mind,* Scholastic (New York, NY), 1997.

*The Secret Life of Mary Anne Spier,* Scholastic (New York, NY), 1997.

*Jessi's Big Break,* Scholastic (New York, NY), 1997.

*Abby and the Best Kid Ever,* Scholastic (New York, NY), 1997.

*Claudia and the Terrible Truth,* Scholastic (New York, NY), 1997.

*Kristy Thomas, Dog Trainer,* Scholastic (New York, NY), 1997.

*Stacey's Ex-Boyfriend,* Scholastic (New York, NY), 1997.

*Mary Anne and the Playground Fight,* Scholastic (New York, NY), 1997.

*Abby in Wonderland,* Scholastic (New York, NY), 1997.

*Kristy in Charge,* Scholastic (New York, NY), 1997.

*Claudia's Big Party,* Scholastic (New York, NY), 1998.

*Stacey McGill . . . Matchmaker?,* Scholastic (New York, NY), 1998.

*Mary Anne in the Middle,* Scholastic (New York, NY), 1998.

*The All-New Mallory Pike,* Scholastic (New York, NY), 1998.

*Abby's Un-Valentine,* Scholastic (New York, NY), 1998.

*Claudia and the Little Liar,* Scholastic (New York, NY), 1999.

*Kristy at Bat,* Scholastic (New York, NY), 1999.

*Stacey's Movie,* Scholastic (New York, NY), 1999.

*The Fire at Mary Anne's House,* Scholastic (New York, NY), 1999.

*Graduation Day,* Scholastic (New York, NY), 2000.

*"FRIENDS FOREVER" SERIES*

*Kristy's Big News,* Scholastic (New York, NY), 1999.

*Stacey vs. Claudia,* Scholastic (New York, NY), 1999.

*Mary Anne's Big Break Up,* Scholastic (New York, NY), 1999.

*Claudia and the Friendship Feud,* Scholastic (New York, NY), 1999.

*Kristy Power,* Scholastic (New York, NY), 1999.

*Stacey and the Boyfriend Trap,* Scholastic (New York, NY), 1999.

*Claudia Gets Her Guy,* Scholastic (New York, NY), 2000.

*Mary Anne's Revenge,* Scholastic (New York, NY), 2000.

*Kristy and the Kidnapper,* Scholastic (New York, NY), 2000.

*Stacey's Problem,* Scholastic (New York, NY), 2000.

*Welcome Home, Mary Anne,* Scholastic (New York, NY), 2000.

*Claudia and the Disaster Date,* Scholastic (New York, NY), 2000.

*"FRIENDS FOREVER SPECIAL" SERIES*

*Everything Changes,* Scholastic (New York, NY), 1999.

*Graduation Day,* Scholastic (New York, NY), 2000.

*"BABY-SITTERS CLUB MYSTERY" SERIES*

*Stacey and the Missing Ring,* Scholastic (New York, NY), 1991.

*Beware, Dawn!,* Scholastic (New York, NY), 1991.

*Mallory and the Ghost Cat,* Scholastic (New York, NY), 1992.

*Kristy and the Missing Child,* Scholastic (New York, NY), 1992.

*Mary Anne and the Secret in the Attic,* Scholastic (New York, NY), 1992.

*The Mystery at Claudia's House,* Scholastic (New York, NY), 1992.

*Dawn and the Disappearing Dogs,* Scholastic (New York, NY), 1993.

*Jessi and the Jewel Thieves,* Scholastic (New York, NY), 1993.

*Kristy and the Haunted Mansion,* Scholastic (New York, NY), 1993.

*Stacey and the Mystery Money,* Scholastic (New York, NY), 1993.

*Claudia and the Mystery at the Museum,* Scholastic (New York, NY), 1993.

*Dawn and the Surfer Ghost,* Scholastic (New York, NY), 1993.

*Mary Anne and the Library Mystery,* Scholastic (New York, NY), 1994.

*Stacey and the Mystery at the Mall,* Scholastic (New York, NY), 1994.

*Kristy and the Vampires,* Scholastic (New York, NY), 1994.

*Claudia and the Clue in the Photograph,* Scholastic (New York, NY), 1994.

*Dawn and the Halloween Mystery,* Scholastic (New York, NY), 1994.

*Stacey and the Mystery at the Empty House,* Scholastic (New York, NY), 1994.

*Kristy and the Missing Fortune,* Scholastic (New York, NY), 1995.

*Mary Anne and the Zoo Mystery,* Scholastic (New York, NY), 1995.

*Claudia and the Recipe for Danger,* Scholastic (New York, NY), 1995.

*Stacey and the Haunted Masquerade,* Scholastic (New York, NY), 1995.
*Abby and the Secret Society,* Scholastic (New York, NY), 1996.
*Mary Anne and the Silent Witness,* Scholastic (New York, NY), 1996.
*Kristy and the Middle School Vandal,* Scholastic (New York, NY), 1996.
*Dawn Schafer, Undercover Baby-Sitter,* Scholastic (New York, NY), 1996.
*Claudia and the Lighthouse Ghost,* Scholastic (New York, NY), 1996.
*Abby and the Mystery Baby,* Scholastic (New York, NY), 1997.
*Stacey and the Fashion Victim,* Scholastic (New York, NY), 1997.
*Kristy and the Mystery Train,* Scholastic (New York, NY), 1997.
*Mary Anne and the Music Box Secret,* Scholastic (New York, NY), 1997.
*Claudia and the Mystery in the Painting,* Scholastic (New York, NY), 1997.
*Stacey and the Stolen Hearts,* Scholastic (New York, NY), 1997.
*Mary Anne and the Haunted Bookstore,* Scholastic (New York, NY), 1997.
*Abby and the Notorious Neighbor,* Scholastic (New York, NY), 1997.
*Kristy and the Cat Burglar,* Scholastic (New York, NY), 1997.

*"BABY-SITTERS CLUB SUPER SPECIALS" SERIES*

*Baby-Sitters on Board!,* Scholastic (New York, NY), 1988.
*Baby-Sitters Summer Vacation,* Scholastic (New York, NY), 1989.
*Baby-Sitters Winter Vacation,* Scholastic (New York, NY), 1989.
*Baby-Sitters Island Adventure,* Scholastic (New York, NY), 1990.
*California Girls!,* Scholastic (New York, NY), 1990.
*New York, New York!,* Scholastic (New York, NY), 1991.
*Snowbound,* Scholastic (New York, NY), 1991.
*Baby-Sitters at Shadow Lake,* Scholastic (New York, NY), 1992.
*Starring the Baby-Sitters Club,* Scholastic (New York, NY), 1992.
*Sea City, Here We Come!,* Scholastic (New York, NY), 1993.
*The Baby-Sitters Remember,* Scholastic (New York, NY), 1994.
*Here Come the Bridesmaids!,* Scholastic (New York, NY), 1994.
*Aloha, Baby-Sitters!,* Scholastic (New York, NY), 1996.

*"BABY-SITTERS LITTLE SISTERS" SERIES*

*Karen's Witch,* Scholastic (New York, NY), 1988.
*Karen's Roller Skates,* Scholastic (New York, NY), 1988.
*Karen's Worst Day,* Scholastic (New York, NY), 1989.
*Karen's Kittycat Club,* Scholastic (New York, NY), 1989.
*Karen's School Picture,* Scholastic (New York, NY), 1989.
*Karen's Little Sister,* Scholastic (New York, NY), 1989.
*Karen's Birthday,* Scholastic (New York, NY), 1990.
*Karen's Haircut,* Scholastic (New York, NY), 1990.
*Karen's Sleepover,* Scholastic (New York, NY), 1990.
*Karen's Grandmothers,* Scholastic (New York, NY), 1990.
*Karen's Prize,* Scholastic (New York, NY), 1990.
*Karen's Ghost,* Scholastic (New York, NY), 1990.
*Karen's Surprise,* Scholastic (New York, NY), 1990.
*Karen's New Year,* Scholastic (New York, NY), 1991.
*Karen's in Love,* Scholastic (New York, NY), 1991.
*Karen's Goldfish,* Scholastic (New York, NY), 1991.
*Karen's Brothers,* Scholastic (New York, NY), 1991.
*Karen's Home Run,* Scholastic (New York, NY), 1991.
*Karen's Good-Bye,* Scholastic (New York, NY), 1991.
*Karen's Carnival,* Scholastic (New York, NY), 1991.
*Karen's New Teacher,* Scholastic (New York, NY), 1991.
*Karen's Little Witch,* Scholastic (New York, NY), 1992.
*Karen's Doll,* Scholastic (New York, NY), 1992.
*Karen's School Trip,* Scholastic (New York, NY), 1992.
*Karen's Pen Pal,* Scholastic (New York, NY), 1992.
*Karen's Ducklings,* Scholastic (New York, NY), 1992.
*Karen's Big Joke,* Scholastic (New York, NY), 1992.
*Karen's Tea Party,* Scholastic (New York, NY), 1992.
*Karen's Cartwheel,* Scholastic (New York, NY), 1992.
*Karen's Kittens,* Scholastic (New York, NY), 1992.
*Karen's Bully,* Scholastic (New York, NY), 1992.
*Karen's Pumpkin Patch,* Scholastic (New York, NY), 1992.
*Karen's Secret,* Scholastic (New York, NY), 1992.
*Karen's Snow Day,* Scholastic (New York, NY), 1993.
*Karen's Doll Hospital,* Scholastic (New York, NY), 1993.
*Karen's New Friend,* Scholastic (New York, NY), 1993.
*Karen's Tuba,* Scholastic (New York, NY), 1993.
*Karen's Big Lie,* Scholastic (New York, NY), 1993.
*Karen's Wedding,* Scholastic (New York, NY), 1993.
*Karen's Newspaper,* Scholastic (New York, NY), 1993.
*Karen's School,* Scholastic (New York, NY), 1993.
*Karen's Pizza Party,* Scholastic (New York, NY), 1993.
*Karen's Toothache,* Scholastic (New York, NY), 1993.
*Karen's Big Weekend,* Scholastic (New York, NY), 1993.
*Karen's Twin,* Scholastic (New York, NY), 1994.
*Karen's Baby-Sitter,* Scholastic (New York, NY), 1994.
*Karen's Kite,* Scholastic (New York, NY), 1994.
*Karen's Two Families,* Scholastic (New York, NY), 1994.
*Karen's Stepmother,* Scholastic (New York, NY), 1994.
*Karen's Lucky Penny,* Scholastic (New York, NY), 1994.
*Karen's Big Top,* Scholastic (New York, NY), 1994.
*Karen's Mermaid,* Scholastic (New York, NY), 1994.
*Karen's School Bus,* Scholastic (New York, NY), 1994.
*Karen's Candy,* Scholastic (New York, NY), 1994.
*Karen's Magician,* Scholastic (New York, NY), 1994.
*Karen's Ice Skates,* Scholastic (New York, NY), 1994.
*Karen's School Mystery,* Scholastic (New York, NY), 1995.
*Karen's Ski Trip,* Scholastic (New York, NY), 1995.
*Karen's Leprechaun,* Scholastic (New York, NY), 1995.
*Karen's Pony,* Scholastic (New York, NY), 1995.
*Karen's Tattletale,* Scholastic (New York, NY), 1995.
*Karen's New Bike,* Scholastic (New York, NY), 1995.
*Karen's Movie,* Scholastic (New York, NY), 1995.
*Karen's Lemonade Stand,* Scholastic (New York, NY), 1995.
*Karen's Toys,* Scholastic (New York, NY), 1995.

*Karen's Monsters,* Scholastic (New York, NY), 1995.
*Karen's Turkey Day,* Scholastic (New York, NY), 1995.
*Karen's Angel,* Scholastic (New York, NY), 1995.
*Karen's Big Sister,* Scholastic (New York, NY), 1996.
*Karen's Grandad,* Scholastic (New York, NY), 1996.
*Karen's Island Adventure,* Scholastic (New York, NY), 1996.
*Karen's New Puppy,* Scholastic (New York, NY), 1996.
*Karen's Dinosaur,* Scholastic (New York, NY), 1996.
*Karen's Softball Mystery,* Scholastic (New York, NY), 1996.
*Karen's County Fair,* Scholastic (New York, NY), 1996.
*Karen's Magic Garden,* Scholastic (New York, NY), 1996.
*Karen's School Surprise,* Scholastic (New York, NY), 1996.
*Karen's Half Birthday,* Scholastic (New York, NY), 1996.
*Karen's Big Fight,* Scholastic (New York, NY), 1996.
*Karen's Christmas Tree,* Scholastic (New York, NY), 1996.
*Karen's Accident,* Scholastic (New York, NY), 1997.
*Karen's Secret Valentine,* Scholastic (New York, NY), 1997.
*Karen's Bunny,* Scholastic (New York, NY), 1997.
*Karen's Big Job,* Scholastic (New York, NY), 1997.
*Karen's Treasure,* Scholastic (New York, NY), 1997.
*Karen's Telephone Trouble,* Scholastic (New York, NY), 1997.
*Karen's Pony Camp,* Scholastic (New York, NY), 1997.
*Karen's Puppet Show,* Scholastic (New York, NY), 1997.
*Karen's Unicorn,* Scholastic (New York, NY), 1997.
*Karen's Haunted House,* Scholastic (New York, NY), 1997.
*Karen's Pilgrim,* Scholastic (New York, NY), 1997.
*Karen's Sleigh Ride,* Scholastic (New York, NY), 1997.
*Karen's Cooking Contest,* Scholastic (New York, NY), 1997.
*Karen's Snow Princess,* Scholastic (New York, NY), 1997.
*Karen's Promise,* Scholastic (New York, NY), 1997.
*Karen's Big Move,* Scholastic (New York, NY), 1997.
*Karen's Paper Route,* Scholastic (New York, NY), 1997.
*Karen's Fishing Trip,* Scholastic (New York, NY), 1997.
*Karen's Big City Mystery,* Scholastic (New York, NY), 1997.
*Karen's Book,* Scholastic (New York, NY), 1997.
*Karen's Chain Letter,* Scholastic (New York, NY), 1997.
*Karen's Black Cat,* Scholastic (New York, NY), 1998.
*Karen's Movie Star,* Scholastic (New York, NY), 1998.
*Karen's Christmas Carol,* Scholastic (New York, NY), 1998.
*Karen's Nanny,* Scholastic (New York, NY), 1998.
*Karen's President,* Scholastic (New York, NY), 1998.
*Karen's Copycat,* Scholastic (New York, NY), 1998.
*Karen's Field Day,* Scholastic (New York, NY), 1998.
*Karen's Show and Share,* Scholastic (New York, NY), 1998.
*Karen's Swim Meet,* Scholastic (New York, NY), 1998.
*Karen's Spy Mystery,* Scholastic (New York, NY), 1998.
*Karen's New Holiday,* Scholastic (New York, NY), 1998.
*Karen's Hurricane,* Scholastic (New York, NY), 1998.
*Karen's Chicken Pox,* Scholastic (New York, NY), 1999.
*Karen's Runaway Turkey,* Scholastic (New York, NY), 1999.
*Karen's Reindeer,* Scholastic (New York, NY), 1999.
*Karen's Mistake,* Scholastic (New York, NY), 2000.
*Karen's Figure Eight,* Scholastic (New York, NY), 2000.
*Karen's Yo-Yo,* Scholastic (New York, NY), 2000.
*Karen's Easter Parade,* Scholastic (New York, NY), 2000.
*Karen's Gift,* Scholastic (New York, NY), 2000.
*Karen's Cowboy,* Scholastic (New York, NY), 2000.

*"BABY-SITTERS LITTLE SISTERS SUPER SPECIAL" SERIES*

*Karen's Wish,* Scholastic (New York, NY), 1990.
*Karen's Plane Trip,* Scholastic (New York, NY), 1991.
*Karen's Mystery,* Scholastic (New York, NY), c. 1991.
*Karen, Hannie, and Nancy: The Three Musketeers,* Scholastic (New York, NY), 1992.
*Karen's Baby,* Scholastic (New York, NY), 1992.
*Karen's Campout,* Scholastic (New York, NY), 1993.

*"BABY-SITTERS CLUB PORTRAIT COLLECTION" SERIES*

*Dawn's Book,* Scholastic (New York, NY), 1993.
*Stacey's Book,* Scholastic (New York, NY), 1994.
*Claudia's Book,* Scholastic (New York, NY), 1995.
*Mary Anne's Book,* Scholastic (New York, NY), 1996.
*Kristy's Book,* Scholastic (New York, NY), 1996.
*Abby's Book,* Scholastic (New York, NY), 1997.

*"BABY-SITTERS CLUB SUPER MYSTERIES" SERIES*

*Baby-Sitters' Haunted House,* Scholastic (New York, NY), 1995.
*Baby-Sitters Beware,* Scholastic (New York, NY), 1995.
*Baby-Sitters' Fright Night,* Scholastic (New York, NY), 1996.

*OTHER "BABY-SITTERS CLUB" SPECIAL EDITIONS*

*Logan Bruno, Boy Baby-Sitter,* Scholastic (New York, NY), 1993.
*Baby-Sitters Little Sister School Scrapbook,* Scholastic (New York, NY), 1993.
*Baby-Sitters Club Guide to Baby-Sitting,* Scholastic (New York, NY), 1993.
*Shannon's Story,* Scholastic (New York, NY), 1994.
*Secret Santa,* Scholastic (New York, NY), 1994.
*Baby-Sitters Little Sister Summer Fill-in Book,* Scholastic (New York, NY), 1995.
*Baby-Sitters Little Sister Jump Rope Rhymes,* Scholastic (New York, NY), 1995.
*Baby-Sitters Little Sister Playground Games,* Scholastic (New York, NY), 1996.
*Complete Guide to the Baby-Sitters Club,* Scholastic (New York, NY), 1996.
*The BSC Notebook,* Scholastic (New York, NY), 1996.
*BSC Chain Letter,* Scholastic (New York, NY), 1996.
*The Baby-Sitters Club Trivia and Puzzle Fun Book,* Scholastic (New York, NY), 1996.
*The Baby-Sitters Club Postcard Book,* Scholastic (New York, NY), 1996.

*Little Sister Photo Scrapbook,* Scholastic (New York, NY), 1997.

*Baby-Sitters Little Sister Secret Diary,* Scholastic (New York, NY), 1997.

*Baby-Sitters Little Sister Laugh Pack,* Scholastic (New York, NY), 1997.

*"THE KIDS IN MS. COLMAN'S CLASS" SERIES; ILLUSTRATED BY CHARLES TANG*

*Teacher's Pet,* Scholastic (New York, NY), 1996.

*Author Day,* Scholastic (New York, NY), 1996.

*Class Play,* Scholastic (New York, NY), 1996.

*The Second Grade Baby,* Scholastic (New York, NY), 1996.

*Snow War,* Scholastic (New York, NY), 1997.

*Twin Trouble,* Scholastic (New York, NY), 1997.

*Science Fair,* Scholastic (New York, NY), 1997.

*Summer Kids,* Scholastic (New York, NY), 1997.

*Halloween Parade,* Scholastic (New York, NY), 1998.

*Holiday Time,* Scholastic (New York, NY), 1998.

*Spelling Bee,* Scholastic (New York, NY), 1998.

*Baby Animal Zoo,* Scholastic (New York, NY), 1998.

*"CALIFORNIA DIARIES" SERIES*

*Dawn,* Scholastic (New York, NY), 1997.

*Sunny,* Scholastic (New York, NY), 1997.

*Maggie,* Scholastic (New York, NY), 1997.

*Amalia,* Scholastic (New York, NY), 1997.

*Ducky,* Scholastic (New York, NY), 1997.

*Dawn Diary Two,* Scholastic (New York, NY), 1998.

*Sunny Diary Two,* Scholastic (New York, NY), 1998.

*Maggie Diary Two,* Scholastic (New York, NY), 1998.

*Amalia Diary Two,* Scholastic (New York, NY), 1998.

*Ducky Diary Two,* Scholastic (New York, NY), 1998.

*Dawn Diary Three,* Scholastic (New York, NY), 1999.

*Sunny Diary Three,* Scholastic (New York, NY), 1999.

*Maggie Diary Three,* Scholastic (New York, NY), 2000.

*Amalia Diary Three,* Scholastic (New York, NY), 2000.

*Ducky Diary Three,* Scholastic (New York, NY), 2001.

*"BABY-SITTERS CLUB" GRAPHIC NOVEL SERIES*

*Kristy's Great Idea,* illustrated by Raina Telgemeier, Scholastic (New York, NY), 2006.

*The Truth about Stacey,* illustrated by Raina Telgemeier, Scholastic (New York, NY), 2006.

*Mary Anne Saves the Day,* illustrated by Raina Telgemeier, Scholastic (New York, NY), 2007.

*Claude and Mean Janine,* illustrated by Raina Telgemeier, Scholastic (New York, NY), 2008.

*"MAIN STREET" SERIES*

*Welcome to Camden Falls,* Scholastic (New York, NY), 2007.

*Needle and Thread,* Scholastic (New York, NY), 2007.

*'Tis the Season,* Scholastic (New York, NY), 2007.

*Best Friends,* Scholastic (New York, NY), 2008.

*The Secret Book Club,* Scholastic (New York, NY), 2008.

*September Surprises,* Scholastic (New York, NY), 2008.

*OTHER*

Martin's books have been translated into several languages. The "Baby-Sitters Club" books have been translated into nineteen languages.

## Adaptations

The *Baby-Sitters Club* television series was produced by Scholastic Productions and broadcast on Home Box Office (HBO) and the Disney Channel; *The Baby-Sitters Club Movie,* co-produced by Scholastic Productions and Beacon Communications, was distributed by Columbia, 1995; a "Baby-Sitters Club" board game has been released by Milton-Bradley; several "Baby-Sitters Club" stories have appeared on video and audio cassette.

## Sidelights

When the curtain came down on the final act of the "Baby-Sitters Club" series in 2000, series author and co-originator Ann M. Martin was one of the best-known

***Cover of Ann M. Martin's middle-grade novel* P.S. Longer Letter Letter, *featuring cover art by Paul Colin.*** (Illustration copyright © 1998 by Paul Colin. Reprinted by permission of Scholastic, Inc.)

names in juvenile publishing. What started in 1986 as an idea for a four-book series to be published over the course of one year had ballooned fourteen years later into a mini-publishing industry with several spin-off titles, a television series, a movie, games, and enough "Baby-Sitters Club" (BSC) merchandise to satisfy the needs of legions of faithful readers. With over 180 million books in print in nineteen languages, the "Baby-Sitters Club" had obviously, as Sally Lodge noted in *Publishers Weekly,* "struck a resounding chord with preteen girls all over the world."

Though Martin bid adieu to her BSC readers with the final volume in the series, *Graduation Day,* she did not say good-bye to publishing. Martin has continued to write for middle-school readers, producing a number of highly regarded novels, including the Newbery Honor Book *A Corner of the Universe.* In 2007 she introduced a new series, "Main Street," which follows the adventures of two orphaned sisters adjusting to life in small-town Massachusetts. "I thought I would never write a series again," Martin admitted to *Chronogram* interviewer Nina Shengold.

Martin's success with the BSC series was a true publishing phenomenon. Millions of teens and pre-teens grew up with the antics and adventures of Kristy, Mary Anne, Stacey, and Claudia, and then found new friends with whom to identify with the addition of Dawn, Jessi, Mallory, and Abby to the club. The spin-off titles include over 130 of the original "Baby-Sitters Club" editions as well as 120 more titles in the "Little Sisters" series, twenty-five books in the "Mystery" series, a baker's dozen in the "BSC Friends Forever" series, another fifteen in the "California Diaries" series, and dozens of titles in super editions, not to mention twelve books in the "Kids in Ms. Colman's Class" series—a spin-off of a spin-off.

Contrary to the way most multi-volume children's book series are produced, Martin penned much of the main series herself, rising at 5:30 each morning to start her writing day and completing nearly two books each month. As the number of series grew, however, it was impossible for her to keep up with the flow of books, and other writers were brought on to help write some of the titles. But after fourteen years both Martin and her publisher, Scholastic, were ready to move on to new projects. Martin already began such a move in 1998 with non-series titles aimed at older juvenile readers and written in collaboration with both Paula Danziger and Laura Godwin.

Born in 1955, Martin grew up in Princeton, New Jersey, in a tight-knit family of parents and one younger sister, Jane. "I grew up in a very imaginative family," Martin once noted. "My mother was a preschool teacher and my father, an artist. Both liked fantasy and children's literature, so my world was one of circuses, animals, Beatrix Potter, *Winnie-the-Pooh, The Wizard of Oz,* elves and gnomes and fairies. It was a lot of fun,

***Cover of* The Doll People, *a fanciful story coauthored by Martin and Laura Godwin and featuring illustrations by Brian Selznick.*** (Illustration copyright © 2000 by Brian Selznick. Reprinted by permission of Hyperion Books for Children. All rights reserved.)

and it stayed with me. I'm often off in some other world, and all my daydreaming goes into my books." Martin was an enterprising child, running a library at one point and charging her friends overdue fines. She also was a babysitter; her oddest "client" was a snake which she had to tend one weekend. The author subsequently modeled many of the events and characters of her popular series from those of her youth, including best friend Beth Perkins who informs much of the character of Kristy, leader of the Baby-Sitters Club.

Reading and writing were among her favorite childhood activities. "I had always enjoyed writing, even as a child," Martin once commented. "Before I could write, I dictated stories to my mother. I took creative writing classes and that sort of thing as a kid, but I wanted desperately to be a teacher, so that was what I prepared for." At Smith College, Martin double-majored in psychology and early childhood education. Out of college, Martin taught elementary school for a year, working with students challenged by learning disabilities such as dyslexia. Soon, however, Martin realized that she wanted to work in children's books rather than in education. Martin cut her literary teeth first on the "other" side of the desk, working as an editorial assistant, then assistant editor, and finally editor and senior editor at publishers including Pocket Books, Scholastic, and Bantam, from 1978 to 1985.

Martin published her first book, *Bummer Summer,* in 1983. A popular story for young readers that focuses on a first overnight camp experience, this debut paved the way for further teen and pre-teen books such as *Inside Out, Stage Fright,* and *Me and Katie (the Pest).* "Some of my books are based on actual experiences," Martin once said, "others are based more on imagination, and memories of feelings. *Me and Katie (the Pest)* is loosely based on riding lessons I took in the third grade. . . . *With You and without You* is about the death of a parent. *Inside Out* was based on my work as a therapist for autistic children; it wasn't really something that happened in my childhood. *Stage Fright* is probably the most autobiographical of my books. I had terrible stage fright when I was a kid, . . . and that was the inspiration for that book."

Increasingly Martin was coming to see herself as a writer rather than an editor. In 1985, Jean Feiwel, editor-in-chief of the book group at Scholastic, came up with the idea of a mini-series about a babysitting cooperative, and she asked Martin to write four stories. When the inaugural title, *Kristy's Great Idea* quickly sold out its 30,000-copy first printing, Feiwel and Martin thought they might just be on to something. The subsequent books were popular enough that Feiwel suggested Martin write two more stories for the series. "Scholastic decided the books were doing exceptionally well when the sixth book of the series hit number one on the B. Dalton Juvenile Bestseller list, sometime in 1987," Martin once noted. "That was when we decided that we really had something. We stepped up the schedule to one book every other month and eventually one every month."

From the outset the series was a collaborative effort, and Martin and Feiwel determined early on that, while sometimes dealing with serious issues such as death, racism, divorce, and peer pressure, the series would not deal with other hot button issues such as child abuse, alcohol or drug abuse, or the death of a parent. Geared at readers aged eight through twelve, the "Baby-Sitters Club" series is intended as entertainment: light, breezy, and conversational. It has often been touted as the perfect introduction to books for reluctant readers. In all of the books, the characters remain the same age. "Two of them are permanently in the sixth grade, and the rest are permanently in the eighth grade," Martin once explained. "I can't let them grow up because the books come out too fast. I try not to allude to birthdays or summer vacations. . . . Otherwise the characters would soon be thirty-five." Martin was also careful to avoid slang and the use of time-fixers such as the names of current rock groups; the "Baby-Sitters Club" books take place in a time capsule, a sort of all-time and any-time.

Books in the series deal with the adventures of a group of girls who band together to operate a child-care business, and individual titles have explored a range of topics. *Kristy and the Secret of Susan* deals with an autistic savant, *Claudia and the Sad Good-bye* is about the death of a grandparent, *Kristy and the Snobs* relates the death of Kristy's pet, and *Jessi's Secret Language* finds Jessi baby-sitting for a deaf boy who communicates only in American Sign Language. Such books demonstrate Martin's own interests and proclivities. Her personal favorite among the books is *Kristy's Big Day.* Martin herself admitted in *Time* magazine that her books are "not great literature," but she has also noted that they "attract kids who are reluctant readers, if not children with definite learning problems such as dyslexia, and turn them into readers. And for kids who are already readers, I don't think there's anything wrong with picking up a series and reading it. I write the books as pure entertainment for myself as well as for the kids, but I am hoping that avid readers who are reading series are reading other things as well, and I also hope that reluctant readers who get hooked on reading through series reading, whether it's the 'Baby-Sitters Club' or another series, will then 'graduate' to other kinds of books."

Over the years, Martin and her editors added new series that would explore different age levels and that might update and enliven the series with a more modern approach. The last such addition was the "Baby-Sitters Club Friends Forever" series, ending with a title in a letters-and-journal-entries format in which the original four members of the club are left to carry on the traditions of their enterprise. The "California Diaries" series, inaugurated in 1997, features Dawn, one of the original baby-sitters, who moves to the West Coast to be with one of her divorced parents full-time. That series is, as the name implies, told in diary format. The eighth-grade girls in this series are involved in somewhat edgier and more sophisticated activities than those found in the original "Baby-Sitters Club" books.

All good things, however, come to an end, and the BSC finally called it a day with *Graduation Day.* Martin was prescient about such a demise. She once noted that "as demographics and tastes change, kids do, too, and maybe in a few years they will find that they want pure fantasy and escape, like the C.S. Lewis books. That might signal the end of the 'Baby-Sitters Club'; I can't really think of the BSC characters traveling to an imaginary kingdom or another planet."

Martin continued publishing hardcover novels during the years she was churning out the BSC. One of her personal favorites of these is *Ten Kids, No Pets,* about the boisterous Rosso family. In a sequel to that book, *Eleven Kids, One Summer,* the Rossos spend the summer on New York's Fire Island. Each chapter puts the lens on the activities of one of the "amiable Rosso offspring," according to a *Publishers Weekly* reviewer, and these young characters range in age from six months to fifteen years. There is a movie being filmed on the island with a handsome star for the eldest Rosso, Abbie, to form a friendship with; there is a house that the sensitive Candy thinks is haunted; and there are plenty of seashells for enterprising Woody to paint and then sell.

"Martin . . . knows well what pleases young readers," the same reviewer concluded, "and this novel is filled with characters, escapades and dialogue that will do just that."

Humor takes center stage in Martin's picture book, *Leo the Magnificat,* a story based on an actual cat who adopted an entire church congregation. The cat in question sauntered into the yard of a Louisville, Kentucky, church one Sunday and remained there for the next twelve years. Martin, in her book, shows how this cat worms its way into the hearts of the entire congregation and surrounding neighborhood, insinuating itself into events from potlucks to church services. When Leo the cat finally passes on, he is buried in the church garden. A reviewer for *Publishers Weekly* dubbed *Leo the Magnificat* a "charmer like its feline hero," and further noted that Martin is a "pro at age-appropriate writing." In *Booklist,* Stephanie Zvirin commented that "Martin's picture book reads just like what it is—a story drawn from life," and concluded that this "gently humorous, poignant (never sentimental)" tale "won't disappoint."

In 1998 Martin teamed up with long-time friend and fellow children's book author, Paula Danziger, to write *P.S. Longer Letter Later.* In this book the two authors, who specialize in writing for young girls, blend their disparate writing styles to create an epistolary novel told from two points of view. When two seventh-grade girls, Elizabeth and Tara*Starr, are separated by a family move, they promise to maintain their friendship through letters. The two girls are a study in contrasts: Tara*Starr is the type to put purple streaks in her hair, to joke incessantly and to write scathingly funny columns for the school paper while staid Elizabeth is into cross-stitching and poetry, and would never think of piercing her ears, let alone her nose. Suddenly Tara*Starr's free-spirited parents become responsible, begin holding regular jobs, think about having another baby, and move to Ohio. Outrageous, flamboyant, creative Tara*Starr—whose letters are written by Danziger—cannot believe the overnight change and subsequently has a hard time adjusting to a new school and finding new friends. Meanwhile the more reserved, introspective, and affluent Elizabeth—her letters written by Martin—undergoes her own transformations. Her father loses his job, turns to alcohol, and then abandons the family as it is on the verge of downsizing to life in a small apartment. In letters that are at once humorous and painful, the two girls maintain their long-distance friendship. They survive tiffs and personal crises and even silence when one or the other fails to write for a time.

"If Danziger and Martin had been childhood pen pals," commented a reviewer for *Publishers Weekly,* "their correspondence might have read much like this strikingly insightful epistolary novel." The same writer further observed of *P.S. Longer Letter Later* that the "venerable authors here do a splendid job of creating a story based on . . . letters." *Booklist* contributor Hazel Rochman felt "the immediacy of the letters format will draw kids in, especially as the tension mounts in Elizabeth's home and her friend replies with humor and heartfelt sympathy." Lynda Drill Comerford, writing in *Publishers Weekly,* commented that the book, "a celebration of friendship, ends on a happy note, with characters overcoming personal conflicts and forgiving each other's shortcomings." Comerford concluded, "For characters and authors alike, it represents the unique meshing of two creative, witty and very different personalities." Renee Steinberg, reviewing the novel in *School Library Journal,* observed that the "authenticity of the well-drawn characters gives life and vitality to the story" and concluded that readers "will thoroughly enjoy this fast-paced story."

In concluding a review of *P.S. Longer Letter Later,* the *Publishers Weekly* writer wished for more: "Given Danziger and Martin's penchant for continuing story lines, readers can only hope that this will be an ongoing correspondence." In 2000 such a hope became a reality with the publication of *Snail Mail No More,* a continuation of Elizabeth and Tara*Starr's correspondence, this time by e-mail. *Booklist* critic Michael Cart dubbed the pair an "epistolary odd couple," and noted that in *Snail Mail No More* "it's business as usual." With her mother pregnant, Tara*Starr is not so sure she wants to be a sister. Meanwhile, Elizabeth's wayward father has shown up again with less-than-positive results. The girls now turn thirteen, and make new friends, including boys. The green-eyed monster pops up between the two for a time, but even jealousy is vanquished by their strong friendship. "Seasoned pros Danziger and Martin couldn't write a dull book if they tried," noted Cart, "and this one . . . is a funny, thought-provoking page-turner that will delight readers and leave them ready for more messages." While *School Library Journal* reviewer Linda Bindner found that *Snail Mail No More* "lacks the energy and freshness" of *P.S. Longer Letter Later,* she also commented that "fans will find it to be an enjoyable sequel." A contributor for *Publishers Weekly* dubbed *Snail Mail No More* a "funny and poignant sequel" and concluded that the "two characters approach life differently enough that there will likely be a response or suggestion that resonates with every reader, and both heroines share one important trait: they are all heart."

Teaming up with Laura Godwin, Martin has also written *The Doll People,* the story of culture clash between members of a Victorian doll household who meet their new, plastic neighbors, the Funcrafts. The staid Victorian world of the doll people is turned upside down by the meeting. The Funcrafts are the birthday present of the younger sister of Kate Palmer, current owner of the Victorian dollhouse and its occupants. Tiffany, the Funcraft doll, is the same age as Annabelle, of the Victorian dollhouse, and the two opposites oddly enough hit it off as they join forces to hunt for the missing Auntie Sarah doll, a longtime resident of the Victorian dollhouse. Kathie Meizner, writing in *School Library Journal,* commented that a "lighthearted touch and a dash of drama make this a satisfying read," while a writer for

*Publishers Weekly* concluded that doll lovers "may well approach their imaginative play with renewed enthusiasm and a sense of wonder after reading this fun-filled adventure."

In a sequel, *The Meanest Doll in the World,* Annabelle and Tiffany stow away in their owner's backpack and inadvertently wind up at the home of Kate's classmate, where they encounter the diabolical Princess Mimi doll. After Annabelle and Tiffany help the household dolls stand up to Mimi, she makes her way back to the Palmers' and threatens the sanctity of the Victorian doll world. The "truly evil nemesis will keep the pages turning," noted *School Library Journal* contributor Eva Mitnick, and Martha V. Parravano stated that the story's "broad humor and action balance with smaller, more personal dramas" in her *Horn Book* review.

Set in the rural South during the 1960s, *Belle Teal* centers on a spunky fifth-grade girl and her experiences in an integrated classroom. When the other white children taunt Darryl, their new African-American schoolmate, Belle reacts with sensitivity, offering her friendship to the boy. Martin's "portrayal of integration in a small school is low key yet quite effective," noted Denise Wilms in *Booklist.* "The writing is graceful and easy, with Belle Teal's narration distinctly and convincingly evoked," Roger Sutton wrote *Horn Book,* while a contributor in *Publishers Weekly* concluded that the youngster's "observations and realizations provide an eye-opening introduction to social and personal injustice."

Martin's award-winning *A Corner of the Universe* was inspired by the tragic story of her Uncle Stephen, her mother's younger brother. As the author told Lynda Brill Comerford in *Publishers Weekly,* "He was diagnosed with schizophrenia at a young age, and he killed himself when he was 23, before my parents met. I remember that what surprised me more than the existence of this uncle and the story behind him was the fact that he had been kept a secret." In the novel, twelve-year-old Hattie Owen meets her Uncle Adam, who suffers from a mental illness, for the first time after he returns to the family's boarding house. Adam's exuberant personality helps shy Hattie come out of her shell, until his problems prove more than she can handle. According to *Kliatt* reviewer Paula Rohrlick, Martin "offers a sympathetic portrait of the mentally ill in this sensitive, tender coming-of-age tale."

Eleven-year-old Flora Northrup and her younger sister, Ruby, are the featured characters in Martin's "Main Street" novels, set in the quiet New England town of Camden Falls. "Though the New England façades of Camden Falls' shops and row houses seem Norman Rockwell timeless," wrote Shengold, "Martin is careful to fill their interiors with lives that are not picture-perfect." After their parents are killed in a car accident, the Northrup girls come to live with their grandmother, Min, who owns a fabric store in town. As the sisters settle into their new environment, they meet a host of intriguing neighbors, including an elderly man caring for his wife, a rebellious teen, and a boy with Down syndrome. Reviewing the series opener, *Welcome to Camden Falls, Booklist* critic Ilene Cooper observed that "Martin's easy style, appealing characters, and obvious love of place will keep readers going." Writing in *School Library Journal,* Kathryn Kosiorek remarked that the "Main Street" books will "appeal to readers more interested in characters and values than true action and adventure."

In addition to writing, Martin is also very active in supporting various community activities. She is co-founder of the Lisa Novak Community Libraries, and founder of the Ann M. Martin Foundation, which benefits children, education and literacy programs, and homeless people and animals. Even without the 'Baby-Sitters Club' on the back burner, it is clear that Martin will not be changing her early rising habits. "I love to feel that every week is full of a lot of different kinds of things," she told Lodge. "I've always worked better when I'm working on many things at one time."

## Biographical and Critical Sources

*BOOKS*

Kjelle, Marylou Morano, *Ann M. Martin,* foreword by Kyle Zimmer, Chelsea House Publishers (Philadelphia, PA), 2005.

*PERIODICALS*

*Booklist,* September 1, 1996, Stephanie Zvirin, review of *Leo the Magnificat,* p. 143; June 1, 1998, Hazel Rochman, review of *P.S. Longer Letter Later,* p. 1765; March 15, 2000, Michael Cart, review of *Snail Mail No More,* p. 1376; August, 2000, Ilene Cooper, review of *The Doll People,* p. 2140; October 1, 2001, Denise Wilms, review of *Belle Teal,* p. 319; December 1, 2002, Ilene Cooper, review of *A Corner of the Universe,* p. 659; November 15, 2005, Hazel Rochman, review of *Friends: Stories about New Friends, Old Friends, and Unexpectedly True Friends,* p. 45; December 1, 2005, Jennifer Mattson, review of *A Dog's Life: The Autobiography of a Stray,* p. 49; August, 2007, Ilene Cooper, review of *Welcome to Camden Falls* and *Needle and Thread,* p. 76.

*Horn Book,* January-February, 2002, Roger Sutton, review of *Belle Teal,* p. 81; November-December, 2003, Martha V. Parravano, review of *The Meanest Doll in the World,* p. 751; November-December, 2004, Susan Dove Lempke, review of *Here Today,* p. 712.

*Kliatt,* November, 2002, Paula Rohrlick, review of *A Corner of the Universe,* p. 12; January, 2007, Jennifer Feigelman, review of *The Truth about Stacey,* p. 32.

*People Weekly,* August 21, 1989, Kristin McMurran, "Ann Martin Stirs up a Tiny Tempest in Preteen Land with Her Bestselling 'Baby-Sitters Club,'" pp. 55-56.

*Publishers Weekly,* August 23, 1991, review of *Eleven Kids, One Summer,* p. 62; September 2, 1996, review of *Leo the Magnificat,* p. 131; September 1, 1997,

Sally Lodge, "Another Busy Season for Ann M. Martin," pp. 31-32; February 16, 1998, review of *P.S. Longer Letter Later,* p. 212; March 9, 1998, Lynda Drill Comerford, "A True Test of Friendship," p. 26; June 7, 1999, review of *P.S. Longer Letter Later,* p. 53; January 10, 2000, review of *Snail Mail No More,* p. 68; July 3, 2000, review of *The Doll People,* p. 71; September 32, 2001, review of *Belle Teal,* p. 88; July 22, 2002, Lynda Brill Comerford, "PW talks with Ann M. Martin," p. 181; April 16, 2007, review of *Welcome to Camden Falls,* p. 51.

*St. Louis Post-Dispatch* (St. Louis, MO), May 6, 2007, Sarah Bryan Miller, "'Baby-Sitters Club' Creator Moves to 'Main Street,'" p. F11.

*School Library Journal,* May, 1998, Renee Steinberg, review of *P.S. Longer Letter Later,* p. 141; March, 2000, Linda Bindner, review of *Snail Mail No More,* p. 234; November, 2000, Kathie Meizner, review of *The Doll People,* p. 128; October, 2003, Eva Mitnick, review of *The Meanest Doll in the World,* p. 130; November, 2005, Laura Scott, review of *A Dog's Life,* p. 142; January, 2006, Nancy P. Reeder, review of *Friends,* p. 138; July, 2006, Ronnie Gordon, review of *Kristy's Great Idea,* p. 128; March, 2007, Sadie Mattox, review of *The Truth about Stacey,* p. 238; August, 2007, Kathryn Kosiorek, reviews of *Welcome to Camden Falls* and *Needle and Thread,* p. 120.

*Time,* June 11, 1990, "Wake-up Call," p. 75.

*ONLINE*

*Chronogram Web site,* http://www.chronogram.com/ (June 26, 2008), Nina Shergold, "Paperback Writer: Ann M. Martin Lifts the Corners."

*Scholastic Web site,* http://www.scholastic.com/annmartin/ (August 15, 2008), "Ann M. Martin."

*OTHER*

*Good Conversation!: A Talk with Ann M. Martin* (video), Tim Podell Productions, 2005.*

* * *

# MARTINEZ, Arturo O. 1933-

## Personal
Born 1933, in TX; son of farmers.

## Addresses
*Home*—Hoboken, NJ.

## Career
Journalist, critic, columnist, editor, and author.

## Awards, Honors
Best Children's Book honor, Texas Institute of Letters, 2007, and Friends of the Austin Public Library Award for Best Children's Book, 2008, both for *Pedrito's World.*

## Writings

*Pedrito's World,* Texas Tech University Press (Lubbock, TX), 2007.

## Biographical and Critical Sources

*PERIODICALS*

*Booklist,* May 1, 2007, Carolyn Phelan, review of *Pedrito's World,* p. 91.

*Bulletin of the Center for Children's Books,* July-August, 2007, Karen Coats, review of *Pedrito's World,* p. 476.*

* * *

# MATSUOKA, Mei 1981-

## Personal
Born March 27, 1981, in Tokyo, Japan; immigrated to England, 1992. *Education:* Kingston University (UK), B.A. (illustration and animation; with honors). *Hobbies and other interests:* Travel, snowboarding, tortoises, collecting podgy characters.

## Addresses
*Home and office*—Buckingham, England; Tokyo, Japan. *Agent*—United Agents, 12-26 Lexington St., London W1F 0LE, England. *E-mail*—meiski@hotmail.com.

## Career
Illustrator and animator.

## Member
Association of Illustrators.

## Awards, Honors
Azora Environmental Picture Book Competition winner, 2004, for *Ten-san, Kame-san, and Muri-san Go on a Journey;* Portsmouth Children's Book Award, 2007, for *Burger Boy.*

## Writings

*SELF-ILLUSTRATED*

*Ten-san, Kame-san, and Muri-san Go on a Journey,* ANA (Japan), 2005.

*Footprints in the Snow,* Andersen Press (London, England), 2007, Henry Holt (New York, NY), 2008.

*ILLUSTRATOR*

Alan Durant, *Burger Boy,* Andersen (London, England), 2005, Clarion (New York, NY), 2006.

Julia Hubery, *Raffi's Surprise,* Simon & Schuster UK (London, England), 2006, published as *A Friend for All Seasons,* Atheneum Books for Young Readers (New York, NY), 2007.

Boris von Smercek and Shimizu Noriko, *Hannibals Marchen,* Shufunotomo (Japan), 2006.

Carl Norac, *Tell Me a Story, Mummy,* Macmillan (London, England), 2007.

***Mei Matsuoka's gentle, softly toned illustrations are a highlight of* A Friend for All Seasons, *a picture book featuring a text by Julia Hubery.***

## Sidelights

Born in Tokyo, Japan, and now making her home in England, Mei Matsuoka is an illustrator and animator whose naive, mixed-media images have appeared in picture books by Julia Hubery, Alan Durant, and Carl Norac. In addition to her work creating illustrations for others, Matsuoka has also created the original picture book *Footprints in the Snow,* which finds a stock big-and-bad story-book villain, Wolf, hoping to rewrite his much-maligned character by penning a story in which the wolf is nice rather than scary.

Matsuoka's distinctive mixed-media art was first seen in *Burger Boy,* a picture-book story by Durant that introduces the hamburger-loving Benny. In fact, Benny eats hamburgers exclusively, much to the consternation of his mother. When the boy actually turns into a hamburger—because, after all, you are what you eat—Durant's amusing tale takes off into a denouement guaranteed to resonate with selective eaters. Calling *Burger Boy* "a tasty and off-kilter romp," a *Kirkus Reviews* writer noted that the book is "embellished with eventful illustrations that are brimming with delightful comic details." In *Booklist* Julie Cummins wrote that Matsuoka's "cartoonlike collage illustrations are the perfect compliment for this cautionary tale," and in *School Library Journal* Rita Hunt Smith concluded that *Burger Boy* is a "rollicking British import" in which the "simple lines and lively colors of the [artist's] acrylic and colored-pencil illustrations add to the kid appeal."

Another illustration project found Matsuoka creating art for Julia Hubery's *A Friend for All Season* (published in England as *Raffi's Surprise*), in which a young raccoon becomes concerned when the tree in which he makes his home, Father Oak, begins to drop its leaves. As the seasons run their course, the raccoon, his squirrel friend, and the reader all learn about the cycle of a year by watching the ongoing transformation of the old tree and its woodsy surroundings, Hubery's gentle story is set off by Matsuoka's "large, stylized" mixed-media pictures that "reflect the changing seasons," according to *School Library Journal* critic Marianne Saccardi. In *Kirkus Reviews,* a critic noted in particular the illustrator's use of "a warm palette of earth tones," dubbing *A Friend for All Seasons* "a gentle tale with a nifty lesson."

Matsuoka told *SATA:* "I love what I get to do as an illustrator and enjoy the challenges of each new picture book. Having grown up in both the UK and Japan, I think that these influences can be seen strongly in my work. I also grew to love the darker side of East European art, which I discovered while studying at Kingston University."

## Biographical and Critical Sources

*PERIODICALS*

*Booklist,* November 15, 2006, Julie Cummins, review of *Burger Boy,* p. 53; July 1, 2007, Hazel Rochman, review of *A Friend for All Seasons,* p. 65.

*Kirkus Reviews,* October 1, 2006, review of *Burger Boy,* p. 1013; July 15, 2007, review of *A Friend for All Seasons.*

*Publishers Weekly,* September 4, 2006, review of *Burger Boy,* p. 66.

*School Library Journal,* October, 2006, Rita Hunt Smith, review of *Burger Boy,* p. 109; August, 2007, Marianne Saccardi, review of *A Friend for All Seasons,* p. 82.

*ONLINE*

*Mei Matsuoka Home Page,* http://www.meimatsuoka.com (August 5, 2008).

* * *

# MAZER, Anne 1953-

## Personal

Born April 2, 1953, in Schenectady, NY; daughter of Harry (a writer) and Norma (a writer) Mazer; children: Max and Mollie Futterman. *Education:* Attended State University of New York at Binghamton, Syracuse University, and University of Paris, Sorbonne.

## Addresses

*Home*—Ithaca, NY. *Agent*—Elaine Markson, Elaine Markson Literary Agency, 44 Greenwich Ave., New York, NY 10011.

## Career

Freelance writer, 1982—. Also worked variously as an au pair, a bank teller, a pill bottle labeler, a receptionist, an English tutor, and an administrative assistant.

## Member

Authors Guild, Authors League of America.

## Awards, Honors

Keystone to Reading Book Award for books for younger children, 1992, ABC Children's Choice Award, Reading Rainbow Feature Selection, and Pick of the Lists, American Booksellers Association, all for *The Salamander Room;* Editor's Choice Award, *Booklist,* 1992, for *Moose Street;* Notable Book designation, American Library Association (ALA), 1993, and Notable Children's Trade Book in the Field of Social Studies citation, National Council for the Social Studies/Children's Book Council, both for *The Oxboy;* finalist, *Hungry Mind* Best Young-Adult Book designation, 1993, and Best Book for the Teen Age selection, New York Public Library, both for *America Street: A Multicultural Anthology of Stories;* Best Book for Teens citation, ALA, 1998, Books for the Teen Age selection, New York Public Library, and Popular Paperbacks for Young Adults selection, ALA, 2000, all for *Working Days: Stories about Teenagers and Work.*

## Writings

*Watch Me,* illustrated by Stacey Schuett, Knopf (New York, NY), 1990.

*The Yellow Button,* illustrated by Judy Pedersen, Knopf (New York, NY), 1990.

*The Salamander Room,* illustrated by Steve Johnson, Knopf (New York, NY), 1991.

*Moose Street,* Knopf (New York, NY), 1992.

*The Oxboy,* Knopf (New York, NY), 1993.

(Editor) *America Street: A Multicultural Anthology of Stories,* Persea Books (New York, NY), 1993.

*The Accidental Witch,* Hyperion (New York, NY), 1995.

(Editor) *Going Where I'm Coming From: Memoirs of American Youth,* Persea Books (New York, NY), 1995.

*Goldfish Charlie and the Case of the Missing Planet,* illustrated by Jerry Harston, Troll Communications (Mahwah, NJ), 1996.

*A Sliver of Glass and Other Uncommon Tales,* Hyperion (New York, NY), 1996.

(Editor) *Working Days: Stories about Teenagers and Work,* Persea Books (New York, NY), 1997.

(Editor) *A Walk in My World: International Short Stories about Youth,* Persea Books (New York, NY), 1998.

*The Fixits,* illustrated by Paul Meisel, Hyperion (New York, NY), 1998.

*The No-Nothings and Their Baby,* illustrated by Ross Collins, Arthur A. Levine Books (New York, NY), 2000.

*"THE AMAZING DAYS OF ABBY HAYES" SERIES*

*Every Cloud Has a Silver Lining,* Scholastic (New York, NY), 2000.

*The Declaration of Independence,* Scholastic (New York, NY), 2000.

*Reach for the Stars,* Scholastic (New York, NY), 2000.

*Have Wheels, Will Travel,* Scholastic (New York, NY), 2001.

*Look before You Leap,* Scholastic (New York, NY), 2001.

*The Pen Is Mightier than the Sword,* Scholastic (New York, NY), 2001.

*Two Heads Are Better than One,* Scholastic (New York, NY), 2002.

*The More, the Merrier,* Scholastic (New York, NY), 2002.

*Out of Sight, Out of Mind,* Scholastic (New York, NY), 2002.

*Everything New under the Sun,* Scholastic (New York, NY), 2003.

*Too Close for Comfort,* Scholastic (New York, NY), 2003.

*Good Things Come in Small Packages,* Scholastic (New York, NY), 2003.

*Some Things Never Change,* Scholastic (New York, NY), 2004.

*The Best Is Yet to Come,* Scholastic (New York, NY), 2004.

*Knowledge Is Power,* Scholastic (New York, NY), 2004.

*It's Music to My Ears,* Scholastic (New York, NY), 2005.

*Now You See It, Now You Don't,* Scholastic (New York, NY), 2005.

*That's the Way the Cookie Crumbles,* Scholastic (New York, NY), 2005.

*Home Is Where the Heart Is,* Scholastic (New York, NY), 2006.

*"SISTER MAGIC" SERIES*

*Violet Makes a Splash,* illustrated by Bill Brown, Scholastic (New York, NY), 2007.

*The Trouble with Violet,* illustrated by Bill Brown, Scholastic (New York, NY), 2007.

*Mabel Makes the Grade,* illustrated by Bill Brown, Scholastic (New York, NY), 2008.

## Sidelights

Raised in a family of children's book authors, Anne Mazer has made her own mark on the field of children's literature, writing several highly praised picture books and young-adult novels. "Mazer writes with such clarity and perception, it can sometimes take your breath away, the same way an unexpected punch does," noted *Booklist* contributor Ilene Cooper of Mazer's young-adult novel, *Moose Street.* Other titles to Mazer's credit include the picture books *The Salamander Room* and *The Fixits* as well as the works in "The Amazing Days of Abby Hayes" series. She has also compiled several anthologies of short fiction for teens that showcase diversity of both socio-economic culture and ethnic heritage.

Mazer has loved books ever since she can remember. As she once told *SATA:* "From the earliest age, I would devour anything that could be read—from comic books to cereal boxes to encyclopedias. I loved boys' books, girls' books, mysteries, adventures, humor, and historical fiction. As a young girl, I stood in front of the shelves of books that lined our walls, and hungrily pulled out volumes. The same scene was repeated countless times in libraries, where I would wander among the stacks almost intoxicated by so many books. When I got older, I crept into my closet late at night, where I stuffed towels under the door and read until well past midnight."

As a teen, Mazer's love of books far surpassed her love of school. She admitted to leaving school after attendance was taken in homeroom and walking the four miles to her town library to spend the day reading. Even though her parents were both published writers by this time, Mazer never considered making the transition from avid reader to writer. "My love of books was private," she recalled.

Following her graduation from high school, Mazer spent several years in Paris where she studied French language and literature and began to write. Her first book, an novel for young adults set in Paris, was never published. After her son was born, she began to write for younger children, and by 1987 had completed three picture books. Her first book, *Watch Me,* was released in 1990.

*Watch Me* was Mazer's reaction to watching her then-two-year-old son playing on her bed. "'Look at me, Mom! Look at me!,'" Mazer recalled him saying. "I wrote the words on my blank piece of paper. In a few minutes 'look at me' had changed to 'watch me,' and I was off." Despite its simple text, Mazer reworked each verse of *Watch Me* numerous times before she felt she had gotten it right. "Some of the verses came out smoothly and easily, but most were the result of hours of trial and error," she recalled. "The phrase 'watch me' seemed such a universal theme for small children that I couldn't believe half a dozen people hadn't thought of it already."

Unlike *Watch Me, The Yellow Button* grew easily out of the author's childhood memories. "When I was a small child, I often tried to encompass infinity within my own mind," Mazer explained. "I would dazzle myself with visions of unlimited space, and then return to my room, my self, my own small, but somehow newly expanded and enlivened reality. This mental game—a kind of contemplation really—used to give me great pleasure. One night I was sitting at the typewriter, when a picture popped into my mind of a button sitting in a pocket. As I wrote down the words, describing the picture I clearly saw, one image seemed to flow from another. In a very short time, the book was written—and I made few changes in it.

*Cover of Anne Mazer's elementary-grade novel* **Mabel Makes the Grade,** *part of the "Sister Magic" series featuring artwork by Bill Brown.* (Illustration copyright © 2007 by Scholastic, Inc. Reprinted by permission.)

"My third book, *The Salamander Room,* was triggered by a remark a little boy made while we were on a nature hike," explained Mazer. "I no longer remember the original conversation, but the boy wanted to bring a salamander home." From the boy's comment, Mazer developed the story of a boy named Brian who is determined to bring home a new pet salamander. Despite his mother's practical questions, like "Where will the salamander sleep?," "Brian's cozy bedroom is gradually transformed into a dark green forest that overflows the pages" as he imagines his pet's ideal home, according to *School Library Journal* contributor Louise L. Sherman. Praising both the story and its illustrations, a *Publishers Weekly* reviewer commented that "Mazer's text offers fitting tribute to a child's perseverance and imagination."

In *The Fixits* a pair of clumsy repair experts wreak havoc on an unsuspecting household. When Augusta and her brother accidentally crack their mother's favorite plate, Tom and Ed Fixit promptly arrive to offer their services. The cheerful duo only serves to make matters worse, and before long the entire house is in shambles. *Booklist* contributor Stephanie Zvirin praised the "wacky, energetic story," and a *Publishers Weekly* contributor stated that Mazer's "boisterous book will have readers wincing and giggling by turns."

A ridiculously dimwitted couple takes charge of a newborn in *The No-Nothings and Their Baby,* another humorous work by Mazer. Upon meeting their daughter, Betty, Bertram, and Doriana No-Nothing attempt to diaper her head, take a swig from her bottle, and place her in the tub for an upcoming "baby shower." After a particularly wild stroller ride, young Betty does the responsible thing and phones for help. Mazer's "deadpan dialogue sets up silly sight gags that reveal the adult No-Nothings' blithe ignorance and their baby's unforeseen smarts," a critic in *Publishers Weekly* remarked.

In addition to picture books, Mazer has written several novels for older readers. In *Moose Street,* eleven-year-old Lena Rosen feels like a loner in her neighborhood because she is the only Jewish child on the block. Her isolation provides her with a different perspective on the people around her, and she shares her heightened sensitivity to people's secret side through a series of interrelated vignettes. Cooper commended Mazer for portraying the "exquisite torture Lena feels when she's made to suffer for a religion she barely believes in, or when she's asked to participate in the torture adolescents excel at, picking on the most vulnerable child around." In another novel, *The Accidental Witch,* Mazer assembles "an imaginative, action-packed plot and a fine cast of characters" in a "light, fun-filled fantasy," according to *Booklist* contributor Lauren Peterson. Fifth-grader Phoebe discovers that she has gained the witch-like powers she always wanted but cannot quite figure out how to focus them in a novel that Anne Connor described in *School Library Journal* as "a lively fantasy [that] creates a world very much like our own," where Phoebe "fulfills her dream through persistence and good will."

In *The Oxboy,* Mazer weaves together fantasy and social commentary to create a world in which animals and humans can marry. The "mixed-bloods" of these unions—which are outlawed by the intolerant humans—must attempt to pass as wholly human because the offspring of such unions, if discovered, are executed. Within this world, a boy whose disguised father is actually a noble ox refuses to oppress other, more obvious mixed-bloods, even though his actions will result in his imprisonment. Mazer's "allegorical world is compelling," noted a *Kirkus Reviews* critic, who found *The Oxboy* to be a "provocative, unusually imaginative tale." According to *Booklist* contributor Hazel Rochman, "Mazer writes with poetic restraint about the glory of pushing boundaries to understand 'the language of stones and stars and moss and roses.'"

"The Amazing Days of Abby Hayes" series, designed to appeal to middle-grade readers, features a spunky fifth-grader who often feels overshadowed by her high-performing siblings. In *Every Cloud Has a Silver Lining* Abby uses a journal to chronicle her misguided efforts to make the soccer team, overlooking her true talent for writing. "Mazer injects some moments of sophisticated, wry humor," observed a reviewer in *Publishers Weekly. Two Heads Are Better than One* centers on Abby's relationship with her science-fair partner, and in *Good Things Come in Small Packages,* she must find a way to salvage a disastrous school project.

In addition to her writing, Mazer has acted on her desire to promote tolerance of cultural differences among young people by editing such anthologies as *Working Days: Stories about Teenagers and Work.* In *A Sliver of Glass and Other Uncommon Tales,* she presents eleven fantasy and horror stories, including a retelling of the King Midas myth. "The best of these stories are told with fine economy," noted Hazel Rochman in *Booklist. Working Days* features tales by such noted young-adult authors as Marilyn Sachs, Victor Martinez, and Graham Salisbury. The collection "dynamically conveys the joys, traumas and discoveries of impressionable teens taking their first leap toward adulthood," a critic in *Publishers Weekly* remarked. In *A Walk in My World: International Short Stories about Youth,* "Mazer invites readers to examine and ponder pearls of wisdom collected from the intimate corners of five continents," observed a *Publishers Weekly* reviewer. The anthology contains stories from Egyptian novelist Naguib Mahfouz, Irish author Frank O'Connor, and Japanese Nobel laureate Yasunari Kawabata.

Although Mazer has expanded her works beyond picture books in recent years, she still respects picture books as a medium far more complicated than it might seem to the casual reader. "Though the text has to be done with the utmost simplicity, I find that I can express many complex and profound emotions such as joy, love and contentment. I also love the spareness of the picture book. There is no waste in a good picture book. Each word counts and each word must be placed exactly right."

## Biographical and Critical Sources

*PERIODICALS*

*Booklist,* November 1, 1992, Ilene Cooper, review of *Moose Street,* p. 510; November 1, 1993, Hazel Rochman, review of *The Oxboy,* p. 523; November 1, 1995, Lauren Peterson, review of *The Accidental Witch,* p. 473; September 15, 1996, Hazel Rochman, review of *A Sliver of Glass and Other Uncommon Tales,* p. 242; July, 1997, Stephanie Zvirin, review of *Working Days: Stories about Teenagers at Work,* p. 1811; January 1, 1999, Hazel Rochman, review of *A Walk in My World: International Short Stories about Youth,* p. 857; April 1, 1999, Stephanie Zvirin, review of *The Fixits,* p. 1421; September 1, 2007, Suzanne Harold, review of *The Trouble with Violet,* p. 118.

*Horn Book,* November-December, 1997, Roger Sutton, review of *Working Days,* p. 682.

*Kirkus Reviews,* December 1, 1993, review of *The Oxboy,* p. 1526.

*Publishers Weekly,* January 11, 1991, review of *The Salamander Room,* p. 101; May 26, 1997, review of *Working Days,* p. 86; December 21, 1998, review of *A Walk In My World,* p. 69; March 8, 1999, review of *The Fixits,* p. 67; July 10, 2000, review of *Every Cloud Has a Silver Lining,* p. 63; September 25, 2000, review of *The No-Nothings and Their Baby,* p. 116.

*School Library Journal,* April, 1991, Louise L. Sherman, review of *The Salamander Room,* p. 100; January, 1996, Anne Connor, review of *The Accidental Witch,* p. 110; November, 2000, Karen James, review of *The No-Nothings and Their Baby,* p. 128; September, 2007, Debbie Whitbeck, review of *The Trouble with Violet,* p. 172.

*ONLINE*

*Anne Mazer Home Page,* http://www.amazingmazer.com (August 15, 2008).

*Scholastic Web site,* http://www2.scholastic.com/ (August 15, 2008), "Anne Mazer."*

* * *

## McCULLOCH, Sarah
## See URE, Jean

* * *

## McDANIELS, Preston 1952-

### Personal

Born 1952.

## Addresses

*Home and office*—Aurora, NE.

## Career

Illustrator.

## Writings

*SELF-ILLUSTRATED*

*A Perfect Snowman,* Simon & Schuster (New York, NY), 2007.

*ILLUSTRATOR*

Jaroslav J. Vajda, *God of the Sparrow,* Morehouse Pub. (Harrisburg, PA), 1999.

Jennie Bishop, *The Princess and the Kiss: A Story of God's Gift of Purity,* Warner Press (Anderson, IN), 1999.

Cecil Frances Alexander, *All Things Bright and Beautiful,* Morehouse Pub. (Harrisburg, PA), 2000.

Caroline Kim Hatton, *Veiro and Philippe,* Front Street (Chicago, IL), 2001.

Sabine Baring-Gould, *Now the Day Is Over,* Morehouse Pub. (Harrisburg, PA), 2001.

Christopher Webber, *Praise the Lord, My Soul: Psalm 104 for Children,* Morehouse Pub. (Harrisburg, PA), 2002.

Cynthia Rylant, *The Lighthouse Family: The Storm,* Simon & Schuster Books for Young Readers (New York, NY), 2002.

Herbert F. Brokering, *Earth and All Stars,* Morehouse Pub. (Harrisburg, PA), 2002.

Cynthia Rylant, *The Lighthouse Family: The Whale,* Simon & Schuster Books for Young Readers (New York, NY), 2003.

Bryce Milligan, *The Prince of Ireland and the Three Magic Stallions,* Holiday House (New York, NY), 2003.

Christopher Webber, *Shout for Joy and Sing!: Psalm 65 for Children,* Morehouse Pub. (Harrisburg, PA), 2003.

Cynthia Rylant, *The Lighthouse Family: The Eagle,* Simon & Schuster Books for Young Readers (New York, NY), 2004.

John W. Stewig, *Whuppity Stoorie,* Holiday House (New York, NY), 2004.

Jennie Bishop, *The Squire and the Scroll: A Tale of the Rewards of a Pure Heart,* Warner Press (Anderson, IN), 2004.

Christopher Webber, *The Lord Is My Shepherd: Psalm 23 for Children,* Morehouse Pub. (Harrisburg, PA), 2004.

Cynthia Rylant, *The Lighthouse Family: The Octopus,* Simon & Schuster Books for Young Readers (New York, NY), 2005.

Cynthia Rylant, *The Lighthouse Family: The Turtle,* Simon & Schuster Books for Young Readers (New York, NY), 2005.

Frances O'Roark Dowell, *Phineas L. MacGuire . . . Erupts!,* Atheneum Books for Young Readers (New York, NY), 2006.

Frances O'Roark Dowell, *Phineas L. MacGuire . . . Gets Slimed!,* Atheneum Books for Young Readers (New York, NY), 2007.

Frances O'Roark Dowell, *Phineas L. MacGuire . . . Blasts Off!,* Atheneum Books for Young Readers (New York, NY), 2008.

## Sidelights

The detailed water color, graphite, and colored-pencil images of Nebraska-based artist Preston McDaniels have been paired with texts by authors ranging from Bryce Milligan and John Warren Stewig to Cynthia Rylant and Christopher Webber. Praising the artist's contribution to Stewig's retelling of a traditional Scottish tale in *Whuppity Stoorie, Booklist* contributor Abby Nolan noted that McDaniels' "flowing, earth-toned illustrations nicely complement the playful turns of the [Scots] language" in Stewig's book. An Irish story, Milligan's *The Prince of Ireland and the Three Magic Stallions,* also benefits from McDaniels' art, according to *Booklist* critic Carolyn Phelan, the critic concluding that the artist's "lively pencil artwork, tinted with watercolor washes," contains "humble details [that] help create an inviting setting."

McDaniels' most frequent collaborations include working with Frances O'Roark Dowell to create art for her "Phineas L. MacGuire" books and bringing to life the "Lighthouse Family" chapter-book series by popular author Rylant. Geared for early elementary readers, Rylant's *The Lighthouse Family: The Storm* and its sequels focus on a cat named Pandora who lives with a dog and several mice in a remote lighthouse. Reviewing the book, *Booklist* critic Karin Snelson wrote that "McDaniels' soft pastel sketches are as lovely and soothing as. . . . [Rylant's] simple, timeless tale," while Dona Ratterree compared the illustrator's "charming illustrations" with the work of noted nineteenth-century author/illustrator Beatrix Potter. In *The Lighthouse Family: The Turtle,* McDaniels depicts the family's reaction when a sea turtle washes up on the rocky shore surrounding their lighthouse, his "elaborate, accomplished graphite drawings exud[ing] . . . personality," according to a *Kirkus Reviews* writer. Describing *The Lighthouse Family: The Whale,* Hazel Rochman concluded in *Booklist* that the book's pastel-and-pencil "drawings are old-fashioned without being fussy and add needed drama" to Rylant's story. Turning to the "Phineas L. MacGuire" books, McDaniels' "amusing black-and-white illustrations add to the fun" of Dowell's middle-grade novel *Phineas L. MacGuire . . . Blasts Off!,* according to *Horn Book* reviewer Robin L. Smith.

In addition to his work for other authors, McDaniels has also written an original, self-illustrated book with a holiday theme. In *A Perfect Snowman* he tells the story of a boy who creates a snowman that then gives up one of his most prized possessions in order to ease the hunger of a family of rabbits. Praising McDaniels' "spacious" sepia-toned pencil drawings, *Booklist* contributor Ilene Cooper added that *A Perfect Snowman* benefits from its author/illustrator's "excellent artistic choices."

## Biographical and Critical Sources

*PERIODICALS*

*Booklist,* November 15, 2002, Karin Snelson, review of *The Lighthouse Family: The Storm,* p. 612; March 15, 2003, Carolyn Phelan, review of *The Prince of Ireland and the Three Magic Stallions,* p. 1322; February 15, 2004, Abby Nolan, review of *Whuppity Stoorie,* p. 1058; October 1, 2005, Hazel Rochman, review of *The Lighthouse Family: The Octopus,* p. 59; August, 2007, Abby Nolan, review of *Phineas L. MacGuire . . . Gets Slimed!,* p. 77; December 1, 2007, Ilene Cooper, review of *A Perfect Snowman,* p. 49.

*Horn Book,* September-October, 2007, Robin Smith, review of *Phineas L. MacGuire . . . Gets Slimed!,* p. 571; July-August, 2008, Robin L. Smith, review of *Phineas L. MacGuire . . . Blasts Off!,* p. 443.

*Kirkus Reviews,* March 1, 2005, review of *Lighthouse Family: The Turtle,* p. 294; July 1, 2007, review of *Phineas L. MacGuire . . . Gets Slimed!;* October 1, 2007, review of *A Perfect Snowman.*

*School Library Journal,* November, 2002, Dona Ratterree, review of *The Lighthouse Family: The Storm,* p. 134; November, 2003, Barbara Buckley, review of *The Lighthouse Family: The Whale,* p. 115; March, 2004, Grace Oliff, review of *Whuppity Stoorie,* p. 200; November, 2004, Debbie Stewart Hoskins, review of *The Lighthouse Family: The Eagle,* p. 117; June, 2006, Wendi Hoffenberg, review of *Phineas L. MacGuire . . . Erupts!,* p. 110.*

* * *

# McDONALD, Jamie
# See HEIDE, Florence Parry

* * *

# McMILLAN, Bruce 1947-

## Personal

Born 1947, in Boston, MA; son of Frank H., Jr., and Virginia M.W. McMillan; married V. Therese Loughran, 1969 (divorced 1989); married Lori Beth Evans, 1997 (divorced, 2000); children: (first marriage) Brett. *Education:* University of Maine—Orono, B.S., 1969.

## Addresses

*Home*—Shapleigh, ME. *E-mail*—bruce@brucemcmillan.com.

## Career

Maine Public Broadcasting Network, Orono, director and photographer, 1969, producer and director, 1969-73; island caretaker, McGee Island, ME, 1973-75; photographic illustrator and writer, 1975—. University of Southern Maine, instructor in children's literature, 1985-97; University of New Hampshire, instructor in children's literature, 1988—. Book Adventures, Inc., puffin tour guide in Iceland, 1997-2000; public speaker, 1980—. Apple Island Books, publisher.

## Member

Authors Guild, Society of Children's Book Writers and Illustrators.

## Awards, Honors

American Booksellers Association (ABA) Pick of the List designation, and *Parents* magazine Best Kid's Book designations, both 1983, both for *Here a Chick, There a Chick;* ABA Pick of the List designation, and Library of Congress Children's Book of the Year, both 1984, both for *Kitten Can . . .;* American Library Association (ALA) Notable Book designation, 1986, for *Counting Wildflowers;* Outstanding Science Trade Book for Children designation, National Science Teachers Association/Children's Book Council (NSTA/CBC), 1986, for *Becca Backward, Becca Frontward; Parenting* certificate of excellence, 1989, for *Super, Super, Superwords; Time to . . .* included among 100 Best Books for Reading and Sharing, New York Public Library, 1989; *Parents* Best Kid's Book designation, and Outstanding Science Trade Book for Children designation, NSTA/CBC, both 1990, and ALA Notable Book designation, 1991, all for *One Sun; Parenting* certificate of excellence, 1990, and Adkin Robinson Award, 1991, both for *Mary Had a Little Lamb;* Library of Congress Children's Book of the Year award, 1991, and *Scientific American* Young Reader's Book Award, 1996, both for *The Weather Sky; Parents* Best Kid's Book designation, 1991, for *Play Day;* ALA Notable Book designation, and *Parents* Best Kid's Book designation, both 1991, both for *Eating Fractions;* ABA Pick of the Lists designation, and Outstanding Science Trade Book for Children designation, NSTA/CBC, 1992, for *The Baby Zoo,* and 1995, for *Puffins Climb, Penguins Rhyme; Parenting* certificate of excellence, 1992, for *One, Two, One Pair!;* Outstanding Science Trade Book for Children designations, NSTA/CBC, 1992, for *Going on a Whale Watch,* 1993, for *Penguins at Home,* and 1995, for *Summer Ice;* John Burroughs Nature Book for Young Readers award, 1993, for *A Beach for the Birds;* ABA Pick of the Lists designations, 1994, for *Sense Suspense,* and 1997, for *Wild Flamingos;* Parents' Choice Honor Book, and Outstanding Science Trade Book for Children designation, NSTA/CBC, both 1995, and ALA Notable Book designation, Maine Librarians Association Lupine Honor Book designation, and named a *Hungry Mind Review* Children's Book of Distinction, all 1996, all for *Nights of the Pufflings; Jelly Beans for Sale* cited among

New York Public Library 100 Best Books for Reading and Sharing, 1996, and ALA Notable Book designation, 1997; Parent's Guide Children's Media Award for nonfiction, 1998, for *Salmon Summer;* Best Children's Book of the Year selection, Bank Street College of Education, 2002, for *Days of the Ducklings;* Notable Social Studies Trade Book, NCSS/CBC, 2006, for *Going Fishing;* Katahdin Award, Main Librarians Association, 2006, for outstanding body of work of children's literature in Maine.

## Writings

*FOR CHILDREN; AND PHOTOGRAPHER*

*Finestkind o'Day: Lobstering in Maine,* Lippincott (Philadelphia, PA), 1977.
*The Alphabet Symphony,* Greenwillow (New York, NY), 1977.
*The Remarkable Riderless Runaway Tricycle,* Houghton Mifflin (Boston, MA), 1978.
*Apples: How They Grow,* Houghton Mifflin (Boston, MA), 1979.
*Making Sneakers,* Houghton Mifflin (Boston, MA), 1980.
(With son, Brett McMillan) *Puniddles,* Houghton Mifflin (Boston, MA), 1982.
*Here a Chick, There a Chick,* Lothrop (New York, NY), 1983.
*Ghost Doll,* Houghton Mifflin (Boston, MA), 1983, revised, Apple Island Books, 1997.
*Kitten Can . . .,* Lothrop (New York, NY), 1984.
*Counting Wildflowers,* Lothrop (New York, NY), 1986.
*Becca Backward, Becca Frontward: A Book of Concept Pairs,* Lothrop (New York, NY), 1986.
*Step by Step,* Lothrop (New York, NY), 1987.
*Dry or Wet?,* Lothrop (New York, NY), 1988.
*Growing Colors,* Lothrop (New York, NY), 1988.
*Fire Engine Shapes,* Lothrop (New York, NY), 1988.
*Super, Super, Superwords,* Lothrop (New York, NY), 1989.
*Time to . . .,* Lothrop (New York, NY), 1989.
*One, Two, One Pair!,* Scholastic (New York, NY), 1990.
*One Sun: A Book of Terse Verse,* Holiday House (New York, NY), 1990.
*The Weather Sky,* Farrar, Straus (New York, NY), 1991.
*Play Day: A Book of Terse Verse,* Holiday House (New York, NY), 1991.
*Eating Fractions,* Scholastic (New York, NY), 1991.
*The Baby Zoo,* Scholastic (New York, NY), 1992.
*Beach Ball—Left, Right,* Holiday House (New York, NY), 1992.
*Going on a Whale Watch,* Scholastic (New York, NY), 1992.
*Mouse Views: What the Class Pet Saw,* Holiday House (New York, NY), 1993.
*A Beach for the Birds,* Houghton Mifflin (Boston, MA), 1993.
*Penguins at Home: Gentoos of Antarctica,* Houghton Mifflin (Boston, MA), 1993.
*Sense Suspense: A Guessing Game for the Five Senses,* Scholastic (New York, NY), 1994.
*Nights of the Pufflings,* Houghton Mifflin (Boston, MA), 1995.
*Puffins Climb, Penguins Rhyme,* Harcourt (San Diego, CA), 1995.
*Summer Ice: Life along the Antarctic Peninsula,* Houghton Mifflin (Boston, MA), 1995.
*Grandfather's Trolley,* Candlewick Press (Cambridge, MA), 1995.
*Jelly Beans for Sale,* Scholastic (New York, NY), 1996.
(With Kathy Mallat) *The Picture That Mom Drew,* Walker (New York, NY), 1997.
*Wild Flamingos,* Houghton Mifflin (Boston, MA), 1997.
*In the Wild, Wild North,* Scholastic (New York, NY), 1997.
*Salmon Summer,* Houghton Mifflin (Boston, MA), 1998.
*Gletta the Foal,* Marshall Cavendish (Freeport, NY), 1998.
*Days of the Ducklings,* Houghton Mifflin (Boston, MA), 2001.
*Going Fishing,* Houghton Mifflin (Boston, MA), 2005.

*OTHER*

*Punography* (adult), Penguin (New York, NY), 1978.
*Punography Too* (adult), Penguin (New York, NY), 1980.
(Photographer) Raffi, *Everything Grows* (children), Crown (New York, NY), 1989.
(Photographer) Sarah Josepha Hale, *Mary Had a Little Lamb* (children), Scholastic (New York, NY), 1990.
*The Problem with Chickens,* illustrated by Gunnella, Houghton Mifflin (Boston, MA), 2005.
*Postcards from the Other Side* (adult), Sulka (Reykjavik, Iceland), 2006.
*Puffins from the Other Side* (adult), Sulka (Reykjavik, Iceland), 2006.
*How the Ladies Stopped the Wind,* illustrated by Gunnella, Houghton Mifflin (Boston, MA), 2007.

Contributor to periodicals, including *Natural History, New Advocate, Down East, Life, US, Scandinavian Review,* and *Yankee.*

## Adaptations

*The Remarkable Riderless Runaway Tricycle* was filmed by Evergreen Productions and Phoenix/BFA Films & Video.

## Sidelights

Photographer and children's author Bruce McMillan specializes in "photo-illustration," which he describes as photographing ideas. "The book as a whole starts in the mind of the illustrator," he once commented. "The book's ideas flow from the illustrator's mind to what he creates in front of him. He paints the scene with light. He sketches the scene with preliminary photos. The finished work flow back into the camera, the photo-illustrator's tool."

Many of McMillan's publications for children are concept books, which illustrate such things as counting, color, money, geometry, growth, opposites, and time, and counting, using a creative approach that invites readers to look at the world around them with fresh eyes. Praising his *Counting Wildflowers* as a "deftly constructed multipurpose concept book" in a review for *Horn Book,* Mary A. Burns added that McMillan "excels in clarity of design and striking representation of an appealing subject." Catherine Wood made a similar assessment of McMillan's work in *School Library Journal,* noting that *Counting Wildflowers* "will be enjoyed by children and can be used in a number of ways by creative educators."

Raised in Maine, McMillan acquired his first camera when he was five, and by the time he reached high school he was proficient enough to be chief photographer for his school newspaper. A university degree in biology reflects his interest in science and the wildlife that has provided the basis for many of his concept books. As McMillan stated on his home page, "*Counting Wildflowers* was about my fascination with wildflowers, and it became my own taxonomy lesson. *Growing Colors* was an extension of my interest in orchards and gardens. *Going on a Whale Watch* was my way of introducing readers to my newfound neighbors, the whales off the coast of Maine."

McMillan's love of the sea found him spending much of his time along the Maine coast, and assignments he received as a freelance photographer for magazines soon found him globe-hopping: from the Antarctic to Venezuela to the Caribbean to California. McMillan developed an interest in writing in his adult years; after a stint with the Maine Public Broadcasting Network, he recalled, "I stayed in Maine as an island caretaker on McGee Island off the coast of Port Clyde, Maine. There was neither electricity nor running water. In the summers I tended the island, and in the winters I taught myself to write." Those skills meshed with his talent as a photographer to make him a successful artist-illustrator for children. "My books demonstrate experiments with different artistic styles and techniques," he noted on his home page. "I photographed *Grandfather's Trolley* in black and white, and then hand tinted the photos with oil colors, just as they did in the trolley era. *Growing Colors* was for me an exploration of color and how far I could take it within the limits of conventional color film. *Mouse Views: What the Class Pet Saw* was a lighting challenge: make the photos look natural so that no reader will realize the entire book is photographed using electronic flash."

McMillan's picture book *Here a Chick, There a Chick* uses the life of a yellow chick from hatching through its discovery of the world as a way of illustrating the concept of opposites. According to a *New York Times Book Review* contributor, "the miracle of new life, almost palpable in these pages, lingers long after the lessons become rote." In *Kitten Can . . .* McMillan uses the antics of a frisky kitten to demonstrate a variety of verbs, from "stare" to "crawl" and "dig." His work prompted *Horn Book* contributor Ann A. Flowers, to note that McMillan's "excellent colored photographs and the engaging calico kitten make an irresistible sequence." *Growing Colors* teaches children to recognize color by matching hues with fruits and vegetables. A *Bulletin of the Center for Children's Books* reviewer deemed *Growing Colors* "consistently well designed," and "a treat for kids and an example of photography as an art form in picture books." *Dry or Wet?* introduces the concepts mentioned in its title, and photographs feature children in before-and-after poses. In *Super, Super, Superwords* McMillan presents a colorful grammar lesson, as a group of children engage in activities kindergartners can relate to—measuring, sitting, carrying, playing—as a way to illustrate the concept of comparison. Another reviewer in the *Bulletin of the Center for Children's Books* stated that the book's author "demonstrates the concept with clarity, humor, and occasional wit."

In addition to concept books, McMillan has been inspired by the beauty of the chillier parts of planet Earth. In *Summer Ice: Life along the Antarctic Peninsula* he captures the wildlife and scenery of this southernmost region during the warm season, when humpback whales, penguins, and seals traverse the icy glaciers. In *Booklist,* Carolyn Phelan called *Summer Ice* a "handsome introduction to the wildlife of the Antarctic Peninsula," while *School Library Journal* contributor Melissa Hudak praised the fact that McMillan's photography—"brilliant in its beauty and attention to detail"—is augmented by information on plants and animals. Other books with a similar focus include *Penguins at Home: Gentoos of Antarctica* and *Going on a Whale Watch,* the latter a documentary of a trip taken by a group of children off the coast of Maine. Praising McMillan's photographs as "bright, intense, and absolutely sparkling," *School Library Journal* contributor Valerie Lennox found *Going on a Whale Watch* "first-rate nonfiction" for young children. "Every choice McMillan makes here is informed by intelligence and an awareness of his audience," added a *Kirkus Reviews* critic.

McMillan has written and photo-illustrated more children's books set in Iceland than any U.S. author. Many trips to Iceland during the 1990s and 2000s provided McMillan with the opportunity to produce such works as *Night of the Pufflings,* his signature book to date, as well as *Gletta the Foal,* and *Going Fishing.* In *My Horse of the North* he introduces nine-year-old Margrét and follows her as she and her Icelandic pony Perla learn to herd sheep in preparation for *réttir*—the annual fall roundup that takes place in the island's rocky, mountainous interior. "The text flows smoothly," noted Carol Schene in *School Library Journal,* "capturing the young girl's activities and also providing informational insights into this way of life." *Gletta the Foal* is a gentle story about a young Icelandic foal—one of the smallest breeds of pony in the world—as it attempts to find the source of a sound it has never before encountered. Praising the "vivid blues and earth tones of the vast Icelandic landscape" captured by McMillan's camera lens,

***Illustrated by Gunella, Bruce McMillan's story* The Problem with Chickens *is inspired by his interest in Icelandic culture and tradition.*** (Illustration 

*School Library Journal* contributor Lee Bock called *Gletta the Foal* a "beautiful, quiet book for youngsters who enjoy solving a simple mystery."

*Days of the Ducklings* follows the efforts of a schoolgirl and her family to reintroduce the endangered eider ducks to a remote island off the coast of Iceland. After gathering more than 200 eggs from adjoining islands, young Drifa must nurture the ducklings to adulthood while ensuring that they retain their self-sufficiency. "McMillan's photographs are of extremely high quality, a wonderful blend of artistry and emotion," remarked *Booklist* contributor Lauren Peterson. In *Going Fishing,* a young boy ventures to a small coastal village to catch cod and lumpfish with his grandfathers. "Both the conversations in the text and the photos have a natural air," remarked *Booklist* contributor Carolyn Phelan, and Kathy Piehl, writing in *School Library Journal,* commented, "All of the images are eye-catching, beautifully composed, and crystal clear."

McMillan has also written a pair of well-received picture books that are set in Iceland. *The Problem with Chickens,* illustrated by Icelandic artist Gunnella (the pseudonym of Gudrun Elin Oladsdottir), concerns a group of women who purchase a flock of hens to stock their town with eggs. When the chickens decide to mimic the ladies instead of laying eggs, however, the women devise an ingenious plan to rehabilitate the birds. "The playful text is both silly and joyous, without a wasted word," noted Mary Hazelton in *School Library Journal,* and a *Publishers Weekly* contributor stated that "the juxtaposition of McMillan's minimal deadpan text . . . and . . . Gunnella's comically literal paintings makes for some unlikely hilarity."

McMillan and Gunnella also collaborate on *How the Ladies Stopped the Wind,* "another amusingly unconventional tale," observed *Horn Book* reviewer Lauren Adams. When strong gusts make it difficult for the ladies to enjoy their daily walks, they decide to plant trees to act as windbreaks. What the women fail to realize, however, is that sheep enjoy the taste of the young plants, and they turn to an unlikely ally—their spirited chickens—for assistance. In the words of a *Kirkus Reviews* contributor, "The homey tale combined with the folksy, funny illustrations makes for an extremely winning combination."

"Three books into my career I realized that I made books with happy endings," McMillan once commented. "It wasn't a conscious decision. It was a reflection of me. I'm a happy person and I love a happy ending. Since then, I've consciously followed this with all my books. My photo-illustrated concept books are a combination of teaching concepts and relating a story—with a happy ending.

"I feel my best work is yet to come. My beloved Iceland continues to be a force in my work. I consider myself to be fortunate to be producing children's photo-illustrated concept books. To date, I'm one of very few people who have produced a body of work in photo-illustrated concept books."

## Biographical and Critical Sources


*BOOKS*

*Popular Nonfiction Authors for Children: A Biographical and Thematic Guide,* edited by Flora R. Wyatt and others, Libraries Unlimited (Englewood, CO), 1998.

*PERIODICALS*

*Arithmetic Teacher,* May, 1994, David J. Whitin, review of *Mouse Views: What the Class Pet Saw,* p. 562.

*Booklist,* May 15, 1992, Deborah Abbott, review of *Beach Ball—Left, Right,* p. 1684; October 15, 1992, Carolyn Phelan, review of *Going on a Whale Watch,* p. 435; April 1, 1993, Kay Weisman, review of *A Beach for the Birds,* p. 1436; November 15, 1993, Elizabeth Bush, review of *Penguins at Home: Gentoos of Antarctica,* p. 620; December 1, 1994, Mary Harris Veeder, review of *Sense Suspense: A Guessing Game for the Five Senses,* p. 675; March 15, 1995, Mary Harris Veeder, review of *Night of the Pufflings,* p. 1331; April 1, 1995, Mary Harris Veeder, review of *Puffins Climb, Penguins Rhyme,* p. 1421; October 15, 1995, Hazel Rochman, review of *Grandfather's Trolley,* p. 412; November 1, 1995, Carolyn Phelan, review of *Summer Ice,* p. 468; September 1, 1996, Lauren Peterson, review of *Jelly Beans for Sale,* p. 139; September 1, 1997, Carolyn Phelan, review of *In the Wild, Wild North,* p. 129; September 15, 1998, Lauren Peterson, review of *Gletta the Foal,* p. 248; September 15, 2001, Lauren Peterson, review of *Days of the Ducklings,* p. 228; March 1, 2005, Carolyn Phelan, review of *Going Fishing,* p. 1190; September 15, 2005, Diane Foote, review of *The Problem with Chickens,* p. 74; October 1, 2007, Julie Cummins, review of *How the Ladies Stopped the Wind,* p. 64.

*Bulletin of the Center for Children's Books,* April, 1988, review of *Dry or Wet?,* p. 162; October 13, 1988, review of *Growing Colors,* p. 48; December, 1995, Roger Sutton, review of *Grandfather's Trolley,* p. 133; October, 1997, Deborah Stevenson, review of *In the Wild, Wild North,* pp. 58-59.

*Christian Science Monitor,* September 25, 1997, Karen Williams, review of *In the Wild, Wild North,* p. 211.

*Horn Book,* October, 1982, Richard Gaugert, review of *The Remarkable Riderless Runaway Tricycle,* pp. 541-542; June, 1983, Nancy Sheridan, review of *Here a Chick, There a Chick,* p. 293; September-October, 1984, Ann A. Flowers, review of *Kitten Can . . .,* p. 583; September-October, 1986, Margaret A. Bush, review of *Counting Wildflowers,* p. 610; November-December, 1987, Margaret A. Bush, review of *Step by Step,* p. 727; July-August, 1991, Maeve Visser Knoth, review of *The Weather Sky,* p. 486; March, 1992, Margaret A. Bush, review of *The Baby Zoo,* p. 217; July-August, 1995, Maeve Visser Knoth, review of *Night of the Pufflings,* p. 480; September, 1997, Margaret A. Bush, review of *Wild Flamingos,* p. 593; May-June, 1998, Ellen Fader, review of *Salmon Summer,* p. 362; January-February, 2002, Danielle J. Ford, review of *Days of the Ducklings,* p. 103; November-December, 2005, Martha V. Parravano, review of *The Problem with Chickens,* p. 708; January-February, 2008, Lauren Adams, review of *How the Ladies Stopped the Wind,* p. 76.

*Kirkus Reviews,* January 1, 1992, review of *The Baby Zoo,* p. 54; July 15, 1992, review of *Going on a Whale Watch,* p. 922; March 15, 1993, review of *Mouse Views,* p. 375; April 1, 1993, review of *A Beach for the Birds,* p. 460; August 1, 1993, review of *Penguins at Home,* p. 1005; August 15, 2001, review of *Days of the Ducklings,* p. 1217; September 1, 2005, review of *The Problem with Chickens,* p. 978; September 1, 2007, review of *How the Ladies Stopped the Wind.*

*Kliatt,* July, 1996, Daniel J. Levinson, review of *The Weather Sky,* p. 35.

*Language Arts,* September, 1989, Janet Hickman, review of *Super, Super, Superwords,* p. 567; January, 1990, Susan Helper, review of *Time to . . .,* p. 79.

*New York Times Book Review,* March 27, 1983, review of *Here a Chick, There a Chick.*

*Publishers Weekly,* March 11, 1983, review of *Here a Chick, There a Chick,* p. 86; October 31, 1986, review of *Becca Backward, Becca Frontward: A Book of Concept Pairs,* p. 63; August 14, 1987, review of *Step by Step,* p. 101; January 15, 1988, review of *Dry or Wet?,* p. 93; May 12, 1989, review of *Super, Super, Superwords,* p. 290; September 29, 1989, review of *Time Two . . .,* p. 66; April 13, 1990, review of *One Sun: A Book of Terse Verse,* p. 62; January 1, 1991, review of *One, Two, One Pair!,* p. 57; October 4, 1991, review of *Eating Fractions,* p. 87; October 25, 1991, review of *Play Day: A Book of Terse Verse,* p. 67; January 30, 1995, review of *Puffins Climb, Penguins Rhyme,* p. 99; August 29, 2005, review of *The Problem with Chickens,* p. 55; July 23, 2007, review of *How the Ladies Stopped the Wind,* p. 67.

*School Library Journal,* January, 1983, William Spangler, review of *The Remarkable Riderless Runaway Tricycle,* p. 44; January, 1984, Leslie Chamberlain, review of *Ghost Doll,* p. 66; December, 1984, Margaret L. Chatham, review of *Kitten Can . . .,* p. 73; August, 1986, Catherine Wood, review of *Counting Wildflowers,* p. 85; October, 1986, Constance A. Mellon, review of *Becca Backward, Becca Frontward,* p. 164; September, 1987, Anna Biagioni Hart, review of *Step by Step,* p. 167; May, 1988, Jennifer Smith, review of *Dry or Wet?,* p. 86; October, 1988, Patricia Dooley, review of *Fire Engine Shapes,* p. 125; April, 1989,

Leda Schubert, review of *Super, Super, Superwords,* p. 86; September, 1989, Lori A. Janick, review of *Time Two . . .,* p. 241; July, 1990, Judith Gloyer, review of *One Sun,* p. 73; February, 1991, Louise L. Sherman, review of *One, Two, One Pair!,* pp. 72-73; May, 1991, Margaret M. Hegel, review of *The Weather Sky,* p. 104; May, 1992, Ellen Fader, review of *The Baby Zoo,* p. 106; June, 1992, Mary Lou Budd, review of *Beach Ball—Left, Right,* p. 110; April, 1993, Myra R. Oleynik, review of *Mouse Views,* p. 100, Valerie Lennox, review of *Going on a Whale Watch,* p. 112, and Diane Nunn, review of *A Beach for the Birds,* p. 137; December, 1993, Lisa Wu Stowe, review of *Penguins at Home,* pp. 128-129; March, 1995, Patricia Manning, review of *Nights of the Pufflings,* p. 198; May, 1995, Dot Minzer, review of *Puffins Climb, Penguins Rhyme,* pp. 100-101; September, 1995, Melissa Hudak, review of *Summer Ice: Life along the Antarctic Peninsula,* p. 212; December, 1995, Virginia Opocensky, review of *Grandfather's Trolley,* p. 86; October, 1996, Beth Tegart, review of *Jelly Beans for Sale,* p. 115; April, 1997, review of *The Picture That Mom Drew,* p. 128; August, 1997, review of *Wild Flamingos,* pp. 148-149; September, 1997, Carol Schene, review of *In the Wild, Wild North,* pp. 204, 206; May, 1998, Susan Oliver, review of *Salmon Summer,* p. 134; December, 1998, Lee Bock, review of *Gletta the Foal,* p. 87; September, 2001, Anne Chapman Callaghan, review of *Days of the Ducklings,* p. 218; May, 2005, Kathy Piehl, review of *Going Fishing,* p. 112; September, 2005, Mary Hazelton, review of *The Problem with Chickens,* p. 177; December, 2007, Marian Drabkin, review of *How the Ladies Stopped the Wind,* p. 94.

*ONLINE*

*Bruce McMillan Home Page,* http://www.brucemcmillan.com (August 5, 2008).

* * *

# MERCER, Sienna [A pseudonym] (Josh Greenhut)

## Personal

Male. *Education:* Haverford College, B.A.; Columbia University, M.B.A.

## Addresses

*Home*—Toronto, Ontario, Canada.

## Career

Advertising copywriter, speechwriter, and novelist. IBM, former executive speechwriter and communications staffer; freelance writer, beginning 2004.

## Writings

*"MY SISTER THE VAMPIRE" NOVEL SERIES*

*Switched,* HarperTrophy (New York, NY), 2007.
*Fangtastic!,* HarperTrophy (New York, NY), 2007.
*Re-Vamped!,* HarperTrophy (New York, NY), 2007.
*Vampalicious!,* HarperTrophy (New York, NY), 2008.

## Biographical and Critical Sources

*PERIODICALS*

*Publishers Weekly,* August 27, 2007, review of *Switched,* p. 90.
*School Library Journal,* January, 2008, Jennifer Huddler, review of *Switched,* p. 124.

*ONLINE*

*Josh Greenhut Home Page,* http://www.36smartpeople.com (September 1, 2008).*

* * *

# MIROCHA, Paul

## Personal

Born in St. Paul, MN; married; wife's name Stina; children: Anna, Claire.

## Addresses

*Home*—Tucson, AZ. *Office*—425 E. 17th St., Tucson, AZ 85701. *Agent*—The Wiley Group, 1535 Green St., Ste. 301, San Francisco, CA 94123. *E-mail*—paul@paulmirocha.com.

## Career

Illustrator and designer. Office of Arid Lands Studies, University of Arizona, Tucson, graphic designer for thirteen years; full-time illustrator, 1990—.

## Awards, Honors

Illustration prize, National Design Art Marker Contest, Eberhard Faber, 1980; John Burroughs Award for Best Natural History Book of 1986, (with Gary Paul Nabhan), for *Gathering the Desert;* Certificate of Merit for Illustrations, Art Directors Club of New York, 65th Annual show, 1985; Arizona Humanities Council grant, 1989; Gold Medal for design, Arizona Press Club, 1991; Publication Design Merit Award, American Association of Museums, 1992; Outstanding Science Trade Books for Children, National Science Teachers Association/

Children's Book Council, 1992, for *Moon of the Wild Pigs;* Bronze Award, Dimensional Illustrators Awards Show, 1995; MPBA/Benjamin Franklin Award for Science and the Environment, 1997, for *The Forgotten Pollinators;* Artist's Project Award, Arizona Commission on the Arts, 1998; Tucson/Pima Arts Council grant, 1999; Skipping Stones Honor Award for ecological and multicultural awareness, and special recognition for Patterson Prize for Books for Young People, 2008, both for *The Bee Tree.*

## Writings

*ILLUSTRATOR*

Gary Paul Nabhan, *Gathering the Desert,* University of Arizona Press (Tucson, AZ) 1985.

*Awesome Animal Actions,* HarperFestival (New York, NY), 1992.

*Freaky Fish Facts,* HarperFestival (New York, NY), 1992.

*Incredible Insect Instincts,* HarperFestival (New York, NY), 1992.

*Baffling Bird Behavior,* HarperFestival (New York, NY), 1992.

Jean Craighead George, *The Moon of the Wild Pigs,* HarperCollins (New York, NY), 1992.

Molly Marr, *I Wonder Where Butterflies Go in Winter and Other Neat Facts about Insects,* Western Publishing (Racine, WI), 1992.

R.M. Alexander, *Exploring Biomechanics: Animals in Motion,* Scientific American Library (New York, NY), 1992.

Annabelle Donati, *Unusual Animals,* Western Publishing (Racine, WI), 1993.

(With Rhod Lauffer) *Back Off!: Animal Defense Behavior,* Scientific American Books for Young Readers (New York, NY), 1994.

(With Rhod Lauffer) *Look Again!: Animal Disguises,* Scientific American Books for Young Readers (New York, NY), 1994.

Melvin Berger, *Oil Spill!,* HarperCollins (New York, NY), 1994.

Barbara Kingsolver, *High Tide in Tucson: Essay from Now or Never,* HarperCollins (New York, NY), 1995.

(With Rhod Lauffer) Susan Lowell, *The Boy with Paper Wings,* Milkweed Editions (Minneapolis, MN), 1995.

Arlene Maguire, *Dinosaur Pop-up ABC,* Little Simon (New York, NY), 1995.

Jean Craighead George, *Acorn Pancakes, Dandelion Salad, and Thirty-eight Other Wild Recipes,* HarperCollins (New York, NY), 1995.

Cindy Kendall, *Butterflies,* Dial Books (New York, NY), 1995.

Cindy Kendall, *Eagles,* Dial Books (New York, NY), 1995.

Annabelle Donati, *Animal Camouflage,* Western Publishing (Racine, WI), 1995.

Stephen L. Buchmann and Gary Paul Nabhan, *The Forgotten Pollinators,* Shearwater Books (Washington, DC), 1995.

Roma Gans, *How Do Birds Find Their Way?,* HarperCollins (New York, NY), 1996.

Aileen Kilgore Henderson, *The Monkey Thief,* Milkweed Editions (Minneapolis, MN), 1997.

Kathleen Weidner Zoehfeld, *The Cactus Café: A Story of the Sonoran Desert,* Soundprints (Norwalk, CT), 1997.

Barbara Kingsolver, *Prodigal Summer,* HarperCollins (New York, NY), 2000.

Mary Batten, *Hungry Plants,* Golden Books (New York, NY), 2000.

Barbara Kingsolver, *Small Wonder,* HarperCollins (New York, NY), 2002.

Diana Cohn, *Mr. Goethe's Garden,* Bell Pond Books (Herndon, VA), 2003.

Ginjer L. Clarke, *Platypus!,* Random House (New York, NY), 2004.

(With Rhod Lauffer) *Do You See What I See?: A Southwest Nature Walk You Read,* Western National Parks Association (Tucson, AZ), 2004.

Abby Mogollon, *A Desert Hello: Welcome to the Sonoran Desert,* Western National Parks Association (Tucson, AZ), 2004.

(With Trudy Nicholson) Sara St. Antoine, editor, *The Great North American Prairie: A Literary Field Guide,* Milkweed Editions (Minneapolis, MN), 2004.

(With Trudy Nicholson) Sara St. Antoine, editor, *The Gulf Coast: A Literary Field Guide,* Milkweed Editions (Minneapolis, MN), 2006.

Stephen Buchmann and Diana Cohn, *The Bee Tree,* Cinco Puntos Press (El Paso, TX), 2007.

Contributor to *The Very Best of Children's Illustration,* Society of Illustrators. Also illustrator of book covers, maps, and catalogues.

## Sidelights

Paul Mirocha often illustrates children's books that examine environmental themes. "I'm fascinated by the world's infinite detail, so my style is naturally realistic," the artist remarked on his home page. Mirocha provided the illustrations for Melvin Berger's *Oil Spill!,* which depicts the causes and effects of these ecological disasters. "Subtle in texture and deep in tone, the colorful artwork effectively illustrates marine animals and oil tankers," observed *Booklist* reviewer Carolyn Phelan. In *The Forgotten Pollinators,* Stephen L. Buchmann and Gary Paul Nabhan look at one of the key roles that bees, moths, and bats play in the ecosystem. According to a *Publishers Weekly* critic, "This important addition to the environmental bookshelf is enlivened by Mirocha's delightful drawings."

Diana Cohn examines the life of eighteenth-century German writer Johann Wolfgang von Goethe, a man who had a keen interest in the natural world, in *Mr. Goethe's Garden.* In *Childhood Education,* Michele Litster praised Mirocha's "breathtaking illustrations," and added, "His vibrant watercolors work beautifully alongside the text." Set in Malayasia, *The Bee Tree,* an award-winning work by Buchmann and Diana Cohn, focuses on traditional hunters Pak Teh and his grandson, Nizam.

***Paul Mirocha's illustration credits include* The Bee Tree, *written by Stephen Buchmann and Diana Cohn.*** (Illustration copyright © 2007 by Paul Mirocha. Reproduced by permission. www.cincopuntos.com.)

To harvest honeycombs, the pair must climb the tualang, a 120-foot-tall tree in which the bees have nested. A critic in *Kirkus Reviews* applauded Mirocha's "wondrous double-spread paintings," and Kathy Piehl, writing in *School Library Journal,* noted that the artist's "illustrations incorporate details of Malaysian culture and the lush landscape of the rainforest."

## Biographical and Critical Sources

*PERIODICALS*

*Booklist,* June 1, 1994, Carolyn Phelan, review of *Oil Spill!,* p. 1824; June 1, 1995, Carolyn Phelan, review of *Acorn Pancakes, Dandelion Salad and Thirty-eight Other Wild Recipes,* p. 1762; February 1, 1996, Stephanie Zvirin, review of *How Do Birds Find Their Way?,* p. 934; May 15, 2000, Shelley Townsend-Hudson, review of *Hungry Plants,* p. 1745; July, 2004, Gillian Engberg, review of *Platypus!,* p. 1850.

*Childhood Education,* summer, 2005, Michele Litster, review of *Mr. Goethe's Garden,* p. 244.

*Kirkus Reviews,* May 1, 2007, review of *The Bee Tree.*

*Publishers Weekly,* July 5, 1993, review of *I Am Lavina Cumming,* p. 74; June 5, 1995, review of *Dinosaur Pop-up ABC,* p. 62; May 13, 1996, review of *The Forgotten Pollinators,* p. 63.

*School Library Journal,* July, 2007, Kathy Piehl, review of *The Bee Tree,* p. 67.

*ONLINE*

*Paul Mirocha Home Page,* http://paulmirocha.com (August 15, 2008).

*Paul's Travel Journal Web log,* http://paulstraveljournal.blogspot.com/ (August 15, 2008).*

* * *

# MISAKO ROCKS!
## [A pseudonym]
## (Misako Takashima)

## Personal

Born April 7, in Japan; immigrated to United States as a teenager; father a police officer, mother a police officer. *Education:* Earned secondary English teacher's certificate in Japan. *Hobbies and other interests:* Bike riding, hip hop, dancing to Michael Jackson's music, reading graphic novels.

## Addresses

*Home*—Brooklyn, NY. *E-mail*—me@misakorocks.com.

## Career

Author and illustrator. Formerly worked as a a puppeteer, face painter, animal balloon maker, and art and manga instructor.

## Awards, Honors

Venice Beach, LA Playwright award, 2008; New York Public Library Books for the Teen Age listee, 2008, for *Rock and Roll Love.*

## Writings

*GRAPHIC NOVELS*

*Biker Girl,* Hyperion Paperbacks (New York, NY), 2006.

*Rock and Roll Love,* Hyperion Paperbacks (New York, NY), 2007.

*Detective Jermain: Volume One,* Henry Holt (New York, NY), 2008.

*OTHER*

Contributor of illustrations to "Savage Love" (column), in *Onion* online. Contributor to periodicals, including *Elle Girl, DFC,* and *New York Times.* Creator of characters and writer for "Archie" comics.

## Sidelights

Misako Rocks! is the pen name of Misako Takashima, the Japanese-born creator of the graphic novels *Biker Girl* and *Rock and Roll Love,* as well as of the "Detective Jermain" series. Educated as a teacher but self-taught as an artist, Misako has always loved manga and comic books, and she created her first original comic as a young teen. After coming to the United States as an exchange student, she decided to make the country her new home and lived in the Midwest while developing a career in puppet theatre. She made the switch to children's books after relocating east to New York City. When her first professional work appeared in the 'zine *Onion,* its popularity allowed Misako to publish book-length works, as well as creating new characters for the popular "Archie" comic-book series. She also was a featured artist in the BBC2 television documentary *Secret of Drawing.*

Misako's first book, *Biker Girl,* focuses on a shy teen named Aki who discovers an unusual bicycle while helping her grandfather clean out his garage. The bike had a special history: it had been ridden by Aki's favorite cousin on the night he was killed by a vicious biker gang. Riding the bike, Aki becomes Biker Girl, a street-smart bike racer with a mission: to avenge her cousin's death. Noting that Misako's "art is very cinematic," *School Library Journal* critic Melissa T. Jenvey called *Biker Girl* "lighthearted and fun," with a "strong protagonist" and fast-moving plot. In *Kirkus Reviews* a writer dubbed the book "manga with a heavy dose of cute," and predicted that Misako's graphic-novel debut "should find a ready crowd of action-oriented shojo fans." Within the pages of "a sassy, spirited romp perfect for middle-schoolers" that is salted with romance, Misako "infuses a light, optimistic story with mange-inspired illustrations that smack of elements of Speed Racer with a dash of Chynna Clugston," according to *Kliatt* critic Jennifer Feigelman.

Admittedly autobiographical, Misako's *Rock and Roll Love* focuses on the author's first romantic relationship after coming to the United States. The book's heroine, appropriately named Misako, finds herself overwhelmed by American popular culture, but Natalie, the daughter of the family she lives with as an exchange student, helps the Japanese-born teen navigate her new Missouri high school and becomes a close friend in the process.

***The spunky, upbeat attitude of Misako Rocks! is evident in her artwork for her "Detective Jermain" series.*** (Illustration by Misako Takashima. Reproduced by permission.)

When Misako meets Zack, the lead singer in a local rock band, the teen is smitten, but should she interpret his flirtation as sincere? Noting that *Rock and Roll Love* pairs a "clean text and a few fairly chaste kisses," Sarah Krygier predicted in *School Library Journal* that the graphic novel would be "a good fit for middle school libraries."

Continuing her focus on teen readers, Misako breaks into new territory with *Detective Jermain: Volume One,* the first book in a planned ongoing series. Inspired by her conversations with teens at a high school Misako visited while living in Madison, Wisconsin, *Detective Jermain* centers on feisty sixteen-year-old Jermain. Her parents worked as high-profile detectives until her father died years before, and Jermain now decides to follow in their footsteps, even though it creates problems with her widowed mom. When some of the teachers and students at school begin to act oddly, the teen decides to investigate, with the help of friends Andy and Travis, both of whom harbor romantic feelings for the determined young sleuth.

Discussing what several critics have observed is her fresh take on the Japanese manga form, Misako explained to online interviewer Brigid Alverson of Good Comics for Kids that her books are better described as teen graphic novels. "Usually manga is about a girl who is waiting for some special boy and they are going to make her happy," Misako explained, "or she is living in her imagination—one girl and ten really good looking boys surrounding her. I am living in America, and I have a lot of American girlfriends here, and obviously those American girls are not like Japanese girls at all. They are not shy, they have their own identity, they have power. I wanted more focus on girls here, and I wanted the readers to share the feeling with my characters."

*Cover of Misako's graphic novel* Rock and Roll Love, *which focuses on a teen's confusing first love.* (Illustration © 2007 by Misako Rocks! Reprinted by permission of Hyperion Books for Children. All rights reserved.)

## Biographical and Critical Sources

*PERIODICALS*

*Booklist,* March 15, 2006, Jennifer Hubert, review of *Biker Girl,* p. 56.

*Kirkus Reviews,* June 1, 2006, review of *Biker Girl,* p. 577.

*Kliatt,* September, 2006, Jennifer Feigelman, review of *Biker Girl,* p. 36.

*School Library Journal,* September, 2006, Melissa T. Jenvey, review of *Biker Girl,* p. 238; September, 2007, Sarah Krygier, review of *Rock and Roll Love,* p. 224.

*ONLINE*

*Good Comics for Kids,* http://www.goodcomicsforkids.com/ (July 7, 2008), Brigid Alverson, interview with Misako.

*Misako Rocks Home Page,* http://www.misakorocks.com/ (August 5, 2008).

* * *

# MOSER, Lisa

## Personal

Born in Fairfield, IA; married; children: one daughter. *Education:* Graduated from University of Iowa. *Hobbies and other interests:* Softball, tennis, volleyball, golf, traveling.

## Addresses

*Home*—Grafton, WI. *E-mail*—lisa@lisamoserbooks.com.

## Career

Author. Taught elementary school in Worthington, OH.

## Member

Society of Children's Book Writers and Illustrators.

## Awards, Honors

Books for Beginning Readers selection, Cooperative Children's Book Center, 2008, for *Squirrel's World.*

***Lisa Moser*** (Courtesy of Lisa Moser.)

## Writings

*PICTURE BOOKS*

*The Monster in the Backpack,* illustrated by Noah Z. Jones, Candlewick Press (Cambridge, MA), 2006.

*Watermelon Wishes,* illustrated by Stacey Schuett, Clarion Books (New York, NY), 2006.

*Squirrel's World,* illustrated by Valeri Gorbachev, Candlewick Press (Cambridge, MA), 2007.

## Sidelights

A former elementary school teacher, Lisa Moser has written a number of well-received picture books. Hailing from a family of readers, Moser developed a love for literature at a young age. She frequently visited her hometown library, and she once read her favorite book, *Little Women,* five times in a single year. Moser's grandmother often created stories that featured Moser and her sister in starring roles. "She would draw pictures to go with them and bind them with bright red yarn," the author noted on her home page. "When I read those stories, I was amazed. From that moment on, I wanted to be a children's author."

A graduate of the University of Iowa, Moser taught fifth grade in Ohio before she became a published author. Her debut work, *The Monster in the Backpack,* was inspired by an incident with one of her students, who had trouble opening a stuck zipper on a backpack. While preparing for school one day, young Annie is startled to find an unexpected visitor hiding in her pink-and-blue-flowered backpack. The monstrous creature proves more troublesome than frightening, however: he proceeds to devour Annie's lunch and put bubble gum in her shoes. He also hates to be left alone, and when an exasperated Annie considers trading her backpack for a new one, the monster finds a messy but heartfelt way to win over his new friend. "The zany story is written in simple, clear language," remarked *School Library Journal* contributor Laura Scott.

In *Watermelon Wishes,* a young boy and his grandfather complete a special project together. When Charlie and Grandpap plant a watermelon patch, Charlie hopes that one seed will grow into a unique watermelon that makes wishes come true. As the summer passes, Charlie and Grandpap tend to the garden regularly, and they reward themselves for their hard work by going fishing, playing cards, and swimming. When the watermelons are ripe, Charlie selects the perfect one and reveals his secret wish to his grandfather. "Moser works in some nice horticultural details," a contributor in *Kirkus Reviews* stated, and Mary Hazelton, writing in *School Library Journal,* noted, "This sweet story is filled with positive images of shared experiences and cooperation."

An incredibly energetic animal is the subject of *Squirrel's World,* a chapter book that "will charm and challenge emergent readers," remarked a *Kirkus Reviews* critic. In the work, Squirrel attempts to lend support to his friends, including sleepy Turtle, hungry Mouse, and frightened Rabbit, though his frenetic antics often create more problems than they solve. "Repetitive text and well-designed pages support the efforts of young readers who will likely enjoy Squirrel's humorous misadventures," Neala Arnold wrote in *School Library Journal.*

"Writing is hard, imperfect work," Moser remarked on her home page. "Sometimes I love what I write. Sometimes I can write all day and only have one good paragraph. I fail more times than I succeed, but that is okay. I know that if I keep at it, I will eventually have a great story."

## Biographical and Critical Sources

*PERIODICALS*

*Horn Book,* November-December, 2006, Betty Carter, review of *The Monster in the Backpack,* p. 721.

*Kirkus Reviews,* November 15, 2006, review of *Watermelon Wishes,* p. 1177; August 15, 2007, review of *Squirrel's World.*

*School Library Journal,* August, 2006, Laura Scott, review of *The Monster in the Backpack,* p. 94; December, 2006, Mary Hazelton, review of *Watermelon Wishes,* p. 110; September, 2007, Neala Arnold, review of *Squirrel's World,* p. 172.

*ONLINE*

*Lisa Moser Home Page,* http://lisamoserbooks.com (August 10, 2008).

* * *

# MURDOCH, Patricia 1957-

## Personal

Born 1957, in Canada.

## Addresses

*Home*—Bradford, Ontario, Canada.

## Career

Author.

## Writings

*Deep Thinker and the Stars* (picture book), illustrated by Kellie Jobson, Three Trees Press (Toronto, Ontario, Canada), 1987.

*Exposure,* Orca Books Publishers (Custer, WA), 2006.

## Sidelights

Patricia Murdoch is a Canadian writer who has written both the picture book *Deep Thinker and the Stars* and the young-adult novel *Exposure,* the latter for Orca's "Soundings" series which focuses on fiction appealing to reluctant readers. In *Exposure* Julie's high-school years are being ruined by the constant insults and bullying she receives at the hand of a popular but mean-spirited classmate named Dana. Then her brother provides her with the ultimate payback: a digital camera full of pictures taken at a keg party that show Dana doing things she shouldn't. As Julie plans the ultimate revenge, her best friend Sammy voices ethical concerns over whether the revenge will be as bad as the torment. For Julie, who narrates the novel, this realization comes too late, and her relationship with Sammy is sacrificed. Noting that the cast of characters in *Exposure* includes teens "YAs can relate to," Stephanie Squicciarini added that Julie is ultimately "forced to face unpleasant truths about herself" in Murdoch's realistic novel. In *Resource Links* Lesley Little praised the author's "auspicious [YA] debut," adding that "Her delivery has an edge that [is] . . . appealing and, perhaps most important, believable."

While *Exposure* was Murdoch's first novel for teen readers, her first published book was written years before. A picture book, *Deep Thinker and the Stars* focuses on a girl named Sharon. Her family is going through a lot of changes: in addition to her mother's departure for the hospital to give birth to a new baby brother, Sharon's beloved grandfather has recently passed, and the girl misses him very much. In her family's Native American traditions, Sharon finds solace by helping her grandmother make beaded stars and prepare for her brother's name-day celebration. Ultimately, the thoughtful girl, whose Indian name is Deep Thinker, finds a connection with the brother she has gained and the grandfather she has lost: they both have the same eyes. Writing that *Deep Thinker and the Stars* will be useful to students learning about Native American family customs, *Canadian Review of Materials* contributor Elizabeth Lockett also noted that the picture book "treats the themes of birth and death in a strong, loving, native family with great sensitivity."

## Biographical and Critical Sources

*PERIODICALS*

*Kliatt,* July, 2006, Stephanie Squicciarini, review of *Exposure,* p. 21.

*Resource Links,* June, 2006, Lesley Little, review of *Exposure,* p. 26.

*School Library Journal,* October, 2006, Michele Capozzella, review of *Exposure,* p. 163.

*ONLINE*

*Canadian Review of Materials Online,* http://www.umanitoba.ca/cm/ (July 1, 1988), Elizabeth Lockett, review of *Deep Thinker and the Stars.**

# P

## PEACOCK, Shane 1957-

### Personal

Born 1957, in Port Arthur, Ontario, Canada; married Sophie Kneisel (a journalist); children: three. *Education:* Trent University, B.A. (English and history); University of Toronto, M.A. (literature). *Hobbies and other interests:* Playing hockey, watching sumo wrestling.

### Addresses

*Home*—Cobourg, Ontario, Canada. *Agent*—Pamela Paul Agency, 12 Westrose Ave., Toronto, Ontario, Canada M8X 1Z2.

### Career

Author, playwright, journalist, and screenwriter. Has also worked for Spruce Falls Power and Paper Company, as a wilderness bush sprayer for Ontario Hydro, and as a box mover for a university bookstore.

### Awards, Honors

National One-Act Play Competition honorable mention, 1985, for "No Heart Punch"; National Magazine Award nomination, 1999, for "Rulers of the Dohyo"; Red Maple Award nomination, and Arthur Ellis Award nomination, both 1999, both for *The Mystery of Ireland's Eye;* Canadian Children's Book Centre select choice, 2000, for *The Secret of the Silver Mines;* National Magazine Award Silver Medal, 2001, for "Team Spirit"; Red Maple Award nomination and Arthur Ellis Award nomination, both 2002, both for *Bone Beds of the Badlands;* Best Bet for 2002 selection, Ontario Library Association, for *Unusual Heroes: Canada's Prime Ministers and Fathers of Confederation;* National Magazine Award nomination, 2002, for "As the Crow Flies"; Junior Library Guild of America Premier Selection Award, 2007, Canadian Library Association Children's Book of the Year Honour Book designation, Canadian Library Association Young Adult-Book of the Year Honour Book designation, and Arthur Ellis Award for best young-adult crime novel in Canada, all 2007, all for *Eye of the Crow: The Boy Sherlock Holmes, His First Case.*

### Writings

*BIOGRAPHIES*

*The Great Farini: The High-wire Life of William Hunt,* Viking (Toronto, Ontario, Canada), 1995.

*Unusual Heroes: Canada's Prime Ministers and Fathers of Confederation,* Puffin Canada (Toronto, Ontario, Canada), 2002.

*"DYLAN MAPLES" ADVENTURE SERIES*

*The Mystery of Ireland's Eye,* Penguin Books Canada (Toronto, Ontario, Canada), 1999.

*The Secret of the Silver Mines,* Penguin Books Canada (Toronto, Ontario, Canada), 2000.

*Bone Beds of the Badlands,* Penguin Books Canada (Toronto, Ontario, Canada), 2001.

*Monster in the Mountains,* Penguin Books Canada (Toronto, Ontario, Canada), 2003.

*"THE BOY SHERLOCK HOLMES" SERIES*

*Eye of the Crow: The Boy Sherlock Holmes, His First Case,* Tundra Books (Plattsburgh, NY), 2007.

*Death in the Air: The Boy Sherlock Holmes, His Second Case,* Tundra Books (Plattsburgh, NY), 2008.

*PLAYS*

*The Great Farini: The Play,* performed in Millbrook, Ontario, Canada, 1994.

*The Devil and Joseph Scriven,* performed in Millbrook, Ontario, Canada, 1999.

*The Art of Silent Killing,* performed in Millbrook, Ontario, Canada, 2006.

Also author of one-act plays produced in Canada.

*TELEVISION DOCUMENTARIES*

*Dangerous Dreams: The Life of The Great Farini* (based on Peacock's play), History Television, 2000.
*The Passion of Joseph Scriven* (based on Peacock's play), History Television, 2001.
(And co-producer) *Team Spirit: The Jordin and Terence Tootoo Story,* CTV National Network, 2004.
(And story editor) *Exhibit Eh!: Exposing Canada,* Travel & Escape Network, 2006.

*OTHER*

Contributor to magazines and newspapers, including *Sports Illustrated, Reader's Digest, Saturday Night, En Route, Toronto Life, Elm Street, Maclean's,* Toronto *Globe & Mail, Ottawa Citizen, Vancouver Sun,* and *National Post.*

## Sidelights

Award-winning Canadian journalist and novelist Shane Peacock is the creator of the "Dylan Maples" adventure series and the critically acclaimed "The Boy Sherlock Holmes" series. Peacock has also written a number of television documentaries, including *Dangerous Dreams: The Life of The Great Farini,* which centers on high-wire artist, discoverer, and inventor William Leonard Hunt, as well as of stage plays, including *The Art of Silent Killing,* a love story set during World War II.

In *Unusual Heroes: Canada's Prime Ministers and Fathers of Confederation* Peacock "brings young adult readers an informative and somewhat entertaining look at the political greats" of that nation, Victoria Pennell stated in *Resource Links.* "Canada is a remarkable, admirable, and unusual country," the author remarked in an interview on the *Puffin Books* Web site. "My book tells kids why it is unique and it shows them that it took some unusual folks to create it and keep it going." The collection, which offers profiles of such leaders as Sir John A. Macdonald, Louis Riel, and Jean Chrétien, "provides a very useful and welcome resource in our quest to make the teaching and understanding of Canadian history and Canadian politics relevant and engaging," noted Alexander Gregor in the *Canadian Review of Materials.*

*The Mystery of Ireland's Eye,* the first work in the "Dylan Maples" series, introduces the young protagonist, an eleven-year-old Canadian boy. During a kayaking trip to Ireland's Eye, an island off the coast of Newfoundland, Dylan and his parents investigate a ghost town. During his explorations, however, Dylan spots a lit cigarette, finds his name carved into an old desk, and witnesses ghostly apparitions. "Peacock weaves a wonderful adventure full of suspense that grasps the reader's attention from the beginning and holds it until the end," a *Resource Links* critic observed. In the *Canadian Review of Materials,* Joan Marshall stated that Dylan's "self-deprecating humour and courage in the face of real and imagined danger make him a character that students will remember."

Dylan returns in *The Secret of the Silver Mines,* set in the small Ontario town of Cobalt. The story "has a distinct Canadian setting," noted a *Resource Links* contributor. Dylan and his friends win a trip to a dinosaur park where they are stalked by an escaped convict in *Bone Beds of the Badlands,* the third work in the series. "The authentic dialogue between the teens" drew praise from Veronica Allen in *Resource Links.* In *Monster in the Mountains,* Dylan meets his eccentric great-uncle who convinces the teen to search for the legendary Sasquatch in British Columbia's Rocky Mountains. According to Marshall, "the action is nonstop and very movie-like, and most young readers will be glued to this book just to find out what happens."

Set in 1867, *Eye of the Crow: The Boy Sherlock Holmes, His First Case* follows the thirteen-year-old budding detective as he investigates a brutal murder in London's East End. Sheila Fiscus, writing in *School Library Journal,* praised the work, stating that "the details of the plot are plausible, the pacing well timed, and the historical setting vividly depicted." *Eye of the Crow* "not only honors the intentions of Doyle's storyworld," David Ward wrote in the *Canadian Review of Materials,* "but it also extends the life of the intrepid detective by exploring the early years of Holmes." In *Death in the Air: The Boy Sherlock Holmes, His Second Case,* Holmes looks into the death of an aerialist whose trapeze equipment was sabotaged. Peacock "has remained true to the original spirit of the Holmes series," observed Ward. "Sherlock's pervasive melancholy and his flirtatious relationship with the underworld of London create yet another authentic mystery."

## Biographical and Critical Sources

*PERIODICALS*

*Booklist,* November 1, 2007, Shelle Rosenfeld, review of *Eye of the Crow: The Boy Sherlock Holmes, His First Case,* p. 44.
*Canadian Review of Materials,* April 14, 2000, Joan Marshall, review of *The Mystery of Ireland's Eye;* December 13, 2002, Alexander Gregor, review of *Unusual Heroes: Canada's Prime Ministers and Fathers of Confederation;* October 3, 2003, Joan Marshall, review of *Monster in the Mountains;* September 14, 2007, David Ward, review of *Eye of the Crow;* April 4, 2008, review of *Death in the Air.*
*Globe & Mail* (Toronto, Ontario, Canada), August 24, 1996, H.J. Kirchhoff, "Finding the Reality in an Illusionist's Life: *The Great Farini: The High-wire Life*

*of William Hunt,*" p. C16; July 31, 1999, Kate Taylor, "Canadian Holy Man's Tale Stranger than Fiction: Peterborough Theatre Teams up with Toronto Author Shane Peacock to Present the Story of 19th-century Preacher Joseph Scriven"; August 16, 2006, Patrick Mullin, review of *The Art of Silent Killing,* p. R8.

*Quill & Quire,* October, 1999, Janet McNaughton, review of *The Mystery of Ireland's Eye;* December, 2002, Laurie Mcneill, review of *Unusual Heroes;* July, 2007, Jeffrey Canton, review of *Eye of the Crow.*

*Resource Links,* December, 1999, review of *The Mystery of Ireland's Eye,* p. 29; October, 2000, review of *Secret of the Silver Mines,* p. 9; December, 2001, Veronica Allen, review of *Bone Beds of the Badlands,* p. 19; February, 2003, Victoria Pennell, review of *Unusual Heroes,* p. 52; October, 2003, Rosemary Anderson, review of *Monster in the Mountains,* p. 18; October, 2007, Leslie L. Kennedy, review of *Eye of the Crow,* p. 37.

*School Library Journal,* November, 2007, Sheila Fiscus, review of *Eye of the Crow,* p. 134.

*ONLINE*

*Puffin Books Web site,* http://www.puffinbooks.ca/ (December, 2002), "An Interview with Shane Peacock on *Unusual Heroes.*"

*Shane Peacock Home Page,* http://www.shanepeacock.ca (August 15, 2008).*

* * *

## PHILLIPS, Suzanne

### Personal

Children: one daughter. *Education:* M.F.A (fiction writing.

### Addresses

*Home*—Santee, CA. *Agent*—Jodie Rhodes Literary Agency, 8840 Villa La Jolla Dr., Ste. 315, La Jolla, CA 92037.

### Career

Author and special education English teacher in CA.

### Writings

*Chloe Doe,* Little, Brown (New York, NY), 2007, published as *Miss America,* Young Picador (London, England), 2007.

*Burn,* Macmillan (New York, NY), 2008.

### Sidelights

In her debut novel *Chloe Doe* Suzanne Phillips draws readers in with what *Booklist* critic Jennifer Hubert described as an "intense and emotional debut" that the critic compared to novels by Patricia McCormick and Ellen Hopkins. Chloe Doe is, at age seventeen, tough, angry, and experienced with life on the streets. Arrested for prostitution, she is sent to the Madeline Parker Institute for Girls, where her meetings with a therapist gradually reveal the reasons for her life's course. Raised in a Hispanic neighborhood, Chloe has always been pragmatic about working the streets, viewing it as a practical way to pay the rent since running away from an abusive home at age eleven. Through her discussions with Dr. Dearborn, and her growing friendships with other girls at the institute, the teen begins to reveal the feelings underlying her tough exterior, however, and slowly readers are made privy to the tragedy that caused her to spin out of control.

Through Chloe's narration, and Phillips' use of stream of consciousness and flashbacks, *Chloe Doe* is "a blisteringly honest portrayal of a good girl who loses, then finds, her way," according to Hubert. While a *Publishers Weekly* critic described the novel as "an exhausting but nonetheless authentic read," the critic also praised the author's "clear understanding of Chloe's tough yet vulnerable character." Phillips' "language is sharp and engaging, even lyrical at times," noted *Kliatt* critic

***Cover of Suzanne Phillips' gritty young-adult novel* Chloe Doe, *which takes readers into the world of a teen trying to survive on the streets.***
(Little, Brown, 2007. Reproduced by permission.)

Myrna Marler, and in *Chloe Doe* the author "completely avoid[s] . . . easy sentimentality." Describing the teen protagonist's narrative voice as "wise beyond her years," a *Kirkus Reviews* contributor predicted that the girl's "spare dialogue and memories" will prove compelling to teen readers.

## Biographical and Critical Sources

*PERIODICALS*

*Booklist,* May 15, 2007, Jennifer Hubert, review of *Chloe Doe,* p. 41.

*Bulletin of the Center for Children's Books,* October, 2007, review of *Chloe Doe,* p. 104.

*Kirkus Reviews,* May 15, 2007, review of *Chloe Doe.*

*Kliatt,* May, 2007, Myrna Marler, review of *Chloe Doe,* p. 18.

*Publishers Weekly,* June 11, 2007, review of *Chloe Doe,* p. 61.

*Voice of Youth Advocates,* August, 2007, Robin Guedel, review of *Chloe Doe,* p. 248.*

* * *

# PRÉVOST, Guillaume 1964-

## Personal

Born 1964, in France; married; children: one son, one daughter. *Hobbies and other interests:* Video games, judo, computer technology.

## Addresses

*Home*—Versailles, France.

## Career

Educator and author. University du Havre, Le Havre, France, instructor in history.

## Writings

*YOUNG-ADULT NOVELS*

*Livre du temps: la pierre sculptée,* Gallimard (Paris, France), 2006, translated by William Rodarmor as *The Book of Time,* Arthur A. Levine (New York, NY), 2007.

*Sept piéces,* translated by William Rodarmor as *The Gate of Days: The Book of Time II,* Arthur A. Levine (New York, NY), 2008.

Author's work has also been translated into German.

*OTHER*

*Les sept crimes de Rome* (fiction), Nil Editions (France), 2000.

Also author of two adult thriller novels published in France: *L'assassin et le prophète* and *Le mystère de la chambre obscure.*

## Adaptations

The "Book of Time" novels were adapted for audiobook by Random House Audio.

## Sidelights

In addition to teaching history at a university in his native France, Guillaume Prévost is also a young-adult novelist. His fantasy trilogy "The Book of Time" includes the novels *The Book of Time* and *The Gate of Days: The Book of Time II,* both of which were originally published in France and were inspired by Prévost's lifelong interest in history and reading.

In *The Book of Time* readers meet fourteen-year-old Sam Faulkner, a boy who has lived with his grandparents ever since his mother was killed in a car accident. Sam's father, Allan, is an antiquarian book dealer. When Allan goes missing, the boy searches his father's bookshop for clues and discovers a secret stone statue that transports him back through time. Soon he is helping to defend Iona from Viking hoards, sleuthing in ancient Egypt in search of a murderer, visiting medieval Belgium, warning residents of pre-Vesuvius Pompeii, and aiding French troops on the front lines during World War I. Aided by his cousin, twelve-year-old Lily, who communicates with him via text-messaging, Sam assists those living in each time period he visits, making a small but crucial mark on history before departing for other eras. He also continues to track his missing father, and in *The Gate of Days* he learns that the bookseller is being held by the evil Vlad the Impaler. Vlad is the same fifteenth-century man who served as the inspiration for Bram Stoker's Dracula, and Sam realizes that the longer his father is trapped in Vlad's castle, the less likely he is to remain alive. To release his father, the teen must quickly travel through time to collect the seven guide coins required to direct the statue in sending him to Vlad's castle.

Reviewing *The Book of Time* in *Horn Book,* Vicky Smith noted that "Prévost keeps the plot moving along at a breakneck pace, giving both Sam and the reader scant moments to catch their breath between time jumps" in his clue-studded tale. The story's "well-drawn characters and a swiftly moving story" keep readers mesmerized, wrote Carolyn Phelan in *Booklist,* the critic predicting that "readers will be scrambling for the second book of the planned trilogy." Calling *The Book of Time* "remarkably inventive," *Kliatt* contributor Cara Chancellor added that "Prévost's real triumph is his stunning historical fiction, which convincingly transports readers" along the same path taken by the novel's adventurous young protagonist.

Discussing his work as a teacher of history, Prévost explained in an interview for *Kidsread.com:* "When talking with my students, I tried to stress the human side of history, to help them understand, for example, that the Greeks who invented democracy in Athens were in some ways different from us, but in many ways, very similar. That's what makes them close to us, and important and useful to know. They still have things to tell us today. And that approach isn't so different from that of *The Book of Time*."

## Biographical and Critical Sources

*PERIODICALS*

*Booklist,* July 1, 2007, Carolyn Phelan, review of *The Book of Time,* p. 59.

*Bulletin of the Center for Children's Books,* September, 2007, Cindy Welch, review of *The Book of Time,* p. 47.

*Horn Book,* September-October, 2007, Vicky Smith, review of *The Book of Time,* p. 587.

*Kirkus Reviews,* July 15, 2007, review of *The Book of Time.*

*Kliatt,* September, 2007, Cara Chancellor, review of *The Book of Time,* p. 17.

*Publishers Weekly,* October 1, 2007, review of *The Book of Time,* p. 57.

*School Library Journal,* November, 2007, Emily R. Brown, review of *The Book of Time,* p. 135.

*ONLINE*

*Kidsreads.com,* http://www.kidreads.com/ (September 1, 2007), interview with Prévost.

*Teenreads.com,* http://www.teenreads.com/ (August 25, 2008), Donna Volkenannt, review of *The Book of Time.**

# R

## REYNOLDS, Adrian 1963-

### Personal

Born 1963, in England.

### Addresses

*Home*—Cambridge, England.

### Career

Illustrator. Formerly worked in a bookstore.

### Awards, Honors

Children's Book Award shortlist, for *Harry and the Bucketful of Dinosaurs* by Ian Whybrow.

### Writings

*SELF-ILLUSTRATED*

*Pete and Polo and the Washday Adventure,* Orchard (London, England), 1997.

*Pete and Polo's Nursery School Adventure,* Orchard (London, England), 1999, published as *Pete and Polo's Big School Adventure,* Orchard (New York, NY), 2000.

*Pete and Polo's Farmyard Adventure,* Orchard (London, England), 2001, Orchard (New York, NY), 2002.

*Pete and Polo's Magical Christmas,* Orchard (London, England), 2002.

*ILLUSTRATOR*

Ragnhild Scamell, *Toby's Doll House,* Levinson (London, England), 1998.

Margaret Ryan, *The Big Sister's Tale,* Hodder Children's (London, England), 1998.

Margaret Ryan, *The Little Brother's Tale,* Hodder Children's (London, England), 1998.

Margaret Ryan, *The Little Sister's Tale,* Hodder Children's (London, England), 1998.

Alan Brown, *Humbugs,* Hodder Children's (London, England), 1998.

Sally Grindley, *Silly Goose and Daft Duck Play Hide-and-Seek,* Dorling Kindersley (London, England), 1999.

Beverley Birch, *Down the Road to Jamie's House,* Hodder Children's (London, England), 1999.

Hiawyn Oram, *What's Naughty?,* Hodder Children's (London, England), 2000.

Michael Lawrence, *Baby Loves Hugs and Kisses,* Dorling Kindersley (London, England), 2000.

Sally Grindley, *Silly Goose and Daft Duck Try to Catch a Rainbow,* Dorling Kindersley (London, England), 2001.

Michael Lawrence, *Baby Loves Visiting,* Dorling Kindersley (London, England), 2002.

Jonathan Emmett, *Someone Bigger,* Oxford University Press (Oxford, England), 2003, Clarion (New York, NY), 2004.

Julia Jarman, *Big Red Bath,* Orchard (London, England), 2004, published as *Big Red Tub,* Scholastic (New York, NY), 2004.

Jonathan Emmett, *If We Had a Sailboat,* Oxford University Press (Oxford, England), 2006.

Jeanne Willis, *Who's in the Bathroom?,* Simon & Schuster (New York, NY), 2007.

Michael Rosen, *Bear's Day Out,* Bloomsbury (New York, NY), 2007.

*ILLUSTRATOR; "HARRY AND THE DINOSAURS" SERIES*

Ian Whybrow, *Harry and the Snow King,* Levinson (London, England), 1997, Sterling, 1999.

Ian Whybrow, *Harry and the Bucket Full of Dinosaurs,* David and Charles (London, England), 1999, published as *Sammy and the Dinosaurs,* Orchard (New York, NY), 1999, adapted as *Harry and the Bucketful of Pop-up Dinosaurs,* Puffin (London, England), 2005.

***Adrian Reynolds teams up with author Michael Lawrence to produce the board book* Baby Loves Hugs and Kisses.** (Illustration copyright © 2000 by Adrian Reynolds. Reprinted by permission of DK Publishing, a member of Penguin Group (USA), Inc.)

Ian Whybrow, *Harry and the Robots,* David and Charles (London, England), 2000, published as *Sammy and the Robots,* Scholastic (New York, NY), 2001.

Ian Whybrow, *Harry and the Dinosaurs Say "Raahh!",* Gullane Children's Books (London, England), 2001, Random House (New York, NY), 2004.

Ian Whybrow, *Harry and the Dinosaurs Play Hide-and-Seek,* Gullane Children's (London, England), 2002.

Ian Whybrow, *Harry and the Dinosaurs Have a Very Busy Day,* Gullane Children's (London, England), 2002.

Ian Whybrow, *Romp in the Swamp,* Gullane Children's (London, England), 2002.

Ian Whybrow, *Harry and the Dinosaurs Make a Christmas Wish,* Puffin (London, England), 2003, Random House (New York, NY), 2004.

Ian Whybrow, *Harry and the Dinosaurs Tell the Time,* Penguin (London, England), 2004.

Ian Whybrow, *Harry and the Dinosaurs at the Museum,* Puffin (London, England), 2004, Random House (New York, NY), 2005.

Ian Whybrow, *Harry and the Dinosaurs Go Wild,* Gullane Children's (London, England), 2005.

Ian Whybrow, *Harry and the Dinosaurs and the Bucketful of Stories* (omnibus), Puffin (London, England), 2005.

Ian Whybrow, *Harry and the Dinosaurs Go to School,* Puffin (London, England), 2006, Random House (New York, NY), 2007.

Ian Whybrow, *Harry and the Dinosaurs Make a Splash,* Puffin (London, England), 2007.

Jean Willis, *Who's in the Bathroom?,* Simon & Schuster (New York, NY), 2007.

Books featuring Reynolds' illustrations have been translated into Welsh.

## Sidelights

British artist Adrian Reynolds was inspired to begin his career as a children's book illustrator while working in a book store in his native England. Among the dozens of books that contain his illustrations are the popular "Harry and the Dinosaurs" series by Ian Whybrow, as well as several original self-illustrated picture books featuring a boy and his stuffed polar bear. In *Pete and Polo&s Big School Adventure,* Pete and toy friend Polo head off to their first day of nursery school, where the white-furred Polo is nervous that the bears of all the other children are brown bears. First-time schoolers will enjoy "a typical school day unfold[ing] through Reynold's cheerful text and bright watercolors," concluded

***Reynolds' most frequent collaborator, Ian Whybrow, produced the text for their humorous picture book*** **Harry and the Dinosaurs at the Museum.** (Illustration copyright © 2004 by Adrian Reynolds. Used by permission of Random House, an imprint of Random House Children' Books, a division of Random House, Inc.)

*Booklist* contributor Lauren Peterson. A visit to grandfather's small farm in rural England is the focus of *Pete and Polo's Farmyard Adventure,* in which the author/illustrator "ably conveys the pleasures of a day in the country" and "makes it real that this is the kind of adventure a kid could have on his own." "The child's-eye view is especially successful; the size and perspective of familiar objects are just as Pete would see them," Carolyn Janssen wrote in a *School Library Journal* review of *Pete and Polo's Farmyard Adventure.*

*Harry and the Bucket Full of Dinosaurs,* which became a best-seller in England and was shortlisted for the Children's Book Award, was published as *Sammy and the Dinosaurs* in the United States and sets the pace for Whybrow's series. In the story, Harry discovers some old toy dinosaurs in the attic of his grandmother's house. Adopting the toys and naming each one, they soon become his favorites, and he takes his dinosaurs everywhere he goes. When the dinosaurs get left behind after Harry takes a train ride, it is left to the boy to avert a potential tragedy and rescue his beloved toys. Praising Whybrow's story as "alternately humorous and poignant, . . . and always right on target," *Horn Book* critic Lolly Robinson added that Reynolds' contribution of "vibrantly colored pen-and-watercolor illustrations" capture "the affection each feels for the other . . . in joyfully expressive drawings that show people and dinosaurs with dot eyes and simple flowing outlines."

Other adventures with Harry have followed, including *Harry and the Dinosaurs Say "Raahh!," Harry and the Dinosaurs at the Museum, Harry and the Dinosaurs Go to School,* and *Harry and the Dinosaurs Go Wild.* In *Harry and the Dinosaurs at the Museum* the boy, his family, and his dinosaurs visit a local museum where the boy finds a dinosaur exhibit that features full-size versions of his dino-friends. In illustrating Whybrow's entertaining lesson in dinosaur history, Reynolds' "bright, sturdy watercolors effectively use ankle-high (toy dinosaur) perspective," according to Robinson. The first day at a new school causes Stegosaurus some qualms in *Harry and the Dinosaurs Go to School,* in which "text and art keep a light touch," according to Robinson, while in *School Library Journal* June Wolfe maintained that Reynolds' "watercolor and line illustrations have more life than the story."

In addition to his work with Whybrow, Reynolds has also created art for texts by other children's book authors, such as Julia Jarman, Margaret Ryan, Michael Rosen, and Jonathan Emmett. He joins Jarman to create *Big Red Bath* (published in the United States as *Big Red Tub*), in which two children playing in a bubble-filled bathtub are joined by a host of animal friends, until a rotund hippo disrupts the crowd of playful bathers. Reynolds' "large, cleanly defined drawings glow with warm washes" and "ratchet . . . up pandemonium before letting the storynote wind down to a cheerful conclusion," observed *Booklist* reviewer Carolyn Phelan. The book's "buoyant pictures make the most of the saturated silliness," concluded a *Publishers Weekly* critic of *Big Red Tub,* adding that the illustrator's "cartooned menagerie exudes an eager mischievousness."

*Someone Bigger,* with a text by Emmett, presents an engaging story that finds a father and son carried away by a frisky homemade kite. Noting Reynolds' use of "unusual aerial perspectives" and a healthy dose of "silliness" in his watercolor cartoon art, *Booklist* contributor Lauren Peterson concluded that the "catchy rhymes and colorful art" in *Someone Bigger* make this a good choice for a spring storytime."

Rosen's *Bear's Day Out,* which focuses on a bear's trek from seashore to city, was praised by *Booklist* contributor Julie Cummins, who wrote that Reynolds' illustrations, with their "vivid colors," "capture the whimsical playfulness of [Rosen's] . . . words." "The illustrator's cityscapes are as chock-full of movement, color and people as the puzzled bear can handle," maintained a *Publishers Weekly* in a laudatory review of *Bear's Day Out.* In *Kirkus Reviews* a critic praised Rosen's rhyming text and added that Reynolds' "large and luscious" cartoons feature "atmospheric and idyllic shore scenes" as well as depictions of bustling city streets.

## Biographical and Critical Sources

*PERIODICALS*

*Booklist,* July, 1999, Carolyn Phelan, review of *Harry and the Snow King,* p. 1956; August, 2002, Carolyn Phelan, review of *Pete and Polo's Farmyard Adventure,* p. 1976; March 1, 2004, Lauren Peterson, review of *Someone Bigger,* p. 1193; January 1, 2005, Carolyn Phelan, review of *Big Red Tub,* p. 869; September 1, 2007, Julie Cummins, review of *Bear's Day Out,* p. 123.

*Horn Book,* September, 1999, Lolly Robinson, review of *Sammy and the Dinosaurs,* p. 602; May-June, 2004, Lolly Robinson, review of *Harry and the Dinosaurs Say "Raahh!",* p. 323; November-December, 2004, Lolly Robinson, review of *Harry and the Dinosaurs Make a Christmas Wish,* p. 666; July-August, 2005, Lolly Robinson, review of *Harry and the Dinosaurs at the Museum,* p. 461; July-August, 2007, Lolly Robinson, review of *Harry and the Dinosaurs Go to School,* p. 387.

*Kirkus Reviews,* April 1, 2002, review of *Pete and Polo's Farmyard Adventure,* p. 298; January 15, 2004, review of *Harry and the Dinosaurs Say "Raahh!",* p. 91; February 15, 2004, review of *Someone Bigger,* p. 176; December 15, 2004, review of *Big Red Tub,* p. 1203; March 1, 2007, review of *Who's in the Bathroom?,* p. 234; October 1, 2007, review of *Bear's Day Out.*

*Publishers Weekly,* June 14, 1999, review of *Toby's Doll House,* p. 69; January 17, 2005, review of *Big Red Tub,* p. 54; October 1, 2007, review of *Bear's Day Out,* p. 56.

*School Library Journal,* December, 2000, Leslie S. Hilverding, review of *Pete and Polo's Big School Adventure,* p. 123; December, 2000, Shanla Brookshire, review of *Baby Loves Hugs and Kisses,* p. 113; July, 2001, DeAnn Tabuchi, review of *Sammy and the Robots,* p. 91; July, 2002, Carolyn Janssen, review of *Pete and Polo's Farmyard Adventure,* p. 97; May, 2004, G. Alyssa Parkinson, review of *Someone Bigger,* p. 109; December, 2004, Julie Roach, review of *Big Red Tub,* p. 110; July, 2005, Jane Barrer, review of *Harry and the Dinosaurs at the Museum,* p. 84; March, 2007, Suzanne Myers Harold, review of *Who's in the Bathroom?,* p. 191; June, 2007, June Wolfe, review of *Harry and the Dinosaurs Go to School,* p. 127.*

* * *

# ROOT, Kimberly Bulcken

## Personal

Married Barry Root (an illustrator); children: Janna, Samuel, Benjamin.

## Addresses

*Home*—Quarryfield, PA.

## Career

Illustrator.

## Awards, Honors

Notable Book for Children selection, American Library Association (ALA), for *Hugh Can Do;* Best Illustrated Book selection, *New York Times,* for *When the Whippoorwill Calls;* Notable Book for Children selection, ALA, for *The Toll-bridge Troll.*

## Writings

*ILLUSTRATOR*

Roger B. Goodman, *A Bed for the Wind,* Simon and Schuster (New York, NY), 1988.

Selma G. Lanes, reteller, *Windows of Gold and Other Golden Tales,* Simon and Schuster (New York, NY), 1989.

Gerald Milnes, *Granny, Will Your Dog Bite and Other Mountain Rhymes,* Knopf (New York, NY), 1990.

Judith Gorog, *In a Messy, Messy Room,* Philomel (New York, NY), 1990.

Eric A. Kimmel, reteller, *Boots and His Brothers: A Norwegian Tale,* Holiday House (New York, NY), 1992.

Jennifer Armstrong, *Hugh Can Do,* Crown (New York, NY), 1992.

Carol Greene, *Beggars, Beasts, and Easter Fire,* Lion Publishing (Batavia, IL), 1993.

Patricia Lakin, *The Palace of Stars,* Tambourine Books (New York, NY), 1993.

Mary Lee Donovan, *Papa's Bedtime Story,* Knopf (New York, NY), 1993.

Reeve Lindbergh, *If I'd Known Then What I Know Now,* Viking (New York, NY), 1994.

Ellin Greene, reteller, *Billy Beg and His Bull: An Irish Tale,* Holiday House (New York, NY), 1994.

Candice F. Ransom, *When the Whippoorwill Calls,* Tambourine Books (New York, NY), 1995.

Margaret Hodges, reteller, *Gulliver in Lilliput: From Gulliver's Travels by Jonathan Swift,* Holiday House (New York, NY), 1995.

Patrica Rae Wolff, *The Toll-bridge Troll,* Browndeer Press (San Diego, CA), 1995.

Alice McLerran, *The Year of the Ranch,* Viking (New York, NY), 1996.

Judith Gorog, *In a Creepy, Creepy Place and Other Scary Stories,* HarperCollins (New York, NY), 1996.

Margaret Hodges, *The True Tale of Johnny Appleseed,* Holiday House (New York, NY), 1997.

Deborah Hopkinson, *Birdie's Lighthouse,* Atheneum (New York, NY), 1997.

Lady Borton, *Junk Pile!,* Philomel (New York, NY), 1997.

Alison Cragin Herzig, *Bronco Busters,* Putnam (New York, NY), 1998.

Dorothy Canfield Fisher, *Understood Betsy,* Holt (New York, NY), 1999.

Maxine Rose Schur, *The Peddler's Gift,* Dial Books (New York, NY), 1999.

Rafe Martin, *The Storytelling Princess,* Putnam (New York, NY), 2001.

Margaret Hodges, reteller, *The Wee Christmas Cabin,* Holiday House (New York, NY), 2001.

Robert D. San Souci, *The Birds of Killingworth: Based on a Poem by Henry Wadsworth Longfellow,* Dial Books (New York, NY), 2002.

Roni Schotter, *In the Piney Woods,* Melanie Kroupa Books (New York, NY), 2003.

Jean Whitehouse Peterson, *Don't Forget Winona,* Joanna Cotler Books (New York, NY), 2004.

Yona Zeldis McDonough, *The Doll with the Yellow Star,* Holt (New York, NY), 2005.

Amy Littlesugar, *Clown Child,* Philomel (New York, NY), 2006.

Susan Fletcher, *Dadblamed Union Army Cow,* Candlewick Press (Cambridge, MA), 2007.

## Sidelights

Kimberly Bulcken Root is an award-winning illustrator of children's books. One of her early efforts, *Granny, Will Your Dog Bite and Other Mountain Rhymes* by Gerald Milnes, contains more than fifty poems from the Appalachian region. Root's watercolor illustrations "extend the action, exuberance and high spirits of the rhymes," noted a contributor to *Publishers Weekly.* The artist also drew praised for her contributions to Eric A. Kimmel's retelling *Boots and His Brothers: A Norwegian Tale.* Root's deeply shadowed, brooding illustrations, reminiscent of Henrik Drescher . . ., add welcome theatrics" to the work, a contributor in *Publishers Weekly* remarked.

Root has more recently provided the artwork for Jennifer Armstrong's debut picture book, *Hugh Can Do,* about a cheerful lad who overcomes a series of challenges to earn his fortune. Here the illustrator "handsomely alternates small spots of Hugh dashing about his tasks with emotive, full-page scenes," noted a *Publishers Weekly* reviewer. A young boy recounts his father's disastrous yet comical attempts at home repair in Reeve Lindbergh's *If I'd Known Then What I Know Now.* The lyrical narrative "is eminently readable, and Root makes hay with it, producing a collection of wonderfully exaggerated, sophisticated illustrations," another *Publishers Weekly* critic remarked.

In Candice F. Ransom's *When the Whippoorwill Calls,* a family of tenant farmers is uprooted from its home in the Blue Ridge Mountains. According to *Booklist* critic Julie Yates Walton, "Root's delicate, muted watercolor illustrations exude nostalgia and deepen the pathos" of Ransom's tale. *The Toll-bridge Troll,* a humorous story by Patricia Rae Wolff, concerns a clever youngster's scheme to outwit a demanding troll. "Root's attractive pen-and-watercolor paintings gracefully blend quaint and contemporary elements," Leone McDermott stated in *Booklist,* and a contributor in *Publishers Weekly* commented that the "visual eccentricities help the reader believe in the fantastical world so deftly created here."

Set in Arizona in 1919, Alice McLerran's *The Year of the Ranch* focuses on a family of homesteaders who must cope with sandstorms and rattlesnakes. "Root's watercolors capture the vibrant and ever-changing palette of bright stars and sumptuous sunsets found in the desert landscape," a *Publishers Weekly* reviewer observed. During a wild storm, a youngster keeps the oil lamps burning when her father falls ill in *Birdie's Lighthouse,* a work by Deborah Hopkinson. Fine, meticulous strokes and a preponderance of shadowy blues and grays give Root's pen-and-ink and watercolor pictures the look of etchings," noted a critic in *Publishers Weekly.*

In *Junk Pile!,* a story by Lady Borton, a shy little girl uses her knowledge of car parts to make a new friend. "Root's line-and-watercolor illustrations perfectly express the intricate glory of the junkyard stuff," observed *Booklist* reviewer Hazel Rochman. A quiet cowboy shows a trio of roughnecks how to tame a pony in Alison Cragin Herzig's *Bronco Busters.* Root's "snapshots of the bronco-busting business in a dusty Wild West palette fairly burst out of their oval," a *Publishers Weekly* contributor stated.

In *The Storytelling Princess,* a work by Rafe Martin, a spunky princess who refuses to participate in an arranged marriage disguises herself as a sailor and finds true love. "Watercolor-and-pencil illustrations in subtle hues with highlights of gold and red cleverly capture the nature of the characters and the essence of the action," wrote *School Library Journal* critic Starr LaTronica.

*Kimberly Bulcken Root's detailed paintings enrich Jeanne Whitehouse Peterson's nostalgic story in* **Don't Forget Winona.** (Illustration copyright © 2004 by Kimberly Bulcken Root. Used by permission of HarperCollins Children's Books, a division of HarperCollins Publishers.)

A fable with an environmental theme, Robert D. San Souci's *The Birds of Killingworth: Based on a Poem by Henry Wadsworth Longfellow* concerns the misguided efforts of colonial villagers to destroy the birds that damage their crops. According to *School Library Journal* contributor Nancy Palmer, Root's pictures "are full of watery color and period detail, enriching the natural setting and tempering the cautionary tale with humor and humanity."

## Biographical and Critical Sources

*PERIODICALS*

*Booklist,* March 1, 1994, Carolyn Phelan, review of *Billy Beg and His Bull: An Irish Tale,* p. 1264; April 15, 1995, Leone McDermott, review of *The Toll-bridge Troll,* p. 1508; April 15, 1995, Hazel Rochman, review of *Gulliver in Lilliput: From Gulliver's Travels by Jonathan Swift,* p. 1500; September 15, 1995, Julie Yates Walton, review of *When the Whippoorwill Calls,* p. 176; July, 1996, Susan Dove Lempke, review of *The Year of the Ranch,* p. 1830; June 1, 1997, Hazel Rochman, review of *Birdie's Lighthouse,* p. 1718; April 15, 1997, Hazel Rochman, review of *Junk Pile!,* p. 1433; July, 1997, Carolyn Phelan, review of *The True Tale of Johnny Appleseed,* p. 1820; September

15, 1998, Kay Weisman, review of *Bronco Busters,* p. 237; October 1, 1999, Hazel Rochman, review of *The Peddler's Gift,* p. 375; July, 2003, Carolyn Phelan, review of *In the Piney Woods,* p. 1898.

*Publishers Weekly,* November 16, 1990, review of *Granny Will Your Dog Bite and Other Mountain Rhymes,* p. 58; Feb 10, 1992, review of *Boots and His Brothers: A Norwegian Tale,* p. 80; June 29, 1992, review of *Hugh Can Do,* p. 62; March 22, 1993, review of *Papa's Bedtime Story,* p. 78; September 13, 1993, review of *The Palace of Stars,* p. 132; May 9, 1994, review of *If I'd Known Then What I Know Now,* p. 71; March 6, 1995, review of *Gulliver in Lilliput,* p. 69; April 17, 1995, review of *The Toll-bridge Troll,* p. 57; June 10, 1996, review of *The Year of the Ranch,* p. 98; February 10, 1997, review of *Junk Pile!,* p. 83; April 14, 1997, review of *Birdie's Lighthouse,* p. 74; September 21, 1998, review of *Bronco Busters,* p. 84; September 27, 1999, review of *The Peddler's Gift,* p. 52; June 25, 2001, review of *The Storytelling Princess,* p. 72; April 15, 2002, review of *The Birds of Killingsworth: Based on a Poem by Henry Wadsworth Longfellow,* p. 63; November 25, 2002, review of *In the Piney Woods,* p. 67.

*School Library Journal,* September, 2001, Starr LaTronica, review of *The Storytelling Princess,* p. 199; August, 2002, Nancy Palmer, *The Birds of Killingworth: Based on a Poem by Henry Wadsworth Longfellow,* p. 168; April, 2003, Jane Marino, review of *In the Piney Woods,* p. 137.

*ONLINE*

*HarperCollins Web site,* http://www.harpercollins.com/ (August 15, 2008), "Kimberly Bulcken Root."*

# S

## SAKAKI, Ichiro 1969-

### Personal

Born 1969, in Japan.

### Addresses

*Home*—Japan.

### Career

Author and creator of anime in Japan. Creator of anime films, including "Strait Jacket," "Mission-E," and "Shinkyoku Sokai Polyphonica" series.

### Writings

*"SCRAPPED PRINCESS" SERIES; GRAPHIC NOVELS*

*Scrapped Princess Novel 1: A Tale of Destiny* (originally published in comic-book format by Kadokawa Shoten, beginning 2002), illustrated by Yukinobu Azumi, translated from the Japanese by Paul Kotta, Tokyopop (Los Angeles, CA), 2006.

*Scrapped Princess Novel 2: Song of the Forgiven* (originally published in comic-book format by Kadokawa Shoten, beginning 2002), illustrated by Yukinobu Azumi, translated from the Japanese by Paul Kotta, Tokyopop (Los Angeles, CA), 2007.

### Biographical and Critical Sources

*PERIODICALS*

*School Library Journal,* January, 2006, Sarah Couri, review of *Scrapped Princess Novel 1: A Tale of Destiny,* p. 167; November, 2006, Jennifer Feigelman, review of *Scrapped Princess Novel 1,* p. 150.

*ONLINE*

*Teenreads Web site,* http://www.teenreads.com/ (August 15, 2008), Eileen Zimmerman Nicol, review of *Scrapped Princess Novel 1.**

* * *

## SAN SOUCI, Daniel 1948-

### Personal

Born October 10, 1948, in San Francisco, CA; married; wife's name Loretta (a children's librarian); children: Yvette, Justin, Noelle. *Education:* Attended California College of Arts and Crafts.

### Addresses

*Home and office*—Oakland, CA. *E-mail*—sansouci@silcon.com.

### Career

Children's book illustrator and author.

### Awards, Honors

*New York Times* Best Illustrated Book designation, 1978, for *The Legend of Scarface;* Western Writers Award, 1985, for *Trapped in the Sliprock Canyon* by Gloria Skurzynski; Gold Medallion, 1986, for *Potter, Come Fly to the First of the Earth* by Walter Wangerin; Aesop Accolade List, American Folklore Society, 1995, for *The Gifts of Wali Dad.*

### Writings

*SELF-ILLUSTRATED*

*North Country Night,* Doubleday (Garden City, NY), 1990.

*Country Road,* Doubleday (Garden City, NY), 1993.

*The Dangerous Snake and Reptile Club,* Tricycle Press (Berkeley, CA), 2004.

*Space Station Mars,* Tricycle Press (Berkeley, CA), 2005.

*The Amazing Ghost Detectives,* Tricycle Press (Berkeley, CA), 2006.

*The Mighty Pigeon Club,* Tricycle Press (Berkeley, CA), 2007.

*ILLUSTRATOR*

Robert D. San Souci, *The Legend of Scarface: A Blackfeet Indian Tale,* Doubleday (Garden City, NY), 1978.

Robert D. San Souci, *Son of Sedna,* Doubleday (Garden City, NY), 1981.

Robert D. San Souci, *The Brave Little Tailor,* Doubleday (Garden City, NY), 1982.

Phyllis Root, *Hidden Places,* Raintree, 1983.

White Deer of Autumn, *Ceremony—In the Circle of Life,* Raintree, 1983.

Gloria Skurzynski, *Trapped in the Sliprock Canyon,* Lothrop (New York, NY), 1984.

Morell Gipson, reteller, *Rip Van Winkle,* Doubleday (New York, NY), 1984.

*The Bedtime Book,* J. Messner, 1985.

Walter Wangerin, *Potter, Come Fly to the First of the Earth,* Chariot Books, 1985.

Freya Littledale, adaptor, *The Little Mermaid,* Scholastic (New York, NY), 1986.

*The Mother Goose Book,* Little Simon (New York, NY), 1986.

Robert D. San Souci, reteller, *The Legend of Sleepy Hollow,* Doubleday (New York, NY), 1986.

Lilian Moore, reteller, *The Ugly Duckling,* Scholastic (New York, NY), 1987.

Diane Arico, compiler and editor, *A Season of Joy: Favorite Stories and Poems for Christmas,* Doubleday (New York, NY), 1987.

Josepha Sherman, *Vassilisa the Wise: A Tale of Medieval Russia,* Harcourt Brace (New York, NY), 1988.

Robert D. San Souci, *The Six Swans,* Simon & Schuster (New York, NY), 1988.

Diane Arico, compiler and editor, *Easter Treasures: Favorite Stories and Poems for the Season,* Doubleday (New York, NY), 1989.

Robert D. San Souci, *The Christmas Ark,* Doubleday (New York, NY), 1991.

Robert D. San Souci, *Feathertop: Based on a Tale by Nathaniel Hawthorne,* Doubleday (New York, NY), 1992.

Margaret Hodges, reteller, *The Golden Deer,* Charles Scribner's Sons (New York, NY), 1992.

Josephine Haskell, *A Possible Tree,* Macmillan (New York, NY), 1993.

William O. Douglas, *Muir of the Mountains,* Sierra Club Books for Children, 1994.

Robert D. San Souci, *Sootface: An Ojibwa Cinderella Story,* Delacorte (New York, NY), 1994.

Aaron Shepard, reteller, *The Gifts of Wali Dad: A Tale of India and Pakistan,* Atheneum (New York, NY), 1995.

David F. Birchman, *Jigsaw Jackson,* Lothrop, Lee & Shepard (New York, NY), 1996.

Jonathan London, *Red Wolf Country,* Dutton (New York, NY), 1996.

Robert D. San Souci, *Young Merlin,* Dell (New York, NY), 1996.

Barbara Mitchell, *Waterman's Child,* Lothrop, Lee & Shepard (New York, NY), 1997.

Jonathan London, *Ice Bear and Little Fox,* Dutton (New York, NY), 1998.

Caroline Stutson, *Cowpokes,* Lothrop, Lee & Shepard (New York, NY), 1999.

Martha Bennett Stiles, *Island Magic,* Atheneum Books for Young Readers (New York, NY), 1999.

Jonathan London, *Mustang Canyon,* Dutton (New York, NY), 2000.

Eric A. Kimmel, *Montezuma and the Fall of the Aztecs,* Holiday House (New York, NY), 2000.

Steven P. Medley, *Antelope, Bison, Cougar: A National Park Wildlife Alphabet Book,* Yosemite Press, 2001.

Sharon Davis, *The Adventure of Capitol Kitty,* Scholastic (New York, NY), 2002.

Jean Craighead George, *Frightful's Daughter,* Dutton (New York, NY), 2002.

Eric A. Kimmel, *The Flying Canoe = La Chasse-Galleiorie: A Christmas Story,* Holiday House (New York, NY), 2003.

Robert D. San Souci, *Sister Tricksters: Rollicking Tales of Clever Females,* August House Little Folk (Atlanta, GA), 2006.

Jean Craighead George, *Frightful's Daughter Meets the Baron Weasel,* Dutton (New York, NY), 2007.

Robert D. San Souci, reteller, *As Luck Would Have It: From the Brothers Grimm,* August House Little Folk (Atlanta, GA), 2008.

*OTHER*

(Reteller) *In the Moonlight Mist: A Korean Tale,* illustrated by Eujin Kim Neilan, Boyds Mills Press (Honesdale, PA), 1999.

(Reteller) *The Rabbit and the Dragon King: Based on a Korean Tale,* illustrated by Eujin Kim Neilan, Boyds Mills Press (Honesdale, PA), 2002.

## Sidelights

Daniel San Souci is a highly regarded children's book illustrator as well as the author of several self-illustrated stories. Frequently praised for the realistic yet expressive water-color paintings depicting the natural world that he has created for such books as Steven P. Medley's *Antelope, Bison, Cougar: A National Park Wildlife Alphabet Book,* San Souci has also garnered positive critical attention for his comical rendering of characters in books such as *Feathertop: Based on a Tale by Nathaniel Hawthorne,* an adaptation by brother Robert D. San Souci, and *The Gifts of Wali Dad: A Tale of India and Pakistan,* a story by author Aaron Shepard. Other books featuring San Souci's artwork include Josepha Sherman's *Vassilisa the Wise,* Jonathan London's *Mustang Canyon,* and Jean Craighead George's *Frightful's Daughter.*

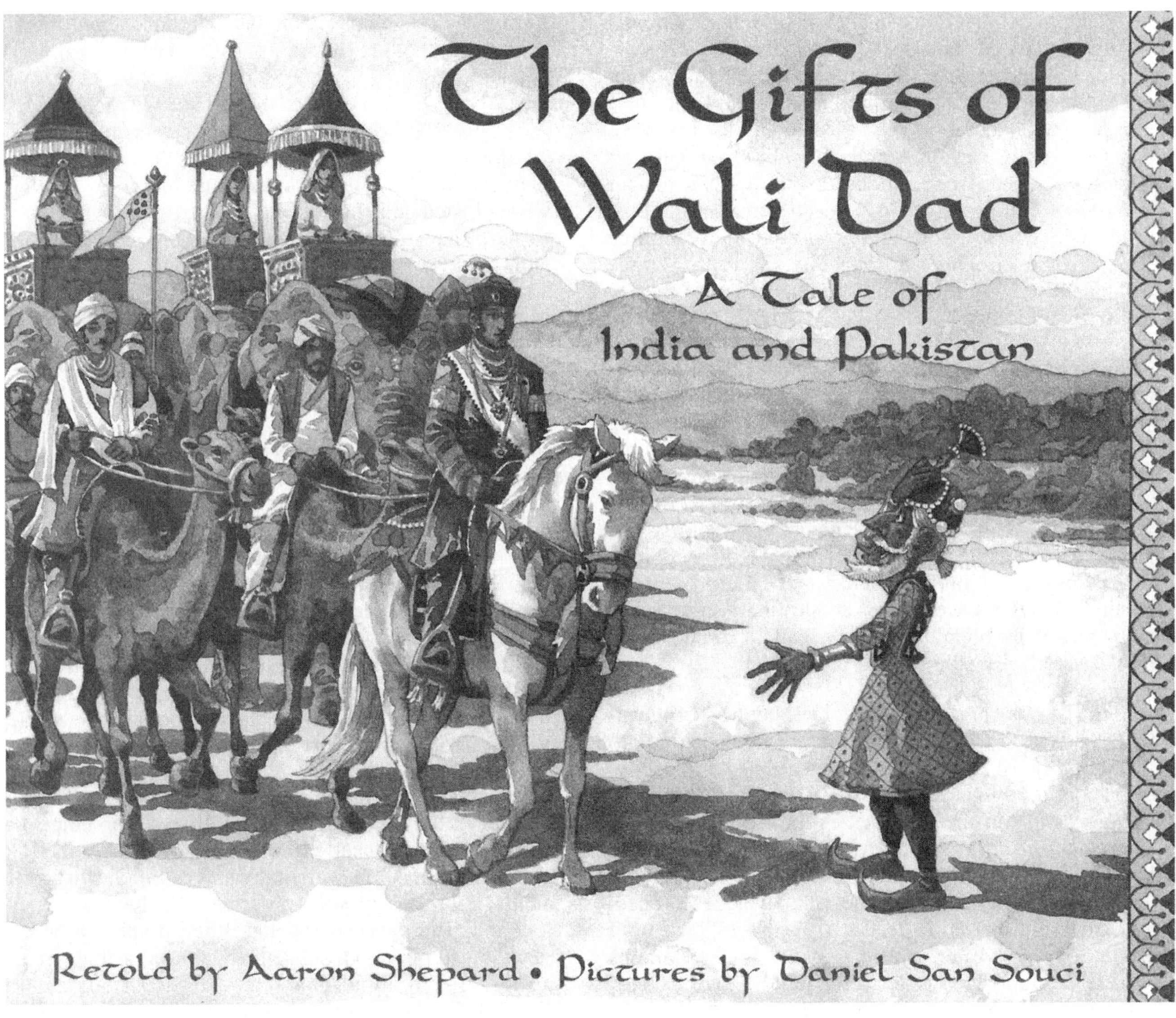


*Cover of Aaron Shepard's retelling* **The Gifts of Wali Dad,** *featuring Daniel San Souci's detailed watercolor art.* (Illustration copyright © 1995 by Daniel San Souci. Reprinted with the permission of Atheneum Books for Young Readers, an imprint of Simon & Schuster Children's Publishing Division.)

In *Vassilisa the Wise,* a folktale set in medieval Russia, a beautiful and clever woman tricks the evil Prince Vladimir into releasing her husband from prison. A *Publishers Weekly* reviewer remarked on the book's "stately watercolors, rich in costume and architectural detail," while Mary M. Burns wrote in *Horn Book* that San Souci's illustrations are "elegant and dynamic, large and authoritative, and reflect the drama and the setting" of Sherman's story. San Souci's watercolor illustrations for Josephine Haskell Aldridge's story *A Possible Tree* were also praised by reviewers. The book presents a number of animals that have been driven away from a farm as pests. Each in turn is drawn to a particular fir tree where they all nest peacefully together throughout the winter. *A Possible Tree* is "a small story made large by well-written prose and exquisite art," remarked Jane Marino in *School Library Journal.*

*The Gifts of Wali Dad* a traditional tale retold by Shepard, is the story of a man whose natural frugality results in his accumulation of some wealth, with which he buys a gold bracelet that he sends to the most noble lady that can be found. She sends a gift back in return, which Wali Dad then sends off to the noblest man. This exchange leads to the eventual marriage of the two gift recipients and Wali Dad's happy return to his simple life as a grass-cutter. San Souci's "illustrations convey an atmosphere of radiating generosity," remarked Mary Harris Veeder in her *Booklist* review of the work, and *School Library Journal* critic Marilyn Taniguchi cited *The Gifts of Wali Dad* for illustrations "full of interesting details . . . [that] . . . support and enlarge upon the text."

Working with London, San Souci has also produced art for *Red Wolf Country, Ice Bear and Little Fox,* and *Mustang Canyon. Red Wolf Country* relates the experiences of two wolves searching for shelter before giving birth to a litter of cubs. "Breathtaking paintings and a dramatic text make this wildlife adventure a real stand-out," enthused Joy Fleishhacker in a *School Library Journal* review of the book. A *Publishers Weekly* contributor wrote that San Souci's "elegant" pictures combine with London's text to produce "perhaps the most compatible collaboration yet." Also widely lauded, *Mustang Canyon* focuses on a herd of wild horses that runs wild through the American desert. San Souci's images "bring . . . children close to the wild herd and the blistering desert heat," noted *Booklist* contributor Gillian Engberg, and in *School Library Journal* Ruth Semrau maintained that the artist's illustrations "capture the joy of the running horses in their desert setting.

San Souci's work for David F. Birchman's *Jigsaw Jackson* results in a lighthearted picture book about a farmer who goes on the road to exhibit his jigsaw-solving prowess one winter. The man finds fame and fortune, but eventually misses his animals and returns home. "Birchman relates the story with gusto, its gleeful excesses mirrored in San Souci's merry watercolors," remarked a reviewer for *Publishers Weekly.* In *School Library Journal,* Christina Linz commented on the author's "hilarious scenarios," adding that "there's just enough fantasy blended with realism to create some pretty hysterical pictures."

*Frightful's Daughter,* a story by Newbery Award-winning writer George, is a picture-book sequel to George's highly popular novel *My Side of the Mountain,* about a boy named Sam and a peregrine falcon he calls Frightful. In the story, set in the Catskills, Frighful's chick, Oksi, grows up with an independent spirit that makes both Frightful and Sam concerned for her safety. "As always, San Souci's . . . well-researched, detailed paintings add greatly to the story," wrote a *Kirkus Reviews* writer, and in *Booklist* Julie Cummins praised the "gorgeous panoramic, aerial scenes" which "will lure children." In *Frightful's Daughter Meets the Baron Weasel* George continues her story about the adventures of Sam, Frightful, and Oksi. Now the mother of chicks of her own, Oksi is as brave as ever, even when her nest is besieged by a local weasel with his own family to feed. San Souci sets the wilderness tale amid what *Booklist* critic John Peters described as "verdant, open forest landscapes," and a *Kirkus Reviews* writer concluded that the book's "realistic watercolors capture the luminous grandeur" of the story's upstate New York setting.

Many of San Souci's illustration projects are collaborations with his brother, author Robert D. San Souci. In *Feathertop,* their adaptation of a tale by noted eighteenth-century writer Nathaniel Hawthorne, Mother Rigby, the town witch, turns her scarecrow into a handsome young man and sends him off to court the judge's daughter as a trick. The trick backfires however, when the scarecrow and the girl fall in love, and the girl must try to convince Mother Rigby to make the transformation permanent. A *Publishers Weekly* contributor noted that Robert San Souci takes constructive liberties with the original tale, and brother Daniel San Souci "effectively capture the garb and architectural details of mid-eighteenth-century New England." The pictures add "brilliant colors and lively action" to the "smoothly flowing oral quality" of the text, according to Shirley Wilton in *School Library Journal.*

Other collaborations by the San Souci brothers include *Sootface: An Ojibwa Cinderella Story,* in which the kindness of good-hearted Sootface wins for her the love of a great invisible warrior. Vanessa Elder, writing in *School Library Journal,* appreciated the book's "lively" text and "full-page watercolors [that] dramatically convey the natural woodland setting" as well as the personalities of individual characters. *Booklist* contributor Carolyn Phelan observed that although the story has

***Jonathan London's* Mustang Canyon *allows readers a window into the life of a young colt living in the wild, courtesy of San Souci's art.*** (Illustration copyright © 2002 by Daniel San Souci. Reproduced by permission of the publisher Candlewick Press, Inc., Somerville, MA.)

been adapted many times, the San Soucis' version is "a satisfying picture book for reading aloud or alone" that could contribute to classroom projects on Native American folklore. In *As Luck Would Have It,* the San Soucis retell the Brothers Grimm's tale "Clever Elsie," and Daniel's illustrations "contribute to the quaint feel of this effort," according a *Kirkus Reviews* writer.

Among San Souci's original books are several self-illustrated stories as well as retellings such as *The Rabbit and the Dragon King: Based on a Korean Folk Tale,* which features artwork by Eujin Kim Neilan. The picture book *Country Road* tells a quiet, contemplative story about a boy's walk through the country with his father. The book features the author/illustrator's "lavish double-page spreads done in realistic watercolors that highlight the animals" father and son encounter on their walk, remarked Valerie Lennox in *School Library Journal.* Noting the minimal text, Hazel Rochman noted in *Booklist* that this may well be San Souci's message to the young reader: pay attention to the visual details of the natural world that the artist captures in his detailed paintings.

Other original texts include *The Dangerous Snake and Reptile Club, Space Station Mars, The Amazing Ghost Detectives,* and *The Mighty Pigeon Club,* a series of stories about three brothers—Bobby, Mike, and Danny—and their adventures growing up in California. Interestingly, the books were inspired by the author/illustrator's memories of growing up with his two real-life brothers. Featuring cartoon art, *Space Station Mars* "captures the wonderful time in children's lives when the line between reality and imagination is blurred," in the words of *School Library Journal* critic Donna Cardon. Featuring details that set the book in a comforting past, *The Amazing Ghost Detectives* was dubbed a "whimsical tale [that] has great child appeal,"according to *School Library Journal* critic Daniellle Nicole Du Puis.

## Biographical and Critical Sources

*PERIODICALS*

*Booklist,* October 1, 1993, Hazel Rochman, review of *Country Road,* p. 354; October 15, 1994, Carolyn Phelan, review of *Sootface: An Ojibwa Cinderella Story,* p. 433; May 1, 1995, Mary Harris Veeder, review of *The Gifts of Wali Dad: A Tale of India and Pakistan,* p. 1578; January 1, 1996, Hazel Rochman, review of *Red Wolf Country,* p. 84; February 1, 2000, Ilene Cooper, review of *Island Magic,* p. 1030; December 15, 2001, Carolyn Phelan, review of *Antelope, Bison, Cougar: A National Park Wildlife Alphabet Book,* p. 729; September 1, 2002, Julie Cummins, review of *Frightful's Daughter,* p. 136; December 1, 2002, Gillian Engberg, review of *Mustang Canyon,* p. 675; September 1, 2007, John Peters, review of *Frightful's Daughter Meets the Baron Weasel,* p. 114, and Ilene Cooper, review of *The Mighty Pigeon Club,* p. 127.

*Horn Book,* July, 1988, Mary M. Burns, review of *Vassilisa the Wise,* p. 507.

*Kirkus Reviews,* August 1, 2002, review of *Mustang Canyon,* p. 1136; August 15, 2002, review of *Frightful's Daughter,* p. 1223; September 15, 2002, review of *The Rabbit and the Dragon King,* p. 1399; September 15, 2006, review of *Sister Tricksters: Rollicking Tales of Clever Females,* p. 966; September 1, 2007, review of *Frightful's Daughter Meets the Baron Weasel;* September 15, 2007, review of *The Mighty Pigeon Club*; August 15, 2008, review of *As Luck Would Have It.*

*Publishers Weekly,* May 13, 1988, review of *Vassilisa the Wise,* p. 374; November 12, 1992, review of *Feathertop,* p. 70; April 15, 1996, review of *Jigsaw Jackson,* p. 68; January 1, 1996, review of *Red Wolf Country,* p. 70.

*School Library Journal,* December, 1992, Shirley Wilton, review of *Feathertop,* p. 90; October, 1993, Jane Marino, review of *A Possible Tree,* p. 41; March, 1994, Valerie Lennox, review of *Country Road,* p. 208; November, 1994, Vanessa Elder, review of *Sootface,* p. 101; August, 1995, Marilyn Taniguchi, review of *The Gifts of Wali Dad,* p. 138; March, 1996, Joy Fleishhacker, review of *Red Wolf Country,* p. 178; July, 1996, Christina Linz, review of *Jigsaw Jackson,* p. 56; October, 2001, Steven Englelfried, review of *Antelope, Bison, Cougar,* p. 144; September, 2002, Margaret Bush, review of *Frightful's Daughter,* p. 192; November, 2002, Margaret Bush, review of *The Rabbit and the Dragon King,* p. 148; August, 2003, Ruth Semrau, review of *Mustang Canyon,* p. 138; December, 2004, Deborah Rothaug, review of *The Dangerous Snake and Reptile Club,* p. 120; October, 2005, Donna Cardon, review of *Space Station Mars,* p. 128; September, 2006, Kirsten Cutler, review of *Sister Tricksters,* p. 196; April, 2007, Danielle Nicole Du Puis, review of *The Amazing Ghost Detectives,* p. 115.

*ONLINE*

*Daniel San Souci Home Page,* http://www.danielsansouci.com (August 5, 2008).*

* * *

# SARDINHA, Rick

## Personal

Born in Paris, France.

## Addresses

*Home and office*—RI. *E-mail*—rick@battleduck.com.

## Career

Artist and illustrator.

## Awards, Honors

First Place Original art award, GenCon, 2006; Best in Show First Place award, DragonCon, 2006; Best Action

Illustration Award runner up, New Masters of Fantasy Awards, 2006, for "Dom of Listonshire"; Chesley Award nomination for Best Gaming-related Illustration, 2006, for "Family Affair," and 2007, for "Coils of Set"; Chesley Award nomination for Best Cover Illustration (Magazine), 2008.

## Illustrator

Nancy Farmer, *The Land of the Silver Apples,* Atheneum (New York, NY), 2007.

Contributor of artwork to periodicals, including *Dungeon.*

## Biographical and Critical Sources

*PERIODICALS*

*Horn Book,* July-August, 2007, Roger Sutton, review of *The Land of the Silver Apples,* p. 394.

*Kirkus Reviews,* July 1, 2007, review of *The Land of the Silver Apples.*

*Kliatt,* July, 2007, Paula Rohrlick, review of *The Land of the Silver Apples,* p. 14.

*School Library Journal,* August, 2007, Beth L. Meister, review of *The Land of the Silver Apples,* p. 114.

*ONLINE*

*Rick Sardinha Home Page,* http://www.battleduck.com (August 5, 2008).

* * *

# SCHERTLE, Alice 1941-

## Personal

Surname rhymes with "turtle"; born April 7, 1941, in Los Angeles, CA; daughter of Floyd C. (a real estate investor) and Marguerite (a teacher) Sanger; married Richard Schertle (a general contractor), December 21, 1963; children: Jennifer, Katherine, John. *Education:* University of Southern California, B.S. (cum laude), 1963.

## Addresses

*Home*—Plainfield, MA.

## Career

Highland School, Inglewood, CA, elementary school teacher, 1963-65; writer, 1965—.

## Member

National Council of Teachers of English, Authors Guild, Authors League, Society of Children's Book Writers and Illustrators.

***Alice Schertle*** (Photograph by Susan Pearson. Reproduced by permission of Alice Schertle.)

## Awards, Honors

Parents' Choice Picture Book Award, 1989, and Christopher Award, 1990, both for *William and Grandpa;* Parents' Choice Picture Book Award, 1991, for *Witch Hazel;* Best Books citation, *School Library Journal,* 1995, for *Advice for a Frog and Other Poems;* National Parenting Publications Award, 1995, for *How Now, Brown Cow?,* and 1996, for *Down the Road;* Notable Children's Books citations, American Library Association, 1996, for both *Advice for a Frog and Other Poems* and *Down the Road;* Oppenheim Toy Portfolio Gold Award, for *All You Need for a Snowman;* Best Books of the Year citation, *Nick Jr.* magazine, 2003, for *¡Pío Peep!;* Children's Books of the Year selection, Bank Street College Children's Book Committee, and Myers Outstanding Book Award honorable mention, Gustavus Myers Center for the Study of Bigotry and Human Rights in North America, both for *We.*

## Writings

*FOR CHILDREN*

*The Gorilla in the Hall,* illustrated by Paul Galdone, Lothrop (New York, NY), 1977.

*The April Fool,* illustrated by Emily Arnold McCully, Lothrop (New York, NY), 1981.

*Hob Goblin and the Skeleton,* illustrated by Katherine Coville, Lothrop (New York, NY), 1982.

*In My Treehouse,* illustrated by Meredith Dunham, Lothrop (New York, NY), 1983.

*Bim Dooley Makes His Move,* illustrated by Victoria Chess, Lothrop (New York, NY), 1984.

*Goodnight, Hattie, My Dearie, My Dove,* illustrated by Linda Strauss, Lothrop (New York, NY), 1985, illustrated by Ted Rand, Harcourt (San Diego, CA), 2002.

*My Two Feet,* illustrated by Meredith Dunham, Lothrop (New York, NY), 1985.

*That Olive!,* illustrated by Cindy Wheeler, Lothrop (New York, NY), 1986.

*Jeremy Bean's St. Patrick's Day,* illustrated by Linda Shute, Lothrop (New York, NY), 1987.

*Bill and the Google-eyed Goblins,* illustrated by Patricia Coombs, Lothrop (New York, NY), 1987.

*Gus Wanders Off,* illustrated by Cheryl Harness, Lothrop (New York, NY), 1988.

*William and Grandpa,* illustrated by Lydia Dabcovich, Lothrop (New York, NY), 1989.

*That's What I Thought,* illustrated by John Wallner, Harper (New York, NY), 1990.

*Witch Hazel,* illustrated by Margot Tomes, Harper (New York, NY), 1991.

*Little Frog's Song,* illustrated by Leonard Everett Fisher, HarperCollins (New York, NY), 1992.

*How Now, Brown Cow?,* illustrated by Amanda Schaffer, Browndeer Press (San Diego, CA), 1994.

*Down the Road,* illustrated by Margot Tomes, HarperCollins (New York, NY), 1994, illustrated by E.B. Lewis, Browndeer Press (San Diego, CA), 1995.

*Maisie,* illustrated by Lydia Dabcovich, Lothrop (New York, NY), 1995.

*Advice for a Frog and Other Poems,* illustrated by Norman Green, Lothrop (New York, NY), 1995.

*Keepers,* illustrated by Ted Rand, Lothrop (New York, NY), 1996.

*I Am the Cat,* illustrated by Mark Buehner, Harcourt (San Diego, CA), 1999.

*A Lucky Thing,* illustrated Wendell Minor, Harcourt (San Diego, CA), 1999.

*All You Need for a Snowman,* illustrated by Barbara Lavallee, Harcourt (San Diego, CA), 2002.

*Teddy Bear, Teddy Bear,* illustrated by Linda Hill Griffith, HarperCollins (New York, NY), 2003.

*When the Moon Is High,* illustrated by Julia Noonan, HarperCollins (New York, NY), 2003.

(Adapter into English) Alma Flor Ada and F. Isabel Campoy, *¡Pío Peep!: Traditional Spanish Nursery Rhymes,* illustrated by Viví Escrivá, HarperCollins (New York, NY), 2003.

*The Skeleton in the Closet,* HarperCollins (New York, NY), 2003.

*All You Need for a Beach,* Harcourt (San Diego, CA), 2004.

*A Very Hairy Bear,* Harcourt (San Diego, CA), 2004.

*One, Two, I Love You,* illustrated by Emily Arnold McCully, Chronicle Books (San Francisco, CA), 2004.

*The Adventures of Old Bo Bear,* illustrated by David Parkins, Chronicle Books (San Francisco, CA), 2006.

*Very Hairy Bear,* illustrated by Matt Phelan, Harcourt (Orlando, FL), 2007.

*We,* illustrated by Kenneth Addison, Lee & Low Books (New York, NY), 2007.

*Button Up!,* illustrated by Petra Mathers, Harcourt (Orlando, FL), 2008.

*Little Blue Truck,* illustrated by Jill McElmurry, Harcourt (Orlando, FL), 2008.

*Jeremy Bean,* illustrated by David Slonim, Chronicle Books (San Francisco, CA), 2008.

*"CATHY AND COMPANY" SERIES*

*Cathy and Company and Mean Mr. Meeker,* illustrated by Cathy Pavia, Children's Press (New York, NY), 1980.

*Cathy and Company and Bumper the Bully,* illustrated by Cathy Pavia, Children's Press (New York, NY), 1980.

*Cathy and Company and the Green Ghost,* illustrated by Cathy Pavia, Children's Press (New York, NY), 1980.

*Cathy and Company and the Nosy Neighbor,* illustrated by Cathy Pavia, Children's Press (New York, NY), 1980.

*Cathy and Company and the Double Dare,* illustrated by Cathy Pavia, Children's Press (New York, NY), 1980.

*Cathy and Company and Hank the Horse,* illustrated by Cathy Pavia, Children's Press (New York, NY), 1980.

## Sidelights

Alice Schertle is the author of more than forty engaging titles for children, including *William and Grandpa, Down the Road,* and *We.* "I write children's books because I love them—always have," Schertle once stated. "The various seasons of my childhood are identified in my memory with the books that were important to me then. There was the year Mary Poppins floated into the lives of Jane and Michael Banks and me. And my sixth grade year I think I spent with the *Black Stallion* and *King of the Wind.*" As an adult helping to provide such moments to new generations of children, Schertle takes her work seriously; as she once asserted, "We who write for young children share the considerable responsibility and the wonderful opportunity of showing them that words can paint pictures too."

Schertle was born and raised in Los Angeles, California. "As a child, I could usually be found folded into some unlikely position (as often as not I was in a tree) either reading a story or trying to write one," she once told *SATA.* "My writing was always very much influenced by the book I was reading at the moment. *The Wizard of Oz* and *Mary Poppins* inspired me to try my hand at fantasy. *The Black Stallion* led to a rash of horse stories. And after a summer of reading Nancy Drew books, I churned out mysteries peppered with words like 'sleuth' and 'chum.'"

She continued: "My early stories did have one thing in common: each got off to a roaring good start and ended abruptly somewhere in the middle. Those beginnings

***Schertle's wintertime tale in* All You Need for a Snowman *is brought to life in Barbara Lavallee's colorful art.*** (Illustration © 2002 by Barbara Lavallee. Reproduced by permission of Houghton Mifflin Harcourt Publishing Company. This material may not be reproduced in any form or by any means without the prior written permission of the publisher. )

were always fun to write, but when it came to developing the plot and bringing it along to a logical conclusion, the whole thing began to smack of work. It still does, sometimes, but I've found it to be a very satisfying kind of work when the tale is told."

After graduating from the University of Southern California in 1963, Schertle married and began teaching elementary school students in Inglewood, California. Following the birth of her first child two years later, she left her teaching job to devote herself full time to raising what would soon be three children. It was not until 1975, when her kids had grown old enough to allow her some free time, that she began writing again. Her first book for children, *The Gorilla in the Hall,* a story about a young boy's vivid imagination, was published in 1977.

Though her first read-aloud book received only mixed reviews from critics, Schertle's next book, *The April Fool,* was pronounced a winner by critics. An amusing story about a curmudgeonly king's search for a pair of shoes that will not hurt his feet, *The April Fool* was described by *School Library Journal* reviewer Patt Hays as "a satisfying story." For Schertle, the story "almost seem[ed] to write itself, from beginning to end. . . . I started with 'Once there was a king whose feet hurt,' and wrote through to 'the end' with scarcely a hitch along the way."

Schertle has often discovered ideas for stories in the activities of her three children. "*In My Treehouse* was inspired by my son's adventures in his own tree house," she once told *SATA*. "As a child, I spent a good deal of time in trees, so I took John up on his invitation to join him in his house in a big fruitless mulberry. In fact, I did a lot of writing up there, though I find they're not making tree houses as big as they used to." With *In My Treehouse,* Schertle translates the experience of being in her son's tree fort into a book about a young boy's love of being apart from the hustle and bustle of the world at large, and about gaining independence.

Living with cats as well as with children provided Schertle the inspiration for *That Olive!,* a picture book about a mischievous kitty that Lucy Young Clem described in *School Library Journal* as "a hall-of-fame cat story." Andy spends a lot of time looking for his cat, Olive, and Olive spends a lot of time playing hide-and-seek with Andy. Only the lure of tuna fish sandwiches brings the elusive Olive out into the open and into Andy's arms.

A book about making friends, *Jeremy Bean's St. Patrick's Day* features a first-grader whose excitement about his school's St. Patrick's Day party withers when he arrives at school and realizes that he has forgotten to put on the green sweater he so excitedly planned to wear the night before. The only one without green on, Jeremy is taunted by his classmates and finally hides in a closet until the school principal discovers him there and loans him the use of his green bow tie for the party. Describing the book's "clear prose and sympathetic observation of small children and their concerns," a *Kirkus Reviews* critic praised *Jeremy Bean's St. Patrick's Day* as a good book about making friends, even with school principals.

The award-winning *William and Grandpa* is another book about the relationship between children and adults, and the friendships that can develop. When Willie comes to stay with his lonely grandfather, the two share a host of simple activities—singing songs, catching shadows, making shaving cream moustaches, and telling old stories about Willie's father—that bond them into a close and loving relationship. "The continuity of generations and the warm relationship between children and the elderly are communicated equally through story and pictures," noted Carolyn Caywood in *School Library Journal.*

In *Witch Hazel,* which a *Publishers Weekly* writer called a "touching story of the triumph of imagination," Schertle tells the story of Johnny, a young boy who is raised by his two grown brothers, Bill and Bart, after the death of their parents. Bill and Bart are farmers who can do without the young boy's help as they work their small farm. When they give their young brother some pumpkin seed and a branch of witch hazel, Johnny plants the seeds and makes a scarecrow lady out of the tree branch, dressing "her" in one of his mother's old dresses. When Bill and Bart leave Johnny and take their crop to market after the fall harvest, Johnny dreams that the scarecrow, "Witch Hazel," has tossed his huge orange pumpkin up into the sky, where it has remained, transformed into a full, round harvest moon.

*Little Frog's Song* tells of the adventures and fears of a young frog who is washed from his lily pad during a fierce rain shower and must now find his way home. "The text . . . is a song, rich with images and the rhythm of repetition reminiscent of the writing of Margaret Wise Brown," commented Katie Cerra in *Five Owls.* Equally lyrical is Schertle's *How Now, Brown Cow?,* a collection of poetry. Everything from milking time to a cow's longing to jump the moon is covered in verses that a *Publishers Weekly* reviewer described as "by turns funny and tender, cheeky and thoughtful" and that *Booklist* critic Ilene Cooper dubbed "beauteously bovine." In *Goodnight, Hattie, My Dearie, My Dove,* Schertle deals with the familiar theme of the bedtime routine. First published in 1985 and reissued with new illustrations in 2002, this picture book describes how Hattie assembles a parade of stuffed animals to take to bed with her, creating a "reassuring and recognizable bedtime (and counting) story," as a *Kirkus Reviews* contributor noted.

A number of Schertle's prose titles deal with family situations, including *Maisie,* which gives an overview of Grandmother Maisie's life, and *Down the Road,* which recounts young Hetty's first experience going to the store alone. When Hetty is asked to go and buy eggs for the family's breakfast, she takes the responsibility seriously. Everything goes fine until, homeward bound, she reaches for apples on an apple tree at the side of the road and accidentally dumps the eggs on the ground. Hetty, afraid to return home empty-handed, climbs the apple tree, where her worried parents eventually find and soothe her. As Martha V. Parravano commented in *Horn Book,* the tale unites the themes of temptation and redemption with "a modern lesson in supportive parenting techniques," thereby creating a "unique story." *Down the Road* is "a fine book that speaks straight to the heart," enthused *Booklist* reviewer Shelley Townsend-Hudson.

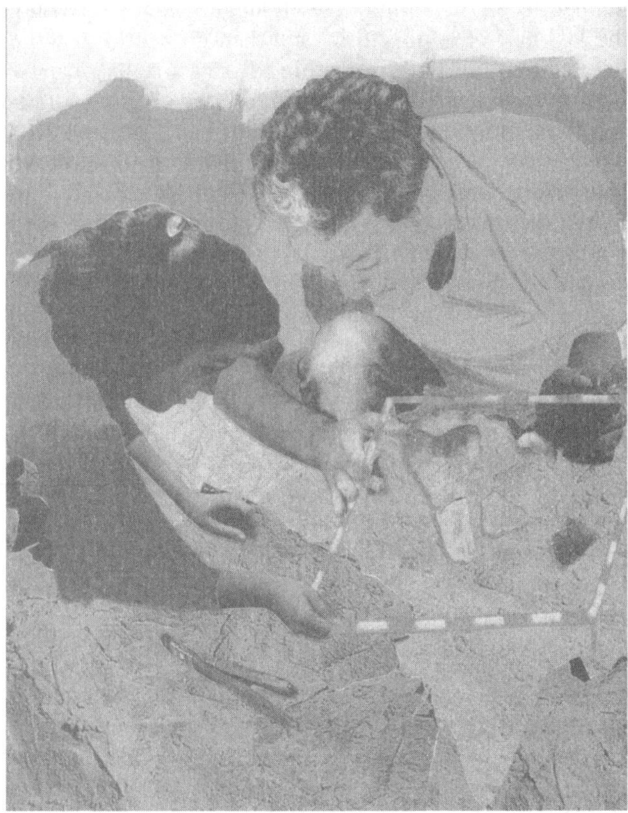

***Schertle's simply titled picture book* We *follows the history of human origins and the evolution of civilized societies throughout the world.*** (Illustration copyright © 2005 by Kenneth Addison. Reproduced by permission of Lee & Low Books, Inc.)

A poetry collection about memories and mementos, *Keepers* elicits a variety of memories in different moods, ranging from comical to pensive. In fact, *Booklist* critic Susan Dove Lempke found many of the poems to be "thought provoking" and suggested that they would be best understood by an audience more sophisticated than the intended one. On the other hand, *I Am the Cat,* a collection of narrative poems and haikus, takes a fresh look at a common subject, demonstrating in "this somewhat surprising book . . . that cats aren't always soft, cuddly felines," to quote Stephanie Zvirin in *Booklist.* A *Publishers Weekly* reviewer remarked that the collection "distills the essence of cat with humor and wry eloquence." A *Horn Book* reviewer cited as noteworthy the poems' "sinous" rhythms, "irony, surprise, and humor," concluding that *I Am the Cat* "holds its own in the cat-poetry category."

Looking at the world with a fresh perspective is often the role of poetry. In *A Lucky Thing,* written for somewhat older readers, Schertle creates a thematically unified and "thoughtful book of poems [that] celebrates the creative process," a *Publishers Weekly* reviewer noted. The work garnered favorable reviews. By reflecting the girl narrator's point of view of life on the farm, Schertle allows children to "see the ordinary with new eyes," commented Lempke, the critic adding that readers might be inspired to write verse of their own. Among the work's other enthusiasts numbered a *Horn Book* reviewer, who appreciated the "humor," "rhythmic assurance," and "robust language" of these fourteen lyric poems. Comparing the verses favorably to those of Nancy Larrick, *Bulletin of the Center for Children's Books* reviewer Deborah Stevenson praised Schertle's book for its "delicate and imaginative precision" and the "unmannered lyricism [that] brings a freshness to oft-elegized subjects." Stevenson even suggested that *A Lucky Thing* might transform some children into poetry lovers.

The companion titles *All You Need for a Snowman* and *All You Need for a Beach* are geared to the preschool crowd. With its "bouncy and light" text describing how to build a snowman, *All You Need for a Snowman* "rolls along like hand-packed snow," wrote Martha Topol in *School Library Journal.* Even with such rhythmic drive, Phelan aserted that the text goes on "without ever falling into lockstep predictability." The word "except" ends each page, encouraging readers and listeners to turn the pages of this "wintertime treat," as a *Publishers Weekly* reviewer dubbed the picture book. Joanna Rudge, in *Horn Book,* predicted that *All You Need for a Snowman* would make "a wonderfully childlike and ebullient addition to the winter repertoire," while a *Kirkus Reviews* contributor suggested that the work would be "read again and again."

In *The Skeleton in the Closet* a bony creature ransacks a little boy's room looking for something to cover his bare bones. A critic in *Kirkus Reviews* praised the "humorous upbeat rhyme," and Lempke pointed out in *Horn Book* that the text does not mention Halloween, making the book useful "to chill and thrill story-hour audiences year-round."

For *¡Pío Peep!: Traditional Spanish Nursery Rhymes,* Schertle provides adaptations of the rhymes into English. It was a project she found absorbing and satisfying, saying, "Since these are not literal translations, but poetic recreations, my challenge was to work out English lines that would fall easily on the ear while retaining the humor and charm and delight of the originals." Ilene Cooper, in *Booklist,* wrote that both the Spanish and English versions "have a sweet, rhythmic simplicity," and Ann Welton called *¡Pío Peep!* "a wonderful reassuring lap book" in her review for *School Library Journal.*

In *One, Two, I Love You,* Schertle's take on the popular "Buckle My Shoe" rhyme, a mother elephant and her young son spend an adventurous day riding a train, playing hide-and-seek, and catching stars. The author's "verse is lyrical and charming," noted *School Library Journal* contributor Jane Barrer, and Phelan wrote in *Booklist* that the work "offers a counting rhyme with an affectionate tone." *The Adventures of Old Bo Bear* centers on a little boy and his well-worn teddy bear. After Bo emerges from the washing machine missing an ear, his owner conjures a number of fanciful scenarios that contributed to his toy's condition, including a battle with pirates, a thrilling ride on a bucking bronco, and a showdown with some outlaws in the Old West. "The tale slyly segues between the real and imagined worlds," a *Publishers Weekly* critic observed.

The yearly cycle of a large brown bear is the focus of *Very Hairy Bear,* "a terrific way to introduce little ones to the seasons," according to Cooper. Schertle follows the creature as it fishes for salmon, forages for berries, and prepares for hibernation. The author's "patterned language sets up a playful cadence," wrote a *Kirkus Reviews* contributor. "Schertle makes frequent use of interior rhymes and alliteration to move the action along," Wendy Lukehart noted in a *School Library Journal* review. *Little Blue Truck,* a "pointed tribute to good hearts and amiable natures everywhere," according to *Booklist* reviewer John Peters, examines themes of kindness and courtesy. As it passes through the countryside each day, Little Blue, a pickup truck, cheerfully greets the rural residents, in stark contrast to rude, noisy, and obnoxious Dump Truck. One rainy day, Dump gets stuck in the mud, and its calls for help go unanswered until Little Blue comes to the rescue. "This old-fashioned picture book has a timeless, if well-trod, message," remarked Kitty Flynn in *Horn Book.* A contributor in *Publishers Weekly* remarked that Schertle's "rhyming stanzas are succinct," and a *Kirkus Reviews* critic noted that the author's "rhythmic text . . . fairly chants itself."

In the award-winning title *We,* Schertle offers a "panoramic, free-verse view of the human story," remarked a contributor in *Kirkus Reviews.* The author traces human evolution from its origins in Africa to the contemporary, and her spare text explores humankind's many achievements in the arts and sciences. According to *Booklist* critic Rochman, Schertle's tale "is about the diffusion of cultures and the rich connections." Writing in *Publishers Weekly,* a critic described *We* as "a compelling work that celebrates humankind's shared beginnings as much as its diversity and achievements."

"When I talk to classes of children and tell them about the unfinished stories I used to write, they usually laugh and say they do the same thing," Schertle once explained to *SATA.* "Sometimes I suggest they try writing the last half of a story first, and then go back and write the beginning. That's something I occasionally do now with my books. Sometimes a funny, or exciting, or ridiculous situation will pop into my head, an idea that would make a good middle of a story. So I'll sit down and write about some characters who find themselves in that situation, though I haven't yet any idea how they got there or what will finally happen to them. Then comes the hard part—writing the beginning and the ending, and making the parts fit together smoothly and logically.

"One of the nicest things about being an author is that it gives me the opportunity to talk to classes of children about books and writing. I always tell them that the best way to learn to write is to read and read and read. It's advice I take myself. There's a tall stack of books precariously balanced on my bedside table, and a good many of them are children's books. One lifetime will never be long enough for me to read all the books I want to read, but it'll be fun to try."

## Biographical and Critical Sources

*PERIODICALS*

*Booklist,* September 15, 1994, Ilene Cooper, review of *How Now, Brown Cow?,* p. 133; April 15, 1995, Stephanie Zvirin, review of *Maisie,* p. 1508; September 15, 1995, Shelley Townsend-Hudson, review of *Down the Road,* p. 161; October 15, 1996, Susan Dove Lempke, review of *Keepers,* p. 428; March 15, 1999, Susan Dove Lempke, review of *A Lucky Thing,* p. 1340; April 1, 1999, Stephanie Zvirin, review of *I Am the Cat,* p. 1417; April 1, 2002, Shelley Townsend-Hudson, review of *Good Night, Hattie, My Dearie, My Dove,* p. 1335; November 15, 2002, Carolyn Phelan, review of *All You Need for a Snowman,* p. 612; October 1, 2004, Carolyn Phelan, review of *One, Two, I Love You,* p. 338; February 1, 2006, Julie Cummins, review of *The Adventures of Old Bo Bear,* p. 57; May 1, 2007, Hazel Rochman, review of *We,* p. 94; October 1, 2007, Ilene Cooper, review of *Very Hairy Bear,* p. 67; April 1, 2008, John Peters, review of *Little Blue Truck,* p. 55.

*Bulletin of the Center for Children's Books,* June, 1999, Deborah Stevenson, review of *A Lucky Thing,* pp. 364-365.

*Five Owls,* April, 1992, Katie Cerra, review of *Little Frog's Song,* pp. 76-77.

*Horn Book,* September-October, 1991, Ann A. Flowers, review of *Witch Hazel,* p. 589; March-April, 1996, Martha V. Parravano, review of *Down the Road,* pp. 191-192; May, 1999, review of *A Lucky Thing,* p. 347; September, 1999, review of *I Am the Cat,* p. 621; November-December, 2002, Joanna Rudge, review of *All You Need for a Snowman,* p. 739; May-June, 2008, Kitty Flynn, review of *Little Blue Truck,* p. 299.

*Kirkus Reviews,* January 15, 1987, review of *Jeremy Bean's St. Patrick's Day,* p. 132; March 1, 1999, review of *I Am the Cat,* pp. 381-382; March 1, 2002, review of *Good Night, Hattie, My Dearie, My Dove,* p. 345; September 15, 2002, review of *All You Need for a Snowman,* pp. 1399-1400; March 1, 2003, review of *When the Moon Is High,* p. 397; April 1, 2003, review of *Teddy Bear, Teddy Bear,* p. 539; April 15, 2003, review of *¡Pío Peep!: Traditional Spanish Nursery Rhymes,* p. 603; July 15, 2003, review of *The Skeleton in the Closet,* p. 968; January 15, 2006, review of *The Adventures of Old Bo Bear, p. 89; April 15, 2007, review of We;* October 1, 2007, review of *Very Hairy Bear;* April 1, 2008, review of *Little Blue Truck.*

*New York Times Book Review,* February 2, 1997, review of *Keepers,* p. 18.

*Publishers Weekly,* January 16, 1981, review of *The April Fool,* p. 80; June 27, 1986, review of *That Olive!,* p. 85; January 16, 1987, review of *Jeremy Bean's St. Patrick's Day,* p. 73; July 10, 1987, review of *Bill and the Google-eyed Goblins,* p. 68; May 19, 1989, review of *William and Grandpa,* p. 82; June 28, 1991, review of *Witch Hazel,* p. 101; September 5, 1994, review of *How Now, Brown Cow?,* pp. 110-111; March 15, 1999, review of *I Am the Cat,* p. 59; May 10, 1999, review of *A Lucky Thing,* p. 68; September 18, 2000, review of *Down the Road,* p. 113; October 21, 2002, review of *All You Need for a Snowman,* p. 73; April 21, 2003, "Pass the Poetry," review of *Teddy Bear, Teddy Bear,* pp. 64-65; August 4, 2003, review of *The Skeleton in the Closet,* p. 80; October 4, 2004, review of *One, Two, I Love You,* p. 86; February 27, 2006, review of *The Adventures of Old Bo Bear,* p. 60; April 30, 2007, review of *We,* p. 160; September 17, 2007, review of *A Very Hairy Bear,* p. 52; April 28, 2008, review of *Little Blue Truck,* p. 137.

*Reading Teacher,* December, 1997, "Memories," review of *Keepers,* p. 330.

*School Library Journal,* August, 1980, Diane Meyer, review of *Cathy and Company and the Nosy Neighbor,* p. 70; October, 1981, Patt Hays, review of *The April Fool,* p. 135; October, 1982, review of *Hob Goblin and the Skeleton,* p. 145; May, 1983, review of *In My Treehouse,* p. 66; May, 1984, Diane S. Rogoff, review of *Bim Dooley Makes His Move,* pp. 71-72; October, 1985, Ginny Caine Cooper, review of *Goodnight, Hattie, My Dearie, My Dove,* p. 162; November, 1985, Joan McGrath, review of *My Two Feet,* p. 77; August, 1986, Lucy Young Clem, review of *That Olive!,* p. 87; October, 1987, David Gale, review of *Jeremy Bean's St. Patrick's Day,* p. 118; January, 1988, Pamela Miller Ness, review of *Bill and the Google-eyed Goblins,* p. 70; March, 1989, Sally R. Dow, review of *Gus Wanders Off,* p. 170; August, 1989, Carolyn Caywood, review of *William and Grandpa,* p. 132; January, 1991, Carolyn Vang Schuler, review of *That's What I Thought,* p. 80; September, 1991, Ruth K. MacDonald, review of *Witch Hazel,* p. 240; July, 1992, Joy Fleishhacker, review of *Little Frog's Song,* p. 64; April, 1995, Jane Gardner Connor, review of *Maisie,* p. 116, and Sue Norris, review of *How Now, Brown Cow?,* p. 129; September, 1995, Ellen Donohue Warwick, review of *Advice for a Frog,* p. 197; April, 1996, Vanessa Elder, review of *Down the Road,* pp. 117-118; December, 1996, Kathleen Whalin, review of *Keepers,* p. 117; June, 1999, Joan Zaleski, review of *A Lucky Thing,* p. 120, and Margaret Bush, review of *I Am the Cat,* p. 120; June, 2002, Heather E. Miller, review of *Goodnight, Hattie, My Dearie, My Dove,* p. 110; December, 2002, Martha Topol, review of *All You Need for a Snowman,* p. 108; July, 2003, Maryann H. Owen, review of *When the Moon Is High,* p. 106, Ann Welton, review of *¡Pío Peep!,* p. 121, and Lee Bock, review of *Teddy Bear, Teddy Bear,* p. 19; September, 2003, Gay Lynn Van Vleck, review of *The Skeleton in the Closet,* p. 190; January, 2005, Jane Barrer, review of *One, Two, I Love You,* p. 97; February, 2006, Marge Loch-Wouters, review of *The Adventures of Old Bo Bear,* p. 109; May, 2007, Marianne Saccardi, review of *We,* p. 124; December, 2007, Wendy Lukehart, review of *Very Hairy Bear,* p. 99; July, 2008, Rachael Vilmar, review of *Little Blue Truck,* p. 81.

*ONLINE*

*Lee & Low Web site,* http://www.leeandlow.com/ (August 15, 2008), "Alice Schertle."

*Teaching PreK-8 Web site,* http://www.teachingk-8.com/ (August 15, 2008), Lee Bennett Hopkins, "Alice Schertle."*

# SELZER, Adam 1980-

## Personal

Born 1980.

## Addresses

*Home*—Chicago, IL. *E-mail*—adam.selzer@gmail.com.

## Career

Writer and musician. Performer with Adam Selzer and His Revolving-Door All-Stars.

## Writings

*How to Get Suspended and Influence People,* Delacorte Press (New York, NY), 2007.

*Pirates of the Retail Wasteland,* Delacorte Press (New York, NY), 2008.

*I Put a Spell on You,* Delacorte Press (New York, NY), 2008.

*Lost and Found,* Delacorte Press (New York, NY), 2009.

Contributor to books, including *Weird Chicago: Forgotten History, Strange Legend, and Mysterious Hauntings of the Windy City,* two volumes.

## Sidelights

Chicago-based writer and musician Adam Selzer is the author of several off-beat books for middle-grade readers, including *How to Get Suspended and Influence People, I Put a Spell on You,* and *Pirates of the Retail Wasteland.* Described as a "farcical mystery" by a *Kirkus Reviews* writer, *I Put a Spell on You* mixes a list of new vocabulary words with an antic story about a middle-school spelling bee that turns vicious. Like Selzer's other books, it also casts young teens in heroic roles and relegates oldsters such as parents, teachers, and school administrators to the status of "overachievement-obsessed lunatics."

In *How to Get Suspended and Influence People* readers meet eighth-grade geek Leon Noside Harris, a boy who suffers from the stigma of being a gifted student of very eccentric but brainy parents. When Mrs. Smollet, the teacher of the Gifted Pool students, agrees to allow him to embark on a filmmaking project, Leon's finished project—an open-minded, Fellini-esque sex documentary for middle-graders—gets him both suspended from school and transformed into a classroom hero. In his humorous text, "Selzer manages to capture the voice of a smarter-than-average young teen," according to a *Kirkus Reviews* writer, and Leon's narrative is rich with what a *Publishers Weekly* critic described as "heavy doses of sarcasm, smart aleck wit and adolescent frustration." In *School Library Journal* critic Pat Scales remarked on Selzer's inclusion of "a lesson or two about free speech" in his "funny, fast-paced novel," and Jennifer Mattson maintained in her *Booklist* review of *How to Get Suspended and Influence People* that "creative" readers "will appreciate the plot's outrageousness and applaud Leon's commitment to his quirky vision."

Leon returns in *Pirates of the Retail Wasteland,* as the students of Mrs. Smollet's Gifted Pool turn their attention to the local branch of mega-coffee-shop Wackfords. Film again becomes the tool of choice as the gifted group stages a takeover of Wackfords that they capture on video in order to raise awareness of the commercial sprawl in their community. As if it is not bad enough to be continually mortified by the antics of his braniac, off-the-chart parents, life becomes even more complicated for Leon when the geeky teen attracts the romantic attention of a persistent female classmate. Selzer's "lighter-than-air comedy" will have a special attraction for "tweener sitcom fans," according to a *Kirkus Reviews* writer, while Paula Rohrlick wrote in *Kliatt* that "the clever repartee and humor" in *Pirates of the Retail Wasteland* "will amuse junior high students."

*Cover of Adam Selzer's* **How to Get Suspended and Influence People,** *featuring artwork by Matt Straub.* (Reproduced by permission of Random House Children's Books, a division of Random House, Inc.)

## Biographical and Critical Sources

*PERIODICALS*

*Booklist,* January 1, 2007, Jennifer Mattson, review of *How to Get Suspended and Influence People,* p. 83.

*Bulletin of the Center for Children's Books,* May, 2007, Karen Coats, review of *How to Get Suspended and Influence People,* p. 385; May, 2008, Karen Coats, review of *Pirates of the Retail Wasteland,* p. 400.

*Kirkus Reviews,* February 1, 2007, review of *How to Get Suspended and Influence People,* p. 128; March 15, 2008, review of *Pirates of the Retail Wasteland;* July 15, 2008, review of *I Put a Spell on You.*

*Kliatt,* January, 2007, Paula Rohrlick, review of *How to Get Suspended and Influence People,* p. 18; March, 2008, Paula Rohrlick, review of *Pirates of the Retail Wasteland,* p. 19.

*Publishers Weekly,* February 26, 2007, review of *How to Get Suspended and Influence People,* p. 91; March, 2007, Pat Scales, review of *How to Get Suspended and Influence People,* p. 218.

*School Library Journal,* March, 2007, Pat Scales, review of *How to Get Suspended and Influence People,* p. 281; July, 2008, Chris Shoemaker, review of *Pirates of the Retail Wasteland,* p. 107.

*Voice of Youth Advocates,* April, 2007, Dave Goodale, review of *How to Get Suspended and Influence People,* p. 56.

*ONLINE*

*Adam Selzer Home Page,* http://www.adamselzer.com/ (August 11, 2008).*

* * *

# SÍS, Peter 1949-

## Personal

Born May 11, 1949, in Brno, Moravia, Czechoslovakia (now Czech Republic); immigrated to United States, 1982, naturalized citizen, 1989; son of Vladimir (a filmmaker and explorer) and Alena (an artist) Sís; married Terry Lajtha (a film editor), October 28, 1990; children: Madeleine, Matej. *Education:* Academy of Applied Arts (Prague, Czechoslovakia), M.A., 1974; attended Royal College of Art (London, England), 1977-78.

## Addresses

*Home*—New York, NY.

## Career

Artist, animator, illustrator, stage designer, and writer. Worked as a disc jockey while in art school. Teacher of art classes at schools in Los Angeles, CA, and New York, NY. *Exhibitions:* Group shows include Interama, Berlin, Germany, 1975; Best of British Illustrators, London, England, 1979; Magical Mystery Tour, Los Angeles, CA, 1982; Expo Art and Metropole, Montréal, Québec, Canada, 1984; Bienalle of Illustrations, Japan, 1985; University of Oregon School of Art, Portland, OR, 1986; International Gallery, San Diego, CA, 1986; Henry Feiwel Gallery, New York, NY, 1990-91; Stedelijk Museum Schiedam, Holland, 1992; Santa Monica Heritage Museum, Santa Monica, CA, 1992-93; New York Public Library, New York, NY, 1994; Gallery MB ART, Stuttgart, Germany, 1995; Storyopolis, Los Angeles, 1996; Chrysler Museum, Norfolk, VA, 1996-97; Salon du Livre de Jeunesse, Montreuil-Paris, France, 1997-98; Katonah Museum of Art, Katonah, NY, 1998; International Youth Library, Blutenburg Castle, Munich, Germany, 1998; Okresni Muzeum a Galerie, Jicin, Czech Republic, 1998; Columbia College Center for Book and Paper Arts, Chicago, IL, 1998; Bohemian Gallery, Astoria-Queens, New York, NY, 1998; "Le immagini della fantasia," Sarmede, Italy, 1998-99; Salon du Livre de Jeunesse, Montreuil-Paris, 1998-99; Tibet House, New York, NY, 1998-99. One-man shows at Gallery Klostermauer, St. Gallen, Switzerland, 1975; Gallery Ploem, Delft, Netherlands, 1977; Gallery Martinska, 1977, and Gallery Rubin, 1979, both in Prague, Czechoslovakia; Gallery Vista Nova, Zurich, Switzerland, 1980; Gallery Medici, London, 1980; Ohio University School of Art, Athens, OH, 1990; Gallery Zeta, Olten, Switzerland, 1990; New York Public Library, 1992; James Cummins Gallery, New York, NY, 1994; Gallery Paseka, Prague, 1995; International Youth Library, Blutenburg Castle, Munich, 1995; Swiss Children's Book Institute and Johanna Spyri Foundation, Zurich, Switzerland, 1995-96; Books & Co., New York, NY, 1996; Salon du Livre de Jeunesse, Montreuil-Paris, 1996-97; Prage Castle-Riding School, Prague, 1997-98; Embassy of the Czech Republic in collaboration with Smithsonian Associates, Washington, DC, 1999. *Military service:* Czechoslovak Army, graphic designer with army's symphony orchestra, 1975-76.

## Member

Association Internationale du Film d'Animation, American Institute of Graphic Arts, Graphic Artists Guild.

## Awards, Honors

Golden Bear Award for best short film, Berlin International Film Festival, 1980, for *Heads;* Grand Prix Toronto, 1981, for short film *Players;* CINÉ Golden Eagle Award, Council on International Non-Theatrical Events, 1983, for *You Gotta Serve Somebody;* Ten Best Illustrated Children's Books for the Year citation, *New York Times,* 1987, for *Rainbow Rhino,* 1990, for *Beach Ball,* 1991, for *Follow the Dream: The Story of Christopher Columbus,* 1993, for *Komodo!,* 1994, for *The Three Golden Keys,* for *The Tree of Life: A Book Depicting the Life of Charles Darwin, Naturalist, Geologist and Thinker,* and for *The Wall: Growing up behind the Iron Curtain;* Gold Medal, Society of Illustrators, 1993, for

*Komodo!; Boston Globe/Horn Book* Honor Award for Picture Books, 1993, for *Komodo!,* and 1994, for *A Small Tall Tale from the Far Far North;* Silver Medal, Society of Illustrators, 1994, for *The Three Golden Keys;* Caldecott Honor Book, American Library Association (ALA), 1997, for *Starry Messenger: Galileo Galilei,* 1999, for *Tibet: Through the Red Box,* and 2008, for *The Wall;* Notable Books for Children citation, ALA, 1999, for *Fire Truck, Tibet, The Tree of Life,* and *The Wall;* Children's Books of Distinction, *Riverbank Review,* and *Boston Globe/Horn Book* Special Citation, both 1999, both for *Tibet;* MacArthur fellow, John D. and Catherine T. MacArthur Foundation, 2003; Ragazzi Nonfiction Award, International Bologna Children's Book Fair, 2004, Best Books for Young Adults selection, ALA, and Outstanding Science Trade Books for Children, National Science Teacher's Association/Children's Book Council, all for *The Tree of Life;* Best Books for Young Adults selection, ALA, 100 Titles for Reading and Sharing selection, New York Public Library, Notable Books for a Global Society, International Reading Association, Notable Trade Book in the Field of Social Studies, National Council for the Social Studies/Children's Book Council, and Robert F. Sibert Informational Book Award, all 2008, all for *The Wall: Growing up behind the Iron Curtain.*

## Writings

*SELF-ILLUSTRATED*

*Rainbow Rhino,* Random House (New York, NY), 1987.
*Waving: A Counting Book,* Greenwillow (New York, NY), 1988.
*Going Up!: A Color Counting Book,* Greenwillow (New York, NY), 1989.
*Beach Ball,* Greenwillow (New York, NY), 1990.
*Follow the Dream: The Story of Christopher Columbus,* Knopf (New York, NY), 1991.
*An Ocean World,* Greenwillow (New York, NY), 1992.
*Komodo!,* Greenwillow (New York, NY), 1993.
*A Small Tall Tale from the Far Far North,* Knopf (New York, NY), 1993.
*The Three Golden Keys,* Doubleday (New York, NY), 1994.
*Starry Messenger: Galileo Galilei,* Farrar, Straus & Giroux (New York, NY), 1996.
*Fire Truck,* Greenwillow (New York, NY), 1998.
*Tibet: Through the Red Box,* Farrar, Straus & Giroux (New York, NY), 1998.
*Trucks, Trucks, Trucks,* Greenwillow (New York, NY), 1999.
*Ship Ahoy!,* Greenwillow (New York, NY), 1999.
*Faust,* Carl Hanser Verlag (Munich, Germany), 1999, translated by Randall Jarrell, Farrar, Straus & Giroux (New York, NY), 2000.
*Dinosaur!,* Greenwillow (New York, NY), 2000.
*Madlenka,* Farrar, Straus & Giroux (New York, NY), 2000.
*Ballerina!,* Greenwillow (New York, NY), 2001.
*Madlenka's Dog,* Farrar, Straus & Giroux (New York, NY), 2002.
*The Tree of Life: A Book Depicting the Life of Charles Darwin, Naturalist, Geologist and Thinker,* Farrar, Straus & Giroux (New York, NY), 2003.
*The Train of States,* Greenwillow (New York, NY), 2004.
*Play, Mozart, Play!,* Greenwillow (New York, NY), 2006.
*The Wall: Growing up behind the Iron Curtain,* Farrar, Straus & Giroux (New York, NY), 2007.

*ILLUSTRATOR*

Jacob and Wilhelm Grimm, *Fairy Tales of the Brothers Grimm,* Albatros (Prague, Czech Republic), Volume 1, 1976, Volume 2, 1977.
Eveline Hasler, *Hexe Lakritze und der Buchstabenkoenig,* Benziger (Zurich, Switzerland), 1977.
*Zizkov Romances,* CSS (Prague, Czechoslovakia), 1978.
Eveline Hasler, *Hexe Lakritze und Rhino Rhinoceros,* Benziger (Zurich, Switzerland), 1979.
*Poetry,* CSS (Prague, Czechoslovakia), 1980.
Milos Maly, reteller, *Tales of the Amber Ring* (Baltic fairy tales), Artia (Prague, Czechoslovakia), 1981, Orbis (London, England), 1985.
Max Bolliger, *Eine Zwergengeschichte* (title means "Little Singer"), Bohem (Zurich, Switzerland), 1982.
George Shannon, *Bean Boy,* Greenwillow (New York, NY), 1984.
George Shannon, *Stories to Solve: Folktales from around the World,* Greenwillow (New York, NY), 1985.
Sid Fleischman, *The Whipping Boy,* Greenwillow (New York, NY), 1986, reissued, HarperTrophy (New York, NY), 2003.
Julia Cunningham, *Oaf,* Knopf (New York, NY), 1986.
Caron Lee Cohen, *Three Yellow Dogs,* Greenwillow (New York, NY), 1986.
Myra Cohn Livingston, *Higgledy-Piggledy: Verses and Pictures,* Atheneum (New York, NY), 1986.
Jean and Claudio Marzollo, *Jed and the Space Bandits,* Dial (New York, NY), 1987.
Monica Mayper, *After Good-Night,* Harper (New York, NY), 1987.
Eve Rice, *City Night,* Greenwillow (New York, NY), 1987.
Sid Fleischman, *The Scarebird,* Greenwillow (New York, NY), 1988.
Kate Banks, *Alphabet Soup,* Knopf (New York, NY), 1988.
Caroline Feller Bauer, editor, *Halloween: Stories and Poems,* Harper (New York, NY), 1989.
Sid Fleischman, *The Ghost in the Noonday Sun,* Greenwillow (New York, NY), 1989.
Louis Decimus Rubin, *The Algonquin Literary Quiz Book,* Algonquin (Chapel Hill, NC), 1990.
Sid Fleischman, *The Midnight Horse,* Greenwillow (New York, NY), 1990.
George Shannon, *More Stories to Solve: Fifteen Folktales from around the World,* Greenwillow (New York, NY), 1990.
Jack Prelutsky, *The Dragons Are Singing Tonight,* Greenwillow (New York, NY), 1993.
George Shannon, *Still More Stories to Solve: Fourteen Folktales from around the World,* Greenwillow (New York, NY), 1994.

Christopher Noel, adapter, *Rumpelstiltskin* (with audiocassette), Rabbit Ears Books (Rowayton, CT), 1995.

Sid Fleischman, *The 13th Floor: A Ghost Story,* Greenwillow (New York, NY), 1995.

Jack Prelutsky, *Monday's Troll,* Greenwillow (New York, NY), 1996.

Miriam Schlein, *Sleep Safe, Little Whale: A Lullaby,* Greenwillow (New York, NY), 1997.

(With Cliff Nelson) Madeleine L'Engle, *Many Waters,* Bantam (New York, NY), 1998.

Jack Prelutsky, *The Gargoyle on the Roof,* Greenwillow (New York, NY), 1999.

José Saramago, *The Tale of the Unknown Island,* translated by Margaret Jull Costa, Harcourt Brace (New York, NY), 1999.

William Nicholson, *The Wind Singer,* Hyperion (New York, NY), 2000.

William Nicholson, *Slaves of the Mastery,* Hyperion (New York, NY), 2001.

Jacques Taravant, *The Little Wing Giver,* translated by Nina Ignatowicz, Holt (New York, NY), 2001.

Jack Prelutsky, *Scranimals,* Greenwillow (New York, NY), 2002.

William Nicholson, *Firesong,* Hyperion (New York, NY), 2002.

Mary Chase, *The Wicked, Wicked Ladies in the Haunted House,* Knopf (New York, NY), 2003.

Diane Ackerman, *Animal Sense,* Knopf (New York, NY), 2003.

Max Bollinger, *The Happy Troll,* translated by Nina Ignatowicz, Holt (New York, NY), 2005.

Carlos María Domínguez, *The House of Paper,* translated by Nick Caistor, Harcourt (Orlando, FL), 2005.

Contributor of illustrations to *American Illustration, New York Times, New York Times Book Review, Atlantic Monthly, Time, Newsweek, House & Garden, Esquire, Forbes, Connoisseur,* and *Print.*

*SHORT FILMS*

*Mimikry,* Academy of Applied Arts (Prague, Czechoslovakia), 1975.

*Island for 6,000 Alarm Clocks,* Kratky Film (Prague, Czechoslovakia), 1977.

*Heads,* Kratky Film (Prague, Czechoslovakia), 1979.

*Players,* Halas & Batchelor (London, England), 1981.

*Hexe Lakritze* (ten parts; title means "Little Witch Licorice"), televised in Zurich, Switzerland, 1982.

*You Gotta Serve Somebody,* Fine Arts (Los Angeles, CA), 1983.

*Aesop's Fables* (two films), Helicon Video, 1984.

*Twelve Months,* Billy Budd Films, 1985.

*Rumpelstiltskin,* Rabbit Ears Productions (Rowayton, CT), 1992.

*Heads* and *Island for 6,000 Alarm Clocks* are part of the permanent film collection of the Museum of Modern Art in New York, NY.

*OTHER*

Also creator of CD-ROM "Eskimo Welzl," about the Czechoslovakian inventor, storyteller, adventurer, and explorer Jan Welzl. Creator of posters for theater, film, institutions, and festivals, including film *Amadeus,* Metropolitan Transportation Authorities in New York City, Children's Book Council, and International Jazz Festival in Rennes, France. Contributor to periodicals, including *Print* and *Parade.*

## Adaptations

*Starry Messenger* was recorded on audio cassette by Recorded Books (Prince Frederick, MD), 1997. *Tibet: Through the Red Box* was adapted by David Henry Hwang as *Tibet through the Red Box: A Drama for Young People,* performed at Seattle Children's Theatre (Seattle, WA), 2004, and published by Playscripts, Inc. (New York, NY), 2006.

## Sidelights

Peter Sís is a distinguished illustrator and writer recognized internationally for his contributions to children's literature. Since the mid-1970s, he has made more than half a dozen short films, illustrated many books for other authors, and written more than twenty self-illustrated children's books, including such award-winning titles as *Komodo!, Tibet: Through the Red Box,* and *The Wall: Growing up behind the Iron Curtain.* In 2003 Sís received a MacArthur Foundation "genius grant," becoming the first illustrator to receive that honor. Stephen Fraser, writing in *Five Owls,* noted that Sís "remains one of the truly distinctive picture-book creators today—quirky, sophisticated, and imaginative."

Born into an artistic family in 1949, Sís grew up in Czechoslovakia at a time when the former Soviet Union ruled his homeland. Because both of his parents were artists (his father was a filmmaker and explorer and his mother, an artist), Sís was surrounded by art as a child. As early as age four or five, Sís began drawing pictures, and within a few years, he became quite serious about his craft. "I was already illustrating regularly by the time I was eight or nine," Sís once told *SATA.* "My father and my mother would give me certain assignments, and I remember I would even have deadlines." Sís credits his parents with providing an appropriate environment to foster his growth as an artist. His talents flourished in an atmosphere that balanced creative freedom with a certain amount of structure and discipline. Above all, he was challenged intellectually as a youth by his parents.

When he had reached his early teens, Sís was convinced that he wanted to pursue a career as a professional artist. Once in formal art school, however, Sís began to experience some frustration in his quest. His family's interest in contemporary art clashed with the traditional ideals of formal artistic training. In spite of these difficulties, Sís earned his master's degree from the

***Peter Sís's work as an illustrator includes the ghost story* The 13th Floor *by Sid Fleischman.*** (Illustration © 1995 by Peter Sís. Used by permission of HarperCollins Children's Books, a division of HarperCollins Publishers.)

Academy of Applied Arts in Prague in 1974 and later attended the Royal College of Art in London, England. He credits his so-called "soft technique," which is still evident in his works, to his traditional art education.

Sís first became involved with animated films in the 1960s, and he cites famous Czech illustrator, animator, and teacher Jiri Trnka as an important role model. By the early 1980s, Sís was already a popular artist and filmmaker in Europe. "Film for me was the passport to the whole world," he once told *SATA.* His short animated film *Heads* earned the Golden Bear at the 1980 Berlin International Film Festival. He was then invited to design and paint illustrations for a Swiss television series called *Hexe Lakritze* ("Little Witch Licorice"). Sís also worked on another film in London. Then, in 1982, he traveled to Los Angeles—the site of the 1984 Olympic Games—to do a film that tied in the theme of the liberation of humanity with the Olympics. However, following the Soviet Union's decision to boycott the 1984 Olympics, other eastern and central European countries, including Czechoslovakia, also withdrew from the competition. The Olympic film project was canceled, but Sís remained in Los Angeles to pursue his career in art.

At first, Sís found life on the West Coast quite challenging. As he once explained to *SATA,* "It was very hard to find my way around in Los Angeles because all of a sudden things were completely different than what I was used to in Europe—the palm trees and lifestyle and everything. I felt completely misplaced and strange." Although Sís had difficulty obtaining film and illustration jobs, he did find work teaching classes in illustration in Los Angeles. In addition, he illustrated two of Aesop's fables for television.

At about the same time, Sís took the advice of a friend who suggested that he send a sample of his work to famous American children's writer and illustrator Maurice Sendak. Sís never expected to get a response, but Sendak was impressed enough with the young artist's work to call him personally and discuss his career aspirations. Several months later, Sendak called again while attending the 1984 American Library Association convention, which was held in Los Angeles. He invited Sís to join him at the convention and introduced him to Ava Weiss, art director of Greenwillow Books, a New York City-based publisher. Sís broke into the American book illustration market on the spot, agreeing to illustrate George Shannon's *Bean Boy.*

Following *Bean Boy* and a move to New York City, Sís illustrated two more books for Greenwillow, Sid Fleischman's juvenile novel *The Whipping Boy,* which won the Newbery Medal in 1985, and *Stories to Solve: Folktales from around the World,* by Shannon. Not long afterwards, Sís became a regular contributor of illustrations to the *New York Times Book Review* and began to write and illustrate his own work. His first self-illustrated work, *Rainbow Rhino,* was listed among the *New York Times* top ten best illustrated children's books of 1987.

By 1991, Sís was well-known in the children's book industry. He had already illustrated almost two dozen works by other authors and created six original works, including the well-received *Follow the Dream: The Story of Christopher Columbus. School Library Journal* contributor Jean H. Zimmerman deemed *Follow the Dream* a "fascinating artistic representation of the discovery of the New World." Excitement surrounding this work stemmed partly from the 500-year anniversary of Columbus's discovery of America and partly from Sís's experimentation with both color and composition. Using oil colors on special plaster-like backgrounds, the artist achieved a textured, authentic old-world look recalling fifteenth-century paintings. Sís was inspired in part by his continuing fascination with his father's exploration and travels and his own journey from a Soviet-dominated country to the new world. As he once explained to *SATA,* "I realized coincidental things with my own life or with somebody who wants to break free from certain situations. With determination and persistence, a person can do it."

In *The Wall* an award-winning autobiographical work, Sís describes life in Czechoslovakia under Communist rule, incorporating black-and-white drawings, period photographs, and excerpts from his childhood journals. According to *New York Times Book Review* contributor Leonard Marcus, "The story unfolds in a word-and-picture montage consisting of a spare, fable-like narrative, introductory and closing notes, a historical timeline, diary excerpts, childhood drawings, family photos and, at the center of it all, a sequence of playful but intense pen-line drawings, many of them arrayed in storyboard panels." *Booklist* reviewer Jennifer Mattson observed that the work would appeal to teen readers "who will grasp both the history and the passionate, youthful rebellions against authority," and Wendy Lukehart, writing in *School Library Journal,* concluded that, "complex, multifaceted, rich in detail, this book shares the artist's specific heritage while connecting to universal longings."

During the 1990s, other of Sís's works also met with success, such as *Komodo!,* the story of boy who travels to Indonesia to visit a famous dragon, and *A Small Tall Tale from the Far Far North,* a story based on the Czech legend of traveler Jan Welzl. He added to his repertoire *The Three Golden Keys,* published in 1994. In this fairy tale, a young man is led by a cat through the city of Prague to find his childhood home, and eventually, the three keys that help him enter it. Writing and illustrating *The Three Golden Keys* proved to be quite intriguing for Sís, and critics and readers alike applauded the book. While *School Library Journal* contributor Julie Cummins felt the work was suited more for older children and adults, she decided that, overall, "the book is intriguing, with visual and textual subtleties interconnecting with cultural and historical ties." Mary M. Burns, commenting in *Horn Book,* also categorized the book as one for an older audience, but praised *The Three Golden Keys* for its "dazzling design, opulent production, [and] meticulous execution," not to mention its "elegantly crafted, breathtaking fine line illustrations."

Turning his attention to biography once again, Sís wrote and illustrated *Starry Messenger: Galileo Galilei,* which the American Library Association named a Caldecott Honor Book in 1997. Like Christopher Columbus in *Follow the Dream,* Galileo set out to prove that the Earth was not what people thought it was—in this case the center of the universe. Unlike Columbus, however, the famous astronomer could only prove his assertion with theories. In this picture book, Sís conveys the finer and darker periods of Galileo's life, alternating simple descriptions in large type for younger readers with more detailed notes in smaller type for older ones. Reviewing this work in the *New York Times Book Review,* Elizabeth Spires commended Sís on how he "manages to tell the relatively complicated story of Galileo in such a simple, straightforward way, accompanied by some of the most gorgeous illustrations imaginable." Wendy Lukehart, writing in *School Library Journal,* added that the "pathos, the painstaking copies of Galileo's famous sketches of the heavens, and the attention to current scholarship make this book a fascinating find."

Sís wrote about the adventures of another explorer—this time his father—in *Tibet.* In the 1950s, the Chinese government recruited Vladimir Sís to record on film the construction of the first highway leading from China into Tibet. While fulfilling his duties, Sís's father witnessed the horrors of China's invasion of Tibet, which act ultimately led to the removal of the Dalai Lama. It was during this two-year period away from home that Vladimir kept a diary. When he returned home, the filmmaker kept the diary locked in a red box, passing on stories about his journey orally to son Peter. In 1994, Vladimir wrote a note to his son saying the diary was his. Sís, in turn, decided to share his father's diary and oral tales with the world by creating a "groundbreaking, creative" picture book, as described by *School Library Journal* contributor Shirley Wilton. Reviewing *Tibet,* a *Publishers Weekly* reviewer wrote that the "luminous colors of the artwork, the panoramas of Tibetan topography and the meticulous intermingling of captivating details . . . make this an extraordinary volume." Caldecott Medal committee members also thought the book was extraordinary, awarding the work a Caldecott Honor in 1999.

Also published in 1998 was Sís's picture book for preschoolers, *Fire Truck.* In this short story, a young boy wakes up to find that he has become a fire truck. He revels in his newly formed body until the smell of pancakes brings him back to reality. "Sís blends simple text with bold pictures to give insight into one boy's vivid imagination," wrote Torrie Hodgson in *School Library Journal.* Two more works that feature vehicles of interest to many children are Sís's *Ship Ahoy!* and *Trucks, Trucks, Trucks,* both of which also use imaginative constructs. In *Ship Ahoy!,* a little boy envisions the blue carpet beneath him as a sea and imagines himself in various vessels. Only a sea monster—in the form of his mother's vacuum cleaner entering his bedroom—jolts the boy back. *Dinosaur!* continues in this same vein, featuring a boy in the bathtub with his toy dinosaur, who suddenly begins to multiply. The tub becomes a primeval pond, and the growing number of dinosaurs then become land creatures. All told, thirteen different prehistoric creatures are depicted, with a glossary at the close. "This imaginative story with wonderful endpapers naming the creatures should appeal to all young dinosaur lovers," remarked JoAnn Jonas in a *School Library Journal* review of *Dinosaur!* In *Ballerina!* little Terry looks into the mirror and imagines herself in some of classical dance's greatest roles. Her costume changes—a towel added, or a scarf—become full-fledged ensembles on the alternate page, where the various aspects of dance—a twirl, the leap—are illustrated for readers. "Sís once again creates a beautifully realized, spot-on view of creative kids at play," commented *Booklist* critic Gillian Engberg.

One's of S´s's more notable collaborations has been with children's poet Jack Prelutsky, a pairing which began in 1993 with *The Dragons Are Singing Tonight.* A follow-up effort, *The Gargoyle on the Roof,* contains poems about werewolves, vampires, trolls, gremlins, and other horrific creatures, but with a lighthearted tone—how does a vampire shave, for example, when he cannot see his own reflection in the mirror? "Sís's cross-hatched oil-and-gouache paintings extend the poems, working especially well to catch the sinister and frightening mood," wrote *Booklist* reviewer Susan Dove Lempke.

"The meisters of madcap are at it again," a reviewer wrote in *Publishers Weekly* when Sís and Prelutsky's fourth collaboration, *Scranimals,* appeared. In *Scranimals,* described as the duo's "best collaboration to date" by *School Library Journal* reviewer Nina Lindsay, the two imagine a world full of crosses between animals and vegetables—such genetic wonders as the Hippopotamushroom, the Orangutangerine, and the Potatoad. Working with black ink and water color, Sís creates "hallucinogenic art" that "takes Prelutsky's ever-clever comic verses in new directions," claimed a critic in *Kirkus Reviews.*

Sís also contributed images to *The Tale of the Unknown Island,* a story by Portuguese Nobel Prize-winning writer José Saramago. The work is a fairy tale for adults that centers on a sailor who finds himself a favorite of the monarch. He tells the king that if he is given a ship, he will search for the unknown island, a place that does not appear on any map. A cleaning woman from the royal household decides to accompany him, and the next morning, after a night in port, they christen their vessel *The Unknown Island.*

Sís began a new series for young readers with *Madlenka,* about a spirited little girl living in New York City. When she realizes that her tooth is about to fall out, Madlenka ventures out onto her block to announce the news to her neighbors. The city's vibrant immigrant culture is the focus of the story, with Madlenka introducing her friends—including a Latin greengrocer, an Indian owner of a news kiosk, and an Italian ice-cream vendor—while the opposing page showing elements of each person's respective culture or homeland. In the end, she has lost the tooth and returns to her worried parents with the blithe assurance that she was merely taking a global walk. Readers, predicted *School Library Journal* reviewer Wendy Lukehart, "will pore over the many details, delighting in the emergence of forms and meaning provided by close inspection," while Engberg commended Sís's "visually stunning spreads."

In *Madlenka's Dog* the girl is again wandering her multicultural neighborhood. This time, she is walking her imaginary dog, an activity that causes the people she meets to reminisce about their own childhood pets. These "resonant intergenerational connections," Roger Sutton wrote in *Horn Book,* "make [*Madlenka's Dog*] an inspired choice for sharing." When Madlenka bumps into her friend Cleopatra, who is out walking her own

***Cover of William Nicholson's novel* The Wind Singer, *featuring artwork by Sís.*** (Artwork copyright © 2000 by Peter Sís. Reprinted by permission of Hyperion Books for Children. All rights reserved.)

imaginary pet, a horse, "the fantasy explodes into beautiful wordless spreads of the two friends soaring through the imagined worlds of their games," explained Engberg. They roam through ancient Egypt, medieval Europe, and the Arctic before Madlenka returns home to find a special surprise awaiting her.

In *The Tree of Life: A Book Depicting the Life of Charles Darwin, Naturalist, Geologist, and Thinker,* Sís offers a biography of the nineteenth-century British scientist who proposed a theory of evolution based on the process of natural selection that he outlined in his 1859 work *On the Origin of Species.* In an interview with *Publishers Weekly* contributor Elizabeth Devereaux, Sís maintained that *The Tree of Life* is "not a book about evolution, it's not about natural selection. It's about a man who sees things differently, how he has this personal fight with his conscience: 'Can I do it? Can I publish my theory?'" *The Tree of Life* "succeeds brilliantly in arresting and educating the eye," wrote Daria Donnelly in the *New York Times Book Review.* "Using a very limited but appealing range of hues, tones and geometric shapes, Sís . . . invites calm and slow movement through his text." "Beautifully conceived and executed, the presentation is a humorous and information tour de force that will absorb and challenge readers," wrote Margaret Bush in *School Library Journal,* and *Horn Book* reviewer Betty Carter stated, "The detailed illustrations and narrative complexities demand of readers the same process Darwin set for himself: observe carefully, make connections, and learn."

Inspired by a visit to the Circus World Museum in Baraboo, Wisconsin, Sís produced *The Train of States,* "a browser's ticket for a cross-country journey and a treat for trivia lovers everywhere," noted Laurie Edwards in *School Library Journal.* Sís depicts each of the fifty United States as a brightly decorated circus wagon, adorned with symbolic images such as the state bird, motto, and tree. "Sís's abundant wit shines through each line-and-watercolor painting," Sutton commented, and Michael Cart, writing in *Booklist,* observed that the "whimsical images" on the wagons "command attention and invite endless, wondering reexamination." Though *New York Times Book Review* critic Bruno Navasky noted a certain sameness to "the procession of facts," he also praised the illustrations, stating, "Every child who can point out the mouse in *Goodnight Moon* or who delights in showing us where Waldo is will love the treasures tucked away on each page of this book."

Famed eighteenth-century classical composer Wolfgang Amadeus Mozart is the subject of *Play, Mozart, Play!,* another well-received picture-book biography. Sís focuses on Mozart's childhood, when he first displayed his prodigious talents, and his relationship with his domineering father. "The tousled, titian-haired young musician is a wide-eyed and sympathetic visual focus," Sutton wrote, and Kate McClelland, reviewing *Play, Mozart, Play!* in *School Library Journal,* remarked that Sís presents the "world master to children in a way that is emotionally resonant, easily understood, and remarkably indelible."

Sís once told *SATA* that through his work, he aims to cultivate free and open thought among children. He firmly believes that an artist's work should challenge a child's imagination. Especially intriguing to him is the wonder and innocence of early elementary-school students. "I really like talking to second graders," he said. "The young kids are wonderful because their minds are completely open. And the feelings children have here are probably the same as children have all over the world. It's amazing to see—in Asia, Thailand, Indonesia, or wherever—how similar the children are, whether they play with a piece of wood, or they play with a very sophisticated computer."

Sís also added: "I think children should have choices, and I would like to participate in their growth." Indeed, he advises young readers who aspire to a career as an artist to persevere and "not be intimidated by anybody." Sís believes that artistic talent should develop naturally, and that young people should be left to "create freely—without any pressure to achieve commercial success."

## Biographical and Critical Sources

*BOOKS*

*Children's Literature Review,* Volume 45, Gale (Detroit, MI), 1998.

Cummins, Julie, editor, *Children's Book Illustration and Design,* Library of Design, PBC International/Rizzoli (New York, NY), 1992.

Silvey, Anita, editor, *Children's Books and Their Creators,* Houghton Mifflin (Boston, MA), 1995.

*PERIODICALS*

*Booklist,* December 1, 1994, Carolyn Phelan, review of *The Three Golden Keys,* p. 687; January 15, 1995, Michael Cart, review of *The Three Golden Keys,* p. 907; October 1, 1995, Ilene Cooper, review of *The 13th Floor: A Ghost Story,* p. 314; October 15, 1996, Carolyn Phelan, review of *Starry Messenger: Galileo Galilei,* p. 423; April 15, 1996, Janice M. Del Negro, review of *Monday's Troll,* p. 1437; November 15, 1997, Susan Dove Lempke, review of *Sleep Safe, Little Whale: A Lullaby,* p. 567; September 15, 1998, Ilene Cooper, review of *Tibet: Through the Red Box,* p. 195, and Kathleen Squires, review of *Fire Truck,* p. 240; June 1, 1999, Kathy Broderick, review of *Trucks, Trucks, Trucks,* p. 1844; September 1, 1999, Lauren Peterson, review of *Ship Ahoy!,* p. 143; October 1, 1999, Susan Dove Lempke, review of *The Gargoyle on the Roof,* p. 355; March 15, 2000, Gillian Engberg, review of *Dinosaur!,* p. 1389; September 1, 2000, Gillian Engberg, review of *Madlenka,* p. 126; April 1, 2001, Gillian Engberg, review of *Ballerina!,* p. 1480; February 15, 2002, Gillian Engberg, review of *Scranimals,* p. 237; April 1, 2002, Gillian Engberg, review of *Madlenka's Dog,* p. 1323; February 15, 2003, Gillian Engberg, review of *Animal Sense,* p. 1068; October 15, 2003, Carolyn Phelan, review of *The Tree of Life: A Book Depicting the Life of Charles Darwin, Naturalist, Geologist, and Thinker,* p. 408; October 15, 2004, Michael Cart, review of *The Train of States,* p. 405; September 1, 2007, Jennifer Mattson, "Peter Sís" (interview), p. 62, and review of *The Wall: Growing up behind the Iron Curtain,* p. 72.

*Commonweal,* April 19, 2002, Daria Donnelly, review of *The Little Wing Giver,* p. 22.

*Five Owls,* May-June, 1993, Stephen Fraser, review of *Komodo!,* pp. 113-114.

*Horn Book,* September-October, 1991, Ellen Fader, review of *Follow the Dream: The Story of Christopher Columbus,* pp. 614-615; January-February, 1994, Ellen Fader, review of *A Small Tall Tale from the Far Far North,* p. 66; March-April, 1995, Mary M. Burns, review of *The Three Golden Keys,* pp. 189-190; May-

June, 1996, Ann A. Flowers, review of *Monday's Troll,* p. 345; January-February, 1997, Roger Sutton, review of *Starry Messenger,* pp. 79-80; March-April, 1998, Peter Sís, "Tiny Pieces of Paint"; September-October, 1998, Marilyn Bousquin, review of *Fire Truck,* pp. 601-602; November, 1998, Roger Sutton, review of *Tibet,* p. 719; May, 1999, Marilyn Bousquin, review of *Trucks, Trucks, Trucks,* p. 322; September, 1999, Lolly Robinson, review of *Ship Ahoy!,* p. 601; July, 2000, review of *Dinosaur!,* p. 445; September, 2000, review of *Madlenka,* p. 558; March-April, 2002, Roger Sutton, review of *Madlenka's Dog,* pp. 205-206; November-December, 2003, Betty Carter, review of *The Tree of Life,* p. 768; July-August, 2006, Roger Sutton, review of *Play, Mozart, Play!,* p. 470; September-October, 2007, Roger Sutton, review of *The Wall,* p. 599.

*Kirkus Reviews,* March 1, 2002, review of *Madlenka's Dog,* p. 345; July 15, 2002, review of *Scranimals,* p. 1042; September 15, 2003, review of *The Tree of Life,* p. 1182.

*New York Times,* December 6, 1996, Christopher Lehmann-Haupt, review of *Starry Messenger,* p. B3; October 13, 1998, Elisabeth Bumiller, "From Fathers to Children, a Twice-Told Tale," p. B2; December 2, 1998, Richard Bernstein, review of *Tibet,* p. E7; December 7, 1998, Christopher Lehmann-Haupt, review of *Fire Truck,* p. E7.

*New York Times Book Review,* November 8, 1987, Janwillem van de Wetering, review of *Rainbow Rhino,* p. 42; November 13, 1988, Liz Rosenberg, "Lonesome John Finds a Friend," p. 56; November 14, 1993, David Small, review of *A Small Tall Tale from the Far Far North,* p. 34; November 13, 1994, Patricia Hampl, review of The *Three Golden Keys,* p. 34; June 2, 1996, Zack Rogow, review of *Monday's Troll,* p. 25; November 10, 1996, Elizabeth Spires, "Stars Were Always on His Mind," p. 32; December 3, 1998, Scott Veale, review of *Tibet,* p. 22; April 11, 1999, Heather Vogel Frederick, review of *Fire Truck,* p. 32; January 16, 2000, Linnea Lannon, review of *The Gargoyle on the Roof,* p. 27; May 14, 2000, J.D. Biersdorfer, review of *Dinosaur!,* p. 18; November 19, 2000, A.O. Scott, review of *Madlenka,* p. 67; June 3, 2001, Adam Liptak, review of *Ballerina!,* p. 49; May 19, 2002, Beth Gutcheon, review of *Madlenka's Dog,* p. 27; December 22, 2002, review of *Scranimals,* p. 18; November 16, 2003, Daria Donnelly, review of *The Tree of Life,* p. 20; November 14, 2004, Bruno Navasky, review of *The Train of States,* p. 40; November 11, 2007, Leonard S. Marcus, "The Cold War Kid," review of *The Wall,* p. 28.

*Print,* November-December, 1998, Julie Lasky, "Mythical Kingdoms," p. 104.

*Publishers Weekly,* August 10, 1990, review of *Beach Ball,* p. 443; October 11, 1993, review of *The Dragons Are Singing Tonight,* p. 88; November 7, 1994, review of *The Three Golden Keys,* p. 76; November 14, 1994, Sally Lodge, "Peter Sís Goes Home Again," p. 26; October 9, 1995, review of *The 13th Floor,* p. 86; March 11, 1996, review of *Monday's Troll,* p. 64; April 29, 1996, Paul Nathan, "Special Handling," p. 25; November 4, 1996, review of *Starry Messenger,* p. 76; August 10, 1998, review of *Tibet,* p. 365; August 17, 1998, Heather Vogel Frederick, "Peter Sís's Red Box Diaries: A Glimpse of Old Tibet," p. 13; April 26, 1999, review of *Trucks, Trucks, Trucks,* p. 81; July 5, 1999, review of *The Gargoyle on the Roof,* p. 71; July 19, 1999, review of *Ship Ahoy!,* p. 193; March 26, 2001, review of *Ballerina!,* p. 92; July 16, 2001, p. 146; September 24, 2001, review of *The Little Wing Giver,* p. 92; June 24, 2002, review of *Scranimals,* p. 54; December 16, 2002, review of *Animal Sense,* p. 67; October 13, 2003, Elizabeth Devereaux, "Discovering the World," interview with Sís, p. 78, and review of *The Tree of Life,* pp. 79-80; July 9, 2007, review of *The Wall,* p. 55.

*School Library Journal,* September, 1990, Michael Cart, review of *The Midnight Horse,* p. 226; September, 1991, Jean H. Zimmerman, review of *Follow the Dream,* p. 249; December, 1993, Julie Cummins, review of *The Three Golden Keys,* p. 87; October, 1996, Wendy Lukehart, review of *Starry Messenger,* p. 118; September, 1998, Torrie Hodgson, review of *Fire Truck,* p. 182; October, 1998, Shirley Wilton, review of *Tibet,* p. 160; June, 2000, JoAnn Jonas, review of *Dinosaur!,* p. 125; October, 2000, Wendy Lukehart, review of *Madlenka,* p. 137; December, 2000, John Peters, review of *The Wind Singer,* p. 146; April, 2001, Patricia Pearl Dole, review of *Ballerina!,* p. 122; April, 2002, Lauralyn Persson, review of *Madlenka's Dog,* pp. 122-123; September, 2002, Nina Lindsay, review of *Scranimals,* p. 217; February, 2003, Lauralyn Persson, review of *Animal Sense,* p. 126; October, 2003, Margaret Bush, review of *The Tree of Life,* p. 204; November, 2004, Laurie Edwards, review of *The Train of States,* p. 130; May, 2006, Kate McClelland, review of *Play, Mozart, Play!,* p. 117; August, 2007, Wendy Lukehart, review of *The Wall,* p. 139.

*ONLINE*

*Peter Sís Home Page,* http://www.petersis.com (August 15, 2008).

*Peter Sís Tibet Web Site,* http://www.petersistibet.com/ (August 15, 2008).*

* * *

## STRYER, Andrea Stenn 1938-

### Personal

Born 1938; married Lubert Stryer (a professor). *Education:* University of Chicago, MA; Southern Connecticut State University, M.L.S.

### Addresses

*Home and office*—Stanford, CA. *E-mail*—andrea@stryer.com.

### Career

Author, educator, and librarian. Worked in public libraries and public and private school libraries for thirty years; taught in elementary and junior high schools.

## Awards, Honors

Schneider Family Book Award, Moonbeam Award, and Bank Street College of Education Best Books designation, all 2008, all for *Kami and the Yaks.*

## Writings

*The Celestial River: Creation Tales of the Milky Way,* August House Publishers (Little Rock, AR), 1998.

*Kami and the Yaks,* illustrated by Bert Dodson, Bay Otter Press (Palo Alto, CA), 2007.

## Sidelights

Andrea Stenn Stryer, a former librarian and educator, is the author of *Kami and the Yaks,* an award-winning picture book set in the Himalayan Mountains. "To reach kids, to involve them in reading, in stories, in facts, and ideas is personally very gratifying and educationally significant," Stryer remarked in an interview on the *Ravenstone Press* Web site.

*Kami and the Yaks* centers on a deaf Sherpa boy who overcomes his physical disability and proves his worth to his family. When Kami notices that his father and brother have trouble locating their herd of yaks, he sets out to discover why the animals have not yet returned that evening. After braving a dangerous climb through a hailstorm, Kami finds the yaks protecting a calf whose leg is caught in the rocks. Once he arrives back home, Kami must communicate the danger to his father, despite his inability to speak. "Many children will recognize Kami's frustration and then pride after he bravely solves a family problem," Gillian Engberg remarked in *Booklist.* "Kami's deafness figures into the story, but it's his grit and resourcefulness that drive the action forward," noted a contributor in *Publishers Weekly,* and Carolyn Janssen, writing in *School Library Journal,* observed that *Kami and the Yaks* "opens the doors to new worlds and gives readers a character to admire."

## Biographical and Critical Sources

*PERIODICALS*

*Astronomy,* May, 1999, review of *The Celestial River: Creation Tales of the Milky Way,* p. 108.

*Booklist,* February 1, 2007, Gillian Engberg, review of *Kami and the Yaks,* p. 49.

*Kirkus Reviews,* March 1, 2007, review of *Kami and the Yaks,* p. 232.

*Publishers Weekly,* May 14, 2007, review of *Kami and the Yaks,* p. 53.

*School Library Journal,* February, 1999, Angela J. Reynolds, review of *The Celestial River,* p. 128; April, 2007, Carolyn Janssen, review of *Kami and the Yaks,* p. 117.

*ONLINE*

*Andrea Stenn Stryer Home Page,* http://www.stryer.com (August 10, 2008).

*Ravenstone Press Web site,* http://www.ravenstonepress.com/ (August 10, 2008), "Authors among Us—Children's Writers Who Are or Who Have Been Librarians."

# T

## TAFURI, Nancy 1946-

### Personal

Born November 14, 1946, in Brooklyn, NY; daughter of Otto George (a retired naval officer and an engineer) and Helen Haase; married Thomas Michael Tafuri (a graphic designer), June 14, 1969; children: Cristina. *Education:* School of Visual Arts (New York, NY), graduated, 1967.

### Addresses

*Home and office*—Roxbury, CT. *E-mail*—tafuri@nancytafuri.net.

### Career

Author and illustrator of children's books. Simon & Schuster (publisher), New York, NY, assistant art director, 1967-69; One Plus One Studio (graphic design firm), Roxbury, CT, cofounder, graphic designer, and illustrator, 1971—. Project Sunshine, member of board of advisors. *Exhibitions:* Work exhibited by Society of Illustrators, 1977; Washington Art Association, 2006; and Mattatuck Museum, 2006.

### Member

Authors Guild, Society of Children's Book Writers and Illustrators, Children's Book Council.

***Nancy Tafuri*** (Photograph by Gary Spector. Reproduce by permission.)

### Awards, Honors

Children's Choice citation, International Reading Association, 1982, for *The Piney Woods Peddler;* Best Books of 1983 citation, *School Library Journal,* 1983, for *Early Morning in the Barn;* Jane Addams Honor Book designation, 1983, for *If I Had a Paka;* Caldecott Honor Book, American Library Association, 1985, for *Have You Seen My Duckling?;* Fanfare Honor Book citation, *Horn Book,* 1986, and Please Touch Museum Book Award, 1987, both for *Who's Counting;* Ten Best Children's Books citation, *Redbook,* 1988, for *Junglewalk;* Recognition of Excellence, California Children's Book and Video Awards, Preschool and Toddler Category, 1990, for *Follow Me!;* Recommended Picture Book Honor, Parents' Choice, 1999, and Oppenheim Toy Portfolio Gold Award, 2000, both for *Snowy, Flowy, Blowy: A Twelve Months Rhyme;* Reading Magic Award, *Parenting* magazine, 2001, for *Silly Little Goose;* Oppenheim Toy Portfolio Gold Award, 2004, for *You Are Special.*

## Writings

*FOR CHILDREN; SELF-ILLUSTRATED*

*All Year Long,* Greenwillow (New York, NY), 1983.
*Early Morning in the Barn,* Greenwillow (New York, NY), 1983.
*Have You Seen My Duckling?,* Greenwillow (New York, NY), 1984.
*Rabbit's Morning,* Greenwillow (New York, NY), 1985.
*Who's Counting,* Greenwillow (New York, NY), 1986.
*In a Red House,* Greenwillow (New York, NY), 1987.
*Where We Sleep,* Greenwillow (New York, NY), 1987.
*My Friends,* Greenwillow (New York, NY), 1987.
*Do Not Disturb,* Greenwillow (New York, NY), 1987.
*Spots, Feathers, and Curly Tails,* Greenwillow (New York, NY), 1988.
*Two New Sneakers,* Greenwillow (New York, NY), 1988.
*One Wet Jacket,* Greenwillow (New York, NY), 1988.
*Junglewalk,* Greenwillow (New York, NY), 1988.
*The Ball Bounced,* Greenwillow (New York, NY), 1989.
*Follow Me!,* Greenwillow (New York, NY), 1990.
*This Is the Farmer,* Greenwillow (New York, NY), 1993.
*The Barn Party,* Greenwillow (New York, NY), 1995.
*The Brass Ring,* Greenwillow (New York, NY), 1996.
*I Love You, Little One,* Scholastic (New York, NY), 1997.
*What the Sun Sees, What the Moon Sees,* Greenwillow (New York, NY), 1997.
*Counting to Christmas,* Scholastic (New York, NY), 1998.
*Snowy Flowy Blowy: A Twelve Months Rhyme,* Scholastic (New York, NY), 1999.
*Will You Be My Friend? A Bunny and Bird Story,* Scholastic (New York, NY), 2000.
*Silly Little Goose!,* Scholastic (New York, NY), 2001.
*Where Did Bunny Go?,* Scholastic (New York, NY), 2001.
*Mama's Little Bears,* Scholastic (New York, NY), 2002.
*The Donkey's Christmas Song,* Scholastic (New York, NY), 2002.
*You Are Special, Little One,* Scholastic (New York, NY), 2003.
*Goodnight, My Duckling,* Scholastic (New York, NY), 2005.
*Five Little Chicks,* Simon & Schuster (New York, NY), 2006.
*Whose Chick Are You?,* Greenwillow (New York, NY), 2007.
*The Busy Little Squirrel,* Simon & Schuster (New York, NY), 2007.
*Blue Goose,* Simon & Schuster (New York, NY), 2008.
*The Very, Big, Scary, Storm,* Simon & Schuster (New York, NY), 2009.

*ILLUSTRATOR*

Jean Holzenthaler, *My Hands Can,* Dutton (New York, NY), 1977.
George Shannon, *The Piney Woods Peddler,* Greenwillow (New York, NY), 1981.
Charlotte Zolotow, *The Song,* Greenwillow (New York, NY), 1982.
Mirra Ginsburg, *Across the Stream,* Greenwillow (New York, NY), 1982.
Charlotte Pomerantz, *If I Had a Paka: Poems in Eleven Languages,* Greenwillow (New York, NY), 1982.
Charlotte Pomerantz, *All Asleep,* Greenwillow (New York, NY), 1984.
Crescent Dragonwagon, *Coconut,* Harper (New York, NY), 1984.
Helen V. Griffith, *Nata,* Greenwillow (New York, NY), 1985.
Mirra Ginsburg, *Four Brave Soldiers,* Greenwillow (New York, NY), 1987.
Charlotte Pomerantz, *Flap Your Wings and Try,* Greenwillow (New York, NY), 1989.
Mirra Ginsburg, *Asleep, Asleep,* Greenwillow (New York, NY), 1992.
Patricia Lillie, *Everything Has a Place,* Greenwillow (New York, NY), 1993.
Kevin Henkes, *The Biggest Boy,* Greenwillow (New York, NY), 1995.
Sharon Phillips Denslow, *In the Snow,* Greenwillow (New York, NY), 2006.

Illustrations included in *Children's Book Illustration and Design,* edited by Julie Cummins; *Literature and the Child,* 2nd edition, by Bernice E. Cullinan; and *1990 Children's Writers and Illustrators Market.* Designer of poster for U.S. National Children's Book Week, Children's Book Council, 1987.

## Sidelights

Artist and writer Nancy Tafuri has been creating books for very young children since the late 1970s. Whether providing illustrations for writers such as Charlotte Pomerantz, Kevin Henkes, and Mirra Ginsburg, or creating art for her original picture-book texts, Tafuri is consistently praised by critics for her simple and uncluttered yet imaginative art. Noting her use of "tiny details," generously sized shapes, and "sunny colors," a *Publishers Weekly* contributor noted that Tafuri's picture book *Five Little Chicks* "proves once again why Tafuri . . . is a favorite with youngsters." *If I Had a Paka: Poems in Eleven Languages,* which Tafuri illustrated for Pomerantz, was selected as a Jane Addams Honor Book, and Tafuri's own *Have You Seen My Duckling?* was runner up for the prestigious Caldecott Medal.

While growing up, Tafuri spent a great deal of time drawing and coloring, and as a teen, she decided on an artistic career. In 1964 she enrolled at the School of Visual Arts in New York City. There she followed a course of studies in journalistic design that included classes in graphic design, type, book design, magazine illustration, and children's book illustration. Although the book-illustration class caught her interest, she still concentrated on her other studies, viewing them as more practical in light of her need to make a living. Tafuri's first job after graduation was as an assistant art director for New York City publisher Simon & Schuster. Two years later, she left this post to marry Thomas Tafuri, a fellow artist whom she had met during her college years.

Working together, the Tafuris opened One Plus One studio in 1971. Although the studio was originally founded in New York City, the Tafuris established enough of a reputation creating book-jacket art to be able move north to rural Roxbury, Connecticut. In addition to working with her husband, Tafuri also built up a portfolio of children's illustrations, then took them around to various publishing houses. "At first," she revealed in *Horn Book,* "publishers felt my images were too graphic, and I got a lot of rejections. Now, when I read my early work, I realize that it wasn't half as good as I thought it was then. I was still learning a craft, the process of putting a book together, but I was determined to make things work."

In 1977 Tafuri received her first illustration assignment: creating art for Jean Holzenthaler's *My Hands Can.* Then came an assignment for Greenwillow Books illustrating *The Piney Woods Peddler* by George Shannon. For this book she modeled her illustrations on her husband and the old Pennsylvania gristmill they were living in at the time. "I had never really concentrated on human shapes until then," Tafuri recalled in *Horn Book.* "Tom helped me. I took photographs of him, and he became the model for the peddler." Tafuri also illustrated Charlotte Zolotow's *The Song* and Charlotte Pomerantz's *If I Had a Paka* for Greenwillow, and in 1983 she gained her first writing credit with her self-illustrated picture book *All Year Long.* Meanwhile, *The Piney Woods Peddler* earned a Children's Choice citation from the International Reading Association, marking the first of several awards Tafuri has received throughout her prolific career.

Several of Tafuri's self-illustrated books have their roots in life on her Roxbury farm. *Early Morning in the Barn* was inspired by her move from New York City to rural New England and *Whose Chick Are You?* is one of many books to focus on farm animals. Tafuri's Caldecott Honor Book *Have You Seen My Duckling?* and its companion volume, *Goodnight, My Duckling,* both stem from a more specific incident. "We have a pond on our property," Tafuri explained in *Horn Book.* "Tom and I went down to look at it one day, and there was a mallard mother and her ducklings. Tom said, 'There's a story here for you, Nancy.' *Have You Seen My Duckling?* came the most easily to me of all my books and was the most pleasurable to work on." A *Parents' Choice* reviewer called *Have You Seen My Duckling?* "beautifully precise, yet emotionally affecting," and a *Horn Book* critic called the book "as fresh as spring—a delightful variation on a familiar theme."

Featuring woodland creatures and a rhyming text, Tafuri's self-illustrated *I Love You, Little One* was praised as a "tender bedtime book" by a reviewer for *Publishers Weekly.* The book features seven little critters who in turn ask their mother, "Do you love me, Mama?" The same reviewer praised Tafuri's "stunningly detailed . . . dusky, downy-coated animals." Tafuri's signature warm animals also star in *Will You Be My Friend?* and its sequel, *Where Did Bunny Go?* In the first book, a "simple yet comforting story," according to Ilene Cooper in *Booklist,* a little bunny wants to become friends with a rather shy bird. The aftermath of a rainstorm finally provide the proper impetus for their friendship to blossom. In the sequel, Bunny and Bird are involved, along with other animals, in a game of hide and seek one snowy day. When Bird becomes fearful that Bunny has run away, the friend lets Bird know that he would not do that. A "reassuring story," *Will You Be My Friend?* "probes both the joys and challenges of developing friendships," as Patricia A. Crawford wrote in *Childhood Education.* A contributor for *Kirkus Reviews* concluded of *Where Did Bunny Go?* that Tafuri's "underlying warmth of tone is as enjoyable as the appealingly depicted wildlife" featured in her self-illustrated picture book.

With their spare, simple texts, Tafuri's books rely primarily on illustrations to show plot and movement. Set in farm country, *Rabbit's Morning* grew out of an encounter Tafuri had with a jackrabbit. *Early Morning in the Barn* employs a similar strategy, with a text featuring animal noises and illustrations featuring baby animals, while *Do Not Disturb* focuses on activities in rural fields and ponds. In *Silly Little Goose!* readers enjoy "a likeable tale about a wayward goose on a quest to find a home," in the words of a *Kirkus Reviews* contributor. Goose needs a place to lay her eggs, but all of the warm, soft, dry spaces have already been taken by other barnyard animals and their babies. Although Goose attempts to settle into each of these spaces, she is repeatedly ejected amid the sounds of the baby animals and the refrain, "Silly little goose!" Eventually, a farmer's hat, which has blown under a bush, becomes the perfect nest for Goose. Tafuri's "large, uncluttered illustrations" combine with her simple text to make the book "perfect for lap-sits and toddler storytimes," in the opinion of *School Library Journal* contributor JoAnn Jonas.

Other stories featuring wild animals include *The Busy Little Squirrel,* in which a small brown squirrel prepares for the coming cold weather, and *Mama's Little Bears,* which finds Mama Bear at watch while her three small cubs venture out into the world surrounding their cozy den. Like *I Love You, Little One, You Are Special, Little One* introduces several different animal relationships—including a human one!—that find a parent encouraging the special qualities of their young. *You Are Special, Little One* "reads like a love song," noted a *Kirkus Reviews* writer, calling the book "a gratifying read to be shared while cuddling." With its clear-toned colored pencil-and-water color art and "soothing" repetitive text, *The Busy Little Squirrel* was deemed "a worthwhile addition to Tafuri's growing treasury of . . . satisfying stories" by *School Library Journal* contributor Martha Topol.

Concepts provide the focus in several books by Tafuri. Counting is the focus of both *Five Little Chicks* and

*Counting to Christmas,* the latter in which holiday rituals are met with numerical skills as an eager child counts down the days to Christmas Day—whle making cards, baking cookies, getting the tree ready, and singing holiday songs in a recital. In *Blue Goose,* Farmer Gray's drab gray farm is colorfully transformed by creative farmyard residents—such as the titular goose, Red Hen, White Duck, and Yellow Chick—after they obtain the colored paints required to complete their barnyard makeover. The months of the year are investigated in rhyme with *Snowy Flowy Blowy: A Twelve Months Rhyme,* a "sumptuous" book, according to a critic for *Publishers Weekly.* "As usual," wrote Shirley Lewis in her *Teacher Librarian* review of *Counting to Christmas,* "Tafuri's artwork is the centerpiece," and *Booklist* critic Carolyn Phelan dubbed the same book a "holiday treat for Tafuri fans." Praising the author/illustrator's "low-key" approach, Phelan noted of *Blue Goose* that the book provides children with "an appealing introduction to primary and secondary colors." With a story line that focuses on creativity, *Blue Goose* allows Tafuri to be "more visually playful . . . than usual," observed a *Publishers Weekly* reviewer, citing the book's upbeat artwork and "pithy text."

Tafuri has received critical acclaim for the artwork she has contributed to texts by other writers. Her illustrations for Ginsburg's *Four Brave Soldiers,* depict four mouse soldiers who cavort while the house cat is asleep. The cat in *Four Brave Soldiers* was the inspiration for the tiger cat in her original self-illustrated *Junglewalk.*

Tafuri is careful to base each of her animal characters on detailed research, commenting that she makes it a priority to "get . . . all the facts correct in my illustrations. Each animal or nature formation has to be correct. Even though my books aren't nonfiction, the feeling of accuracy has to be there." "My main concern is always how the book will look when it is printed," she explained in *Horn Book.* "I think about the final form—that is the training that doing [book] jackets provided for me. I like being able to pick out my own typefaces for books and work the illustrations around the type. . . . One of my major thoughts is how I'm going to work text and art together."

## Biographical and Critical Sources

*PERIODICALS*

*Booklist,* May 1, 1993, Ilene Cooper, review of *Everything Has a Place,* p. 1595; October 1, 1996, Susan Dove Lempke, review of *The Brass Ring,* p. 360; November 15, 1997, Susan Dove Lempke, review of *What the Sun Sees, What the Moon Sees,* pp. 567-568; February 1, 1998, GraceAnne A. DeCandido, review of *I Love You, Little One,* p. 924; September 15, 1998, Carolyn Phelan, review of *Counting to Christmas,* p. 240; January 1, 2000, Ilene Cooper, review of *Will You Be My Friend?,* p. 938; February 1, 2001, Marta Segal, review of *Silly Little Goose!,* p. 1058; December 1, 2001, Ilene Cooper, review of *Where Did Bunny Go?,* p. 651; March 1, 2002, Ellen Mandell, review of *Mama's Little Bears,* p. 1144; September 15, 2002, Hazel Rochman, review of *The Donkey's Christmas Song,* p. 247; November 1, 2003, Karin Snelson, review of *You Are Special, Little One,* p. 506; January 1, 2005, Julie Cummins, review of *Goodnight, My Duckling,* p. 875; December 15, 2005, Hazel Rochman, review of *Five Little Chicks,* and Julie Cummins, review of *Whose Chick Are You?,* both p. 52; June 1, 2007, Gillian Engberg, review of *The Busy Little Squirrel,* p. 80; November 15, 2007, Carolyn Phelan, review of *Blue Goose,* p. 47.

*Childhood Education,* winter, 2000, Patricia A. Crawford, review of *Will You Be My Friend?,* p. 110.

*Horn Book,* April, 1984, review of *Have You Seen My Duckling?,* p. 188; November-December, 1989, Nancy Tafuri, "The Artist at Work: Books for the Very Young," pp. 732-735; May-June, 1992, Elizabeth S. Watson, review of *Asleep, Asleep,* p. 326; May-June, 1993, Mary M. Burns, review of *Everything Has a Place,* pp. 321-322; September-October, 1994, Martha V. Parravano, review of *This Is the Farmer,* p. 582; May-June, 1995, Hanna B. Zeiger, review of *The Biggest Boy,* p. 325; March-April, 2002, Christine M. Heppermann, review of *Mama's Little Bears,* p. 206.

*Kirkus Reviews,* March 1, 2001, review of *Silly Little Goose!;* September 15, 2001, review of *Where Did Bunny Go?,* p. 1369; November 1, 2002, review of *The Donkey's Christmas Song,* p. 1626; August 1, 2003, review of *You Are Special, Little One,* p. 1024; January 15, 2005, review of *Goodnight, My Duckling,* p. 126; November 15, 2005, review of *Five Little Chicks,* p. 1236; July 15, 2007, review of *The Busy Little Squirrel;* December 15, 2007, review of *Blue Goose.*

*Library Talk,* March-April, 2001, Susan Shaver, review of *Silly Little Goose!*

*Publishers Weekly,* April 26, 1993, review of *Everything Has a Place,* p. 76; September 1, 1997, review of *What the Sun Sees, What the Moon Sees,* p. 103; January 5, 1998, review of *I Love You, Little One,* p. 67; November 8, 1999, review of *Snowy Flowy Blowy: A Twelve Months Rhyme,* p. 67; January 10, 2000, review of *Will You Be My Friend?,* p. 67; March 12, 2001, review of *Silly Little Goose!,* p. 88; September 15, 2003, review of *You Are Special, Little One,* p. 67; February 13, 2006, review of *Five Little Chicks,* p. 87; December 10, 2007, review of *Blue Goose,* p. 54.

*School Library Journal,* May, 1994, Lee Bock, review of *This Is the Farmer,* p. 105; March, 1998, Marianne Saccardi, review of *I Love You, Little One,* p. 188; October, 1998, Lisa Falk, review of *Counting to Christmas,* p. 45; March, 2000, Karen James, review of *Will You Be My Friend?,* p. 214; April, 2001, JoAnn Jonas, review of *Silly Little Goose!,* p. 123; October, 2002, Linda Israelson, review of *The Donkey's Christmas,* p. 64; October, 2003, Jane Barrer, review of *You Are Special, Little One,* p. 140; February, 2006, Marge Loch-Wouters, review of *Five Little Chicks,* p. 110;

February, 2007, Susan Weitz, review of *Whose Chick Are You?,* p. 98; November, 2007, Martha Topol, review of *The Busy Little Squirrel,* p. 101.

*Teacher Librarian,* November, 1998, Shirley Lewis, review of *Counting to Christmas,* p. 48.

*ONLINE*

*Nancy Tafuri Home Page,* http://www.nancytafuri.net (January 10, 2008).

*Autobiography Feature*

# Nancy Tafuri

Nancy Tafuri contributed the following autobiographical essay to *SATA:*

Having a child makes you look back on your own childhood . . . remembering how it was to be young and growing up with all its special beginnings and trials, but most of all remembering the good and bad that have helped you be the person you are today.

This process started for me after Cristina was born, when I would sit with her for hours: rocking, talking, reading, and sleeping with her in my arms, realizing what a special person I had been transformed into—a mother—and how it must have been for my mother when I was born some forty-two years ago on a fall day in November 1946. My father was a career officer in the navy and spent most of my childhood overseas. Which meant I was an important part of my mother's life and she was *my* life. We lived during my first years in an apartment in Ridgewood, New York, which was in the borough of Brooklyn. I had a little French friend named Joseph, and we made the halls, the stairs, and basement of an ordinary building into the most fascinating place, sharing secrets and exploring together. How different that will be for Cristina. We are all together—father, mother, and child—in a natural setting in the midst of an orchard. Pond, meadows, and woods make up our Connecticut world, surrounding us with everything I love to paint and write about, everything I want to expose the young child to through my books.

***Nancy Tafuri in 1947*** (Courtesy of Nancy Tafuri.)

I don't really know how all that began in me, that extreme love of nature, the feel of the seasons, the yearning: to draw animals and, actually, not always for myself, but for children.

When we moved from Ridgewood, Brooklyn, to Richmond Hill, Queens—still a borough in New York—I was nearly five years old. Now we were near parks with sprinklers, sand, and trees. But my favorite pastime was coloring and drawing. My mornings were spent very happily making a white page glow with color. Our neighbor's child could never understand this devotion, but I could—it was my time. Actually, mornings are still very important to me and now, with Cristina, even more so. It's the kind of quiet time we need to cuddle, play, read, and color, the last being a great favorite of Cristina's also, even at this young age.

Like Cristina, I was an only child . . . but that all changed when my father retired from the service. I was ten years old and our family started to grow. First came my brother, Douglas, and my sister, Dianne, shortly after . . . and then a move to the country to a small town in northern New Jersey.

It was a big change for all of us. Gradually we each adjusted at our own rate. I think my mother was the one that had the most change: a husband home from the service, a new family, and a location so foreign from her New York City background. We really didn't have as much time to give each other and I missed that. Starting in a new school and making friends, on top of getting used to my new big-sister status, was all so challenging. My dad worked hard to tie us all together and also adjust to civilian life.

As we became accustomed to our new roles, the opportunity to share time with my mother returned . . . and in high school when the time came to decide what direction to take, it was my mother who encouraged the

*Nancy with her father, Otto Haase, in 1950* (Courtesy of Nancy Tafuri.)

art field and helped persuade my German father. In high school I took every opportunity to involve myself in art. I even persuaded my home economics teacher to let me paint a mural in her classroom instead of the assignment of sewing a new spring outfit! I gathered paintings à la Modigliani—sketches of horses (my favorite animal), life studies, etc.—to form my first portfolio. It weighed forty pounds. Off I went to the School of Visual Arts, by Third Avenue on Manhattan's Twenty-third Street. With moist palms and arms aching from the extra baggage, I sat watching my inner soul being thumbed through by the school's director. He was encouraging, but you had to be reviewed and that took six weeks. I was working in a dress shop at the time, and every chance I had I'd call home to hear if I was accepted. It was torture. Six weeks was starting to turn into six years.

The day came in July when I called home and had Mom rip the envelope open to find that I had been accepted. My art training would begin in September and my major would be children's book illustration. Just the thought of having a major that would deal in creating books for young children was overwhelmingly exciting.

I commuted into New York City from Kinnelon, New Jersey. The trip was a long one, so rise-and-shine time was generally around five in the morning, even before the roosters. I'd meet the bus along the side of the highway with pads, portfolio, and canvases wrapped under my arms. But just to enter the school with its smell of oil, paint, and turpentine lingering through the halls made it worth all the travel. I thrived in the environment. I had never been exposed to anything quite like it before, and it managed to shape my entire life. The people, the teachers, the informality were all so different from anything I had ever experienced.

You were the shaper of your own destiny, you were in control, the harder you worked the greater your chances were in finding new ways to do the same thing—it was all experimental, all new. Just to see how differently we could all see and interpret was exhilarating. Painting, design, typography, media, children's book illustration, and academic classes were but a few of the many courses I took during my art school years.

*

The first part of my second year I found myself in love with a boy my own age. Tom was quiet and soft-spoken, he won me over. He was a dedicated student and I admired his determination. Tom lived not too far from the Richmond Hill area that I grew up in and actually was born in Brooklyn five months earlier than myself. We dated all through school, making trips up to New Jersey and down to Queens. It was a commuters' romance. We shared all the artists' haunts, the galleries, museums, and shows. Manhattan was our campus and we relished the thought of being successful artists some day.

After fantasizing how it would be once we graduated, the day finally came and when it was over and the dust had settled, I hustled out into the world to show publishing what I had learned. Tom rented a studio in Union Square and started illustrating and painting.

My first job was freelancing at Random House, doing pasteups and mechanicals for their educational book department for young readers. It was a summer job and it was preparing me for the nine-to-five world I knew I needed to experience to enter.

With the knowledge I gained from freelancing, I answered an ad through an agency for assisting an art director of trade-book jackets at Simon & Schuster. The appointment was set and I gathered together samples of pasteups and mechanicals from my freelance job and my art-school works concerning graphic design. The interview was successful and I started my first real full-time, art-related job the following Monday.

The salary was minimal and the commute a long one, but I knew I'd never receive the type of experience locally that I would obtain in Manhattan. I relaxed and found myself more and more comfortable with design and type, and fascinated by book jackets—each one a small poster of art wrapped around a piece of literature, drawing the reader into its grip. My excitement influenced Tom and he, too, enjoyed working with me on freelance projects from the publisher until he also branched out into the world of graphic book design.

We worked together building our portfolios, making them strong in the hopes of someday forming our own graphic design studio.

Three years after Tom and I graduated from the School of Visual Arts, we were married on a rainy day in June of 1969. For us rain was good fortune!

***Nancy with her mother, Helen Kruger Haase, in 1951*** (Courtesy of Nancy Tafuri.)

We made our home in Forest Hills, New York, minutes from Manhattan, and started our own graphic art studio, One Plus One Studio. Tom would go around during the day gathering freelance projects, and we would work every chance we got to complete our jobs. Business was coming along slowly. We really had enough clients to keep just one of us very busy, so when Tom received a very promising position as assistant art director at a top paperback publisher, he took the job. After a couple of years, our client list started growing. Tom would come home now and the two of us would have our dinner and go right back to work.

Then fate stepped in one afternoon. I was going to have lunch with Tom in Manhattan and was a bit early, so I decided to walk to the Museum of Modern Art. On the way I noticed a row of brownstone buildings with some vacant apartments. I looked up and started to imagine how wonderful it would be to have a studio right in the middle of New York City. I entered the art store to ask with what agency one would inquire about a possible rental. My heart was pounding. Tom and I often spoke of moving to the city with the studio and giving up his full-time position, but until now it had been only a dream. I proceeded to the penthouse door of Aeon Realty and I was face-to-face with the rental agent. She informed me that there was one front apartment available left that was on hold for a photographer, and I should call back in a few days. Being optimistic, I took all the information down and ran to tell Tom. Several days passed and I called to find out the photographer had passed on the space and it could be opened for us to look at.

The superintendent met Tom and me in front of the building and we rushed up what felt like a thousand steps into an apartment that required much-needed repair. We walked through the two front rooms with visions of how the unit could be transformed into our ultimate dream. The floors were so blackened from grime and soot, it was a shock to find out that they were wood parquet. The fireplace was boarded and plastered over. The kitchen area had been ripped out, but the bathroom was there (dirty, but there at any rate). A large closet which a previous owner had divided for his shirts stood in the entry area. We looked with such delight. What a perfect place for all our type and art books: WE'LL TAKE IT!

A big plunge, but we did it. We jumped into a complete lifestyle change. We started renovation on the studio after all the necessary arrangements were made with rent and leases.

Tom left his full-time assistant's position at New American Library, and we now had One Plus One Studio running again in full gear. Our dear mascot, a Keeshond dog that couldn't or wouldn't be left alone, came with us on our city commute every day. A short ride into a metropolis can very often be transformed into hours of impatience, exhaustion, and wasted time. So after a

***"With my sister, Dianne, and brother, Doug," 1959*** (Courtesy of Nancy Tafuri.)

year of coming home to take-out and a dark apartment, Tom and I lit up when we discovered a rental available on the top floor of an adjacent building. Just about forgetting all the work we had completed on our studio, we walked into this new space with open hearts. It seemed like heaven—of course it could have been . . . it was a five-flight walk up!

When I walked in, it was hard to believe I was still in Manhattan. The ceilings were low with windows encased in shutters, giving them a built-in feeling. The floors were wood, not parquet like the studio, but in running widths. There were two fireplaces, one in what became our living room and another in one of the two bedrooms. It was an open but very cozy feel, and we just knew it was perfect for us.

By this time we were starting to be real hands at plastering, painting, and woodworking. We stripped off bags of plaster to expose the brick on the chimneys and kitchen-wall area. We had been collecting American antiques along the way, so this floor, having been part of the maid's quarters at the turn of the twentieth century, really lent itself to the warmth of the furniture.

We started to grow there . . . Tom with his designing and then me with illustrating. Living in New York City helped us develop our ideas and become independent.

Combing galleries and visiting museums, libraries, and bookstores made me yearn for the children's book field. Even though my publishing credits now included a picture book I had illustrated for E.P. Dutton—*My Hands Can* written by Jean Holzenthaler—as well as a coloring book for Dover Publications of Robert Louis Stevenson's *A Child's Garden of Verses* and several small illustration assignments, recognition was still very slow in coming.

The studio was becoming successful now. The time had come when I could devote my energies to just illustration. But the illustration I found myself doing wasn't really what I had seen being published. I adored shapes—big, round, inviting shapes. My work was being drawn into the world of large, sparse, and colorful, which I felt would be perfect for the very young. But in the late seventies the youngest reader was not a priority. Getting somewhat discouraged, I put my work down for a time only to find myself drawn back to it with the same devotion.

*

It wasn't until the spring of 1980 that my career in children's books took a wonderful turn. I had been working on my portfolio of samples for a time and had made several appointments with publishers in New York City, one of them being Greenwillow Books. Their parent company was William Morrow & Company. At this time, Greenwillow was a relatively new house devoting much of their list to the very young child. Ava Weiss, the art director, had given us several adult trade-book jackets when she was at Macmillan Publishing. So when I called to set up an appointment, she was warm and inviting and asked to see me right away. I was so thrilled, I couldn't get out of the door and into a cab fast enough. Our greetings were joyful, even though my heart was up around my throat. Ava listened to every word and looked at every piece. Then, taking several pieces with her, she disappeared for a time. I sat and told my hopes not to get too high. When she returned, it was with a manuscript for *The Piney Woods Peddler* by George Shannon. Shannon had retold an American folktale from the Appalachian region, and the direction Greenwillow wanted this book to go in was one with humor, an early American feeling, and a strong structure. One artist had attempted to illustrate this manuscript already, so right there I knew this was going to be a tough one. That, coupled with the fact that my experience with the human figure wasn't the strongest . . . but I had to take it, I had to try, even though Ava said if I didn't there would be other chances. At that moment I felt it was a now-or-never situation. Beaming with joy, I scooped up my work and flew back to the studio in record time to share the good news with Tom, ringing the buzzer to our studio and running up one hundred steps yelling, "I've got a book—I've got a book!"

What followed weeks later was an ideal situation. Tom and I were just about to rent an old gristmill in the midst of Amish farmland in Pennsylvania, in a town called Millbach. The owners were moving across the road into an early restoration and needed someone to care for the old mill. We knew it would be a great place to work and antique, so we took the offer. I knew it would make working on *The Piney Woods Peddler* authentic, but I needed a peddler, someone I could sketch and pose to really give this book a special flair. Moments later I saw Tom coming out of one of the back rooms with a large straw hat, pants pushed up, a finger in the air, and a smile on his face: my peddler!

Before Tom would leave for Manhattan on Mondays, I made sure to take enough poses and gestures to carry me through the week. It was exhilarating for me to be working on a book that I could be putting my real design feelings into. Even if it didn't get accepted, I would still know the feeling of trying to make it work.

I completed eight pages and a cover sketch for approval. I mounted my vellum tissue sketches on a folded dummy, simulating the correct size of the book, slipped it into a manila envelope, and off I went . . . for the verdict.

Susan Hirschman (editor-in-chief), Elizabeth Shub (senior editor), and Ava Weiss were all there to greet me. Our hellos were all cordial, and then out came the sketches from their manila home. I looked at their faces while they looked at what I was hoping to be my next book. When the words "May we give you a contract?" rang out from Susan, my breath came back and my voice managed a "yes." "Well," she said, "we'll draw one up right away."

The summer of 1980 marked the true start of my illustrating career. Working on *The Piney Woods Peddler,* pulling in people from the rural area to model, gave me that self-assurance I needed to make me confident that this was the path I wanted to take professionally. To know that a publisher had given me the chance to prove that meant everything. I spent the summer sketching people from this rural area, walking the outstretched roads, passing cornfields and farms, antiquing with Tom, and cooking Pennsylvania German meals from the area. It was a summer I'll never forget. So much has passed since then, but a part of me still reacts the same every time I sit down at the drawing board to start a new book. It's that exuberance which comes over me, making every book just like the first one.

During our stay at Millbach House, Tom and I received news that our studio building had been taken over by new owners, and we were given notice to find different space. At first the news was heartbreaking, and going back and forth from Pennsylvania difficult; but we were able to find space in a building not far from our home apartment that would suit our needs. That first studio, however, has always held a special place in our past, as where it all started for One Plus One.

After the completion of *The Piney Woods Peddler* and the move back to Manhattan, my hopes were high as to the possibility of receiving another manuscript for a picture book. When *The Piney Woods Peddler* was completed, it was a preseparated book. The color was indicated with shades of gray on vellum overlays in degrees of percentages. It involved a certain amount of guess work and a great deal of patience, unlike today when one can do separate colorful paintings for each spread. Due to printing advancements and more demand for children's books, the prices have become more competitive, enabling artists to project their images more freely.

*The Piney Woods Peddler* was printed in the U.S.A. at a plant in New Jersey, and Ava asked if I could go! You bet! What a thrill to watch the presses rolling off large sheets of Tom—the smiling trader. It was also educational watching Ava working with the printers, lightening, darkening, aligning, and cleaning every page under her watchful eye; and rewarding to see the care that went into the printing. I'm happy I was able to see the process, since most of my books from 1986 on have been printed in Hong Kong and overseeing them is impossible. Proofs are always sent, however, and checked and rechecked here with Ava. Results are compared to original art and treated with the utmost care, as if you were there in person. Ava goes over to Hong Kong twice a year and personally oversees every book on Greenwillow's ever-growing list.

For me *The Piney Woods Peddler* was the book that opened the starting-gate doors. Since then, my relationship with Greenwillow has been a strong one. The books that have followed include *The Song* by Charlotte Zolotow, *If I Had a Paka* by Charlotte Pomerantz, and *Across the Stream* by Mirra Ginsburg. Each one in its own right helped stabilize me in the field of books, but *Across the Stream* enabled me to take animals (in this situation a fox, hen, chicks, a duck and her ducklings) and project them through an entire book with feeling, humor, and kindness.

So, *Across the Stream* was another milestone in my illustrating career, culminating in uniting illustration with writing, which started to surface in 1983 with *All Year Long,* a book combining the months of the year with the days of the week. Mixing numbers, colors, holidays, and seasons with an open-ended almanac adds to learning fun for the youngest reader.

*

As I was working on *All Year Long,* Tom and I found the country house of our dreams. After combing the countryside with maps, clippings, and guidance from realtors, we found our dwelling. We knew it as soon as we saw it—an old, center-chimney colonial, built in 1800, which sat on fields with an orchard and barn. Our realtor was not familiar with the house, since it had been on an exclusive listing and just went on multiple. So going through the house together and exploring the possibilities was just as new to her as it was to us both. When we responded, "We really love it," she turned to us with a surprised "You do?"

Tom and I never saw the house the way it actually was—we envisioned it the way it is now. It was right for us, since the owners had never touched any of the original details. The floors, fireplaces, windows were all there, and in an old house that's quite rare. No one had built huge additions that made the house too large for us, or put in new bathrooms or a kitchen just to sell. No, it was in a rough stage, a stage that took some getting used to since we were so settled in New York. But the change was truly worth it. We took one day at a time and adjusted accordingly. At first we went back and forth, bringing our most cherished belongings along with us.

We cleaned one area and stored everything in that space, then proceeded, as in the four apartments before, to take one room at a time and tackle the scraping, plastering, sanding, painting—techniques we had become so proficient in along the way. So, in the middle of chaos, a jewel emerged as "the dining room." We had just painted the floors tan with a red border stripe, the windows and doors with warm grey trim, and the freshly plastered and painted walls in buff white. One at a time, with sighs of pleasure and exhaustion, we placed each piece of our collection in. Carefully measuring and nailing in place the appropriate paintings, watercolors, and theorems, we transformed the room into the vision we had both imagined that cold December day when we first stepped into it.

Work on the house went slowly—I had completed *All Year Long* just prior to moving. I was even able to place drawings of the house in several spots throughout the book, which, of course, made me glow. Now I waited anxiously for its outcome in the reviewers' columns.

At home we cleared space for me to work with good light and the right surfaces to be able to spread everything out. At this point I was working on a book about a barn . . . being so excited about our big barn structure and, of course, loving the farmyard aspect. Knowing how much I enjoyed *Across the Stream,* the birth of *Early Morning in the Barn* came about quite naturally with its feisty rooster arousing all the barnyard critters with his cock-a-doodle doo, and the little chicks taking their morning jog through the barn to greet all their friends.

Midway through the completion of *Early Morning in the Barn,* our own barn went up in flames. It was 11:30 on the eve of Halloween, 1982, when the blaze lit up the entire hill. We were awakened by pounding on the front door—weekenders who were unable to pass due to the blaze and who, by glancing at the house, knew we were totally unaware of what was happening.

*The author in 1964* (Courtesy of Nancy Tafuri.)

At the pounding, we jolted out of bed to see, straight ahead, right outside our own bedroom window, the entire corner of our big old brown barn aflame. It was an experience I feel no one should go through. That night, only five months after the purchase of our new home, was the worst I had ever experienced. The flames blanketed the two-thousand-square-foot structure like bees making honey. The conflagration was fast and furious. The barn was covered with a tight new roof and, with its breezy vents of siding and disjointed windows, it was virtually a hot box, topped with hundreds of bales of hay for the horses and two cords of wood I had just stacked myself. So there wasn't a chance (even though the volunteer fire department answered only nine minutes later), that our barn would survive. Hoses were stretched to reach the north side of the house to stop the paint from blistering under the heat. Then, amidst this tragedy, on the horizon a large glow appeared . . . another fire. This occurrence led everyone to believe arson was the cause. The distant flames were coming from a farm in the next town belonging to an old resident farmer who worked the hills and meadows with his cows to supply the local dairy with his milk.

As the sun rose the following morning, our hearts sank. Our land had been violated, and our feelings numbed by thoughtlessness and disregard.

In the following weeks we stood up and dusted ourselves off. We decided that this was where we wanted to stay and proceeded to turn our lives around. Insurance forms were filled out; excavators leveled land and planted seed. Our house now stood alone on top of the hill as plans for another barn were being made.

That winter passed quickly. Rides into the surrounding towns to search for old structures to erect on the barn site proved fruitful. One was found in New York State just over the Connecticut/New York line.

*Early Morning in the Barn* was completed in full color with black line overlays. Reviews of *All Year Long* were favorable, and a new manuscript by Charlotte Pomerantz, *All Asleep,* was on my drawing board ready to be worked on.

Tom was designing and holding up the studio name in New York on weekdays, then zooming up to Connecticut every chance he could. We hated being apart, but knew until we made some headway on the place it was the only way.

As plans were being made on the construction of our new (old) barn, I was also searching for a new book idea of my own. Nature around our perimeters was alive with wonderment to my country-starved eyes. Walks into outstretched meadows past the pond and into the nearby woods were so easy on mind and body. One crisp, early spring day, when Tom and I were nearing the pond's edge, we heard rustling and then a splash. As we approached, we came upon a brightly colored mallard with its mate, swimming contentedly among the reeds. We sat quietly watching their every move. Then Tom turned with a smile and said, "There's a book here for you, Nancy." A book—I wondered—could there be? I loved all the elements, but one needs more than objects and location. Yet I knew he was right. I felt it, too. There was so much in this small body of water waiting to be captured.

I visited the pond site continuously for several weeks after discovering our feathered residents; and I was rewarded by a grand finale. What Mama and Papa had been preparing themselves for these long weeks was the hatching of fluffy brownish yellow babies: eight fine ducklings.

I started to sketch, putting down my thoughts for a book called "The Pond," having our feathered mother delightedly showing off her young babies to all the pond residents. Since I had just completed *All Asleep,* I was enthusiastic over this idea and dashed into New York to share it with Susan and Libby. Their lack of enthusiasm wasn't what I had expected and I knew something must be missing. I really wanted to make it work. The appropriate self-doubt entered my thoughts but then left, leaving me with only seven ducklings. Where was the eighth duckling? Back to the drawing board to hide the adventurous fuzzy offspring from Mama, but not from the young viewers' eyes.

I was optimistic about the way the dummy was coming along and couldn't wait until its completion to share it with my publisher. As the time neared, I needed a title and *Have You Seen My Duckling?* seemed a natural. I was greeted back at Greenwillow with excitement and so was *Have You Seen My Duckling?* . . . I was on my way!

And so was the construction of the barn. Its foundation was dug (much closer to the house than the original) and plans for a potting shed, work area, and garage were incorporated into a 1,100-square-foot frame. Dating from approximately the same time time period as our home, the barn had been carefully disassembled from its New York State location and trucked to its new site. Photos of Tom were taken atop one of the twenty-foot hand-hewn beams just after positioning. What a change from midtown Manhattan! Our world truly had shifted, and we were experiencing all of its challenges.

*

The stimulation of our environment and our work continued. *Duckling* was going to be a full-color picture book. My line needn't be separated and I was both excited and apprehensive of its outcome, although once I started working on the friendly, warm, round, fuzzy bodies with watercolor, pastels, and ink, I soon lost my fear and enjoyed the results. When the book was finally finished, I missed having the ducklings on my board, greeting me every morning. *Have You Seen My Duckling?* has rewarded me through its pleasantries. In January of 1985 it was chosen as a Caldecott Honor Book, which was a thrill and an incredible moment for me.

It was midweek and I was in the midst of training our two-month-old Keeshond puppy, Tavo, named after dear Tara who had passed away in December. I was huddled up in muffler, hat, and sweaters while running to the phone just after a snowy escapade with the furry youngster.

When the voice on the other end announced my name and started in with the formal dialect, it was somewhat muffled through the many layers of clothing still on my head. Being polite and listening carefully while catching my breath, I couldn't believe my ears. I had to ask, "Is that the silver seal?" "Yes, it is," answered the friendly voice of Karen Hoyle, chair of the Caldecott committee.

What a moment, what a thrill! The awards were given in Chicago that year in July and the experience of meeting teachers and librarians from across the country was really an enriching experience, not to say a heck of a lot of fun . . . and something I sure wouldn't mind doing again!

The barn was finished, but excavation around its outside continued—a stone wall leading to the house connecting the two structures, a graveled driveway, and an herb garden tucked below with raised beds that would be planned in the winter for early spring planting.

The herb garden became the backdrop for *Nata,* Helen V. Griffith's work about an unusual fairy. The format and layout of *Nata* was very different for me. Having designed dust jackets, I was at home with rules and spacing type. I placed *Nata* in a miniature garden on the right while her story was held together by decorative rules and bees on the left. Quite different from my large double spreads in *Have You Seen My Duckling?,* a format to which I returned in *Rabbit's Morning.*

One very early morning, as Tom was leaving for the week, he found one of our side apple trees coming down with a fungus. Its leaves had all turned yellow and were falling. In order for the fungus not to spread to any of the trees in the orchard, Tom wanted me to rake up the leaves as soon as possible.

That misty, wet morning is when it happened: I heard a pounding and then, out of thin air, a huge jackrabbit appeared not more than three feet from my rake. His leaps were outstretched, his direction zigzag and very playful. Not more than seconds later, a second rabbit followed in his tracks. What a morning—they dashed up the hill and down and around. What fun . . . for them and me! They danced in the wet foliage, performed for nature, and then disappeared as quickly as they had appeared.

That night I sat trying to put the morning's experience down on paper. A rabbit, let's see, one rabbit's morning, yes, a rabbit's morning—and *Rabbit's Morning* was born. Slowly I felt him explore the countryside and pass families, lots of families, until he, too, came to his own home with his own family.

While I was working on *Rabbit's Morning,* Tom and I talked about fixing up a small building on the property. It had been used as a chicken shed by the previous farmer and had been turned into a rental apartment by the last owner; now we wanted to make it into a studio so that One Plus One could incorporate itself back into its original working status. Tom had been giving thought to leaving New York City, and when our landlord gave us a new rental increase, we figured the time was right. We could always find space if need be—if it didn't work.

The construction was barely over when Tom and I moved into this lovely space, which looked out into the orchard and fields and up to the hills. Nervous at first, but encountering less interruption and feeling a sense of calmness, Tom felt it would work. And work it did, some six years later. With the aid of a stat machine, fax, and express mailings, working outside the city became a reality, long before computers. We enjoyed working together again—and being involved in each other's projects and careers.

*"The house after completion," Roxbury, Connecticut, 1985* (Courtesy of Nancy Tafuri.)

My first book in the new studio was *Who's Counting?* Tavo, our exuberant puppy, gave me all the needed reference for that book . . . large watercolor paintings of an adventurous puppy teaching us all the numbers in big bold letters.

*Do Not Disturb,* an environmental book for the very young, came next—a brightly colored book showing a family as they reach a campsite and proceed to set up their tent, start a fire, lay out a blanket, and change into their bathing gear to begin their outdoor day. But little do they know that along the way many woodland inhabitants are being disturbed, until the tables are turned after nightfall and the reader gets a surprise and a chuckle when the animals show them whose home it really is!

It had been a while since I had had a Mirra Ginsburg manuscript on my drawing board, and now I was enthusiastic about drawing up sketches for *Four Brave Sailors*—a tale of four fearless sailors in a white ship. Their adventure started out in my mind on a shelf in a young child's room and slipped off into a large blue wave on an open sea of imagination. Animals and birds I had always wanted to place in a book came to life in *Four Brave Sailors.* Fearless as they were, our furry mouse sailors only feared the child's tiger cat.

That tiger cat planted himself in my mind and turned himself into the tiger in *Junglewalk.* In this book a dream transforms an ordinary night into an adventure for both cat and boy through the animal-and bird-infested rain forest, ending with a warm hug and a walk to share his adventure-filled book with a friend.

After *Junglewalk,* Susan had a wonderful suggestion: a series of board books for the very young child. The thought was appealing, but what should the subject matter be? "Animals," Susan replied. Well, wouldn't that be fun! So, my thoughts turned to farmyard animals on my long bus ride home. Bunnies, a fawn, a puppy, a kitten, chicks, a colt, a piglet, and a lamb are all babies . . . all babies like me! That's it, what a great ending . . . then I could put a round smiling infant on the last page. And the title *My Friends* was all it needed.

*My Friends* needed a couple of companion books: *In a Red House,* a book containing all the familiar objects in a young child's room, and *Where We Sleep,* holding images of all the cozy places where bunnies, fawns, puppies, kittens, ducklings, chicks, lambs, cubs, and babies sleep!

I was so enthusiastic over the series that after *Spots, Feathers, and Curly Tails,* a barnyard question-and-answer book, I started to work on two more in the board book series: *Two New Sneakers,* about a little boy putting on all of his new clothes to go outside, and *One Wet Jacket,* in which a little girl takes off all her wet clothes before her bath.

Back at the house, a bathroom was added downstairs, taking from one area and giving to another. The kitchen came next, a rather messy job but so rewarding when the commercial range was placed into position. Tom's eyes glowed with delight and my mouth watered. Tom's culinary abilities are superb. He started to feel an interest in cooking when we experimented with foods from the market areas in New York City, duplicating some of the entrees from the varied restaurants we'd search out in and around the city. Even now Tom grows a garden that with proper preparation lasts us until winter. I'm in charge of the herbs and flowers, the first being a treat to dry and enjoy all through the inclement weather; the flowers are a joy just to look at and cut for the house.

The rooms were all starting to come together now and our collection was filling them up with the right amount of objects. Our policy has always been one of "less is more," with a cozy feel.

Just like Tom, I was trying to bring our new life together with love, respect, and lots of hard work. My

***Nancy and six-month-old Cristina, with Margo, 1990*** (Courtesy of Nancy Tafuri.)

new manuscript by Charlotte Pomerantz, *Flap Your Wings and Try,* was about that same topic, simplified but straight to the point. After reading the text, I focused on a large, round sea gull for my lead. Knowing this may be a bit unusual, I approached Susan to see if she, too, could imagine my large feathered friend and his seashore home for *Flap Your Wings and Try.* Her reply was an exuberant "Yes!" . . . and my awkward young sea gull was soaring through the skies before you knew it.

Working on children's books, whether totally my own or another author's, has always been one of life's joys for me . . . being able to take short lines of text or, in some cases, none at all and turn them into a package that can be held by small hands is so rewarding. My author appearances in many parts of the country are especially enjoyable when they involve the children that my books are intended for.

*

My work, my life with Tom, our country surroundings, the dogs, our friends and families, all make up me. But a time came in my life when I unselfishly wanted more. Tom and I both wanted someone else to share in all of this with us. We wanted a child.

But unlike apartments or houses and books, wanting and trying are not always the answer, and many years passed along with many disappointments. There was just enough encouragement, however, to make us feel assured we would someday be rewarded for all of our efforts.

My nurturing emotions were starting to overflow when *Follow Me!* made its way to the drawing board. A young baby seal taking a nap under Mama's flipper finds herself distracted by a red crab passing by. Anxious to cohort with a friend, she slips away and follows the crab through groups of sea gulls, hills of rocks, tidal pools of sea urchins, crayfish, and others. But unknowingly, Mama is always keeping a watchful eye on her adventurous young explorer. And it turns out that the young seal's crab joins up with many, many more crabs on the shore, so many more that her nearly new friend is lost in the group and then soon swims out to sea. Such a disappointment for the young seal.

Saddened by her loss, baby turns to discover what we knew all along. Mama was always with her and, after consoling her, Mama knows just what she needs—a group of young seal friends for her to be a part of—and with a smile on her face, our young seal stands surrounded by friends.

The summer *Follow Me!* was being conceived, we found out that our daughter, Cristina, was, too! A feeling of much joy filled the house, along with a little anxiety as to whether we could fill our roles as parents

***Tom, Cristina, and Nancy with Tavo and Margo in the apple orchard, 1991*** (Courtesy of Nancy Tafuri.)

in the years to come. But that soon passed and a glow of excitement filled our hearts and souls in the following nine months.

Work on *Follow Me!* seemed more realistic. I was actually starting to feel like that mama seal, sitting at my drawing board and enthusiastically completing the book before its due date . . . and Cristina's.

May 9, 1989, I walked into Greenwillow with the completed pages for *Follow Me!* What joy we all shared—it was wonderful being in the fold again after what seemed so long an absence. Great anticipation was in the air, not only for the book, but also for the nearing arrival of still another "little reader."

We laughed and talked, looked at *Follow Me!* again and again, until the time came for kisses and departing good wishes and home again to the house that held the warm "little room" waiting for Cristina.

The wait was not long. Cristina started entering this world that same week and blessed us with her arrival on the eve of Mothers Day with wide eyes, dark hair, and a delicate little six-pound, fifteen-ounce body. Her birth was an experience matched by none. Exalted emotions filled us with pride, love, and endearment.

The months ahead were made up of Tom and I getting to know Cristina with tender touches and warm embraces, smiling and talking and just looking at the miracle that was before us.

My life immediately changed. Priorities shifted and our little infant moved to the top of the list. To this day; two years later, that hasn't changed, but Cristina's life integrated into ours so that we're all living and working entirely in sync with one another.

I find I need to plan ahead more, work stranger hours, put some things on hold. But when I place myself at that drawing table now, I'm a different person from before. I feel that what I'm doing is more important; what I'm trying to say means more. My life has more depth, more responsibility, more meaning.

I feel honored to be creating literature for young children. Seeing how very important the early years are in a person's life, I can only hope that my books can contribute in some small way to that growth through line, color, shape, and story.

Since Cristina's birth, my books have taken on a different feel. Now I have a model to work into my drawings . . . and a very patient one at that. Mirra Ginsburg's manuscript for *Asleep, Asleep* was a perfect book to put me back at the drawing board, a perfect book at the perfect time. Talk about really feeling your part! Sleep habits seemed my only concern. So when this gentle book came into my hands, I was eager to begin. Tender and rhythmic, it could lull you to sleep. There were times I wished it were completed and printed so I, too, could lull my bouncy baby to sleep. Cristina's modeling debut can be found on the last pages of this twenty-four page, full-color, nighttime journey.

During the first year of babyhood, I could see the fondness Cristina had for farmyard animals . . . the sounds they made, their looks, and where they lived. Since we are right in the middle of lots of farms, she would point to the different creatures and make the appropriate moos and baas. That made the wheels want to start turning, but, boy, did they need oil. I couldn't repeat *Early Morning in the Barn* and didn't want to come close to *Spots, Feathers, and Curly Tails.* I wanted more words, but without becoming too complicated. First I started with the sun, the sun coming up; no, the rooster should be first; no, that's what I did in *Early Morning in the Barn.* Then I forgot about it, put the thoughts out of my head, and just waited.

I waited so long that I forgot what I was waiting for, and then he appeared, The Farmer . . . on a big blank page of my tissue pad. Along with his wife and dog and cat and ducks and donkey and cow. One right after another, all helping me form one great big long sentence.

I was thrilled with the outcome and couldn't wait until Susan read it. But unlike the days before Cristina, hopping on a bus to discuss a book had become a luxury now. So, with a phone call and a fax, I waited for the reply quite anxiously. Susan and Libby met and went over my lines and got back to me with a positive response. I was so pleased because now I could look forward to another book somewhere down the line that would be entirely my own. *This Is the Farmer* has the farmer that cuts our fields for hay as the lead, along with local animals and structures to add color to this barnyard tale.

***The author at her drawing board, 1992*** (Courtesy of Nancy Tafuri.)

In the interim I had begun taking photos of Cristina for Patricia Lillie's book, *Everything Has a Place.* When the lines were read to me over the phone, even before my reply to accept, visions of the pages were flashing in my mind's eye.

At that moment, I knew Cristina would be just the model for this very young picture book. I was happy to say I wanted to illustrate Patricia Lillie's book and Susan was thrilled. Contracts were drawn up and work began on *Everything Has a Place.*

Taking photos of an eighteen month old for a twenty-four-page book was a task in itself. It actually stretched out for months. Changing positions, changing ideas, and editorial changes are all part of putting even what seems like the easiest of books together.

I've been most successful working with tissue overlays. My first attempt at visualizing a book begins with a small storyboard on a large tissue pad, picturing the size best suited for the book, oblong or upright. When size is decided, vellum pages (a heavier type of tissue) are ruled up. Then research begins. Since photos of situations were being used for *Everything Has a Place,* I used the three-by-five snapshots as reference for my drawings, along with the proper props for the different situations. In such cases as *Have You Seen My Duckling?, Junglewalk,* or *Follow Me,* for instance, area, location, animals, plant life, and bird life all need careful consideration before being placed in a book. Then, working on separate smaller sheets of tissue, I sketch my drawings and slide them under my vellum frame for the proper placement. If a finished drawing does not meet my page requirement, I then make a black-and-white stat to enlarge or reduce my image. So tissues are worked around my pages until they obtain the graphic image I would like to project. With tissues in place, a finished sketch is then transferred onto the vellum overlay. When this process is repeated through the twenty-four or thirty-two pages, plus cover, title page, and sometimes endpaper format, the book dummy is completed and ready for editorial and art approval.

A meeting is set up and we all go over the completed dummy. If any changes are to be made, this is the best time to do them since the next step is color.

To date, most of my books have been in watercolor with a black Rapidograph pen line or Pigma Micron pens in varying widths. Some added pastel touches are needed at times for effect. I place the vellum drawing on my lightbox and transfer it onto the ruled-to-size watercolor paper (140-pound hot-press D'Arches). I do this for the entire book. Then I go through the entire book again with my black line outline. In the case of *Junglewalk,* during the dream sequence the black line was eliminated and a pastel line was integrated after the watercolor wash was put down.

When I have all the colors chosen and mixed for the page, I begin with the largest area of a single color and start washing clear, cool water over the entire surface, making certain no water bleeds into any other area. If so, the color, when put down, would seep into another section. I have been using water color inks or dyes for most of my work. The color is very luminescent and color reproduction has been very true to the original. It has been noted by some to fade after extensive time in a framed situation, but I have been very successful in this area, just by avoiding direct sunlight and fluorescent bulbs. I like using gouache, pastels, colored pencils, and watercolor in tube form for accenting purposes. Very often I write my formulas down when mixing, so at a later date, when the mind fades, I still have a record of colors used earlier on that page.

I enjoy working with type in combination with my illustrations. I find working images around type a challenge. I also enjoy the way the printed letter form complements the colorful images. The cover always needs special attention, since its impact will attract a child, parent, librarian, etc., at first glance. The format is smaller than a double spread, with added type for author, illustrator, title, etc. So it's very important to make it a strong element of design. I always like to do a separate piece of art for the cover so it works in the allotted space given, with type that will balance with the art.

I've often been asked if I enjoy working on another author's work as much as my own. I truly enjoy working on both. Many books I've taken on have been a challenge and have enabled me to grow both as an artist and a writer of picture books for young children. I look forward to growing more, improving my skills, in the years to come, and adopting new techniques.

Being involved in children's literature has been a special part of my life. I encourage anyone who feels strongly about entering the world of books for the natural world around me and, in turn, I hope I can help young children to do the same.

Tafuri contributed the following update to *SATA* in 2007:

Fifteen years have passed since I was asked to write my original autobiography. And now I am being asked to add a decade and a half to the series in chronological order. I'm not a journal writer; my books have always been the markers in my life. They have become my bench marks. When I completed my autobiography fifteen years ago, I had cast Cristina as the little toddler in Patricia Lillie's *Everything Has a Place. This Is the Farmer* was also underway.

When delivering the completed artwork for *This Is the Farmer,* I was bubbling with enthusiasm over the plans for Cristina's upcoming fourth birthday party. I explained that we were having the same farmer and his wife from *This Is the Farmer,* come to our barn with their resident animals—rooster, rabbits, ducks, sheep, hens with chicks, and one goat, to help Cristina celebrate turning four!

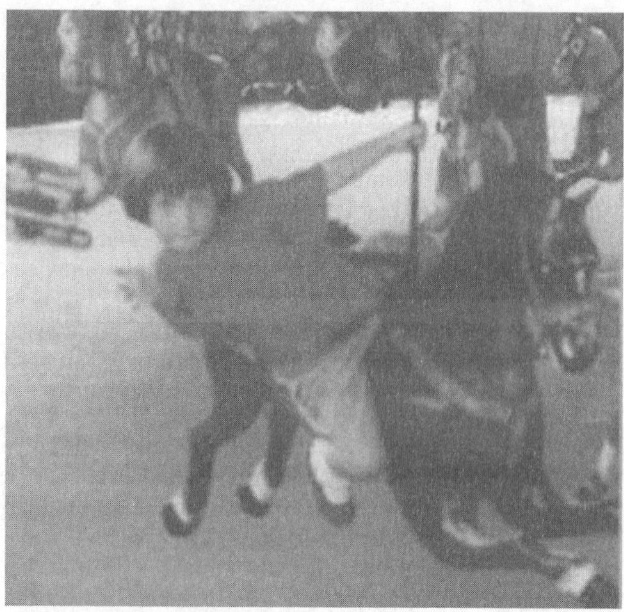

*Cristina, reaching for the brass ring, in Watch Hill, Rhode Island* (Courtesy of Nancy Tafuri.)

After listening to all the details, my editors exclaimed that they would make a terrific book! So in 1996 Cristina's fourth birthday party was documented in *The Barn Party,* and in the story that lone goat is the one to add to the surprise ending.

My next book had a very similar beginning. Since Cristina was a toddler we had gone to a small seaside town in Rhode Island called Weekapaug for our summer holiday. We would stay in an old inn, which had been reconstructed after the 1938 hurricane. It had been placed on the neighboring salt pond, away from the ocean's strong tides. After several years of shell picking, wave hopping, and sand castle building, Cristina was old enough to ride the historic flying-horse carousel in the nearby town of Watch Hill. She was strapped in place and mother was asked to stand on the other side of the white picket fence. Cristina was to go it alone. Away she went, with a smile on her face. Holding on tightly, she took off on her first ride on the country's oldest carousel. Every year since, she would reach for the brass ring. Ride after ride, the carousel arm would come down, loaded with the shiny silver rings with only a single golden brass piece that, if grasped, would entitle the bearer to a free ride. Winner or not, Cristina's ride on the Watch Hill carousel became the ultimate summer tradition, and in my book *The Brass Ring* I documented these childhood summer holidays. The book was very popular in coastal southern New England, since the carousel is such an endearing landmark, but the sales were not strong enough in the rest of the country to warrant reprinting. *The Brass Ring* went out of print.

As time passed, Tom and I received continued requests for the local book, until we decided to publish *The Brass Ring* ourselves. After many phone calls and written permission letters, the rights were released and we searched for a printer. In 2005, *The Brass Ring* was published under our imprint, Duck Pond Press. In this way, we became publishers. Storing, signing, packing and sending out yet another printing of *The Brass Ring!*

Along with *The Brass Ring* and *The Barn Party,* Cristina also appeared in another book, but not as a girl. This time she was a very eager little boy in Kevin Henkes' *The Biggest Boy.* This book was too delicious to pass up. Cristina was the perfect age to become the story's growing protagonist, a boy who has puppies and kittens living in his pockets while wearing a house for a jacket. I fastened Cristina's short bob back with hair clips, found her short jeans and a pair of suspenders, and she was ready to model yet again. It's so tender knowing I have these sweet shots of her being so patient and expressionist during her young life . . . and knowing that *The Biggest Boy* is really a little girl!

Cristina has definitely had a strong influence in the creation of my books. One night, after reading several of her favorite stories, she had finally fallen asleep. It was an evening with a full moon, and it was shining directly across her body. She was encased in a silvery glow. I sat looking at her in admiration and muttered the line, "What the moon sees." *What the Moon Sees . . .* what a great title!

A title and a vision for the last page do not make a book, so the wheels started turning. What if I divided the book into two sections, reserving one half of the book for the daytime—*What the Sun Sees*—and then close the book, turn it around, and open it to show a similar situation in the nighttime for *What the Moon Sees*? Then at the end I can put the visual that started the whole book: Cristina's moonlit body. *What the Sun Sees, What the Moon Sees* was published in 1997.

During the time I was working on *What the Sun Sees, What the Moon Sees,* I received a package from an editor at Scholastic Press. It contained numerous promotional posters and cards to show that they were a house that promoted their authors and illustrators. It also contained a manuscript titled *Deep in the Woods.*

What a tempting approach. In the past, when I had received a request to illustrate a book from another publisher, I would decline. Those were the days when loyalties prevailed, and an author or illustrator stayed with the publisher they began their career with. But then I started to read the words, "Yes, little one, I love you as the pond loves you, forever and ever and always." The visuals were that of deer, ducks, rabbits, mice, bears, owls, and a child. The book began to unfold in my mind as I read each page. I was hooked. *Deep in the Woods* became *I Love You, Little One,* my first illustrated book for Scholastic.

Truth be told, I had been having growing pains for some time, and working with a new house was exhilarating. It was the spark I needed to take some chances and experiment with medias along with ideas.

The hardcover edition of *I Love You, Little One* was eventually reduced to board-book size for those little hands to handle.

I always wanted to do a Christmas book, but never had a concrete foundation for an idea. Then one year I was watching Cristina doing a craft project during the holidays when the idea struck: Creating an advent calendar of events and crafts that lead up to that all-important day: the 25th of December. The book was titled *Counting to Christmas.* It contains recipes for spicy gingerbread cookies, pomander treats for outside wildlife, yuletide cards, and popcorn-cranberry garlands to decorate the Christmas tree. As the days pass by, readers watch the excitement grow through all the activities and events occurring in preparation for the big day. And the finale is found on the last page, which shows all the outdoor animals enjoying the treats the book's young protagonist have prepared for them.

*Counting to Christmas* was the last book Cristina was able to model for. But while growing out of my books, our daughter was turning into a young lady. And amid this bittersweet turn into the next decade, a wonderful turn of events evolved.

Cristina and I began traveling together. My husband had seen the itinerary for Rose Tree Cottage Tours in *Victoria* magazine. It was a literature tour covering the northern section of England. The tour would include visiting the homes and surrounding countryside, villages, and cities of writers from Wordsworth to Beatrix Potter, from Jane Austen to the Brontës. Along the way, participants would visit Chatsworth, the home of the Duchess of Devonshire.

We were thrilled with the prospect of exploring a new world together. We were able to walk along Beatrix Potter's stone garden paths, have tea in the parlor of William Wordsworth, and peek into the study of John Ruskin, along with visiting the stables and office of James Herriot and peering into the room where the Brontë sisters—Charlotte, Emily, and Anne—wrote their memorable books. This was the first of many trips for the two of us—we were bitten.

For Cristina, it was enriching for her to see life outside her Roxbury home. The experiences she has had have helped her grow into the confident young lady she is today. For me, our travels have not only contributed to my work as an illustrator and lover of nature, but have

*Cristina, making popcorn garlands in preparation for* **Counting to Christmas** (Courtesy of Nancy Tafuri.)

***Nancy and Cristina at Hill Top, the hometown of Beatrix Potter, 1999*** (Courtesy of Nancy Tafuri.)

also forged friendships along the way that I know I will have for a lifetime. Not to mention the memories Cristina and I have to look back on. Thank you, Tom!

Now that my young model has grown up on me, she asked if I could just draw animals instead. I love drawing animals, especially round ones! From 1994 to the present, 2008, I have completed forty-eight books. My characters have ranged from bunnies to bears and donkeys to chicks. I enjoy working with the different shapes and personalities of animals, but I know now that if other little child models came along for my books, Cristina would be right there to guide them.

I am sitting in my studio seventeen years after its completion. It is filled with the many books, notes, and memorabilia that come with life. It's still my favorite place to be. I look forward to coming over here every day. My work still presents its challenges but I'm not growing tired of creating books for the youngest reader. At times it's somewhat daunting thinking in pure, simple terms in a world that is so complex. But drawing shapes and writing words that can be read to a small child is still very rewarding.

And when I go to a reading and I finish a story and I hear "Read it again"—I just smile.

Maybe in some way I've helped create another reader.

## TAKASHIMA, Misako
## See MISAKO ROCKS!

* * *

## TAYLOR, Sean 1965-

### Personal

Born 1965, in Fetcham, Surrey, England; married; wife's name Adriana; children: Joey. *Education:* Cambridge University, degree (English literature).

### Addresses

*Home*—England; São Paulo, Brazil. *Agent*—Ceila Catchpole, celiacatchpoleyahoo.co.uk. *E-mail*—sean@seantaylorstories.com.

### Career

Author and storyteller. Pluto Press, London, England, former member of staff; former freelance journalist; formerly worked in writing development for East London, England.

### Awards, Honors

Independent/Scholastic Story of the Year award, 1994.

### Writings

*FOR CHILDREN*

(Reteller) *Silly Stories from Here, There, and Everywhere,* illustrated by Eric Smith, Brett Hudson, and Nick Schon, Heineman (London, England), 2000.

*Headfirst into the Porridge,* illustrated by Carla Daly, Rigby (London, England), 2001.

*The Woodcutter and the Bear,* illustrated by Bill Bolton, Rigby Educational (London, England), 2001.

*Brer Rabbit's Trickbag,* illustrated by Dave McTaggart, Oxford University Press (Oxford, England), 2002, new edition, 2007.

*The Huge and Horrible Beast,* illustrated by Tim Archbold, Oxford University Press (Oxford, England), 2003.

*Carnival King,* illustrated by Emma Shaw Smith, Oxford University Press (Oxford, England), 2003.

*Aligator Swamp,* illustrated by Neil Chapman, Pearson Longman (London, England), 2003.

*Small Bad Wolf,* illustrated by Jan Lewis, Kingfisher (London, England), 2003, Kingfisher (Boston, MA), 2004.

*The Genie of the Bottle Bank,* illustrated by Ella Okstad, Ginn (London, England), 2004.

*Boing!,* illustrated by Bruce Ingman, Candlewick Press (Cambridge, MA), 2004.

*Mojo and Weeza and the Funny Thing,* illustrated by Julian Mosedale, Collins Educational (London, England), 2004.

*The Stone Cutter,* illustrated by Serena Curmi, Collins (London, England), 2005.

*Too Much Talk!,* illustrated by Ofra Amit, Rigby Educational (London, England), 2005.

*Booooo!,* illustrated by Joanne Partis, Rigby (London, England), 2005.

*Purple Class and the Flying Spider,* illustrated by Helen Bate, Frances Lincoln (London, England), 2006.

*Purple Class and the Skelington, and Other Stories,* illustrated by Helen Bate, Frances Lincoln (London, England), 2006.

*When a Monster Is Born,* illustrated by Nick Sharratt, Orchard (London, England), 2006, Roaring Brook Press (New Milford, CT), 2007.

*Mojo and Weeza and the New Hat,* illustrated by Julian Mosedale, Collins Educational (London, England), 2007.

*The Great Snake: Stories from the Amazon,* illustrated by Fernando Vilela, Frances Lincoln (London, England), 2008.

*The Bopping Big Band,* illustrated by Christyan Fox, Scholastic UK (London, England), 2008.

*The Ring Went Zing!,* illustrated by Jill Barton, Dial Books for Young Readers (New York, NY), 2009.

Contributor of short fiction to *Skin Deep,* edited by Tony Bradman, Puffin (London, England), 2004, and *Like Father like Son,* edited by Bradman, Puffin, 2006.

*OTHER*

(Editor) *Cheese and Chips Are Related to the Moon* (poetry), Eastside Books (London, England), 1992.

*Take It from Me* (poetry), Basement Writers (London, England), 1992.

### Sidelights

Sean Taylor started writing poetry in the 1990s, but his sense of whimsy, paired with his interest and talent for storytelling, motivated him to shift to writing for children. Specializing in stories that appeal to pre-and beginning readers, Taylor teams up with a number of illustrators to produce brightly colored books designed to appeal to younger children. Among his books are *Small Bad Wolf,* with humorous art by Jan Lewis; *Boing!,* illustrated by Bruce Ingman; and *When a Monster Is Born,* featuring cartoon art by popular illustrator Nick Sharratt.

In *Boing!* Taylor and Ingman tells a story about a man who loves to jump. Calling himself the Great Elastic Marvel, the man is a five-time trampoline champion. During one of his many trampoline practices, he miscalculates while executing a quadruple flip. After bouncing out of his apartment window, the springy trampolinist bounds, hops, and springs from one scary situation to another. Author and illustrator "get the hero from one slapstick scrape to the next, with plenty of fun—and the greatest of ease," concluded a *Publishers Weekly* contributor in a review of *Boing!* Praising Taylor's "lively" story in her *School Library Journal* review, Shawn Bro-

***Sean Taylor's amusing monster story* When a Monster Is Born *is brought to life in droll cartoons by British illustrator Nick Sharratt.*** (Illustration copyright © 2006 by Nick Sharratt. Reprinted by permission of Henry Holt and Company, LLC. in the US. Reproduced by permission of Orchard Books.)

mmer noted that the author's use of "repeated phrases add consistency and rhythm" to animate young listeners. Michael Cart wrote in *Booklist* that Ingman's "sketchy" paintings complement Taylor's "simple but zany tale."

Taylor's sense of whimsy is enhanced by Sharratt's colorful art in *When a Monster Is Born,* which *Booklist* contributor Gillian Engberg described as "just the thing for a sugared-up, restless story-hour crowd." A parody of many picture books about the birth of a new infant, Taylor's tale quickly introduces the new arrival: a roly-poly creature with mismatched blue and orange eyes, fuchsia horns, and funny teeth. As the tale continues, readers are given a sequence of two alternatives as the monster grows up, one monstrous and one silly but benign. By choosing the most human of the options, the monster eventually goes to school, grows up, and has a baby monster of his own. The story's "hilarious possibilities . . . make [*When a Monster Is Born*] . . . a great choice for storytime," according to *Booklist* contributor Susan Dove Lempke, while a *Kirkus Reviews* writer predicted that Taylor's "circular tale" has enough appeal to make the book "a storytime staple."

## Biographical and Critical Sources

*PERIODICALS*

*Booklist,* August, 2004, Michael Cart, review of *Boing!,* p. 1946; June 1, 2007, Gillian Engberg, review of *When a Monster Is Born,* p. 86.

*Horn Book,* July-August, 2007, Susan Dove Lempke, review of *When a Monster Is Born,* p. 386.

*Kirkus Reviews,* June 15, 2004, review of *Boing!,* p. 582; May 1, 2007, review of *When a Monster Is Born.*

*Publishers Weekly,* July 12, 2004, review of *Boing!,* p. 63.

*School Library Journal,* August, 2004, Anne Knickerbocker, review of *Brown Bear Gets in Shape,* p. 86; August, 2004, Shawn Brommer, review of *Boing!,* p. 96; June, 2007, Suzanne Myers Harold, review of *When a Monster Is Born,* p. 126.

*ONLINE*

*Sean Taylor Home Page,* http://www.seantaylorstories.com (August 15, 2008).*

* * *

## THÉ TJONG-KHING

See KHING, T.T.

* * *

## TOMLINSON, Heather

### Personal

Born in Redlands, CA; married; children: one son. *Education:* Graduated from Wellesley College. *Hobbies and other interests:* Books, cats, children's literature, fairy tales, fantasy, France, quilting, sailing.

### Addresses

*Home and office*—Southern CA. *E-mail*—heather@tomlinson.com.

### Career

Writer. Worked in book distribution for ten year; has taught English in Paris, France, and French in the United States.

### Member

Society of Children's Book Writers and Illustrators, Authors Guild.

### Writings

*NOVELS*

*The Swan Maiden,* Holt (New York, NY, 2007.

*Aurelie: A Faerie Tale,* Holt (New York, NY, 2008.

### Sidelights

Heather Tomlinson, who has a degree in French literature and taught English for several years in Paris, is the author of *The Swan Maiden,* a novel inspired by French fairy tales. In a *Class of 2k7* interview with Sarah Beth Durst, Tomlinson remarked of writing her first novel: "I was reading Paul Delarue's excellent book *Le conte populaire Français,* and found a story called "The Devil's Daughter." It had many, many versions in French—over 120, I think—so I knew there'd be lots of possible shapes the story could take. Plus disobedient daughters, lots of magic, and a central mystery. Writing gold!"

A native of California, Tomlinson developed an interest in fantastic literature at a young age. "As a kid, I collected all the Andrew Lang colored fairy tale books," she told Durst. "Another favorite was Iona and Peter Opie's *The Classic Fairy Tales,* with colored plates by great illustrators: [Arthur] Rackham, [Edmund] Dulac, [Walter] Crane, [Gustave] Doré. I think seeing how each artist was able to create a different mood, setting,

*Cover of Heather Tomlinson's* **The Swan Maiden,** *featuring cover art by Julia Breckenreid.* (Copyright © 2007 by Heather Tomlinson. Reprinted by permission of Henry Holt and Company, LLC.)

and characterization for the same tale made a deep impression on me, though of course I'm just realizing that now."

The Swan Maiden centers on Doucette, the sixteen-year-old daughter of the count and countess of Aigleron. The girl envies the magical powers possessed by her swan maiden sisters, Azelais and Cecilia. When Doucette finds her own swan skin hidden beneath a mattress, she realizes that her parents have deceived her and she becomes determined to claim her birthright and marry her true love, the shepherd boy Jaume. "Layered, elegantly written, and filled with unexpected twists and turns, *The Swan Maiden* soars with grace and power," observed *Booklist* contributor Frances Bradburn, and Neala Arnold, writing in *School Library Journal,* commented that the author "skillfully weaves a satisfying and enchanting tale that flows quickly and immerses readers in a charming, rustic setting."

"To me, writing feels like joining a great conversation, where you can enjoy what other people have to say and make your own contribution," Tomlinson stated in her *Class of 2k7* interview. "Books have given me so much pleasure through the years that I hope to share some of it with new readers."

## Biographical and Critical Sources

*PERIODICALS*

*Booklist,* October 1, 2007, Frances Bradburn, review of *The Swan Maiden,* p. 58.

*Kirkus Reviews,* July 15, 2007, review of *The Swan Maiden.*

*Publishers Weekly,* August 27, 2007, review of *The Swan Maiden,* p. 91.

*School Library Journal,* December, 2007, Neala Arnold, review of *The Swan Maiden,* p. 146.

*ONLINE*

*Class of 2k7 Blog,* http://community.livejournal.com/classof2k7/ (November 26, 2007), Sarah Beth Durst, interview with Tomlinson.

*Class of 2k7 Web site,* http://classof2k7.com/ (August 10, 2008), "Heather Tomlinson."

*Heather Tomlinson Home Page,* http://heathertomlinson.com (August 10, 2008).

*Heather Tomlinson Web log,* http://calepin.livejournal.com (August 10, 2008).

# U

## URE, Jean 1943-
## (Ann Colin, Jean Gregory, Sarah McCulloch)

### Personal

Surname sounds like "ewer"; born January 1, 1943, in Surrey, England; daughter of William (an insurance officer) and Vera Ure; married Leonard Gregory (an actor and writer), 1967. *Education:* Attended Webber-Douglas Academy of Dramatic Art, 1965-67. *Hobbies and other interests:* Reading, writing letters, walking dogs, playing with cats, music, working for animal rights.

### Addresses

*Home*—Croydon, Surrey, England. *Agent*—Caroline Sheldon, Caroline Sheldon Literary Agency, Thorley Manor Farm, Thorley, Yarmouth PO41 0SJ, England. *E-mail*—jeanure@talktalk.net.

### Career

Writer. Has worked as a waitress, cook, washer-up, nursing assistant, newspaper seller, shop assistant, theater usherette, temporary shorthand-typist, translator, secretary with NATO and UNESCO, and television production assistant.

### Member

Society of Authors.

### Awards, Honors

American Library Association Best Book for Young Adults citation, 1983, for *See You Thursday;* long-listed for *Guardian* Award for Children's Fiction, 2003, for *Bad Alice.*

### Writings

FICTION; FOR YOUNG READERS

*Ballet Dance for Two,* F. Watts (New York, NY), 1960, published as *Dance for Two,* illustrated by Richard Kennedy, Harrap (London, England), 1960.

***Jean Ure*** (Photograph by Hilary Palmer. Reproduced by permission.)

*A Proper Little Nooryeff,* Bodley Head (London, England), 1982, published as *What If They Saw Me Now?,* Delacorte (New York, NY), 1984.

*If It Weren't for Sebastian,* Bodley Head (London, England), 1982, Delacorte (New York, NY), 1985.

*Hi There, Supermouse!,* illustrated by Martin White, Hutchinson (London, England), 1983, published as *Supermouse,* illustrated by Ellen Eagle, Morrow (New York, NY), 1984.

*You Win Some, You Lose Some,* Bodley Head (London, England), 1984, Delacorte (New York, NY), 1987.

*You Two,* illustrated by Ellen Eagle, Morrow (New York, NY), 1984, published as *The You-Two,* illustrated by Martin White, Hutchinson (London, England), 1984.

*Nicola Mimosa,* illustrated by Martin White, Hutchinson (London, England), 1985, published as *The Most Important Thing,* illustrated by Ellen Eagle, Morrow (New York, NY), 1986.

*Megastar,* Blackie (Glasgow, Scotland), 1985.

*Swings and Roundabouts,* Blackie (Glasgow, Scotland), 1986.

*A Bottled Cherry Angel,* Hutchinson (London, England), 1986.

*Brenda the Bold,* illustrated by Glenys Ambrus, Heinemann (London, England), 1986.

*The Other Side of the Fence,* Bodley Head (London, England), 1986, Delacorte (New York, NY), 1988.

*One Green Leaf,* Bodley Head (London, England), 1987, Delacorte (New York, NY), 1989.

*Tea-Leaf on the Roof,* illustrated by Val Sassoon, Blackie (Glasgow, Scotland), 1987.

*War with Old Mouldy!,* illustrated by Alice Englander, Methuen (London, England), 1987.

*Who's Talking?,* Orchard (New York, NY), 1987.

*Frankie's Dad,* Hutchinson (London, England), 1988.

(With Michael Lewis) *A Muddy Kind of Magic,* Blackie (Glasgow, Scotland), 1988.

(With Michael Lewis) *Two Men in a Boat,* Blackie (Glasgow, Scotland), 1988.

*Play Nimrod for Him,* Bodley Head (London, England), 1990.

*Cool Simon,* Orchard (New York, NY), 1990.

*William in Love,* Blackie (Glasgow, Scotland), 1991.

*Dreaming of Larry,* Doubleday (New York, NY), 1991.

*A Place to Scream,* Doubleday (New York, NY), 1992.

*Spooky Cottage,* Heinemann (London, England), 1992.

*The Unknown Planet,* Walker (London, England), 1992.

*The Ghost That Lives on the Hill,* Methuen (London, England), 1992.

*Captain Cranko and the Crybaby,* Walker (London, England), 1993.

*The Phantom Knicker Nicker,* Blackie (London, England), 1993.

*Always Sebastian,* Bodley Head (London, England), 1993.

*Seven for a Secret,* Blackie Children's (London, England), 1993.

*Night Fright,* Blackie Children's (London, England), 1994.

*Who Says Animals Don't Have Rights?,* Puffin (London, England), 1994.

*Faces at the Window,* Corgi Freeway (London, England), 1994.

*Howzat, Gordon!,* Black Children's Books (London, England), 1994.

*Horrible Baby,* Longman (Harlow, England), 1994.

*Jug Ears,* Longman (Harlow, England), 1994.

*Help! It's Harriet,* Collins Children's Books (London, England), 1995.

*Demons in Disguise,* Ginn (Aylesbury, England), 1995.

*Has Anyone Seen This Girl?,* Bodley Head (London, England), 1996.

*Love Is Forever,* Orchard (London, England), 1996.

*Whatever Happened to Katy-Jane?,* Walker (London, England), 1996.

*Dance with Death,* Scholastic (New York, NY), 1996.

*The Gools,* Ginn (Aylesbury, England), 1996.

*The Children Next Door,* Scholastic (New York, NY), 1996.

*Harriet Strikes Again!,* Collins (London, England), 1996.

*The Collins Book of Ballet and Dance Stories,* Collins (London, England), 1996.

*Whistle and I'll Come,* Scholastic (New York, NY), 1997.

*The Big Time,* Ginn (Aylesbury, England), 1997.

*Danny Dynamite,* Transworld, 1998.

*Three-in-One Ballet Stories,* Red Fox (London, England), 1998.

*Girl in the Blue Tunic,* Scholastic (New York, NY), 1998.

*Puppy Present,* Collins (London, England), 1998, HarperCollins (New York, NY), 2000.

*Big Head,* Walker (London, England), 1999.

*Secret Simon,* Hodder Children's Books (London, England), 1999.

*A Twist in Time,* Walker (London, England), 1999.

*Just Sixteen,* Orchard (London, England), 1999.

*Family Fan Club,* HarperCollins (New York, NY), 2000.

*Big Tom,* HarperCollins (New York, NY), 2000.

*Monster in the Mirror,* HarperCollins (New York, NY), 2000.

*Get a Life!,* Orchard (London, England), 2001.

*Boys on the Brain,* HarperCollins (New York, NY), 2002.

*Daisy May,* Collins (London, England), 2002.

*Dazzling Danny,* Roaring Good Reads (London, England), 2003.

*Bad Alice,* Hodder (London, England), 2003.

*Ballet Stories: "Hi There, Supermouse!," "Proper Little Nooryeff," "Star Turn,"* Red Fox (London, England), 2004.

*Is Anybody There?: Seeing Is Believing,* HarperCollins Children's Books (London, England), 2004.

*The Tutti-Frutti Collection* (short stories), HarperCollins Children's Books (London, England), 2005.

*Sugar and Spice,* HarperCollins (London, England), 2005.

*Over the Moon,* HarperCollins Children's Books (London, England), 2006.

*The Flower Power Collection,* HarperCollins Children's Books (London, England), 2006.

*Gone Missing,* HarperCollins Children's Books (London, England), 2007.

*Hunky Dory,* HarperCollins Children's Books (London, England), 2007.

*Star Crazy,* HarperCollins Children's Books (London, England), 2007.

*Just Sixteen,* Orchard (London, England), 2007.

*Love Is Forever,* Orchard (London, England), 2008.

*Fortune Cookie,* HarperCollins Children's Books (London, England), 2009.

Contributor to anthology *The Animals' Bedtime Storybook,* Orion Children's Books, 2000.

*"THURSDAY" TRILOGY*

*See You Thursday,* Kestrel (London, England), 1981, Delacorte (New York, NY), 1983.

*After Thursday,* Kestrel (London, England), 1985, Delacorte (New York, NY), 1987.

*Tomorrow Is Also a Day,* Methuen (London, England), 1989.

*"WOODSIDE SCHOOL" SERIES*

*The Fright,* Orchard Books (New York, NY), 1987.
*Loud Mouth,* Orchard Books (New York, NY), 1988.
*Soppy Birthday,* Orchard Books (New York, NY), 1988.
*King of Spuds,* Orchard Books (New York, NY), 1989.
*Who's for the Zoo?,* Orchard Books (New York, NY), 1989.
*Who's for the Zoo?; Loud Mouth: Two Plays,* Longman (Harlow, England), 1994.

*"VANESSA" TRILOGY*

*Trouble with Vanessa,* Transworld (London, England), 1988.
*There's Always Danny,* Transworld (London, England), 1989.
*Say Goodbye,* Transworld (London, England), 1989.

*"PLAGUE" SERIES*

*Plague 99,* Methuen (London, England), 1989, published as *Plague,* Harcourt (New York, NY), 1991.
*After the Plague,* Methuen (London, England), 1992.
*Watchers at the Shrine,* Methuen (London, England), 1992
*Come Lucky April,* Methuen (London, England), 1992.

*"PETER HIGH SCHOOL" SERIES*

*Jo in the Middle,* Hutchinson (London, England), 1990.
*Bossyboots,* Hutchinson (London, England), 1991.
*Fat Lollipop,* Hutchinson (London, England), 1991.
*Jam Today,* Hutchinson (London, England), 1992.
*The Matchmakers,* Hutchinson (London, England), 1992.

*"WIZARD" SERIES*

*The Wizard in the Woods,* illustrated by David Anstley, Walker (London, England), 1990, Candlewick Press (New York, NY), 1992.
*Wizard in Wonderland,* illustrated by David Anstley, Walker (London, England), 1991, Candlewick Press (Cambridge, MA), 1993.
*The Wizard and the Witch,* Walker (London, England), 1995.

*"DANCING DREAM" SERIES*

*Star Turn,* Hutchinson (London, England), 1993.
*A Dream Come True,* Hutchinson (London, England), 1994.
*Fandango!,* Hutchinson (London, England), 1995.

*"COMETS" SERIES*

(With John Blake, David Clayton, Mick Gowar, Ian Gregory, Sam McBratney, and Stephanie Moody) *Comets Pack: 1,* Collins Educational (London, England), 1995.
(With John Blake, David Clayton, Mick Gowar, Ian Gregory, Sam McBratney, and Stephanie Moody) *Comets Pack: 2,* Collins Educational (London, England), 1996.
*The Great Safe Blag,* Collins Educational (London, England), 1996.

*"DIARY" SERIES*

*Skinny Melon and Me,* illustrated by Chris Fisher and Peter Bailey, Holt (New York, NY), 1996.
*Becky Bananas: This Is Your Life!,* HarperCollins (New York, NY), 1997.
*Fruit and Nutcase,* HarperCollins (New York, NY), 1998.
*Secret Life of Sally Tomato,* HarperCollins (New York, NY), 2000.
*Shrinking Violet,* HarperCollins (New York, NY), 2002.
*Pumpkin Pie,* Collins (London, England), 2002.
*Passion Flower: Wars of the Roses,* HarperCollins (London, England), 2003.
*Secret Meeting,* HarperCollins (London, England), 2004.
*Boys Beware,* HarperCollins Children's Books (London, England), 2005.

*"PET PALS" SERIES*

*Lucky Pup,* Orchard (London, England), 1997.
*Lucky,* Orchard (London, England), 1998.

*"SANDY SIMMONS" SERIES*

*Sandy Simmons and the Spotlight Spook,* Orchard (London, England), 1998.
*Sandy Simmons, Star Struck!,* Orchard (London, England), 1998.
*Sandy Simmons: Saves the Day,* Orchard (London, England), 1999.
*Sandy Simmons, Show Stealer,* Orchard (London, England), 1999.
*Sandy Simmons: Superstar,* Orchard (London, England), 1999.
*Sandy Simmons: Sweet Success,* Orchard (London, England), 1999.

*"WE LOVE ANIMALS" SERIES*

*Brave Warrior,* Scholastic Hippo (London, England), 1998.
*Daffy Down Donkey,* Scholastic Hippo (London, England), 1998, Barron's Educational Series (Happauge, NY), 1999.
*Foxglove,* Scholastic Hippo (London, England), 1998, Barron's Educational Series (Happauge, NY), 1999.
*Muddy Four Paws,* Scholastic Hippo (London, England), 1998, Barron's Educational Series (Happauge, NY), 1999.
*Snow Kittens,* Scholastic Hippo (London, England), 1998, Barron's Educational Series (Happauge, NY), 1999.
*Honey Bun,* Scholastic Hippo (London, England), 1999.

*"FOSTER FAMILY" SERIES*

*Foster Family,* Hodder Children's Books (London, England), 1999.
*Here Comes Ellen,* Hodder Children's Books (London, England), 1999.
*Meet the Radish,* Hodder Children's Books (London, England), 1999.
*My Sister Sam,* Hodder Children's Books (London, England), 1999.
*Babycakes,* Hodder Children's Books (London, England), 2000.
*Little Miss Perfect,* Hodder Children's Books (London, England), 2000.

*"CHUMS" SERIES*

*Bella,* HarperCollins (New York, NY), 2000.
*Buster,* HarperCollins (New York, NY), 2000.
*Bouncer,* HarperCollins (New York, NY), 2000.
*Bonnie,* HarperCollins (New York, NY), 2000.

*"GIRLS" SERIES*

*Boys Are OK!,* Orchard (London, England), 2002.
*Girls Are Groovy!,* Orchard (London, England), 2002.
*Girls Stick Together!,* Orchard (London, England), 2002.
*Pink Knickers Aren't Cool!,* Orchard (London, England), 2002.

*"STREETWISE" SERIES*

*Literacy Land,* Longman (London, England), 2003.
*Prince Pantyhose,* Longman (London, England), 2003.

*"STEVIE SILVER" SERIES*

*Stage Struck,* Orchard (London, England), 2006.
*Star Light,* Orchard (London, England), 2006.

*FOR ADULTS*

*The Other Theater,* Transworld (London, England), 1966.
*The Test of Love,* Corgi (London, England), 1968.
*If You Speak Love,* Corgi (London, England), 1972.
*Had We but World Enough and Time,* Corgi (London, England), 1972.
*The Farther Off from England,* White Lion, 1973.
*Daybreak,* Corgi (London, England), 1974.
*All Thy Love,* Corgi (London, England), 1975.
*Marriage of True Minds,* Corgi (London, England), 1975.
*No Precious Time,* Corgi (London, England), 1976.
*Hear No Evil,* Corgi (London, England), 1976.
*Curtain Fall,* Corgi (London, England), 1978.
*Masquerade,* Corgi (London, England), 1979.
*A Girl like That,* Corgi (London, England), 1979.
(Under pseudonym Ann Colin) *A Different Class of Doctor,* Corgi (London, England), 1980.
(Under pseudonym Ann Colin) *Doctor Jamie,* Corgi (London, England), 1980.
(Under name Jean Gregory) *Love beyond Telling,* Corgi (London, England), 1986.

*"RIVERSIDE THEATER ROMANCE" SERIES; FOR ADULTS*

*Early Stages,* Corgi (London, England), 1977.
*Dress Rehearsal,* Corgi (London, England), 1977.
*All in a Summer Season,* Corgi (London, England), 1977.
*Bid Time Return,* Corgi (London, England), 1978.

*GEORGIAN ROMANCES; UNDER PSEUDONYM SARAH McCULLOCH; FOR ADULTS*

*Not Quite a Lady,* Corgi (London, England), 1980, Fawcett (New York, NY), 1981.
*A Most Insistent Lady,* Corgi (London, England), 1981.
*A Lady for Ludovic,* Corgi (London, England), 1981.
*Merely a Gentleman,* Corgi (London, England), 1982.
*A Perfect Gentleman,* Corgi (London, England), 1982.

*TRANSLATOR*

(And compiler and editor) *Pacala and Tandala, and Other Rumanian Folk Tales,* illustrated by Charles Mozley, Methuen (London, England), 1960, published as *Rumanian Folk Tales,* Franklin Watts (New York, NY), 1961.
Henri Vernes, *City of a Thousand Drums,* Corgi (London, England), 1966.
Henri Vernes, *The Dinosaur Hunters,* Corgi (London, England), 1966.
Henri Vernes, *The Yellow Shadow,* Corgi (London, England), 1966.
Jean Bruce, *Cold Spell,* Corgi (London, England), 1967.
Jean Bruce, *Top Secret,* Corgi (London, England), 1967.
Henri Vernes, *Treasure of the Golcondas,* Corgi (London, England), 1967.
Henri Vernes, *The White Gorilla,* Corgi (London, England), 1967.
Henri Vernes, *Operation Parrot,* Corgi (London, England), 1968.
Jean Bruce, *Strip Tease,* Corgi (London, England), 1968.
Noel Calef, *The Snare,* Souvenir Press, 1969.
Sven Hassel, *March Battalion,* Corgi (London, England), 1970.
Sven Hassel, *Assignment Gestapo,* Corgi (London, England), 1971.
Laszlo Havas, *Hitler's Plot to Kill the Big Three,* Corgi (London, England), 1971.
Sven Hassel, *S.S. General,* Corgi (London, England), 1972.
Sven Hassel, *Reign of Hell,* Corgi (London, England), 1973.

Contributor to television series *Dramarama,* 1983. Contributor of articles to periodicals, including *Vegan, Writers' Monthly, Books for Keeps,* and *School Librarian.*

## Sidelights

While Jean Ure has written fiction for audiences of all ages, she is best known for her young-adult books, in which she combines her lively sense of humor with unique stories that feature off-beat situations and characters. Ure is a vegetarian who is avid about animal rights, and while her books make references to these tendencies among her characters, they are not considered preachy. Class struggles, homosexuality, sexual wakenings, and feminism are among Ure's topics, all of which she discusses with freshness and immediacy.

Ure does not remember a time when she did not want to be a writer. While growing up in Surrey, England, she would steal notebooks from her school to fill with imaginative stories. She was also happy to read poetry or dance in front of a room of adoring relatives.

Going to school, however, was painful for Ure. She constantly felt that she did not fit in. Being outside of the popular crowd caused her to fantasize about many things, including being in love and dancing. Being a compulsive writer, Ure wrote down these fantasies. She sent the manuscript off to a publisher and, at the age of sixteen, she became a published writer with *Dance for Two.* Writing the novel "was a very cathartic exercise and brought me great solace," she once recalled. "I almost managed to believe that . . . I really *did* have a sweetheart called Noel, that I really *was* a ballet dancer."

Ambition and not wanting to continue with the pain of school life were reasons why Ure chose to try writing as a profession rather than go to college, and she worked several menial jobs while trying to get her work published. Discouraged by her lack of success, she enrolled in a drama class and found that she had a talent for entertaining. While attending drama school, she met her husband, Leonard Gregory, at one of the few parties she attended, and he became a major influence in her life. Shortly afterward, Ure's writing career suddenly took off, and she started writing romance novels and translating books. While these did not stimulate her intellectually, they helped her learn her craft and earn a living at the same time. After a few years, however, she began to feel that she was compromising herself by writing such books.

Her book *See You Thursday* was a turning point for Ure. The novel focuses on a blind pianist named Abe and a sixteen-year-old rebel named Marianne. Although Abe is eight years older, wiser, and from a different background than Marianne, the pair become attracted to each other, and the relationship blossoms as Marianne sheds her shyness and finds a new maturity. In *After Thursday,* the sequel that followed, the romance of Abe and Marianne is further tested by their differing perspectives on independence.

Ure was extremely happy to have found a fresh audience for her writing. "The reason I turned to writing for young adults was, basically, that it offered a freedom which 'genre' writing does not allow," she later related. She also commented: "When I created Abe, my blind pianist, I did the very minimum of research into blindness, but was able to gain direct knowledge, albeit to a severely limited extent, of how it would be to be blind by tying a scarf about my eyes and blundering around the house." *See You Thursday* won the American Library Association's Best Book for Young Adults citation in 1983.

Ure returns to the themes of autonomy and awakening sexuality in the "Vanessa" trilogy, which includes *Trouble with Vanessa, There's Always Danny,* and *Say Goodbye,* as well as in *The Other Side of the Fence.* Describing the first two books of the "Vanessa" trilogy as more than a romantic tale, Stephanie Nettell in the *Times Literary Supplement* labeled Ure's novels "intelligent, spiky and imaginative." Similarly enthusiastic about *The Other Side of the Fence,* reviewers such as *Bulletin of the Center for Children's Books* contributor Zena Sutherland praised the same novel as a "mature and sensitive" work that is "told with both momentum and nuance." This romance is unusual, however, because it concerns a young homosexual, Richard, who meets and finds friendship with Bonny, a girl who is attracted to him but cannot understand, until the end, why her sexual interest is not returned. Although *School Library Journal* writer Karen K. Radtke questioned Bonny's "naiveté" regarding Richard when she is otherwise street-smart, the critic also admitted that the novel may be satisfying to teenagers who "harbor secret fantasies about . . . flaunting parental authority."

Ure's sensitive treatment of relationships is often praised by critics. The special rivalry among sisters is explored in *Supermouse,* as a shy but talented girl, Nicola, is offered a dancing role over her more favored younger sister, Rose. Mary M. Burns wrote in *Horn Book* that even though the story is told from the point of view of an eleven year old, "the author has managed to suggest subtle emotions which underlie the family's values and actions." The story is continued in *The Most Important Thing* as Nicola, now age fourteen, must decide whether her future career will include ballet or whether she should concentrate instead on science and become a doctor. Cynthia K. Leibold concluded in *School Library Journal* that "Ure is skillful at creating colorful characters . . . and her characters execute their roles perfectly."

Using insight and sometimes humor, Ure's novels often question values and touch upon subjects such as social standards. In one such book, *What If They Saw Me Now?,* an athletic young man is caught in an amusing dilemma when he is asked to dance the male lead in a ballet. Described by Zena Sutherland in the *Bulletin of the Center for Children's Books* as "a funny and liberating" tale, Ure's novel may appeal to both boys and girls as they appreciate Jamie's predicament: how to overcome his own and others' "macho" stereotypes.

Coping with illness is the theme of two of Ure's contemporary works, *If It Weren't for Sebastian* and *One Green Leaf,* the first focusing on mental illness, and the latter on a fatal physical sickness. In *If It Weren't for Sebastian,* the title character is an intense, but peace-loving, young man whose "strangeness" is an object of scorn and misunderstanding to others. Maggie becomes his friend and soon discovers that Sebastian is being treated as an outpatient at a mental health clinic. Ure "explores the borderline psychotic and his relationships with great sensitivity and understanding," declared Zena Sutherland in a *Bulletin of the Center for Children's Books* review. Fatal illness is treated with similar sympathy and skill in *One Green Leaf.* After an unsuccessful surgery, it becomes obvious that David's cancer is terminal. Ure's emphasis, however, is on how David copes, and on the affection of his friends during his illness. According to Tess McKellen in *School Library Journal,* the author "dramatizes successfully the effect of unexpected tragedy on young minds and emotions" in the novel.

*Always Sebastian* brings back the unique character from *If It Weren't for Sebastian* and follows the relationship between Sebastian, now deeply involved in the animal-rights movement, and Maggie, a single parent with two daughters. That same year, Ure also authored a science-fiction thriller for teens, *A Place to Scream.* The work is set in 2015, a near future in which social problems caused by incautious economic policies have worsened immensely. The protagonist is the teenage Gillian, who has been fortunate enough to grow up in an affluent household, but feels overwhelmed by the world outside. Her involvement with a maverick new friend brings both romance and a sense of purpose to her life.

Ure's teen novel *Has Anyone Seen This Girl?* is told in diary form. The book begins with fourteen-year-old Caroline riding in a train to her new boarding school. Aboard the train, she meets Rachel and the two become fast friends. At school, however, the quirky Rachel is relegated to the role of outcast, and Caroline is torn between peer pressure to reject her and a sense of loyalty to her first friend. Rachel makes friendship difficult, however, as she proves to be a demanding, asocial friend, and Caroline suffers tremendous guilt when Rachel runs away from the school. "Ure once again writes with a sympathetic understanding of young people," attested Maggie Bignell in *Quill & Quire.*

Ure won critical plaudits for her "Plague" series, which includes the postapocalyptic tales *Plague 99* (published in the United States as *Plague*), *Come Lucky April,* and *Watchers at the Shrine. Plague 99* opens in the twentieth century in a world where biological warfare germs have triggered a contagious and deadly illness. Returning from camp, Fran Latimer finds both of her parents dead and her best friend looking to her for help. The two girls team up with Shahid, a schoolmate and, as the plague worsens in their hometown, with death seemingly everywhere, they journey across London in search of Shahid's brother, only to find the family there decimated as well. When Shahid becomes sick, Fran nurses him as they hide out in an old bookstore until he recovers enough for them to once more begin their journey to safety. As *Plague 99* concludes, they are on their way to distant Cornwall, where Fran's grandmother lives.

*Plague 99* proved to be so popular with teens that Ure decided to continue the story. *After the Plague* follows Fran and Shahid's great-grandson, Daniel. A hundred years after the fateful flight to Cornwall, Daniel learns of the existence of Fran's fascinating journal, which she wrote during the plague. He travels to Croydon where the ms. was left, but the London suburb is now an entirely feminist-governed community in which new births are the result of artificial insemination, and male offspring in Croydon are routinely castrated. A virtual outlaw in this community by reason of his gender, Daniel falls in love with one of its members, April, and she must choose between remaining in her society or leaving with him and entering the outside world.

*Watchers at the Shrine,* Ure's third installment in the "Plague" series, reveals that in 2099 April did not leave Croydon, but remained behind and gave birth to a son, Hal. When Halnears puberty, he is sent to Cornwall to escape castration, but he has trouble adjusting to the vastly different patriarchal community. A large number of birth defects occur in Cornwall since an abandoned nuclear power plant nearby is still emitting radiation. Hal is shocked to discover that people both in the greater Cornwall community and those inside the odd religious sect known as the Watchers, with whom he is sent to live, display an ignorance of history and science, and, in contrast to Croydon, women are treated quite brutally. He falls in love with a Watcher's daughter who, born with a birth defect, will soon be relegated to the community's brigade of officially sanctioned prostitutes. Instead, the pair escape to Croydon where a crisis has brought some positive changes to the feminist community's system of social order. In a review of *Watchers at the Shrine,* a *Junior Bookshelf* critic commended Ure's powers of description in creating a desolate, postplague Britain, as "intriguing as well as shocking and forbidding, and she contrives associations for Hal which increase the horror of societies which have lost their way."

Other topics benefitting from Ure's creative energy often center around her passions: music, vegetarianism, animal rights, books, and theater. Her main motive is not to convert people, but to stimulate thought. Having published many books during her career, she offered this advice to aspiring writers on her home page: "Basically, try to become as a child. Think as a child thinks. See through a child's eyes. Experience a child's feelings. Keep the adult part of yourself in the background—whilst always making sure that you keep a tight hold on the reins. In other words, let the child in you do the speaking while the adult shapes the words."

Ure's goal as a writer, she maintained on the *Conversations with Writers* blog, remains "to entertain. I see no point in indulging and amusing myself if no children are going to read what I write. I *do* want to indulge and amuse myself, but I also want readers to identify with my books, to recognise the concerns of the characters as *their* concerns, to take heart, gain solace, to laugh, to cry and maybe, along the way, to learn a bit about life."

## Biographical and Critical Sources


*BOOKS*

*Children's Literature Review,* Volume 34, Gale (Detroit, MI), 1994.

*St. James Guide to Young Adult Writers,* 2nd edition, St. James Press (Detroit, MI), 1999.

*PERIODICALS*

*Booklist,* January 1, 1996, Hazel Rochman, review of *The Children Next Door,* p. 836; January 1, 2001, Ilene Cooper, review of *Skinny Melon and Me,* p. 961; December 15, 2001, Ilene Cooper, review of *Plague,* p. 729.

*Bulletin of the Center for Children's Books,* June, 1984, Zena Sutherland, review of *What If They Saw Me Now?,* p. 195; June, 1986, Zena Sutherland, review of *If It Weren't for Sebastian,* p. 198; February, 1988, Zena Sutherland, review of *The Other Side of the Fence,* p. 127.

*Horn Book,* June, 1984, Mary M. Burns, review of *Supermouse,* p. 334.

*Junior Bookshelf,* October, 1994, review of *Watchers at the Shrine,* p. 191.

*Publishers Weekly,* September 27, 1991, review of *Plague,* p. 59; November 27, 2000, review of *Skinny Melon and Me,* p. 77.

*Quill & Quire,* August, 1996, Maggie Bignell, review of *Has Anyone Seen This Girl?,* p. 121.

*School Library Journal,* May, 1986, Cynthia K. Leibold, review of *The Most Important Thing,* p. 110; April, 1988, Karen K. Radtke, review of *The Other Side of the Fence,* p. 114; May, 1989, Tess McKellen, review of *One Green Leaf,* p. 128; January, 2001, Ashley Larsen, review of *Skinny Melon and Me,* p. 134.

*Times Literary Supplement,* June 9, 1989, Stephanie Nettell, reviews of *Trouble with Vanessa* and *There's Always Danny,* p. 648.

*ONLINE*

*Conversations with Writers,* http://conversationswithwriters.blogspot.com/ (December 4, 2006), "Interview with Children's Author Jean Ure."

*Jean Ure Home Page,* http://www.jeanure.com (September 29, 2008).

## *Autobiography Feature*

# Jean Ure

Jean Ure contributed the following autobiographical essay to *SATA:*

If there is one thing I find tiresome when reading a biography it's having to wade through an entire first chapter dealing with a person's antecedents before coming to the actual person herself. For this reason, dearly though I loved both of my parents, I am going to devote no more than a few short paragraphs to family history. I know they would understand—my father because he was a very modest, retiring, truly *gentle* man, my mother because she was of an impulsive turn of mind, always eager to get on with things, impatient of preambles.

Briefly, therefore, I will say that my grandparents on my father's side—Wee Granny and Grandpa—were working-class Scots who came south of the border during the Depression. Wee Grandpa was short, dumpy, and phlegmatic—to the point where he once sat contentedly puffing on his pipe on the family's one remaining chair whilst the bailiffs stripped the house bare and poor Wee Granny wrung her hands and cried that the shame would kill her. Phlegmatic also to the point of standing in the kitchen shouting, "Sarah, Sarah, the milk's boiling over!" whilst the milk did indeed do just that.

Wee Granny was just the opposite: also short, but thin and wiry, ceaselessly on the go, up and down twenty times during the course of any meal, gaily sliding down the banisters at the age of eighty. Too excitable, also, to be quite as diplomatic as she might. I don't think, for a start, that it was altogether diplomatic to christen her only daughter Agnes Proven Benny Bleakley, nor to saddle her youngest son with the name of Alexander Workman. When Agnes Proven Benny Bleakley married and became Agnes Proven Benny Bleakley Dredge and went on a crash diet to prepare for the great day, Wee Granny really ought not, in response to her daughter's anxious "I didn't want to slim down *too* much," have come back with her unthinking "Och, no! It would look silly with that great fat face." Many family upsets were caused by Wee Granny's tactless tongue. It must, I am sure, have been a source of great sadness to my peace-loving and family-oriented father that for the last ten years of his mother's life my own mother refused to speak to her or have her in the house.

My grandparents on my mother's side—Big Granny and Grandpa, or Popsy—definitely considered them-

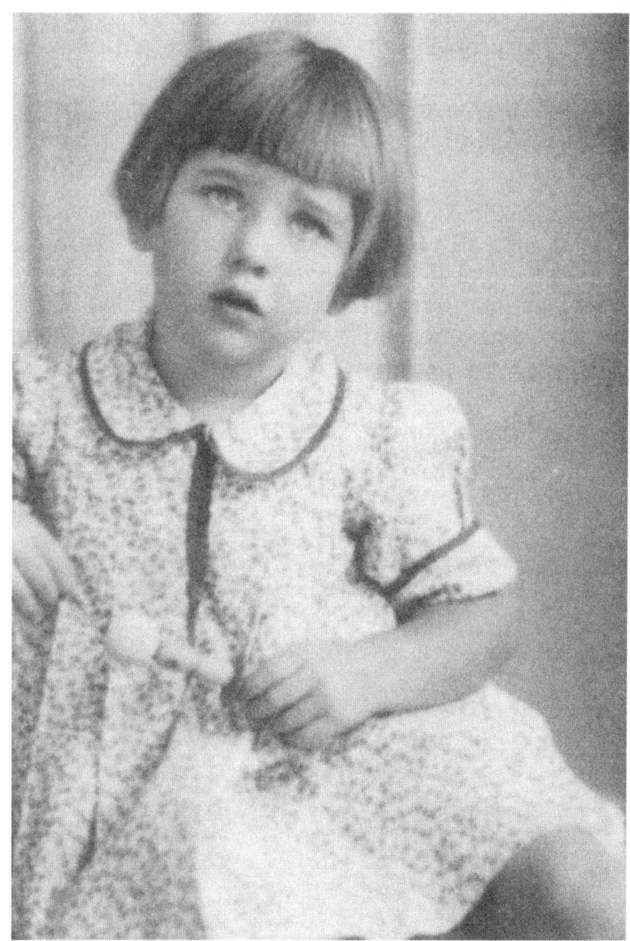

***Jean Ure—"with a stomachache"*** (Reproduced by permission.)

selves a cut above the working class. Popsy was an official of the Bank of England (not just a bank clerk: an *official*—though I am never quite sure what the difference was supposed to be). He was also a church warden; a most honest and upright man whom as a child I always strove to impress. He had been gassed and shell-shocked in the First World War and died, alas, when I was only eleven. He left me his *Roget's Thesaurus,* annotated in his own hand. I treasure it to this day.

Of my parents, I have always felt closer in spirit to my father than to my mother, though in temperament I am an amalgam of both. By nature a scholarly man, whose education was cut short by economic circumstances, my father always encouraged me in my early efforts at writing. Today's feminist ideology would, I think, bemuse him. I'm pretty certain he would consider it "against nature." By both class and upbringing he has to be labeled a male chauvinist, yet never in the sense of believing men to be superior to women. Superiority formed no part of his makeup. But he had been taught, and genuinely believed, that it was a man's duty to provide for his family and that any man whose wife had to go out to work had failed in that duty. [He came] from an unbroken line of labourers ("Workman" was a family surname). For his part, after years of correspondence courses dutifully Undertaken—and patiently endured, it has to be said, by my mother, who sat reading or knitting in silence whilst he studied: totally against *her* nature—he succeeded in making a career for himself in a specialised branch of insurance, but it was not the career he would have chosen. The law was what interested him.

My father died of stress-induced emphysema when I was in my early twenties, and I have never ceased to regret that I knew him so little. He was a shy man, and I was too immature, and made too awkward by his shyness, to break through the barrier. There are a wealth of subjects I should dearly loved to have discussed with him.

My mother, though subscribing, as her class and generation did, to the notion that a woman's place was in the home, was nonetheless in many ways a stronger, certainly more resilient figure, than my father. She had no great depth, either emotionally or intellectually, but was a born fighter and incurable optimist, forever cheerful in the face of adversity, particularly at the end of her life. Her courage in her last days has immeasurably enriched my memory of her.

***"Wee Granny and Grandpa with my father"*** (Reproduced by permission.)

I had a happy, totally unremarkable childhood, born in 1943 in Surrey, brought up in London suburbs—North London until the age of eleven, South London until I left home at the age of eighteen. I wish I could have been raised amongst scenes of either architectural or scenic beauty, for then I should perhaps have more sense of "place" in my books. London suburbs are dreary and monochrome—endless streets full of endless houses, all very much the same as one another. As a teenager I was filled with angry contempt for the suburban, lower-middle-class way of life. Bourgeois, I thought it small-minded and complacent. I realise now that small-mindedness and complacency are not confined to either the middle classes or the suburbs. I appreciate, which I did not when I was younger, the struggle that it took for my father to pull himself from the pit of working-class poverty in which he began. He could not have done it without the support of my mother; and if he had not done it then I very much doubt whether I should be writing this autobiographical sketch today.

During the years of my early childhood—my father believing passionately, as he did, in the value of education: my mother, somewhat less exaltedly, but no less passionately, in the value of learning how to speak nicely—they denied themselves not only luxuries but even, sometimes, necessities to send me to what they considered a "good school." As a socialist I might possibly consider this misguided, but it was certainly well meant; and who knows whether it might not have been thanks to that "good school," with its Latin and its French and its emphasis on academic excellence, that I was awarded a scholarship at the age of eleven to go to yet another "good school," where, alas, I turned out to be a total misfit for reasons quite unconnected with either class or academic achievement. I am inclined to believe now that I would have been a misfit at any educational establishment, but my parents were not to know that. I am sure it was no fault of theirs.

One other member of my family, apart from a succession of beloved dogs, whom I have not yet mentioned is my brother. He is two years younger than I am, and as children we fought almost continuously whilst yet remaining the best of friends. I have a vivid memory of us kicking each other quite viciously under the table as my parents attempted to eat their dinner with some semblance of dignity, and of my poor long-suffering father saying piteously to my mother, "They're at it again!" (It was my mother's job to discipline us: he left child rearing strictly to her.) My brother tells me that as a child he was jealous of me for seeming to be more of an academic high flyer than he was, yet by dint of application he has ended up with a university degree whilst I was totally profligate of every educational opportunity offered me. I only confessed recently that I in my turn was jealous of his social prowess. "Perfectly normal teenage behaviour," he says; and so it was—and how I yearned after it!

Looking back, I see our relationship as being one of school-teacherly bossiness on my side, brazen rebellion on his; but it is possible that had I not had a brother I should find it difficult to get under the skin of my male characters and write with any degree of insight about them. As it is, my brother appears in many of my books under various guises, though generally, it has to be said, as a rather revolting small boy.

One of my most enduring, and happiest, memories from childhood is the ritual gathering of the clans at Christmastime. The gathering always took place in one of my parents' houses—though when I say *one,* it must not be imagined that we grandly had several residences all at once, only that my mother had inherited Big Granny's propensity for buying and selling, with the result that we rarely lived anywhere for more than a couple of years. These were the days before the rupture with Wee Granny, when all the Scots side of the family would meet to make mayhem and play games, in which my very private and reserved father, surprisingly enough, was a leading light. Charades was our favourite. I still cherish the memory of portly and dignified Aunt Aggie disporting herself in a frilly lampshade and a red silk bedspread. I have put this scene into one of my books, *You Win Some, You Lose Some.* I have also plundered it for *The Most Important Thing* (the sequel to *Hi There, Supermouse!* and known in the U.K. as *Nicola Mimosa*).

I was brought up in a tradition of writing, inasmuch as my father's family were inveterate ode writers, sending one another long screeds of poetry on every possible occasion. They also, for several years, ran a family drama group, writing and staging their own plays. I was no stranger, therefore, either to the idea of setting pen to paper or of showing off, which I did repulsively and precociously and at the drop of a hat, feeling no shame, for instance, at reciting Burns's "Ode to a Mouse" in a Scots accent before an audience of genuine Scots, or treating them to a dance of my own invention whilst belting out one of Wee Granny's favourite songs, "My Am Folk," at the top of my not-very-melodious voice. Memories of Shirley Temple still lingered on, and such loathsome behaviour was not only tolerated but actually encouraged.

I started my writing career at a fairly young age, being about four or five when I produced my first opus. This was a poem, observed from the life:

M'Daddy had a boot lace,

M'Daddy did lose it.

***"Big Granny and Popsy with a wee me"*** (Reproduced by permission.)

And when the rain began to pour,

There it was a-hanging on the door.

I stopped writing poetry pretty soon after that and took up the novel instead. I wrote my first novel when I was six. It was about a little girl called Carol who went off to collect her friends for a party. The novel went on for two pages and consisted of a long list of all my favourite names—Carlotta, Bianca, Natasha, Patricia. (I regret to say that no boys were invited to the party: at six years old I was instinctively sexist.)

This story was written in an outsize scrapbook which my Auntie Grace, who had once wanted to be a nun but had gone to live in Chicago instead, had brought back with her on a visit, but most of my early writings were done in tiny spiral-bound notebooks bought from Woolworth's. Later, when I was at senior school, I graduated to proper exercise books filched from the school stationery cupboard. Down in the cellar I still have a vast pile of such books with the name of my school printed on the label and the name of one of my stories written beneath it in inks of various hues. (I went in for inks. One particular story, "The Big One," is written in no fewer than fifteen exercise books in a whole variety of different colours: radiant blue, blue

*"My brother, John, the Marxist Economist"* (Reproduced by permission.)

black, red, brown, green, magenta . . . all part of the creative process. To this day I write all my preliminary drafts by hand.)

I must always, I think, have wanted to be a writer, though I am not sure I considered it a matter in which I had any choice. I wrote instinctively: it seemed to me as natural as eating or sleeping. But I also had ambitions. Some might say, overweening ambitions. At the age of nine, I told my first writer's lie: I told a little friend (who was rightly sceptical) that I had had a story published in a magazine. The story was called Jam Pot Jane. Maybe one of these days I shall actually get around to writing it. . . .

Most of my MSS from those early days have been lost over the years. Of the few which survive, there is "The Big One"—*he was a very big one: he stood 6'6" in his big bare feet*—written in its variegated inks. "The Big One" is a spoof detective story whose style derives partly from Caryl Brahms and S.J. Simon (*No Bed for Bacon, A Bullet in the Ballet*) and partly from the tabloid press—*Last night an odious thug arrived at London Airport. A bright red tie leapt from his neck like a burst blood vessel.* The odious thug was called Keef Guggisberg, and at the risk of souring international relations I have to reveal that he came from America and was a *crook.*

Other MSS down in the cellar are "Me"; "Form Prefect," 109 pages of unmitigated boredom, written in the style of an author called Joanna Cannan (all my early books were written in the style of other authors); "Hump's Diary" (a direct crib from Jerome K. Jerome's *Three Men in a Boat,* a Ruritanian novel, whose chapters are pretentiously numbered [in] Latin, which I doubtless felt bestowed an air of quality, and whose characters have a quaint habit of drinking "powerful potents"; and "Women's (Very) Cheaply, Xmas Edition," an extended joke of unrelieved corniness. Amongst the contents are "The Man with the Gong," by J.R. Thrank; "Abstractions," by D. Pinthorte; "Hairy Styles for Xina," by Mr. Squeeiy Deezy; "Off the Disc," by D. Fenning-Row; "The Wind in the Chimbley," by Kathy du Laurier; and "On Second Thoughts," by Candy Stripe—yes, well, I *was* only eleven!

Thinking back to my childhood it seems I must have spent far more of my time scribbling in my filched notebooks than going out and enjoying the more routine pursuits of my peers—parties, youth clubs, pop concerts. Indeed, I can remember Big Granny complaining that "it's not natural, shutting herself away in her room all the time. Why doesn't she get out and join the Girl Guides?" Under pressure I did join the Girl Guides, for about a month, but it was not my scene. Throughout my youth I had a total inability to go with the crowd. I still have it today, but today it doesn't bother me. When I was young it troubled me most desperately. I felt I was doomed to be perpetually excluded, to peer forever through the windows at the party going on inside and never being asked to join in. The problem was that on the occasions when I was asked to join in I ended up even more miserable than before, because if there is one thing worse than *not* being at the party it's being at the party and not fitting in. I never fitted in.

I have often pondered the reason for this, and I believe I have finally come up with the answer. One of the questions people often ask writers in their mature years is, "What were your major influences?" Meaning, in other words, who or what helped make you the person you are today, treading the particular path that you have trodden. A frequent answer is, "I had this most wonderful English teacher." Well, I had a pretty good English teacher, and doubtless I owe her a great deal, but she was by no means the main influence on me. I'm willing to bet that my answer to this question is unique: my main influence was *hair.* Ordinary, common, or garden hair that you wear on your head. In my case, very common or garden.

I have had this hair all my life long. It has plagued me ever since I can remember. It is fine hair, it is straight hair, and it is mousey hair, and its overwhelming preference is to hang about in lank, lethargic wads doing nothing. Indeed, hanging about doing nothing is virtually its only activity. It refuses even the most minimal attempt at cooperation: beat it, coax it, curl it, brush it, it simply sinks back, sighing, into its normal state of energy-drained torpor.

*Trouble with hair* has been the recurring theme of my life. When I was at school it was the fashion to be home-permed. Home perms, however, did not work with my particular brand of hair. Twink, Twonk, Toni, and all the rest, they simply transform it into a dismal dry frizz. Whilst others paraded with luscious thick waves, I hid in the corner looking as if I had a pot scourer attached to my head. But to be without a kink of some kind in one's hair was unthinkable. When not home permed and pot-scoured, therefore, I suffered torture by night in metal rollers secured to my scalp with inch-long spikes—and torture by day as slowly but surely my beautiful curls unraveled themselves, drooping ever lower as the hours passed by. And oh! the misery of a misty morning! A thirty-minute bicycle ride through fog and drizzle and there was my precious coiffure all limp and soggy, not a trace of curl to be seen. But even worse was a day which started dry and treacherously turned wet halfway through a game of net-ball . . . the hideous and ghastly shame of it! To have bounced out on court all carefully crimped, only to slink back again forty minutes later be-sodden and rats'-tailed, thus to remain for the rest of the day. *Knowing* that everyone was looking at you. Whispering about you. "Her hair's come out of curl. . . ."In fact, as old school photographs all too plainly show, even when it was *in* curl it was hardly anything to write home about.

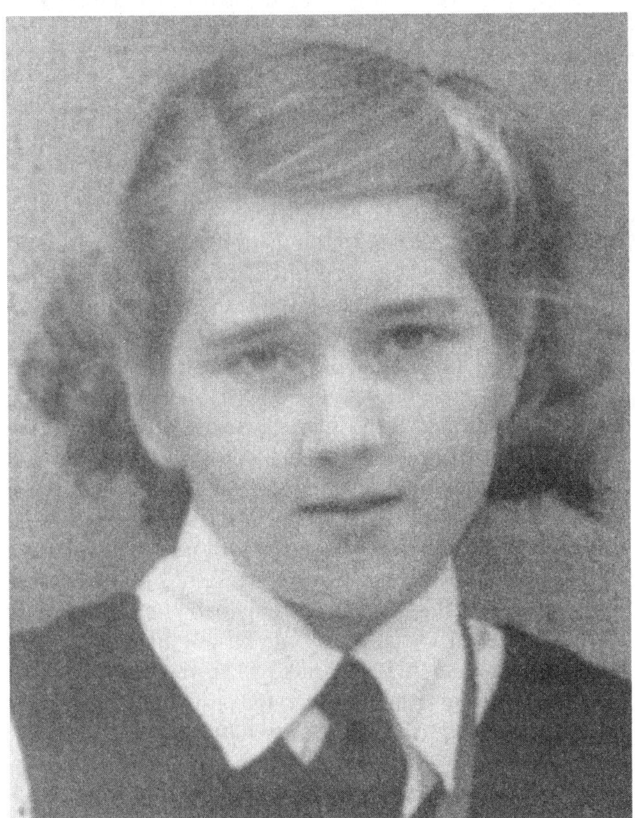

*"Me, with the hair," at eleven years old* (Reproduced by permission.)

Dead straight it hung, until the final half inch, which just occasionally turned under but more often stuck out at right angles, or, having escaped during the night, continued on its journey straight down. On more than one occasion, such were the depths of self-consciousness and despair into which I was plunged; I took refuge in the sick room with unspecified aches and pains. All I wanted was to dig a hole and bury myself.

Decades have passed since then. Decades of wanting to dig holes and bury myself. I have learnt that my hair goes in cycles. *Cycle I* lasts, on average, for about a week. During this week my hair looks almost presentable. I gain confidence; I am almost happy with it. No longer do I feel the need to be forever touching at it, patting at it, holding it down in high winds, fluffing it up in damp weather. But, alas, and all too speedily, we pass to *Cycle II. Cycle II* can either set in insidiously, or it can begin quite abruptly and without any warning: the hair which yesterday looked almost presentable has become, overnight, unmanageable and grotesque. Wash it, brush it, beat it, comb it . . . something has happened to it. Something has gone wrong. This cannot continue! It is time something is done, once and for all. *This hair trouble must be remedied.*

At this stage, one of two things can happen. Either one panics and reaches for the scissors, or one plucks up one's courage and marches oneself down the road to a hairdresser. (A hairdresser, you note: not *the* hairdresser. One wouldn't have the nerve to go anywhere more than once.) Whichever course of action one takes is really immaterial, since either way the result is the same: in brief, disaster. Faced with hair like mine, even the professionals tend to panic. Many is the time I have slunk from the salon with the words of the hairdresser ringing nervously in my ear: "It'll look all right when it settles down. . . ." It doesn't, of course. You can't make a good roof out of inferior thatch. By now, we are well launched into the third cycle. This is the cycle where we wish to dig holes and bury ourselves. (I address myself now to fellow sufferers. I never seem to see any of them—I only ever seem to see people with hair that is immaculate—but surely there must be some? *Some* where? Or are they all living in their holes underground?)

*Cycle III* can last anywhere from a month, if one is lucky, up to half year if one is not. The half-a-year jobs are caused mainly by attempts at perming (does one never learn? It seems not. Blind optimism springs eternal). The lesser catastrophes are caused by a too-cavalier use of the scissor. Between chance and design I must by now have sampled just about every kind of hairdo that has ever been invented. By design I have been bubble cut and razor cut, club cut, feather cut, layered, lacquered, shaved, shorn, permed, frizzled, plaited, pleated, beehived, bunned, and ponytailed. By chance (self-inflicted) I have had what might be termed "the frilly cut," "the upward slope," "the off-the-head look," and, a particular favourite, "the crenellated effect." Punk has got nothing on what I can achieve with a pair of scissors. I haven't yet resorted to dyeing what little is left to me after the carnage in multicoloured strips, but then I reckon I don't need to: the effect is quite startling enough without.

The more I think about it, the more it seems to me that hair was the root cause of all my problems; I am almost seriously persuaded that had it not been for hair I would have gone to the party along with everyone else. I would have done what was expected of me and trotted meekly off to read English at university. I make the excuse now—and this shows how one can rewrite the story of one's life—that the reason I didn't go to university was that I had my first book published while I was still at school and that this prompted me to turn my back on formal education and go hawk myself around the marketplace.

It is perfectly true that I had my first book published while I was at school, but to blame this for my failure to pursue my studies is to rationalise. I didn't leave school to compete in the marketplace (a venue I have always abhorred) but purely and simply to escape from the, to me, hell of communal living. I'd been watching the party go by for seventeen years; what hope of ever joining it now? And if I hadn't been able to join the party going on at school, what chance of joining the bigger and better party that would be going on in the halls of academe? If only I had not had the hair. . . .

Not surprisingly, my characters' hair is very important to me. Heroes and heroines alike are always exceedingly well-endowed. Only one character has been saddled with my limp locks, and that is poor Nicola from *Hi There, Supermouse*! and *The Most Important Thing: "Her sister Rose's hair was bright chestnut and springy. Nicola's was dark, and limp, and straggled."*

Nicola is largely an embodiment of me. Many of my female characters, and indeed quite a few of my male ones, are aspects of myself—rebellious, prickly Marianne, from the "Thursday" books, for example: self-conscious, introspective Christopher from *Play Nimrod for Him.* Colleen, on the other hand, in the book I published while I was still at school—*Ballet Dance for Two* (just *Dance for Two* in the U.K.)—goes one stage further and is not so much an embodiment as a wish-fulfillment.

At the age of eleven I was taken for the first time to the ballet, to see *Coppélia,* and knew instantly that it was my destination to become a ballet dancer. Week after week (after month after month) I begged my mother to let me take ballet lessons. The answer was always the same: "I'm sorry, we can't afford it."

Were my parents really as hard up as all that? Money was not plentiful, I know; but oh, I did so long to do ballet! Big Granny, like some Greek chorus in the background, did nothing to help my case. "Take no notice of her," she advised my mother. "It's only a phase she's going through."

Everything was "a phase." It was "a phase" when I wanted to have piano lessons. When I was finally given an old piano by one of my aunts—funny little Auntie Kitty, known in her youth as Little Miss Dingle Dangle from her habit of smothering herself in jewelry—my joy knew no bounds. I was at that piano day and night, no doubt driving the family mad, for they were not musical. I had just taught myself, by means of a gramophone record, to play the opening bars of Debussy's *Cakewalk,* when my mother happened to look through a magnifying glass and horror of horrors discovered a *woodworm.* Everyone knows that where there is one woodworm there will shortly be ten thousand woodworms, they will eat up the floors and the walls and the ceiling and before you can say Jack Robinson the house will be down about your ears. . . . Result: piano chopped up. Taken into garden and burnt. I never did get to have my piano lessons.

Nor did I ever get to have my ballet lessons. (Not until I went to drama school, some years later, but by then I was too old.) And so, to solace myself, I wrote *Dance for Two,* which is all about Colleen, who is desperate to learn ballet but is not allowed to on account of the family finances being straitened. Colleen, of course, is me; but being a wish-fulfillment she gets lucky: she ends up dancing the lead role in *Coppélia* with her childhood sweetheart (the Hero).

Colleen's childhood sweetheart was also my childhood sweetheart. I spent the years from fourteen to fifteen, which were the years when I wrote the book, being passionately in love with one of my own characters. It is true to say that he was more real to me than any boyfriend I could have had—I say could have had advisedly, since all the time I was at school I never knew any boys. Too shy, too introverted, and *trouble with hair.* I did, however, have lots of passions. My first (peculiar) passion as an extremely small child was for a film star called George Raft. My next was for Roy Rogers, and my next for a balding, freckled English cricketer, of no conceivable charm that I can now see, called Tony Lock. Following closely on his heels came Mary Bigg, the school sports captain (such names! George Raft, Tony Lock, Mary Bigg . . .) followed, although at this distance I am not quite sure of the running order, by Dirk Bogarde, Sir Malcolm Sargent (Flash Harry was his nickname amongst musicians and he was *very* flash), a ballet dancer, David Blair, my own hero, Noël, from *Dance for Two,* the Spanish dancer Antonio, and the French singer Gerard Souzay, who opened my ears to the beauty of lieder and chanson, and of Strauss and Fauré in particular, and who remained the Great Love of my Life until I went to drama school and fell in love with my husband, with whom I have remained in love ever since. A rich romantic life for one who never properly kissed a boy till she was over twenty-one!

Writing *Dance for Two* was a very cathartic exercise and brought me great solace. I almost managed to believe that I *was* Colleen, that I really *did* have a sweet-

***"My parents, William and Vera Ure"*** (Reproduced by permission.)

heart called Noël, that I really *was* a ballet dancer . . . such is the intense power of make-believe that I even carved the name Noël into the top of my desk lid and inked it in on my ruler. I recently met up with an old school friend who remembered that I had had "a foreign boyfriend, called something like Noël. . . ."

The book was published in the U.K. when I was sixteen, and in the States a year or so later. In the U.K. version, for what strange psychological reason I cannot even begin to guess, I describe my hero as being short of stature: in the American version this had to be deleted. In America in the sixties it seemed that heroes could not be small.

Having a book published while I was still at school was a bit of a double-edged blessing since it gave me the excuse I needed for running away from that party I never seemed able to join. Pride would never have allowed me to admit my miserable inability to lead a normal social life with my peers. It was with immense pride, however, that at the age of seventeen I rose up, grandly declaring myself a writer—*A Writer*—and flounced out into the world to pursue this vocation.

Over the next few years, "being a writer" consisted mainly of scrubbing floors, waiting at table, selling groceries, having fits of temperament in people's offices. . . . I also did a short spell at nursing, a short spell at the BBC, a short spell at NATO, a short spell at UNESCO, a short spell as a translator, a short spell at pretty well everything that didn't require any actual qualifications. Even today, when I look back on it over a distance of three decades, I can still all too clearly recall the sense of desolation and, yes, of *terror,* which all too often engulfed me in the years of my young womanhood. The party still went on—and I still wasn't at it. The low-grade jobs I was forced to do not only bored and insulted me but contracted my already none-too-healthy ego to the size of a pinhead. Before ever I entered a room full of people I would recite, like a litany, "I am Jean Ure and I am a writer," to bolster my flagging courage.

But was I a writer? How could I call myself such when I had had nothing but rejections ever since *Dance for Two* and was rapidly discovering that I really didn't have anything very much left to write about? Frenziedly I would force myself to start books which fizzled out after only a couple of chapters for want of anywhere to go. (The character Christopher, from *Play Nimrod for Him,* cropped up frequently in these abortive attempts: Christopher, angry, scared, and isolated,

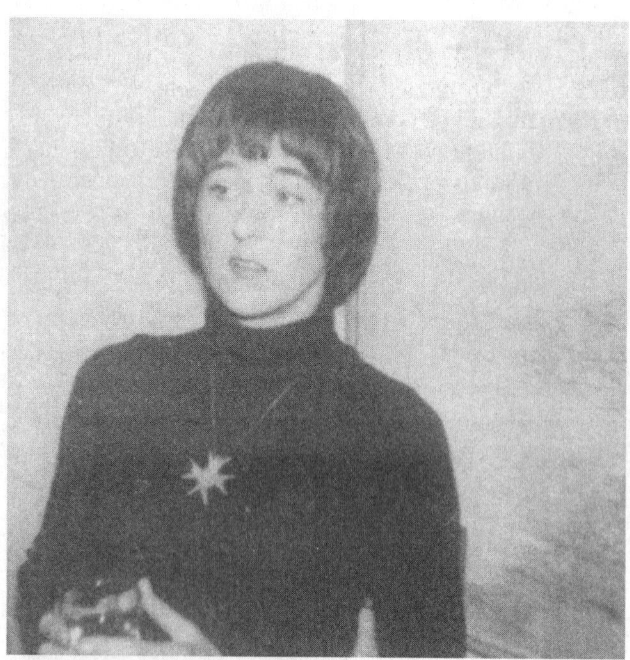

***Jean Ure, 1973*** (Reproduced by permission.)

seemingly arrogant, totally confused, was me in masculine guise. When I wrote *Nimrod* a couple of years ago and looked back to see if I could plunder any of those early writings, I found them, for all their immaturity, still extraordinarily raw and painful.)

Panic set in. I had visions of ending up, alone, unloved, and unlovely, starving in a garret at the age of fifty . . . This is a piece of sub-T.S. Eliot from those years:

*The Lament of a Rebel with Cold Feet*

How do people do it?
They stay there forty years
Or more. The same place
Day in, day out. Why
Don't they go mad? How
Is it they keep alive?
Or do they? In reality,
Perhaps they're all a little
Dead, a little near
grave.

Very sub!

Fortunately, I did not totally inherit my father's rather defeatist nature. I had just enough of my mother's spark to pick myself up and realise, finally, that no one was going to come along and lead me *by* the hand. If I were ever going to make anything of my life, it had to be up to me. As a start along the road, I enrolled for a part-time drama course. Amateur acting is an excellent way for misfits to join the party, even if under slightly false colours. It takes you out of yourself, as my Wee Granny would have said. Flushed with success as an amateur, I decided to try for a full-time course. No one was more amazed than I when I was accepted for the grandly named and highly respected Webber-Douglas Academy of Dramatic Art, Gloucester Road, London.

From that point on, I can truly say that life blossomed. To begin with I discovered in myself an unsuspected talent to amuse. As a straight actress, certainly as a *dramatic* actress, I was pretty well a disaster. I remember the principal, a terrifying man, snarling at me because I wouldn't open up. "Scared of emotions!" he snarled. He was doubtless quite right. My way of handling emotion was, and to an extent still is, to turn everything into a joke. This is why, although many of my books handle subjects which can only be described as weighty—in *One Green Leaf* for instance, the hero, David, has a leg amputated because of cancer—humour is always one of the chief ingredients. Thus all my best parts at drama school were character cameos—Miss Prism, in *The Importance of Being Earnest,* Verges, the ancient night watchman, in *Much Ado about Nothing,* Mrs. Dainty Fidget, in the restoration comedy *The Country Wife.*

It was this minor talent to make people laugh which kept me afloat, as it has so many other of society's misfits. I still wasn't at the party; I still couldn't truthfully be described even as a writer, never mind *A Writer,* but I felt that I was at last beginning to acquire the protective covering of some sort of normality.

Two things happened while I was at drama school which influenced the future course of my life. The first was that I put some of my post-school experiences to good use and wrote a book about a girl who was a nurse and fell in love with a boy who was an actor. This was supposed to be a book for teenagers, but my agent (I acquired a literary agent right at the beginning, with *Dance for Two*), no doubt hoping she might have a future Barbara Cartland on her hands—even agents can get it wrong!—sent it to Transworld, who said that if I were willing to beef it up a bit and put some more romance in, they would be willing to publish it.

Desperate as I was to get back into print, I stuffed romance in at every pore. It was published as *The Other Theatre,* and today I would much prefer to forget it, along with the two or three which followed. They are what might best be described as "pre-feminist." I had not yet thrown off the influence of my very conventional upbringing. *The Other Theatre* led, however, not only to a succession of contracts for more novels but also to a great deal of lucrative translating work. The reason the translations were so lucrative was that they were paid per thousand words. It was pretty low-grade stuff (though still in the bookshops even today) and thus I had no compunction, having finished a book, in going back and doing a bit of creative writing on my own account. "Just enough to cover the rent, to clear up the overdraft. . . ."

The other thing that happened was, and remains, the best thing that has ever happened, the thing that has shaped my life more than anything else: I met my husband. The first time we actually noticed each other, being in different classes, was, ironically enough, at a party. I so nearly didn't go to that party. I had promised a classmate that I would, but as I arrived on the doorstep all the old familiar feelings of inadequacy swamped over me and I turned and walked away. If my life were a romantic novel I should no doubt say that it was at this point that a mysterious something called me back, but in fact it wasn't a mysterious something so much as a sense of shame. And also anger at my own feebleness. I stood on the pavement, in the Earls Court Road, and lectured myself: "You can't spend all your life running away. There comes a time when you have to face up to things."

And so for once I did, and have been thanking my lucky stars ever since. Even today we sometimes go cold when we speculate where we should both be if we hadn't gone to the party, for Leonard also, for different reasons, very nearly didn't make it, and after twenty-five years of being together, and despite all our right-on views—"so far left," my mother once complained, "they're nearly out of sight"—we still manage to be that strange old-fashioned and now-endangered species, the happy couple. Even happier now than we were then. A rarity indeed in the theatrical profession, but I had never seriously wanted to become a working actress and as soon as we graduated from drama school I left the acting to Leonard whilst I got on with my writing.

***Husband, Leonard, about 1973*** (Reproduced by permission.)

For many years, to keep us afloat as Leonard moved from rep to rep and had the usual "resting" periods, without which no actor's life is complete, I continued to translate French novels into English and write my so-called romantic novels—so-called because things happened in them which were not supposed to happen. Not in the romantic novel; not in those days. It worried my poor editor tremendously. "Jean, you can't say that!" she used to wail. "You'll upset Mrs. Jones from Saffron Walden!"

No one ever knew who Mrs. Jones from Saffron Walden was, but whoever she was she sat on my shoulder like a malignant parrot, squawking her distaste. Ultimately I found the formula just too frustrating, but not before I had managed to slip a few unorthodoxies past the glittering eye of the Saffron Walden parrot. I don't expect, even today, there are many romantic novels with homosexual heroes, or heroes who have multiple sclerosis. How the parrot squawked!

But if romantic novels eventually wore out their charm, at least they taught me my craft. They didn't make me rich, but to be rich was never my aim. I should like to be rich now, as this would allow me to fulfill another and more recent ambition, to open an animal sanctuary, but in those days to be able to earn my living as a writer was all I ever asked.

Following my romantic-novel period, which lasted from the late sixties through most of the seventies, I wrote a series of Georgian romances using my Wee Scots Granny's name of Sarah McCulloch. (Much better than Jean Ure, incidentally, if only for the practical reason that M is in the middle of the alphabet and thus generally comes in the middle of the shelves, rather than down at floor level where nobody ever stoops. We T's and U's and W's also suffer from the fact that most people seem to get eye fatigue as they work through the alphabet. I have a writing friend who swears his next novel is going to be under the name of Aaron Aardvark. . . .)

I greatly enjoyed writing my Georgian romances as they allowed me to pretend that I was Jane Austen. Whenever I go to give talks in schools I am asked the question, "Who is your favourite author?" and I always reply, "Jane Austen." This mystifies today's thirteen year olds, as most of them have never heard of her. One young lad recently was under the impression that she was a tennis player. *Plus ça change, plus ce n'est pas la même chose. . . .* Conversely, the thirteen year olds I speak to are far more aware of world affairs, of animal rights, of feminism, of all the really important issues than I was at their age, so it is not all loss.

It wasn't until 1980 that I really emerged as myself, with a book for young adults called *See You Thursday.* The characters of Abe, the blind pianist schoolteacher, and Marianne, the sixteen-year-old rebel, are still my personal favourites. I have since written two sequels, *After Thursday* and *Tomorrow Is Also a Day.* The reason I turned to writing for young adults was, basically that it offered a freedom which "genre" writing does not allow. No parrots these days sit on my shoulder, though I have noticed an ominous gathering of psittacine creatures over these last few years. I first noticed it when I started to be published in the States, when my American editors would request the deletion or changing of certain words or phrase to suit the demands of the moral majority. It is a truism, but none the less true for all that, that what happens today in the U.S. happens tomorrow in the U.K. I begin to fear that tomorrow may already have arrived, especially in the field of younger fiction, where my publishers are receiving more and more letters complaining of language—"the custard tasted like horrible yellow snot," to take just one recent example. "To find this sort of language," writes Outraged of Chatham, "in a young child's book is beyond belief." I was told that one parent recently confiscated one of my books for eleven year olds because it contained the word "bum." This is worrying, enforcing as it does a censorship on authors. I have no desire to have my eleven year olds go round mouthing obscenities, but if they are to be sanitised into saintliness they will bear no relation whatsoever to any living child, and no living child worth its salt will wish to read about them. Perhaps more importantly, no living writer worthy of the name will wish to write about them. In essence, it is not so much morals which are at stake here as monetary considerations. I have never met an *editor* who wishes to produce books so vapid, so shorn of all subversive matter, that they will offend none and fulfill the same emotional function as Muzak. It is those who hold the moneybags who insist on publishing literary wallpaper.

I am very much a writer who writes from within rather than without, by which I mean that I tend to look inwards for my inspiration. As a result, I can write only about those things which instinctively interest me, or about which I know. I could not, for instance, go and research a subject about which I had no firsthand knowledge and then write about it. When I created Abe, my blind pianist, I did the very minimum of research into blindness but was able to gain direct knowledge, albeit to a severely limited extent, of how it would be to be blind by tying a scarf about my eyes and blundering around the house. This taught me more than any amount of talking to blind people or studying blind people. My most passionate interests, other than reading, are music and animals. For this reason, many of my characters are musicians, or at any rate musical—Abe, of course; Nick, in *Play Nimrod*; Larry, in *Dreaming of Larry*—and the subject of animal rights and/or vegetarianism crops up frequently.

I became a vegetarian, and subsequently a vegan, several years ago, and most of my characters in recent books have a tendency to follow suit, and eschew both the eating and wearing of murdered animals. I have, however, written only one book, *If It Weren't for Sebastian,* which deals directly with the subject. One of the most gratifying letters I have ever had from a reader came from a fourteen-year-old schoolgirl who wrote that "reading *Sebastian* has made me become a vegetarian!" Not that I set out with the deliberate intent to convert, as I don't believe this is the way to write books. What I do set out to do is to make people think: to make them examine their motives and question their assumptions. Someone once described my books as "good campaigning books," but they are never, I hope, didactic.

Other subjects which tend to recur in my work are ballet and theatre, obviously because I know about them. I have lost my youthful passion for the ballet, but it still intrigues me as a subject to write about—I find the discipline and dedication of its practitioners as fascinating as those of nuns in a nunnery, another perennial source of wonderment to the uninitiated. I am somewhat less starry-eyed about the straight theatre, having a far closer acquaintance with it, and it is a fact that none of the books that I have written with a theatrical background—mainly the "Vanessa" trilogy, *Trouble with Vanessa, There's Always Danny,* and *Say Goodbye*—have quite the same joyous naivety as, for instance, *Dance for Two* or *What If They Saw Me Now?* (published in the U.K. as *A Proper Little Nooryeff*).

Whatever the background subject, however, I am mostly interested in writing about young people who are striving either to achieve something or to make something of themselves, not necessarily in a worldly sense and certainly not in any monetary sense. I find it difficult to empathise with those who have no aims or ambitions. I can sympathise; but I cannot enter into their personality and imaginatively experience their experiences, and thus I cannot write about them.

Having shaken the dust of South London off my feet forever (as I thought, at the age of eighteen), ten years later I found myself back here by necessity, I may say, rather than by design. Penniless writer married to penniless actor equals not very much choice in the matter of roof over head. To begin with we rented accommodation—one room and a kitchen in an old house, subsequently purchased by the local authority and scheduled for demolition. This meant that whether we liked it or not we were now tenants of the local authority. Still being penniless, we did our best to fight for our rights, protesting most strongly at the suggestion we be rehoused in a concrete tower block. The ideal solution was found: the sprawling top floor, complete with secret passage, of a Victorian mansion. The authority were glad to be rid of it, while we felt we could happily stay there for life. It was not to be. Five years on and the authority came marching in again with yet another demolition order. Battle resumes. . . .

We live in a conurbation of steel and glass, the Home Office towering on concrete stilts, multistorey car parks, flyovers and underpasses. It is a town devoted almost entirely to the pursuit of Mammon, in which any building more than fifty years old is almost routinely demolished. We are now currently in possession of the one—the one—that got away. Built in 1690 and condemned as uninhabitable, it had been compulsorily purchased by the authorities as far back as 1938 for a local road widening which never took place. We were told that we could "buy it if you really want," the implication being that we were stark mad.

Over the years we have lovingly restored the house to its original condition, until now it is a listed building, under government protection, safe (almost) from demolition, a perfect specimen of its period. There is only one problem; it is in the middle of a town, where we no longer wish to be.

We have until very recently been resistant to the idea of moving, partly for love of the house, partly for the convenience of being only twenty minutes away from the heart of London. Charing Cross, Trafalgar Square, Westminster Abbey, the Houses of Parliament . . . who could ask for more? When I first discovered London, the real London, the London of bookshops and record shops, of Covent Garden and the ballet, of Shaftesbury Avenue and the theatre, at the age of about fourteen, I thought it the most wondrous and exciting place on earth. Dr. Johnson once famously said that when a man is tired of London, he is tired of life. I hesitate to disagree with the great doctor, but I have long grown tired of what the eighteenth-century writer and lover of the countryside, William Cobbett, was wont to refer to as the Great Wen, whereas I am not in the least bit tired of life. But I yearn now, we both yearn, for green fields rather than tarmac, for fresh air rather than petrol fumes, for bird song rather than the constant roar of traffic. The quality of city life has been degraded to a point where even Dr. Johnson, I feel, would be disenchanted. Our ambition, in any case, is to start up our animal sanctuary.

We already have seven animals of our own—two rescued cats, both pure white, called Humphrey and Smudger; three rescued dogs, Benny, Beth, and Gusset; and our two original smooth-haired fox terriers, William and Becky. Benny and Humphrey were both born deaf. Humphrey is a thug, Benny is a goon; both crave

***"The house"*** (Reproduced by permission.)

***Jean Ure with Humphrey, 1985*** (Reproduced by permission.)

affection. Smudger is a cat of immense consequence, with a highly developed sense of his own importance. Gusset, named after her puppyhood penchant for chewing people's underwear, is a tiny pop-eyed muppet. Beth is an overexcitable Border collie of great intelligence and charm. Little Becky is a worrier, who takes life rather seriously, while William, variously known as Bill, Billy, the Beast, is the boss dog who keeps them all in order. If we could only move to the country, we could have half a dozen more. . . .

Our animals are, I suppose, our greatest joy in life. Some of our happiest hours are spent walking with the dogs, and we think it is about time we started to walk in open fields rather than in city parks. Maybe then my books would cease to be quite so clamorous, quite so rebarbative, full of disgusting urban words such as snot and bum, and acquire a more decorous rurality. They might even achieve a sense of place.

But wherever I live and whatever I write about, it will always be my characters who interest me the most; and my aim, if conscious aim I have—though it becomes conscious only when I force myself to stop and think about it—will still be to stimulate and entertain, and hopefully, for the receptive few, to unlock the door to that same lifetime of spiritual and intellectual nourishment which was unlocked for me nearly forty years ago by a book called *Little Women* . . . as dear to me now as it ever was then!

Ure contributed the following update to *SATA* in 2007:

## *Postscript*

It must be getting on for fifteen years since I wrote my first installment for *SATA*. It seems a lifetime ago! When I look back at the books I was writing then, they might almost have been written by a different person, and yet there have been no dramatic changes in my life. I am still, for instance, married to the same husband, we still live in the same house, I still have the same hair, we still have a large family of rescued animals.

*Husband* is no longer an actor. Having decided that he wished to exercise rather more control over the direction his life was taking, he finally turned an absorbing passion into a highly successful business venture and now operates internationally as *The Cartridge Man,* a specialist in the field of top-end hi fi—strictly analog. This means that my study is no longer exclusively my study, and that my sea of paper and husband's stacks of boxes are now in line for a head-on collision, but there you go. I do occasionally rise up in self-righteous rage, but husband sternly reminds me that Jane Austen didn't even have her own private corner, never mind half a study, so who am I to complain?

As for *House,* this was on the market for so long we actually forgot we had ever put it up for sale, until the day we received a telephone call from persons unknown and upon inquiring "Who exactly are you?" were informed in injured tones that "We're your estate agents!" Whereupon we gazed at all the accumulation of clutter and cravenly decided it would be far simpler just to stay put.

We also gazed at *Animals,* whose number has now increased to eleven: seven dogs, and four cats. None of the original crew, alas, but just as beloved. Anyone, however, who has tried showing prospective purchasers round a house with a horde of excited canines—including two outraged Jack Russells—yammering to get out and be part of the fun will possibly understand the sudden waning of enthusiasm.

And then we come to *Hair,* and here, perhaps, there has been a bit of a change. *I have not taken the scissors to it for six whole months.* For the record, *that is a record.* And as a result, I now have absolutely no sympathy whatsoever with smokers. Breaking the nicotine habit has nothing on managing to keep one's hands off a pair of scissors. Yup! I am feeling pretty proud of myself. If I could now just stop pulling out the gray hairs—well, if I don't I shall probably go bald, so that means yet another battle. Dear God, is there no end to it?

Seemingly not. In the early days I myself was a smoker; couldn't possibly write without a fag in my hand. Then I quit smoking and moved on to chocolate: couldn't write without a constant supply of the stuff. With the advent of middle age and the dreaded *spread,* the chocolate had to go and the scissors came in. Now it's the tweezers.

It would be easier to cure myself, I guess, if I were to do what most authors do and write directly on to a computer. I still sit at the kitchen table, surrounded by animals (and tweezers). Partly this is habit, partly it's because I enjoy the organic feel of pen on paper, but mostly it's a cunning ploy to kid myself that I am *just having fun.* To sit down, formally, in front of the computer, would be too much like admitting that Writing is Work.

But at least, and at last, I did succumb to the lure of the PC. A couple of years ago I even caved in and got myself a Web site (www.jeanure.com), which has transformed my relationship with readers.

"All those e-mails!" said a non-writing friend recently. "All from your fans! It must be so gratifying."

I agreed that it was; it would have been churlish not to. And, besides, it *can* be gratifying, and indeed mostly is. I still have a warm glow of satisfaction when some eleven year old tells me she's my number 1 fan, or she's read all my books, or better yet has bought all my books. Of course I do! I love it. Yet there is no denying, e-mails from young readers can be a bit of a mixed blessing. You need to be strong. E-mails from adults are, on the whole, more temperate, less blunt, rather more *discreet.* Eleven year olds just come straight out with it.

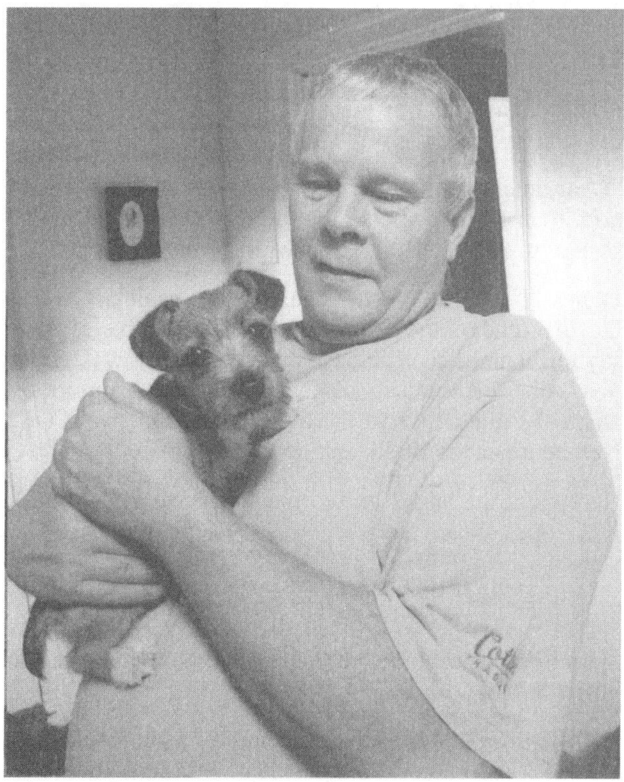

***Jean's husband with dog Gertie*** (Reproduced by permission.)

***Jean with one of her seven dogs*** (Reproduced by permission.)

"Hi, Jean Ure! You're my fave author. Do you know J.K. Rowling?

"Dear Jean Ure, I'm your no.1 fan. I was wondering can you give me J.K. Rowling's e-mail address?

"Dear Jean, Your books are great. Me and my friend both love them. We also love J.K. Rowling. We would so like to meet her! Can you arrange this?

I guess I receive at least one J.K.R. e-mail per week. On the other hand I do occasionally receive e-mails saying "I used to read Harry Potter, but now I prefer you," or "I like your books better 'cos they're more realistic." I don't receive these quite so often. Well, OK! Nowhere near as often. But now and again.

Here from the bag of mixed blessings, are a few non-J. K.R. ones which have come in during the past few weeks.

"My friend says you watch porno. Is this true?"

"Have you heard of Ellen Potter? She is my all time favorite author."

"Why haven't you ever turned any of your books into movies? You should think about it. I'm sure you could if you tried your best."

"Are you rich? You must be rich because if you were not rich you would not be able to publish books."

"I went into a shop today and saw a copy of your new book but it was too late to buy it as I had spent all of my money."

And, of course, the famous "My teacher said we had to write to authors and I got you."

Sometimes I find myself caught up in mad exchanges. This from a reader in Malaysia:

"Hi, Jean Ure, Wot UR opinion of your book *Boys Beware*?

(me) "My opinion is that it is funny. What is your opinion?"

"No, I want UR opinion."

(me) "I just gave you my opinion! Why not give me yours?"

"I want know whats UR opinion Tash 'n Emily" (characters in the book)

(me) "Give me your opinion first and then I'll give you mine. Your opinion is more important than mine."

"My opinion is UR very lazy person."

OK, OK! I surrender. Had the computer been in such everyday use fifteen years ago as it is now, would I still have received such shoals of e-mails from readers? Somehow, I doubt it. In those days I wrote mainly for older teens and young adults. My reputation was high, but my sales were low, yet still I clung on, reluctant to move down the age ladder. And then I had an epiphany. Or perhaps, on second thoughts, the words *salutary experience* might better describe it.

I went with a fellow author to visit a school on an American airbase in the east of England. I was talking to Year Nine students, my fellow author to Year Six. My fellow author sold so many books after the event that a fresh supply had to be hastily brought in from the nearest bookshop. I sold precisely *one*—and that was to a member of the teaching staff.

It is received wisdom that teenagers do not buy books. I had always been aware of this, but had chosen to ignore it. I loved writing for teenagers! And teenagers loved my books! The few who read them. On that day at the American air base the truth was brutally and humiliatingly brought home to me: it was only the few who read them.

I knew, then, that I had to make a decision, but desperately not wanting to make it I would probably have hung on had I not, in the end, been pushed. From having been enthusiastically embraced in the 1980s, teen/YA fiction was now falling like flies from publishers' lists. A book I had been contracted to write—had indeed written—was axed, others looked like going out of print. Change was forced on me whether I liked it or not. I allowed myself a short period of mourning, then somewhat aggressively embarked on a new phase of my writing life. From now on, I would concentrate on the preteens. The Year Fives, the Year Sixes. I had an Ideas Folder bulging with ideas—for YA books—which I was determined not to waste. The authorial mind needs to be flexible, so I went with the flow and made the, to me, surprising discovery that almost any idea can be adapted for younger readers.

For instance, a gritty plotline about two girls who run away from home and get drawn into prostitution turned into my latest book, *Gone Missing.* The prostitution had to go, but that still left me plenty to explore.

An Internet idea, a girl and her best friend meeting someone in a chat room and being enticed into meeting him only to discover they have put themselves in deadly peril, became *Secret Meeting.* The girls are slightly younger, and the "him" has become a "her," so that the sexual angle has gone, but they still manage to end up in a dangerous situation.

The adventures and misdeeds of three sixteen year olds sharing an apartment gave me a bit of a battle. How to turn my sixteen-year-olds into thirteen year olds and still maintain plausibility? I wrestled with this one for several months, reluctant to give up on a book I had long wanted to write. But no problem is insoluble, as *Boys Beware* will testify.

In essence, I am writing the same kind of books as I have always written, the kind of books I love to write and which best suit both my ability and my temperament. Quirky, realistic, and character-led. Sometimes lighthearted, as in *The Secret Life of Sally Tomato;* sometimes tragic, as in *Becky Bananas;* but always with humour, always accessible, always with the odd unexpected word or turn of phrase to keep readers on their toes. I have frequent tussles with my editors on the subject of language. "Teenagers wouldn't *use* that word!" they wail. No? Well, tough! Mine do. I refuse to write in unregenerate teenspeak. Not only is it manifestly impossible to keep up with the latest in-phrase, which in any case would almost certainly be well on its way out long before publication date, it also makes for a threadbare text: unimaginative and unchallenging. It is perhaps for this reason that I have never been comfortable writing for the very youngest readers, where it is not always the case of using the *best* word so much as the *simplest* word; and, of course, where story has to be paramount. I think I have never been a story-teller *per se.* For me, it is the characters who provide the inspiration: any action flows directly from them.

One happy result of writing lower down the age range is that my school visits are now mainly centered on years Four through Seven. I remember when I wrote my first YA novel, back in the dim and distant 1980s, I actually had this vision of eager, enthusiastic, book-loving Year Nines queuing up to read it. I remember how my agent—who possibly at that stage shared my rose-tinted vision—arranged for me to travel up to the wilds of the English Lake District to do a talk in a large secondary school. I had never done a book talk before, I hadn't set foot in a school since I was eighteen, and I was frankly so petrified with fear that my entire life was blighted for days beforehand. All that buoyed me up was the thought of those eager, enthusiastic, book-loving fourteen year olds hanging on my every word.

Well, the big day came and off I went, sweating at every pore. It was November, I recall, and pitch black when I got off the train at some deserted wayside halt where a teacher was supposed to meet me. But where was the teacher? Where was anybody? Not a soul in sight! No phone on the platform, and this was before the days of mobiles. Panic speedily set in. I am a Londoner, born and bred, and all this sinister open space, surrounded by darkness, was most alarming. But there's nothing worse than kicking one's heels and doing nothing, so by and by I struck out blindly into the night, turning left for no better reason than that is the way I instinctively turn. I could have gone right, and then where would I have ended up? The northernmost tip of Scotland, maybe. Who knows? Fortunately, left led me to a bit of habitation, including—oh, bliss!—a pub. I understand about pubs.

When I finally tore myself away from the open hearth to use the telephone, I found that "my" teacher was in the middle of his dinner, having forgotten the time I was due to arrive. Not a good start to my speaking career. Still, those kids in the Lake District, being out in the sticks, were at least pretty meek and mild. They showed no interest in reading my book, but at least they didn't boo or hiss or throw things at me. Over the next few years I became rather better acquainted with the denizens of Year Nine, especially the inner-city variety. The ones who conduct private conversations while you're talking to them. The ones who paint their nails or do their neighbour's hair. The ones who fight each other. The ones who ostentatiously go to sleep. The ones who shout out four-letter words, knowing that you can't shout them back.

And then there are the teachers . . . the poor, defeated teachers. The ones who scowl, forbiddingly, throughout your session. The ones who stare into space, seemingly brain-dead. The ones who totally ignore you and get on with marking homework. The one who greeted me with, "I can't say I've ever heard of you, but someone said you'd be good." The one who solemnly informed me that "I've shut them in the hall. I didn't tell them you were coming, in case they bunked off." The one who introduced me to the class as "This lady who has come to talk to you. I don't know who she is, but I'm sure she'll tell you." The one who jovially inquired whether

***Jean talking to a class of Year Sixes*** (Reproduced by permission.)

I was famous, and jovially supplied the answer: "Well, no, I suppose you can't be, or I wouldn't have to ask, would I?" Ha ha. Even the kids thought that was a bit off.

Oh, I have suffered for my art! But no experience is ever wasted. One particularly forbidding school I went to, where the walls were topped with razor-wire and covered in graffiti and I literally had to shout to make myself heard above the continuing hubbub, became the inspiration for a recent book, *Sugar and Spice.* There is the school, in all its glory: razor-wire, graffiti, rampaging pupils—and one small, sad, eleven year old whose ambitions are slowly being crushed. I once met such an eleven year old, and she has remained in my memory ever since. I should like to think she found an ally and managed to pull through, as Ruth does in *Sugar and Spice.*

Maybe, upon reflection, the only downside to visiting junior schools is that they tend to be friendly, welcoming places, with—on the whole—friendly, welcoming kids who are both willing and eager to be pleased. There is not a lot of *material* there. But lots of readers!

The first of my "new generation" of books, *Skinny Melon and Me,* was published in 1996. What goes around, comes around, and teen/YA fiction is now back with a vengeance. Most of the prizes, most of the reviews, almost all of the kudos are reserved for this section of the market. Books which appeal to nine-through-thirteen-year-old boys are eagerly sought after and much lauded and magnified—and, of course, made into rip-roaring movies. Books, however, which appeal to girls in that age group are very largely ignored, or even slightly sneered at. Girl stuff! I would seriously suggest that there is still a lot of rampant sexism about.

So, with the YA market back in full swing, am I ever tempted to return to my first love? The answer is a very definite no. I can live without reviews, I can live without kudos, but I cannot live without my readers! For all that I sometimes smile, and sometimes groan, at the flood of eager e-mails, I wouldn't be without them. Just this very morning I had an e-mail from an eleven-year-old girl who told me that her mum wanted to thank me for getting her into reading. "I never used to read at all but then I discovered your books and now I can't stop." It makes it all worthwhile!

# V-W

## VELASQUEZ, Eric

### Personal

Born in New York, NY. *Education:* School of Visual Arts, B.F.A., 1983; studied with Harvey Dinnerstein at Art Students League, 1984.

### Addresses

*Home and office*—Hartsdale, NY. *E-mail*—eric@ericvelasquez.com.

### Career

Illustrator.

### Member

Art Student's League.

### Awards, Honors

Coretta-Scott King/John Steptoe Award for New Talent, 1999, for *The Piano Man;* Carter G. Woodson Award, National Council for the Social Studies/Children's Book Council, 2001, for *The Sound That Jazz Makes.*

### Writings

(Self-illustrated) *Grandma's Records,* Walker & Company (New York, NY), 2001.

*ILLUSTRATOR*

Beverley Naidoo, *Journey to Jo'burg: A South African Story,* Lippincott (Philadelphia, PA), 1985.

Lesley Koplow, *Tanya and the Tobo Man: A Story for Children Entering Therapy/Tanya y el hombre Tobo: Una historia para niños que empiezan terapia,* Spanish translation by Alexander Contos, Magination Press (New York, NY), 1991.

Gary Soto, *The Skirt,* Delacorte (New York, NY), 1992.

Eleanora E. Tate, *Front Porch Stories at the One-Room School,* Bantam (New York, NY), 1992.

Kim L. Siegelson, *The Terrible, Wonderful Tellin' at Hog Hammock,* HarperCollins (New York, NY), 1996.

Gary Soto, *Off and Running,* Delacorte (New York, NY), 1996.

Debbi Chocolate, *The Piano Man,* Walker & Company (New York, NY), 1998.

Sharon Shavers Gayle, *Escape!: A Story of the Underground Railroad,* Soundprints (Norwalk, CT), 1999.

Carole Boston Weatherford, *The Sound That Jazz Makes,* Walker & Company (New York, NY), 2000.

David "Panama" Francis and Bob Reiser, *David Gets His Drum,* Marshall Cavendish (New York, NY), 2002.

Jim Haskins, *Champion: The Story of Muhammad Ali,* Walker & Company (New York, NY), 2002.

Candice Ransom, *Liberty Street,* Walker & Company (New York, NY), 2003.

Sharon Shavers Gayle, *Emma's Escape: A Story of America's Underground Railroad,* Soundprints (Norwalk, CT), 2003.

Linda Walvoord, *Rosetta, Rosetta, Sit by Me!,* Marshall Cavendish (New York, NY), 2004.

Kathleen Krull, *Houdini: World's Greatest Mystery Man and Escape King,* Walker & Company (New York, NY), 2005.

Charisse K. Richardson, *The Real Lucky Charm,* Dial Books (New York, NY), 2005.

Angela Johnson, *A Sweet Smell of Roses,* Simon & Schuster (New York, NY), 2005.

Regina Hanson, *A Season for Mangoes,* Clarion Books (New York, NY), 2005.

Carole Boston Weatherford, *Jesse Owens: The Fastest Man Alive,* Walker & Company (New York, NY), 2006.

Hugh Brewster, *The Other Mozart: The Life of the Famous Chevalier de Saint-George,* Abrams Books (New York, NY), 2007.

Gary Soto, *The Skirt,* Yearling (New York, NY), 2008.

Carole Boston Weatherford, *I, Matthew Henson: Polar Explorer,* Walker & Company (New York, NY), 2008.

Carole Boston Weatherford, *Racing against the Odds: Wendell Scott, African American Stock Car Champion,* Marshall Cavendish (New York, NY), 2008.

Addie K. Boswell, *The Rain Stomper,* Marshall Cavendish (New York, NY), 2008.

Also illustrator of book covers, including "Encyclopedia Brown" series, "You Be the Jury" series, "Ghost Writers" series, and "Apple Classics" series.

## Sidelights

During his career as a freelance illustrator, Eric Velasquez has provided the artwork for more than 300 book covers and book interiors. Growing up in New York City's Spanish Harlem neighborhood, Velasquez was greatly influenced by his grandmother's love of music and his father's love of film, and his mother encouraged his interest in drawing and sketching. "Becoming an artist was a natural choice for me," Velasquez stated on his home page. "I have never thought of being anything else."

Velasquez made his picture-book debut in 1985, serving as the illustrator for Beverley Naidoo's *Journey to Jo'burg: A South African Story.* He later collaborated with Debbi Chocolate on *The Piano Man,* a tribute to an African American musician. Velasquez's "subtle characterization of faces gives warmth and individuality to the main characters," observed *Booklist* reviewer Carolyn Phelan. Carole Boston Weatherford's award-winning *The Sound That Jazz Makes* traces the evolution of the American art form through the musicians who contributed to its development. The illustrator's "portraits emphasize the dignity and pride of his subjects," remarked a *Publishers Weekly* contributor. In a self-illustrated title, *Grandma's Records,* Velasquez recalls a special concert he attended with his grandmother. "Velasquez's touching yet simply told memoir of this tender relationship is lovingly captured in his illustrations," wrote Alicia Eames in *School Library Journal.*

Angela Johnson's *A Sweet Smell of Roses* follows two young girls as they join a civil rights march led by Dr. Martin Luther King, Jr. "Velasquez's red-accented pencil illustrations capture the sweep and emotion of the march," Martha V. Parravano stated in *Horn Book.* Set in Jamaica, Regina Hanson's *A Season for Mangoes* focuses on a youngster's memories of her late grandmother during an all-night "sit-up," a type of wake. "Rich, naturalistic, full-color oil paintings fill the pages," observed Nancy Palmer in *School Library Journal.* "They reflect emotions well, succeeding most often in their close-up, almost portrait-like faces."

Velasquez has also illustrated several critically acclaimed biographies. *Champion: The Story of Muhammad Ali,* a work by Jim Haskins, explores the life of the boxing legend. "Velasquez's lush oils dominate the page in monumental fashion," a *Kirkus Reviews* critic stated. "They frequently appear as montages or in sequences of

***Among the many books featuring Eric Velasquez's detailed paintings is* Houdini, *written by Kathleen Krull.*** (Illustration copyright © 2005 by Eric Velasquez. Reprinted by permission of Walker & Co.)

stop-action frames, for a truly cinematic effect." Celebrated illusionist, stunt performer, and escape artist Harry Houdini is the subject of Kathleen Krull's *Houdini: World's Greatest Mystery Man and Escape King.* In the words of *School Library Journal* critic Heide Piehler, "Velasquez's impressive framed, posed oil paintings portray the magician's intensity and sense of showmanship." In *The Other Mozart: The Life of the Famous Chevalier de Saint-George,* Hugh Brewster looks at an accomplished eighteenth-century French composer who was born into slavery in Guadeloupe. According to *Booklist* reviewer Gillian Engberg, "Velasquez's arresting full-page portraits" for this profile "will captivate many young readers."

Velasquez and Weatherford teamed up again on *Jesse Owens: The Fastest Man Alive,* a biography of the famed sprinter who won four gold medals at the 1936 Olympic Games. The illustrator's "pleasingly grainy pastels easily convey the movement and speed, determination and triumph at the core of Owens's uplifting story," a critic wrote in *Publishers Weekly.* In *I, Matthew Henson: Polar Explorer,* Weatherford offers a portrait of the African-American adventurer who journeyed to the North Pole with Robert Peary. The "full-spread pastel illustrations" Velasquez contributes here "use a palette of white, gray, pale blue, and brown to show the vast, icy landscape," remarked a contributor in *Kirkus Reviews.*

## Biographical and Critical Sources

*PERIODICALS*

*Booklist,* February 15, 1998, Carolyn Phelan, review of *The Piano Man,* p. 1018; September 1, 2005, Ilene Cooper, review of *The Real Lucky Charm,* p. 119; February 1, 2007, Gillian Engberg, review of *The Other Mozart: The Life of the Famous Chevalier de Saint-George,* p. 56.

*Horn Book,* January-February, 2005, Martha V. Parravano, review of *A Sweet Smell of Roses,* p. 79.

*Kirkus Reviews,* April 15, 2002, review of *Champion: The Story of Muhammad Ali,* p. 569; March 1, 2005, review of *Houdini: World's Greatest Mystery Man and Escape King,* p. 289; April 1, 2005, review of *A Season for Mangoes,* p. 417; December 1, 2006, review of *Jesse Owens: Fastest Man Alive,* p. 1226; December 15, 2006, review of *The Other Mozart,* p. 1265; December 1, 2007, review of *I, Matthew Henson: Polar Explorer.*

*Publishers Weekly,* November 24, 1997, review of *The Piano Man,* p. 73; May 15, 2000, review of *The Sound That Jazz Makes,* p. 115; January 3, 2005, review of *A Sweet Smell of Roses,* p. 55; January 1, 2007, reviews of *The Other Mozart* and *Jesse Owens,* p. 49; January 28, 2008, review of *I, Matthew Henson,* p. 67.

*School Library Journal,* July, 2000, Ginny Gustin, review of *The Sound That Jazz Makes,* p. 99; September, 2001, Alicia Eames, review of *Grandma's Records,* p. 207; July, 2002, Alicia Eames, review of *Champion,* p. 136; November, 2004, Tracy Bell, review of *Rosetta, Rosetta, Sit by Me!,* p. 120; April, 2005, Heide Piehler, review of *Houdini,* p. 124; May, 2005, Nancy Palmer, review of *A Season for Mangoes,* p. 84; October, 2005, Mary N. Oluonye, review of *The Real Lucky Charm,* p. 126; March, 2007, Suzanne Myers Harold, review of *Jesse Owens,* p. 236; June, 2007, Emily R. Brown, review of *The Other Mozart,* p. 166; January, 2008, Barbara Auerbach, review of *I, Matthew Henson,* p. 112.

*ONLINE*

*Eric Velasquez Home Page,* http://www.ericvelasquez.com (August 10, 2008).*

* * *

# WAKIYAMA, Hanako 1966-

## Personal

Born 1966, in Tokyo, Japan; immigrated to United States, 1984; married; children: one daughter. *Education:* Attended art school.

## Addresses

*Home*—San Francisco, CA.

## Career

Illustrator.

## Illustrator

Wendy Tokuda, *Humphrey, the Lost Whale: A True Story,* Heian (Union City, CA), 1986.

Claire Masurel, *Too Big!,* Chronicle Books (San Francisco, CA), 1999.

Erin Dealey, *Goldie Locks Has Chicken Pox,* Atheneum Books for Young Readers (New York, NY), 2002.

Maribeth Boelts, *When It's the Last Day of School,* G.P. Putnam's Sons (New York, NY), 2004.

David LaRochelle, *The Best Pet of All,* Dutton Children's Books (New York, NY), 2004.

Erin Dealey, *Little Bo Peep Can't Get to Sleep,* Atheneum Books for Young Readers (New York, NY), 2005.

Peggy Archer, *From Dawn to Dreams: Poems for Busy Babies,* Candlewick Press (Cambridge, MA), 2007.

## Sidelights

San Francisco-based illustrator Hanako Wakiyama spent her childhood in Tokyo, Japan, then moved with her family to California during her teen years. She had developed a love of art early on, and her first illustration project, Wendy Tokuda's *Humphrey, the Lost Whale: A True Story,* was published shortly after she completed college. She developed her unique retro style as a means of making her artwork stand out from the illustration work then in vogue, and it caught the attention of an editor at Chronicle Books, who assigned her to create the illustrations for Claire Masurel's *Too Big!* Praising the book, about a boy who receives a giant toy dinosaur as his prize for winning a carnival game, Susan Dove Lempke concluded in *Booklist* that Wakiyama's "paintings glow with soft light and capture the story's gently whimsical tone." While comparing her work to that of author/illustrator William Joyce, a *Publishers Weekly* critic added of Wakiyama that her "use of unexpected perspectives [in *Too Big!*] is all her own" and her "delightfully peculiar artwork . . . fits the fantasy of animated toys especially well."

Wakiyama's colorful oil paintings for *Too Big!* reflect her early-twentieth-century aesthetic, a style that can be seen in her more-recent work, which includes Erin Dealey's *Goldie Locks Has Chicken Pox, The Best Pet of All* by David LaRochelle, and Peggy Archer's *From Dawn to Dreams: Poems for Busy Babies.* In *Goldie Locks Has Chicken Pox* the illustrator imbues Dealey's text with what Carol Anne Wilson described in *School Library Journal* as "a decidedly retro feel," the critic adding that "observant viewers will have fun with the visual references to fairy-tale events." Another collaboration with Dealey, *Little Bo Peep Can't Get to Sleep,* features "playful, retro-style" paintings in "vivid saturated colors" that "keep . . . the book fresh and childlike," according to *School Library Journal* critic Angela J. Reynolds. The illustrator's decision to combine "modern and traditional elements" in her illustrations for the

***Hanako Wakiyama creates colorful and stylized art for Maribeth Boelts' picture book* When It's the Last Day of School.** (Illustration copyright © 2004 by Hanako Wakiyama, Used by permission of G.P. Putnam's Sons, a division of Penguin Putnam Books for Young Readers.)

book will satisfy "younger viewers, who will have no trouble identifying the nursery-rhyme characters," in the opinion of a *Kirkus Reviews* writer.

Reviewing *The Best Pet of All* for *Kirkus Reviews,* a contributor concluded that Wakiyama's "insouciant retro-looking illustrations add sly touches of humor" to LaRochelle's story, while *Booklist* critic Karin Snelson cited the artist's "candy-colored palette, clever use of thought bubbles, and comical touches." In *From Dawn to Dreams* Wakiyama's retro style gives a nostalgic spin to infanthood as she brings to life Archer's poems about busy babies and toddlers of all sorts. From first steps to bubble baths, the active parts of a baby's day come to life in the artist's clear-toned oil paintings. Praising the illustrations as featuring a '50s aesthetic, *School Library Journal* contributor Maryanne H. Owen dubbed *From Dawn to Dreams* "a sweet tribute to young children," while in *Kirkus Reviews* a contributor noted that Wakiyama combines "vintage colors, Kewpie-doll faces and '40s-inspired motifs to cheery effect."

## Biographical and Critical Sources

*PERIODICALS*

*Booklist,* August, 1999, Susan Dove Lempke, review of *Too Big!,* p. 2065; January 1, 2004, Karin Snelson, review of *The Best Pet of All,* p. 1731; April 15, 2004, Carolyn Phelan, review of *When It's the Last Day of School,* p. 1445.

*Kirkus Reviews,* January 15, 2002, review of *Goldie Locks Has Chicken Pox,* p. 103; January 15, 2004, review of *When It's the Last Day of School,* p. 80; April 15, 2004, review of *The Best Pet of All,* p. 396; February 1, 2005, review of *Little Bo Peep Can't Get to Sleep,* p. 175; June 1, 2007, review of *From Dawn to Dreams: Poems for Busy Babies.*

*Publishers Weekly,* April 26, 1999, review of *Too Big!,* p. 80; January 21, 2002, review of *Goldie Locks Has Chicken Pox,* p. 88; July 12, 2004, review of *The Best Pet of All,* p. 63.

*School Library Journal,* February, 2002, Carol Ann Wilson, review of *Goldie Locks Has Chicken Pox,* p. 97; April, 2004, Lisa Gangemi Kropp, review of *When It's the Last Day of School,* p. 102; July, 2004, Jane Barrer, review of *The Best Pet of All,* p. 80; March, 2005, Angela J. Reynolds, review of *Little Bo Peep Can't Get to Sleep,* p. 170; July, 2007, Maryann H. Owne, review of *From Dawn to Dreams,* p. 88.

*ONLINE*

*Chronicle Books Web site,* http://www.chroniclebooks.com/ (August 19, 2008), Garda Parker, interview with Wakiyama.*

* * *

# WEATHERLY, Lee 1967-
# (Titania Woods)

## Personal

Born 1967, in Little Rock, AR; married; husband's name Pete. *Hobbies and other interests:* Reading, dancing, cooking, walking.

## Addresses

*Home*—Hampshire, England. *Agent*—Caroline Sheldon Literary Agency, carolinesheldon@carolinesheldon.co.uk. *E-mail*—writetolee@ntlworld.com.

## Career

Writer and editor. Founder of Flying Frogs (writing consultancy). Worked variously as a restaurant hostess, desk clerk, gift-shop clerk, receptionist, and secretary.

## Awards, Honors

Sheffield Children's Book Award, 2003, and Quick Picks for Reluctant Readers selection, American Library Association, both for *Child X;* Edgar Allan Poe Award shortlist, Mystery Writers of America, for *Missing Abby;* Stockport Children's Book Award, 2007, for *Kat Got Your Tongue.*

## Writings

*NOVELS*

*Child X,* David Fickling Books (New York, NY), 2002.
*Missing Abby,* David Fickling Books (New York, NY), 2004.
*Breakfast at Sadie's,* David Fickling Books (New York, NY), 2005.
*Them,* Barrington Stoke (Edinburgh, Scotland), 2006.
*Kat Got Your Tongue,* David Fickling Books (New York, NY), 2006.
*Watcher,* Barrington Stoke (Edinburgh, Scotland), 2007.

*"GLITTERWINGS ACADEMY" SERIES; UNDER NAME TITANIA WOODS*

*Midnight Feast,* Bloomsbury (London, England), 2007.
*Friends Forever,* Bloomsbury (London, England), 2007.
*Fairy Dust,* Bloomsbury (London, England), 2007.
*Fledge Star,* Bloomsbury (London, England), 2007.
*Term-time Trouble,* Bloomsbury (London, England), 2007.
*New Girl,* Bloomsbury (London, England), 2007.
*Seedling Exams,* Bloomsbury (London, England), 2007.
*Flying High,* Bloomsbury (London, England), 2008.

*OTHER*

(With Helen Corner) *How to Write a Blockbuster,* McGraw-Hill (Blacklick, OH), 2006.

Also author of picture books *Pigwitchery* and *Hic!*

## Sidelights

Lee Weatherly, an American-born writer living in England, is the author of the young-adult novels *Child X* and *Kat Got Your Tongue.* Publishing under the pseudonym Titania Woods, Weatherly has also produced several works in the "Glitterwings Academy" series of fantasy tales for younger readers. Being a full-time writer "has its ups and downs like any job, but in general, I feel very, very lucky to make my living doing something I enjoy so much," the author remarked on her home page.

Weatherly's debut novel, *Child X,* concerns Jules Cheney, a British teen whose adoring father, Ben, abruptly leaves their home and cuts off all contact with Jules after a horrible argument with his wife. Later, while reading the newspaper, Jules learns that Ben is not her biological father and that he has filed a lawsuit against her mother, demanding financial restitution for his years of parenting. To protect her identity, news reports refer to Jules as "Child X," though she quickly becomes the focus of a media circus. "The effects of divorce are particularly well honed and believable," noted *School Library Journal* reviewer Daniel L. Darigan, and Lori Atkins Goodson, writing in the *Journal of Adolescent & Adult Literacy,* called *Child X* "a story of families and lies and how those lies can devastate everyone around them, no matter when or how the truth emerges."

*Missing Abby* centers on Emma, an insecure thirteen year old who was the last person to see her friend, Abby Ryzner, before she disappeared. Though Emma and Abby once shared a love of fantasy role-playing games, the girls drifted apart after Emma, who was bullied by classmates, transferred schools and distanced herself from Abby. Joining the search for the missing girl, Emma must now earn the trust and respect of Abby's goth friends. A *Kirkus Reviews* critic wrote that the novel "focuses on Emma's growth in emotional maturity," and *School Library Journal* critic Susan W. Hunter observed that Emma "gradually gains strength to surmount shameful memories and learns to accept her own uniqueness."

In *Breakfast at Sadie's* a British teenager unexpectedly finds herself running a bed-and-breakfast. The work was inspired by an incident Weatherly came across while reading *500 Mile Walkies,* a travel book by Mark Wallington. "While hiking the Cornish Coastal trail, Mark stayed at a B&B that, so far as he could tell, was being run by a 10-year old girl, with no adults in sight," Weatherly stated on her home page. In the work, Sadie takes charge of the family business after her mother becomes ill and her aunt runs off. "Sadie is an endearing character who learns how strong she really is," Janet Hilbun remarked in *School Library Journal.*

An amnesia victim attempts to piece her life back together in *Kat Got Your Tongue.* After running into the street and being struck by a car, thirteen-year-old Kathy loses her memories of her family and friends, as well as her sense of identity. Adopting the nickname "Kat," the teen hopes to find answers to several unsettling questions about her past, including the reasons why her former best friends now dislike her. Weatherly "offers insight to the girl's troubled state of mind before the accident and simultaneously traces her difficult reentry into a world full of strangers," noted a *Publishers Weekly* contributor, and Amy S. Pattee, writing in *School Library Journal,* commented that "readers are asked to consider the ultimate mystery: who any of us really are."

## Biographical and Critical Sources

*PERIODICALS*

*Booklist,* July, 2002, Frances Bradburn, review of *Child X,* p. 1850; January 1, 2005, Gillian Engberg, review of *Missing Abby,* p. 847; August, 2007, Francisca Goldsmith, review of *Kat Got Your Tongue,* p. 64.

***Cover of Lee Weatherly's young-adult novel* Kat Got Your Tongue, *featuring cover art by Tracey Hurst.*** (Illustration copyright © 2006 by Tracey Hurst/Jerry Paris. Used by permission of Random House Children's Books, a division of Random House, Inc.)

*Journal of Adolescent & Adult Literacy,* February, 2003, Lori Atkins Goodson, review of *Child X,* p. 448.

*Kirkus Reviews,* June 1, 2002, review of *Child X,* p. 812; November 1, 2004, review of *Missing Abby,* p. 1047; May 15, 2007, review of *Kat Got Your Tongue.*

*Kliatt,* May, 2004, Barbara McKee, review of *Child X,* p. 24.

*Publishers Weekly,* July 29, 2002, review of *Child X,* p. 72; June 4, 2007, review of *Kat Got Your Tongue,* p. 51.

*School Library Journal,* June, 2002, Daniel L. Darigan, review of *Child X,* p. 148; September, 2006, Janet Hilbun, review of *Breakfast at Sadie's,* p. 221; September, 2007, Amy S. Pattee, review of *Kat Got Your Tongue,* p. 210.

*ONLINE*

*Lee Weatherly Home Page,* http://www.leeweatherly.com (August 10, 2008).

*Wordpool Web site,* http://www.wordpool.co.uk/ (August 10, 2008), "Author Profiles: Lee Weatherly."*

## WESTWOOD, Jennifer 1940-2008 (Jennifer Chandler, Jennifer Fulcher)

*OBITUARY NOTICE—*

See index for *SATA* sketch: Born May 1, 1940, in Norton Subcourse, a village of Norfolk, England; died of cancer May 12, 2008. Folklorist, educator, television and radio personality, tour guide, children's writer, and author. Westwood's expertise and interests lay in the areas where history, folklore, and legend are mostly likely to meet. It all began, she once commented, when her son craved stories. As a university student of Old and Middle English and Anglo-Saxon, the stories that came to mind were very old, but her son enjoyed them, and it occurred to her that others might also enjoy modern renditions of these ancient tales. Old English led to Old Norse, medieval England led to the Dark Ages, and legends led to the historical background from which they had emerged. Westwood spent her career teaching "lost languages," presenting children's programs for the British Broadcasting Corporation and publishing books of history, tales, and legends. Her special interest was folklore—the body of oral tradition passed down over the centuries by nameless people unable to record their stories in writing—with a side interest in the landscape and artifacts of old England. For a time she conducted "Magical Britain" tours from a base in Glastonbury, England, a community on the Isle of Avalon and the reputed burial place of the legendary King Arthur. Westwood published more than a dozen books, including *Medieval Tales* (1967), *Albion: A Guide to Legendary Britain* (1985), *The Atlas of Mysterious Places: The World's Unexplained Sacred Sites, Symbolic Landscapes, Ancient Cities, and Lost Lands* (1987), *Sacred Journeys: An Illustrated Guide to Pilgrimages around the World* (1997), and *The Lore of the Land: A Guide to England's Legends, from Spring-heeled Jack to the Witches of Warboys* (2005). At the time of her death, she was reportedly finishing a book on Scottish folklore and preparing for a work on the folklore of sailors and the sea, both of which were expected to be completed by others.

*OBITUARIES AND OTHER SOURCES:*

*PERIODICALS*

*Times* (London, England), May 26, 2008, p. 45.

* * *

## WILD, Kate 1954-

### Personal

Born 1954, in Leicester, England; partner of Henri (a designer and video producer); children: two sons.

## Addresses

*Home*—Leicester, England. *Agent*—Darley Anderson, Darley Anderson Literary, TV, and Film Agency; darley@darleyanderson.com. *E-mail*—kate@katewild.co.uk.

## Career

Author and filmmaker. Has also worked at a casino and for a video production company.

## Writings

*Fight Game* (novel), Chicken House/Scholastic (New York, NY), 2007.

Also author of scripts for videos and documentary films.

## Sidelights

British filmmaker and screenwriter Kate Wild is the author of *Fight Game,* a "dark, action-packed tale," according to Paula Rohrlick in *Kliatt.* The inspiration for the novel came to Wild in 1996 as she worked on a documentary about gypsies and travelers. "Whilst filming two boys whose great uncle was a fighter called the Gypsy King," she noted on her home page, "I had an idea for a story about a traveller boy and fighting."

*Fight Game* centers on Freedom Smith, a fifteen-year-old Gypsy with superhuman strength and incredible combat skills, which he inherited from his ancestor, Hercules Smith, a legendary bare-knuckles fighter. After defending his family against a group of skinheads, Freedom is arrested but avoids prison by agreeing to go undercover and infiltrate a shadowy, illegal fighting organization run by Darcus Knight. Freedom soon discovers a subterranean complex known as the Bear Pit where brainwashed, steroid-enhanced runaways battle one another for the amusement of wealthy bettors. Freedom, "a truly peculiar yet likable character, should hold in readers' memories," noted *Booklist* contributor Ian Chipman, and a *Publishers Weekly* reviewer observed that the author "imbues her roguish hero with an appealing voice . . ., and despite the far-fetched elements, the tension produces some authentic thrills."

## Biographical and Critical Sources

*PERIODICALS*

*Booklist,* September 15, 2007, Ian Chipman, review of *Fight Game,* p. 59.

*Kirkus Reviews,* July 1, 2007, review of *Fight Game.*

*Kliatt,* July, 2007, Paula Rohrlick, review of *Fight Game,* p. 21.

*Publishers Weekly,* July 30, 2007, review of *Fight Game,* p. 83.

*School Library Journal,* December, 2007, Douglas P. Davey, review of *Fight Game,* p. 148.

*ONLINE*

*Chicken House Web site,* http://www.doublecluck.com/ (August 10, 2008), "Kate Wild."

*Darley Anderson Web site,* http://www.darleyanderson childrens.com/ (August 10, 2008), interview with Wild.

*Kate Wild Home Page,* http://www.katewild.com (August 10, 2008).

* * *

# WOLF, Allan 1963-

## Personal

Born February 26, 1963, in Storrs, CT; married; children: three. *Education:* Virginia Tech, B.A., M.A. *Hobbies and other interests:* Reading, writing, drawing, basketball, music, books.

## Addresses

*Home and office*—Asheville, NC. *E-mail*—allanwolf@earthlink.net.

## Career

Author, poet, performer, and educator. Virginia Tech, Blacksburg, instructor in writing and composition, beginning c. 2005; Poetry Alive!, Asheville, NC, educational director and coordinator of national residency program, 1990-2003. Artist-in-residence at school in Seoul, South Korea. Member of The Dead Poets (poetry band).

## Awards, Honors

Richard L. Hoffman Teaching Award, Virginia Tech; Best Book for Young Adults selection, American Library Association, Children's Book Award Notable Book selection, International Reading Association, and Southeastern Booksellers' Association Poetry Award finalist, all 2004, all for *New Found Land: Lewis and Clark's Voyage of Discovery.*

## Writings

*POETRY*

*Something Is Going to Happen: Poem Performance for the Classroom,* Poetry Alive! (Asheville, NC), 1990.

*It's Show Time: Poetry from the Page to the Stage,* Poetry Alive! (Asheville, NC), 1993.

*The Blood-hungry Spleen and Other Poems about Our Parts,* illustrated by Greg Clarke, Candlewick Press (Cambridge, MA), 2003.

*Immersed in Verse: An Informative, Slightly Irreverent and Totally Tremendous Guide to Living the Poet's Life,* illustrated by Tuesday Mourning, Lark Books (New York, NY), 2006.

*Haiku Stickies: 100 Haiku to Write and Leave Behind,* Lark Books (New York, NY), 2007.

(With Sara Holbrook) *More than Friends: Poems from Him and Her,* Wordsong (Honesdale, PA), 2008.

*NOVELS*

*New Found Land: Lewis and Clark's Voyage of Discovery,* Candlewick Press (Cambridge, MA), 2004.

*Zane's Trace,* Candlewick Press (Cambridge, MA), 2007.

## Sidelights

Allan Wolf is a full-time poet and performer who conducts more than one hundred presentations each year. A former college instructor, Wolf joined Poetry Alive!, a traveling troupe of theatrical poets, in 1990 and served as the group's educational director for more than a decade. He is also the author of such works as *The Blood-hungry Spleen and Other Poems about Our Parts* and *Zane's Trace,* the latter a young-adult novel.

Born in 1963 in Connecticut, Wolf was raised in Blacksburg, Virginia. At the age of twelve, he began experiencing episodes of hypergraphia, an overwhelming compulsion to write. Wolf wrote on his bedroom walls, first in pencil, then in permanent marker. "My walls became a diary upon which I recorded the events of my life," he noted on his home page. "I wrote on my walls every day for years until my room had become one huge continual tattoo of words and pictures that spread over all four walls, the ceiling, the floor, even some of the furniture." After graduating from high school, Wolf earned a master's degree from Virginia Tech and taught writing and composition there before taking a position with Poetry Alive!

In 2003 Wolf published *The Blood-hungry Spleen and Other Poems about Our Parts,* his first work for young readers. A collection of humorous verse about the human anatomy, the book contains such poems as "Shy Silent Rivers," which explores the function of the circulatory system, and "Moving Food Along," a tribute to the intestines. According to a contributor in *Publishers Weekly,* "Wolf's debut . . . is sure to tickle the funny bone (one body part that isn't covered here)."

Wolf offers a how-to for young authors in *Immersed in Verse: An Informative, Slightly Irreverent and Totally Tremendous Guide to Living the Poet's Life.* Wolf advises budding poets on such topics as poetry forms, choosing an appropriate subject, and revising work, and he includes selections from Langston Hughes and Shel Silverstein, among others. "The information is intensive without being overwhelming, wise without being didactic," observed Teresa Pfeifer in *School Library Journal.* In the words of *Booklist* critic Hazel Rochman, *Immersed in Verse* "makes writing and reading poetry cool."

Wolf's novel-in-verse, *New Found Land: Lewis and Clark's Voyage of Discovery,* presents an account of Meriwether Lewis and William Clark's journey to the Pacific Ocean through the voices of fourteen narrators. Wolf told *Publishers Weekly* interviewer Sally Lodge that "the idea of multiple voices was a kind of theatrical thing for me. By creating the character's monologues I was able to have each of them speak their own minds and give their own descriptions of events and of other characters, leaving the reader to do the linking up." In the work, Wolf "manages something fresh and alive," observed a *Kirkus Reviews* contributor, and Patricia Moore, writing in *Kliatt,* stated that *New Found Land* "is a book of poetry; it is a book of history; it is a tour de force."

A distraught, epileptic teen is the focus of *Zane's Trace,* a novel for young adults. After his mother commits suicide, seventeen-year-old Zane Guesswind steals his brother's car and heads to her grave site in Ohio, where he plans to end his own life. His journey is interrupted by the spirits of his ancestors, who counsel the troubled

***Cover of Allan Wolf's verse saga* New Found Land, *featuring artwork by Max Grafe.*** (Illustration copyright © 2004 by Max Grafe. Reproduced by permission of the publisher Candlewick Press, Inc., Somerville, MA.)

teen, as well as by Libba, a mysterious hitchhiker. "Wolf successfully straddles the line between magical realism and unreliable narration, keeping each possibility alive to enrich the other," noted *Horn Book* reviewer Claire E. Gross. "Eventually we realize that [in *Zane's Trace*] Wolf is weaving an unexpectedly complex tale, one that speaks to the vagaries of American history and the 'twisted, crazy-beautiful' family trees so many of us have," observed Katie Haegele in the *Philadelphia Inquirer.*

## Biographical and Critical Sources

*PERIODICALS*

*Booklist,* October 15, 2003, Karin Snelson, review of *The Blood-hungry Spleen and Other Poems about Our Parts,* p. 410; May 15, 2006, Hazel Rochman, review of *Immersed in Verse: An Informative, Slightly Irreverent, and Totally Tremendous Guide to Living the Poet's Life,* p. 44; October 15, 2007, Lynn Rutan, review of *Zane's Trace,* p. 48.

*Horn Book,* September-October, 2007, Claire E. Gross, review of *Zane's Trace,* p. 592.

*Kirkus Reviews,* July 1, 2003, review of *The Blood-hungry Spleen and Other Poems about Our Parts,* p. 917; July 15, 2004, review of *New Found Land: Lewis and Clark's Voyage of Discovery,* p. 695; September 1, 2007, review of *Zane's Trace.*

*Kliatt,* January, 2008, Patricia Moore, review of *New Found Land,* p. 18.

*Philadelphia Inquirer,* October 3, 2007, Katie Haegele, "*Zane's Trace:* Teen Boy Has a Compulsion to Write, and a Death Wish."

*Publishers Weekly,* August 4, 2003, review of *The Blood-hungry Spleen and Other Poems about Our Parts,* p. 80; October 25, 2004, Sally Lodge, "Allan Wolf: The Lewis and Clark Expedition in 14 Voices," p. 20; November 1, 2004, review of *New Found Land,* p. 63.

*School Library Journal,* October, 2003, Dona Ratterree, review of *The Blood-hungry Spleen and Other Poems about Our Parts,* p. 206; September, 2004, Renee Steinberg, review of *New Found Land,* p. 220; June, 2006, Teresa Pfeifer, review of *Immersed in Verse,* p. 190.

*ONLINE*

*Allan Wolf Home Page,* http://www.allanwolf.com (August 10, 2008).

*Poetry Alive! Web site,* http://www.poetryalive.com/ (August 10, 2008), "Allan Wolf."

* * *

## WOODS, Titania
## See WEATHERLY, Lee

* * *

## WRIGHT, Elinor
## See LYON, Elinor

# Y-Z

## YACCARINO, Dan 1965-

### Personal

Born May 20, 1965, in Monclair, NJ; married; children: two. *Education:* Parsons School of Design, B.F.A., 1987.

### Addresses

*Home and office*—New York, NY. *E-mail*—dan@danyaccarino.com.

### Career

Illustrator, artist, author, animator, and producer. Created art for advertising campaigns, including Cotton, Inc., AT&T, Gardenburger, Sony, and Nikkei. *Exhibitions:* Sculptures and large-scale paintings exhibited in galleries in New York, NY; Tokyo, Japan; Los Angeles, CA; and Rome, Italy.

### Awards, Honors

ADDE Award, Society of Illustrators—Los Angeles; AIGA Award, Association of Educational Publishers; Parent's Choice Award; American Library Association Notable Book designation and Parent Guide award; illustration awards from Society of Illustrators, *Communication Arts,* and *American Illustration;* invited to read his books at 2002 Easter festivities at the White House; *New York Times* Ten Best Illustrated Books, 2007, for *Every Friday.*

### Writings

SELF-ILLUSTRATED; FOR CHILDREN

*Big Brother Mike,* Hyperion (New York, NY), 1993.
*If I Had a Robot,* Viking (New York, NY), 1996.
*An Octopus Followed Me Home,* Viking (New York, NY), 1997.

***Dan Yaccarino*** (Reproduced by permission.)

*Good Night, Mr. Night,* Harcourt (San Diego, CA), 1997.
*Zoom! Zoom! Zoom! I'm off to the Moon,* Scholastic, Inc. (New York, NY), 1997.
*Five Little Pumpkins,* HarperFestival (New York, NY), 1998.
*Deep in the Jungle,* Atheneum (New York, NY), 2000.
*Oswald,* Atheneum (New York, NY), 2001.
*Unlovable,* Holt (New York, NY), 2001.
*So Big!,* HarperFestival (New York, NY), 2001.
*I Met a Bear,* HarperFestival (New York, NY), 2002.
*Dan Yaccarino's Mother Goose,* Little Golden Books (New York, NY), 2003.
*Where the Four Winds Blow,* Joanna Cotler Books (New York, NY), 2003.
*Oswald,* Simon Spotlight (New York, NY), 2004.
*Good Night, Mr. Night,* Harcourt (San Diego, CA), 2004.
*The Birthday Fish,* Henry Holt (New York, NY), 2005.

*Five Little Ducks,* HarperFestival (New York, NY), 2005.
*The 12 Days of Christmas,* HarperFestival (New York, NY), 2005.
*Every Friday,* Henry Holt (New York, NY), 2007.
*Go, Go America,* Scholastic (New York, NY), 2008.
*The Fantastic Undersea Life of Jacques Cousteau,* Alfred A. Knopf (New York, NY), 2009.

*FOR CHILDREN*

*The Lima Bean Monster,* illustrated by Adam McCauley, Walker & Company (New York, NY), 2001.
*Oswald's Sleepover,* illustrated by Gregg Schigiel, Simon Spotlight (New York, NY), 2003.
*Oswald's Camping Trip,* illustrated by Jennifer Oxley, Simon Spotlight (New York, NY), 2003.
*A Little Nap,* illustrated by Antonie Guilbaud, Scholastic (New York, NY), 2003.

Coauthor, with Lisa Desimini, David Ricceri, and Sara Schwartz, of *All Year Round: A Book to Benefit Children in Need,* Scholastic.

*"BLAST-OFF BOY AND BLORP" SERIES; SELF-ILLUSTRATED*

*First Day on a Strange New Planet,* Hyperion (New York, NY), 2000.
*New Pet,* Hyperion (New York, NY), 2001.
*The Big Science Fair,* Hyperion (New York, NY), 2002.

*ILLUSTRATOR*

Catherine Friend, *The Sawfin Stickleback: A Very Fishy Story,* Hyperion (New York, NY), 1994.
Eve Merriam, *Bam! Bam! Bam!,* Holt (New York, NY), 1995.
M.C. Helldorfer, *Carnival,* Viking (New York, NY), 1996.
W. Nikola-Lisa, *One Hole in the Road,* Holt (New York, NY), 1996.
Kevin Henkes, *Circle Dogs,* Greenwillow Press (New York, NY), 1998.
Laura Godwin, *Little White Dog,* Hyperion (New York, NY), 1998.
Andrea Zimmerman and David Clemesha, *Trashy Town,* HarperCollins (New York, NY), 1999.
Rebecca Kai Dotlich, *Away We Go!,* HarperFestival (New York, NY), 2000.
Naomi Shihab Nye, *Come with Me: Poems for a Journey,* Greenwillow Books (New York, NY), 2000.
Laurie Myers, *Surviving Brick Johnson,* Clarion Books (New York), 2000.
Robert Burleigh, *I Love Going through This Book,* HarperCollins (New York, NY), 2001.
Abigail Tabby, *Baby Face,* HarperFestival (New York, NY), 2001.
Jack Prelutsky, *Halloween Countdown,* HarperFestival (New York, NY), 2002.
Margaret Wise Brown, *The Good Little Bad Little Pig,* Hyperion (New York, NY), 2002.
Patricia MacLachlan, *Bittle,* Joanna Cotler Books (New York, NY), 2006.
Dee Lillegard, *Who Will Sing a Lullaby?,* Alfred A. Knopf (New York, NY), 2007.

Illustrator of *Discover 2000: The New York State 2000 Summer Reading Program,* by Lisa von Drasek, and of "Play and Learn" kits *Move It!* and *Bugs,* published by Running Press. Contributor of illustrations to periodicals, including *Rolling Stone, Playboy, New York,* and *Fast Company.*

## Adaptations

*Oswald* was adapted for an animated television series produced by Nickelodeon, 2001. *An Octopus Followed Me Home* was adapted as the animated television series *Willa's Wild Life,* produced on the Discovery Channel. Yaccarino's characters have been made into plush toys.

## Sidelights

Dan Yaccarino is a children's book writer and illustrator who first broke into print with his self-illustrated picture book *Big Brother Mike,* a "visually offbeat take on sibling rivalry," according to a reviewer for *Publishers Weekly.* Since that time, he has authored many books of his own as well as creating art for numerous texts by writers such as Jack Prelutsky, Margaret Wise Brown, Naomi Shihab Nye, and Robert Burleigh. Best known for his picture book *Oswald,* which was adapted as an animated series on the Nickelodeon television network, Yaccarino has also penned a trio of books about Blast-Off Boy and Blorp, a pair of "unlikely intergalactic exchange students," according to a contributor for *Kirkus Reviews.* Other books from the versatile and prolific author/artist include *Deep in the Jungle, Good Night, Mr. Night, Where the Four Winds Blow, Unlovable,* and *Go, Go America.* Writing in the *Bulletin of the Center for Children's Books,* Deborah Stevenson applauded the "retro" style of Yaccarino's work. "There's no glamorized, adult-appealing nostalgia here," the critic commented. "Rather there's a robustness reminiscent of the energetic illustrative work of the colorful 1950s and even at times . . . of [Mexican muralist] Diego Rivera's glistening monumental figures." Employing bold, bright colors and sturdy figures, Yaccarino's illustrations have a "refreshing unfussiness," Stevenson added.

In Yaccarino's first original self-illustrated picture book, *Big Brother Mike,* he tells a story of sibling relationships, including the usual ups and downs between brothers. Even though older brother Mike comes to the aid of the young narrator when bullies threaten or help is needed in burying a pet hamster, the older boy can also be irritating to his younger sibling when battling for the television remote control. A reviewer for *Publishers Weekly* called *Big Brother Mike* a "spunky first book." In *Booklist* Lisa Napoli cited Yaccarino's "ability to use color, form and composition to show feelings," while a *Kirkus Reviews* critic praised *Big Brother Mike* for featuring "vibrantly expressive illustrations, with emotion-indicative colors."

In *If I Had a Robot,* young Phil dreams of having a machine that can handle everything distasteful, from finishing up his vegetables at dinner to going to school and doing homework. Reviewers focused on Yaccarino's "visually emphatic" illustrations, as John Peters characterized them in *School Library Journal.* In *Booklist* Susan Dove Lempke also commented on the author/illustrator's "retro-style artwork . . . [which] carries through the time-honored concept" of childish wish-fulfillment. A contributor for *Publishers Weekly* likewise felt that the "main appeal" of *If I Had a Robot* "comes from the quirky sci-fi illustrations." Yaccarino returns to a similar premise in *The Lima Bean Monster,* in which Sammy unwittingly unleashes a monster while trying to dispose of a dreaded legume. Lima beans need to be discretely emptied from the boy's plate, and Sammy does so by slipping them into his sock and then burying them in a vacant lot. When a Lima Bean Monster sprouts from the site and starts to eat all the adults in the neighborhood, Sammy and the other kids protect their parents by gathering around the monster and eating it up. Sally R. Dow, writing in *School Library Journal,* described *The Lima Bean Monster* as a "fast-paced story . . . [with] surefire appeal for youngsters who won't touch their vegetables."

*Yaccarino's artwork appears on the covers of several books by Wendelin Van Draanen, among them* **Sammy Keyes and the Hotel Thief.** (Cover art © 1998 by Dan Yaccarino. Used by permission of Alfred A. Knopf, an imprint of Random House Children's Books, a division of Random House, Inc.)

Yaccarino presents a bowler-hatted Mr. Night, who puts the world to bed and also helps children fall asleep, in the picture book *Good Night, Mr. Night,* as "simple forms and Matisse-like colors match the innocence of the story, told in a series of simple lines," according to a *Kirkus Reviews* critic. Writing in the *Bulletin of the Center for Children's Books,* Janice M. Del Negro commented on Yaccarino's "Rousseauian landscape," and dubbed *Good Night, Mr. Night* a "storytime natural" due to its "controlled text and flamingly colorful illustrations." Similarly, a reviewer for *Publishers Weekly* called the book a "calming bedtime tale" and further remarked that Yaccarino's "quiet narration and undulating illustrations have an almost hypnotic quality." Lauren Peterson, writing in *Booklist,* called *Good Night, Mr. Night* a "gentle bedtime tale that stirs the imagination" and went on to praise Yaccarino's "rich, vibrant" double-page spreads, which "complement the text beautifully."

Moon exploration is the focus of *Zoom! Zoom! Zoom! I'm off to the Moon,* about a boy astronaut who takes an adventurous trip into space. The text of Yaccarino's rhyming narrative climbs diagonally up the page, reducing in size as the boy's spaceship takes off and gains altitude. A contributor for *Publishers Weekly* called this an "effervescent" picture book that readers could use as a "launch pad for their own imaginations," and *Horn Book* critic Roger Sutton deemed *Zoom! Zoom! Zoom!* "a perfect space story for the toddler realm." Sutton also commented on Yaccarino's use of signature "rounded retro shapes" in his illustrations, shapes reminiscent of 1950s toys. Shelley Townsend-Hudson, reviewing the same title in *Booklist,* wrote that the book's "fanciful illustrations pull children into this exuberant picture book and make the launch a special event."

More rhyming text is presented in *An Octopus Followed Me Home,* in which a child whines to be allowed to keep the stray octopus that has followed her home. Then her father reminds the girl of all the other animals that have followed her home, including the crocodile under the bed and the giraffe with its neck up the chimney. No more, says Dad, but readers wonder when they reach the last page and see an even more monstrous critter following the girl home. In *Booklist* Rochman noted that the verses and "bright illustrations give an uproarious spin" to the usual tale of a kid pleading to keep a stray. A reviewer for *Publishers Weekly* maintained that Yaccarino "specializes in simple text and whimsically distorted shapes," and in *Newsweek* Malcolm Jones, Jr., dubbed *An Octopus Followed Me Home* a "beguilingly simple can-I-keep-it story."

A reviewer for *Publishers Weekly* called Yaccarino's *Deep in the Jungle* "perhaps his best book yet," and a "tongue-in-cheek look at an arrogant king of beasts." Tricked one day into leaving the jungle for the confines of a zoo, the lion decides he does not really care for captivity, nor for a taste of the medicine he regularly dosed out to underlings in the jungle. After eating his

*A family tradition shared by father and son inspired Yaccarino's self-illustrated picture book* **Every Friday.** (Copyright © 2007 by Dan Yaccarino. Reprinted by permission of Henry Holt and Company, LLC.)

tamer, the king of beasts returns home and helps the other jungle animals outsmart another trickster attempting to trap them at the zoo. In *Booklist* Connie Fletcher wrote that the author/illustrator's "bright and cartoony" illustrations help take the "bite out of the tale."

Straying far from Earth, Yaccarino has created three books about an earthling student, Johnny Smith, and an alien boy from the planet Meep, Blorp Gorp, who trade places. Smith—dubbed Blast-Off Boy—is chosen from millions of applicants to represent Earth on Meep; at the same time Blorp, all green except for his black eyes, tries to adjust to his new life at Blast-Off Boy's former elementary school. *First Day on a Strange Planet* chronicles the outset of this strange arrangement. While Blast-Off Boy becomes the center of attention on Meep, Blorp is put in detention. A reviewer for *Publishers Weekly* felt that Yaccarino "puts a fresh and funny spin on ordinary events like lunchtime and gym class" in *First Day on a Strange Planet,* while Stevenson found the book to be "an enjoyable armchair excursion into space."

Blorp is living with the Smiths and Blast-Off Boy resides with Blorp's family on Meep in the second title of the series, *New Pet.* A critic for *Kirkus Reviews* thought that while this second book "won't send any young readers into orbit, it will appeal to those who adore aliens of any variety." John Peters, writing in *Booklist,* had higher praise for the book, commending Yaccarino's "daffy spin on familiar themes" and noting that the author/illustrator once again "deftly intertwin[es] his two story lines." The dual story line continues in *The Big Science Fair,* and both students are preparing for fairs on each planet: Blorp with real exuberance and Blast-Off Boy with more of a sense of dread, faced with "all the brainy aliens [who] are planning their macaroni models of hydrogen molecules," as a contributor for *Kirkus Reviews* noted. The same critic concluded that the series is a "welcome addition to the library of those just blasting off out of easy readers." Marlene Gawron, writing in *School Library Journal,* thought that Yaccarino's name should be added to the list of those authors "who have nailed the schoolroom scene."

Other picture books by Yaccarino include *Oswald, The Birthday Fish, Every Friday,* and *Go, Go America,* as well as his own self-illustrated version of the stories of Mother Goose. Illustrated with computer-generated images, *Oswald* is a cumulative story that follows Oswald and his dog, Weenie, as they move to a new city where they have no friends. Attempting to catch a runaway piano, they begin to meet a cast of odd new locals, including trees that can walk and hat-wearing eggs. Gillian Engberg, writing in *Booklist,* felt that youngsters three to seven would enjoy the "zany, random comedy."

In *The Birthday Fish* Cynthia wants a pony for her birthday and has already given her new pet a name. When her new pet turns out to be a goldfish, she decides to toss it down the drain in protest. However, when the goldfish begs to be tossed into a nearby lake instead, the girl loads the fish bowl onto her doll stroller and heads off on her relocation mission. The trip proves longer than planned, however, and by the time the travelers reach the lake shore girl and fish have bonded as friends. In *Kirkus Reviews* a writer called *The Birthday Fish* "deceptively simple," and praised the book's "retro look," while *School Library Journal* critic Wendy Woodfill cited Yaccarino's "highly stylized" art as "a perfect complement to the amiable story." In *Booklist,* Jennifer Mattson predicted that young children will easily perceive the book's message: "about withholding judgment and finding friendship in unexpected places."

A more urban neighborhood is the backdrop for *Every Friday,* which was inspired by the time the author and his son set aside each week to spend with each other. The story is narrated by a young boy who describes the father-and-son routine step by step, from greeting the doorman to stopping at favorite shop windows and eating breakfast at a favorite local diner where the waitress welcomes them each Friday with a hearty greeting. Illustrated in Yaccarino's characteristic retro style, *Every Friday* "shows a cozy plan tailored to urban life, yet suggests the rewards are transferable anywhere," according to a *Publishers Weekly.* Observing that "the story is simple but sweet," Daisy Porter added in *School Library Journal* that the young narrator's "excitement about the time spent with his dad is obvious throughout" Yaccarino's cozy tale, and a *Kirkus Reviews* writer deemed *Every Friday* a "sweet tribute to the unparalleled connection between parent and child."

Featuring a different state on every page, Yaccarino's energetic touring guide *Go, Go America* follows the enthusiastic, tourist-minded Farley Family on their whirlwind tour of the fifty states, revealing a wealth of trivia. From state mottos to festivals, sports, landmarks, history, and unique foods, the book tucks myriad facts within its pastel-toned, image-packed pages. "Browsers will find this hard to put down," maintained a *Kirkus Reviews* writer, and in *School Library Journal* Lynda Ritterman wrote that Yaccarino's "busy but energetic" page design incorporates maps, cartoons, and factoids to produce a book that "is loads of fun and . . . certain to stimulate interest in the U.S." The "old-fashioned road trip" presented in the pages of *Go, Go America* "integrates text and eye-popping art to highlight ridiculous but true tidbits about each state," concluded a *Publishers Weekly* critic.

## Biographical and Critical Sources

*PERIODICALS*

*Booklist,* March 15, 1993, Lisa Napoli, review of *Big Brother Mike,* p. 1363; July, 1996, Susan Dove Lempke, review of *If I Had a Robot,* p. 1831; August, 1997, Hazel Rochman, review of *An Octopus Followed Me Home,* p. 1908; November 1, 1997, Lauren Peterson, review of *Good Night, Mr. Night,* p. 485; November 15, 1997, Shelley Townsend-Hudson, review of *Zoom! Zoom! Zoom! I'm off to the Moon,* p. 568; December 15, 1998, Carolyn Phelan, review of *Five Little Pumpkins,* p. 754; March 1, 2000, Connie Fletcher, review of *Deep in the Jungle,* p. 1253; July, 2001, Gillian Engberg, review of *Oswald,* p. 2022; September 1, 2001, John Peters, review of *The Lima Bean Monster,* p. 118; December 1, 2001, John Peters, review of *New Pet,* p. 645; November 15, 2003, Ed Sullivan, review of *When the Four Winds Blow,* p. 611; October 15, 2004, Jennifer Mattson, review of *Mother Goose,* p. 409; May 15, 2005, Jennifer Mattson, review of *The Birthday Fish,* p. 1667; February 1, 2007, Gillian Engberg, review of *Every Friday,* p. 47; December 1, 2007, Krista Hutley, review of *Little Boy with a Big Horn,* p. 49; March 1, 2008, GraceAnne A. DeCandido, review of *Go, Go America,* p. 64.

*Bulletin of the Center for Children's Books,* September 1, 1998, Deborah Stevenson, "Rising Star: Dan Yaccarino"; January, 1998, Janice M. Del Negro, review of *Good Night, Mr. Night,* p. 182; December, 2000, Deborah Stevenson, review of *First Day on a Strange New Planet,* p. 167; June, 2001, Deborah Stevenson, review of *Oswald,* pp. 392-393.

*Horn Book,* September-October 1997, Roger Sutton, review of *Zoom! Zoom! Zoom!,* p. 567; March-April, 2000, Jennifer M. Brabander, review of *Deep in the Jungle,* p. 191; July-August, 2005, Kitty Flynn, review of *The Birthday Fish,* p. 462.

*Kirkus Reviews,* March 1, 1993, review of *Big Brother Mike,* p. 308; August 15, 1997, review of *Good Night, Mr. Night,* p. 1315; December 15, 2000, review of *So Big!,* p. 1768; September 1, 2001, review of *New Pet,* p. 1304; November 1, 2001, review of *Unlovable,* p. 1556; October 1, 2002, review of *The Big Science Fair,* p. 1484; April 15, 2003, review of *Where the Four Winds Blow,* p. 614; September 1, 2004, review of *Mother Goose,* p. 875; May 15, 2005, review of *The Birthday Fish,* p. 597; August 15, 2007, review of *Every Friday;* August 15, 2007, review of *Who Will Sing a Lullaby?;* December 1, 2007, review of *Little Boy with a Big Horn;* March 1, 2008, review of *Go, Go America.*

*Newsweek,* December 1, 1997, Malcolm Jones, Jr., review of *An Octopus Followed Me Home,* p. 78.

*Publishers Weekly,* March 15, 1993, review of *Big Brother Mike,* p. 85; June 24, 1996, review of *If I Had a Robot,* p. 58; July 21, 1997, review of *Good Night, Mr. Night,* and *Zoom! Zoom! Zoom!,* p. 200; October 20, 1997, review of *An Octopus Followed Me Home,* pp. 74-75; January 3, 2000, review of *Deep in the Jungle,* p. 75; October 30, 2000, review of *First Day on a Strange New Planet,* p. 75; July 30, 2001, review of *The Lima Bean Monster,* p. 84; December 17, 2001, review of *Unlovable,* pp. 89-90; September 6, 2004, review of *Mother Goose,* p. 61; May 30, 2005, review of *The Birthday Fish,* p. 59; March 12, 2007, review of *Every Friday,* p. 56; April 14, 2008, review of *Go, Go America,* p. 54.

*School Library Journal,* September, 1996, John Peters, review of *If I Had a Robot,* p. 195; December, 1997, Susan M. Moore, review of *Zoom! Zoom! Zoom!,* p. 103; February, 1999, Blair Christolon, review of *Five Little Pumpkins,* pp. 83-84; February, 2000, Joy Fleishhacker, review of *Deep in the Jungle,* p. 106; July, 2001, Linda M. Kenton, review of *Oswald,* p. 91; September, 2001, Sally R. Dow, review of *The Lima Bean Monster,* p. 209; December, 2001, Gay Lynn Van Vleck, review of *New Pet,* p. 116; January, 2002, Karen Land, review of *Unlovable,* p. 114; December, 2002, Marlene Gawron, review of *The Big Science Fair,* p. 114; November, 2003, Susan Lissim, review of *Where the Four Winds Blow,* p. 120; October, 2004, Judith Constantinides, review of *Mother Goose,* p. 152; July, 2005, Wendy Woodfill, review of *The Birthday Fish,* p. 85; June, 2007, Daisy Porter, review of *Every Friday,* p. 128; March, 2008, Lynda Ritterman, review of *Go, Go America,* p. 192; March, 2008, Ieva Bates, review of *Little Boy with a Big Horn,* p. 154.

*ONLINE*

*Dan Yaccarino Home Page,* http://www.yaccarinostudio.com (August 7, 2008).

# ZARIN, Cynthia 1959-

## Personal

Born July 9, 1959, in New York, NY; daughter of Michael (a lawyer) and Renee (an administrator) Zarin; married Michael Seccareccia, January 24, 1988 (divorced, 1996); married Joseph Goddu (an art dealer), December 6, 1997; children: Rose; stepchildren: Anna, Jack. *Education:* Radcliffe College, B.A., 1981; Columbia University, M.F.A., 1984.

## Addresses

*Home*—New York, NY. *Office*—Yale University, Department of English, 63 High St., Room 109, P.O. Box 208302, New Haven, CT 06520-8302. *E-mail*—cynthia.zarin@yale.edu.

## Career

*New Yorker* magazine, New York, NY, staff writer, 1984-94, 2004—; Princeton University, Princeton, NJ, lecturer in creative writing, 1993-97; Cathedral of St. John the Divine, New York, NY, artist-in-residence, 1994—; Yale University, New Haven, CT, instructor in English, 2008—. Columbia University, New York, NY, adjunct faculty; Johns Hopkins Writing Seminars, Baltimore, MD, visiting poet, 1998.

## Member

PEN.

## Awards, Honors

Ingram Merrill Award, 1989, for *The Swordfish Tooth;* Lavan Award, Academy of American Poets, 1994; National Endowment for the Arts Award, 1997; *Los Angeles Times Book Award,* 2002, for *The Watercourse;* Front Page Award, 2006, Newswomen's Club of New York, for "Not Nice: Maurice Sendak and the Perils of Childhood"; Richard T. Liddicoat Award, Consumer National Reporting, 2006, for "Seeing Things: The Art of Olafur Eliasson."

## Writings

*PICTURE BOOKS*

*Rose and Sebastian,* illustrated by Sarah Durham, Houghton Mifflin (Boston, MA), 1997.

*What Do You See When You Shut Your Eyes?,* illustrated by Sarah Durham, Houghton Mifflin (Boston, MA), 1998.

*Wallace Hoskins, the Boy Who Grew Down,* illustrated by Martin Matje, DK Ink (New York, NY), 1999.

*Albert, the Dog Who Liked to Ride in Taxis,* illustrated by Pierre Pratt, Atheneum (New York, NY), 2004.

***Cynthia Zarin*** (Photograph by Joseph Goddu. Copyright © 1997 by Cynthia Zarin. Reprinted by permission of SLL/Sterling Lord Literistic, Inc.)

*Saints among the Animals,* illustrated by Leonid Gore, Atheneum (New York, NY), 2005.

*POETRY*

*The Swordfish Tooth,* Knopf (New York, NY), 1989.

*Fire Lyric,* Knopf (New York, NY), 1993.

*The Watercourse,* Knopf (New York, NY), 2002.

*OTHER*

Contributing editor at *Gourmet.* Contributor to *Architectural Digest, New York Times Book Review, New York Times Magazine,* and *Paris Review.*

## Sidelights

Cynthia Zarin, a staff writer at the *New Yorker* and an instructor at Yale University, is the author of three highly regarded books of poetry, including *Fire Lyric* and *The Watercourse.* Zarin's poems, according to *Boldtype* online contributor Ernest Hilbert, "tend toward the symmetrical: orderly stanzaic patterns, metrical figures, and regular rhymes," and they offer a purity of language and a slightly offbeat perspective on mundane, typically overlooked topics. Her books for children, including *Rose and Sebastian, Albert, the Dog Who Liked to Ride in Taxis,* and *Saints among the Animals,* encourage young readers to look at things from a fresh perspective.

In *Rose and Sebastian,* Zarin's debut picture book, Rose is a young child who is used to the noisiness of New York, where she lives in an apartment with her mother. The noises made by Sebastian, the rowdy boy who lives upstairs, are a different story, however—they are scary. Summoning her courage, Rose goes upstairs to confront her fear and meet Sebastian. To her delight, she learns to appreciate the exuberance of a noisy new friend. "Zarin offers not only a glimpse of apartment life, but establishes Rose as a captivating heroine who wants to overcome her fears, and does," remarked a critic in *Kirkus Reviews.* Susan Hepler, a reviewer for *School Library Journal,* likewise called *Rose and Sebastian* "a nice supplement to the preschool read-aloud shelf on overcoming fears."

*What Do You See When You Shut Your Eyes?* is less a storybook than a humorous game. Rhyming questions and answers encourage children to use their five senses and their imaginations to participate in the fun. Zarin's text "expresses a poet's sensibility," asserted a reviewer for *Publishers Weekly,* "an ability to observe, a sense of the absurd, an affection for the everyday, an eye for juxtaposition." Noting that the author ends with a question about dreams, *School Library Journal* contributor

***Cover of Zarin's picture book* Rose and Sebastian, *featuring cover art by Sarah Durham.*** (Illustration copyright © 1997 by Sarah Durham. Reprinted by permission of Houghton Mifflin Harcourt Publishing Company. All rights reserved.)

Olga R. Barnes called *What Do You See When You Shut Your Eyes?* "a pleasant addition to a lesson on imagination or the senses."

A youngster's bizarre physical appearance is the focus of *Wallace Hoskins, the Boy Who Grew Down,* a "convoluted tall tale," in the words of a *Publishers Weekly* reviewer. Eight-year-old Wallace, whose red fireman's helmet never leaves his head, has stopped growing for a number of years, much to the dismay of his mother, Gladys. When Wallace finally sprouts because his legs—and no other part of him—are getting longer, Gladys pays a visit to Nanny Heppleweather. Taking the wise old woman's advice, Gladys removes the helmet one night and picks the toadstool that grows beneath it. *Wallace Hoskins, the Boy Who Grew Down* earned mixed reviews. Though some critics faulted the work for the complexity of its language, *Booklist* contributor Tim Arnold noted that the "highly original, clever tale is a gentle reminder that children need some adult help from time to time."

In *Albert, the Dog Who Liked to Ride in Taxis,* a dachshund embarks on an adventure in the big city. Albert loves to ride along with his owner, Mrs. Crabtree, as she taxis around New York, but when the canine spies an opportunity to travel solo, he begins hopping from cab to cab. While touring the town, Albert is invited to the Kalahari Desert by an elderly woman, and he later accepts a ride to the airport from two youths bound for California. Arriving at the terminal, Albert is greeted by a startled and amazed Mr. Crabtree, who has just returned from a business trip. "As much as what happens, equally enjoyable is the way Zarin tells it," observed *Booklist* reviewer Ilene Cooper, and a critic in *Kirkus Reviews* stated that the author "tells the tale in an offhand, tongue-in-cheek tone." According to a *Publishers Weekly* contributor, "Zarin's story blends realism and fiction with quirky verve, and the memorable Albert is Fred Astaire-suave."

Inspired by Margaret Ward Cole's 1905 book of the same title, Zarin's *Saints among the Animals* contains ten stories that explore the often remarkable relationship between a holy figure and a wild creature. In one familiar tale, Saint Francis tames a wolf that was terrorizing the townspeople of Gubbio, and in another, Saint Jerome pulls a thorn from a lion's paw. Zarin also includes the stories of Saint Werburge, an English abbess who orders a flock of geese to stop destroying her crops; Saint Brendan, an abbot who is rescued by a whale when his boat catches fire on the Irish Sea; and Saint Hilda, who prevents an infestation of serpents. Zarin's "folksy, matter-of-fact telling roots the iconic figures firmly in the natural world, emphasizing their humanity," wrote *Horn Book* contributor Lauren Adams. "The tales are neatly told," Cooper stated, and a *Publishers Weekly* reviewer commented that the "entries reflect a sense of wonderment and mystery, something that will likely enchant readers."

## Biographical and Critical Sources

*PERIODICALS*

*Antioch Review,* fall, 2002, John Taylor, review of *The Watercourse,* p. 714.

*Booklist,* October 15 1999, Tim Arnold, review of *Wallace Hoskins, the Boy Who Grew Down,* p. 457; December 15, 2003, Ilene Cooper, review of *Albert, the Dog Who Liked to Ride in Taxis,* p. 749; December 1, 2006, Ilene Cooper, review of *Saints among the Animals,* p. 44.

*Horn Book,* January-February, 2006, Lauren Adams, review of *Saints among the Animals,* p. 87.

*Kirkus Reviews,* August 15, 1997, review of *Rose and Sebastian,* p. 1316; January 1, 2004, review of *Albert, the Dog Who Liked to Ride in Taxis,* p. 43.

*New York Times Book Review,* March 31, 2002, Ken Tucker, "Address to a Hot, Wet Place," review of *The Watercourse,* p. 17.

*Publishers Weekly,* August 17, 1998, review of *What Do You See When You Shut Your Eyes?,* p. 71; August 16, 1999, review of *Wallace Hoskins, the Boy Who Grew Down,* p. 84; January 21, 2002, review of *The Watercourse,* p. 87; January 19, 2004, review of *Albert, the Dog Who Liked to Ride in Taxis,* p. 74; October 20, 2006, review of *Saints among the Animals,* p. 65.

*School Library Journal,* September, 1997, Susan Hepler, review of *Rose and Sebastian,* p. 198; September, 1998, Olga R. Barnes, review of *What Do You See When You Shut Your Eyes?,* p. 186; September, 1999, John Sigwald, review of *Wallace Hoskins, the Boy Who Grew Down,* p. 210; February, 2004, Mary Ann Carcich, review of *Albert, the Dog Who Liked to Ride in Taxis,* p. 125; January, 2007, Linda L. Walkins, review of *Saints among the Animals,* p. 121.

*ONLINE*

*New Yorker Web site,* http://www.newyorker.com/ (August 15, 2008), "Cynthia Zarin."

*Boldtype Web site,* http://www.randomhouse.com/boldtype/ (May 17, 2006), Ernest Hilbert, "Cynthia Zarin."*

* * *

# ZIMMERMAN, Andrea 1950-
# (Andrea Griffing Zimmerman)

## Personal

Born December 2, 1950, in Akron, OH; daughter of Leland (a business consultant) and Mignon (an auditor) Zimmerman; married David J. Clemesha (an author), 1973; children: Alex, Christian, Chase. *Education:* California State University, Los Angeles, B.A., 1979; University of California, Los Angeles, D.D.S., 1988. *Hobbies and other interests:* Gardening, travel.

## Addresses

*Home*—San Diego, CA. *E-mail*—email@andreaand david.com.

## Career

Author. Also worked as a dentist.

## Member

Society of Children's Book Writers and Illustrators.

## Awards, Honors

Blue Ribbon selection, *Bulletin of the Center for Children's Books,* 1999, "One Hundred Picture Books Everyone Should Know" citation, New York Public Library, and Notable Books for Children selection, American Library Association, 2000, all for *Trashy Town;* Oppenheim Toy Portfolio Gold Award, and Best Children's Books designation, Bank Street College of Education, both 2000, both for *My Dog Toby;* Oppenheim Toy Portfolio Gold Award, 2003, for *Digger Man.*

## Writings

*FOR CHILDREN*

(As Andrea Griffing Zimmerman) *Yetta the Trickster,* illustrated by Harold Berson, Clarion Books (Boston, MA), 1978.

(As Andrea Griffing Zimmerman) *The Riddle Zoo,* illustrated by Giulio Maestro, Dutton (New York, NY), 1981.

*SELF-ILLUSTRATED; WITH HUSBAND, DAVID CLEMESHA*

(As Andrea Griffing Zimmerman) *Rattle Your Bones: Skeleton Drawing Fun,* Scholastic (New York, NY), 1991.

*Digger Man,* Holt (New York, NY), 2003.

*Fire Engine Man,* Holt (New York, NY), 2007.

*FOR CHILDREN; WITH HUSBAND, DAVID CLEMESHA*

*The Cow Buzzed,* illustrated by Paul Meisel, HarperCollins (New York, NY), 1993.

*Trashy Town,* illustrated by Dan Yaccarino, HarperCollins (New York, NY), 1999.

*My Dog Toby,* illustrated by True Kelley, Harcourt (San Diego, CA), 2000.

*Fire! Fire! Hurry! Hurry!,* illustrated by Karen Barbour, Greenwillow (New York, NY), 2003.

*Dig!,* illustrated by Marc Rosenthal, Harcourt (Orlando, FL), 2004.

*Manatee Mom,* illustrated by Michael-Che Swisher, Millbrook Press (Minneapolis, MN), 2006.

## Sidelights

Andrea Zimmerman is the author of the children's books *Yetta the Trickster* and *The Riddle Zoo.* In addition, she has collaborated with her husband, author David Clemesha, on several more titles for young readers, among them *Digger Man, Trashy Town,* and *My Dog Toby.*

In *Yetta the Trickster,* Zimmerman's first story for children, the title protagonist enjoys playing practical jokes so much that she does not care if she is the player or the victim. Set in an eastern European village, the narrative follows Yetta through numerous pranks, including one in which the village turns the tables on the young jokester. *Booklist* reviewer Barbara Elleman commented that each of the book's "four short chapters . . . ripple with spirit and humor." Mary I. Purucker, writing in the *School Library Journal,* praised illustrator Harold Berson's "pen-and-ink wit and humor," and found Zimmerman's depiction of Yetta's adventures to be "human, childlike, and universal."

In *The Cow Buzzed,* the second Zimmerman-Clemesha collaboration, farm animals pass a cold from one creature to the next—along with each animal's signature noise. Thus the cow catches not only the bee's cold, but his buzz as well. The confusion is made worse when the farmer feeds each animal according to his/her noise, so that they all end up with the wrong food. In the end, the cold is stopped by a rabbit who covers his mouth when he sneezes, and the animals ultimately discover the origins of the illness when the bee unexpectedly roars. A *Kirkus Reviews* contributor called this tale "deliciously silly" with "clever new rhymes worked into each repetition of the tricky, catchy rhythm." A *Publishers Weekly* critic noted that "the book's humor is even more infectious than the bee's cold."

In *Trashy Town* the husband-and-wife team offer readers a glimpse of a day in the life of Mr. Gilly, the trashman, as he and his two rat sidekicks clean up the town's trash with the cheerful refrain: "Dump it in, smash it down, drive around the Trashy Town!" At the end of his day, Mr. Gilly unloads the trash at the dump, then goes home for a bath. Writing in *Horn Book,* Nancy Vasilakis complimented Zimmerman, Clemesha, and illustrator Dan Yaccarino for creating a "well-designed picture book that does a lot with a simple concept." Calling the narrative "an overdue salute to an unsung hero," a *Publishers Weekly* reviewer remarked that "despite the smelly and slimy aspects of garbage collecting, Zimmerman and Clemesha make Mr. Gilly's job seem satisfying." Comparing *Trashy Town* to "Margaret Wise Brown's best work," *Booklist* critic Linda Perkins praised the book as "right on the mark for young children."

Zimmerman and Clemesha's *My Dog Toby* earned similarly positive reviews. In this story, a young girl is convinced of her basset hound's intelligence, despite his inability to learn tricks. Even though the girl's brother suggests that the dog might be "dumb," she perseveres and eventually teaches her pet to sit, leading her brother to agree with Toby's intelligence after all. Commenting in *Booklist,* Carolyn Phelan commented on "the understated humor of the text," and summarized the work as "a warm, witty picture book celebrating the mutual devotion of dogs and their owners." *New York Times Book*

*Among Andrea Zimmerman and David Clemesha's picture-book collaborations is* My Dog Toby, *featuring cartoon art by True Kelley.*

*Review* critic Adam Liptak observed that "[Zimmerman and Clemesha] infuse the story with some gentle lessons about appreciating dogs—and people—for what they are."

A group of firefighters are kept busy during mealtime in *Fire! Fire! Hurry! Hurry!*, "a joyful celebration of team work [that is] . . . sure to please the preschool set," noted a critic in *Kirkus Reviews.* Each time Captain Kelly and his animal cohorts, including a green elephant and a striped cat, sit down for dinner, they receive an urgent call to tackle a blaze. "This construction is both funny and judicious: it gives kids a sense of control over what would otherwise be chaotic," observed a *Publishers Weekly* reviewer. "The repetitive text lends itself well to reading aloud," Leslie Barban noted in *School Library Journal.*

*Dig!* follows Mr. Rally, a backhoe driver, and his loyal canine companion, Lightning, during a busy day on the job. The verse narrative describes the efforts of Mr. Rally to move rocks from a bridge, create a drainage ditch, and level a plot of land. According to *New York Times Book Review* contributor Jess Bruder, the authors "use their familiar style and structure to explore new terrain. Sentences jounce along from one construction site to the next." Marian Creamer, writing in *School Library Journal,* maintained that "the pace, repetition, and word choices make the book appropriate for beginning readers." "Full of action and rhythm," wrote *Booklist* critic Gillian Engberg, *Dig!* "will delight preschoolers who dream of their own big-engine, dirt-digging adventures."

Zimmerman and Clemesha have also collaborated on a number of self-illustrated titles. While playing in his sandbox, a little boy imagines himself behind the controls of a huge digging machine handling massive construction projects in *Digger Man,* a "lively, sure-to-please winner," according to Andrea Tarr in *School Library Journal.* Ellen Mandel, writing in *Booklist,* applauded the "joyful acrylic illustrations and the sparse, confident text," and a *Publishers Weekly* reviewer also complimented the artwork, stating that in one scene Zimmerman and Clemesha "construct a characteristic spread of bold shapes in bright colors, then splendiferously splatter it with chocolate-brown acrylic paint."

In a companion volume, *Fire Engine Man,* a youngster shares his dream of becoming a firefighter with his infant brother as he pictures himself putting out a fire and preparing a meal for his coworkers. According to *Booklist* critic Shelle Rosenfeld, Zimmerman and Clemesha's story "highlights firefighter duties, safety, and a caring sibling relationship." The duo's illustrations also garnered praise. In *School Library Journal* Linda M. Kenton remarked that "colorful acrylic illustrations greet readers," and a contributor in *Kirkus Reviews* stated that "the cheery paints depict sturdy firefighters and proud engines."

Zimmerman once commented: "I enjoy making books to amuse young children. I try to place myself in the mind of a child to see the world as children do and to write about what interests them in a way they will find most entertaining. My husband, David, and I work together, inspired by our own children, our own childhoods, and the other children we meet. We are now illustrating some of our books, as well as writing them. We love the thirty-two-page format of picture books for its simplicity and wide potential."

## Biographical and Critical Sources

*PERIODICALS*

*Booklist,* December 1, 1978, Barbara Elleman, review of *Yetta the Trickster,* p. 621; January 15, 1982, Ilene Cooper, review of *The Riddle Zoo,* p. 656; May 1, 1993, Ilene Cooper, review of *The Cow Buzzed,* p. 1606; August, 1999, Linda Perkins, review of *Trashy Town,* p. 2067; May 1, 2000, Carolyn Phelan, review of *My Dog Toby,* p. 1666; September 1, 2003, Ellen Mandel, review of *Digger Man,* p. 132; May 15, 2004, Gillian Engberg, review of *Dig!,* p. 1627; May 1, 2007, Shelle Rosenfeld, review of *Fire Engine Man,* p. 101.

*Horn Book,* March, 1999, Nancy Vasilakis, review of *Trashy Town,* p. 204.

*Kirkus Reviews,* June 1, 1993, review of *The Cow Buzzed,* p. 730; September 1, 2003, review of *Digger Man,* p. 1133; April 15, 2007, review of *Fire Engine Man.*

*New York Times Book Review,* May 14, 2000, Adam Liptak, "It's a Dog's Life," p. 29; September 19, 2004, Jess Bruder, review of *Dig!*

*Publishers Weekly,* May 24, 1993, review of *The Cow Buzzed,* p. 84; April 26, 1999, review of *Trashy Town,* p. 82; May 10, 2004, review of *Dig!,* p. 57; September 15, 2003, review of *Digger Man,* p. 63.

*School Library Journal,* January, 1979, Mary I. Purucker, review of *Yetta the Trickster,* p. 49; February, 1982, Lois Kimmelman, review of *The Riddle Zoo,* p. 72; May, 1999, Lisa Dennis, review of *Trashy Town,* p. 102; May, 2000, Holly Belli, review of *My Dog Toby,* p. 159; April, 2003, Leslie Barban, review of *Fire! Fire! Hurry! Hurry!,* p. 144; December, 2003, Andrea Tarr, review of *Digger Man,* p. 131; July, 2004, Marian Creamer, review of *Dig!,* p. 90; July, 2007, Linda M. Kenton, review of *Fire Engine Man,* p. 88.

*ONLINE*

*Andrea Zimmerman and David Clemesha Home Page,* http://www.andreaanddavid.com (August 5, 2008).

* * *

## ZIMMERMAN, Andrea Griffing
See ZIMMERMAN, Andrea